Working Americans 1880–1999

Volume IV: Their Children

Working Americans 1880–1999

Volume IV: Their Children

by Scott Derks

A Universal Reference Book

MILLERTON, NY 12546

PUBLISHER: Leslie Mackenzie
EDITORIAL DIRECTOR: Laura Mars-Proietti
EDITORIAL ASSISTANT: Pamela Michaud
MARKETING DIRECTOR: Jessica Moody

AUTHOR: Scott Derks
CONTRIBUTOR: Greg Flowers
EDITORIAL ASSISTANT to the author: Linda Kelly

COPYEDITOR: Elaine Alibrandi
COMPOSITION & DESIGN: Stratford Publishing Services

A Universal Reference Book
Grey House Publishing, Inc.
185 Millerton Road
Millerton, NY 12546
518.789.8700
800-562-2139
FAX 518.789.0545
www.greyhouse.com
e-mail: books @greyhouse.com

First edition published 2002

Printed in the USA

10 9 8 7 6 5 4 3 2

ISBN 1-930956-35-5 hardcover

Table of Contents

INTRODUCTION

Working Americans 1880–1999 Volume IV: Their Children is the fourth volume of an open-ended multi-volume series. Like its predecessors, *Volume I: The Working Class, Volume II: The Middle Class,* and *Volume III: The Upper Class,* this volume looks, decade by decade, into the lives of Americans. This fourth volume focuses on children—of all ages, from all backgrounds, and from all across the country. We've included children from a wide range of backgrounds, from children of migrant workers to those born into privileged families; from kids who play stickball after school to those who work in their family's Chinese restaurant; from teenage debutantes to video game junkies. *Working Americans: Volume IV: Their Children* presents a socio-economic picture of 20th century America, including the last decade of the 19th century, through the eyes and ears of its children.

Praise for earlier volumes:

> "*. . . The accounts of the families make compelling reading . . . this volume is unique in that it puts a human face on the statistics. This volume "promises to enhance our understanding of the growth and development of the working class over more than a century." It capably fulfills this promise. . .*"
>
> ARBA 2001

> " *. . . Overall, this volume engages and informs, contributing significantly and meaningfully to the historiography of the working class in America. . .*"
>
> Library Journal

> "*. . . This is no dull statistical compilation of economic history. It is a very interesting, readable account of life in the United States for the worker or laborer . . .*"
>
> Journal of Business & Finance Librarianship

Children's Profiles

Working Americans 1880–1999 Volume IV: Their Children contains 11 chapters, each comprising a decade. Every decade includes at least three profiles focusing on the working, middle or upper class, as identified in the previous volumes of this series.

All 33 profiles examine life at home, life at school, and life in the community. These profiles span not only the economic spectrum, but also a wide range of ages, ethnic backgrounds, and residential settings, from small towns to large urban centers.

Information is presented in narrative form, but hard facts and real life situations back up each story. The basis of the profiles come from a variety of sources, including diaries, private print books, personal interviews, family histories, estate documents, and magazine articles.

As in previous volumes, we have given each prototyped child a name to help readers identify with them. Ora McFadden is a 13-year old from Memphis, who lost both parents in 1882 to the yellow fever epidemic; 9-year old Ovo Novajovsky lives in Brooklyn in 1926, and dreams of meeting his hero, Babe Ruth; Raymond Walker, at 14 years old, works as a caddie in Baltimore in 1962; Betty Elizabeth Putnam, in 1981, migrates up and down the east coast, as she and her family pick fruits and vegetables for a living; and Cordelia Dorffman, in 1992, lives a privileged life on her parent's Texas ranch.

Economic Profiles

Each chapter also includes an Economic Profile. These are a series of statistical comparisons designed to put the child's lifestyle in perspective. Enhancing some of the chapters are examinations of important issues faced by not just children and their families, but society as well, such as how Americans coped with war and the civil rights movement.

In addition to the detailed economic and social data for each family, each chapter is further enriched with Historical Snapshots, News Profiles, articles from local media, and illustrations derived from popular printed materials of the day: clippings from cereal boxes, campaign buttons, postcards, and posters. Each graphic was carefully selected to add depth to the understanding of the world that the families lived in.

In more than 600 pages, *Working Americans 1880–1999 Volume IV: Their Children* covers dozens of ethnic backgrounds including Welsh, Russian, Italian, Chinese, Sardinian, Croatian, Native American, African American, and Laotian. Geographically, the text travels the entire country, from New Jersey to California.

The Table of Contents provides a clear guide through each chapter, and a comprehensive index includes thousands of terms.

Next in this series is *Working Americans 1880–1999 Volume V: At War.* This volume will explore the various ways officers, enlisted personnel, and civilians handled Americans at war, including declared conflicts, one-time military actions, protests, or preparation for future wars, during the 20th century.

Preface

Welcome to the fourth volume in a series focused on the social and economic lives of working Americans. The first volume, *Working Americans: 1880–1999,* examined the struggles of the working class through the eyes and wallets of more than three dozen families. With pictures, stories and statistics, it studied their jobs, wages, family life, expenditures, and hobbies throughout the decades. The second volume captured the struggles of the middle class in a similar but sometimes subtly different way, profiling the lives of everyday families that played a quiet role in building the day-to-day economy of America from 1880 to 1999. Few were heroes, all felt the pressures of life, and most wanted better for themselves and their families. The third volume examined the fascinating and often complex world of the upper class. Through hard work, grit, good luck or inheritance, these people were elevated to the highest pinnacle of economic prosperity. All were wealthy, though not all were well off.

This fourth volume builds upon the concepts and social issues explored in the previous three volumes—this time examining the lives of children of working Americans, whether they came from the working, middle or upper classes. Through more than three dozen profiles, *Working Americans IV: Their Children* looks at the issues of growing up: parents, homework, child labor, education, peer pressure, food, first jobs, fads, and fun with friends. In the course of this book, children are loved, orphaned, sent away for their own safety or trucked from town to town while their parents seek work. The study of children from all economic levels adds depth and texture to this social/economic series, allowing time and space to be devoted to stories ranging from a girl's first trip in 1904 to Coney Island, the sale of the family farm during the Great Depression, and the experience of a white, middle class park ranger's son attending Yale on a full scholarship in a 1950s attempt at diversity.

Each story is unique, as each of us is unique, but hauntingly similar. Whether we are rich or poor, we harbor that confusing gumbo-mix of joy and fear when preparing to attend our first junior high school dance or take our first driving lesson. Clearly, every generation endows a certain level of romance to the age gone by, especially if it included a first date, a first kiss, a baseball game in Yankee Stadium or the chance to learn how to play the saxophone. This book includes these experiences and more: the little girl who joyfully sells handmade paper butterflies to buy her mother Easter shoes, the insecure bravado of the Baltimore socialite during her Grand Tour, the Denver boy who publishes his own science fiction magazine, or the fruit tramp girl who simply wants to get off the road and finish school.

During this youth-filled stroll through time, we are able to experience, as these children did, what it was like to read in reputable publications that girls were ill-equipped to play basketball because their hearts were too small and temperaments too weak. We can relive the dreams of a teenage boy intent on inventing the perfect automobile in 1909, or simply remember what it was like to be an eight-year-old girl discovering the wicked joy of going to the drive-in movies dressed in her pajamas.

All of the profiles were modeled on real people and events, although, as in the previous books in the series, the families' actual names have been changed and some details have been added—such as the television shows they watched—based on statistics, popularity and writings of that particular time. Otherwise, every effort has been made to create profiles that reflect the youths' home life, school experiences and community. To ensure that all other details accurately reflect the mood of each decade, diaries, biographies, interviews and high school annuals were consulted. The newspaper and magazine stories strategically placed throughout the book are intended to remind us how much and how little some issues have changed—especially when it comes to boy/girl interactions, our relationships with our parents, and the desire to feel a part of the community. In many cases, the subjects' lives reflect national trends, but not always, and not always to the same level as statistical models would have us believe. It is the people, events and actions of American families—along with their investments, spending decisions, time commitments, jobs and energies—that shape society and the economy.

It is my prayer that in conjunction with my earlier work, *The Value of a Dollar,* this series on working Americans will offer the student of history a few salient and tangible clues toward understanding the history, the economy and social issues of the United States. Although the work of others may provide a more comprehensive picture of Americans, few other books, I submit, will be as much fun or as useful in finding ourselves through these portraits from the past.

Scott Derks

Working Americans Volume IV, focused on the lives of children, is lovingly dedicated to Jan and Robin for all they have done for all God's children through the years.

ACKNOWLEDGMENTS

The author wishes to thank and recognize the work of Greg Flowers, whose research skills, innate curiosity and love of knowledge made this book more valuable. Thanks also go to Linda Kelly, whose editorial assistance and dedication to this book about children persisted even after her first grandchild was born. For the fourth and hopefully not the final time, thanks are extended to Elaine Alibrandi, whose joy in making every word shine emanates through these pages. In addition, thanks are extended to the many friends whose donation of pictures, stories, advice and critiques was critical to this process. They include Caroline Gottlieb, Kathy Glidden, Bobby Long, Laura Mars-Proietti, Robin Brown, Ellen Hanckel and Marshall Derks. The author must also thank Susan Tracy at Miss Porter's School for providing both information and photographs. Finally, thanks are extended to the staff of the Reference Department of the University of South Carolina's Thomas Cooper Library, who showed unrelenting good humor in the face of a barrage of offbeat queries: department head Virginia Weathers; librarians Marilee Birchfield, Kate Boyd, Paul Cammarata, Gary Geer, Tom Marcil, Rose Marshall, Sharon Verba; former staff members Brette Barron, Michael Macan; and graduate assistants Trish Raque and Karen Williams.

Lungs
Position
Structure

1880–1899

The last two decades of the nineteenth century danced in the reflected glow of the Gilded Age, when the wealth of a tiny percentage of Americans knew no bounds. Children of the working class routinely left school in their teens to work beside their parents; the middle class was small, and college was largely an institution reserved for the élite and wealthy of America. It was also a time marked by an abundance of emerging technology and changing opportunities, symbolizing the restless spirit of the American people. The highly popular children's books featuring Horatio Alger reinforced the notion that opportunity and wealth lurked around every corner for every child who worked hard enough and believed long enough in America's prosperity. At the same time, child labor laws were largely nonexistent, and on-the-job injuries were common, even expected.

The rapid expansion of railroads opened up the nation to new industries, new markets and the formation of monopolistic trusts that catapulted a handful of corporations into positions of unprecedented power and wealth. This expanding technology also triggered the movement of workers from farm to factory, the rapid expansion of wage labor, and the explosive growth of cities. Farmers, merchants and small-town artisans found themselves increasingly dependent on regional and national market forces. The shift in the concentrations of power was unprecedented in American history. At the same time, professionally trained workers were reshaping America's economy alongside business managers or entrepreneurs eager to capture their piece of the American pie. It was an economy on a roll with few rudders or regulations.

Across America the economy—along with its work force—was running away from the land. Before the Civil War, the United States was overwhelmingly an agricultural nation. By the end of the century, non-agricultural occupations employed nearly two thirds of the workers. As important, two of every three Americans came to rely on wages instead of self-employment as farmers or artisans. At the same time, industrial growth began to center around cities, where wealth accumulated for a few who understood how to harness and use railroads, create new consumer markets, and manage a ready supply of cheap, trainable labor. Jobs, offering steady wages and the promise of a better life for workers' children, drew people from the farms into the cities, which grew at twice the rate of the nation as a whole. A modern, industrially-based work force emerged from the traditional farmlands, led by men skilled at managing others and the complicated flow of materials required to keep a factory operating. This led to an increasing demand for attorneys, bankers, and physicians to handle the complexity of the emerging urban economy. In 1890, newspaper editor Horace Greeley remarked, "We cannot all live in cities, yet nearly all seem determined to do so."

The new cities of America were home to great wealth and poverty—both produced by the massive migrations and influx of immigrants willing to work at any price. It was a time symbolized by Andrew Carnegie's steel mills, John D. Rockefeller's organization of the Standard Oil monopoly, and the manufacture of Alexander Graham Bell's wonderful invention, the telephone. By 1894, the United States had become the world's leading industrial power, producing more than England, France, and Germany—its three largest competitors—combined. For much of this period, the nation's industrial energy focused on the need for railroads requiring large quantities of labor, iron, steel, stone, and lumber. In 1883, nine tenths of the nation's entire production of steel went into rails. The most important invention of the period—in an era of tremendous change and innovation—may have been the Bessemer converter, which transformed pig iron into steel at a relatively low cost, increasing steel output 10 times from 1877 to 1892.

The greatest economic event during the last two decades of the nineteenth century was the great wave of immigration that swept America. It is believed to be the largest worldwide population movement in human history, bringing more than 10 million people to the United States to fill the expanding need for workers. In the 1880s alone, 5.25 million immigrants arrived, more than in the first six decades of the nineteenth century. This wave was dominated by Irish, German, and English workers. Scandinavia, Italy, and China sent scores of eager workers, normally men, to fill the expanding labor needs of the United States. To attract this much-needed labor force, railroad and steamship companies advertised throughout Europe and China the glories of American life. To an economically depressed world, it was a welcome call.

Despite all the signs of economic growth and prosperity, America's late-nineteenth-century economy was profoundly unstable. Industrial expansion was undercut by a depression from 1882 to 1885, followed in 1893 by a five-year-long economic collapse that devastated rural and urban communities across America. As a result, job security for workers just climbing onto the industrial stage was often fleeting. Few wage-earners found full-time work for the entire year. The unevenness in the economy was caused both by the level of change under way and irresponsible speculation, but more generally to the stubborn adherence of the federal government to a highly inflexible gold standard as the basis of value for currency.

Between the very wealthy and the very poor emerged a new middle stratum, whose appearance was one of the distinctive features of late-nineteenth-century America. The new middle class fueled the purchase of one million light bulbs a year by 1890, even though the first electric light was only 11 years old. It was the middle class also that flocked to buy Royal Baking Powder, (which was easier to use and faster than yeast) and supported the emergence and spread of department stores that were sprouting up across the nation.

1882 Profile

Middle Class

Thirteen-year-old Ora McFadden and his two sisters lost their parents and a middle-class lifestyle when yellow fever swept through Memphis, Tennessee. The three children now live in the Catholic Orphan Asylum.

Ora dreams of his home before the fever arrived.

Life at Home

- At night Ora often dreams about the house he lived in before he and his sisters, Iris and Rose, came to the orphanage four years ago.
- He had a bedroom of his own just up the stairs from the kitchen, where good smells originated.
- He had a dog and friends, a mother who tucked him in at night and a father who loved to tell stories.
- Then, the yellow fever epidemic hit Memphis, and everything changed.
- A New Orleans steamboat deckhand was the first person to die of yellow fever during the outbreak of 1878.
- He was followed by Mrs. Kate Bionda, who operated a snack shop patronized by river men, and then James McConnell, a policeman.
- More than 20,000 citizens—half the city—then staged a hysterical exodus.
- The *Public Ledger* observed, "At no time within the history of our city has there been such a sudden or effective panic among the people of Memphis. Our community is in a state of great alarm, and all who can leave are doing so."

Ora's grandmother dies trying to save her son-in-law from the fever.

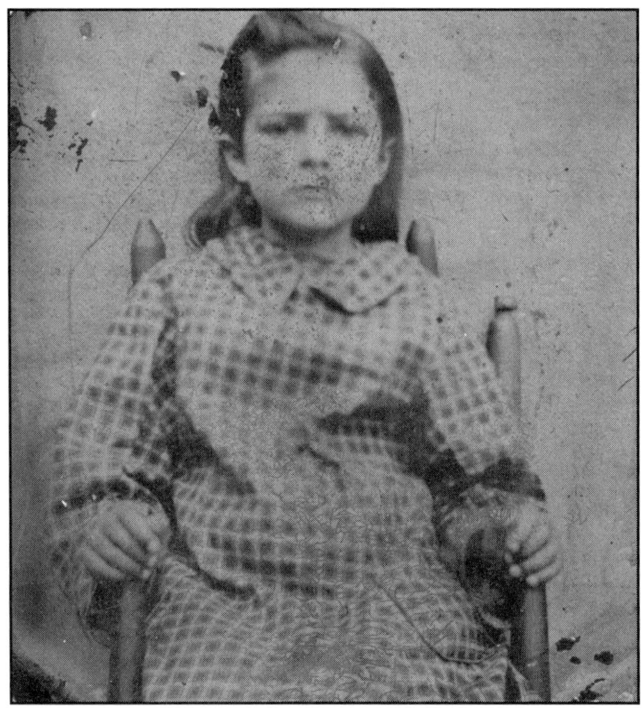

Rose becomes an orphan in a city full of homeless children.

- When the yellow fever outbreak began, Ora's father, a bank clerk, sent the family north, while he stayed behind in Memphis to provide necessary travel funds to fleeing residents.
- The family took the Louisville & Nashville train north 100 miles to the country home of Ora's aging grandmother; railroad cars had to be added to accommodate all the extra passengers leaving Memphis.
- It was a frightening time, and the three children clung tightly to their mother for most of the trip; no one felt the need to appear brave.
- *The Daily Appeal* said, "The ordinary courtesies of life were ignored; politeness gave way to selfishness and the desire for personal safety broke through the social amenities."
- To further assist the citizens of Memphis, Ora's father joined the Citizen's Relief Committee, which had two white members and one black member from each of the city's 10 wards.
- Space was set aside in the hospital for indigents, while schools were converted to hospitals.
- Of the 40,000 original residents of Memphis, only 7,000 whites and 13,000 blacks stayed in the city.
- Most who remained in the city's four square miles were either volunteers, the sick, or those who felt they were immune.
- It was generally believed that African-Americans had a higher resistance to yellow fever than did whites.
- Once the epidemic began, the Howard Association employed 3,000 nurses to care for the sick, two-thirds of whom were black or white males from Memphis.
- In addition, 500 nurses came from outside the city to help—volunteers from Catholic, Protestant and Hebrew groups—along with many who were employed by fraternal organizations such as the Odd Fellows and the Masons.
- Hundreds of nurses died caring for patients.
- During the first week of September, the city government and Board of Health ceased to function.
- That same week, Ora's father became ill with yellow fever.
- He was immediately given the "Creole treatment," consisting of small doses of castor oil or calomel to keep the bowels open, sponge baths to reduce fever, adequate covering in the event of chills, and absolute rest of mind and body.
- When Ora's mother learned that her husband was sick, she and the children's grandmother returned to Memphis.
- During the next two weeks, they all caught yellow fever and died within days of each other.
- Suddenly, Ora, Iris and Rose were orphans in a city full of wandering, homeless children.
- More than 4,000 people in Memphis died.
- For $2 a day, black grave diggers labored day and night, but still could not keep up with the mountain of coffins.

- When Ora and his sisters returned to Memphis, as instructed by the authorities, they were placed in a Catholic Orphan Asylum, where they have remained for four years, but they have never forgotten how nice their mother smelled when she tucked them in at night.

Ora's father stays behind to help his customers.

Life at School and the Orphanage

- Every evening while lying in his bed in the orphan asylum, Ora pulls out the ferrotype pictures taken when the family was still together.
- He remembers the pictures were taken on a Saturday afternoon; father's barber had proudly set up a photography studio, complete with desks, chairs and props.
- They were some of the photographer's first customers; father and mother even got dressed for the occasion, although the children did not.
- Pictures were taken of Ora at age eight, and his sisters, along with his father, mother and grandmother.
- It was a great afternoon of fun; he was unsure if he could remain standing completely still for 30 seconds so the photograph would not be spoiled, but he did.
- The photos of his mother and sister Iris were lost when the children were taken to the orphanage.
- He still likes to look at the pictures, even when they make him sad; he is determined he will always remember what his mother, father and grandmother looked like before they died.
- The orphan asylum is filled with children who lost their parents four years ago.

The nuns nurse the children during the fever.

Funeral carts roll from house to house.

- As the oldest child, he felt it was his job to lead the children into the asylum for the first time, though he was frightened beyond words.
- Everyone was very nice, but the house was extremely chaotic then.
- Too many children had come too quickly, and few Sisters remained to care for them; now it is better and everyone knows what is expected.
- Many children came to the orphanage after living on the streets for months, begging for food from house to house before being invited to the asylum.
- Until the hard winter came in January, many of the street children did not want to stay at the orphan asylum because so many nuns had died during the fever.
- Currently, 125 children live in the asylum, 47 of whom are boys.
- Everyone in Memphis thought God would make the Sisters safe; now, four years later, many of the nuns are like Ora, arriving since the fever.
- He hopes the fever never comes back.
- Many of the nuns believe that if they can control the influences that make up a child's life and thoughts, he won't ever be a truant or disrespectful, or run with a gang.
- His English lessons are taught from *Graded Lessons in English*; his younger sisters use the McGuffy Reader, which has many delightful pictures.
- First published in 1836, the McGuffy Readers are now the basic schoolbook in 37 states, with more than two million copies sold each year.
- Little Rose loves to repeat the alphabet as she learned it from the first reader—from A is for axe, B is for box, cat, dog—all the way to Y is for yoke and Z is for zoo.

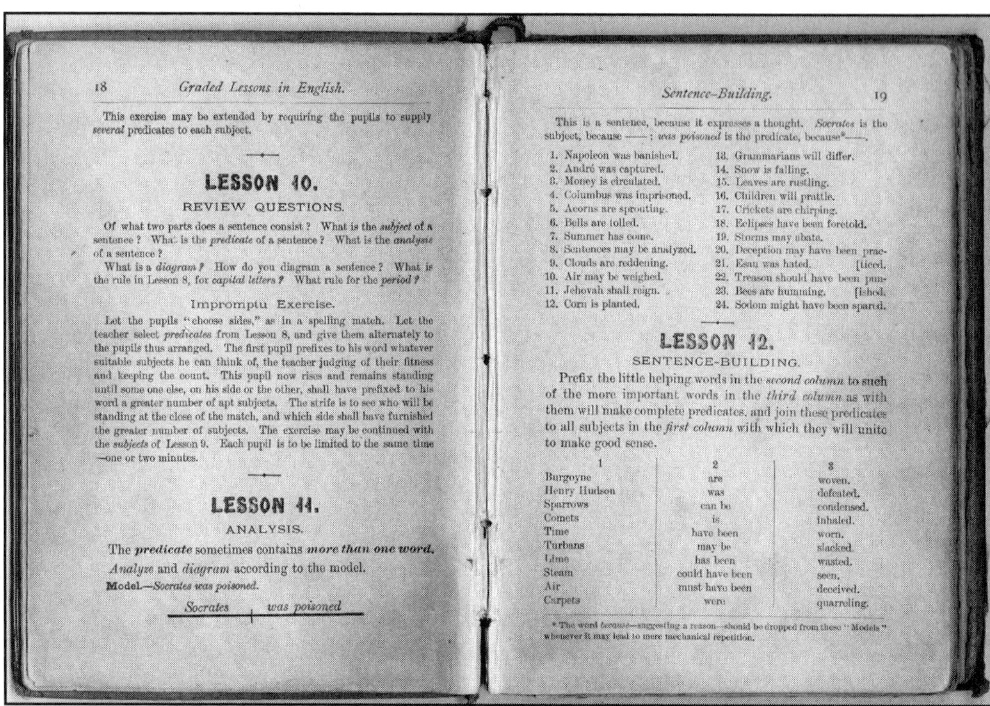

18 *Graded Lessons in English.*

This exercise may be extended by requiring the pupils to supply *several* predicates to each subject.

LESSON 10.

REVIEW QUESTIONS.

Of what two parts does a sentence consist? What is the *subject* of a sentence? What is the *predicate* of a sentence? What is the *analysis* of a sentence?

What is a *diagram?* How do you diagram a sentence? What is the rule in Lesson 8, for *capital letters?* What rule for the *period?*

Impromptu Exercise.

Let the pupils "choose sides," as in a spelling match. Let the teacher select *predicates* from Lesson 8, and give them alternately to the pupils thus arranged. The first pupil prefixes to his word whatever suitable subjects he can think of, the teacher judging of their fitness and keeping the count. This pupil now rises and remains standing until some one else, on his side or the other, shall have prefixed to his word a greater number of apt subjects. The strife is to see who will be standing at the close of the match, and which side shall have furnished the greater number of subjects. The exercise may be continued with the *subjects* of Lesson 9. Each pupil is to be limited to the same time —one or two minutes.

LESSON 11.

ANALYSIS.

The ***predicate*** sometimes contains ***more than one word.***

Analyze and *diagram* according to the model.

Model.—*Socrates was poisoned.*

Socrates | *was poisoned*

Sentence-Building. 19

This is a sentence, because it expresses a thought. *Socrates* is the subject, because ——; *was poisoned* is the predicate, because*——.

1. Napoleon was banished.
2. André was captured.
3. Money is circulated.
4. Columbus was imprisoned.
5. Acorns are sprouting.
6. Bells are tolled.
7. Summer has come.
8. Sentences may be analyzed.
9. Clouds are reddening.
10. Air may be weighed.
11. Jehovah shall reign.
12. Corn is planted.
13. Grammarians will differ.
14. Snow is falling.
15. Leaves are rustling.
16. Children will prattle.
17. Crickets are chirping.
18. Eclipses have been foretold.
19. Storms may abate.
20. Deception may have been practiced.
21. Esau was hated.
22. Treason should have been punished.
23. Bees are humming.
24. Sodom might have been spared.

LESSON 12.

SENTENCE-BUILDING.

Prefix the little helping words in the *second column* to such of the more important words in the *third column* as with them will make complete predicates, and join these predicates to all subjects in the *first column* with which they will unite to make good sense.

1	2	3
Burgoyne	are	woven.
Henry Hudson	was	defeated.
Sparrows	can be	condensed.
Comets	is	inhaled.
Time	have been	worn.
Turbans	may be	slacked.
Lime	has been	wasted.
Steam	could have been	seen.
Air	must have been	deceived.
Carpets	were	quarreling.

* The word *because*—suggesting a reason—should be dropped from these "Models" whenever it may lead to mere mechanical repetition.

"How Yap Got the Slipper," *The Knoxville Tennessee Chronicle*, March 22, 1882:

Molly was so happy playing with her doll baby that she had no time to notice Yap.

That little dog was jealous. He barked yap! yap! very loudly, and now sat looking at Molly out of the corners of his eyes, wondering what mischief he could get into, and so worry her into playing with him. Suddenly he trotted off, his mind quite made up as to what to do.

"Molly, Molly," called mamma.

"Mamma, don't call so loud," whispered Molly. "My little doll baby is sleeping."

"Molly," called mamma again, "make haste and see what Yap is after. I am sure he is in my room."

"Oh, what a bad doggie," sighed Molly, with her face in a pucker, but she put her baby down, and went to see after the dog.

There he was on the staircase, with mamma's slipper in his mouth. When he saw Molly he dropped the slipper, and ran past her, looking very much as if he was laughing.

Molly shook her finger at him, and laughing, too, picked up the slipper and carried it to mamma.

But Yap was too smart to be cheated out of his fun in that way. So he ran into the yard and began to bark furiously at Puss. Mrs. Puss cared little for his barking, and soon he stopped. Then Molly looked out of the window and said, "Yap and Puss look as if they were talking to each other, mamma." And so they were.

"Oh, you beautiful darling," said Molly, taking her baby against her, and hugging it tight; "Come and let us take a walk." Then she sat down to put on the doll's best clothes, and while she was very busy and almost ready for the walk, she thought she heard a sound, tip tip, on the staircase, and ran to see what was the matter.

"Mamma," she screamed, "come here—oh, do come!" and mamma hurried out to see Pussy bringing the slipper down to Yap, who was waiting at the foot of the stairs.

How they laughed when Pussy dropped the slipper under Yap's nose, and he trotted off in a grand way!

Molly ran after him, and found him ready to bury it with some other treasures at the end of the yard.

"Mamma," said Molly, when she returned to the house with the second slipper, "do you think dogs and cats can talk? Do."

And Molly thinks so to this day.

- The books are filled with pictures of boys with hoops, kites and skates; the girls happily play with dolls, sleds and jumping ropes.
- The children are also instructed in the French language.
- Girls are taught to sew, wash, iron and cook; sewing is taken in to support the institution and encourage the industrial education of the children.
- About half of the girls are in the sewing department, half in the mending department.
- Boys are trained in breadmaking, farm work and blacksmithing.
- Ora has found great joy in the bakery, but knows his destiny is to work on the docks where he can make enough money to buy back his childhood home.
- The asylum's chapel, fitted with seats of natural wood and decorated with walnut moldings, is capable of accommodating 250 people.
- The nuns insist that everyone attend chapel regularly; the boys are lectured on temperance and told to pledge that they will never use alcohol or tobacco.
- The cost of housing the children is generally $5 a month.

- The Catholic churches of the area provide additional support; $116 was provided last year for the sustenance of 15 Sisters, while an additional $423 went toward the upkeep of the 125 children.
- The dormitories are furnished with single iron beds and straw mattresses.
- In addition to sewing, Iris has been taught to iron, which she likes because it means she gets to be around the nuns; one Sister talks just like her mother.
- Under the mattress of her bed, in the only place that is private, she keeps her collection of trading cards which advertise Soapine soap products.
- She especially likes cards decorated with a gold rim depicting little girls like her.
- Mr. Anderson at the corner store, a man who knew her father and mother well, saves them for her, as a special reminder of home.
- On Sunday afternoons the Sisters read aloud to the orphans, often from the newspaper, which carries features just for children such as "How Yap Got the Slipper."
- Some nights, the three children climb to the roof of the asylum and look toward the Mississippi River; Ora then imagines the day he will be working there.
- Some nights he pretends he can see his father walking from his station at the bank to the Cotton Exchange as he did every day.
- When Ora turns 14 next year, he must leave the orphanage and support himself; the girls can stay until they are 16.
- He believes if he can buy back his parents' home one day by working on the cotton docks, he and his sisters can live there again and be happy.

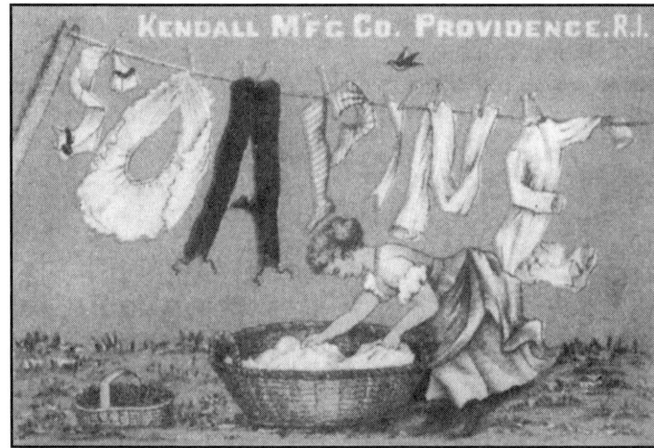

Iris keeps her collection of Soapine cards under the mattress of her bed.

Song sheet dedication for "Let Me Kiss Him for His Mother," concerning the Southern yellow fever epidemic of 1878:

During the ravages of the yellow fever in New Orleans, a young man from the state of Maine was attacked by that dreadful disease and soon died, with no relative to watch by his bedside, or soothe him with that sympathy which none but those of our own "dear kindred" can feel or manifest. He died among strangers, and was buried by them. When the funeral service was over, and the strange friends who ministered to him were about to close the coffin, an old lady who stood by stopped them and said, "Let me kiss him for his mother."

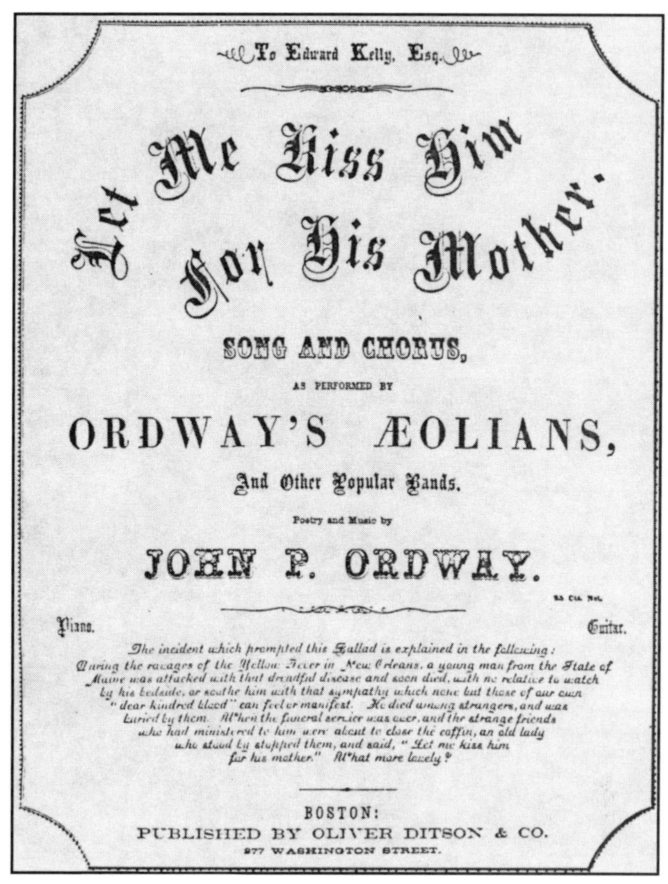

Life in the Community: Memphis, Tennessee

- Since the yellow fever epidemic four years ago, doctors throughout the city have been advocating better sanitation methods to prevent another outbreak.
- Even in the best of neighborhoods, the streets contain animal droppings, most homes have backyard privies, windows are unscreened against flies and mosquitoes and water is often contaminated.
- To improve conditions, the city has ordered that unconfined goats and hogs in the city be impounded.
- New regulations have been created concerning the dumping of dead animals and the proper ways to empty privies.
- An extensive sewer construction effort is now under way, with 30 miles of lines built in 1880 and 1881.
- Worldwide, more than $4.5 million was contributed to Southern cities hit by the fever; $1 million has been donated to Memphis alone, $45,000 of which came from New York City.
- Additional contributions have come from all across America, Europe, Asia, Australia and South America.
- The epidemic was also the last economic straw for the struggling city—Memphis is now bankrupt.
- When the yellow fever struck, over a million dollars in back taxes were due, most of it now uncollectible.

Ora's father worked in the cotton business along the city's docks.

- Currently, residents continue to leave the city, some through fear of a new outbreak of yellow fever, others simply fleeing a dying city that offers few opportunities.
- In addition, Memphis is battling a flood that has disrupted one of its key economic elements—the shipping of cotton on the Mississippi River.
- Since 1873 Memphis has operated a spot market for cotton through The Cotton Exchange; here, cotton is bought and sold on the spot in contrast to a futures market, in which cotton is purchased based on the expectation of its value.
- Ora's father, as a bank clerk, was heavily involved in the city's cotton business, often serving as middleman between buyer and seller, and handling the financial exchange of goods; the bank received a commission for its services.

Historical Snapshot 1882–1883

- An internal combustion engine powered by gasoline was invented by German engineer Gottlieb Daimler
- In Chicago, electric cable cars were installed, travelling 20 blocks and averaging a speed of less than two miles per hour
- Only two percent of New York homes had water connections
- The Andrew Jergens Company was founded to produce soaps, cosmetics and lotions
- Canadian Club whiskey was introduced by the Hiram Walker Distillery
- Van Camp Packing Company produced six million cans of pork and beans for shipment to Europe and U.S. markets
- Brooklyn Bridge opened
- *Ladies' Home Journal* began publication, with Cyrus H. K. Curtis as its publisher
- Thomas Edison invented the radio tube
- The first malted milk was produced in Racine, Wisconsin
- The first peapodder machine was installed in Owasco, New York, replacing 600 cannery workers
- The American Baseball Association was established
- The United States banned Chinese immigration for 10 years
- The three-mile limit for territorial waters was agreed upon at the Hague Convention
- Robert Lewis Stevenson's *Treasure Island* was first published
- Boxer John L. Sullivan defeated Paddy Ryan to win the heavyweight boxing crown
- The first skyscraper was built in Chicago, topping out at 10 stories
- Robert Koch described a method of preventative inoculation against anthrax

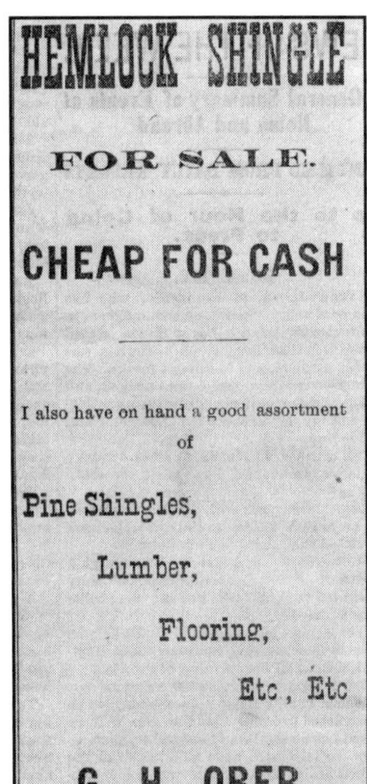

1882 Economic Profile

Selected Prices

Chair, Oak, Highback	$1.00
Detergent, Boraxine	$0.10
Diaper	$0.65
Knee Pants, Boy's	$0.75
Linoleum, Yard	$0.80
Molasses, Gallon	$0.10
Necktie, Man's	$0.10
Piano Lessons, 24	$8.00
Pork and Beans	$0.06
Railroad Fare, 107 Miles, Round-Trip	$1.00
Rice, Pound	$0.04
Rifle, Remington	$30.00
Song Sheet	$0.30
Suspenders	$0.05
Tooth Soap	$0.25

Recitations And How to Recite.

Social... Evening Entertainments.

Our new Pamphlet, "Recitations and How to Recite," consists of a large collection of Famous and Favorite Recitations, both for Adults and Children, and includes some Novelties in the way of Poems and Monologues sure to meet with the Approval of Everyone interested in Elocutionary Entertainments.

Unique Features are the Prefatory Remarks and Suggestions, by which the Reciter is Instructed not only comprehensively in the Art of Elocution, but Specially in whatever Number he Selects for Personal Recitation before an Audience. The Collection is an Eminently Satisfactory one from which to choose Recitations for the Parlor, for School Exhibitions or Church Entertainments, or for benefits for Individual or other Charitable Objects.

Every Scholar at School should have a Copy of "Recitations and How to Recite"; every Elocutionist, Professional or Amateur, will find it Most Useful; and no Library can Afford to omit it from the List of Up-To-Date Books of Recitations.

The Pamphlet, "Social Evening Entertainments," is issued in response to many letters asking for Suggestions for Entertainments that are Novel, Original, Amusing and Instructive, and *not* of the *Purely Conventional Types* requiring *Full Dress, Dancing* and *Luxurious Refreshments.* It meets Every Requirement of our Correspondents, and at the same time offers Pleasing Suggestions to those who desire to vary their Grand Entertainments by an occasional Simpler One. A few of the many Entertainments offered are: A Literary Charade Party, A Witch Party, A Ghost Ball, A Hallowe'en German, A Novel Card Party, A Midsummer Night's Entertainment, A Flower Party, A Fancy-Dress Kris Kringle Entertainment, The Bowers' Chrismas Tree, A St. Valentine's Masquerade Entertainment, etc., etc.

"Social Evening Entertainments" is just the thing for a Neighborhood Full of Party-Giving, Fun-Loving Young People.

PRICE of each of these Pamphlets, Twenty-Five Cents.

THE BUTTERICK PUBLISHING CO. (Limited), 7 to 17 West Thirteenth Street, New York.

"Wayside Gatherings," wise sayings from *The Yorkville Enquirer*, 1882:

- A cremated body leaves a residuum of only ounces; all besides is stored in the gaseous elements
- A deacon in Indiana has four boys, the youngest of whom is named Doxology, because he's the last of the hims
- The microscopists say that a mosquito has 22 teeth in the end of its bill, 11 above and the same number below
- It is said that of the total working expenses of the railroads, over 60 percent goes in various ways to the wage-earners
- If one's hands perspire easily when doing delicate work, they should be bathed in a few drops of cologne occasionally
- It would take 40 years for all the water in the great lakes to pour over Niagara at the rate of one million cubic feet a second
- The expressions "Hallelujah" and "Amen" are said to have been introduced into Christian worship by St. Jerome, about A.D. 390
- Instantaneous photography has revealed the fact that the former method of representing electricity as a fiery zigzag was entirely false
- The tensile strength of a wet rope is only one-third the strength of the rope when dry, while a rope saturated with grease or soap is weaker still

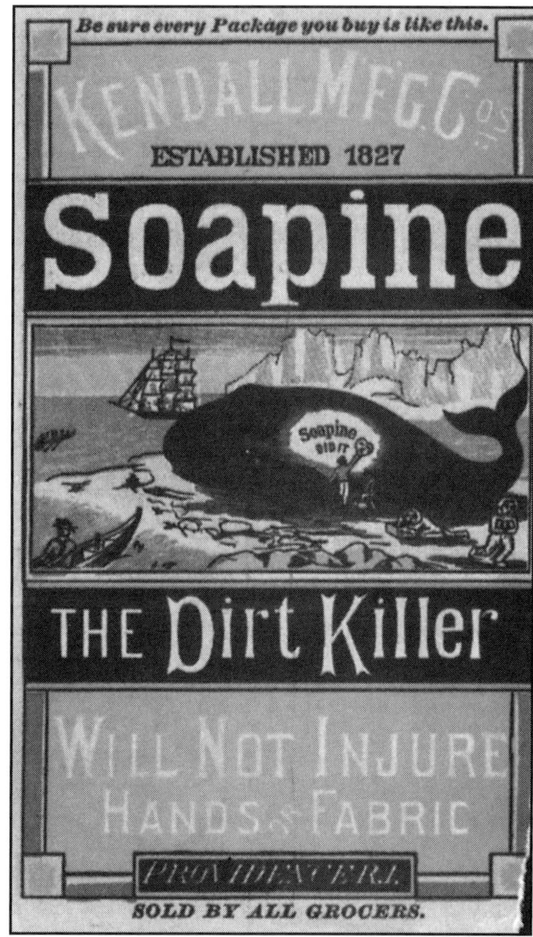

The Yellow Fever Epidemic

- During the summer of 1878, yellow fever spread upriver from New Orleans as far north as Gallipolis, Ohio, and as far east as Chattanooga, Tennessee, claiming nearly 20,000 victims.
- The economic loss was estimated at $200 million.
- Although Memphis, Tennessee, had experienced minor outbreaks of yellow fever in 1828 and 1848, until 1855 most Memphis residents believed they lived safely beyond the fever line.
- This proved untrue; 220 lives were lost in 1855, 550 in 1867, and 2,000 in 1873.
- Yellow fever first appeared in North America in 1668 in New York and hit Philadelphia the following year.
- In the eighteenth century, "yellow jack" struck Boston, Charleston and other cities on the Atlantic Coast; New Orleans suffered its first epidemic in 1796.
- By the nineteenth century, the pattern of epidemics shifted away from the Atlantic Coast to the Gulf Coast area, extending up the Mississippi River.
- In 1853 New Orleans lost almost 9,000 people.
- Yellow fever attacks the liver, kidneys and digestive tract, bringing extremely high temperatures and jaundice, the latter giving the disease its name.
- The symptoms are similar to those of other ailments such as dengue fever.
- The onset of yellow fever is marked by headache, backache, weakness, loss of appetite and increased thirst.

Letter by Julia Raine to her infant daughter during the yellow fever epidemic, October 8, 1878:

My Darling Little Daughter,

We are in the midst of death and desolation; today we are alive but tomorrow may find us dead—victims of the most terrible plagues that ever desolated any country. Your father and myself with you in our arms left Memphis on the fourteenth of August for this place which we then thought was a place of safety. Since our arrival hundreds upon hundreds have died in Memphis and now the disease has spread to every town upon the railroad—for miles and miles, the mortality, sickness and distress being almost too horrible to contemplate. Nothing seems to stop the progress of this Grim Destroyer. Frost is our only hope, which seems far in the distance as tonight is as warm as the middle of July. We are hemmed in on every side—there seems no escape. We have not the money to obtain trains to go far into the mountains and the railroad cars are as dangerous as can be. This is our position tonight, my Baby. Tomorrow we may be numbered with the many hundreds who have already departed—victims, victims of this loathsome disease.... I can see you now as you lie in your cradle fast asleep, unconscious, unheeding of the great storm that is lowering so darkly o'er our heads, and I pray that God will always keep you just as innocent as you are now of all dark things, and that that loving smile of yours at the Great Day be found among his chosen ones, an inheritor forever of the beautiful mansions above. Goodnight, my darling, darling Daughter. A Father and Mother's love and blessing are yours forever.

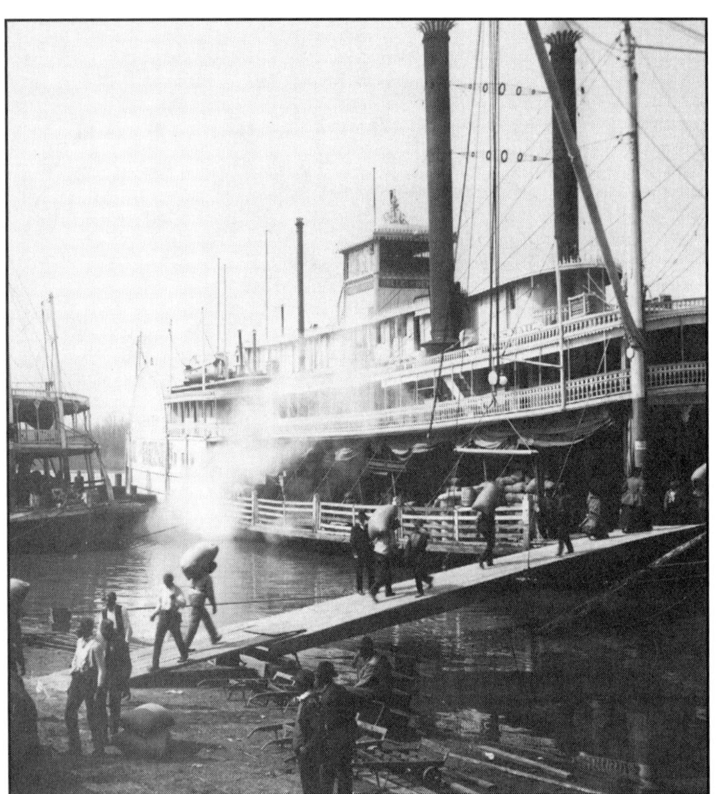

The docks are essential to the economy of Memphis.

- Restlessness, chills, fever and vomiting also occur during the initial stages.
- On the third day, the fever typically subsides and the pulse slows as the crisis is reached.
- Fortunate patients begin to recover; others relapse into kidney failure and begin the black vomiting.
- Following the fever of 1878, the medical community was divided on its treatment; many believed yellow fever to be non-contagious, while others demanded that victims be quarantined and stricter sanitation methods be employed.

1883 News Feature

"Dress at Home and Abroad, Letters to My Daughter," by Jenny June, *Demorest's Monthly Magazine*, April 1883:

Since the inventive genius of our first mother found in fig leaves a basis of operations, dress has served more or less to occupy the thoughts and attention of mankind, until now, when it is probably the most fruitful subject for tongue and pen that can be found in the domain of social and individual life.

Everyone writes, everyone talks, about dress. Women especially find in it their principal resource and occupation; nor do I see why they should be so severely blamed for it. When they have been taught better, and the world itself has learned to value the man or woman for themselves rather than the cost and cut of their garments, the subject of clothing, in the minds of women as well as men, will occupy its proper place.

At present, even the right-minded girl is perplexed by the many contradictory opinions she hears, and appalled by the severity of the condemnation passed upon those of her own sex who represent the most diverse habits and conditions. The "Girl of the Period," with her small airs and exaggerations of all the caprices of *la mode*, has been used *ad nauseam* for brainless paragraphists to sharpen their dull wits upon, while the same empty conceit would be just as ready to exercise itself upon women whose devotion to principle had induced them to sacrifice the natural love of appearing at their best to what they considered a worthier object.

Out of a dozen people, no two will be found to express the same ideas of the duty of women in regard to dress. With some, a high moral obligation is involved in always dressing "well," that is to say, fashionably. It is a woman's business to "look well," and she cannot look well, according to this code, unless her skirt, waist, train or sleeves are shortened or lengthened in exact accordance with the prevailing mode, and are of the color and material prescribed by fashion.

Others, equally zealous, ignore, or would have women ignore fashion altogether. With these, fashion is an unreasoning and always unreasonable tyrant, whose dictates no woman of sense would obey.

Few women have been accustomed to think enough to form opinions of their own, or rather to think that they ought to express opinions of their own; so the mass of them, even the women of experience, mothers, are swayed by the impressions made upon them by the

authors which they read, the circle in which they move, and the habits engendered by their social conditions and opportunities. Some mothers, compelled to pinching economy, will yet strain every nerve to exhibit their small, spindle-legged, flat-chested darlings in white kid boots, low bodice, and distended skirts at dancing school or party, while others, the wives of millionaires, will wardrobe their 20-year-old daughters to the most modest limits, preferring for them a Quaker-like severity to the modern indulgence in the senseless changes and extravagances of *les modes*.

The strength of fashion grows out of the common faculty of imitation—few can originate, but many can follow—and the majority just accept what they find, without an inquiry as to whether it is necessary or best for them to do so, until someone comes who discovers a better thing, and gradually persuades the world into its adoption.

1892 Profile

Upper Class

Seventeen-year-old Clarissa Strobel has found great freedom and friendship at Miss Porter's, a private girls' school in Farmington, Connecticut, known for developing women of character and intellect.

Life at Home

- For the past two years, Clarissa has been summering with her mother, attending Miss Porter's School, and thinking about her future.
- Her mother is often mystified by Clarissa's serious thoughts, mingled with a mischievous nature.
- Secretly she is happy that she doesn't know everything her daughter, the last of three, is up to.
- Clarissa and her mother summered in York Harbor, renting one of the Twin Dominick Cottages, where they were able to play tennis in bright sunshine, "while our friends on the ocean are in a damp fog," her mother liked to say.
- In addition to tennis, Clarissa has learned to swim, mastering various strokes with the help of a friend and a new book on swimming.
- Her father, a major industrialist, has earned millions since the end of the Civil War; her mother is talking about building a place of her own.
- Clarissa loves taking pictures, which everyone calls Kodaks; she believes that the modern camera is so easy to use, anyone can do it, but her mother seems reluctant to try.
- The film is loaded into the camera at the factory, and after taking 12 pictures, the photographer sends the entire camera straight to Kodak, where the pictures are developed,

Clarissa Strobel enjoys the companionship at Miss Porter's School.

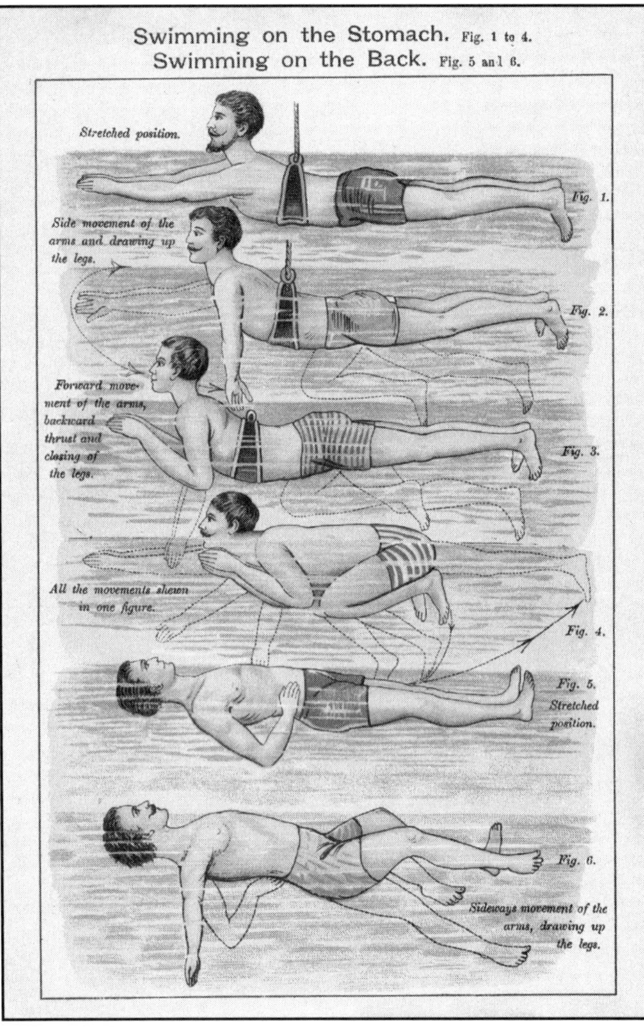

printed and returned by mail along with the camera, newly loaded with film.

- Recently, Clarissa took pictures of her friend Mary Sprague and was most upset that a young man who admires Mary took one of the Kodaks without her permission.
- She is not only angry about the theft, but also feels bad that the boy now has a picture of her friend, which is not proper in the least unless Mary gives her consent; it might give the wrong impression.
- In addition to her camera, one of Clarissa's prize possessions is a delicate doll with a bisque head known as Miss Elizabeth, which she dresses in a white silk gown.
- When she returned to Miss Porter's School last fall, the doll was carefully boxed and wrapped, but her head was broken during the trip; after several trips to Hartford, her father was able to locate a new head so that Miss Elizabeth could be put whole again.
- In Farmington, where fashion is always important, the girls are now wearing sweaters.
- Clarissa has discovered that sweaters can be found in red, white and black, but chiefly in dark blue.
- Most of the sweaters were originally made for small men, she believes, but at least one girl at school enjoys the dis-

Some Kodak Sense.

A wooden box with a pin hole at one end and a groove for holding a glass plate at the other will take a picture—after a fashion. With slight modifications this box becomes a "camera". It takes a fair *size* picture and sells for a small sum. **That's one kind of camera.**

Another kind has the Film Cartridge system by which it can be **Loaded in Daylight.** Has carefully tested lenses. We test all those used in our cameras and none but good lenses can pass our inspection. Has sets of three stops, improved rotary shutters, finders and tripod sockets, is well made and beautifully finished—**that's the Kodak Kind.**

Pocket Kodaks, Bullets and Bulls-Eyes

Have these features. Pocket Kodaks and Bullets use either film cartridges or glass plates. Other cameras do not have these features—we hold the patents.

Our booklet **"Cartridge Photography,"** *tells all about it.* **Postal gets it.**

EASTMAN KODAK CO.

Pocket Kodaks, Bullets, Bulls-Eyes. $5.00 to $15.00

Rochester, N. Y.

tinction of owning a sweater that was made to order and obtained through Harvard by a friend on the varsity team.

- It is dark red, with an extremely wide double collar, which is open with lacing a few inches from the throat.
- In addition to her many skills, Clarissa is an accomplished palmist, and is believed by many to be capable of telling fortunes.
- During visits home, on more than one occasion, she has been called upon during gatherings to tell someone's fortune and character by looking at the shapes, lines and suppleness of the person's hands, which she firmly believes are a window to the soul.

Spring Costumes.
Jasintha Waist. Orra Drapery.
Ernesta Jacket. (Back.)—Hermione Waist. Freda Drapery.

Life at School

- Clarissa's room at Miss Porter's School is decorated with great care; she is using a Spanish theme, dominated by Spanish shawls and pictures taken by a cousin while traveling in Spain.
- She hopes to include Spain on her traveling itinerary when she takes her grand tour of Europe next year.
- For most of last semester, she used an elaborate assortment of Japanese fans to spark up the room, but that grew boring.
- Her room is also filled with fresh flowers, which she buys almost daily.
- Flowers, she and her roommates agree, make life more pleasant and the room a joy.

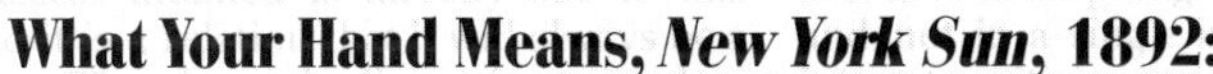

What Your Hand Means, *New York Sun*, 1892:

A soft hand, said Mr. Heron-Allen, in his lecture, indicated a fervent but fickle lover, while a hard hand denoted a long, enduring, though possibly smothering, love. A spatula hand, wherein the tips of the fingers are broad and flat, denoted inconstancy, desire for change and love of locomotion. It was found in jockeys and colonists. A hand with conically tipped fingers indicated inspiration, instinct, Bohemianism and generosity.

A hand with squarely built fingertips showed order and arrangement, particularly when the joints throughout were prominent. A scientific hand was irregular to a marked degree, the joints lumpy and highly developed—altogether a malformed conglomeration of knots and twists. This sort of hand is invariably small, while the analytic hand is large. The hand of the idealist is the most symmetrical of all and the most useless in every sense.

A supple hand indicates generosity. A hand, the fingers of which, when placed together and held to the light, exhibit transparency, and between which no rays of light penetrate, shows avarice or, in other words, closeness. Fingers submitted to the same test which will not fit alongside each other without openings and which are denser, indicate curiosity and loquacity. People with hands that are always white are egotistical and have no sympathy.

DEMOREST'S FAMILY MAGAZINE.

What Women are Doing.

Eleven women in Santa Clara, California, run and manage prune orchards.

Miss Amelia B. Edwards has promised not to write a book about America.

Mary J. Holmes, the novelist, received royalties on seventy-seven thousand copies of her books sold in 1889.

Miss Gertrude Magill, daughter of the President of Swarthmore College, is about to enter the Christian ministry.

Eight colored women recently served as pall-bearers at the funeral of a colored woman in Paris, Kentucky.

Mrs. Ida A. Harper is editor-in-chief of the largest daily paper published in Terre Haute, Indiana.

The Queen Regent of Spain can converse in Spanish, French, German, and English. She is fond of music and literature.

The Woman's Relief Corps, Department of Vermont, expended last year $1,011.95 in charity, assisting three hundred and fifteen old soldiers and families of soldiers.

Dr. Jessie B. Woodside, of Futleguhr, India, recently delivered an address in New York City, on "Medical Missionary Work Among the Women and Children of India."

Two hundred girls are now being educated in the medical schools of India. Madras has already supplied six fully qualified female doctors for the northern part of the country.

Miss Clara Conway, of Memphis, is offering a $300 prize to the pupil in her college preparatory department whose examination is the best. This is done with a view to encouraging girls to take the higher courses.

Rosa Bonheur is sixty-seven years old. She says she still has work enough in her mind to fill two lifetimes. She sold her latest picture for more than $10,000.

Dr. King, an American woman, occupies the somewhat enviable position of physician-in-ordinary to one of the most distinguished statesmen in China. Her practice in Shanghai is large and valuable, and some of her successful surgical operations have elicited the warmest praise from her brother physicians.

Miss Hankey, the first woman ever graduated at Columbia, is to be commemorated by a window in the college library. The design is an allegorical representation of her career as a scholar, cut short by death. There are three principal figures, those of Science, an angel, and a student.

A young colored woman, who had passed a good examination, received an appointment in the Bureau of Printing and Engraving, at Washington, D. C., being selected simply from the position of her name on the list. The young man to whose assistance she was assigned refusing to work with her, he was promptly discharged.

Mrs. George Kennan, wife of the author, is a thorough business woman, and devotes all her time to her husband's interests. Each day finds her at work re-copying manuscript, reading proofs, translating some Russian piece, or going over the receipts from his work and seeing to their investment or deposit.

Mrs. Annie Louise Cary Raymond has organized a ladies' quartette which she is now training for Sunday work in the hospitals of New York. Mrs. Raymond will sing in the quartette, and the music selected will be simple, familiar airs, and sung softly, so as not to unpleasantly affect nervous patients.

Maud Banks, the gifted daughter of Gen. Banks, is a beautiful and distinguished looking girl about twenty-six years of age, but she looks younger. During her residence abroad she studied various languages, and at one time, in Paris, was the only lady at an embassy reception who could speak modern Greek with some diplomats present.

Mrs. Marshall Field, wife of the Chicago dry-goods prince, employs a cultivated and intelligent young lady to dispense her charity. To her all applications for assistance are referred, and a personal investigation is made in every case: if worthy, immediate assistance of the necessary kind is afforded; if fraudulent, the particulars are entered in a book of frauds, for future reference.

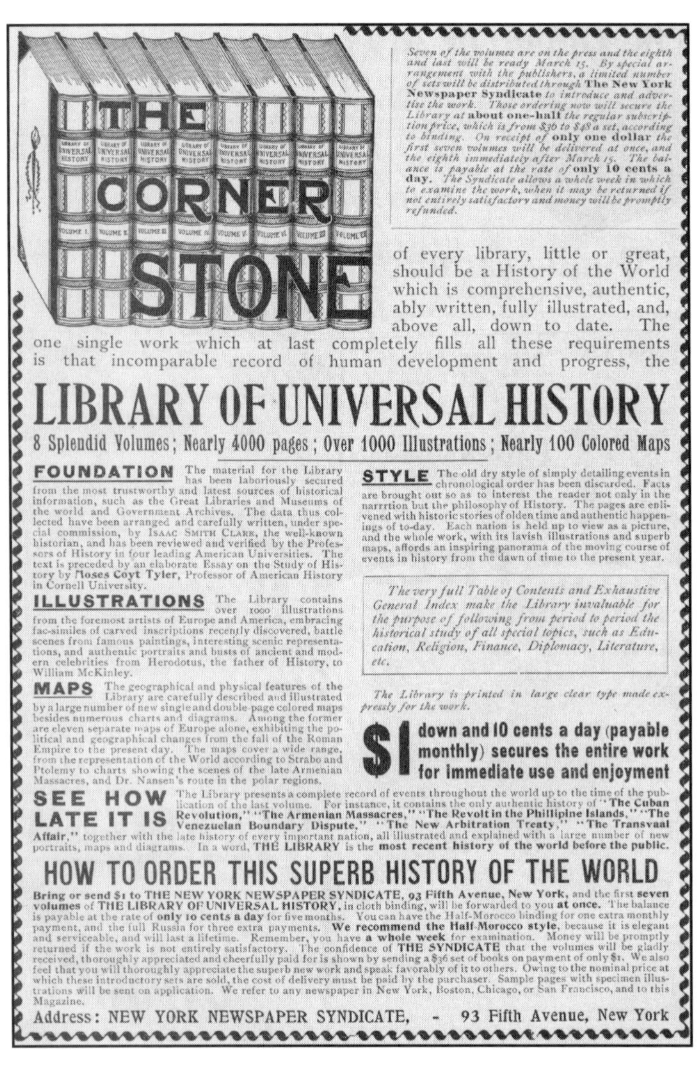

Clarissa is currently helping to select a new reading for her book club.

- Currently, she is attempting to help select a new reading for her book club, which she and several friends started last term, and which now consists of six members.
- Others are asking to join the group, but she believes that restricting the size of the club is important.
- For pleasure, they read *The Dancer's Jewels*, *The Witch of Prague* and *Laut Plario*.
- They are now reading *Villette*, but it will be finished soon.
- With the onset of winter snow in Connecticut, she and her friend Louise were able to go coasting, or sledding, on the hills near the school.
- Directly after dinner, they donned leggings and undertights, and went straight away to the stable for a sled.
- Unfortunately, only two were available, both rather high and long, which made them more suitable for gentle slopes than daunting hills; Clarissa, who had not been on a sled in seven years, was timid at first.
- Louise offered to take her along on her sled for the first trip, but she declined; she likes to learn quickly and by experience.
- When Louise prepared herself to go down the hill, Clarissa watched carefully as her friend gathered the rope in one hand, rested a hand on either side of the sled, then ran a step or two before throwing herself full-length on the clipper for the trip down the slope.
- She thought Louise's legs looked comical sticking up in the air as she zoomed down the hill.
- When Clarissa took her turn, she found it easy and exhilarating, discovering how quickly she could gain more speed, and left the slopes feeling quite proud of herself.
- Although her height is five feet, four inches, she is often considered small at Miss Porter's because her three roommates are all five feet, eight inches tall.
- She does not like to be compared to them, and sometimes gets so angry that she does not even like to hear compliments about her many good features, such as her voice.
- She loves pink ribbons, placing them on every possible article of clothing she owns; during a recent round of goodnight calls within the dormitory, she wore a very dainty pink jacket with long pink ribbons.
- She planned for the calls to take only a moment, but found her friend Lucy

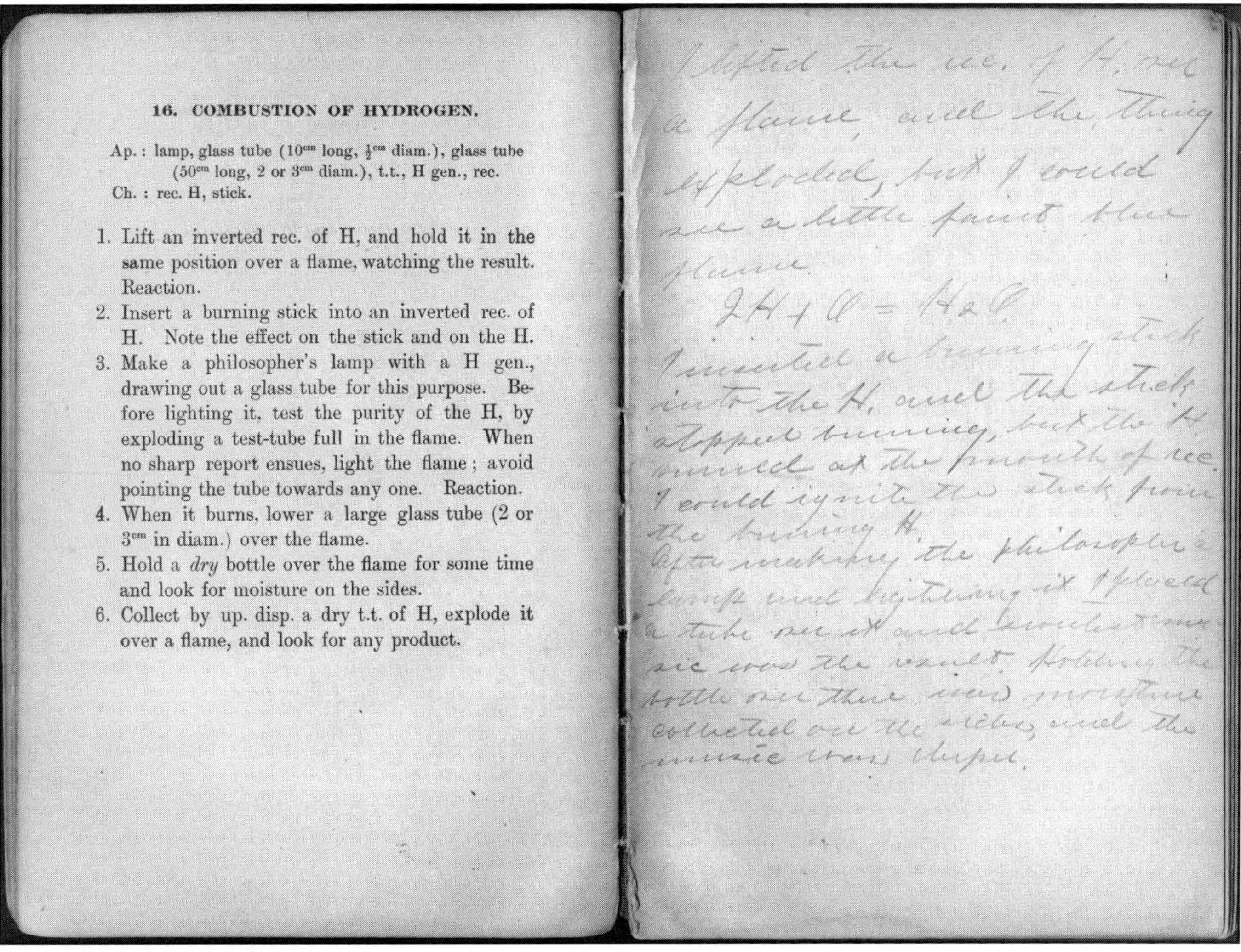

16. COMBUSTION OF HYDROGEN.

Ap. : lamp, glass tube (10^{cm} long, $\frac{1}{2}^{cm}$ diam.), glass tube (50^{cm} long, 2 or 3^{cm} diam.), t.t., H gen., rec.
Ch. : rec. H, stick.

1. Lift an inverted rec. of H, and hold it in the same position over a flame, watching the result. Reaction.
2. Insert a burning stick into an inverted rec. of H. Note the effect on the stick and on the H.
3. Make a philosopher's lamp with a H gen., drawing out a glass tube for this purpose. Before lighting it, test the purity of the H, by exploding a test-tube full in the flame. When no sharp report ensues, light the flame; avoid pointing the tube towards any one. Reaction.
4. When it burns, lower a large glass tube (2 or 3^{cm} in diam.) over the flame.
5. Hold a *dry* bottle over the flame for some time and look for moisture on the sides.
6. Collect by up. disp. a dry t.t. of H, explode it over a flame, and look for any product.

I lifted the rec. of H. over a flame, and the thing exploded, but I could see a little faint blue flame.
$2H + O = H_2O$.
I inserted a burning stick into the H. and the stick stopped burning, but the H. burned at the mouth of rec. I could ignite the stick from the burning H.
After making the philosopher's lamp and lightening it I placed a tube over it and [illegible] was the result. Holding the bottle over there was moisture collected on the sides, and the music was [illegible].

busily sewing and in need of help; Lucy's brother has written her asking for a gown to wear to a dance given at Williams College.

- He also asked for gloves, a fan and a handkerchief; both girls agree that he will look quite amusing in white muslin.
- Although Miss Sarah Porter is still involved with the school, occasionally conducting a class when a teacher falls ill, the day-to-day leadership of the school falls to Mrs. Mary E. Dow, Miss Porter's trusted associate of many years.
- In recent years, critics have said Miss Porter's School has paid small heed to the requirements of a modern education.
- Instead the school has endured by ensuring that its students carried away the ideals of the meaning of life, appreciation of culture, love for the place and the traditions that are found in a natural home.
- Approximately 125 girls attend the school, many of them daughters and relatives of the "ancients" or graduates who came before.
- Because of demand and limited space, admission is a privilege extended to few outside the immediate family circle.

The "AHS" in a Girls' School, John Chinaman Illustrates a Lecture, *New York Semi-Weekly Tribune*, June 18, 1892:

FARMINGTON, CONN., JUNE 18—Everyone knows about the prosperous school for young ladies which is so conspicuous a feature of the life of this New England village. At least everyone who knows of Farmington must know the school, for the school is Farmington. Without it, the village would be quiet and staid enough. Having it, the village possesses an animation and spirit which seems to fire even the woods and mountains with purpose. It lies back in the hills a few miles from the railroad station, secluded among great groves of elms and maples and oaks, where the bracing air bears no other freight than the perfumes of flowers and the songs and birds, and where nothing interferes with the spirit of education and refinement which this school has cultivated during half a century.

Its proprietress, Miss Porter, the sister of the former president of Yale College, is a progressive woman. She utilizes everything and everybody that can serve to improve the minds of her pupils or to throw light upon their studies. Perhaps nothing better illustrates this fact than the lectures on music which her musical director, Mr. Boekelman, has instituted. The last of these, delivered on Tuesday evening by Mr. H. E. Krohbiel, was on the subject of Chinese music, a theme that, at first sight, scarcely looks suggestive of much that could assist the study of the musical art in its present stage, and yet before he was done, the lecturer made it clear that the lowly Wings and Hos and Kiangs and Tiems of the Celestial Empire, the home of His August Mightiness, the Son of Heaven, know a good deal about music.

- Clarissa writes daily in her diary, taking care to detail her day so that later she can enjoy it all over again; several of her roommates envy her discipline and have discouraged her from working in her theme book so frequently.
- For her, writing is a task and a joy; her thoughts flow fluidly from her pen no matter how tired she might be, and the writing process itself seems to give her new energy and many personal insights.
- Recently a young woman entered Miss Porter's from Ohio, arriving at the school with her entire family.
- Clarissa realized quickly that the new girl was not accustomed to restraint and did not understand that her actions must be more circumspect in a town such as Farmington.
- The new girl is 16 and thinks men useful only as dancing partners, but make poor substitutes when feminine society can be found.
- She was quickly and clearly informed by the girls that men are the only enjoyment in life; a girl who could not boast of at least two or three admirers was considered a "stick" by her girlfriends and other men.

- On George Washington's birthday, Clarissa was assigned the task of writing about the celebration, but she has grown discouraged.
- Even though there is a flag in the hall downstairs and the homes in the village are decorated, she finds most people rather unpatriotic, or at least undemonstrative of their loyalty to the Stars and Stripes.
- As the spring grew warmer and the flowers bloomed, she and her roommates organized a daisy party; for an entire afternoon they picked fresh daisies in a field, decorated hats, ate lunch and even made a daisy banner with a large "92" crafted in flowers.

Life in the Community: Farmington, Connecticut

- Farmington, located only nine miles from the center of Hartford, is considered one of the mother towns of Connecticut because it formerly included land that has been divided into nine other towns.
- Land for the settlement was purchased from the Tunxis Indians in 1640; by 1645, enough people lived in the area to apply for incorporation and the name designation of Farmington.
- In the summer of 1841, the 37 freed slaves of the ship *Amistad* lived in the village, awaiting return to Africa.
- A school was maintained for them, and seats provided at church services, which they attended as a group.
- For most of the century, Farmington has been renowned for the quality of its private schools, including Miss Porter's.
- The village is also known for its historic sites, including the Elm Tree Inn, erected around a seventeenth-century house in 1865 by Philip Lewis, and the Congregational Church, built in 1771, with its tall steeple topped with an open-belfry spire.
- Until recently, a free library started by a public-spirited lady was housed in an old building on one end of town; two years ago it was consolidated with the village library.
- Efforts are under way to revitalize some parts of Farmington; running water has been introduced, sewers are being constructed, and highways have been graded and, in part, macadamized.
- When attempts were made to cut trees in the village to make way for a trolley line through Main Street, the people rose almost en masse and halted the project.

Current fashion emphasizes a tiny waist.

Historical Snapshot
1892

- To meet the needs of the automotive industry, an improved carburetor was invented
- Violence erupted during a steelworker's strike at Carnegie-Phipps Mill in Homestead, Pennsylvania
- The General Electric Company was created through a merger of Edison General Electric Company and Thomson-Houston Electric Company
- The $1 Ingersoll pocketwatch was introduced
- Chicago's first elevated railway went into operation to begin the famous Loop
- The first U.S. motorcar was produced in Springfield, Massachusetts, by Duryea Brothers
- The Hamilton Watch Company was founded
- The United States boasted 4,000 millionaires
- New York's 13-story Waldorf Hotel was under construction
- The first successful gasoline tractor was produced by a farmer in Waterloo, Iowa
- Thousands of Kansas farmers were bankrupted by tight money conditions
- The first full-service advertising agency was established in New York City
- "Gentleman Jim" Corbett defeated John L. Sullivan for the heavyweight boxing title
- William Ewart Gladstone became prime minister of Great Britain, Prince Ito was made premier of Japan, and Grover Cleveland was elected president of the United States
- America's first automatic telephone switchboard was introduced

1892 Economic Profile

Selected Prices

Aquarium Ticket $0.50
Buggy Carriage $135.00
Cape, Woman's $8.25
Cross-Stitch Book $0.50
Dental Extraction $0.25
Dress Shield $0.25
Extract of Beef $0.10
Hair Curler $1.00
Japanese Fan $0.02
Oil Heater $12.00
Piano Lessons, 24 . . . . $8.00
Scarf Pins, Silver $0.15
Sleeve Buttons, Ivory and
Pearl, Pair $3.00
Sugar, Pound $0.04
Writing Paper, Linen,
72 Sheets and Envelopes $0.75

On receipt of ten cents we will mail a trial bottle containing sufficient **FLUID BEEF** to make a quart of delicious soup, or enough for six persons. Our handsome pamphlet, "A FEW FINE SOUPS," mailed to any address upon application. Your grocer either has our goods, or will get them for you.

THE NUTRIMENT COMPANY,
Chicago, Ill.

Proper Food.

Unnatural food and drink gradually undermine the stomach and the nervous system, and somewhere in the body the trouble shows, which drugs will not heal. It may be dyspepsia, constipation, heart trouble, kidney complaint or lung trouble, or it may show in bad blood, tumors, piles, weak eyes, etc.; these are caused by stomach and nervous disorder, and they cannot exist when stomach and nerves work properly.

Coffee is a polished villain that has undermined millions of systems and brought no end of misery and suffering. Hundreds of thousands of stomachs have been made well and healthy after years of distress when coffee was abandoned and **POSTUM CEREAL FOOD COFFEE** used at meals. If coffee is heavy on your stomach, try POSTUM.

See that you get POSTUM, and only POSTUM. Grocers sell it at

. . . . . 15 AND 25 CENTS A PACKAGE . . . . .

POSTUM CEREAL CO., Limited,

BATTLE CREEK, MICH.

Miss Porter's School fosters an appreciation of culture as well as skill in the arts of the home.

Miss Porter's School

- Miss Porter's was founded in the summer of 1842 when Sarah Porter borrowed $32.94 from her family, added some funds of her own, and set about to equip a school.
- Initially she bought nine desks and chairs, a bench, a blackboard, a bowl, two pails and some carpet.
- The first classroom was in rented rooms over a store on the main street of Farmington, Connecticut.
- By the end of her first year, she had 18 pupils.
- By the 1850s the school was attracting students from Chicago and San Francisco, as well as from Natchez, Mississippi.
- Unlike many seminaries for young ladies, the curriculum at Miss Porter's School did not confine itself to the ladylike accomplishments of the times such as embroidery, filigree and quill work.
- Miss Porter's students learned the sewing arts as part of a total education focused on becoming good Christians, good wives and good mothers.
- The daughter of a minister and sister of the president of Yale, Miss Porter not only expected her students to learn their lessons, but to understand what they read and acquaint themselves with higher culture.
- Lessons included history, art history, language and literature, studied as guides to understanding people and their civilizations.
- Students housed at the school slept two to a bed and four to a room; girls were reprimanded for waving at passing boys, and in the spring of 1860, two students were expelled for flirting.
- By the 1870s, Miss Porter's had become a favorite destination of the daughters of a new class of rich industrialists, bankers and entrepreneurs who emerged after the Civil War.
- In 1874 alone, booming Chicago sent to the school the daughters of merchant Samuel B. Kimball, lawyer Henry S. Monroe and railroad executives Perry Smith and James M. Walker.

Advertisement:

Miss Sarah Porter will reopen a School for Young Ladies in the village of Farmington, on the first of May next. There will be three terms in a year of 14 weeks each. The course of instruction will comprehend the branches usually taught in seminaries for young ladies, including the Latin, French and German languages. The number of pupils will be limited, that each will be under the personal instruction of Miss Porter.

The price of tuition will be $10.00 for pupils over 12 years of age, and $5.00 for those under that age. Instruction on the piano will be furnished to such as desire it at an extra charge.

Board may be obtained in the village on moderate terms. A few pupils can be received as boarders with the principal, and be under her constant supervision and care. To such the charge for board and tuition will be $55 a term, one half payable in advance, and the remainder at the end of the term.

Farmington, Connecticut

- Despite the excesses of the gilded age, Miss Porter's continued to teach responsibility, simplicity and kindness.
- Sarah Porter saw the wealth enjoyed by some of her students as a temptation, but as an opportunity for virtue as well.

Expenses of Isabella Goodrich, Miss Porter's student, 1892

October 9

Rocking Chair	$8.50
Mirror	3.00
Cocoa	0.40
Beef Extract	0.45

October 11

Flowers	0.25
Flowers	1.50

October 15 and 16

Tintypes	1.00

October 17

Flowers	1.05
Flowers	1.50
Soda Water	0.15
Flowers	0.50

October 31

Flowers, Momma & Mrs. D	4.50
Estate	1.06
Chocolate	0.30
Maple Sugar	0.10
Fee, Katie	0.50
Fee, Ellen	2.00
Fancy Dress, Becky Sharp	5.00
Washing	2.00
Stamps	0.50
Special Delivery Stamp	0.10

Miss Porter's School is located on a tree-lined street in Farmington Connecticut.

- She also kept the religious life of the girls structured, including frequent prayers and Sundays composed of Bible lessons as well as both morning and after-dinner church services.
- Sunday evenings, students were expected to discuss the subjects of that day's sermons.
- By the 1890s, the curriculum included natural philosophy composed of physics, chemistry and geometry; political economy which included French, German and Latin; and the mental philosophy courses, incorporating psychology.
- Many girls continued their education after leaving Miss Porter's by traveling through England and the European continent; travel was considered essential preparation for young women before they married and took their place in society.
- To further assist her students, Sarah Porter often read aloud, chose girls to read aloud, and hired scholars to read Shakespeare and give elocution lessons.
- The school's reputation also attracted famous authors of the times such as Mark Twain, Charles Dudley Warner and Harriet Beecher Stowe.

Diary of Isabella Goodrich, a student at Miss Porter's School

January 14, 1891:

Last night Ellen and Mrs. Rice gave a party. They asked me—soon after dinner—and I accepted their invitation with glee. At half past six the "Black Maria" was to come for us, for the walking was very bad.

I got downstairs at about 20 minutes before seven, and was horrified to see not carriage nor girls. Learning the party had gone without me, I was about to retrace my steps, when two other girls in their wraps came leaping downstairs, and ran to the door. They, too, were disappointed. They, too, had been left behind. Matters were looking higher, now that I was not the only one late. Just then Louise came, saying, "It does not take them a long time to go and return from the inn."

"What! Are we not late?"

"Oh, no! There are to be two loads. You are just on time."

February 4, 1892:

Last night, after lights out, as I came back to my room after my goodnight visits, an inspiration seized me—an inspiration for a valentine. It was very dark in the room, and I fumbled about among some loose papers on the table and finally wrote down enough of my verse to recall the rest the next morning. Then I scrambled into bed. When I got up to dress for breakfast, I glanced over my verse and found, to my horror, that I had written it on a pamphlet, and not a block of paper, as I had intended. The treatise was one of several deep asides that Adela has, and I found I had scribbled a valentine on Realism!

February 9, 1892:

We were discussing Professor Ladd at the dinner table, and Miss Hawley, who knew him, was giving us some account of his manner when out of the lecture room. She spoke of his low idea of woman's intellectual abilities. It seemed to be a judgement on him that he should have two stupid sons, good enough in their way, but by no means like their brilliant father, while his only daughter is wonderfully bright and clever with good reasoning power. Miss Hawley spoke of his wife, saying she was a charming woman to meet in society and yet was an intelligent companion for her husband.

February 17, 1892:

How it irritates when a person answers, "Don't know." When I get it, I am tempted to answer: "You should then," but it would be useless. A girl that can answer merely "Don't know" to a civil and opportune question, must be singularly lacking in interest in you and your affairs, and, may say, singularly absorbed in her own.

She must be, too, of a disagreeable, rather snarlish and haughty temper, and with all have a grudge against her English language. Else she would scarcely abbreviate her remarks to four words, "I do not know."

March 4, 1892:

What a thing it must be to be popular. That word has always had an affirmative ring to me. I dare say it's my innate "lowness" of nature that makes me long for the approval of the multitude.

March 7, 1892:

Adela says it makes her uneasy to see me scribbling away every night before I go to bed; she thinks this writing is doing me more harm than good. I wonder if she's right, and I don't know. At all events it may amuse me, in the future, to read this over, and from what older people are forever telling us, we shall have need of all the amusements we can get when we are old and perhaps wise.

March 12, 1892:

Mrs. Donn talked to us the other night about our responsibility as "old girls" and about the influence we must exercise, whether we wish or not, so that we should see to it that we stand for law and order, against lawless noisiness and rule-breaking. She was very sweet in her tactful fibbing of things, and the girls resolved to reform that night. Not a creature shined from her room after the bell rang. The next day there was a subdued air about the school, and no girl thumped "upstairs" that night; however, the reversed goodness began to wear off. After lights out, one double-gowned figure after another stole out into the dimly lighted hall, each very surprised to see the other, but glad to find herself not the only malefactor. But the halls are still quiet.

1896 News Feature

"Kindergarten Papers," by Mrs. Sara Miller Kirby, *The Delineator, A Journal of Fashion, Culture and Fine Arts*, April 1896:

There should be a general outline, though not a castiron plan, for the year's work in the kindergarten. It should be made out, if possible, before the school year begins after the kindergartner has informed herself as to the main points of each subject, collected materials, and learned the songs and games to be used. It is an excellent plan for the mother or kindergartner to keep a notebook, jotting down subjects as they come to her from outside reading or as they arise from the children's conversations and questionings. The season of the year and the climate, with their characteristics, products and occupations, must necessarily be considered when making plans. Do not forget that the kindergarten is for the child and not the child for the kindergarten. It is sometimes wise for the kindergartner to drop her own preconceived plan for the time being and take up the subject suggested by the child. . . .

For Autumn

Preparations for the cold.
Fall fruits and nuts. Summer fruits, how preserved.
Exercises with the senses in this connection.
Jack Frost and his work.
Preparations on the part of people, indoors and out-of-doors.
Farmer, miner, miller, baker.
Preparation by animals, as squirrels, etc. Migration of birds.
Preparation of plants, buds formed for following year, falling leaves, etc.
Idea of the world as a ball.
Ideas of place, direction, distance, time; record for the weather commenced.
Ideas of weight, form and color commenced.
Develop ideas of animal, mineral and vegetable substances.
Thanksgiving. Patriotism. Loving and giving.
Mother-play songs of bird's nest and flower basket. . . .

For Winter

Christmas.

Winter clothing. Vegetable substances used for clothing, as straw, cotton, hemp, flax, India rubber. Animal substances used for clothing, as silk, fur, wool, leather and hair.

Animal and vegetable substances used in manufacturing.

Food: Plants, fruits, etc., used for food; animal substances used for food.

Substances used for fuel.

Occupations: Carpenter, shoemaker, weaver, tailor.

Transportation: Sledges, wheelbarrows, wagons, streetcars, railroads, ships. . . .

Things transported. Condiments and fruits brought from other countries.

Exercises for the senses as to these eatables.

Moon and stars.

Other countries compared with the home country: difference in living, clothing, occupation and climate.

Jane Anderson's "Seven Little Sisters Who Live in the Round Ball That Floats in the Air," would prove excellent for this work. . . .

For Spring

Wind and its work for plants. Commence the germination of seeds. Bursting of buds, sap flowing, manufacture of maple sugar.

Egg and chicken, cocoon and butterfly.

Sunshine and its work (heat and light).

Coming of birds, building of nests. Young animals. New life.

Occupations: Farmer, blacksmith, gardener, housecleaning.

Color, by spectrum and color top. . . .

Sample Lessons: Grass Mowing

Coming on to summer, we study that wonderful food—milk—from Froebel's Mother-play song, "Grass Mowing." To fulfill the law of unity we show first a bunch of grass, milk, butter and a child's picture. Collect pictures of meadows, farmhouses, and haying and dairying utensils with songs and games related to them. Represent, first by gift and occupation, the meadow with the grass growing, the farmer cutting and curing hay, the children playing nearby at making daisy chains. Next, show the farmyard with barn, hay mow, cow stable and water trough; then, milking, the milking pail, the milk pan, the cooler and skimming; then, the child drinking milk; last, churning and preparing the butter. With rolls from the baker we now have bread, butter and milk for the child's supper. The songs are: "All's Gone," "Grass Mowing," "The Farmyard Gate" and "Alice's Supper."

1898 Profile

Working Class

Gwen Shanklin, a 16-year-old Welsh girl, works as a maid for a wealthy Philadelphia family that is trying hard to copy many of the manners, patterns and routines of the English.

Life at Home

- Originally from Bethesda, Wales, a region known for the quality of its quarries, Gwen Shanklin loves working in America, where there is plenty of food to eat and the homes are heated.
- In Wales, her father often treated her like a servant, demanding that she care for him, especially after her mother died when she was 13 years old.
- Finally, convinced that she was too lazy to be of any use to him, he sent her to London when she was 14, where she was employed as a servant girl to a wealthy family.
- In London she learned the rules of a grand house and how to handle the needs of a large crowd.
- Answering a newspaper advertisement, she came to Philadelphia a year ago to escape the dampness of London for the promise of America.
- She found Philadelphia to have a pervasive brownness, thanks to innumerable furnaces burning the soft coal of Pennsylvania.
- In this wealthy American household, being a child is paradise: her employer's five daughters seem to get whatever they ask for from their father, Mr. Pfannebake—from new dresses to a carriage ride.
- Permission for the girls to travel or attend social functions and parties, however, is left entirely to Mrs. Pfannebake.

Gwen Shanklin loves working in America.

Mr. Pfannebake loves to indulge his five daughters.

- When Gwen first took the job, she found the smells of the kitchen so incredible, she felt she could eat the air.
- Like most large Philadelphia homes, this house is constructed of dark red brick with white marble steps, and accented with white mantels and shutters on the first floor and green on the second.
- Even though the house is massive, comprising 24 bedrooms, she now feels comfortable, as long as she sticks to a routine.
- Like many homes of wealthy Philadelphians, it is the interior quality, not the exterior appearance of the house, that is most prized.
- The house contains many beautiful objects—many made in England; a matching pair of china doorstops in the main living room particularly fascinates Gwen.
- One doorstop features a cat dressed as a woman holding a parasol and wearing a fancy hat with a red band tied under the chin and a frilly blue dress and apron; the second doorstop depicts a dog dressed as a man carrying a walking stick in one paw and wearing a tan suit with green waistcoat, watch chain and gold buttons, and sporting a tall hat on his head.
- Seeing them in the early morning light always gives Gwen a smile.
- The head of the household, Mr. Pfannebake, is very different from her father; when possible and appropriate, she watches him closely.
- He is a rich, staunch Republican, and not nearly so mean as the newspapers report.
- In addition, he is German and a mill owner, both characteristics about which she has been warned, yet he is kind to his daughters and does not molest the servants.
- The second daughter, Louise, who is the same age as Gwen, owns a beautiful music box bearing 12 musicians who dance along with the music while they stroke the violin, bang the drum or blow a horn.

Before coming to America, Gwen worked for a family in London.

- Gwen loves to watch the musicians dance to the music; it is so romantic!
- Each of the daughters is different: Louise is a bookworm, and her father loves to brag that her memory is colossal and her brains are the best in the family; he tells everyone that she takes after him.
- The third daughter has the style in the family; she cares about clothes, and her sashes and hair ribbons are always tied better and are more chic than those of her sisters.
- The youngest child goes from mother to father to sisters until she gets what she wants; Gwen thinks she is terribly spoiled, but says nothing, even to the other servants, some of whom can be terrible gossips.

Life at Work

- Having worked for a time in London, Gwen is grateful that American houses are well-heated, and has few regrets about leaving the cold-water discipline of the English upper classes.
- The most difficult part of her 17-hour day is the morning.
- As a maid, her workday begins at 5:30 a.m., when she must clean the kitchen floors and heat water.
- By 6:30 a.m. she wakes the more senior staff and helps lay and relight the fires in the 12 fireplaces located throughout the house.

"Household Helps and New Ideas," *Ladies' Home Journal*, April 1898:

The deep cutting in fine glass requires special care to keep it clean and brilliant. A brush is now sold for polishing and drying cut glass. It is made of the finest Russian bristles and does the work speedily and well.

- Afterward, she helps start the other servants' breakfast and deliver breakfast to the upstairs maid, who works in the nursery.
- At 7:30 a.m., dressed in a print dress, she goes upstairs with jugs of fresh water and tea trays to wake the five girls; at the same time, she takes away the chamber pots and empties the contents that have accumulated during the night.
- The chamber pots will be emptied and replaced three or four times during the day; in addition, some of the senior servants have their own chamber pots, but most relieve themselves at an outhouse located 28 steps from the back kitchen.
- Currently, the only flushing water closet in the house is off the master's bedroom.
- The servants' breakfast is at 7:45 a.m.
- Three days a week, the woman of the house insists that everyone, including servants, participate in morning prayer services in the parlor, followed by the family breakfast and then cleanup.
- At noon the servants eat lunch, and at 1 p.m. Gwen helps to serve lunch, having changed into a black dress with white lace cap and white apron.
- She makes the dresses herself and always ensures they are clean and well-starched.
- By 2:30 lunch ends and she often takes a nap before the 4:30 p.m. tea time for the household.
- Before Mrs. Pfannebake toured England, the family rarely observed afternoon tea; now, convinced that high tea is the epitome of civilization, she insists that all work cease at 4:30 p.m. for tea.
- By 6 p.m. Gwen helps set the banquet table for dinner and helps in the kitchen until 7 p.m., when the meal begins.
- As part of her preparation for dinner, she and one other maid must arrange the table linen, which is very heavy and beautifully monogrammed.
- At each plate, she carefully lays oversized table napkins that measure 30 inches square; afterward she helps serve or assist in the kitchen until the meal ends.
- Most nights the family dresses formally for the multicourse dinner.
- Once it is over, cleanup normally takes until 9 p.m., when she and the rest of the servants eat dinner before retiring at 10 p.m.
- She is frequently delighted by the foods available to the servants, once the household has been served.
- She has dined often on a combination of chicken salad and fried oysters (one of Mr. Pfannebake's favorites), oyster croquettes, fresh shad, soft-shell crabs, Philadelphia ice cream, cream cheese, terrapin and snapper soup.
- European wines are often served with dinner, but are rarely included in the servants' meals.
- Despite all the good food, she is cautious about what she eats.
- She knows for a fact that swallowing grape seeds will cause appendicitis, which actually happened to a friend of hers.

> The things that truly last when men and times have passed, they are all in Pennsylvania this morning!
>
> —Rudyard Kipling

"Bacteria, the Progress of Science," by Bertha Gerneaux Davis, *The Cosmopolitan*, March 1897:

Zoologists and botanists alike laid claim to the bacteria until comparatively recent years, but the zoologists were forced to yield to their botanical brethren, and the curious little organisms popularly known as "microbes" are now classified, almost without question, among the simplest of the plant forms, and as near relatives of algae. The common form of bacteria is rod-shaped, though others are spiral, spherical and egg-shaped. In size they vary considerably. Some of the larger forms are 20/25,000 of an inch in length, while one of the smallest is about 1/50,000 of an inch. To give a rather more definite idea of the minuteness of some of these organisms, imagine 1,500 placed end to end, hardly reaching across a pinhead. Extremely powerful lenses must consequently be brought to bear upon them before they will yield up the secret of their life history and workings; and, as the little bodies are almost transparent, the microscopist is obliged to stain them with some dye to render them anything but shadowy and indistinct.

- Some foods are restricted in the house; Mrs. Pfannebake has banned all soft drinks, declaring them to be "common" —despite the pleas of her daughters.
- Until recently, maids had no days off; now Gwen is allowed most Sunday afternoons free unless guests are expected at the home.
- Her biggest breaks take place in the summer when the family takes the rail to their country estate a few miles outside the city.

A stereoscopic view of fine dining in an affluent household.

Every guest is offered a piece of butterscotch candy purchased in England.

- While the family is away, they only need 10 servants, so Gwen takes on different duties such as washing the walk each Saturday, polishing silver or receiving supplies for the kitchen.
- At these times she is allowed to take long walks, since the demands of the house are fewer.
- On one such trip, she discovered Fairmount Park, which looks like a 12-mile-long valley in the center of the city.
- While out, she often buys shaved ice at the numerous apothecary stores and goes window-shopping at the many fine stores.
- While on a recent trip, a handsome young man spoke to her favorably; she often thinks about that encounter, but has not seen him since, even though she often walks the same route.
- For most of her life, Gwen has worn her hair free around her shoulders; upon employment she was instructed always to have her hair braided while at work.
- Another maid, who came from Scotland, helped her fix her hair in braids and pin them to the back of her head.
- Recently, she decided to have her hair cut short in preparation for a studio picture of herself.
- She loves the new look, and wants to send the picture home to show everyone that she is doing well.
- The madam of the house insists that the household follows English customs, and for that reason only hires servants from the Isles.
- Following Mrs. Pfannebake's most recent trip to Britain, the madam's friends whispered, "She is more English than the English."

Letter written by Lafcadio Hearn

Philadelphia is a city very peculiar, isolated by custom, antique, but having a good, solid morality, and much peace. It has its own dry, drab newspapers which are not like any other newspapers in the world, and contain nothing not immediately concerning Philadelphia. Consequently, no echo from New York enters here—not any from anywhere else.... But it's the best old city in the whole world all the same.

"Risks of Modern Life," *The Youth's Companion*, February 17, 1898:

Most of the appliances of modern civilization bring risks as well as advantages. The people who lived a hundred years ago could not travel so rapidly nor communicate with each other across great distances so conveniently as we do; but on the other hand, they were strangers to some perils which are familiar nowadays.

Their journeys were slow and serious affairs; but they were in no danger of being blown up on a steamboat, or tumbled over a railway embankment, or even of being run over by a trolley car or a "scorching" wheelman. Their houses were not lighted by electricity or by gas; but they were not burned up by reason of badly insulated wires or asphyxiated in their beds. They knew nothing of 15-story buildings, but they also knew nothing of elevator accidents.

Nevertheless, it is doubtful if more lives are lost by accident in travel, in proportion to the number of people travelling, than was the case a century ago.

Hundreds of people travel by water now than did so then; but ocean travel has been made relatively more safe, as well as more swift and comfortable, by modern appliances. There are still possibilities of collision or of striking a reef in a fog, but it almost never happens that a modern, seaworthy vessel founders through stress of weather. One steamship company which has sent its steamers back and forth across the Atlantic for more than 50 years is able to boast that it has never lost the life of a passenger in the service.

As to the railways, in 1896, 181 passengers were killed on the railways of the United States, and nearly 2,900 were injured. When these figures are compared with the amount of passenger traffic, it appears that the railways carried nearly three million passengers for every one who was killed and about 180,000 passengers for every passenger injured.

A famous humorist once compared the number of people killed in railway accidents with the number dying in their beds, and reached the conclusion that it was several thousand times more risky to lie in bed than to travel on a railway. It was a playful exaggeration; but it is true that, if modern discovery and invention have resulted in new hazards to human life, they have also supplied new safeguards and preventives.

- Her fascination with England does not end with work routines and observing afternoon tea; she also loves to serve English foods.
- It is now obligatory that every guest be offered a piece of Callard & Bowser's Butter-Scotch Candy out of the tin box she bought in England.
- The box features a hen and her chicks, and Gwen has taken great care never to mention that normally in Britain, this particular design is reserved for the nursery or the sick-room, nor does she snicker when the madam talks about the aristocracy of Philadelphia, meaning the very rich—not the titled, as in Europe.
- Coffee comes to the house in large straw and canvas sacks, one sack of mocha, the other of Java, a blend being made according to quarter measure, after which the beans are parched in the kitchen, one panful at a time.
- The beans are then ground in a hand coffee mill, a day's supply at a grinding.
- Recently, a merchant brought around a mandarin orange, which he called "the kid glove orange" because it could be peeled without removing one's gloves.

"Fruits as Foods and Fruits as Poisons," by S. T. Rorer, *Ladies' Home Journal*, June 1898:

Fruits Which I Allow on My Table

It may be interesting to know that the fruits allowed on my table are fresh figs, dried ones carefully cooked, guavas canned without sugar, guava jelly, orange marmalade made by special home recipe, dates both raw and cooked with almonds, persimmons, bananas cooked, and an occasional dish of prunes with the skins removed, blackberries and dewberries, slightly cooked, strained and made into flummery. The objection to the latter [sic] fruit, however, is the addition of starch and sugar, which is prone to fermentation. All fruits, whether cooked or raw, should be used without sugar. It must be remembered that sugar in no way neutralizes an acid; for this an alkali must be used. Sugar sprinkled over an acid fruit masks the objectionable and severe acid until it slips by the "guard-keeper," the palate. Once in the stomach, however, it regains its own position and grants the same to the irritating acid.

Acid Fruits Have No Food Value

Acid fruits are used by the great majority to stimulate the appetite, that they must eat what is called "breakfast," miscalled, however, for really there is no fast to break. It is well to observe that the person who eats a heavy luncheon at or near midnight is the same who eats one or two good-sized oranges or a dish of strawberries to give him an appetite the next morning.

Another fact of no small importance is that starches are digested and sugars converted only in an alkaline medium. What, then, becomes of the bowl of cereals taken immediately after these acid fruits for breakfast, taking no account of the sugar that is usually sprinkled over it? The intestinal tract must sooner or later become irritated by these fermenting foods. The blood loses its alkalinity, and a train of diseases, already only too well-established in the system, follows such a diet.

Fruits and bread and butter are very common mixtures for those who have at the end of the day a supper. One can see at a glance that such combinations are not wise.

- Last Christmas, the fruiterer who supplies the house year 'round sent a handsome basket of fruit as a gift, including oranges, both red and yellow apples, bananas, assorted nuts and Malaga grapes.
- The whole basket was dripping with gold and silver tinsel, and tucked in the corners were firecrackers, a box of candy and balloons for the children.
- On Christmas Day, Gwen received a gift of cloth for a new dress from the family, and then joined the entire staff for an afternoon of singing Christmas carols in the parlor.

- Currently, the household is buzzing about a new invention that could protect them from illness; Mr. Pfannebake purchased a Ralston new-process water-still that sterilizes water with heat to destroy the bacteria, then re-aerates the water with sterilized air.
- Everyone in the house feels safer from invading microbes now, though the fear of yellow fever and other diseases always lingers in Philadelphia; this is one of the reasons the family maintains its own garden, especially for the cultivation of healthful vegetables.
- Work in the massive garden is often done by three men and a mule; the tools used include small steel plows, hand tools and a horse-driven Zephanian Breed Weeder, which has proven invaluable in improving crop production.
- Recently, most of the staff was allowed to stop work for the afternoon to watch a balloon ascension.
- Gwen joined the five sisters on the third-floor balcony, where they could see the balloon being inflated with gas, then witness a man climb into a large, woven basket.
- As the ropes were untied, he waved his hands wildly to the crowd and slowly floated upward into the air and out of sight.
- The other joy of city life is the ice cream cart; several times a week the ice cream vendors peddle ice cream blocks in push carts.
- Ringing a large dinner bell, they wend their way down the streets selling vanilla, chocolate, pineapple and lemon, each wrapped in wax paper; the price is $0.05.
- Gwen looks forward to a lemon ice cream break, especially in the afternoons.

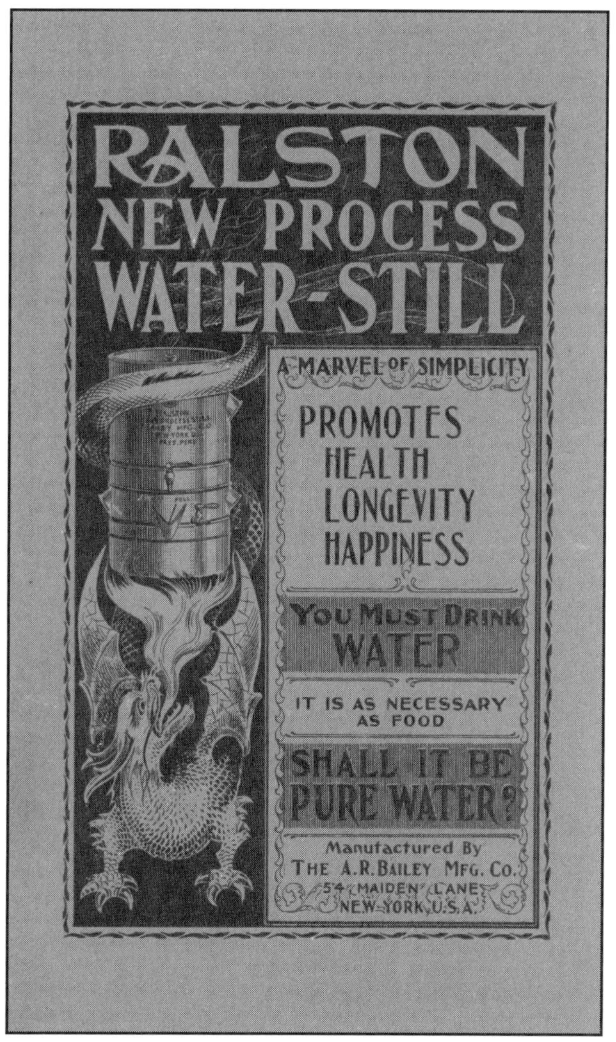

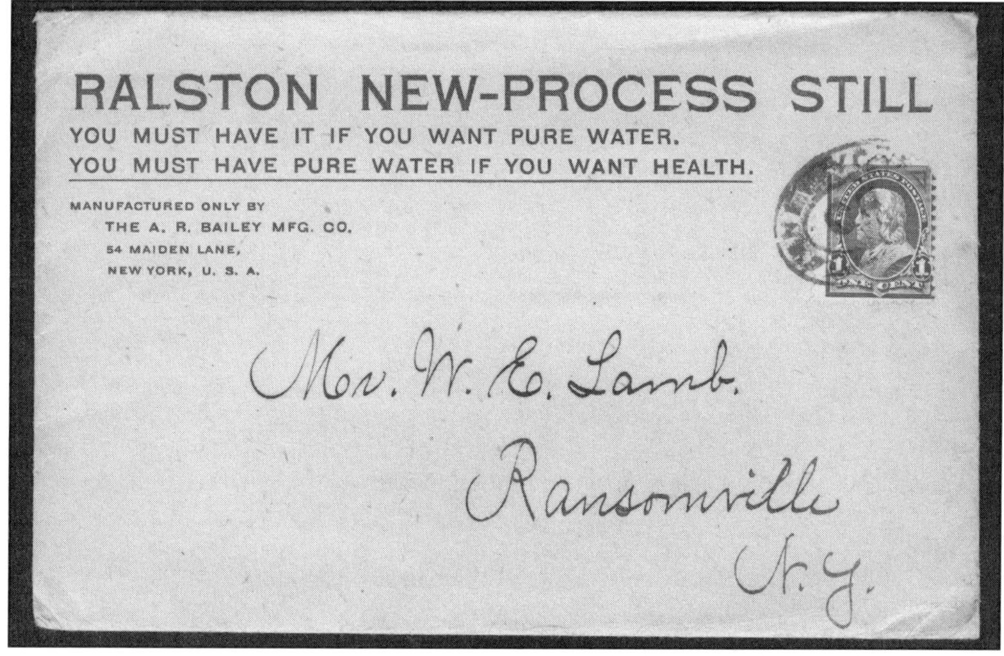

The household is now protected from microbes by the Ralston water-still.

WATER-DRINKING.

WHEN it is considered that the body is made up very largely of water it can readily be understood how important to health is a constant supply of this fluid. Many people have a notion that the drinking of water in any amount beyond that actually necessary to quench thirst is injurious, and acting on this belief they endeavor to drink as little as possible. The notion, however, is wide of the truth. Drinking freely of pure water is a most efficacious means not only of preserving health, but often of restoring it when failing.

All the tissues of the body need water, and water in abundance is necessary also for the proper performance of every vital function. Cleanliness of the tissues within the body is as necessary to health and comfort as cleanliness of the skin, and water tends to insure the one as truly as it does the other It dissolves the waste material, which would otherwise collect in the body, and removes it in the various excretions.

These waste materials are often actual poisons, and many a headache, many rheumatic pains and aches, many sleepless nights and listless days, and many attacks of the "blues" are due solely to the circulation in the blood or deposit in the tissues of these waste materials, which cannot be got rid of because of an insufficient supply of water

Water is accused of making fat, and people with a tendency to corpulence avoid it for that reason. But this is not strictly true It does undoubtedly often increase the weight, but it does so because it improves the digestion and therefore more of the food eaten is utilized and turned into fat and flesh. But excessive fat, what we call corpulence, is not a sign of health but of faulty digestion and assimilation, and systematic water-drinking is often employed as a means of reducing the superfluous fat—which it sometimes does with astonishing rapidity.

It is impossible to recount in a few words all the benefits which may result from the taking of pure water in sufficient quantity, but the discussion of this subject will be resumed in a future number of the *Companion*.

Life in the Community: Philadelphia, Pennsylvania

- The city's principal boulevards are wide; Broad Street, especially its northern portion, is wider than the great boulevards of Paris or the Ringstrassen of Central Europe.
- Philadelphia has about 1.3 million residents, making it the third-largest American city and one of the 10 largest cities in the world.
- In all, it encompasses 130 square miles—more than London—thanks to the Consolidation Act of 1854.
- Because so much property was included in the city limits under this Act, people still go fox hunting within the city's municipal boundaries.
- Although Philadelphia has experienced significant growth during the past decade, the percentage of foreign-born residents at 23 percent is lower than New York's 38 percent and Boston's 35 percent.
- Currently, the Jewish population, many who are immigrants from Russia and Rumania, is growing rapidly.
- Unlike New York, whose streets appear to be constantly in motion, Philadelphia is slower-moving, without the fierce rhythms of other American cities.
- Philadelphia has few landmarks that it can boast are recognizable to people who are not from the city, and even fewer renowned vistas.
- The solitary exception is City Hall, with an enormous statue of William Penn topping its tower.
- There, 547 feet above the street, visitors can obtain a view of the city, and even use a Kodak camera to capture the scene.
- Some consider the statue, constructed by Alexander Milne Calder in 1894, a Philadelphian Statue of Liberty.
- Real-estate prices are reasonable, compared with other urban areas; a middle-class house containing seven rooms can be rented for $15 a month.
- Between 1886 and 1893, 50,000 houses were built in west and northern Philadelphia, most of them financed by the 450 neighborhood savings and loan associations.
- Currently, more people own their houses in Philadelphia than in any other city in the world.
- The city also enjoys a sense of spaciousness; typically, 100 houses in Philadelphia accommodate an average of 550 people, while in New York, the same number of homes harbor 1,650 inhabitants, according to census figures.
- Philadelphia is known for its shops and local wares: Dexter's for cakes, Margerum's for beef, Fluke's for dainties, Dreka's for stationery, Sautter's for ice cream, Jones's for oysters and Leary's for books.
- Leary's, owned by Mayor Edwin S. Stuart, is considered one of the finest bookshops in the United States.
- A cherished tradition of the city, especially among the more élite families, is for the men to be involved in cooking special dishes; wealthy businessmen are often seen at the market selecting meat, and many take great pride in their ability to make mayonnaise.

Historical Snapshot
1898–1899

- The first shots of the Spanish-American War were fired
- The Louisiana "grandfather clause" restricted most blacks from voting
- The Union Carbide Company was founded
- Motorcar production reached 1,000 vehicles per year in 1898; production topped 2,500 in 1899
- Goodyear Tire and Rubber Company was founded
- *The New York Times* dropped its price from $0.03 daily to $0.01; as a result, circulation tripled
- Pepsi-Cola was introduced by pharmacist Caleb D. "Doc" Bradham in New Bern, North Carolina
- Uneeda Biscuits was created
- J. P. Stevens & Company was founded in New York
- Shiga Kiyoshi, a Japanese bacteriologist, discovered the Shigella bacillus, responsible for dysentery and named after him
- Trolley cars replaced horse cars in Boston
- Wesson Oil was developed
- The United Mine Workers of America was founded
- The first concrete grain elevator was erected near Minneapolis
- A very destructive insect, the boll weevil, began spreading across cotton-growing Southern states

1898 Economic Profile

Selected Prices

Bedroom Suite, Four-Piece, Antique	$11.00
Chocolate, Pound	$0.20
Cloth, Shirting Percale	$0.13
Coffee, Pound	$0.25
Dinner Set, English Porcelain, 100 Pieces	$14.00
Face Powder	$0.25
Gloves, Man's Kid	$1.50
Hotel Room, Columbia, SC	$2.50
Insecticide, Quart	$1.00
Magazine, *Ladies' Home Journal*	$0.10
Music Box	$6.00
Piano, Steinway	$200.00
Pocket Watch	$12.00
Tea, Breakfast	$0.65

"Protection from Flies," *Southern Poultry and Stockman's Guide*, September 1898:

An old, tried-and-true remedy for flies is pine tar and grease, says the Progressive Farmer. Many a fisherman has found this a welcome protection to his own person whilst pursuing his art destructive to the finny tribe. For our cows can be found no more effective remedy for the attack of flies and probably no cheaper one than pine tar one part and crude cottonseed oil two parts. If too thick add more oil, but the more expensive and less dirty it makes the cows. We have used two parts of oil to one of tar, being careful to brush it on with a piece of coarse burlap and not use enough to make the hair very sticky, but enough so about two applications per week will keep flies looking elsewhere than on cattle thus smeared for a free lunch.

The best protection against flies yet tried at the Experimental Farm has been clutches of chickens used in combination with care to clean up the cow yard regularly. All droppings are brought daily to the manure pit, and near this the chicks have had their homes, so they find fruitful scratching ground and grow fat on fly larvae.

PLEASE PRESERVE THIS CIRCULAR. YOU WILL WANT IT SOMETIME.

ZEPHANIAH BREE

OFFICE OF

THE Z. BREED WEEDER CO.

26 MERCHANTS ROW,

BOSTON, MASS.

Zephaniah Breed was bor
right farm which he now occu
other officers of our Company.
the saloon, that curse of all cu
He has written a great d
Journal of Agriculture until
farmer testifies to-day of the
For the last ten years he
level culture, conservation of n
fruitful indeed, and the "Zeph
Although seventy-eight ye
and with his Weeder, his late
than he did in his younger d
results of his experimental wor
vast amount of labor which th
the soil.

We presume that you, as
believe in purchasing all thos
accompanying circulars your c
slowly read them, and from th
Now, if you have a little s
Are you not raising some
do what we say it will? Do
cabbages, tomatoes, celery, as
combination to the extent of o
that much, and if you are in th
Now if you never have see
work of which many other we
shall have to say in their favo
(Wm. O. Breed) "knows how
and what it would do, he repl
a crop plant, and which to ta
He did not consider that the r

OFFICE OF

THE Z. BREED WEEDER CO.,

26 Merchants Row, Boston.

Season of 1898.

DEAR SIR:

Do you own a Weeder yet? If not, then why not?

The question is not CAN YOU AFFORD TO BUY A WEEDER, but can you afford NOT to do so?

Can you afford, with your old-style cultivator, to expend from twice to six times the time and labor that would be required when using a Weeder?

Can you afford to do with your hoe or hands any work that can be done by a machine at a small fraction of the cost of hoe or hand work? We think that you will agree with us that you CANNOT.

Can you afford to do without the ten to fifty per cent increase of crop which is sure to follow the timely use of a Weeder?

Can you afford to grow weeds in your crops when a Weeder will keep the fields free from them?

A Z. Breed Weeder (in one form or another) is something you should have if you are either farming, market gardening, or even if you have only a small family garden to care for.

If you are a farmer, one or more of our Nos. 1, 2, 3, or 4, is what you should

If not delivered in 5 days return to

Our Weeders save time. Time is money.

THE Z. BREED WEEDER CO.,
26 Merchants Row, Boston, Mass.

Ransomville
N.Y.

W. E. Lamb

Never put off until to-morrow that which you ought to do to-day. Send your order **to-day.**

No Farmer or Gardener makes a mistake when he orders a Zephaniah Breed Weeder.

83
BROKERS

1900–1909

The first decade of the twentieth century was not only marked by dramatic innovation, but an emerging awareness of the changing role of children in American society. Educational philosophies began to shift, school consolidations programs began, cities focused on the creation of parks, and issues-related child welfare began to receive national attention. America's men and women were gaining a sense of the country's potential on the world stage as they competed to invent a better automobile, devise the perfect soft drink or invent a new candy. At the same time, the number of inventions and changes spawned by the power of electricity was revolutionary. Factories converted to the new energy force, staying open longer and employing entire families, including children as young as 10. A bottle-making machine patented in 1903 virtually eliminated the hand-blowing of glass bottles; another innovation mechanized the production of window glass. A rotating kiln manufactured in 1899 supplied large quantities of cheap, standardized cement, just in time for a nation ready to leave behind the bicycle fad and fall madly in love with the automobile. Thanks to this spirit of innovation and experimentation, the United States led the world in productivity, exceeding the vast empires of France and Britain combined.

In the eyes of the world, America was the land of opportunity. Millions of immigrants flooded to the United States, often finding work in the new factories of the New World—many managed by the men who came two generations before from countries like England or Germany or Wales. When Theodore Roosevelt proudly proclaimed in 1902, "The typical American is accumulating money more rapidly than any other man on earth," he described accurately both the joy of newcomers and the prosperity of the emerging middle class. Elevated by their education, profession, inventiveness, or capital, the managerial class found numerous opportunities to flourish in the rapidly changing world of a new economy.

At the beginning of the century, the 1900 U.S. population, comprising 45 states, stood at 76 million, an increase of 21 percent since 1890; 10.6 million residents were foreign-born and more were coming every day. The number of immigrants in the first decade of the twentieth century was double the number for the previous decade, exceeding one million annually in four of the 10 years, the highest level in U.S. history. Business and industry were convinced that unrestricted immigration was the fuel that drove the growth of American industry. Labor was equally certain that the influx of foreigners continually undermined the economic status of native workers and kept wages low.

The change in productivity and consumerism came with a price: the character of American life. Manufacturing plants drew people from the country into the cities. The traditional farm patterns were disrupted by the lure of urban life. Ministers complained that lifelong churchgoers who moved to the city often found less time and fewer social pressures to attend worship regularly. Between 1900 and 1920, urban population increased by 80 percent compared to just over 12 percent for rural areas. During the same time, the non-farming work force went from 783,000 to 2.2 million. Unlike farmers, these workers drew a regular paycheck, and spent it.

With this movement of people, technology, and ideas, nationalism took on a new meaning in America. Railroad expansion in the middle of the nineteenth century had made it possible to move goods quickly and efficiently throughout the country. As a result, commerce, which had been based largely on local production of goods for local consumption, found new markets. Ambitious merchants expanded their businesses by appealing to broader markets.

In 1900, America claimed 58 businesses with more than one retail outlet called "chain stores"; by 1910, that number had more than tripled, and by 1920, the total had risen to 808. The number of clothing chains alone rose from seven to 125 during the period. Department stores such as R. H. Macy in New York and Marshall Field in Chicago offered vast arrays of merchandise along with free services and the opportunity to "shop" without purchasing. Ready-made clothing drove down prices, but also promoted fashion booms that reduced the class distinctions of dress. In rural America the mail order catalogs of Sears, Roebuck and Company reached deep into the pocket of the common man and made dreaming and consuming more feasible.

All was not well, however. A brew of labor struggles, political unrest, and tragic factory accidents demonstrated the excesses of industrial capitalism so worshipped in the Gilded Age. The labor-reform movements of the 1880s and 1890s culminated in the newly formed American Federation of Labor as the chief labor advocate. By 1904, 18 years after it was founded, the AFL claimed 1.676 million of 2.07 million total union members nationwide. The reforms of the labor movement called for an eight-hour workday, child-labor regulation, and cooperatives of owners and workers. The progressive bent of the times also focused attention on factory safety, tainted food and drugs, political corruption, and unchecked economic monopolies. At the same time, progress was not being made by all. For black Americans, many of the gains of reconstruction were being wiped away by regressive Jim Crow laws, particularly in the South. Cherished voting privileges were being systematically taken away. When President Roosevelt asked renowned black educator Booker T. Washington to dine at the White House, the invitation sparked deadly riots. Although less visible, the systematic repression of the Chinese was well under way on the West Coast.

1902 Profile

Working Class

Twelve-year-old Mary Egan, along with her father and brother, moved to Chicago two years ago after her mother died. She lives in a crowded apartment, attending school in the mornings and helping her father in his commercial sign painting business in the afternoons.

After her mother's death, Mary Egan moved to Chicago.

Life at Home

- This Irish family of three moved to Chicago two years after her mother died a very slow and sad death.
- Mary has just turned 12, and her brother Kenny is 15; they currently live near Forquer Street in one of the most crowded sections of Chicago.
- Their one-room tenement apartment is in the back of the building and has no windows; they have little furniture, so nearly everything they own hangs from pegs on the walls—hats, kettles, pans, partly consumed Bologna sausages, and Mary's clothes.
- The apartment does not have a bathtub or hot water, so a neighbor lets her take a bath every other Saturday, along with her own four children.
- To handle the brutal winters of Chicago, Mary has covered her bed with some old carpets she found on the street to keep her warm at night.

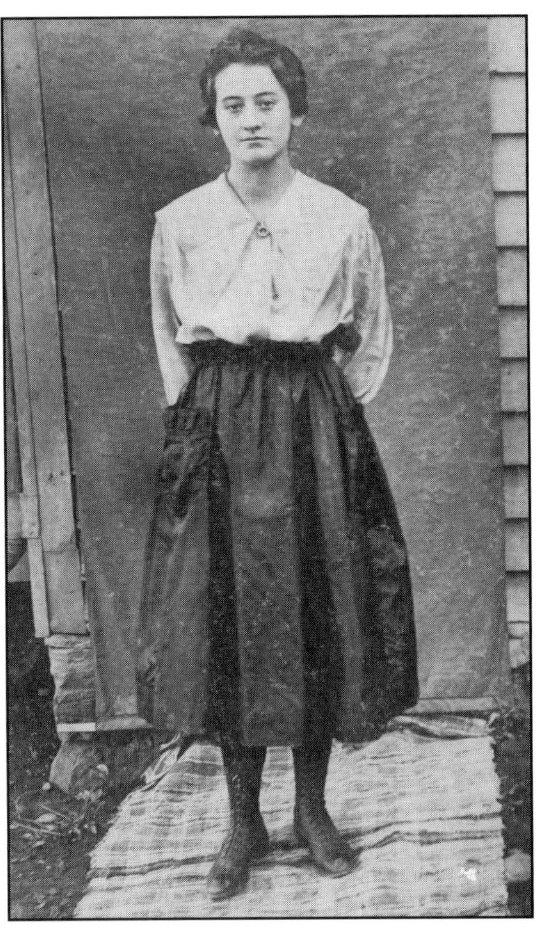

Mary's mother worked in a match factory before her death.

- Evenings, after visiting the outhouse and lighting a small candle, she uses a pair of scissors she found to cut pictures from magazines and create her very own paper doll family—complete with mother, father and five children.
- She is especially delighted when she finds a copy of *Ladies' Home Journal* in the trash because it has so many pictures of ladies in dress-up clothes.
- She does not like to be out alone at night, having heard dozens of stories about the white slave traffic in Chicago; hundreds of girls, she has been told, have been kidnapped from their homes and forced into prostitution.
- She is shocked that many people seem unaware that there is an active trade in the ruin of girls, as though they were cattle or sheep.
- At the end of many days, when the family has little energy to eat, meals often consist of black bread and sausage.
- Mary has learned that when money is available, cornmeal, Van Camp's Pork and Beans and Jell-O will fill them up, though nothing satisfies her brother, who always complains and always wants more.
- Many nights he doesn't come home; refusing to attend school in Chicago, he roams the streets, stealing from vendors and begging for money.
- Some afternoons during a factory shift change, he will take in $1.50 or more in coin—the city is his own personal park.
- When the horses that draw carts up and down the streets die and are left along the curb, it often takes the city several days to remove the carcasses.

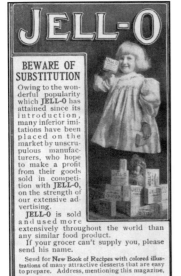

"Life under the Shadows," ***Chicago and Its Cess-Pools of Infamy*****, by Samuel Paynter Wilson, 1915:**

It is a terrible thing to be poor in any part of the world. In Chicago, poverty is simply a living death. The city is full of suffering and misery. Some of the wretched people who endure it have, no doubt, brought it upon themselves by drink, by idleness, or by other faults, but a large majority is simply unfortunate. Their poverty has come upon them through no fault of their own; they struggle bravely against it, and would better their condition if they could only find employment. They are held down by an iron hand, however, and vainly endeavor to rise out of their misery. They dwell in wretched tenement houses, in cellars of buildings in the most thickly populated parts of the city, and in shanties and hovels in almost every quarter of the city. A few families, even in the midst of their suffering, manage to keep their poor quarters clean and neat, but the majority live in squalor and filth.

Mary and her family live in one of Chicago's most crowded sections.

- Kenny and his buddies find great sport in jumping on the dead horses, especially their bellies, sometimes breaking their bladders and producing a terrible smell.
- Mary doesn't like for her brother to steal, but when he does, her favorite treat is a box of Cracker Jack; the caramel-covered popcorn has been a favorite in Chicago since it was first invented by a popcorn vendor and sold at the World's Columbian Exposition a decade earlier.
- Before she died, Mary's mother worked for the Federal Match Company in Paterson, New Jersey; Mary's aunt, who had always worked for this same company, also died recently.
- Efforts are now under way to ban the use of white or yellow phosphorus in match-making because so many workers have become ill.

"Evils of the Match Industry," *Scientific America*, October 22, 1898:

In the manufacture of the ubiquitous match, as is well-known, the use of phosphorus entails many miseries and discomforts upon those engaged in the manufacture, they being mostly women and girls. Existing lesions of any kind are thereby likely to become aggravated, owing to the fumes of the phosphorus that arise from the "dipping" trough, fumes that are highly irritating to eyes and throat, to lung tissue, and that by permeating the cavities of the teeth, frequently provoke diseases of the jaw, leading to hideous deformities, perhaps even fatality.

- The most common symptom is necrosis, in which the worker's bones become so fragile they break without warning or develop unattractive deformities.
- For Mary's mother, the illness spread through the cavities of her teeth, the doctors said, first causing severe disfigurement, and then death.
- Before her death, she gave Mary her most prized possession—an elegant woman's watch—along with a picture of herself.
- Mary had vowed to keep the watch always, but it disappeared into one of Chicago's pawn shops more than a year ago to pay the rent.
- Nearly everything they own has been to pawn at least once, except her father's kit of fine paint brushes, all with their own special names and uses.
- The tools of his profession include crow-quill pencils in various sizes, a large goose-hair pencil, and at the large end, the eagle pen.
- Her father is constantly fatigued, especially after a long day of standing on scaffolding to paint massive advertisements on the sides of buildings.
- In recent months a black line has formed beneath his gums—a condition many of the commercial painters develop.
- As a young man he dreamed of becoming a famous artist, and talks at length about his dream when drinking with friends.
- His current sign-painting assignment for a giant department store requires him to work three stories up, but he likes being up that high and able to see the city below.
- When work is steady, he makes $5 a week, but health, weather and temperament affect his income, so he only made about $180 last year.
- Since coming to Chicago two years ago, the Egans have been evicted for nonpayment of rent three times; his frequent worrying often translates into more drinking.

Before her death, Mary's mother gave her an elegant watch.

Kenny refuses to attend school, spending most of the day on the street.

- Most of the houses in the area are small wooden residences inhabited by three or more families, and were constructed quickly and cheaply to accommodate the thousands of new residents flooding into America's second-largest city.
- These structures are often attached to dilapidated outhouses with broken sewer pipes, all littered with garbage said to be alive with disease.
- At the back of some houses, it is customary for the lower floor to be used as a stable and outhouse, while the upper rooms serve entire families as a place for eating, sleeping, bearing children and dying.
- If there are alleys adjacent to the buildings, the refuse and manure are sometimes removed; otherwise, it accumulates.
- Fruit stands and ice cream carts clutter the streets.
- In this section of Chicago, the faces and manners, one writer says, are "very foreign"; in all, 18 nations are represented in this small slice of the city.
- The area includes 81 saloons, not including restaurants and cigar stores that also sell liquor.
- Heat during the Illinois winters is provided by coal; earlier in the year, 150 wagons ordinarily employed by the Street Cleaning Department were engaged in hauling coal to the needy families of the city, including the Egans.
- Unlike most major cities, Chicago has few absentee landlords; many live in the neighborhoods in which their tenements are located.

"Tears to Coax the Cash, How Chicago's Boy Beggars Impose on Sympathetic Ones," *Chicago Tribune*, August 1, 1902:

Tricks that surpass the wiles of the adult beggars have been used with success by child mendicants on Chicago's streets. At the detention home for delinquent children it has been found that the 40 youthful beggars turned over to them by representatives of the Visitation and Aid Society all have been even more cunning than most of the older fraudulent seekers of alms.

Two boys, who apparently are no more than seven or eight years old, for weeks have plied a paying venture in beggary on the corner of Madison and State streets. Fiore and Amiel Pappa, who have records in the juvenile court for misdemeanors, have wept bitterly on the street corner in mock terror, while kindhearted pedestrians have paused to thrust nickels and dimes in their pockets. Not since the juvenile "beggar trust" was broken up about two years ago by agents of the Visitation and Aid Society has such a successful "sympathy game" been plied by youthful experts.

Eyes made sore by rubbing with dirt aid the children in crying at will, according to Officer E. E. Goggin of the Visitation and Aid Society detail who has followed the career of the crafty Pappa family for months. A discarded newspaper picked up on the street also serves as part of the stock and trade for the most popular and successful "play" of the child mendicants.

"Please buy the paper, mister. I'll get a beatin' if I go home without the money," is a favorite salutation of the child beggar, whose tears rarely fail to coax money from a passerby.

Life at School and Work

- Mary attends school from 8 a.m. to noon five days a week; her classroom has 47 students, not all of whom speak English.
- Her school has too many children for an all-day program, so the children have been separated into two shifts to accommodate the influx of new students.
- The city recently purchased 26 portables—small, wooden shacks temporarily placed on the school site—to ease the crowded classroom conditions.
- Mary spends the mornings learning to read, doing sums and studying some science; afternoons are reserved for helping her father with his work—when he is well enough to work all day.
- Across the city, 11,000 children voluntarily attend classes for only half a day so they can help their families in the afternoons.
- When she turns 14, she plans to quit school; lots of jobs are open to young girls in frame-gilding, button-holing and working in the paint factories of the city.
- She figures she can make more money working on her own than by helping her father, since his health does not seem to be getting any better.
- She has even considered going into match-making like her mother, but remembers how disfigured her mother's face became before she died.
- Chicago is emerging as one of the nation's match-making centers, especially now that machinery is speeding up the process, improving the technology and requiring less labor.

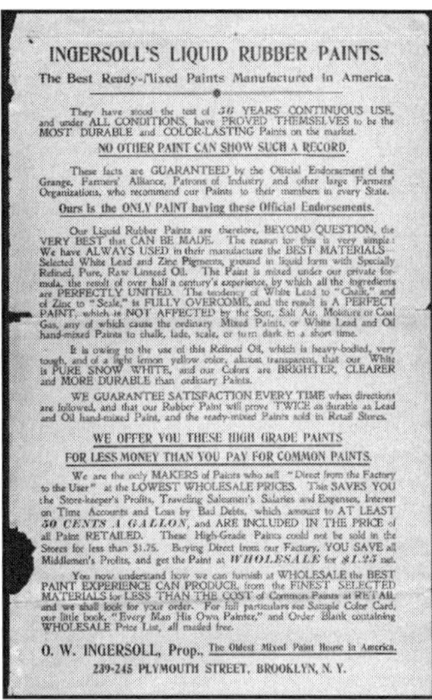

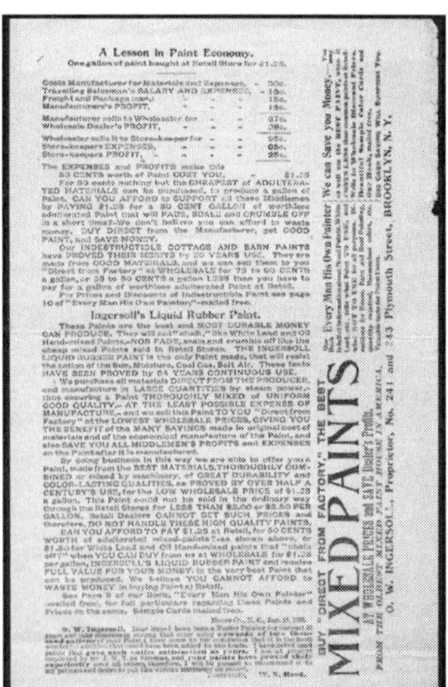

"Boys Should Play Football, Says Chancellor Andrews," *Chicago Tribune*, August 12, 1902:

Chancellor E. Benjamin Andrews of the University of Nebraska startled the summer coeds and pedagogues at the University of Chicago yesterday afternoon by an emphatic indorsement [sic] of football. No more enthusiastic defense of the gridiron game could have been given by the most rabid rooter.

"Every son of mine," said the chancellor, "if I had a hundred, I should be glad to have play football and play it lustily."

The occasion of this expression came in a letter on "The Monogamous Family," in which Dr. Andrews stated as one of the chief advantages of such a family relation that under it the child was trained by the father as well as the mother.

In his morning lecture on "The Ideal of Womanliness," Chancellor Andrews told what he thought were the essential qualities of the ideal woman. "She should be beautiful," he said. "To be beautiful is a sacred obligation upon women. This does not necessarily mean that she must have physical beauty. She must have beauty of character. She must be physically strong. She must be trained in consecutive thinking. In the lack of this ability often lies woman's greatest defect. Therefore, she should study geometry."

Mary's father paints signs on windows and walls of commercial buildings.

- The 200 billion wooden safety matches produced daily in the United States for world-wide distribution are largely produced by a series of machines.
- On the days when her father can't paint or climb upon scaffolding, she spends her afternoons in the tiny city park, where there are trees and birds—like at their old home back in New Jersey.
- The city has created the Chicago Small Parks Commission to help bring country life and fresh air to the city.
- In other sections of Chicago, shower baths, swimming pools, reading rooms and gymnasiums are being built and enjoyed, but Mary is happy to sit on a swing and watch the ice cream vendors go by.
- The Chicago Relief and Aid Society believes strongly that more fresh air in the most densely populated sections of the city will improve health, reduce infant mortality and aid in learning.
- On those days when he cannot work, her father normally starts drinking earlier than usual.
- Twice since coming to Chicago, Mary has used a precious nickel to buy a balcony seat at the vaudeville theater where she can watch moving picture shows all day; laughing is fun and she feels safe in the darkness of the theater, even without her father.

"A Family Budget," *Charities Magazine*, September 5, 1902:

In the hope of inducing or compelling her refractory husband to take a reasonable view of her housekeeping, as well as put a check on his personal extravagances, Mrs. N____ has kept a strict account of her household expenses, which may incidentally prove of interest to besides herself. The family is French, consisting of Mr. and Mrs. N__, their two children, one and five years old, respectively, and Mrs. N's mother. . . .

Her expenditures for food for the month were as follows:

Meat	$3.95
Crackers	$0.57
Bread	$1.75
Butter	$1.28
Milk	$2.24
Buttermilk	$2.07
Potatoes	$1.40
Sugar	$0.90
Ice	$0.85
Coffee	$0.64
Lard	$0.50
Eggs	$0.35
Tomatoes	$1.67
Macaroni	$0.30
Cabbage	$0.30
Beans	$0.60
Soup Vegetables	$1.05
Chicory	$0.14
Condiments	$0.45
Oatmeal	$0.20
Flour	$0.03
Lemons and Oranges	$0.09
Soda and Ice Cream	$0.33
Total	$21.66

Other Items:

Fuel and Light	$1.89
Soap, Starch, etc.	$0.40
Clothes Line	$0.56
Pulley	$0.05
Clothes Pins	$0.15
Acid Oxalide	$0.05
Chloride Lime	$0.05
Stove Wick	$0.04
Scissors Sharpened	$0.10
Can Opener	$0.08
Sponge	$0.05
Baby Powder	$0.10
Castoria	$0.25
Peruna	$1.50
French Newspaper	$0.40
Snuff	$0.30
Children's Bank	$0.07

- Currently, tuberculosis is common in Chicago, and doctors have begun recommending against licking postage stamps or wetting one's finger to turn the page of a book.
- Her father jokes that since he is illiterate and can never write letters or read a book, he will be safe from the great modern plague.
- The Chicago papers are also filled with news concerning a typhoid epidemic that has killed 402 persons so far; health experts are warning residents: "Do not eat raw and unclean vegetables, don't buy cheap dairy products, and sterilize the milk."
- The health department believes that this time, water is not to blame for the last 50 deaths, and have turned their attention to raw cabbage and celery which are often eaten without being washed, and milk that is often kept in foul iceboxes.
- Earlier in the year, Jane Addams of Hull House began a crusade against the dangers of foul water and its potential for causing disease.

Chicago is the nation's second-largest city; currently 250,000 children attend the city's public schools.

- "When the water of Chicago is foul," she says, "the prosperous buy water bottled at distant springs, while the poor have no alternative but the typhoid fever that comes from using the city's supply."

Life in the Community: Chicago, Illinois

- With a population exceeding two million, Chicago is the nation's second-largest city; currently, 250,000 children attend the city's public schools.

> The day must come when electricity will be for everyone, as the waters of the rivers and the wind of heaven. It should not merely be supplied, but lavished, that men may use it at their will, as the air they breathe.
>
> —French novelist Emile Zola

The excitement and industry of Chicago have attracted a flood of immigrants.

- Seven new school buildings costing $700,000 are currently under construction to accommodate 6,000 additional students.
- The construction is expected to eliminate the many rented rooms now used by the School Board and greatly reduce the number of children who have been forced into half-day school sessions.
- Nationwide, 21.4 million of the country's 72.3 million citizens are of school age—from five to 18.
- The average annual school session is 143 days, with some states such as North Carolina and Arkansas having sessions only 68 days long.
- The average monthly salary of male teachers is $45.16, and for women, $38.74.
- During the past 40 years the average salary has increased 86 percent.
- The average school expenditures per capita are $2.67; per pupil, they average $18.86, with teachers' salaries absorbing 64 percent of total school expenditures.
- Charities of various types exist throughout Chicago, ranging from Hull House and its programs for uplifting the poor to the unemployed workers' relief operated by the Judd Street Jewish Synagogue, originally created for the Hebrew poor but now available to all.
- Chicago's Hull House, run by Jane Addams, includes a women's club, day nursery, gymnasium, the Hull House Players, and the Plato Club, where guests like John Dewey and Clarence Darrow convene.
- Eighteen months ago, a group called the City Homes Association, also headed by Jane Addams, began a full investigation of the tenement districts of Chicago.
- The resulting study showed that these tenements house 900 people per acre.
- The average tenancy throughout the districts is three families to a house; most houses have three rooms.
- The average rent paid by an Italian family for an apartment is $4.92 a month; for a Bohemian family, it is $5.93 a month, and for a Jewish family, $8.28.
- Most of the houses sit on lots 25 feet wide and 120 feet deep.
- Miss Addams is very interested in the efforts under way in Philadelphia to install gardens, playgrounds and gymnasiums on the tops of buildings; she believes it would benefit the poor children of Chicago, but is skeptical that it will be done there.

Historical Snapshot
1902

- President Teddy Roosevelt's settlement of the coal miner strike was hailed as "the greatest single event affecting capitalism and labor in the history of America"
- The window envelope was invented by Chicagoan Americus F. Callahan, who called the window an "outlook"
- The University of Chicago segregated the sexes during their first two years of college for "educational benefits"
- American Federation of Labor (AFL) union membership surpassed one million for the first time; Maryland passed the first Workman's Compensation law
- Cuba was declared a republic, as the last U.S. troops withdrew following the Spanish-American War of 1898
- "If Money Talks, It Ain't on Speaking Terms with Me," was a popular song
- The sixth running of the Boston Marathon was won in two hours, 43 minutes and 12 seconds
- Joseph Conrad published *Heart of Darkness*, Jane Addams released *Democracy and Social Ethics*, and Professor Woodrow Wilson wrote *A History of the American People*
- Professional baseball's popularity continued to soar; more than 3.9 million fans attended games
- America's escape artist Harry Houdini was a worldwide phenomenon
- The medical community protested as unhealthy the continued use of restrictive metal strips within women's corsets, designed to create the wasp-waisted look
- Seven of the 11 players named to the College All-American Football team were from Yale
- New York City, which passed the Tenement House Act of 1901, began enforcing the requirement that every room receive direct air and sunlight and, more significant, that indoor toilets be installed
- Crayola crayons, radio telephones on ships, AAA and the brassiere all made their first appearance
- Savannah, Cincinnati, and San Francisco all adopted an 8-mph speed limit for automobiles
- The train known as the Twentieth Century Limited traveled from New York City to Chicago in 20 hours
- New York's Lower East Side, occupied largely by Jewish immigrants, was believed to be the most densely populated square mile in the world
- The speed of trolley cars increased to 12 miles per hour—twice the pace of a horse

"Hull House Basketball," *The Chicago Chronicle*, May 25, 1902:

Basketball is more than a fad and a craze with the girls of Chicago. It has come to stay and grows more in favor every year. It has more than the fun of the thing to recommend it to its devotees, for it not only affords good exercise and plenty of excellent sport, but—what is much more in the eyes of its followers—conduces to beauty of form and gracefulness of carriage. And then, it is a game girls can play.

1902 Economic Profile

Selected Prices

Item	Price
Almonds, Two Pounds	$0.25
Blanket	$0.50
Bromo Quinine Laxative	$0.10
Cigar	$0.05
Corset	$0.50
Carter's Liver Pills	$0.25
Ghirardelli Chocolate, One Pound	$0.05
Hoosier Kitchen Cabinet	$14.00
Rice, per Pound	$0.07
Shirt, Man's Madras	$0.94
Shotgun	$27.75
Underwear, Child's Jersey	$0.15
Wart Remover	$0.10
Waterproof Baby Pants	$0.05
Whiskey, per Quart	$1.00

It often takes the city several days to remove cart-horse carcasses left on the streets.

Changing America

- Levi Strauss, the inventor of blue jeans, died at age 73, leaving an estate of $6 million, the bulk of which was left to four nephews, the Pacific Hebrew Orphan Asylum, the Home for Aged Israelites, the Roman Catholic and Protestant Orphan Asylums, the Eureka Benevolent Society and the Emanu-El Sisterhood.
- Robert Hunter's book *Poverty* estimated that 20 million American families made less than $460 annually, the amount he considered a minimum subsistence income.
- U.S. citizenship was granted to the "Five Civilized Tribes"—the Cherokee, Creek, Choctaw, Chicasaw and Seminole—the previous year.
- Domestic service was the single largest nonagricultural job category in the United States.
- Forty-one years after the start of the Civil War, six theatrical companies still toured the play *Uncle Tom's Cabin* to continuing commercial success.
- John Dewey proposed a new method of education that emphasized functionality and "learning by doing" as opposed to rote memorization; Dewey opened his first child-centered school at the University of Chicago.
- The New York Child Labor Committee was pushing several industrial states, including New York, to reduce the number of hours a week children under age 16 could work from 60 to 56.
- The Salvation Army had more than 3,000 officers across the nation, many in the slums providing food, shelter and camaraderie, all tied to moral uplift.
- Carrie Chapman Catt, of the National American Woman Suffrage Association, wrote: "The world taught women nothing skillful and then said her work was valueless. . . . It taught her that every pleasure must come as a favor from men, and . . . when she decked herself in paint and fine feathers, as she had been taught to do, it called her vain."
- The United States and Mexico became the first nations to use the Hague Peace Court to settle an international dispute.
- Ivan Pavlov proposed the law of conditioned reflexes after observing that a dog repeatedly given food along with the sound of a bell will salivate in response to the sound alone.
- The U.S. reported nearly 350,000 cases of typhoid fever, resulting in approximately 35,000 deaths.

"Babes in Wood Go Broke, Then Come Their Papas and 'Good Time' Ends," *Chicago Tribune*, August 6, 1902:

Three prodigal sons, aged 11, eight and six years, weary after 24 hours of riotous living on a $5 bill, went home with their papas on the streetcars yesterday to the fatted veal.

In those 24 hours they had more of the sweets of life, more popcorn and peanuts, more soda water, pony rides, swings and other delights than the average boy gets in a month. But then came the husks—and their fathers.

H. L. William, 4120 Vincennes Avenue, one of the worried parents, found his son Robert, aged 11, with his two companions, Marshall Jones, aged eight, and Albert Jones, aged six, of 4112 Vincennes Avenue, wandering near Washington Park. The boys disappeared Monday afternoon with the $5.

"Robbie" was the bank. He had been given the money to buy peaches and told to come home with the change. But "Robbie" did not come. He flaunted the $5 before the eyes of his two bosom buddies and they started out for a taste of the high life. If "Robbie" had not lost half the cash assets of the trio, the husks would not have come so soon. They figured they had enough money for a week, but they went "bust" in a day at a south side summer garden.

This shows the extravagant life they led and the way they spent their fortune:

Summer Garden............................$0.45
Merry-Go-Round..........................$0.60
Boat Ride....................................$0.30
Cracker Jack...............................$0.20
Swings..$0.30
Cookies.......................................$0.03
Miniature Railroad.......................$0.30
Peanuts.......................................$0.15
Pony Ride....................................$0.20
Soda Water..................................$0.30
Lost during Pony Ride..................$2.07

When the money was lost the boys realized that adversity had come on them and prepared for a night in the park. The fathers of the runaways were hunting for them, and their mothers were spending a sleepless night. Mrs. Jones fainted when she saw her two prodigals coming back.

This is the chronicle of the eventful day as told by Marshall Jones:

"We went out to stay a week, but the money did not last. Robbie carried it and he lost it while he was running a race on a pony with a boy in a goat wagon. Robbie said that his aunt had given him the money to have a good time on. We thought it would last about a week.

"We went out to the park and Robbie paid for everything. He got the money changed at a store before we went in. We had a good time all right. Robbie took a ride on a pony in the park, but he didn't buy us any ride. Albert was too little to stick on, anyway.

"A boy was driving a goat wagon and he dared Robbie to race. He raced him and won, but all the money bounced out of his pocket. When we found he had lost the money we looked for it, but couldn't find it."

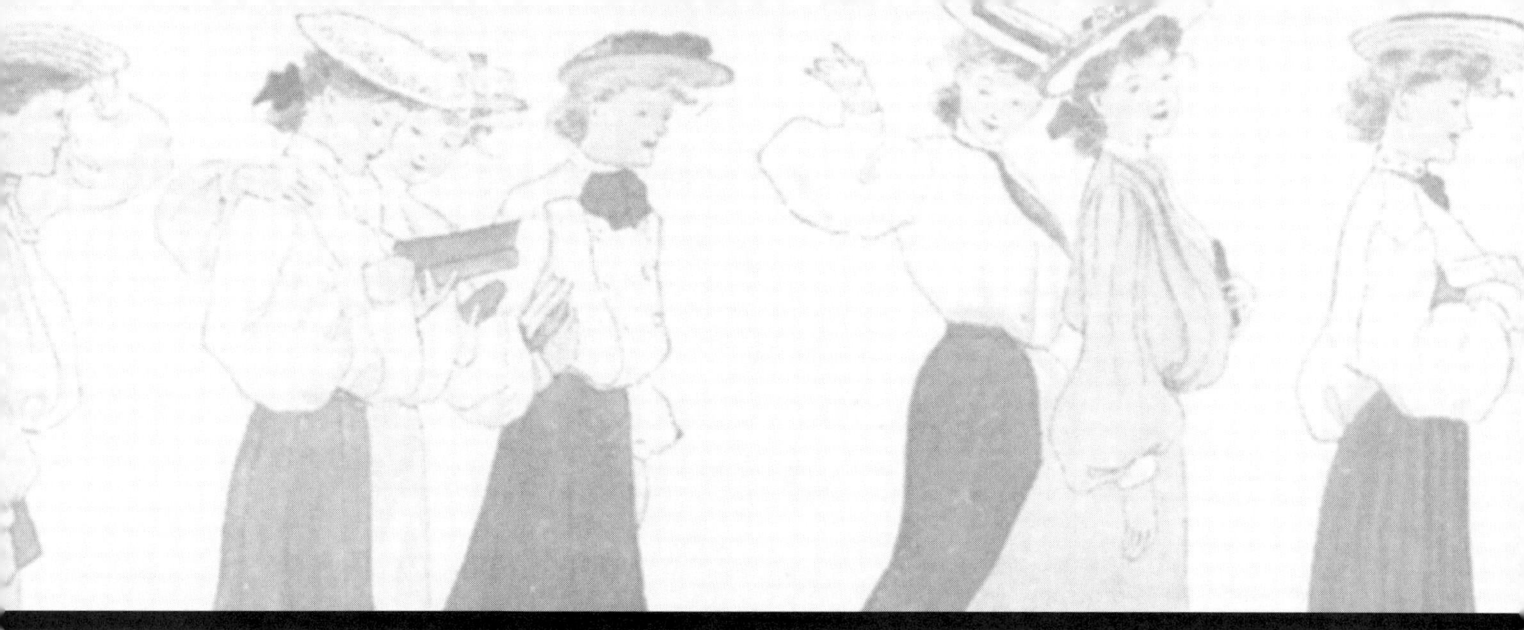

1904 Profile

Middle Class

For months, the Shlake family of Burlington, Vermont, has been planning a trip to Coney Island. It is a dream-come-true, especially for nine-year-old Edna.

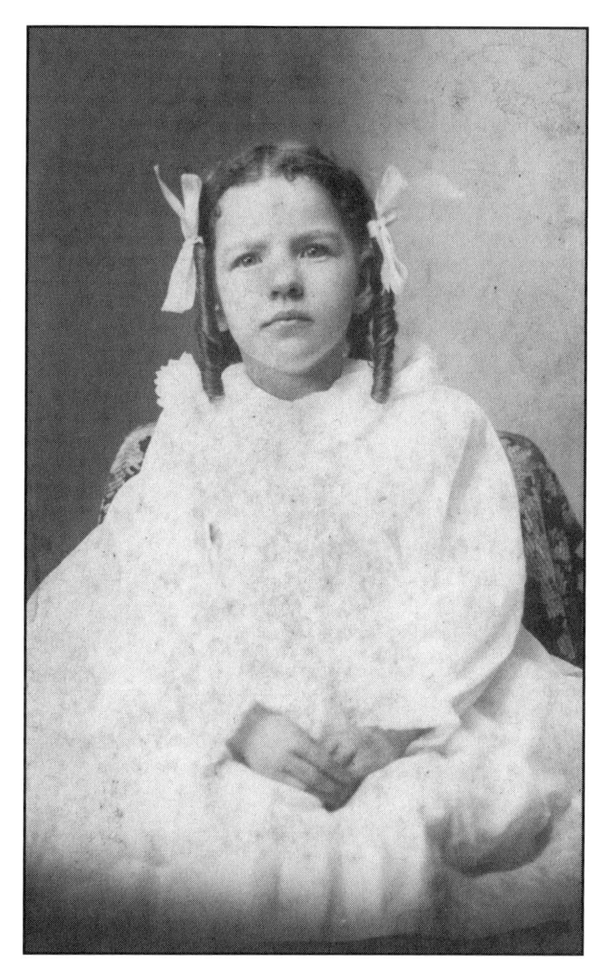

Edna has been looking forward to visiting Coney Island for years.

Life at Home

- Nine-year-old Edna Shlake and her family live outside progressive Burlington, Vermont, in the community of Winooski.
- Edna's father claims it combines the best of all worlds—the joy of being in the woods along with the convenience of a modern city—and Edna agrees with her Papa.
- She thinks her father looks very distinguished in a beard, and she just knows she is his favorite; after all, her older sister is such a brat, no one could like her.
- If they had to wait for her sister to be good so they could take a holiday at Coney Island, it would never happen.
- Edna had been disappointed recently to learn that the school she attended from the first to the fifth grade will be closing.
- All the one-room schools in her area are consolidating into one to provide better education; Edna doesn't want a better education, she just wants her school back.
- Many of the young teachers at her school come fresh from the nearby University of Vermont, which has a reputation for supporting public education across the state.
- Edna wishes they also had a commitment to being nicer to her when she can't keep quiet in class any longer and simply has to talk.
- Last Christmas the family got two collections of stereograph cards for viewing—one featuring faraway lands, and the other all about children.

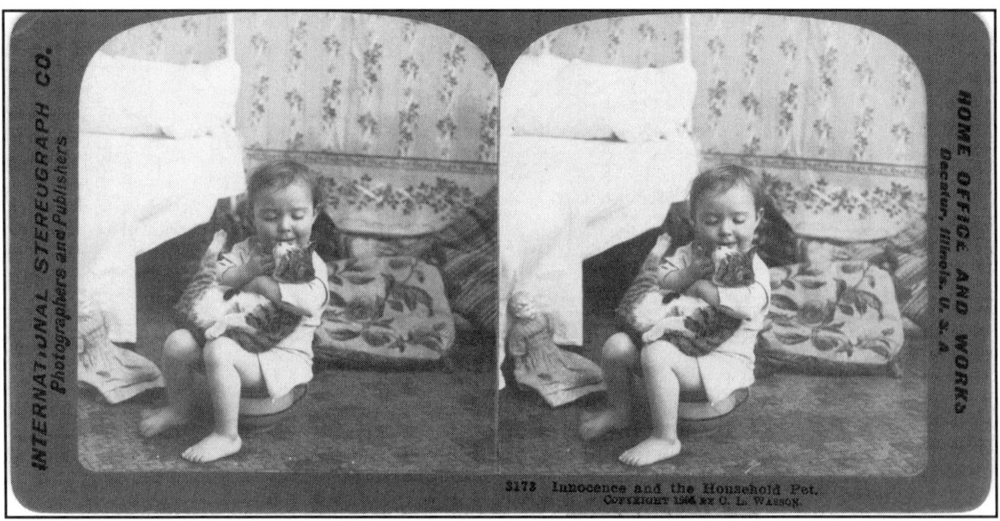

Looking at stereoscopic cards is a treasured pastime.

- On cold days, she loves to pull out the stereoscope and spend hours pulling the pictures in and out of focus, always marveling at the way the images pop into three dimensions when perfectly aligned.
- When she is blue, a picture of the little child with the cat always makes her feel better; the picture of the boy having his pants re-sewn makes her laugh.
- On Saturday afternoons, after Papa gets off work, they try to visit the Fletcher Free Library, which he says is one of the libraries funded by Mr. Carnegie.
- Saturday is always special if Papa has time to take them to the library, which has thousands of books, many with pictures of people from around the world.
- Sundays are spent at the Congregationalist church; with 210 churches, it is the largest denomination in Vermont.

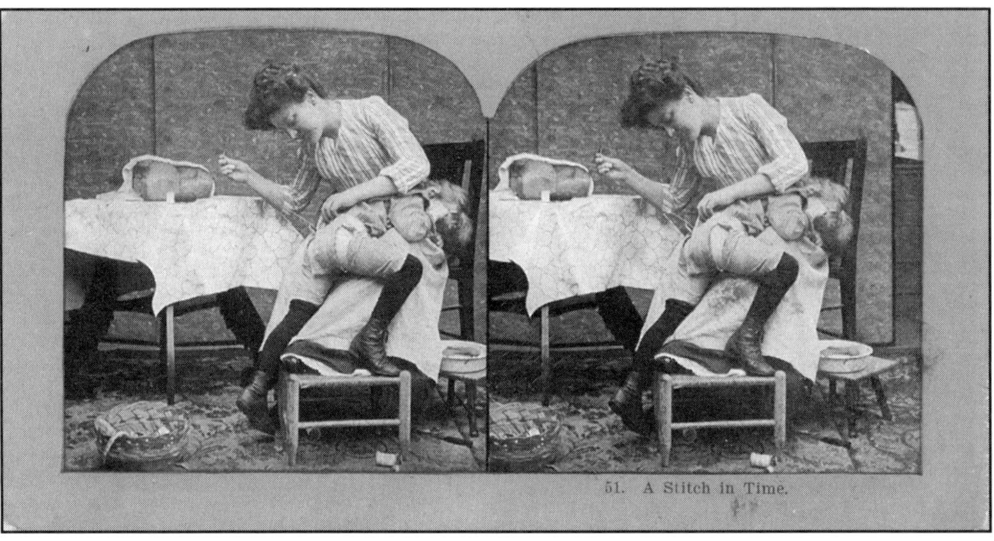

On Vacation: Coney Island, New York

- Everyone has dressed very carefully for the train trip and two days at Coney Island.
- Papa is wearing his best jacket with his Sunday tie and hat, while Momma has bought a new dress with matching parasol for the outing.
- No new dresses were purchased for Edna or her older sister, but great care was taken in ironing their outfits so they looked just right.
- Both girls did, however, receive new summer straw hats for the trip; Edna's is trimmed with a bright red satin ribbon.
- For months she has been looking forward to this trip to Coney Island; she has seen pictures of the Steeplechase Race, and Papa has said she could ride.
- She cannot wait to climb on the mechanical horse and gallop down the rail to the finish line—she is sure she will be first!
- Papa has also promised that she can go on the Ferris wheel if she dares; secretly, he thinks it is too high, even for the world's bravest nine-year-old.
- She knows that each ride costs a dime and she must not spend up all of Papa's hard-earned money, although she knows there is much to do.
- Friends have warned Edna about the Blowhole Theater, where concealed compressed air jets send hats and skirts flying upward.

Edna thinks her Papa looks distinguished in a beard.

Swimmers and their clinging bathing costumes are a bit embarrassing for Edna.

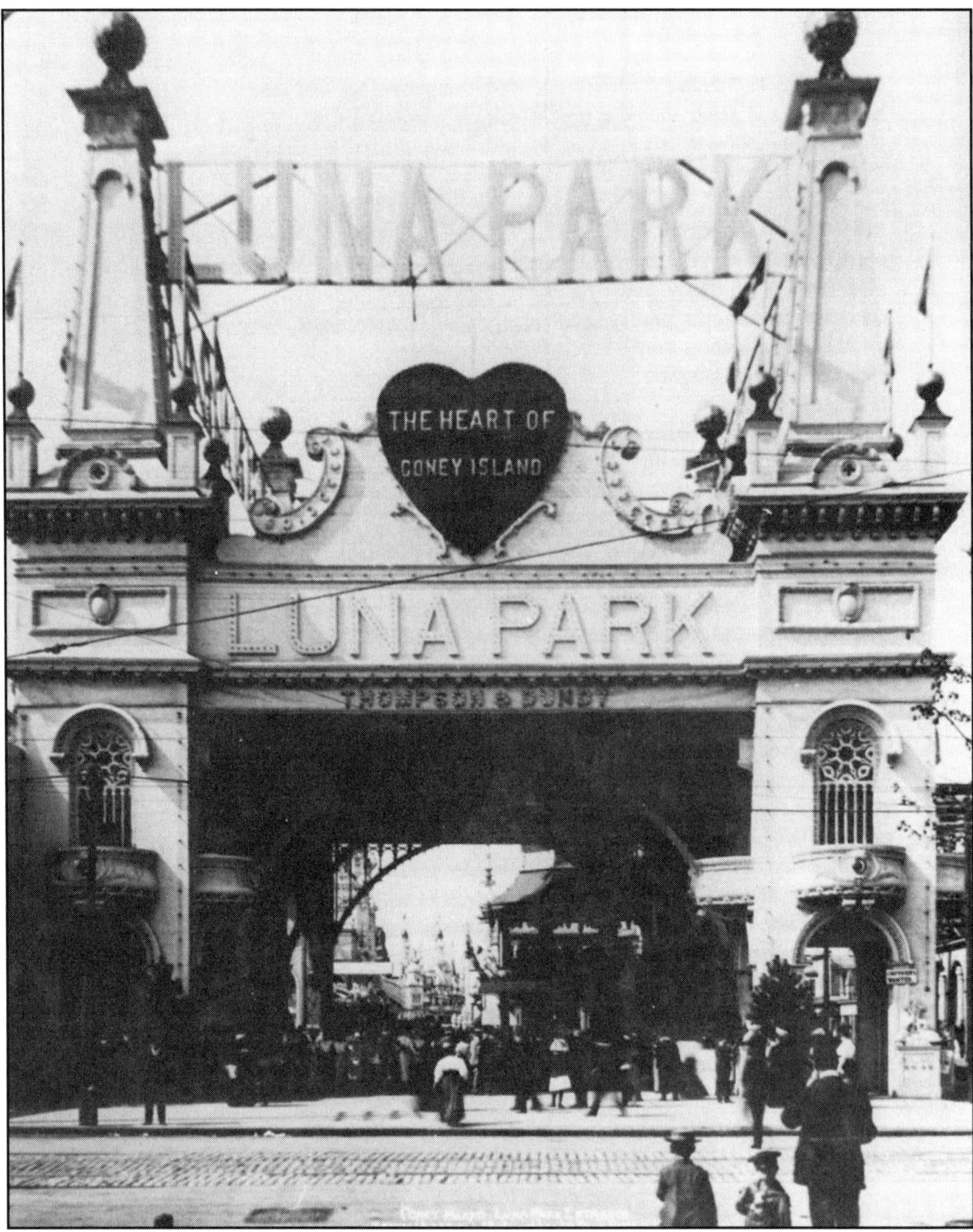

The beauty of Coney Island surpasses Edna's vivid imagination.

- She does not want strangers to laugh at her and has made Papa promise three times not to go near the Blowhole.
- But it wasn't until she arrived at Luna Park on Coney Island that her fantasies were fulfilled; Edna literally rubbed her eyes in disbelief when they arrived at Luna Park, the heart of Coney Island—not that she isn't an experienced traveler, of course.
- On a previous trip, they took a train to Niagara Falls in the middle of the winter to see the sights.
- Edna was surprised that so many people would come out in the cold just to witness falls frozen like giant icicles, she says every time she tells the story.
- Yet, Coney Island surpassed her vivid imagination; everything was so beautiful, and she had never expected to see this many people all at once.

The real magic starts when night falls and a quarter of a million lights spring to life.

- The developer of Luna Park, Frederic Thompson, was a former architectural student whose vision for a pleasure park included grand buildings with rich ornamentation that shut out the rest of the world.
- So much was going on at once, and so fast; Edna felt as though she were on a gigantic stage set and it was her job to be part of everything, not just to watch.
- Almost breathless, she and her family went from the Venetian city, complete with gondoliers, to the Japanese garden, then the island village, the Eskimo village, past the Dutch windmill and on to the Chinese theater.
- The real magic started when night fell, and the entire sky was transformed by a quarter of a million electric lights springing to life, outlining the buildings and exhibits with a soft glow.

"The New Coney Island," by Albert Bigelow Paine, *Century Magazine*, August 1904:

Once inside, the crowds "discovered an enchanted, storybook land of trellises, columns, domes, minarets, lagoons and lofty aerial flights. And everywhere was life—a pageant of happy people; and everywhere was color—a wide harmony of orange and white and gold.... It was a world removed—shut away from the sordid clatter and turmoil of the street.

Tall towers that had grown dim suddenly broke forth in electric outlines and gas rosettes of color, as the living spark of light traveled hither and thither, until the place was transformed into an enchanted garden, of such a sort as Aladdin never dreamed.

- At home, the streets are lit with gas, and her house by electricity—but rarely more than one bulb per room; this many lights were overwhelmingly beautiful.
- Momma has collected a dozen picture postcards of Coney Island and plans to write all her neighbors immediately; she wants the cards posted quickly so they will arrive back home before the family does.
- Only a few years ago, the post office began allowing picture postcards to be sent through the mail, and now everyone sends them.
- At her older sister's insistence, they visited the iron pier where people were swimming.
- Hundreds of people were in the water playing in the waves, making their bathing costumes wet; Edna was embarrassed that Papa might see the women's swimming dresses clinging to their limbs that way.
- On the second day they got to see the sideshows; although Edna didn't like the barkers talking about Little Egypt dancing the hootchy-kootchy for everyone to see, she loved feeding the elephants.
- She only agreed to ride the elephant when Papa said he would come, too.
- It was bumpy and fun and scary, and she can't wait to tell her friend, Iris.

Coney Island Barker on the "Streets of Cairo," 1904:

This way for the Streets of Cairo! One hundred and fifty Oriental beauties! The warmest spectacle on earth! See her dance the hootchy-kootchy! Anywhere else but in the ocean breezes of Coney Island she would be consumed by her own fire! Don't crowd! Plenty of seats for all!

- The most amazing sight was the re-creation of the fall of Pompeii, including the eruption of Mount Vesuvius and the death of 40,000 people; right after that, Edna watched a four-story building set ablaze while firemen heroically battled the inferno.
- She is sure she will include Mount Vesuvius in her school report about her summer vacation, as well as the elephant and the Ferris wheel and the train trip and the new hat.
- If she works hard enough on her report she could even get another Reward of Merit from her teacher.

Edna plans to write a story about her adventures at Coney Island.

Life in the Community: Burlington, Vermont

- The Shlake family lives outside Burlington, Vermont, whose population has reached nearly 19,000.
- As the principal city on Lake Champlain, the community has been a magnet for new industry during the past several years.
- With the addition of heavy manufacturing to its employment base, Burlington's reliance on lumbering has decreased.
- One of these manufacturers, the Porter Screen Company, is America's largest window screen company, producing 9,600 window screens each day.
- Their custom-made screens are stretched to drumhead tension, making a smooth and beautiful finish.
- The Baldwin Refrigerator Company, also located in Burlington, is currently shipping its product worldwide, including China, Africa and South America.

"The Consolidation of Rural Schools," Editorial Department, *The Educational Era*, April 1904:

Of all the plans for the improvement of rural schools, the establishment of the township central graded and high school we believe to be the most promising. The theory is perfectly intelligible, and as a practical scheme, is supported by success where it has been tried . . .

An article in *The School Journal* (June 27, 1903) gives a full account of the successful working of the plan in Ohio, where nearly 40 townships up to that time had adopted it. A few extracts from this article will supplement:

The local schools are abolished under this system. A school in a central position is selected. The pupils are transported at the public expense from their homes to the school. The general result is better schools, more interesting schools, increased attendance and decreased expense.

This solution to a troublesome problem is all the more satisfactory because the system is practically applicable everywhere. In Ohio, for instance, there are probably no townships that support any system of subdistrict schools, which could not support a system of centralized schools.

The first effect of the consolidated schools visible to the taxpayer is the increased size of the schoolhouse. What a contrast the centralized school building of two stories, many rooms, steam heat and commodious stables is with the log or slight frame district school, with one room, a stove and lean-to shed!

The contrast has been well-illustrated in Green Township, Ohio. Before 1900 there were seven or eight boxlike, one-room structures distributed over the township. The township is five miles square, 11 miles from one railroad and six from another. A central school was voted in, and a two-story brick structure was built. It contains six schoolrooms, a library, and an office. A basement is equipped as a laboratory and gymnasium. There are three acres of land around it. Shade trees, schoolroom decorations and a library are a few of the things unknown before its appearance. Here, eight wagons bring the children of the entire township where they enjoy the benefits of sanitary seating, lighting, heating and ventilation.

The attendance of transported pupils is almost perfect, for it suffers little from the weather, and it is a great increase over the number enrolled in the old schools. This is a logical result of the plan.

The item of expense has been the great stumbling block in the way of the expansion of the system. It means that a new schoolhouse must be built, and transportation provided. It has worked out that the expense of the separated schools is only a small amount less than with the central school; there is, for instance, a saving of a large amount of fuel, and the expenses of repairs on fences, pumps, walks and roofs are reduced 75 percent.

The educational advantages of the scheme are self-evident. Classification of pupils is possible. Larger classes stimulate interest. Progress can be made by the pupils. Better teachers can be engaged.

Such are the advantages claimed for the township high school . . . the main argument in favor of this consolidation and grading of the rural school is that, with little or no increase of expense, incalculably better schools will be provided. The children of the country shall have as good opportunities as the children of the cities.

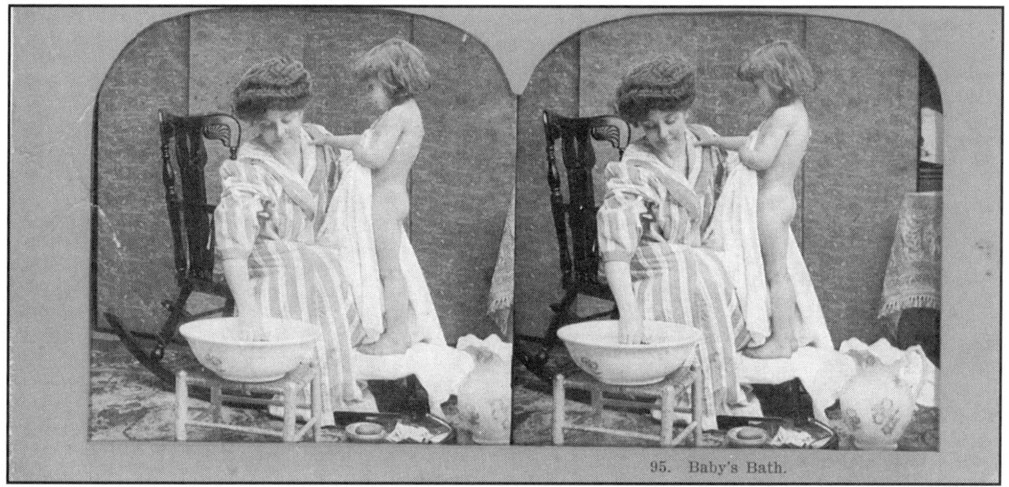

- On the market for 30 years, the Baldwin Refrigerator uses dry air circulation, zinc, porcelain and opal glass-lined interiors, and a hardwood finish to create a thoroughly hygienic refrigerator.
- Corporation taxes pay all the expenses of the state; recently, Vermont eliminated all other direct taxes.
- In addition to being the home of the largest patent-medicine factory in America, Burlington is also the site of one of the four oldest universities in New England, the University of Vermont, founded in 1791.
- Focused on continued growth, the university recently completed construction of a new medical building, considered one of the most perfectly equipped buildings of its kind in the country.
- A writer assigned to describe the town said, "We feel justified in saying that, not excepting Boston itself, Burlington is one of the least provincial cities in New England."
- Battery Park is located along the lakefront, an attractive green commemorating the site of a fortification that resisted an invading British fleet in 1812.
- The stability of the town has been assured by the three quality banks, including Burlington Savings Bank, which was chartered in 1847; currently, it has $12 million in deposits, making it one of the largest institutions of its kind in New England.
- According to a bevy of magazine authors, Vermont itself is best known to the world at large for its pretty girls and fine horses.
- It is also the state that gave America Ethan Allen, maple sugar, Clark of the Oregon and the Green Mountain Boys, and was the first state to abolish human slavery.
- Vermont has 860 licensed automobiles, 26 public libraries, nine newspapers and 65 brass bands.
- Several years ago, Vermont experimented with the prohibition of liquor, but abandoned the effort and eventually repealed the law; however, Burlington, the biggest city in the state, continues to be dry.

Vermont is known for its pretty girls.

Historical Snapshot
1904

- Malaria and yellow fever disappeared from the Panama Canal after army surgeons discovered the link to mosquitoes and developed successful disease control
- The sixth moon of Jupiter was sighted
- Marie Curie discovered two new radioactive elements in uranium ore—radium and polonium
- *The Shame of the Cities* by Lincoln Steffens and *History of the Standard Oil Company* by Ida Tarbell were published
- Carl Sandburg published *In Reckless Ecstasy*
- Laura Ziegler held a grand opening for her brothel in Fort Smith, Arkansas, hosted by the mayor and other dignitaries; the cost at the brothel was $3 an event, higher than the $1 charged at most establishments
- To celebrate the centennial of the Louisiana Purchase, St. Louis staged a World's Fair that attracted 18.7 million
- Montgomery Ward mailed three million catalogs to people free of charge; many were examined as religiously as the Bible
- President Teddy Roosevelt ruled that Civil War veterans over 62 years were eligible to receive a pension
- Central heating, the ultraviolet lamp, Dr. Scholl arch supports, E. F. Hutton, the Caterpillar Tractor Company and offset printing all made their first appearance
- Thorstein Veblen coined the phrase "conspicuous consumption" to describe the useless spending habits of the rich in his book, *Theory of Business Enterprise*
- The counterweight elevator was designed by the Otis Company, replacing the hydraulic elevator and allowing buildings to rise more than 20 stories
- The United States paid $40 million to purchase French property in the Panama Canal region
- The New York subway opened, with more than 100,000 people taking a trip on the first day
- Popular songs included "Give My Regards to Broadway," "Meet Me in St. Louis, Louis" and "Come Take a Trip in My Air-Ship"
- A massive fire in Baltimore destroyed 26,000 buildings
- The Olympics were held in St. Louis as part of the St. Louis Exposition; basketball was presented as a demonstration sport
- Novocain, the crash helmet, snow chains and the vacuum tube were invented

1904 Economic Profile

Selected Prices

Acme Refrigerator $27.50
Alarm Clock $2.50
Black Taffeta Petticoat $12.00
Broadcloth, 52 Inches, per Yard $1.00
Child's Folding Go-cart $8.50
Coca-Cola, per Glass $0.05
English Baby Carriage $25.00
Eyeglasses $2.50
Fireworks, Roman Candle $0.06
Graphophone Talking Machine $5.00
Human Hair Wig $2.50
Karo Corn Syrup $0.25
Peerless Disc Records $0.30
Pencils, per Dozen $0.05
Swiss Milk Cocoa $0.15

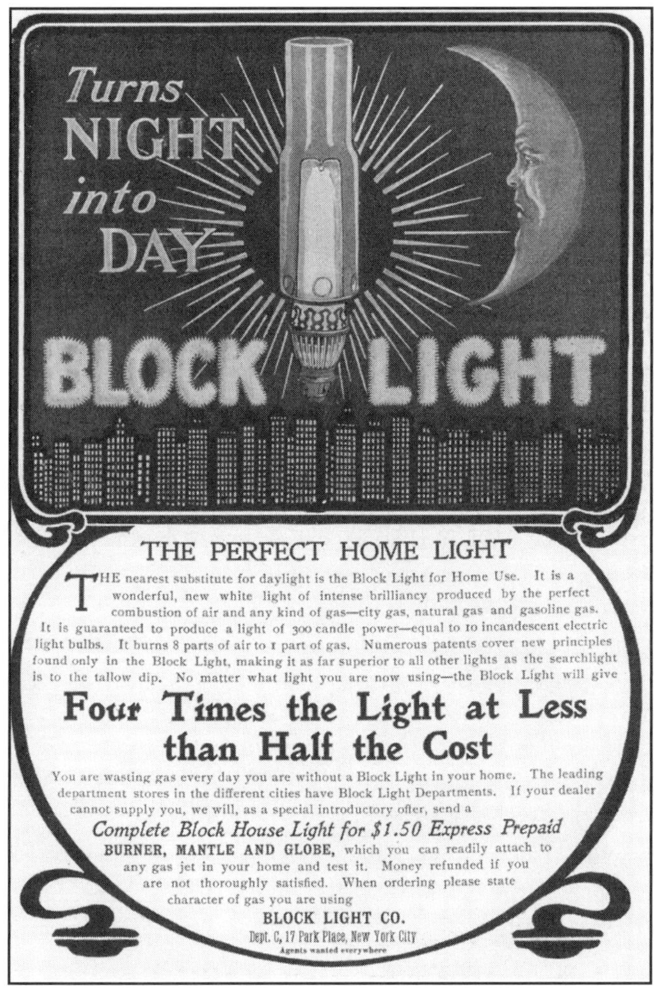

The thoughts of immigrant Virginia Parsons, born in 1899 as the middle child in a family of nine children, describing rural life in 1904 and beyond:

The woods was right close to where we lived, so we would all go. We'd get these big oak leaves, and we would see which ones could make the prettiest hats. And the broom sage that grows out in the field, you could break it off and make straws out of it. And we'd break it off about as long as a toothpick. And that's what we could glue this together with. And we made beautiful hats and decorated them with daisies and just the leaves that grew in the field. Well. we'd spend just our whole afternoon up there.

And I never will forget the first day that I went to school. Every time I saw my mother come to the well. I raised my hand to be excused. I wanted to go out and see her because I hated to leave her so bad that I didn't know what to do. I wanted to go to school, but if she hadn't had to come to the well, and I hadn't seen her, I would have been all aright. But I was in the first year of school. And the teacher, she caught on to what it was. So she always pretended. She knew where I was going. . . . I went to work in Burlington when I was 12 years old. I stood on a stool in what they called the warp room and tied knots on the warp that came down from the machines. I made $0.50 a day and I was the proudest thing that you ever saw.

Changing America

- Helen Adams Keller wrote for women's magazines about blindness, a previously forbidden subject.
- In some American cities, including New York City, women were being arrested for smoking cigarettes in public.
- Polls indicated that most Americans sided with Japan in the Russo-Japanese War.
- Saks published a 270-page catalog devoted to clothes to wear when motoring about the countryside.

"Mrs. Ralston's Answers," *Ladies' Home Journal*, May 1904:

How shall I make the every-day summer dresses for my two girls, 12 and 14 years of age, respectively, and of what materials? The materials must be inexpensive and serviceable.

—*A Mother*

Dark, washable linens and striped calicos would be both serviceable and inexpensive materials for the younger girl. Suits for girls of 12 are usually made with separate gored skirts, and blouses of a Russian tunic shape, which extend from three to four inches below the belt-line; otherwise, they are made exactly like little boys' Russian bloused suits. For your daughter of 14, I should also advise a plain gored skirt and a full gathered waist finished with a belt of the material attached to the skirt. One-piece play dresses are better and more becoming to girls of her age than separate blouses and skirts. Make the waist with clusters of side or box plaits and with full bishop sleeves, trimming the cuffs and collar with folds of narrow muslin or organdy.

"Daily Program of Gift and Occupation Work," by Carolyn Bailey and Clara M. Lewis, 1904:

Sample list of books that could be read to kindergarten children, month by month

September

Dust under the Rug	Maud Lindsay
Mrs. Tabby Gray	Maud Lindsay
Adventures of a Brownie	Miss Mulock
Mr. Sun	Richard Le Gallienne
Legend of Jack and Jill and the Moon	Dewey and Cady

October

The Ugly Duckling	Hans Anderson
The Ant and the Grasshopper	Aesop
The Lost Chicken	Emilie Poulsson
Contented Earthworm	Child's World
The Big Red Apple	Kindergarten Review, 1902

November

The Anxious Leaf	Henry Ward Beecher
The Porcelain Stove	Nora Smith
How Patty Gave Thanks	Emilie Poulsson
The Pumpkin Glory	William Dean Howells
Persephone	Flora Cook

- The Supreme Court ruled that Puerto Ricans could not be refused admission to the United States even though they were not citizens.
- Nationwide, the average school term was 143 days, though the average number of days attended per student was 99.
- Britain offered the country of Uganda as a national homeland for Jews.
- More than 3.2 million immigrants had come to America during the past four years.
- The military rejected the notion of using heavier-than-air flying machines during wartime.
- The Edison Company produced a short movie called *The Land Beyond the Sunset*, about slum youngsters taken on an outing.
- The Metropolitan Opera stopped leasing itself to independent impresarios and established itself as a stock company.
- Steerage rates for immigrants coming to the United States were cut to only $10 a person.

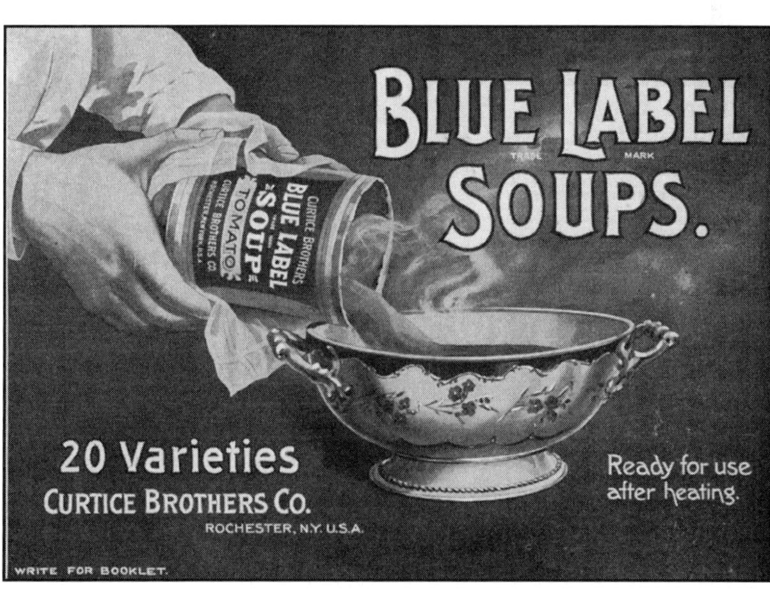

"What's the Matter with Vermont?" by Frank Putnam, *New England Magazine*, September 1904:

The Western man is surprised to learn that in Vermont, a state more than a century old, high schools have only recently come within the province of free public education. There have been many seminaries and academies in the state, some of them very old, which did the work of high schools, but these were not part of the public school system. The state until lately provided only primary education free. There was no mandatory high school law requiring towns and cities to provide free high school education until 1896. There are today 75 high schools and free academies doing high school work. There are, in addition, 17 private seminaries and academies doing high school and college preparatory work.

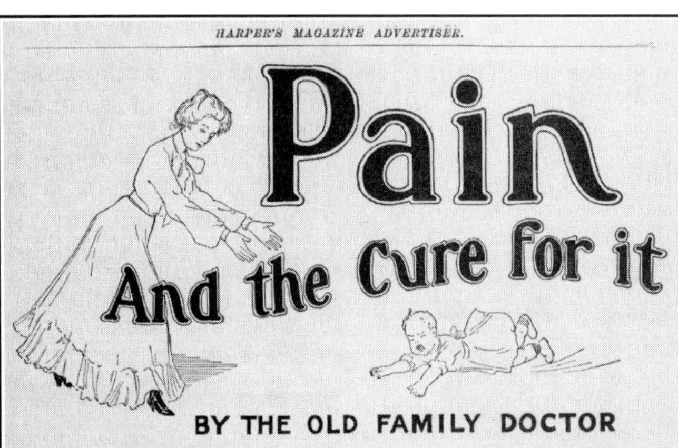

BY THE OLD FAMILY DOCTOR

EVERY home should have its medicine chest and be prepared for emergencies. As the "first aid" on the battlefield helps the surgeons to save thousands of lives, so, likewise, may the first aid in the home help the doctor.

An indiscriminate collection of remedies, patent medicines and old prescriptions on the medicine shelf is not only useless, but positively dangerous. All the emergency remedy needed in the home is a bottle of that good old pain preventive, Pond's Extract, the pure extract of Hamamelis. For ages physicians have recognized the value of this remedy as an anodyne, antiseptic and astringent.

For reducing inflammation, alleviating pain, preventing soreness, stopping bleeding; for the bumps and bruises of childhood; the burns and scalds of womanhood and the serious injuries of manhood, there is no relief so effective as Pond's Extract. Indeed, there are so many ills in which Pond's Extract is valuable that it often supplies for years every medicinal need of a family. For piles, ulcers or sores; for toothache, earache, neuralgia; for sore throat, sore eyes, stiff joints, back lameness, rheumatism, and all painful ailments of local nature, it is not only invaluable but perfectly safe and harmless. This is why physicians do not hesitate to recommend Pond's Extract for home use and to sound a warning against the use of the common substitute—witch hazel.

Chemical analysis discloses that wood alcohol is used in still further cheapening the production of witch hazel. This being a deadly poison, the danger of using common store witch hazel, without knowledge of its origin or purity, is readily understood.

To say that witch hazel is the same as Pond's Extract is like saying that colored water resembles rare old wine. In fact, ordinary witch hazel is nearly all water, while Pond's Extract is the pure extract of Hamamelis, distilled from the tender shoots of the plant when the sap is flowing and afterward aged for years to give it greater strength and purity. This is the reason Pond's Extract is used by physicians in the hospitals, on battlefields and wherever men get hurt and require quick attention.

For over sixty years this famous extract has been sold in the curious shortnecked bottles, with the same buff colored wrappers to identify the remedy that relieves the suffering of mankind.

1904 News Feature

"Little People in Their Play Clothes," by Mrs. Ralston, *The Ladies' Home Journal*, May 1904:

Play clothes, as all mothers know, mean plain clothes, strong clothes, clothes that will wear, wash and iron, and, in addition to all this, are inexpensive and pretty. Undoubtedly the materials which have proven most serviceable for play clothes for general wear are the better grades of gingham and linens. This does not, of course, mean that all the lovely thin materials, such as batiste and nainsook, are not nice for children's clothes, because they are; but I mean that, especially for the stouter clothes for hard play wear, the heavier cotton materials are the best. Clothes of this character are prettier and far more sensible when made up altogether without accessories or trimmings. For little girls to play in, the one-piece dress is the best; it is more comfortable and far more easy to wash and iron than the one which is made in two pieces. The one-piece dresses are worn by little girls from their tiniest days until they reach at least 12 years of age, and are especially pretty when made in the brown Holland linens with plaited backs and fronts, and the plaits varying in width; the simplest and easiest way is to have the plaits rather wide. Sometimes these one-piece dresses are made with very wide box plaits, the edges of which are generally stitched.

Another nice way to make little girls' play dresses is after the fashion of the coat worn the past winter, known as the "Buster Brown" style, with one very wide double box plait down the centre front. So wide is the plait that it really covers the greater part of the front; the edges of the plait are stitched and finished with a row of buttons that form the fastening of the dress. . . .

For boys from four to six years of age, very nice little play suits are made with tunics. In fact, it is difficult to say whether they are tunics or coats: they seem to be a little of each; however, they are very nice particularly when made in the washable summer materials. These little coats or tunics, whichever you please to call them, are quite short, reaching not more than three inches below the waist, and thus show much more of the bloomers than the original tunic, which as a rule almost altogether covered them. You may be quite sure that these little coats which show so much of the bloomers will please the small boys very well. They are made quite plainly both after the style of the sailor and Russian blouse tunic suits; or again, they are made with box backs and fronts, the fronts being double–breasted after

Page 52 — The Ladies' Home Journal for May 1904

LITTLE PEOPLE IN THEIR PLAY CLOTHES

By Mrs. Ralston

the fashion of a coat. They are worn either with turnover linen collars or with very narrow little straight collar bands. The collar and the cuff bands, as a rule, are trimmed with narrow folds of white tape or white muslin to give them just a touch of white as a finish. . . .

One very pretty model of a plain coat for a girl about 12 years of age has a wide box plait down the centre back, two double box plaits down the front—one from each shoulder—the centre front being made quite plain and the fastening of the coat hidden under the left side box plait. The collar is a low, rolling one, and the sleeves are box plaited and finished with wide, rolling cuffs. . . .

The fashions for little men seem to change but little. The only real new note to be seen in their summer clothes, and particularly in those intended for real service, is in the extra length of the shoulders, this being a note apparently directly copied from their mothers' clothes. These play dresses for the little men are made always with the tunic coat and bloomer trousers. The tunics and the trousers are always the same shade, but not necessarily of the same material; for instance, some of the older boys have tunics of brown linen and bloomers of brown velveteen or corduroy. This, of course, is only for economy and service, as the suits look better for dressier occasions when made with bloomers to match.

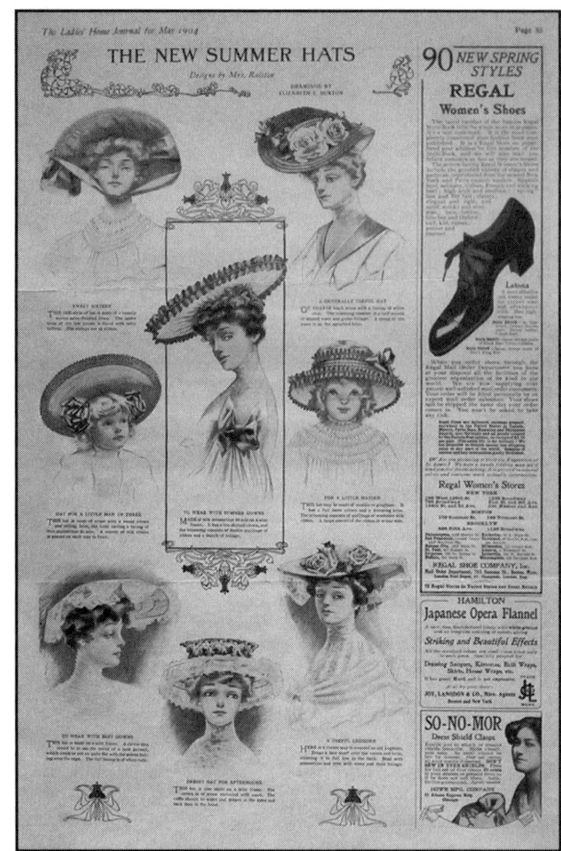

The Ladies' Home Journal for May 1904

THE NEW SUMMER HATS

Designs by Mrs. Ralston

The Outlook

1907 News Feature

"A Better Chance for Children of the Slums," by Charles W. Eliot, President of Harvard University, *The Outlook*, August 10, 1907:

Well-to-do people, having found it very difficult to bring up their children satisfactorily in closely built towns and cities, have invented two different means of securing a healthy life for them while at school. One means is the patronage of academies or schools situated in the country, but conducted by accomplished teachers who know how to provide for the intellectual and moral, as well as the physical, needs of children in their charge; hence the prosperity of the partially endowed academies of New England, and of the more recent private country schools which provide board and lodging as well as instruction. The second means is the provision of day schools well-situated in the country, within easy reach of the city, so that the children can easily come out of their city homes to the country every morning, and return near the close of the afternoon. This is a comparatively recent invention used with satisfaction by parents who do not wish their children to be wholly separated from them. The families who use one or other of these two means are well-to-do, live in the cleanest and most wholesome parts of the crowded cities, and can provide their children at home with such facilities for out-of-door exercises as cities afford.

The children of the slums need the fresh air and light of large open spaces much more than the well-to-do children, but the noisy, obscure and dirty streets of the poorest quarters of the city are their only resort.

In the interest of these poor children, a Boston architect, Mr. J. Randolph Coolidge, has lately made to the Boston School Committee a new proposal with regard to the location of public school buildings. He suggests that grammar schoolhouses for the children who live in congested districts be placed on the edge of one or more of the city parks, and that the pupils be carried out to the schoolhouses so situated in the morning and brought home again at night in streetcars, at the public expense, five days in the week, so that on school days the children shall no longer play in the streets or study at home.

There can be no doubt that this arrangement would be highly advantageous to the children who should be thus brought out from the slums five days in the week, and kept under supervision nine or 10 hours a day. They would have the adjoining park to play in, and each schoolhouse could be provided with a large yard and plenty of light and air.

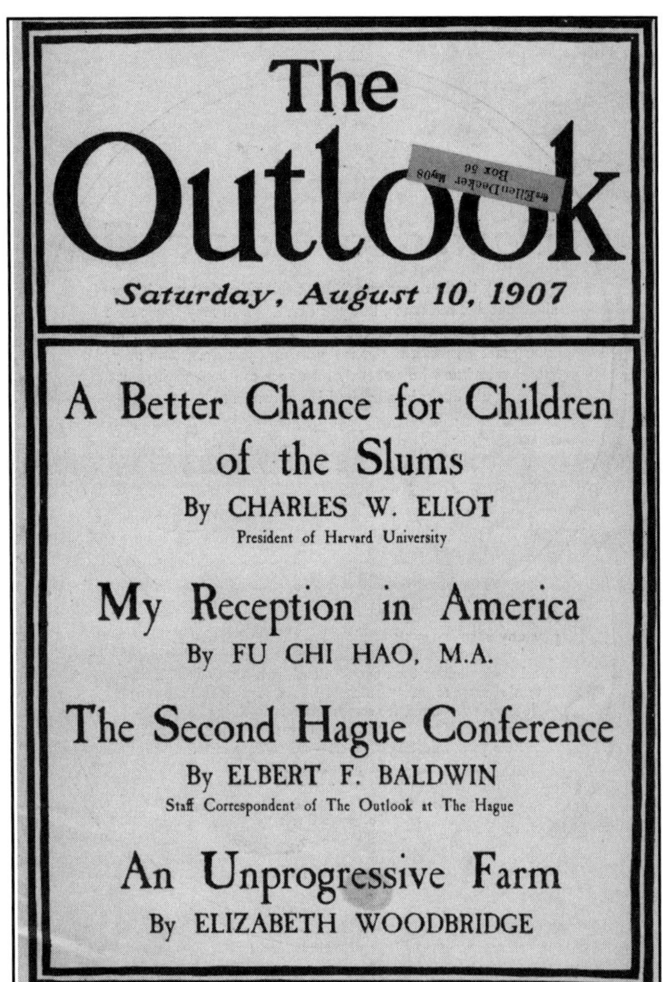

The Outlook

Saturday, August 10, 1907

A Better Chance for Children of the Slums

By CHARLES W. ELIOT

President of Harvard University

My Reception in America

By FU CHI HAO, M.A.

The Second Hague Conference

By ELBERT F. BALDWIN

Staff Correspondent of The Outlook at The Hague

An Unprogressive Farm

By ELIZABETH WOODBRIDGE

If it be assumed that the fathers and mothers in the slums will be willing, or more than willing, to have their children treated in this way, the only objection to this excellent proposal is that it would cost the city something more than the city now spends on these children. There would be two new items of expense: (1) the transportation of the children, and (2) the supervision of the children's play hours. If cars could be used running the opposite direction from that of the greatest traffic during the busiest hours, the transportation companies might make the children's fare very low and yet lose no money. The supervision of the play and study hours of the children would be a clear additional expense which would be different in different localities, but might easily cost $5,000 a year for each school of 1,000 children. These extra charges would be partially met by the interest on the difference in cost between a schoolhouse site in the heart of the city and a schoolhouse site taken on the comparatively cheap land of the suburb adjoining a large country park. This difference in cost would be very considerable in many American cities. About 40,000 square feet is the least suitable area for a schoolhouse to accommodate 1,000 children. Such an area might easily cost in Boston, for example, $50,000, whereas the same area opposite one of the large Boston or metropolitan parks might be procured for $5,000. The park sites would also have the advantage of being permanent, as well as thoroughly suitable in all respects. In the closely built parts of a city, the shifting of population so infrequently makes it necessary to sell an old site and procure at great cost a new one.

This plan is not applicable to young or delicate children, or to children whose services at home for part of the day are absolutely required. It is proposed for healthy children, not less than 10 years old, who are not required to work for their families in the afternoon. These country public schools should have facilities for exercise, occupation or games under cover in stormy weather; in good weather the children's games and exercise should take place in the open air, partly in the park and partly in the large schoolyard. It is not proposed to give away any food at the country schoolhouse. Food brought from home would be warmed, and food would be sold over a counter at cost.

This proposal is certainly very attractive to the humanitarian, the sanitarian and the economist, for it would give the children of the slums a far better chance for a healthy and happy childhood, and for the future serviceableness at adult age. The general plan would have to be adapted in its details to each locality which should determine to try it, for the transportation problem would be different in different cities, and the cost of adequate supervision would vary in different localities. The amount of money to be saved on the difference of cost between schoolhouse sites in the congested districts and sites near the parks would also vary widely in the different localities. It is an advantage of the plan that it can be tried with one schoolhouse at a time. That the method is strictly analogous to the methods being adopted by well-to-do people for the benefit of their children should additionally commend it to the democracy for trial.

1909 Profile

Upper Class

Nathan Federov is the son of affluent Russian Jews whose ancestors came to Iowa 50 years ago. Nathan is obsessed with cars and all things mechanical; it is his destiny, he believes, to help shape the automobile age.

Life at Home

- Fifteen-year-old Nathan Federov loves to tinker: If an object has moving parts, Nathan can tear it apart and put it back together—just ask him.
- When only seven, he dismantled his mother's sewing machine and insisted he could put it back together.
- It did little good; his mother was so mad she sent him to the woods to select a limber whipping stick.
- He loves spending time at his father's motorcar garage and sales store working on cars, motorcycles, boats—anything that has an engine.
- The garage is the sales and repair depot for the entire region; if it's new and innovative, it can be found there.
- Nathan just received plans from *Scientific American* describing how to convert a horse-drawn buggy into a motorcar for less than $300; he thinks this is a great way to introduce people to the joys of owning a car.
- His father thinks little of his son's idea, believing it to be just another way for local Luddites to avoid buying a real car and joining the modern transportation era.
- Since the automobile revolution began, Nathan's father has owned half a dozen cars, a motorcycle and a motor boat.
- Two of the cars were wrecked on country roads after getting caught in a rut and tossed into a ditch; the 18-foot gasoline launch is used on a nearby lake.
- Currently, Nathan's favorite vehicle is a motorized cycle, or Motoracoche, which weighs 66 pounds; he built it himself.

Fifteen-year-old Nathan Federov loves to tinker with machinery.

Nathan's father and two uncles own various businesses in town.

"The Automobile of Tomorrow," by Herbert Ladd Towle, *Scribner's Magazine*, May 1909:

The automobile has not yet found itself. In the crude mechanical sense it has nearly—not quite—arrived. Legally it is still in the Dark Ages, doing penance for the sins of its graceless youth. Socially it is a fad, a blatant crier of surplus wealth, a separator—automatic and horribly efficient—of the Fool and his Money, a double-barreled troublemaker that is always loaded.

The daughter of a Baptist minister has caught his eye.

- Using six wing nuts, he was able to attach the Motoracoche to his bicycle, just under the bar.
- A twisted belt was passed through a grooved pulley and clamped onto the spokes of the rear wheel to transmit the power of the motor, which weighs 15 pounds and delivers one-quarter horsepower.
- The carburetor, weighing nine pounds, uses either gasoline or alcohol, while two cells of battery storage supply current for ignition; the gas tank has a capacity of three pints—enough for a 60-mile trip.
- Almost 40 years ago, Nathan's family came to Ottumwa, Iowa.
- His grandfather, a Jewish immigrant from Russia, was a traveling peddlar who pulled a wagon of kitchen utensils from village to village.
- Then, in the early 1870s, after his wagon broke down and his third son was born, he settled in Ottumwa and opened a livery stable, which expanded to include a blacksmith shop, then a garage and lodge for travelers.
- Eventually, the final transformation was a garage and sales studio for the emerging automobile.
- Nathan's uncle, the oldest in the family, now runs the family hotel—the largest one in Ottumwa—while Nathan's father handles motorcars, repairs and tire sales; the third son now runs the livery stable and blacksmith shop.
- Thanks to hard work, they all own homes and have raised large families.
- Nathan is the oldest of six children, and the only boy.
- To serve the expanding Jewish population of the region, a new, larger synagogue is under construction; Nathan's mother is in the center of getting it built.

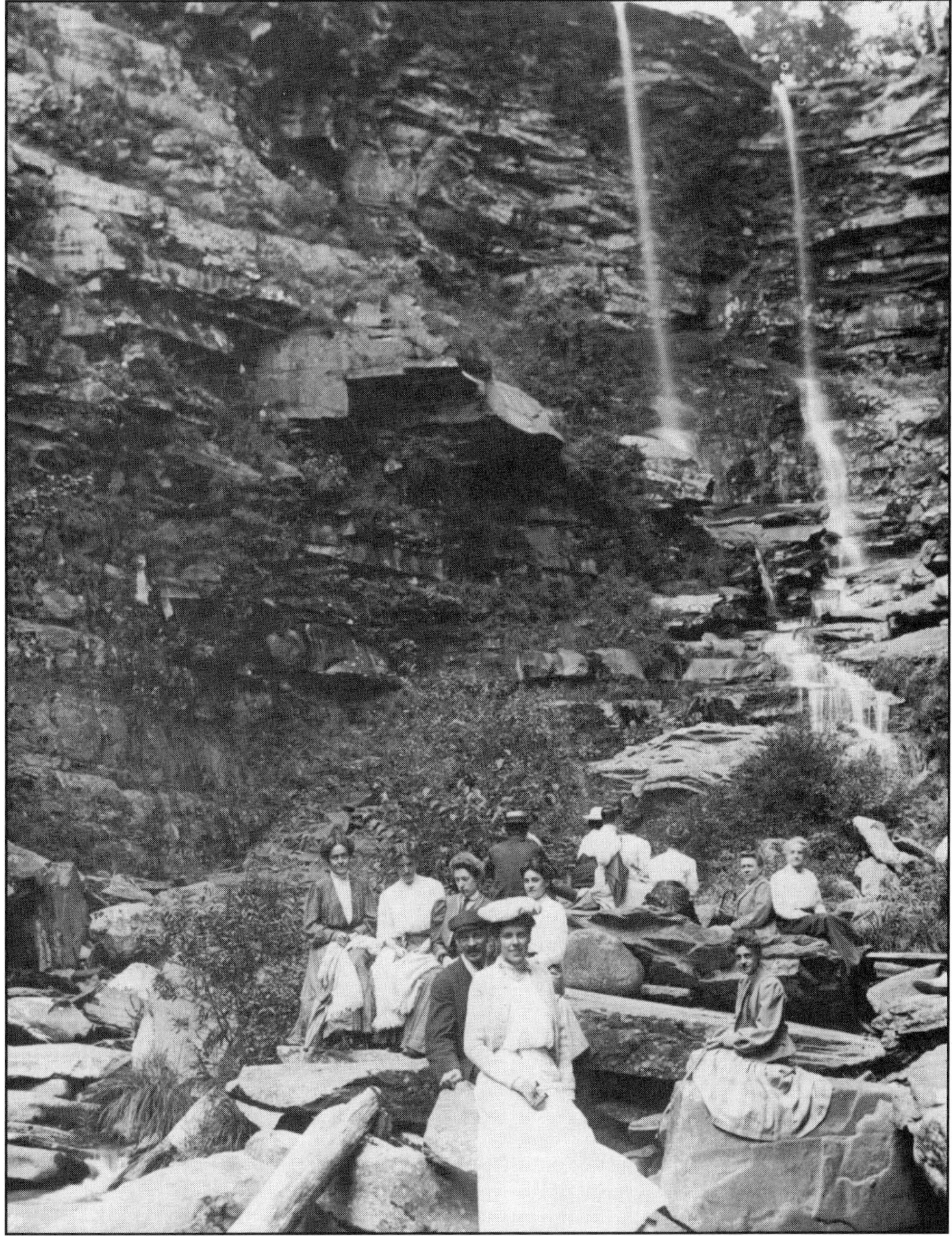

Thanks to the automobile, the Federov family and friends take trips into the countryside.

Life at School and Work

- Nathan wants to be a mechanic and help run his father's motorcar showroom, but his father wants him to go East to attend college, possibly at an Ivy League school.
- It is an old argument: what kind of education does Nathan need?
- His father wants him to be worldly, but still return to Iowa to help run the business; Nathan does not want to fool with Shakespeare and Europe's various King Henrys and Louies when he could be a part of defining the mechanics of the American automobile.
- At school Nathan is bored by the classes and in love with the girls.
- As one of the richest boys in town, he is watched closely by many of the pretty girls; as one of the few Jewish boys in Ottumwa, he is regarded with curiosity.

"Moving Picture Drama for the Multitude," by George Ethelbert Walsh, *The Independent*, February 6, 1909:

The moving picture drama furnishes entertainment for the millions, literally reproducing comic, tragic and great events to some 16 million people a week at a nominal cost of a nickel or a dime. The effect of this new form of pictorial drama on the public is without parallel in modern history, for it more graphically illustrates the panorama of life than the photographs and texts of the daily newspaper and intrudes upon the legitimate theater through the actual dramatization of plays that have had a good run. The moving picture drama is for the multitude, attracting thousands who never go to the theater, and is particularly appealing to children.

All of this has been developed within half a dozen years, and the remarkable growth of the industry is due to the perfection of the biograph, vitagraph, kinetosope or cinematograph—whichever name the moving picture machine goes by—within the last year or two. Edison first invented the moving picture machine, but he did not perfect it, and others rushed in to secure patents on its improvements which gave them certain protective rights....

In the last two years "nickelodeons," or moving picture theaters or exhibition halls, have opened in nearly every town and village in the country, and every city from the Klondike to Florida and from Maine to California supports from two or three to several hundred. Millions of dollars have been invested in the shows, and it is estimated that, on average, two or three million people in this country attend the shows every day of the week.

A considerable class of pantomime actors depends entirely upon the film companies for their living. They receive all the way from $15 to $40 a week for their services. Then, too, the story writer comes in for a share of the profits of the new profession. A good story suitable for moving picture reproduction may sell from $5 to $30 or even more. The story is not written out in magazine form, but is a brief description of scenes and acts which have a well-defined plot. Some of the companies are experimenting with the phonograph in connection with the moving pictures, by means of which the actors in the scenes will actually speak and declaim as the various pantomime scenes are thrown on the screen.

- He has his eye on one girl in particular, the daughter of a Baptist minister; he is sure they would get along if he could work up the courage to talk with her, but he is unsure of what to say or what her father might think.
- He is thinking about sending her a postcard as a means of introduction—but is worried that it might be too forward.
- His goal is to take her to a moving picture show, now that a theater has opened in Ottumwa.
- Recently, he watched as trains roared across the screen and even seemed to fly into the audience; yes, an invitation to the moving pictures might be just the thing to capture her heart.
- At the motorcar store where he spends every afternoon, 1909 is shaping up to be a good year.
- Nationwide, automobile sales have increased from $8 million in 1903 to $105 million five years later; the auto industry now employs 110,000 people in manufacturing and sales.
- Today, 250 firms are engaged in automobile construction, producing approximately 52,000 cars last year alone; currently, 320,000 motorcars are on America's roads.

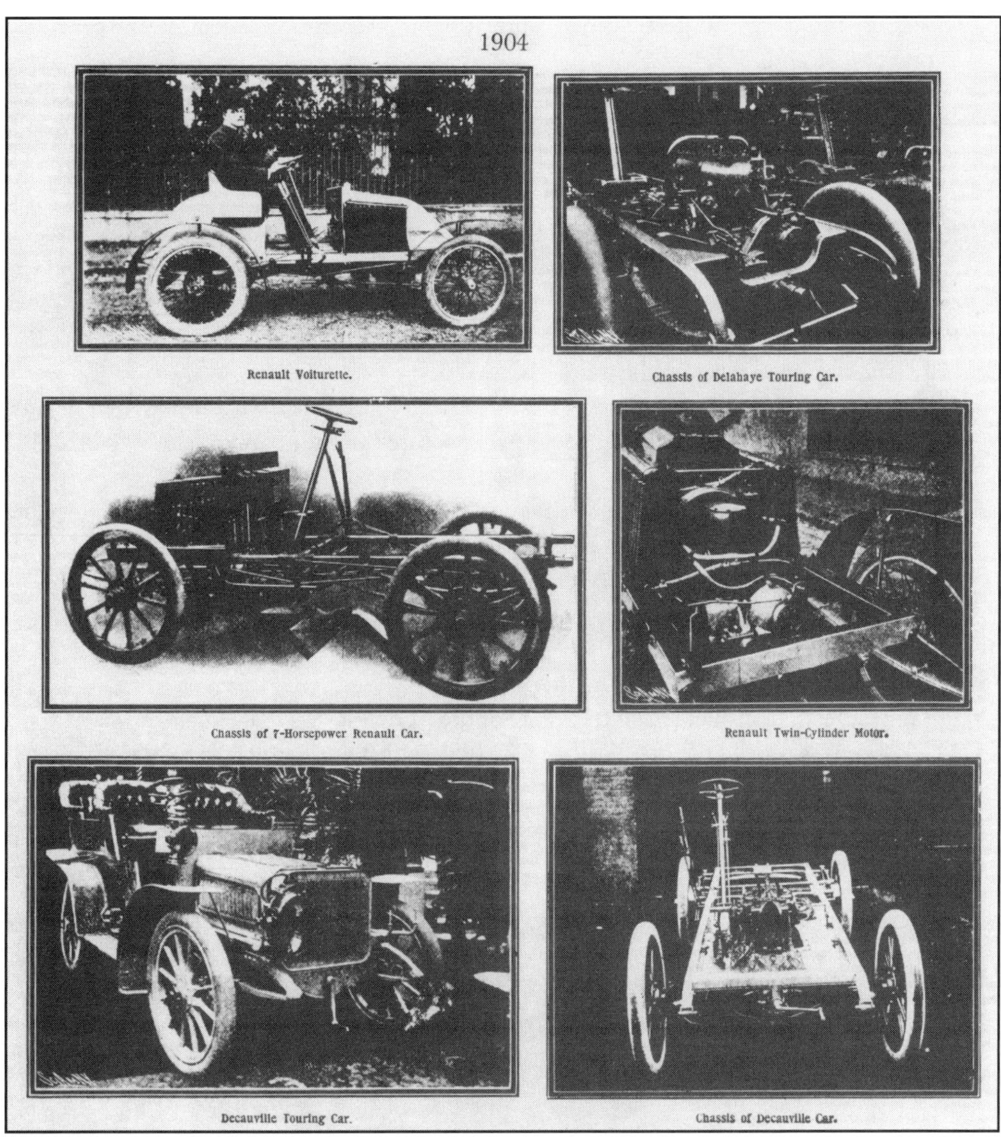
1904

Renault Voiturette.

Chassis of Delahaye Touring Car.

Chassis of 7-Horsepower Renault Car.

Renault Twin-Cylinder Motor.

Decauville Touring Car.

Chassis of Decauville Car.

Nationwide, 250 firms are engaged in automobile construction.

- American manufacturing has been so successful, the importation of cars has rapidly declined, falling to 28 million in 1908.
- A typical four-cylinder automobile producing 20 to 30 horsepower costs around $1,500 at his father's garage.
- Buyers come from miles around to talk about motorcars, buy tires and get repairs done.
- Innovation is in the air; just in the past six months the price of tires has fallen from $97 to as low as $37 each, thanks to improvements in manufacturing.
- This year's car models feature a magneto ignition, water-cooled cylinders, forced-feed lubrication and direct shaft drive, including three forward gears and one reverse.
- Recently, Nathan found an article in *Scientific American* that detailed the cost of running an automobile to 8.8 cents per mile; his father was so pleased he uses it in his sales talks with customers.
- According to the article, which was based on the experience of an automobile owner who drove his seven-passenger car 30,000 miles in two and a half years, the cost per mile

was: tires, 5 cents; gasoline, 2.7 cents; lubricating oil, 0.2 cents; incidentals, 0.9 cents, for a total of 8.8 cents.

- If a car owner drives 1,000 miles a month, the car's annual cost is: tires, $500; gasoline, oil, acetylene and repairs, $500; chauffeur and rental of private garages, $1,300—total: $2,300.
- The dealership is beginning to specialize in rough and rugged motorcars that can withstand the mud, ruts and stumps of the area.
- Automobiles are now being designed with 36-inch diameter tires to improve road clearance; the cars also have a double chain drive with a 52-tooth sprocket on the two rear wheels, and 8-tooth sprockets on the jackshaft, which give considerable leverage for heavy pulling when stuck in the mud.
- A special, more elastic transmission for Midwestern roads is being created so that in hard pulls and heavy mud, it can be set to stop just before the strain approaches the breaking point.
- Recently, Nathan was thrilled when his father bought him his own car—the juvenile, foot-propelled auto made by the Toledo Metal Wheel Company in Toledo, Ohio, which also makes 25 models of automobiles.

Life in the Community: Ottumwa, Iowa

- Ottumwa, Iowa, considers itself to be one of the Midwest's great business cities.
- The last census pegged the population at 22,000, with a vibrant farming community that swells the population even more.
- As a railroad and manufacturing center, Ottumwa boasts many quality retail stores, competing well with cities of comparable size across the country.

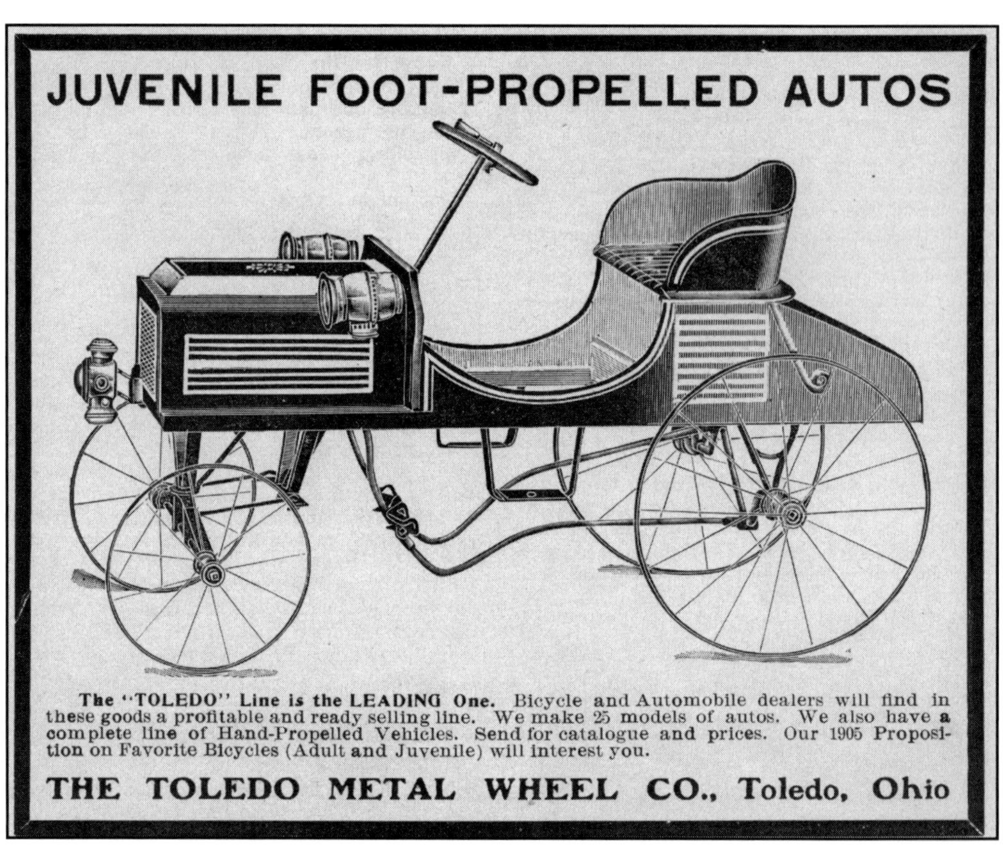

"Conquerors of the Road, A Forecast of Automobilism," by William Frederick Dix, *The Independent*, November 7, 1909:

If one will look over the advertising pages of the magazines of five or six years ago, the pictures of the automobiles then sold will strikingly illustrate the development since then of this modern sport. At that time the manufacturers seemed to have an ambition to conceal the fact, as far as possible, that their vehicles were machines. They made buggies and surreys with the engines hidden away beneath the seats and flooring, and a new topic was given to the joke writers and cartoonists—that of the motorist lying on his back in the dusty or muddy road, tinkering awkwardly at the most inaccessible inner parts above him. The world still regarded these vehicles as "horseless carriages," and it was several years after they came into use before the makers realized that they should forsake the designs of the carriage manufacturers and treat the cars as engines.

Gradually, bicycle wheels and light bodies were discarded, the engines were taken from their ignominious position under the body and placed forward under a protecting bonnet, where they might be easily reached; the chassis became suitably heavy, and the modern motor-car emerged triumphant as an engine of locomotion. Today it no longer sails under false colors; it looks the world in the face, an enfranchised motorcar.

- In all, the city has four railway trunk lines leading into Ottumwa, and a division point on three of them.
- Industries include the manufacturing of farm and mining implements, as well as cigar and candy production; jobbers also consider Ottumwa a quality distribution point for wholesale hardware, dry goods, groceries, drugs and fruit.
- Two factories recently relocated to the town, one moving from Moline, Illinois, the other from Davenport, Iowa.
- The city has begun to develop its water power on the Des Moines River, which is wide enough for the navigation of large boats.
- Ottumwa boosters brag that from Des Moines to Keokuk, the Des Moines River has a fall of 369 feet, and that Ottumwa is halfway between these two points, generating enough power to run factories.
- Currently, the city generates enough electric power to begin lighting the surrounding countryside as well.
- A commercial college now operates, and a large college is planned, based on the city's potential as an agricultural center, not only for Iowa, but for Omaha, Minneapolis, Kansas City and Springfield, Illinois.
- Boosters say, "In these places are millions of mouths to be fed, and Iowa is the garden for all of them."

Historical Snapshot
1909

- Windsor McCay's cartoon, *Gertie the Dinosaur*, became the first animated film produced in the United States
- Congress passed the 16th Amendment, permitting federal income taxation
- The song, "I Wonder Who's Kissing Her Now" soared in popularity
- Cigarette smoking increased dramatically, with production topping eight billion units
- The modern plastic age was born when Leo Baekland created Bakelite, which was hard, impervious to heat and could be dyed in bright colors
- President Howard Taft set aside three million acres of Western land for conservation
- Congress banned the importation of opium except for medical uses
- The Rockefeller Sanitary Commission led a nationwide fight to eradicate hookworm, especially in poor children
- Automobile production doubled from the previous year to 127,731 cars; 34 states adopted laws setting the speed limits at 25 miles per hour
- Nationwide, more than a million people attended various ceremonies celebrating the birth of Abraham Lincoln
- The new penny imprinted with Abraham Lincoln's image replaced the Indian head penny, in circulation since 1864
- General Electric advertised an electric kitchen range that had 30 plugs and switches embedded in a wooden table, powering an oven, broiler, pots, pans and even a waffle iron
- The Kewpie doll, the electric toaster, the gyroscope, gasoline cigarette lighters and *Vogue* magazine all made their first appearance
- During the college football season, 33 players died, heightening safety concerns

1909 Economic Profile

Selected Prices

Acme Lawn Mower	$5.89
Bicycle	$14.95
Cigarettes, 10	$0.05
Elgin Pocketwatch	$8.15
English Day Clock	$6.66
Gillette Safety Razor	$5.00
Motorcycle, Seven Horsepower	$275.00
Petroleum Jelly, Two Ounces	$0.03
Pistol, Automatic	$3.75
Playing Cards	$0.25
Sak's Men's Suit, Tropical Weight	$15.00
Sardines, per Can	$0.35
Scientific American, One Year	$3.00
Suspenders	$0.50
Wrestling Match Tickets, Balcony	$0.50

"Because You're a Jew," by Sydney Reid, *The Independent*, November 26, 1909:

Some little time ago, a very bright Southern lady, writing in the columns of *The Independent*, twitted us of the North because, while we held up our hands in horror at evidences of what we called race prejudice displayed by Southern folks against the Negroes, we ourselves were entertaining what, she insisted, was quite as virulent and much more absurd race prejudice against highly intellectual, highly polished and entirely harmless people called Jews. . .

Listen to the voice of a leading Rabbi of Brooklyn, who has made a study of anti-Jewish feeling among Gentiles:

"In spite of the fact that many of the great department stores are owned by Hebrews and patronized chiefly by Gentiles, I hear that there is a little commercial prejudice against Jews—that many Gentiles say, 'We won't go to a Jew store.' But the leading manifestations of anti-Judaism are social—the fraternal societies particularly—societies whose very foundation is the promotion of universal brotherhood make use of all sorts of excuses to keep out Jews. Most Masonic lodges keep out Jews, though there are some lodges that are almost entirely composed of our people, thus segregating them from the general brotherhood of Masons. So it is throughout the other fraternities, and though we have fraternities of our own, we find it mortifying and humiliating that we are excluded from the general social body.

"Jews are admitted into the great colleges and universities of the country. In fact, so far as the authorities are concerned—the faculties and university officials—I never heard of a case of discrimination. They set a good example of liberality. But among the students it is different. They draw aloof from their Jewish comrade, and to a greater or lesser extent, send him to Coventry. He finds he can't get into the fraternities. He finds he can't get on the athletic teams, no matter how competent an athlete. He doesn't like that at all, for he has the same social instincts as others. But if he inquires why, and manages to secure from any quarter an honest answer, it is 'Because you're a Jew.'

"Many of the leading private schools refuse outright to receive young Jews as pupils, and others again will take them if their names are not 'too Jewy. . . ' The school would admit any young Jews whose names might be Gentile Germana, or Russian, or English, but not a Levi, a Cohen, a Moses or a Solomon."

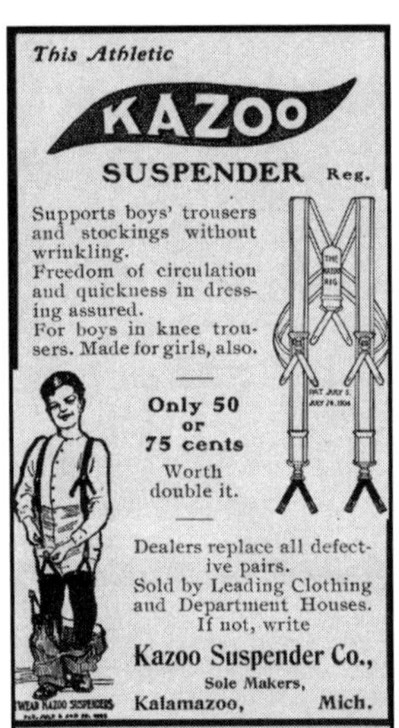

Changing America

- Approximately 8,500 women received college degrees, up from 2,500 in 1890.
- Introduced and developed by Thomas Edison, 35mm film became the accepted film size for movie-making.
- Jell-O, the wildly popular packaged gelatin food, advertised itself as "the American dessert."
- The average price of a beef steer was $6.80, up from $5.15 at the turn of the century.
- The Niagara Movement joined with white liberals to form the National Association for the Advancement of Colored People; leaders included W. E. B. Du Bois, John Dewey, Lincoln Steffens, Clarence Darrow and Rabbi Stephen Wise.
- During the previous five years, 4.9 million immigrants came to America.
- Former President Teddy Roosevelt recommended that the Pearl Harbor Naval Station in Hawaii be used to defend the United States against the Japanese.
- The incandescent light was beginning to replace the carbine flame jets used for automobile headlights.

"Why There Are So Few Women Automobilists," by Mrs. Andrew Cuneo, *Country Life in America*, March 1909:

There must be some good reason why so few women drive automobiles. It may partially be accounted for by the fact that the automobile manufacturers are not building cars that are especially adapted to women's use; then, too, considerable strength is required to crank a car and to attend to tire troubles; the unpleasant attitude of other drivers may have something to do with it, also the difficulty that most women experience in understanding machinery, and their natural disinclination to do any work that will soil hands or clothing. Perhaps the principal reason is that they lack confidence in their ability to drive a car.

- A Broadway play titled *The Melting Pot* examined the disappearance of Jewish tradition when Jews became assimilated into the New World.
- A bison refuge was created near Boise, Idaho.
- Wilbur Wright designed an airplane for the United States Army that carried two passengers and reached a top speed of 40 miles per hour.
- U.S. President Howard Taft's salary was increased from $50,000 a year to $75,000.

"The Children's Library in Cleveland," *Charities and the Common Welfare*, November 21, 1909:

The Perkins Children's Library, recently established by the Cleveland Public Library, is an interesting instance of cooperation between two civic institutions. It was made possible by the Day Nursery and Free Kindergarten Association which leased to the library, free of rent, a small frame house adjacent to the Perkins Day Nursery. The expense of remodeling was borne by the library. . . .

The result is a room which seats 70 children and a story hour room which seats 50. The furniture cost about $1,200. There are about 3,000 books which cost about $2,000. A small collection of adult books which adults may draw upon, and which may be given to children to take home to their parents, will be provided. . . .

The library is in the vicinity of iron foundries, a clock factory and a large casket factory. The people are German, Bohemian and Ukrainian. They are housed in small buildings, two and three deep, and under very unsanitary conditions. The neighborhood is rapidly growing more congested.

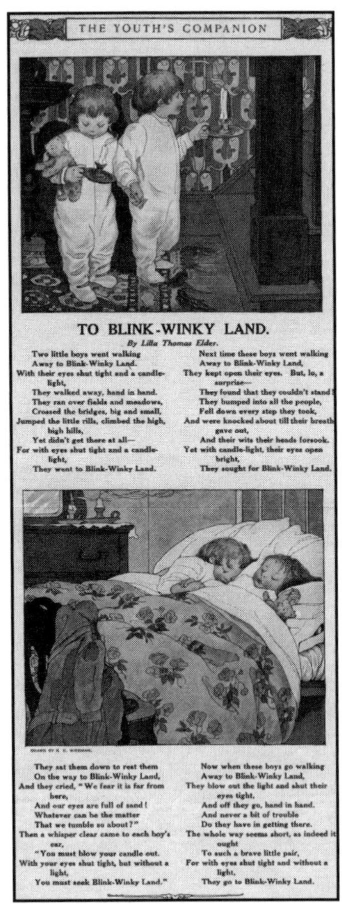

THE YOUTH'S COMPANION

TO BLINK-WINKY LAND.

By Lilla Thomas Elder.

Two little boys went walking
Away to Blink-Winky Land,
With their eyes shut tight and a candle-light,
They walked away, hand in hand.
They ran over fields and meadows,
Crossed the bridges, big and small,
Jumped the little rills, climbed the high, high hills,
Yet didn't get there at all—
For with eyes shut tight and a candle-light,
They went to Blink-Winky Land.

They sat them down to rest them
On the way to Blink-Winky Land,
And they cried, "We fear it is far from here,
And our eyes are full of sand!
Whatever can be the matter
That we tumble so about?"
Then a whisper clear came to each boy's ear,
"You must blow your candle out.
With your eyes shut tight, but without a light,
You must seek Blink-Winky Land."

Next time these boys went walking
Away to Blink-Winky Land,
They kept open their eyes. But, lo, a surprise—
They found that they couldn't stand!
They bumped into all the people,
Fell down every step they took,
And were knocked about till their breath gave out,
And their wits their heads forsook.
Yet with candle-light, their eyes open bright,
They sought for Blink-Winky Land.

Now when these boys go walking
Away to Blink-Winky Land,
They blow out the light and shut their eyes tight,
And off they go, hand in hand.
And never a bit of trouble
Do they have in getting there.
The whole way seems short, as indeed it ought
To such a brave little pair,
For with eyes shut tight and without a light,
They go to Blink-Winky Land.

"Fighting Tuberculosis," *The Youth's Companion*, March 18, 1909:

It has always been recognized that in warfare, a knowledge of the enemy's weak points confers immense tactical advantage. This was never truer than in the tremendous crusade that mankind is banding together to wage against that dreaded foe, tuberculosis.

A few decades ago, this particular enemy of the human race was not believed to have any vulnerable spots. It was thought by all to be invincible, and that its mere touch meant death. Then it was gradually discovered that, after all, certain weapons were at hand by means of which mankind could give fight; that before sunlight, fresh air and proper food, this foe would recoil like Mephistopheles before the crucifix. . . .

The good news was taken to the tenements and crowded parts of great cities, where sunshine and fresh air are not secured without a struggle, but where they are just as efficacious as in the haunts of the wealthy.

The free exhibits given by the International Tuberculosis Exhibition are of immense value in this educational crusade, and the charity that takes the form of paying carfare in order that the poor of the tenements may not miss this invaluable object-lesson is a very real one. Here, the mother trying to save her stricken child in two rooms in a tenement district is shown those two rooms as they probably are and as they may be. In the first instance, dirty, cluttered up with useless rubbish, with every crack through which air may filter carefully stuffed with unclean rags. Then side by side with this picture, the same rooms cleaned and purified, with windows which will open wide and stay open, and with nothing in sight that cannot be made clean and kept clean.

The great lesson is taught in capital letters that comfort and stuffiness are not synonymous terms; that whitewash is a thousand times better than ancient, germ-laden wallpaper, and can be applied by anyone, and as often as is desirable; that a floor that can be washed daily with soap and water feels better and looks better than the same floor covered with scraps of microbe-infested carpet; and that sanitary receptacles can be had for the asking, which make it possible to expectorate without endangering the lives of a whole family.

It would be well indeed if these exhibitions could be given in every town and village in the country.

"A Good Catch, The Little Folks Play Department," *Little Folks*, June 1909:

It was a rainy day. Nurse thought and thought. Nurse always had to think hard on rainy days because Teddy and Freddy, the twins, got tired of their playthings, and wanted new games every few minutes.

Mother and nurse began to talk secrets—something was surely going to happen!

"Now, boys," said the mother, "how would you like to go fishing?"

The twins jumped up and down with delight. Their chubby faces were covered with smiles and dimples.

Mother opened a cupboard drawer, brought out a big blue crumb-cloth (a sheet, shawl, blanket or large papers can be used for the purpose), and spread it over the carpet.

"Gee! That's make-believe water!" whispered Teddy to Freddy.

"Now, Teddy," said mother, "go to the hall for papa's cane, and Freddy, you will find the yardstick in the sewing-room. They're to be your fishing poles."

The boys ran for their poles, then stood waiting for what was to happen next.

First, nurse came in with packages of gray and white cotton batting, two extra-large pins, some coarse linen thread, pieces of red worsted and a wad of tin foil.

Teddy and Freddy watched closely while nurse rolled the pieces of cotton batting lightly between her hands till they looked almost like sure-enough fish—gray trout and white perch. One by one, they dropped into the blue pond.

"Fishermen, now for some rocks," called out mother merrily—"big rocks to stand on when you want to fish way out in the deep water."

The two hassocks were lifted from their corners on either side of the hearth, and placed close to the edge of the fishing banks.

The boys were so anxious to begin that they jumped on top of the colored rocks before things were quite ready.

Mother bent one end of each pin into a hook, tied on the linen thread for lines, and fastened the lines to the homemade poles. Small wads of tin foil, twisted and placed above the hooks, made first-rate sinkers.

Even the "worms" were not forgotten. They were made from the red worsted cut into one-inch strips. Of course, in this kind of fishing, the bait couldn't cover the end of the hook, or the fish mightn't bite!

Then Freddy left his rock, and off flew the two towards the kitchen for the baskets, before mother had finished telling them where to find them.

All was ready. Hurrah for the new game!

Mother and nurse made believe to go away, for they knew the small boys (and girls, too) could have much more fun if big folks were not around. But you may be sure they were near enough to see the youngsters were going to enjoy the rainy day frolic. Of course they had to keep very quiet.

The eyes of the young fishermen sparkled as each held up a finger to his mouth and said, "Hush!" creeping softly on tiptoe towards the pond—as the fish would really be scared away, you know!

Current thinking has it that women lack the confidence to drive cars.

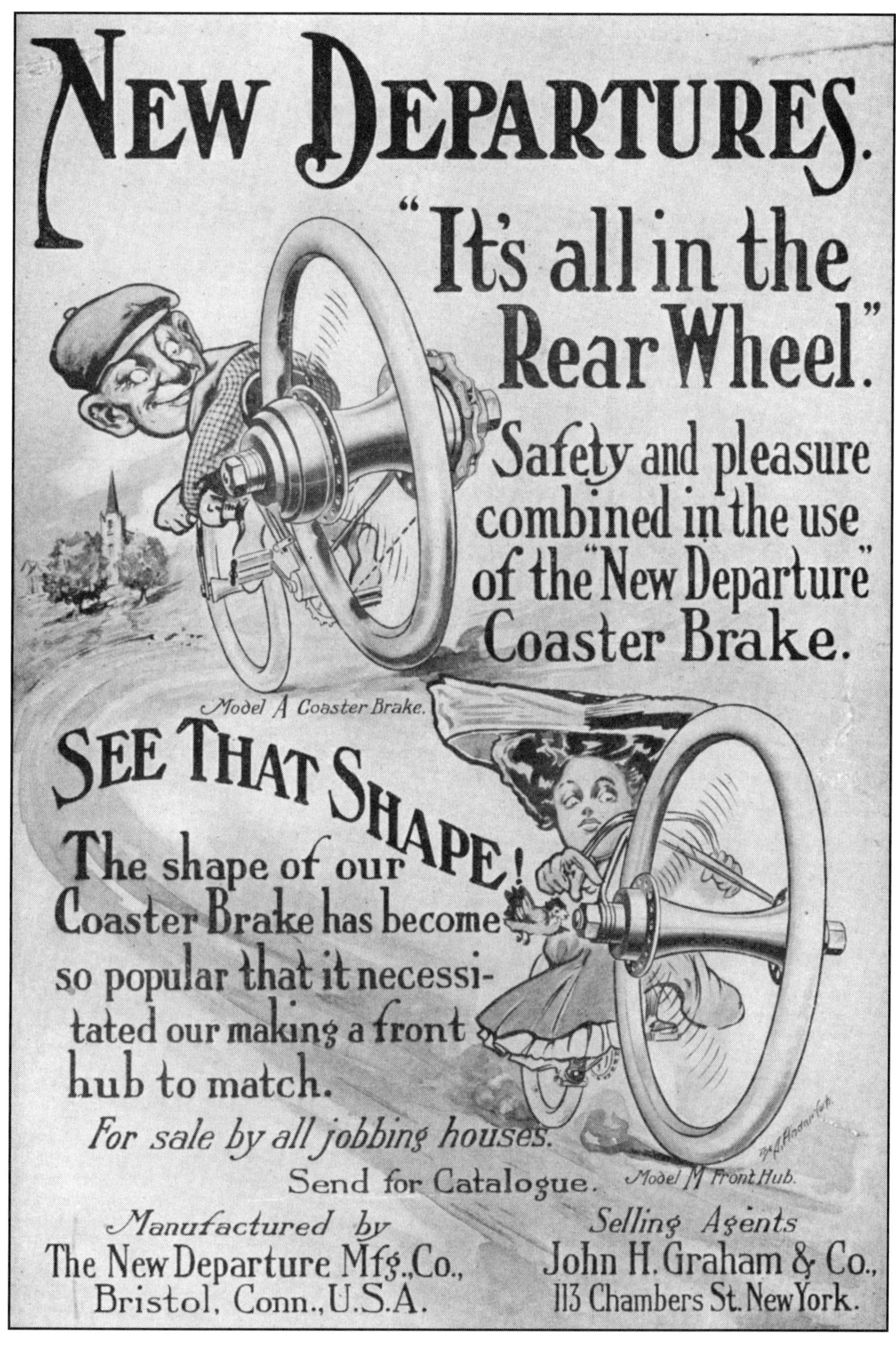
NEW DEPARTURES.
"It's all in the Rear Wheel."
Safety and pleasure combined in the use of the "New Departure" Coaster Brake.
Model A Coaster Brake.
SEE THAT SHAPE!
The shape of our Coaster Brake has become so popular that it necessitated our making a front hub to match.
For sale by all jobbing houses.
Send for Catalogue.
Model M Front Hub.
Manufactured by
The New Departure Mfg. Co., Bristol, Conn., U.S.A.
Selling Agents
John H. Graham & Co., 113 Chambers St. New York.

1910–1919

The second decade of the century marked a changed role for America's children. As the middle class expanded, education reform took new prominence, children's wellness clubs prospered, and even America's quilting designs and story book pictures began featuring children gleefully at play, not simply as small adults in family portraits. At the same time, the emerging middle class was proving that it was capable of carrying a greater load of managerial decisions, freeing factory owners and stockholders to travel, experiment, and study ways to cure the ills of the poor. Millions of dollars were poured into libraries, parks and literacy classes designed to uplift the immigrant masses flooding to American shores. America was prospering and, at the same time, the country's élite were reevaluating America's role as an emerging world power which no longer had to look to Britain for approval.

Immigration continued at a pace of one million annually in the first four years of the decade. Between 1910 and 1913, some 11 million immigrants—an all-time record—entered the United States. The wages of unskilled workers fell, but the number of jobs expanded dramatically. Manufacturing employment rose by 3.3 million, or close to six percent in a year during the period. At the same time, earnings of skilled workers rose substantially and resulted in a backlash focused on protecting American workers' jobs. As a result, a series of anti-immigration laws was passed culminating in 1917 with permanent bars to the free flow of immigrants into the United States. From the beginning of World War I until 1919, the number of new immigrants fell sharply while the war effort was demanding more and more workers. As a result, wages for low-skilled work rose rapidly, forcing the managerial class—often represented by the middle class—to find new and more streamlined ways to get the jobs done—often by employing less labor or more technology.

In the midst of these dynamics, the Progressive Movement, largely a product of the rising middle class, began to shape the decade, raising questions about work safety, the rights of individuals, the need for clean air and fewer work hours. It was a people's movement that grasped the immediate impact of linking the media to its cause. The results were significant and widespread. South Carolina prohibited the employment of children under 12 in mines, factories, and textile mills; Delaware began to frame employer's liability laws; the direct election of U.S. senators was approved; and nationwide communities argued loudly over the right and ability of women to vote and the need and lawfulness of alcohol consumption.

During the decade, motorized tractors changed the lives of farmers, and electricity extended the day of urban dwellers. Powered trolley cars, vacuum cleaners, hair dryers, and electric ranges moved onto the modern scene. Wireless communications bridged San Francisco to New York and New York to Paris; in 1915, the Bell system alone operated six million telephones, which were considered essential in most middle class homes as the decade drew to a close. As the sale of parlor pianos hit a new high, more than two billion copies of sheet music were sold as ragtime neared its peak. Thousands of Bibles were placed in hotel bedrooms by the Gideon Organization of Christian Commercial Travelers, reflecting both the emerging role of the traveling "drummer" or salesman and the evangelical nature of the Progressive Movement.

Yet in the midst of blazing prosperity, the nation was changing too rapidly for many—demographically, economically, and morally. Divorce was on the rise. One in 12 marriages ended in divorce in 1911, compared with one in 85 only six years earlier. The discovery of a quick treatment for syphilis was hailed as both a miracle and an enticement to sin. As the technology and sophistication of silent movies improved yearly, the Missouri Christian Endeavor Society tried to ban films that included any kissing. At the same time, the rapidly expanding economy, largely without government regulation, began producing marked inequities of wealth—affluence for the few and hardship for the many. The average salary of $750 a year was rising, but not fast enough for many.

But one of the biggest stories was America's unabashed love affair with the automobile. By 1916, the Model T cost less than half its 1908 price, and nearly everyone dreamed of owning a car. Movies were also maturing during the period, growing rapidly as an essential entertainment for the poor. Some 25 percent of the population, including many newly arrived immigrants, went weekly to the nickelodeon to marvel at the exploits of Charlie Chaplin, Mary Pickford, and Douglas Fairbanks, Sr.—each drawing big salaries in the silent days of movies.

The second half of the decade was marked by the Great War, later to be known as the First World War. Worldwide, it cost more than nine million lives and swept away four empires—the German, the Austro-Hungarian, the Russian, and the Ottoman—and with them the traditional aristocratic style of leadership in Europe. It bled the treasuries of Europe dry and brought the United States forward as the richest country in the world.

When the war broke out in Europe, American exports were required to support the Allied war effort, driving the well-oiled American industrial engine into high gear. Then, when America's intervention in 1917 required the drafting of two million men, women were given their first taste of economic independence. Millions stepped forward to produce the materials needed by a nation. As a result, when the men came back from Europe, America was a changed place for both the well-traveled soldier and the newly trained female worker. Each had acquired an expanded view of the world. Yet women possessed full suffrage in only Wyoming, Colorado, Utah, and Idaho.

The war forced Americans to confront one more important transformation. The United States had become a full participant in the world economy; tariffs on imported goods were reduced and exports reached all-time highs in 1919, further stimulating the American economy.

1911 Profile

Upper Class

Jonas Bergman is the son of a major mill owner in Everett, Washington. He is obsessed with all things connected with football, which he believes to be his destiny.

Life at Home

- Sixteen-year-old Jonas Bergman loves being the oldest son in a family of seven, which includes eight-year-old twin sisters.
- He thinks it is great to be the leader and dream up plans for everyone, especially at Christmastime.
- Every year when he, his sisters and brothers decorate the giant Christmas tree, he gets to decide who puts which ornaments on the tree.
- It is the special job of the youngest and the oldest to put on the first string of popcorn and berries along the lower limbs of the fir tree, but Jonas alone gets to place the angel on the top.
- His mother tells everyone that her children are the finest tree trimmers in the Western states.
- At Easter, he also takes a lead role in reading *Ben-Hur, A Tale of the Christ* to the smaller children.
- Most of the year, a well-illustrated edition of *Ben-Hur* sits next to the Bible; during the Christian season of Lent a nightly reading is held.
- Both his mother and father were raised on a tradition of reading this historical romance novel written in 1880 by Lew Wallace.
- The book, which tells the effect of the life and death of Christ on a Hebrew merchant, quickly became a national bestseller and evolved into an Easter tradition in many homes.
- Two years ago a touring company actually staged the theatrical version of *Ben-Hur*, which was attended by the entire family.
- Jonas also loves to pass along his secrets, and is currently showing his five-year-old brother how to twiddle his thumbs; for the little boy, the challenge is to twiddle backward and forward with his eyes closed and not fall over.

Jonas Bergman is obsessed with football.

Everett is a great town for boys who love hopping logs and swimming to the sandbars.

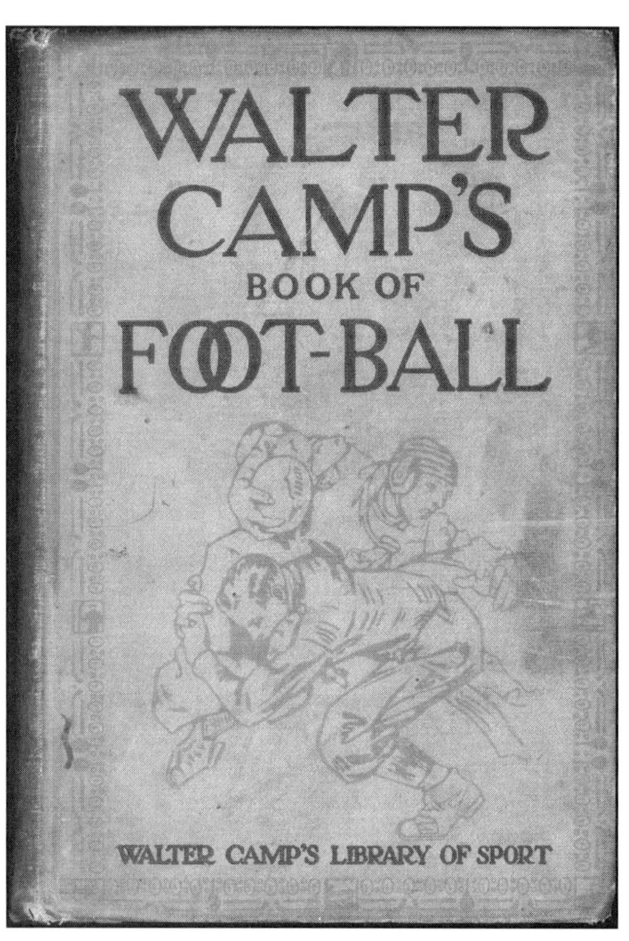

- In this home, the evening meal is an important family time, and no excuses are accepted for not being in attendance.
- Jonas, his sisters and brothers stand behind their chairs at opposite sides of the table until their parents take their seats, one at each end of the table.
- Then, all heads are bowed as father says grace.
- Invariably, in front of father are 10 dinner plates—blue willow on weekdays and Haviland china on Sundays.
- If the main course is roast or fowl, father does the carving and serves the food on everyone's plate.
- Always to his left sits a bowl of potatoes or stuffing, while on his right is a bowl of fresh or home-canned vegetables, depending on the season.
- The children are not allowed to say if they don't like something being served; if a child indicates a certain food is not his favorite, father puts less on his or her plate, but the child must eat it all.
- In front of mother sits the salad or fruit of the day, and at her left is a pot of hot tea in a highly glazed black pottery teapot with enameled flowers—for the adults only.
- All of the family's milk comes from Hembree, the family cow, even though quality milk is now available year 'round in Everett.
- Jonas's father was born in Sweden and raised in rural Wisconsin.
- He married a fellow Swede and immersed himself in the timber industry, jumping at the opportunity to move West where thousands of acres of virgin forest still existed.

Red cedar shingles are one of the lumber industry's most profitable products.

- He now manages investments in Everett for John D. Rockefeller, and serves as co-owner of the largest shingle-manufacturing mill in the United States.
- During the past decade, red cedar shingles milled for distribution nationwide have been one of the lumber industry's most profitable products, though it is often subject to wide price swings based on competition and availability.
- The shingle plant is doing well, comparable to the business year of 1906, when the earthquake and fires of San Francisco—and the city's rebuilding—opened up considerable demand for shingles; in one year, the price of logs, lumber and shingles doubled.
- Jonas's father employs 165 shingle weavers who produce more than a million shingles during each 10-hour shift.
- In Everett, the term "shingle weaver" applies to sawyers, filers and packers who work as a crew to produce cedar roofing shingles.
- Stacking the slices of cedar into overlapping bundles, a skilled packer works so rapidly he appears to be weaving the shingles together—thus, the name "shingle weaver."
- Since the mid-1880s, investors from the East, including John D. Rockefeller, have speculated heavily in the possibilities offered by Everett, Washington; many succeed in their ventures, but few succeed for long in this rough market.
- Growing up in Everett, Jonas has enjoyed the freedom afforded by the town, his father's position and his intrepid spirit.
- Everett is a great town for adventurous boys—they can hop onto logs that float down the Snohomish River, swim out to the sandbar in mid-channel or catch snakes along the riverbank.
- Like many boys in the area, Jonas takes great pride in his ability to identify the various mill whistles along the waterfront—the Ferry-Baker, the Clough-Hartley, the Hulbert, the Eclipse and others all have a distinctive sound.
- At the noontime whistle, when other young boys in the town run pails filled with their fathers' lunches to the mill, Jonas eats at home with his father, who takes a nap after lunch before returning to work.

"Ring-a-Ring o' Roses"

Ring-a-ring o' roses
A pocket full of posies
Ashes! Ashes!
We all fall down.

EDWARD H. COY
Yale
THOMAS L. SHEVLIN
Yale
WALTER W. HEFFELFINGER
Yale

Jonas longs to be a star quarterback at Yale.

- His mother often spends her afternoons taking a walk; she is still wearing black in mourning for her baby, Garrison, who died last year when the measles epidemic swept through the northwest, claiming 17 children in Everett under the age of two.
- The town's best photographer was hired to shoot a picture of Garrison as he lay in his casket; Jonas's mother keeps the picture by her bed, which is also draped in black.
- Several days a week the mothers of the victims walk to the cemetery together to put flowers on their children's graves.

Life at School

- Jonas enjoys school, but is obsessed with football, believing it represents his future.
- Ever since he read *Walter Camp's Book of Foot-ball*, he is convinced he should play in college, maybe at Yale.
- He longs to be the star quarterback, especially now that the rules have been changed to allow the quarterback to cross the line of scrimmage whenever he pleases.
- For the past 25 years, football's rules said: "The quarterback is obligated, when running the ball across the line of scrimmage, to be at least five yards away from the center."
- That has now been changed, and it is not the only significant rule shift, although not all of the changes are positive.
- According to the 1910 rules, flying tackles are now prohibited, because of so many injuries to both tackler and runner.
- The new rule states, "A player in tackling must have at least one foot on the ground."
- Jonas agrees with Walter Camp's comment on this new rule: "If a man, therefore, is endeavoring to go around an end and a (defensive) halfback is running at full speed to reach him, it is going to be a very difficult question as to what will happen, for we all know that a man running at speed has both feet off the ground at once, and if it is a close thing, either the halfback must tackle when he is on the run, or lose his man if he stops."
- The second rule causing trouble is the new one on passing, stating: "No player of either side while in the act of catching a forward pass shall be tackled, thrown, pushed, pulled, shouldered or straight-armed until he shall have caught the ball and taken more than one step in any direction."
- Jonas believes this rule must be changed; after all, interference is the keynote of American football, and crucial to preventing the other player from catching the ball.
- At night Jonas and his father work together on designing "weight plays," such as Harvard's flying wedge, which concentrate the weight of the attack upon a point in the opponent's line that could not be as quickly supported.
- To support Jonas's fascination with the sport, his father has cleared a large field near his mill and helped create an industrial league.
- Most of the other players are the mill's sawyers and lumbermen who give and take pain with great pleasure.
- Now that a field is available, industrial teams are forming at many of the mills in the area, with games always scheduled for Sunday afternoons—the workers' only day for recreation.

Recent rule changes give the quarterback more freedom of movement.

"The New Foot-ball," *The Book of Foot-ball*, by Walter Camp, 1910:

There is really much to be said in favor of football, and much has been said and explains why the game has acquired its tenacious hold upon players and spectators. History shows that the game of football has been severely criticized and denounced and even forbidden by law, but with singular insistence it continues to assert its vitality, and it never was more popular in America [than it is] today. East and west, north and south, it spreads. Whatever objection there may be to it—or rather, to the abuse of it—the history of the sport would indicate that it is "here to stay," and the wisdom on the part of both its advocates and its critics would seem to consist in endeavoring to eliminate the objectionable features. . .

The physical and mental development produced in the individual player is not all that may be cited in its support. Those who look beneath the surface find in football in the United States something to supply that lack of rigid discipline for which the American youth, except possibly at West Point and Annapolis, suffer in comparison with those of other peoples. Not only does the rigid training establish self-control in those who play, but the game holds up a standard of discipline to those who observe it. And it must be admitted that this side of the argument is a strong one, while the fact that it offers almost the ideal measure of effort followed by immediate relaxation renders it far less a tax on the vital organs than the majority of our contests.

A quarter of the people in Everett are foreign-born.

On Sundays, Jonas plays football in the industrial league against lumberjacks who delight in the roughness of the game.

- Spirited competition, fights and rivalries are now forming, with more than one broken arm or leg resulting from these Sunday outings.
- Jonas, one of the few who has actually read the rules, attempts to explain them before each game; everyone, including massive-bodied lumberjacks, listens to the boss's boy.
- They have also agreed that he should be the quarterback.
- His high school has a team as well, but the industrial league is more competitive and fun for a boy getting ready to go East to college.
- Even though his grades are poor, he is sure that when he graduates from the eleventh grade next year, Yale will be more than happy to accept him; after all, his uncle graduated from Yale, and his father has lots of money.
- Besides, playing for a school whose mascot is a bulldog seems right; like the cheer says, "Bulldog, bulldog, bow, wow, wow!"

Life in the Community: Everett, Washington

- Six days a week, the mills' whistles blow at six in the morning, giving a working man an hour to build a fire, have his breakfast and smoke his pipe before embarking on a 10-hour day in the lumber industry.

2765 - View of Harbor, Everett, Washington.

The town of Everett boasts 95 manufacturing plants, mostly involved with lumber.

- Currently, Everett boasts 95 manufacturing plants, including 11 lumber mills, 16 shingle mills, 17 combination lumber-shingle mills, a paper mill, an iron factory, several makers of logging and milling machinery, shipyards, an arsenic plant, breweries and dozens of companies related to the sawdust economy.
- More than 5,000 of the city's 35,000 men, women and children earn their wages in mills and factories—a ratio more similar to the industrial East than to the rural West.
- A quarter of the people in the city are foreign-born, while another quarter are of foreign parentage; on the streets of Everett, Norwegian, Swedish, German, Italian and Greek can be heard.
- Two years ago the Norwegians agreed to close their private school when the public schools introduced the Norwegian language as a regular part of the high school curriculum.
- Most homes have been built on 25-foot lots offered by the Everett Improvement Company—two lots if the family is affluent—and are designed by the carpenters who build them, a tradition that has inspired considerable creativity as carpenters compete with one another to build the most interesting house.
- Everett has 40 churches, many based around nationality more than theology.
- Of the six large Lutheran congregations, only one holds services in English; the others are conducted in German, Norwegian and Swedish.
- Everett has four fraternal lodges—most of them with women's auxiliaries—25 labor unions, dozens of reform clubs, political clubs, women's clubs, book clubs, historical societies and professional organizations, most of which hold regular meetings, picnics, smokers, clambakes, dances and parties.
- In addition, the YMCA has classes in English, bookkeeping and arithmetic.

Tues'day, tiūz'dę̂, *not* Tooz'day (tūz'dę̂) *nor* Chewz'-day (chiūz'dę̂). The full sound of the English long *u* (iū) as in *dew*, *few*, *new*, is a little difficult to give after *t*; hence, to speak it correctly is a mark of education and culture. Let any one attempt to say rapidly, "I will *meet you*," and he will find a strong tendency to say, "I will *meechoo* (mī'chū)," the initial *y* sound of the *you* fusing with the preceding *t*. The same tendency leads some persons, in the attempt to be very accurate, to say *Chewz'day* (chiūz'dę̂), while others harshly say *Tooz'day* (tūz'dę̂). "Will those shoes be ready by *Chewzday?*" asked the exquisite. "No, sir, not before *Churzday*," replied the shoemaker. The true pronunciation is very easy; simply put a *y* before the *ū*; this may be represented to the eye thus: Tʸuesday; or in the scientific alphabet tiūz'dę̂.

The lumberjacks are heavily unionized, including the radical Industrial Workers of the World.

- The city is already heavily unionized; currently the Wobblies—the Industrial Workers of the World—are actively recruiting members among lumber workers.
- Recently, shingle weavers began sending money to help assist IWW members arrested in Spokane, Washington, for organizing workers.
- Union men in Everett address each other as "brother," and when one union member falls ill, support is typically provided by many, including aid for the family.
- Help is often needed; shingle-making is dangerous work.
- To cut a cedar log into bolts that can fit the carriage of the shingle saw, a man pushes the log forward at waist height with his knee and hands, risking the danger of falling into the blade.
- The sawyer on the upright machine faces similar danger from two whirling blades; the blade on his left slices the blocks that come automatically from the bolter, ripping 60 slices a minute.
- To make the operation work, the sawyer clears his saw with his left hand, then passes the slices of wood over to his right hand, with which he then shapes the shingle on the trimmer saw and passes it down a chute to the packer.
- During the operation, sawdust clouds his eyes, nose and throat, yet a good sawyer takes great pride in his ability to cut and trim 30,000 shingles in a 10-hour shift.

Everett has built its growth and fortune around timbering.

- Despite the dangers, shingle weaver jobs are prized; the average $4.50 a day is significantly higher than the $2.25 that lumber mill workers make.
- Everett got its start in the 1880s after the Northern Pacific Railroad linked its rails from Lake Superior to the Columbia River, and then to Puget Sound, attracting nearly 100,000 people to the region during a two-year period.
- Washington achieved statehood in 1889, as thousands roamed the new territory looking for fortunes in lumber, wheat, gold and new development.
- Speculation was so rampant that a piece of land selling in 1891 for $4,000 was quickly resold for $128,000, and eventually $500,000 as 1892 drew to a close.
- But the early speculation turned to despair in the Panic of 1893, when wages fell 60 percent and the schools that survived had only enough funds to operate for three months; thousands were driven into bankruptcy and fled the city.
- Today, a new city has formed around the railroads of James J. Hill, the lumbering might of Frederick Weyerhaeuser and the investments of Rockefeller.

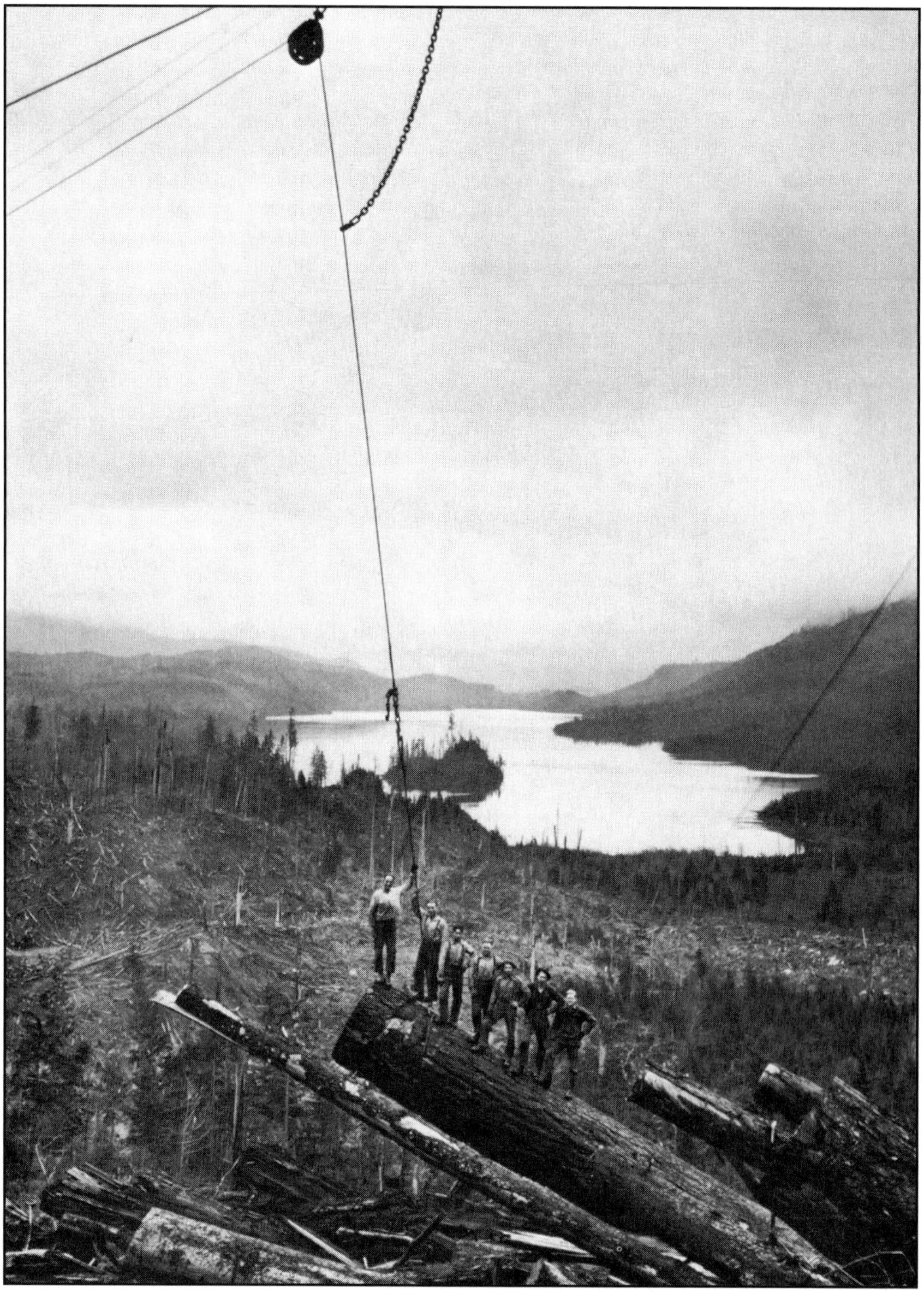

The West offers a seemingly endless supply of trees.

- In 1900, Weyerhaeuser purchased 900,000 acres of timber from the Northern Pacific land grants at $6.00 an acre, or about $0.10 per thousand feet of wood.
- The resulting lumber mill is the largest in the world, currently processing 70 million feet of timber a year.

Historical Snapshot 1911

- The Triangle Shirtwaist Factory fire in New York City ignited a nationwide demand for better working conditions; the single exit door had been locked to keep the 146 girls from stealing thread
- The rising divorce rate—one in 12 marriages compared with one in 85 just six years earlier—was condemned nationwide
- Dr. Boris Sidis proclaimed that "early training is responsible for precocity," after his 11-year-old son entered Harvard with advanced standing
- Sixty thousand Bibles were placed in hotel bedrooms by the Gideon Organization of Christian Commercial Travelers
- South Carolina prohibited children under 16 from working between 8 p.m. and 6 a.m.; children under 12 were restricted from working in mines, factories or textile establishments
- Demand was rising for a public parcel post system, since it often cost more to mail an item to a neighboring town than to another country
- An estimated 40 million Christian worshipers attended summer "Chautauquas" featuring opera singers, orchestras, yodelers, Hawaiian crooners, American Indian artists and inspirational lecturers
- John Muir's *My First Summer in the Sierra* and *South Sea Tales* by Jack London were published
- Domino brand sugar, Skidmore College for Women, tide-predicting machines, Lee denim work clothes and the Appalachian Forest Reserve Act all made their first appearance
- The United States Supreme Court dissolved the Rockefeller Standard Oil Trust
- The *Mona Lisa* was stolen from the Louvre in France
- Songs such as "I Want a Girl Just Like the Girl That Married Dear Old Dad," "When I Was Twenty-One and You Were Sweet Sixteen" and "Be My Little Bumble-Bee" were extremely popular
- The U.S., Japan, Britain and Russia signed a 15-year treaty to regulate seal hunting
- President Howard Taft's weight went from 340 to 267 pounds
- Protests erupted when Marie Curie—after winning an unprecedented second Nobel prize—was still refused admission to the prestigious French Academy of Science
- Author Jacob Riis advocated that city youth gangs could be minimized by teaching children hands-on skills, not just book-learning

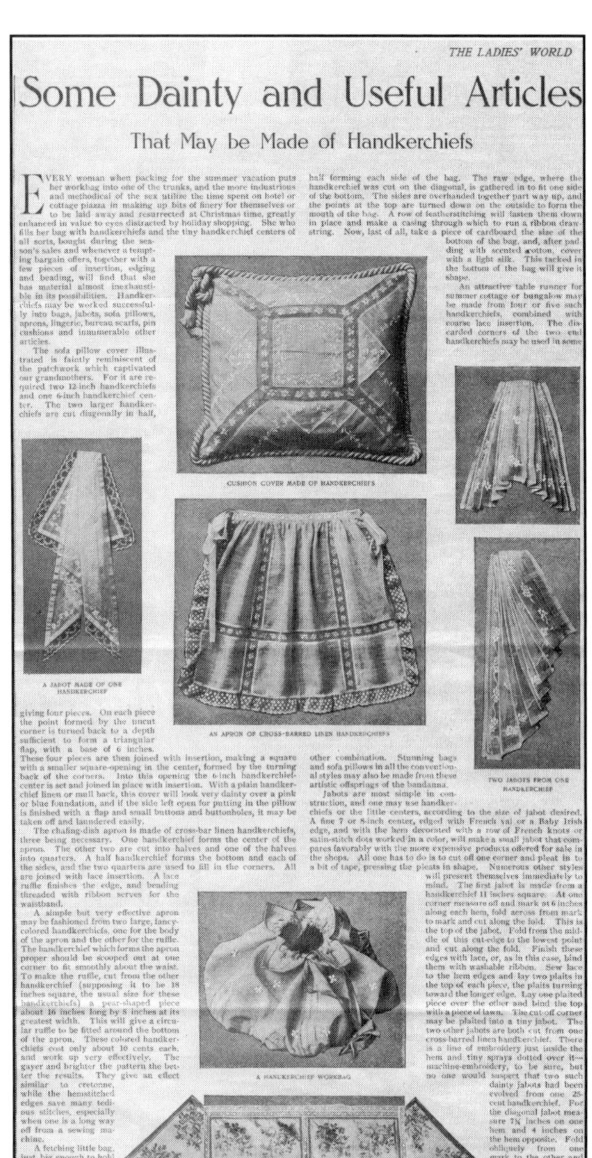

THE LADIES' WORLD

Some Dainty and Useful Articles

That May be Made of Handkerchiefs

EVERY woman when packing for the summer vacation puts her workbag into one of the trunks, and the more industrious and methodical of the sex utilize the time spent on hotel or cottage piazza in making up bits of finery for themselves or to be laid away and resurrected at Christmas time, greatly enhanced in value to eyes distracted by holiday shopping. She who fills her bag with handkerchiefs and the tiny handkerchief centers of all sorts, bought during the season's sales and whenever a tempting bargain offers, together with a few pieces of insertion, edging and beading, will find that she has material almost inexhaustible in its possibilities. Handkerchiefs may be worked successfully into bags, jabots, sofa pillows, aprons, lingerie, bureau scarfs, pin cushions and innumerable other articles.

The sofa pillow cover illustrated is faintly reminiscent of the patchwork which captivated our grandmothers. For it are required two 12-inch handkerchiefs and one 6-inch handkerchief center. The two larger handkerchiefs are cut diagonally in half, giving four pieces. On each piece the point formed by the uncut corner is turned back to a depth sufficient to form a triangular flap, with a base of 6 inches. These four pieces are then joined with insertion, making a square with a smaller square-opening in the center, formed by the turning back of the corners. Into this opening the 6-inch handkerchief-center is set and joined in place with insertion. With a plain handkerchief linen or mull back, this cover will look very dainty over a pink or blue foundation, and if the side left open for putting in the pillow is finished with a flap and small buttons and buttonholes, it may be taken off and laundered easily.

The chafing-dish apron is made of cross-bar linen handkerchiefs, three being necessary. One handkerchief forms the center of the apron. The other two are cut into halves and one of the halves into quarters. A half handkerchief forms the bottom and each of the sides, and the two quarters are used to fill in the corners. All are joined with lace insertion. A lace ruffle finishes the edge, and beading threaded with ribbon serves for the waistband.

A simple but very effective apron may be fashioned from two large, fancy-colored handkerchiefs, one for the body of the apron and the other for the ruffle. The handkerchief which forms the apron proper should be scooped out at one corner to fit smoothly about the waist. To make the ruffle, cut from the other handkerchief (supposing it to be 18 inches square, the usual size for these handkerchiefs) a pear-shaped piece about 16 inches long by 8 inches at its greatest width. This will give a circular ruffle to be fitted around the bottom of the apron. These colored handkerchiefs cost only about 10 cents each, and work up very effectively. The gayer and brighter the pattern the better the results. They give an effect similar to cretonne, while the hemstitched edges save many tedious stitches, especially when one is a long way off from a sewing machine.

A fetching little bag, just big enough to hold the crocheting of the summer girl, can be evolved out of a small center and two handkerchiefs of ordinary size. The center is used for the bottom of the bag. The handkerchiefs are cut diagonally in half, half forming each side of the bag. The raw edge, where the handkerchief was cut on the diagonal, is gathered in to fit one side of the bottom. The sides are overhanded together part way up, and the points at the top are turned down on the outside to form the mouth of the bag. A row of featherstitching will fasten them down in place and make a casing through which to run a ribbon draw-string. Now, last of all, take a piece of cardboard the size of the bottom of the bag, and, after padding with scented cotton, cover with a light silk. This tacked in the bottom of the bag will give it shape.

An attractive table runner for summer cottage or bungalow may be made from four or five such handkerchiefs, combined with coarse lace insertion. The discarded corners of the two end handkerchiefs may be used in some other combination. Stunning bags and sofa pillows in all the conventional styles may also be made from these artistic offsprings of the bandanna.

Jabots are most simple in construction, and one may use handkerchiefs or the little centers, according to the size of jabot desired. A fine 7 or 8-inch center, edged with French val or a Baby Irish edge, and with the hem decorated with a row of French knots or satin-stitch dots worked in a color, will make a small jabot that compares favorably with the more expensive products offered for sale in the shops. All one has to do is to cut off one corner and pleat in to a bit of tape, pressing the pleats in shape. Numerous other styles will present themselves immediately to mind. The first jabot is made from a handkerchief 11 inches square. At one corner measure off and mark at 6 inches along each hem, fold across from mark to mark and cut along the fold. This is the top of the jabot. Fold from the middle of this cut-edge to the lowest point and cut along the fold. Finish these edges with lace, or, as in this case, bind them with washable ribbon. Sew lace to the hem edges and lay two plaits in the top of each piece, the plaits turning toward the longer edge. Lay one plaited piece over the other and bind the top with a piece of lawn. The cut-off corner may be plaited into a tiny jabot. The two other jabots are both cut from one cross-barred linen handkerchief. There is a line of embroidery just inside the hem and tiny sprays dotted over it—machine-embroidery, to be sure, but no one would suspect that two such dainty jabots had been evolved from one 25-cent handkerchief. For the diagonal jabot measure 7¾ inches on one hem and 4 inches on the hem opposite. Fold obliquely from one mark to the other and cut in the fold. Lay small, close plaits along the cut-edge. The other jabot measures 4½ inches at each side-hem (it was a 12-inch handkerchief), and is sloped to 3½ inches at the center, then plaited.

CUSHION COVER MADE OF HANDKERCHIEFS

A JABOT MADE OF ONE HANDKERCHIEF

AN APRON OF CROSS-BARRED LINEN HANDKERCHIEFS

TWO JABOTS FROM ONE HANDKERCHIEF

A HANDKERCHIEF WORKBAG

A TABLE SCARF MADE OF FOUR GAYLY PRINTED HANDKERCHIEFS WITH BLUE BORDERS

1911 Economic Profile

Selected Prices

Climbing Monkey Toy	$0.21
Eureka Vacuum Cleaner	$35.00
Florsheim Shoes	$5.00
Hair Net	$0.15
Knee Pants, Boy's	$0.45
Marshmallows, 200	$0.42
Mahogany Sleigh Bed	$39.50
Muff, Opossum Fur	$8.25
Player Piano	$1,050.00
Rambler Automobile	$1,800.00
Steamship Ticket, San Francisco to Los Angeles, Roundtrip	$12.00
Telephone with Two Dry Batteries	$10.20
Tooth Soap, Three Ounces	$0.10
Tuition, Harvard, per Year	$150.00
Umbrella	$2.74

Changing America

- As a result of the European immigration movement to the United States, 15 percent of Americans were foreign-born.
- Fingerprinting was gaining widespread use in crime prevention.
- A white line painted down the middle of the road to divide the lanes was introduced.
- Dutch physicist Heike Kamerlingh Onnes discovered that at very low temperatures some metal alloys lose all resistance to electricity and become superconductors, moving electricity without any loss of heat or energy.
- Electric food mixers and kitchen ranges with heat-resistant, glass-paneled oven doors were becoming available.
- The average household in America had 4.6 persons; 23 percent of the population were under 10 years of age, while 4.4 percent were over 65.
- The U.S. Supreme Court placed forest reserves under federal, not state, authority.
- President Howard Taft vetoed a bill requiring literacy tests for immigrants aimed at slowing the tide of new workers coming to America.
- The term "phone" for telephone became popular with the release of the song "A Ring on the Finger Is Worth Two on the Phone."

Suffragist Banner, San Francisco, 1911:

Forward out of error
Leave behind the night
Forward through the darkness
Forward into light

Telephone Etiquette

Co-operation is the keynote of telephone success.

For good service there must be perfect co-operation between the party calling, the party called, and the trained operator who connects these two.

Suggestions for the use of the telephone may be found in the directory and are worthy of study, but the principles of telephone etiquette are found in everyday life.

One who is courteous face to face should also be courteous when he bridges distance by means of the telephone wire.

He will not knock at the telephone door and run away, but will hold himself in readiness to speak as soon as the door is opened.

The 100,000 employees of the Bell system and the 25,000,000 telephone users constitute the great telephone democracy.

The success of the telephone democracy depends upon the ability and willingness of each individual to do his part.

AMERICAN TELEPHONE AND TELEGRAPH COMPANY AND ASSOCIATED COMPANIES

One Policy ***One System*** ***Universal Service***

When writing to Advertisers kindly mention "THE WORLD TO-DAY."

Ivy League Autumns, by Richard Goldstein, 1996:

In the autumn of 1909, college football experienced a dark moment, a reminder that all those reform efforts aimed at curing the game's brutality could still fall short. . . . Hamilton Fish, Harvard's all-American tackle and captain, had been playing opposite Icy Byrne, Army's acting captain. Fish could remember that Byrne was exhausted, yet insisted on staying in because a player could not return once he had been removed.

"Our line went into a shift," Fish recalled. "I was lined up about four yards away from Icy when—bam—our 200-pound fullback smashed over my tackle position and straight into Byrne. Icy stiffened, held his ground, but the impact was too much. His neck was broken; the game was immediately stopped. He died in the hospital later that evening."

Yale is a football powerhouse.

"The Nervous and Determined Child, Family Problems," a letter from Mrs. C. B. H. to *The Ladies' World*, August 1910:

I have solved the problem of my eldest boy, who inherited an extremely nervous disposition. The least sound would startle him, and he would not get over a severe fright for several days, sometimes almost going into convulsions.

My friends advised me to be very firm and insist that he must overcome this so-called "unreasonable fear," but I soon found this heroic treatment had the opposite effect to that desired.

As far as possible, by diet and care, I kept him in good health. When afraid, I would soothe and quiet him, then attract his attention by talking about something pleasant and very different from the object that had startled him.

His play and playthings were arranged to be of a quiet rather than an exciting nature, and I was careful that no scary stories were told in his hearing at bedtime.

He was never shut in dark closets, and dire punishments were never threatened. He was allowed a light in his bedroom till after he fell asleep, and if nervous or restless at bedtime I would sit by his bedside and talk of brave people and how sad it was to be cowardly. In this way he was encouraged to overcome his nervous fears. Now, at 10 years of age, while he has a sensitive temperament, he is as brave a little fellow as one could wish to see.

Obedience is required from my children, but I want the obedience that comes from love and not from fear. My boys have never had a "sound whipping"—but many compliments have come to me on my "manly, obedient little sons."

My main problem, at present, is an affectionate but very determined little fellow of seven years. I want to so train him that the perseverance and determination that are paramount in his character may be directed in the proper channels, and I should like to hear from experienced mothers on this subject.

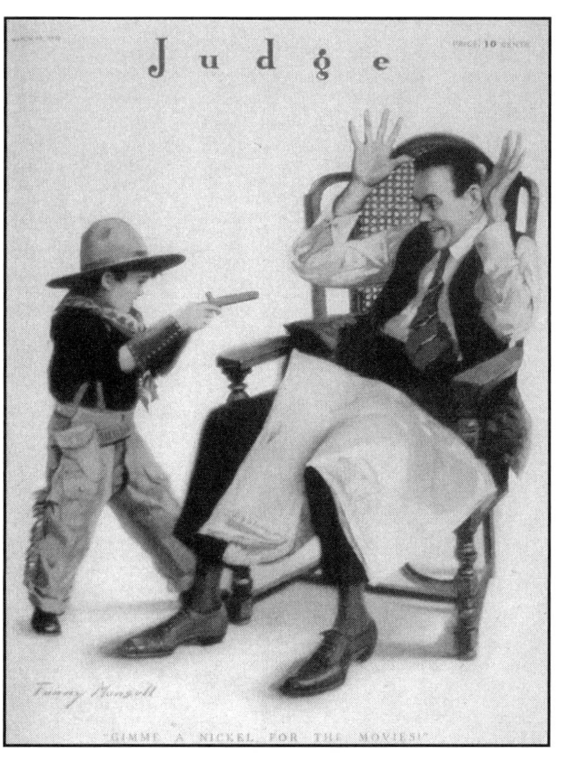

Preamble adopted by the 1908 Convention of the Industrial Workers of the World (Wobblies):

It is the historic mission of the working class to do away with capitalism. The army of production must be organized, not only for the everyday struggle with capitalists, but also to carry on production when capitalism shall have been overthrown. By organizing industrially we are forming the structure of the new society within the shell of the old."

Excerpts from *Helpful Hints in English*, by James C. Fernald, Funk and Wagnalls Company, 1911:

I don't think so. Never say, "I don't think," exclaims the purist. "Any rational person is always thinking." Doubtless, my dear purist, but, not always thinking the same way that you do. Consult your dictionary and you will find that "think" has more than one meaning; it may mean "to carry on the process of thought" in which sense we are "always thinking"; or it may mean "to entertain a particular opinion," in which sense I may never think your way. You think that tree is a maple; I do not think (entertain the opinion) that it is; in other words, "I don't think so." In that case, would it not be better to say, "I think not"? That depends on what you mean. The two expressions are not identical; "I don't think so" means I am doubtful of the affirmative; "I think not" means I am almost sure of the negative.

Woman, women: With reference to organizations and movements, the singular (woman) is commonly preferred, as "The Woman's (not Women's) Christian Temperance Union"; "woman suffrage," not "women suffrage." Woman, so used, is generic, denoting all "womankind," just as man is generic in the sentence "Man is mortal." But we say, "Votes for women"; there are to be as many women as there are votes for them; "Votes for woman" might suggest plural voting; but "The ballot for woman" is correct. We may say either "A woman's college" or "A college for women," but not a "Women's college." "Woman's nature"; is the nature inseparable from womanhood? "Women's opinions" are the opinions of a large part of the sex, thought of as individuals.

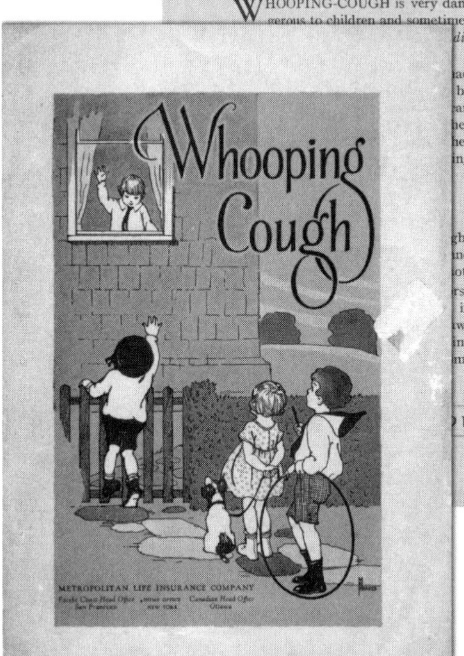

Whooping-Cough

A DANGEROUS DISEASE TO CHILDREN AND GROWN-UPS
HOW TO KNOW IT AND TO TREAT SUFFERERS FROM IT

WHOOPING-COUGH is very dangerous to children and sometimes ...

In mild cases, the child will have four or five coughing fits a day; in severe cases, many more than that.

Call the Doctor

If your child shows the first signs of whooping-cough, call the doctor, and follow his directions absolutely.

The child frequently vomits because of the hard coughing. As a result many children lose weight and become very weak. In this condition they easily get tuberculosis, pneumonia, or other serious diseases.

Do not give the child heavy foods. Give him those that are easily digested. Milk and eggs are very good.

Give him an egg well beaten in milk every time he loses his meal. This drink can be made attractive by adding a little sugar and vanilla.

Carelessness Spreads Disease

All matter that comes from the mouth and nose while the child is sick should be received in a piece of clean old linen or rags, and burned. It is through carelessness in this that the disease is spread. Keep separate cups, glasses, plates, and spoons for the child while it is sick.

See that the child gets plenty of fresh air. Keep the room well aired night and day. Unless it is raining, take him out EVERY DAY, on the roof, in the yard, or into the park.

Keep the Child Away From Others

Even after the "whoop" has stopped, he can give the disease to others. Wait until the Doctor says he is well.

Remember that whooping-cough is very catching. Be sure that your child does not spread disease and possible death to others.

...WS SIGNS OF WHOOPING-COUGH, CALL A DOCTOR!

"Boy Scouting—What It Really Is," by F. A. Crosby, *The World To-day*, February 1911:

"Be Prepared," the motto of the "Boy Scout," signifies fully the purpose of the scout movement as it is being grafted from the parent English stock, where it first took shape, to that more live and adaptable, but perhaps less sturdy shoot, the American boy. Whether it is to be ready in will and training to help an old lady safely cross a busy crossing; to give "first aid" to an injured companion; or to repel an invasion by a hostile nation, the American youth may well take as his slogan, "Be Prepared." This does not mean merely gaining a fund of information from the leader, book and nature, but unconsciously developing a resourcefulness which will always stand him in stead and which our average city-bred boy lacks to a great degree.

The American boy used to live in the country, or in close proximity to it, and a healthy environment and nature's schooling gave him a practical knowledge and a resourcefulness which have brought forth empire-builders. This boy could ride, swim, hunt and skate; he was handy with tools; knew nature's secrets in field and wood; had chores to do. He was self-reliant and well-developed in body and brain. Because of a careful rearing in a real home he was respectful and obedient, the right material from which to build a nation, and from which come nation-builders.

There is the danger of our losing this type of boy through the change due to modern social and industrial conditions. Modern standards of living may conduce to a higher type of civilization, but the adolescent boy, with his many semi-barbarous instincts, is being forced onward too rapidly, like a hothouse plant, toward and into this stage of refinement, to the exclusion of his natural impulses. His wide interest in nature—persons, beasts, plants at work—is being dwarfed by narrow nature study from books; his personal interest in athletics is being superseded by a mania for "beating" in spectacular contests; his desire to make things and see them work is in danger of being smothered by too much theoretical instruction. Likewise, the normal boy's natural religious instincts, his altruistic impulses are too crude and deep-seated to be found and nurtured by many of our modern religious forms and prejudices.

Any scheme of ideas that will help to bring back to our city boy's life his inherent rights and desires of achievement, adventure, observation and knowledge of nature, is well worth careful study. The Boy Scout movement is such a scheme. Although its ideals can better be attained in the country, yet its adaptation to the city has been proved, and is only in its beginnings. Scouting is an educational movement, to be promoted by and in conjunction with other institutions, not an independent organization.

ENGLISH BOY SCOUTS GETTING DINNER READY

Jonas's father was excited to move West, where thousands of acres of virgin forest still existed.

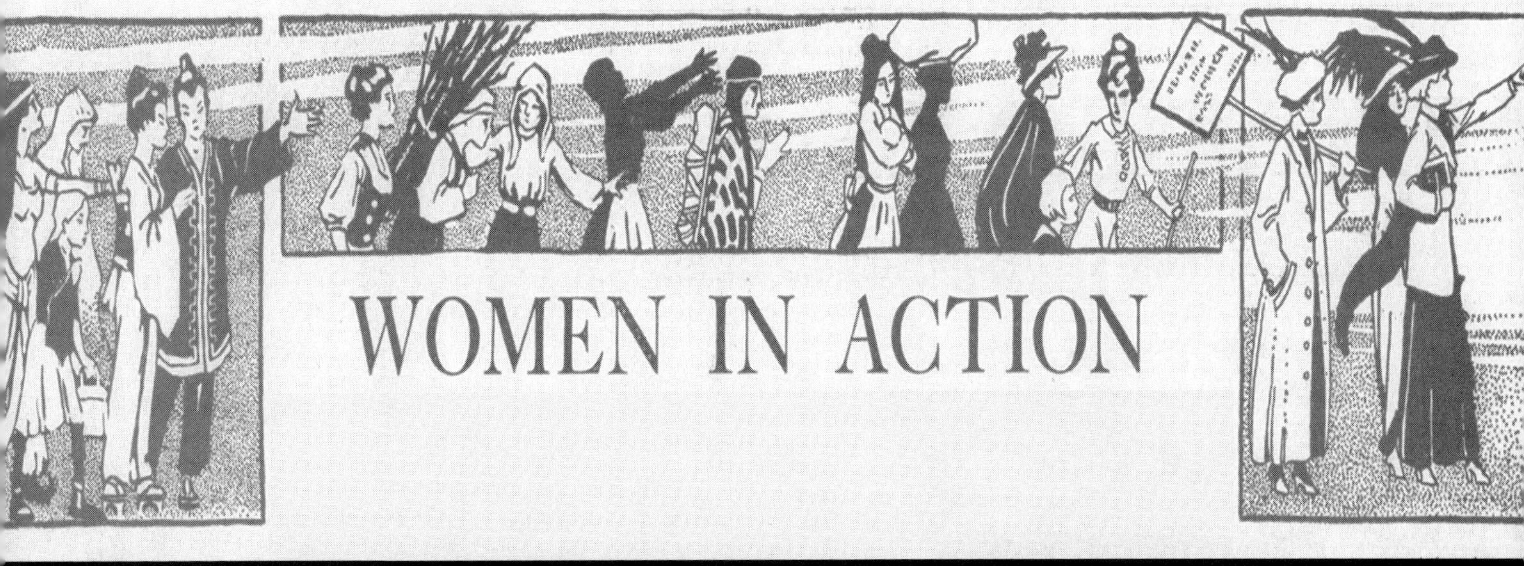

1914 News Feature

"Light through Work, The Dawn of New Hope for the Blind," by Ethel M. Colson, *Today's Housewife*, January 1914:

"Please tell the mayor that I have six blind babies outside. I am going to hit them in the head with a sledge hammer and drop them over Brooklyn Bridge and I want him to take some responsibility for it."

Mrs. Cynthia Westover Alden didn't look like a murderous crank on the morning that she sent in this gentle message to the mayor of New York seven years ago, but in less than three minutes she had gained that difficult thing, access to the mayor's private office. "It would be better to put them out of their misery with one blow," she told the city's chief executive calmly, "than to continue letting them die by inches as is now the case."

Then Mrs. Alden, sure of a startled and attentive listener, communicated her discovery to the mayor, that nowhere in the city or in the United States was there a place for a blind orphan baby under eight years old.

Sick babies, well babies, crippled babies, orphan babies, feeble-minded babies, cats, dogs, birds, for every other kind, shape and variety of helpless little animal, it would seem, human love and charity had provided havens; but of blind babies no one, apparently, had thought.

Yet the earliest years of the blind child are the most important. Time lost then can never be regained.

In a tiny flat that cost but three dollars a week, the International Sunshine Branch for the Blind started. From the county poorhouse, where the blind babies of the very poor were classed with the feeble-minded, since no other provision or classification had been arranged, were "borrowed" six tiny creatures for six months. Almost at once it was seen that miracles could be accomplished in their behalf, but when the time was up, the children were "called back" by the county officials.

Mrs. Alden, the moving spirit, had realized that unless something radical was done, the hard, good work would go for naught, but the mayor of New York, upon whom the situation depended, was a busy man, difficult to secure speech with. At last the earnest woman had hit upon the plan that brought her into his presence.

The shocked and startled mayor promised all the help in his power, and four years later redeemed the promise by signing the bill appropriating funds for the care of dependent blind babies. A similar bill is now pending in Illinois, having its object the "care, maintenance and education of blind babies in the state of Illinois from the day they are blinded." Similar bills should be passed in every state, since proper care in infancy means independence later. It is a short-sighted policy that neglects the blind babies, then passes appropriations—frequently, too, quite inadequate—for the assistance of the adult blind.

The "light-hunger" of a blind baby is so great that instead of sucking its thumb like the seeing baby, it rubs and digs and pokes at its poor closed eyes until the eyes are injured and the baby often dies of blood poisoning. And even if it lives, it usually comes to the worse fate of imbecility because nobody understands how to treat it.

The brains and physical development of blind children are often normal at birth; but, receiving no exercise or training, the little wits become stupid; not seeing the light the little heads droop; helpless and timid, the poor little blind sufferers become unreasonably shy and retiring, huddle away in corners and shrink against the wall. Properly taught, they acquire confidence, learn to be much as other children, grow properly, stand erect.

The establishment of the first Blind Babies' Home—Mrs. Alden raised almost $100,000 to render the work properly effective—was followed by a winning fight to have the Home Kindergarten made a part of the public school system. This was a long step in advance, since blind children, in the opinion of those who know most about them, should be treated as much like normal children as possible, right from the start. Then came work for proper state support of the Home, now, after various moves and vicissitudes, established in a beautiful house in Dyker Heights, Brooklyn. At last the desired law went through Albany without one opposing vote.

This law, which provides for the maintenance of blind children in the International Sunshine Home for the Blind at a rate of $1 a day, should be duplicated in every state in the Union, substituting, of course, local institutions for the Sunshine Home whenever advisable. New Jersey already has a law committing the New Jersey blind babies to the Arthur Sunshine Home at Summit, New Jersey, at the rate of $330 a year for each child. Children from other states are joyously admitted to the Brooklyn Home at the rate of $1 a day, the Sunshine Society frequently, as in the case of a little blind lad from Peoria, Illinois, making up any necessary deficit. For the child mentioned the county pays $10 monthly toward his support, the Sunshine Society contributing the monthly deficit of $20. This is done in order to keep the little ones under the necessary training until they are old enough to attend the blind schools of their various states.

The children of the rich are welcome, because, under the most promising of ordinary conditions, they are as helpless and needy as those of the poor. The blind denizen of a luxurious nursery learns little more, unless supplied with a specially trained attendant, than the child of the poor mother who must leave it alone during long working hours daily.

1916 Profile

Working Class

After a lifetime of working on his father's tobacco farm, Wilfred Mathieson has been given the opportunity to become the first person in his family to graduate high school, but only by leaving home and attending school in a neighboring Kentucky town.

Wilfred Mathieson wants to be the first in his family to finish high school.

Life at Home

- Born at home in his parents' bed, 16-year-old Wilfred Mathieson has begun attending high school in a neighboring community, over his father's strong objections.
- His father has assumed for the past two years that his son would quit school when he finished the eighth grade and help on the tobacco farm.
- He expects the other children to do likewise, and does not want to give any of them the wrong impression concerning their duty to the family.
- "The boy's become too valuable on the farm to be going off to school and looking at a book," he overheard his father tell his mother.
- Wilfred's father left school in the fourth grade to help tend the family farm—and because of the fight he had with a new teacher over rock throwing.
- Wilfred's mother was determined that her son would be the first person in the family to complete high school, and she arranged for him to live with her second cousin, Buford Forbes, in the neighboring community of Greenburg, Kentucky.
- Before Wilfred left for school, he gave away some of his possessions; little brother Buford got a slingshot, Sarah got

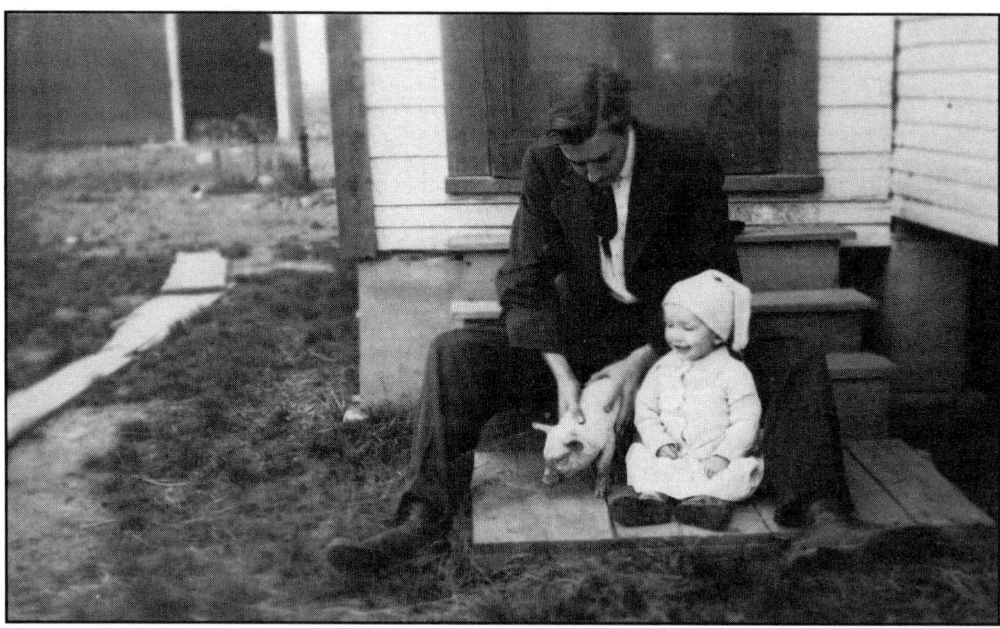

The youngest child, Talbert, was given a piglet when Wilfred went off to school.

his gardening trowel, and to Talbert, the youngest child, he gave a piglet that had just been born to one of his prize sows.

- Like most of the families in the neighborhood, the Mathiesons are small-scale farmers—the one-horse kind who depend on Burley tobacco for money and vegetables for food.
- Wilfred began farming with his parents at age six, just like his five brothers and sisters; his first job was planting, which requires considerable stooping—a skill well-suited to children of about this age.
- Plants are set out in rows about three feet apart, wide enough for a horse or mule to pass through.
- Wilfred would bend over and push a peg into the ground, pull a plant from a bucket, push it into the hole and drag dirt around it; next, he would move two feet and stoop again.
- After planting comes weeding with a hoe and worming, the removal of tobacco worms by hand.
- Sometimes, Wilfred would pull the three-inch-long worms off the leaf in a way that caused the innards to squirt out; it relieved the boredom.
- Last tobacco season, to show off for a girl, he pulled a worm off the leaf, put it in his mouth and bit the head off.
- She was impressed, he believes.
- Even though he has been around tobacco his entire life, he does not smoke; his mother warned him that if he drank coffee or smoked cigarettes, he would turn as black as the field hands with whom he worked.
- After a lifetime of hand-me-down shirts and homemade pants, often constructed of denim material so hard it wouldn't bend, he got store-bought clothes for the first time, including a Sunday suit when he went off to school.
- Until recently, he wore his homemade pants at a three-quarter length—six inches below the knee—to protect his stockings, which were entirely homemade, including the carding, spinning, dyeing, and knitting.
- His oblong handkerchiefs are made by his mother from flour sacks, which normally yield two or three handkerchiefs each.

Even though he has been around tobacco his entire life, Wilfred does not smoke cigarettes.

- His hats are made from wool in a way that assumes the shape of a cone when wet, referred to on the farm as "going to seed."
- He wears a stiff-bottomed, brogan-type shoe made of rough leather held together in front with a buckle.

***A Dutch Fork Farm Boy*, a memoir by J. M. Eleanor:**

The finest milk cow we ever had got her neck broken while being driven to water. The water hole was down below the barn in a clump of cedars. She had been hitched out that day and a colored boy on horseback was driving her to water before taking her in that afternoon. When he hit the cedars he started chasing her full speed with her chain dragging. The galloping horse stepped on the chain, tripped her and broke her neck.

To the old folks, that was a tragedy of the first rank. But not to us kids. Hidden in the dense cedars, we watched the buzzards there for days, until nothing but a clean skeleton remained.

We saw none of the gruesomeness of it. Our observations were of a sort of scientific nature. To us that was a marvel of nature. It would have taken at least two mules that we did not have to pull her away. And much work to dig a hole big enough to bury her in the stone hills. So the buzzards came along and saved us all of that.

When we tired of watching the busy gang of them on the carcass, we would lie on our backs on the grass behind the cedars and look into the languid May skies. At first we would see only a dot. Then it grew larger into a buzzard. It would glide around and around, seldom flapping a wing, gradually descending. And when it landed there was always a slight flurry among the scores that were already there, as it dived into the feast.

Wilfred loves to entertain his little brother and sister by fishing for chickens or carving whistles.

- Because his mother did not want him walking a mile to the nearest school alone, Wilfred started school when his younger brother turned six and the boys were able to go together.
- The elementary school includes eight grades in two rooms for 48 children, and is considered a modern school because the children are divided by skill level and age.
- The school term runs for three months, or about 61 days each year; the rest of the time, the building is used for storing farm supplies, including feed and fertilizer.
- From the beginning, Wilfred loved going to school, and at the end of the first grade, he received a New Testament Bible for perfect attendance.
- Since his earliest years, his special talent has been growing herbs, especially mint, which can be used with water to create a beverage to treat stomach troubles, or as a flavoring for candy.

"Meeting the Child Labor Problem," by Mabel Potter Daggett, In the Spotlight, Women and Events in the World Drama, *Today's Woman*, January 1914:

When we put on the statute books the law against child labor, we found ourselves confronted with a new difficulty. What about the child who must work or starve? There have been various expedients to meet this situation. Sometimes a woman's club has provided a "scholarship" that paid the child a factory wage when he was taken from work to school. In some states now this assistance is regularly arranged by the Department of Education that buys a child's time in which he may go to school, just as for a long while it has been customary to buy his schoolbooks at public expense. United States Commissioner of Education, Hon. P. O. Claxton, has recently proposed another plan. He would offset the need for the child's wage by an increase in the family purse through home gardening. He suggests that the school term be increased to 12 months and that half of each day be devoted to teaching the child to raise vegetables, chickens, cows and pigs, the instruction to be given in the home backyard. These home agricultural products, by the savings effected in the daily marketing, would more than compensate for the loss of the child's factory wage.

The plan, it appears, would work until it reaches the cities where there aren't any backyards. High up in the tenements there wouldn't be room for the pig and the cow and the chickens and for but very few vegetables in the limited area of a window garden where the slum geranium grows. We have recently been finding out that all of the child labor isn't confined to cotton mills. Children as young as three years of age in the New York tenements are engaged with the rest of the family in making artificial forget-me-nots at a rate of 540 for $0.05. In over 30,000 licensed tenement houses in New York, little girls and boys are making flowers and feathers and dolls' clothes for the trade.

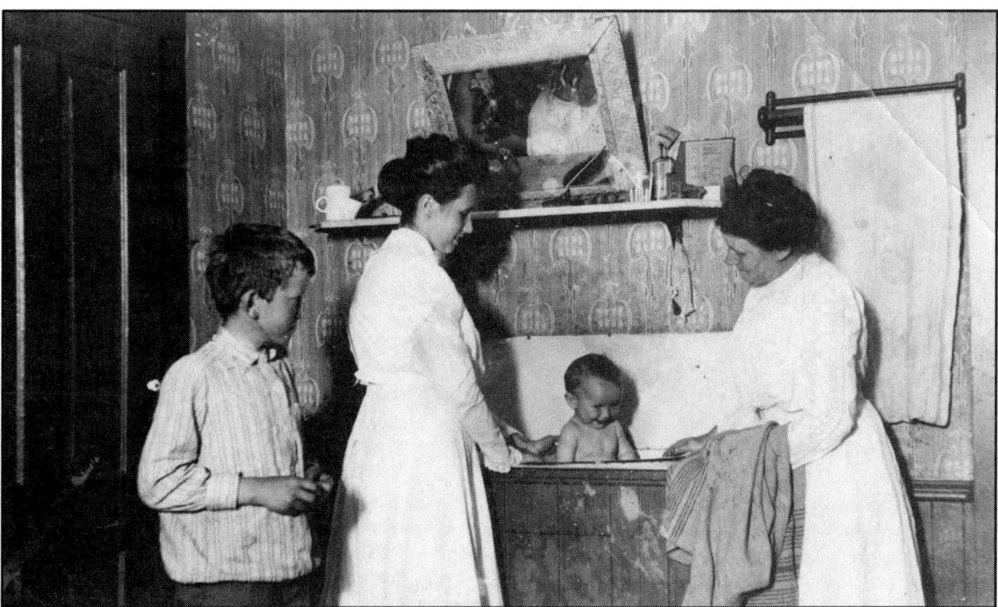

Wilfred comes from a large farm family accustomed to taking care of itself.

- Sage is grown for seasoning meats and for making a soothing tea for the sick.
- Wilfred also learned to grow medicines such as catnip for colic, and especially prides himself on his ability to create the perfect asthma medicine used by his little sister; it is made from jimsonweed which, when dried, mixed with saltpeter, burned and then inhaled, brings relief.
- But in this modern era, growing herbs for homemade medicine is obsolete, since everyone can now go to the store and get the farmer's universal remedy—Goody Headache Powder.
- To entertain the younger children before leaving for school, Wilfred showed them how to "fish" for chickens; with the little ones gathered all around him, he cut a notch in a grain of corn, tied it to a piece of cotton thread and tossed it to the family chickens.
- Every time one of the chickens swallowed the corn, Wilfred would give the string a jerk and out popped the grain of corn.
- The boys fell on the ground laughing.
- Some hungry but confused chickens swallowed the corn several times before abandoning the potential meal.
- The game was a roaring success until the family rooster, objecting to losing his supper, flew at the children with his wings ferociously beating, scaring little Talbert.
- Wilfred also likes to entertain the little ones by whittling popguns when the chinaberries are right, or wooden whistles when the hickory bark slips.
- Before he left home, his granny, who also lives at the farm, pulled him aside and said, "Don't forget the Lord when you get to the city."
- She gave him a Bible with his name engraved on the cover.
- Now that he is away, his father has the younger brothers looking for snakes, because a fresh-killed snake laid across a limb is guaranteed to bring rain—something his farm desperately needs right now.
- He also knows from experience that a black snake hung in a persimmon tree brings the best luck of all.

The term of the new school runs a full seven months.

Life at Work and School

- The new school is a big, brick building, boasting two stories; best of all, the term goes for seven full months.
- The school even has a small chemistry lab, and offers courses in English literature and algebra.
- Wilfred sweeps floors, washes dishes and does odd jobs to earn his room and board at the Forbes's house; the Forbes also rent the upstairs rooms to three old maids to earn extra money.
- After meals he helps clear the table, and dries the dishes with dishtowels made from feed bags.
- He sleeps on a cot in the living room and walks to school each day.
- Mr. Forbes is a successful cotton salesman, and believes that any young man who has "get up and go" can prosper.

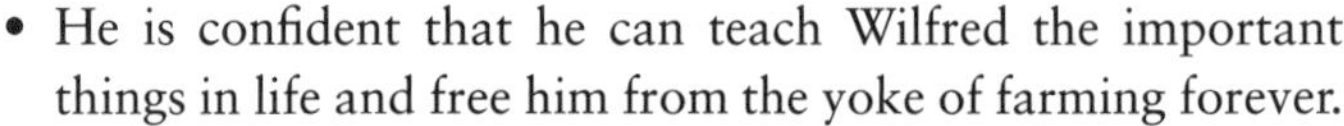

- He is confident that he can teach Wilfred the important things in life and free him from the yoke of farming forever.
- At the Forbes's home, the boy is surrounded by books; the family even subscribes to publications such as *American Magazine*, filled with stories on how to be successful in business and life.
- A special benefit of the move to Greenburg is the Saturday movies; since arriving he has seen a dozen two-reelers of runaway trains and chase scenes and cowboy fights, all of which have been wonderful.
- Recently, when Wilfred watched the movie *The Birth of a Nation*, the farmer next to him got so excited during certain scenes he pulled out a loaded pistol and waved it around.
- Wilfred was sure the man would shoot at the screen at any moment.

Since he was a little boy he has hunted for arrowheads in the fields near his home.

- But some changes have been startling and hard to accept at Greenburg High School.
- Growing up, Wilfred spent many afternoons listening to old-timers tell about how the South whipped up on the Yankees during the "war of northern aggression."
- As a border state, Kentucky divided its allegiance, giving more recruits to the Union than did Ohio, and more to the Confederacy than Florida.
- He was surprised when he was told during history class at Greenburg High School that despite all the stories, which always ended in victory, the South had lost the war.
- Wilfred's other problem is girls—they all treat him like a farm hick and won't have anything to do with him—all except Sara, a very sweet, churchgoing girl who lets him walk her home some days.
- Twice he has been allowed to sit with her on her front porch swing—while her mother was home—and once he caught a June bug for her.
- He tied a thread to its leg and they both laughed themselves silly while the June bug flew around and around making a determined buzzing sound.
- Still, he's convinced that if he were only smarter or owned more than two pairs of pants, the other girls would like him better.
- Starting when he was a little boy working in the fields, Wilfred has been collecting flint points and arrowheads from the freshly plowed furrows.
- His father has bragged for years that his oldest son is the best rock hound in Kentucky, and that his boy is capable of spotting quality arrowheads in a hailstorm.

Wilfred's grandmother gave him a bible when he went away.

To make himself less lonely, Wilfred took many of his best points to Greenburg.

- A shoebox full of arrowheads is the one possession he took with him to Greenburg to keep from being too lonely.
- Shortly after coming here, though, Wilfred discovered he is not the only person in the world interested in ancient Indian arrowheads.
- Several other boys have impressive collections that include arrowheads from as far away as Ohio and Illinois; already he has swapped dozens of his childhood finds for big, carefully carved, dovetail points that take his breath away.
- When he is lonely, he has also found it comforting to sit with the old men at the country store that also serves as a post office, three blocks away from the school.
- Even though he doesn't know these men well, their tales are a familiar reminder of home, as are their gentle running arguments, such as whose mule has the most pulling power, which hog is the biggest, and who grows the finest sorghum cane.

Life in the Community: Greenburg, Kentucky

- Educational reform is evident throughout Kentucky, with the number of high schools alone more than tripling in the past decade from 50 in 1908 to over 160 today.
- Within that time the state has passed truancy laws to increase the percentage of children attending school, standardized the educational requirement of teachers, created a state textbook commission, fixed the minimum salary of public school teachers at $75 a month, and enlarged the power of school boards.
- For many years, lumbering was a critical industry in the Green River region, with many of the area's hardwood trees used as cross ties for the ever-growing railroads.

"A Pile of Bones and Broken Pots—the Record of a Race," by Bessie T. Conkwright, *The Courier-Journal*, Sesquicentennial Edition, January 1, 1942:

When the first white traders came to Kentucky, more than four decades before statehood, there were few Indian residents, but there was evidence of habitation by large numbers of aborigines for countless centuries.

Even in the great forests, mounds were a distinctive feature of the landscape in many sections until cultivation reduced or obliterated them. In the caves where explorers pursued game or took shelter were the ashes of ancient campfires and often bones of the early occupants. Along the rivers and on the hillsides, erosion had exposed ancient village sites, the stone walls of graves, innumerable flints, pot shards, stone, bone and shell implements, and human bones.

Curiosity, if not scientific interest, led the early settlers to ask Indians with whom they came in contact about the origin of the old fortifications and mounds. The answers varied, but the gist was that they belonged to an ancient, different people. From these many garbled stories came the tales of "white Indians," "Welch Indians," a great "race" of Mound Builders of high culture, extensive catacombs beneath the present site of Lexington, and of a great battle on an island at the Falls of the Ohio in which the "white" race was finally wiped out by the red.

- Since the 1890s, steamboat travelers on the Green River have been gradually increasing from a few thousand annually to nearly 20,000 a year.
- Passengers include women going to Evansville to shop, businessmen on fishing trips, young people going to Massey Springs on the Barren River to dance, athletic teams meeting their rivals, and drummers bound for various Kentucky towns to peddle their wares.

Kentucky Tales:

Down our way we can never forgive Mrs. Harriet Beecher Stowe for writing *Uncle Tom's Cabin*, not because she painted Southern slavery in such black colors but because she has Eliza crossing the Ohio River to get out of Kentucky. To this day, we hold that Eliza made the mistake of her life.

—Irvin S. Cobb, *American Magazine*, 1916

The people of Kentucky are determined that when the next census is taken, there shall not be found one man or woman in the state who cannot read and write. They are fighting illiteracy as they might some terrible plague. In fact, they have come to realize that illiteracy is a plague, and that to allow it to exist is dangerous to the commonwealth.

—William F. De Moss, *Illustrated World*, 1916

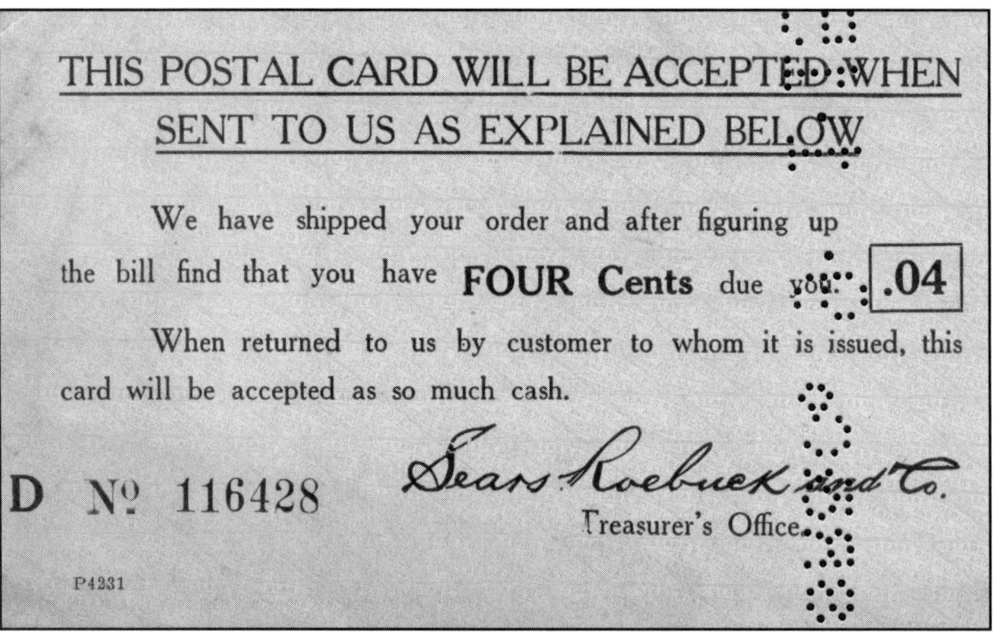
THIS POSTAL CARD WILL BE ACCEPTED WHEN SENT TO US AS EXPLAINED BELOW

We have shipped your order and after figuring up the bill find that you have **FOUR Cents** due you. **.04**

When returned to us by customer to whom it is issued, this card will be accepted as so much cash.

D No. 116428

Sears Roebuck and Co.
Treasurer's Office.

P4231

- Many come to the western portion of the state to see Mammoth Cave, a major tourist attraction; some even take the four-day trip to the natural phenomenon for $8.00, which includes steamboat transportation, entertainment, meals and cave tours.
- Currently, many children in the area are suffering from pellagra, whose hallmark is a butterfly rash that can spread across the victim's face.
- Most farmers in the area believe pellagra is caused by eating moldy corn, though a few have heard it is caused by the flood of Italians who have been coming to America, bringing unknown diseases with them.
- Across the South, 75,000 to 165,000 cases are suspected out of a population of 32.5 million; about five percent of those who have pellagra will die from dementia or from dehydration caused by diarrhea.
- Joseph Goldberger, a doctor known for his work with malaria, came through the region a while back, doing research concerning what he called "the three-M Southern diet of meal, molasses and meat"—which is cheap, fast and filling.
- He claims the diet may cause the disease, but no one trusts what he says in these parts.
- Based on the 1910 national census, 5,516,163 people cannot read in the United States—more than the entire population of Denmark.
- Since 1911, dozens of counties in Kentucky have opened their schoolhouses to adult education in a program called "Moonlight Schools," designed to eliminate illiteracy from the state by the 1920 census.
- So far, 1,600 men and women have enrolled in the program.
- Arithmetic, geography, history, civics, agriculture, horticulture, home economics and road building are among the subjects taught, while reading assignments deal with topics such as seed-testing, crop rotation, plumbing, the value of a daily bath, extermination of the fly, and ways of cooking.
- Progress is also being made in the building of good roads; throughout the state the newspapers are calling for Kentucky to join the automobile age by constructing hard-surface roads fit for car travel.

HISTORICAL SNAPSHOT
1916

- After Mexico requested that the United States remove its troops during the Mexican Civil War, 17 Americans and 38 Mexicans died in a clash
- The U.S. bought the Virgin Islands from Denmark for $25 million
- Railway workers gained the right to an eight-hour day, preventing a nationwide strike
- Ring Lardner published *You Know Me Al: A Busher's Letters*, John Dewey wrote *Democracy and Education* and Carl Sandburg's *Chicago Poems* was released
- The Federal Land Bank System was created to aid farmers in acquiring loans
- Popular songs of the day included "Ireland Must Be Heaven for My Mother Came from There" and "There's a Little Bit of Bad in Every Good Little Girl"
- Orange Crush, Nathan's hotdogs, Lincoln Logs and mechanical windshield wipers all made their first appearance
- Henry Ford chartered a Peace Ship to stop the war in Europe, caused, he said, by international Jews and Wall Street
- Margaret Sanger opened the first birth control clinic in the country, distributing information in English, Italian and Yiddish
- The Mercury dime and Liberty fifty-cent piece went into circulation
- High school dropout Norman Rockwell published his first illustration in *The Saturday Evening Post*
- Actor Charlie Chaplin signed with Mutual for a record $675,000 salary
- Multimillionaire businessman Rodman Wanamaker organized the Professional Golfers Association of America
- South Carolina raised the minimum working age of children from 12 to 14
- Lucky Strike Cigarettes were introduced, costing $0.10 for a pack of 20
- Stanford Terman introduced the first test for measuring intelligence, coining the term "IQ" for intelligence quotient

1916 Economic Profile

Selected Prices

Automobile, Willys-Knight Touring Sedan	$1,950.00
Boots, Man's Elk	$21.00
Candy, Pep-O-Mint Lifesavers, Roll	$0.05
Card Game, Rook	$0.42
Chair, Reclining	$37.00
Child's Suit	$2.95
Macaroni, Skinner's	$0.25
Magazine, *Vanity Fair*	$0.25
Oil, 3-in-1	$0.25
Printing Press	$765.00
Shotgun, Remington	$32.70
Talcum Powder	$0.25
Telephone Call, New York to San Francisco, Three Minutes	$20.70
Typewriter, Underwood	43.85

Changing America

- Encouraged by the success of his movie *Birth of a Nation*, which had grossed $18 million, D. W. Griffith produced the ambitious film *Intolerance*.
- President Woodrow Wilson signed into law a "Good Roads Bill," for state road-building projects.
- America boasted 951 four-year colleges, up from 700 a decade earlier.
- James L. Kraft discovered how to pasteurize cheese for canning, assuring a long shelf life without refrigeration.
- Half of the Irish families on Manhattan's West Side—an area rife with crime and poverty—were fatherless.
- Enamel bathtubs were beginning to replace the traditional claw-footed, cast-iron tubs in many homes.
- America now had 21,000 movie theaters charging an average of $0.05 to $0.10 per show.
- While the popular Model T cost $360, the average cost of a new car was $600; more than 3.5 million cars were on the nation's highways.
- The Prohibition movement continued to gain ground, with 24 states voting against the sale of alcoholic beverages.
- The First Rose Bowl football game was played between Washington State College and Brown University; Washington won 14-0.
- Taxicabs, charging a nickel per ride, appeared on urban streets.
- Piggly Wiggly introduced do-it-yourself shopping in Tennessee with a self-serve grocery store.

"A Wonderful Discovery," *The Youth's Companion*, November 1, 1916:

When Roentgen announced his discovery of what has since become known as x-rays, no one could anticipate the value of the instrument that he placed in the hands of physicians and surgeons. But great as the value of that instrument is, it is strictly limited. Although it gives correct and most useful views of the bones of our frame, it delineates unsatisfactorily the soft parts of the body; and in a great number of cases a complete knowledge of those is of supreme importance.

Now news comes from England of an invention and discovery much more remarkable than any of Roentgen's. By an ingenious use of the electric current generated within the body in combination with two other electric currents in x-ray tubes, the living tissues are made to make their own pictures. They actuate a needle, which makes a diagram of any desired organ on a revolving cylinder covered with waxed paper. . . . The story seems well-nigh incredible, but is well-authenticated. It is accepted as true by the *British Medical Journal*, one of the best medical authorities in England.

"Nationwide Mortality Probe," *Child Betterment*, June 1914:

About 300,000 babies under one year of age die yearly in the United States. Fully 150,000 of these could be saved by applying methods of care already known and widely practiced. But while the death rate for the entire population is slowly but surely declining, the death rate for children under one year is, if anything, rising. One babe in every eight born in this country dies before it is a year old. In certain localities the ratio is far worse than that. In one American city, for which statistics have been gathered, babies die in the poor neighborhoods at the rate of 373 per 1,000 born, or more than one in every three; while in the good residence districts in the same city, the rate is 154 per 1,000. Even that is high compared to the death rate in New Zealand, where for babies under one year it is only 68 for each 1,000. We have, therefore, in infant mortality a nationwide problem, and it is to have a nationwide probe. The new Children's Bureau of the Department of Commerce and Labor will make one of its chief activities for some time to come the study of infant mortality. With the new year, it will begin a house-to-house canvass of the entire nation, to verify numbers, scan conditions, seek causes, and obtain a basis on which to formulate remedies. Among the special matters to be studied is the housing of families, the feeding of infants, the sanitary conditions of neighborhoods, and the physical and mental health of parents as well as children. No doubt great results will follow this careful and scientific study of the main problems relating to the causes of illness and death among juveniles.

Joke:

Is your husband at home?

Yes, what do you want with him?

I'm revising the voting list and I just want to inquire which party he belongs to.

Do yer? Well, I'm the party wot'e belongs to!

1919 Profile

Middle Class

After being pronounced dead last year during the Spanish flu epidemic, and then found alive by his father at the morgue, Arthur Ledbetter is now a freshman at North Carolina State University where he is studying animal husbandry.

Arthur Ledbetter is now attending college at North Carolina State University.

Life at Home

- Less than a year after nearly dying during the great influenza epidemic, 20-year-old Arthur Ledbetter now attends North Carolina State University.
- When America sent its troops into the Great War, Arthur joined dozens of his friends to fight in the army.
- At Camp McClellan, an army boot camp in Alabama, he was overtaken by the flu epidemic sweeping the nation.
- When the flu struck, Arthur suffered a sudden onset of chills, severe headache, back pains, a general malaise, flushed face, some soreness of the throat and a roaring fever in excess of 104 degrees.
- This rapidly progressed into bronchitis, for which the treatment included bed rest, free movement of the bowels and a light diet.
- Within days of falling ill, he lapsed into unconsciousness, and in the confusion of the crisis, was pronounced dead.
- When his father arrived at the camp to claim the body of his oldest son, he was sent to the camp morgue where, while leaning over his son, he felt a breath—Arthur was alive!
- Subsequently revived and nursed back to health, he was discharged from the army and immediately entered North

The two Ledbetter boys are strong-willed and competitive.

Carolina State University in Raleigh to major in his long-standing interest—animal husbandry.

- At home in Hendersonville, North Carolina, his father is worried; the economy is in a tailspin following the war's end and inflation is eating up his profits and hard-earned savings.
- He is determined to find enough money so his son can attend college, especially after he came so close to dying.
- To save money, the annual shopping trip to Charleston, South Carolina, has been cancelled; last year's fashions will have to do.
- For Thanksgiving dinner, the family is having cod because, as his mother says, even a king could not afford turkey this year.
- She is also planting a larger vegetable garden so that nearly all of the family's food can be homegrown.
- Her greatest fear is not inflation, but that one of her children will catch the flu again and die.
- Some days, when the air is heavy, she insists that the entire family wear masks—just in case the epidemic returns.
- The 1918 outbreak impacted many nations, including America, Europe, India, China and Australia.
- *The Literary Digest* said future generations would view the epidemic of 1918–19 in the same way previous generations had regarded the Great Plague of London in 1665.
- About 25 percent of all Americans caught the flu, and approximately 548,000 died.

"War Reports from the Influenza Front,"
***The Literary Digest*, February 22, 1919:**

A war here in the United States, a war that reached into practically every community in the country and took a toll of American lives twice as great as that taken by the war overseas, has raged through the early winter months. In the fight against influenza, which is not yet finished, devoted women have served in the front ranks, many of them inspired by the interest and honor that helped the dough-boy to act the hero, and have gone down to death, if not unwept, at least unsung. "The women of America have been pretty heroic in France," writes an official of the Visiting Nurses' Association of Chicago, "but they have been none the less so at home, volunteers as well as professionals, and honorable mention would perhaps bring the situation a bit more closely home to many of us. . . ."

- The name "Spanish influenza" was bestowed in the mistaken belief that the disease started in Spain, prominent medical journals now report.
- Arthur was one of many pronounced dead, but the only one awaiting burial to be found alive.
- He was born in South Carolina in 1899 to a mother enormously proud of her Huguenot background.
- The daughter of a state senator, she enjoyed a French governess and tutors as a child and many privileges growing up.
- A graduate of Mercer College in Macon, Georgia, Arthur's father is a tall, spare, beak-nosed man with one eye; the other one was shot out by a black sharecropper during a fight in which the latter was convinced Arthur's father was "having his way" with the sharecropper's wife.

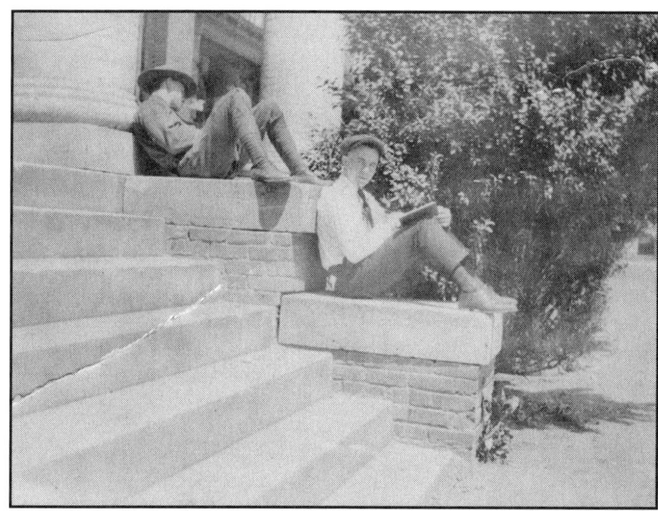

While in the military, Arthur contracted the flu and nearly died.

- The family moved to Hendersonville, North Carolina, when Arthur was five, after doctors recommended the move to relieve his sister's severe asthma.
- Arthur and his younger brother attended the Blue Ridge School, a private institution in Hendersonville for both boarding and day students.
- The two boys were so strong-willed and competitive that their father was forced to construct a board down the middle of the bed they shared to keep them from fighting.
- Their sister currently attends a finishing school in Virginia.
- Her father's favorite picture of her was taken during a Methodist church play in which she was a daisy and her best friend played a fairy.

Life at School

- Having waited years for the chance to be away from home and free of supervision, Arthur loves being in college and afforded the chance to learn.
- His classes are in either Patterson Hall, the main agricultural building, or in the animal husbandry building.
- Patterson Hall is a buff brick structure with two stories and a basement; the lower floor is used as a dairy with washrooms and sterilization chamber, while the first floor provides room for the experimental station offices and classrooms for agronomy, horticulture, soils and agricultural experimentation.
- The second floor accommodates the departments of botany and plant pathology, physiology and veterinary medicine.
- There are also rooms for the poultry department and stock judging, as well as zoology and entomology.
- The centerpiece of North Carolina State's animal husbandry program is a dairy herd of over 80 head, a flock of sheep, and a number of hogs and Percheron horses.
- To earn extra money, Arthur spends weekends racing his Indian motorcycle at county fairs in the area, where he can sometimes make $10 or more.

Hendersonville is a magnet for tourists.

North Carolina State Itemized Expenses by Month, 1918–1919, North Carolina State Catalog:

September: Room rent, and fuel and lights, $15; incidental fee, $2; medical and hospital fee, $3; lecture fee, $1; library fee, $1; furniture fee, $1; physical culture fee, $3; Y.M.C.A. fee, $1; military equipment deposit, $15; waste and breakage deposit, $5; board for September, $16—a total of $63 to be paid to the College. Tuition for one-half session, $22.50, may be paid at this time, which will make a total of $85.50 to be paid to the College. Thirty-five dollars will be required to buy books and drawing instruments, and for incidentals.

October: Board, $16.

November: Board, $16; tuition, if it was not paid in September, $22.50.

December: Board, $10, through the nineteenth.

January: Tuition, $22.50; lodging, and fuel and lights, $15; medical and hospital fee, $3; furniture fee, $1; physical culture fee, $3; Y.M.C.A. fee, $1; board, $14. A total of $59.50.

February: Board, $16.

March: Board, $16.

April: Board, $16.

May: Board, $16.

- The total cost for a freshman is calculated at $325, including board, tuition, lodging, fuel and lights, fees and deposits, books, drawing instruments, laundry and a moderate allowance for incidentals.
- The college advises that "the allowances which parents make their sons for contingencies and spending money, it is suggested, should be kept small, for small allowances take away temptation to unwise living."
- His classes during his freshman year consist of botany, chemistry, agricultural drawing, mechanical engineering, shop, mathematics, zoology, animal husbandry and farm crops.
- In his sophomore year he will take dairying, organic chemistry, military art, English, soil geology, comparative physiology, veterinary medicine, plant propagation, horticulture and agricultural physics.
- During the school year he also has access to the college's machine shop, which has lathes, shapers, drill presses, grinders and planers.

The total cost for a freshman at N.C. State is $325.

Description of Courses, Animal Husbandry and Dairying, North Carolina State College of Agriculture and Engineering, Course Catalog, 1918–1919:

101 or 102. Types and Market Classes of Livestock. A survey of the development of the livestock industry, with special reference to present condition. Consideration is given to the fundamental principles of livestock judging; the relation of form to function, or production; the combination of characters indicating constitutional strength, temperament, capacity and sexuality necessary in the development of animals for special purposes as milk, meat, work and speed production. Time is devoted to the market requirements of livestock and adaptation of the different types. Both terms, two periods. Required of freshmen. Professor Reed, Mr. McCluer.

- He used some discarded lumber to rebuild his dorm room bed, and has recently been recruited by a local theater to help build scenery for an upcoming play.
- It did not pass his notice that the play calls for nearly all of the actresses to be young and pretty, but he knows he must be careful in selecting his friends; he has been promised a gold watch if he neither drinks nor smokes before he is 21—a goal that is only one year away.
- He realizes, however, many young men—and women—do not share this goal, and has told his Pa these are not just city kids either; the boys from the farms also seem inclined toward easy pleasures.
- His dorm room has electric lights and steam heat; room assignments were made by the military department when he registered.
- Under the provisions of a 1916 act of Congress, a unit of the Reserve Officers' Training Corps was established at the college in 1917.
- As a member of the Corps, Arthur receives a government uniform and will spend four weeks in a training camp during the summer.
- During his freshman and sophomore years, three hours a week are devoted to military training; during his junior and senior years, the requirement is that no less than five hours a week be allotted to military training.
- In addition to his uniform allowance, Arthur receives $100 per year for his participation in the Corps.
- After graduation, he will be placed on a list of reserve officers of the United States Army for 10 years.

The local theater recruits young, pretty actresses.

Life in the Community: Hendersonville, North Carolina, and North Carolina State in Raleigh

- When Arthur's family moved to Hendersonville to alleviate his sister's asthma, few people in the community could afford an automobile except the tourists who arrived each summer from such diverse places as Chicago, Charleston and New Orleans.

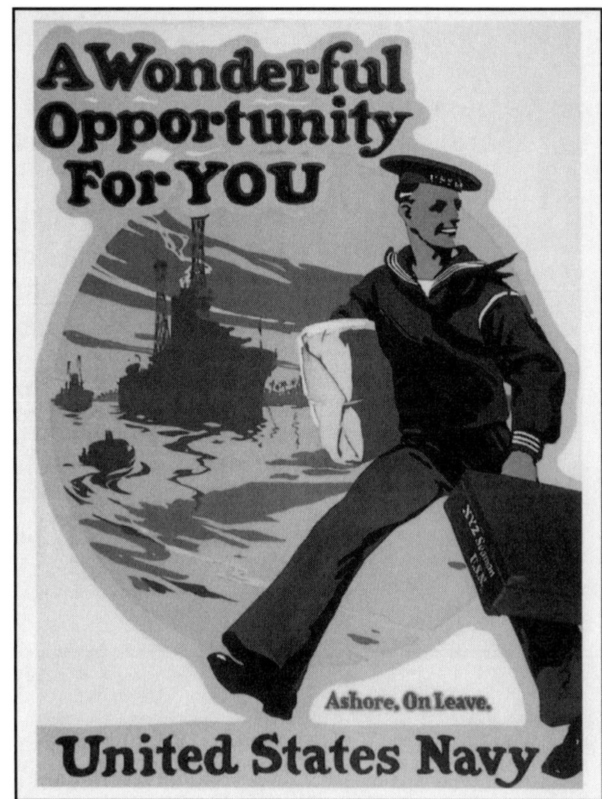

- During the summer months, the St. John's Hotel in Hendersonville is often a blaze of lights as guests sit in the porch rocking chairs to watch a handful of cars and millions of fireflies go by.
- The neighboring communities of Black Mountain, Saluda, Montreat and Junaluska are all building a sound reputation as assembly grounds for religious services of all kinds—one of the reasons the state is placing a high priority on building roads, particularly hard-surface roads.
- Of the 349 miles of road scheduled to be added or improved, 240 miles are to be built of gravel, sand and other materials, while 109 miles will be of hard-surface construction.
- The average North Carolina teacher's annual salary is $284, below Mississippi's average by $7 and South Carolina's by $31; nationally, the average is $635.
- According to the publication *School and Society*, most North Carolina teachers are paid less than it "costs to feed and house prisoners in the county jail."
- North Carolina still has 63,000 landless, tenant farmers.
- In Raleigh, where Arthur attends school, the college is an important institution.
- It was created by the North Carolina legislature in 1887 as a land grant for an agricultural and mechanical college, and opened two years later with 70 students taught by six full-time faculty and two assistants; the college roster for 1919 lists 651 freshmen—many of whom are WWI veterans who delayed college to fight in France—123 sophomores, 73 juniors, 41 seniors and eight graduate students.
- The college rests on 486 acres in the western suburbs of Raleigh, approximately one mile and a quarter from the state capital.
- The college library, open from 9 a.m. to 6 p.m., contains 8,000 volumes.

Historical Snapshot 1919

- The Paris Peace Conference was held in Versailles, where President Woodrow Wilson proposed the creation of a League of Nations
- A poll of newspaper editors indicated that 77 percent of those surveyed favored ratification of the peace treaty, including its League of Nations provision
- Labor unrest was at its most turbulent since 1890; inflation triggered 2,665 strikes involving over four million workers
- More than 500,000 union workers staged a strike in Chicago, resulting in riots and 36 deaths, while 300,000 organized a strike in New York City
- U.S. World War I casualties were declared to be 116,516; battle deaths totaled 53,402, while other deaths, including those from disease, numbered 55,114; total wounded was tallied at 204,002, and worldwide fatalities totaled 10 million
- More than $7.8 million was raised at the Victory Liberty Loan concert at the Metropolitan Opera
- The rate of inflation reached 8.9 percent
- The first nonstop transatlantic flight from Newfoundland to Ireland was made by J. W. Alcock and A. Whitten in 16 hours and 27 minutes
- *The Economic Consequences of the Peace* by J. M. Keynes, *Ten Days That Shook the World* by John Reed, and *Winesburg, Ohio* by Sherwood Anderson were all published
- The Eighteenth Amendment, prohibiting the sale of alcoholic beverages, was approved to take effect in 1920
- Seventy lynchings occurred in the South as membership in the Klan increased to 100,000 across 27 states
- Herbert Hoover was named director of the U.S. Commission for Relief to aid liberated countries, both neutral and enemy
- Peter Paul's Konobar, a dial telephone, the Drake Hotel in Chicago and a state gas tax (in Oregon) all made their first appearance
- Attorney General Mitchell Palmer instructed the FBI to round up 249 known communists, who were then deported on the Soviet Ark to Finland
- Hockey's Stanley Cup championship was cancelled after one player died and many others were stricken with the deadly flu
- The wildly popular vaudeville was featured at 4,000 theaters nationwide

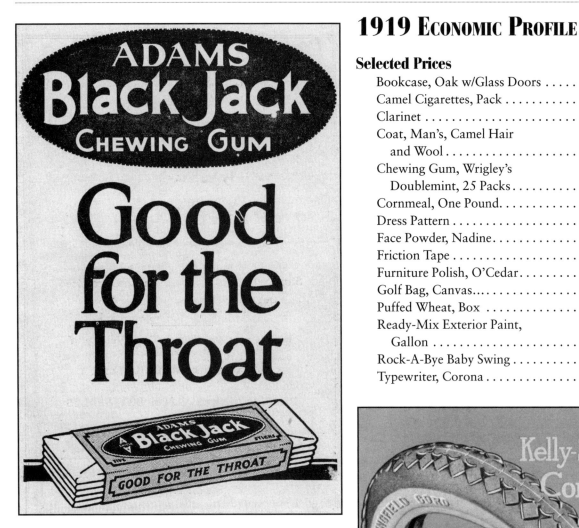

1919 Economic Profile

Selected Prices

Bookcase, Oak w/Glass Doors $8.00
Camel Cigarettes, Pack $0.18
Clarinet $18.45
Coat, Man's, Camel Hair and Wool $4.85
Chewing Gum, Wrigley's Doublemint, 25 Packs $0.73
Cornmeal, One Pound. $2.70
Dress Pattern $0.10
Face Powder, Nadine. $0.50
Friction Tape $0.02
Furniture Polish, O'Cedar. $0.25
Golf Bag, Canvas.... . . . . $3.45
Puffed Wheat, Box $0.15
Ready-Mix Exterior Paint, Gallon $2.95
Rock-A-Bye Baby Swing $1.00
Typewriter, Corona $50.00

"Housing and Reconstruction," by Clarence Stein, *Journal of the Institute of Architects*, October 1918:

The public now, for the first time in this century, is seeing housing undertaken on a large scale for the good of those to be housed and not for the profit of the real-estate speculator or builder. The memory of the American public is short, and it is while we are carrying on war housing that we must prepare for similar peace-problems.

Changing America

- Devoted to self-improvement, the General Federation of Women's Clubs, formed in 1890, now claimed more than one million members in 17 states.
- To keep the price of a pack of Lucky Strikes at a dime in the face of increased cigarette taxes, R. J. Reynolds cut the number of cigarettes per pack from 20 to 12.
- Almost 10 million telephones had been installed, up from 195,000 in 1888, including one on nearly every businessman's desk.
- Ernest Rutherford reported the first manmade atomic fission.
- Ten percent of draftees and volunteers in World War I were rejected for neuropsychiatric disorders—usually alcoholism.
- The average school term nationwide was 161 days, while the average number of days attended per pupil was 121.
- The number of farms operated by landless tenants increased from 15 percent 40 years earlier to 38 percent today.
- Scientist Robert Goddard proposed using rockets to send a vehicle to the moon.
- Camels were the soldier's favorite brand of cigarette.
- More than 30,000 Jews marched in Baltimore to protest pogroms in Poland and elsewhere.
- Socialist Eugene Debs was jailed for sedition for calling Lenin and Trotsky the "foremost statesmen of the age."

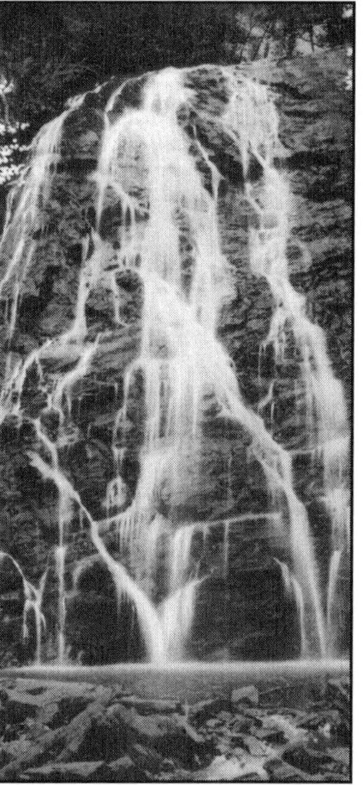

Level land is scarce in the mountain areas of North Carolina.

"The Steamship Outrivaled," *The Literary Digest*, May 29, 1919:

A real rival to the steamship has appeared on the scene for the first time since steam-driven vessels succeeded in crossing the Atlantic. The rival is the motorship, propelled by the Diesel engine. Dr. Charles Edward Lucke, professor of mechanical engineering at Columbia University, is quoted as endorsing in the highest terms this seagoing agent of rapid transportation.

For the first time in its history the steamship has a real rival which may compete with it on the sea as effectively as motor-driven vehicles compete with railroads on land. This does not mean that the motorship will drive the steamship from the seas, any more than the motorcar has driven the steam-locomotive from the rails, but it does mean that the motorship will make for itself as important a place in the world of shipping as the motorcar has achieved on land in relation to the steam railroad.

The fundamental element of the motorship, the element that is responsible for all of its characteristic economic qualities, is the Diesel oil-engine, which is used both in large units for propelling vessels directly and also in small units for driving electric generators, the current from which operates all auxiliary machinery. This type of internal combustion engine is now completing a period of 25 years of development for all purposes, and, therefore, as such cannot be regarded as a novelty.

"The Mountains Go to School," ***The Land of Saddle-bags, A Study of the Mountain People of Appalachia*****, by James Watt Raine, 1924:**

Today, of course, every district has a schoolhouse of some fashion. But the schoolhouse, the length of the school term, and the teachings are too often, one or all, very inadequate.

Level land is so scarce in the Mountain area that it is usually preempted for the family garden, which must furnish the major part of the food supply. Even if it were not thus seized, schoolhouses would not be built thereupon, for it is safer to have the children higher up, out of the reach of sudden tides, or high waters that roar in torrents down the creeks after heavy rains or melting snow.

The little schoolhouse, therefore, is usually built on a steep slope, one side set up on stilts. It is seldom fenced or planted with grass. It is to be used only a few months in the year, so it is made as cheap and ugly as possible, and its surroundings are unbelievably bare and depressing. There are no outhouses and no playground.

Such a schoolhouse is not always furnished with desks. Its blackboards are often worn colorless, and chalk is frequently lacking. Often there is no chair for the teacher, and the stove pipe is likely to rust down or disappear between sessions. The school term is often discouragingly short. A few years ago a three-months school was very common. But for most of the pupils that seldom meant 60 days' attendance. The average attendance in the district was often less than 30 days. Where would you and I have been with only 30 nonconsecutive days of instruction in a year?

Recent years have seen great improvements in education. Schools for five months are now as common as the three-months schools used to be. And though many districts have still only a three- or four-months school, a great number have gradually increased the term to five or six months, and a few are heroically supporting seven or eight. The average attendance computed by counties runs from 20 days' attendance in a year to 90. Ninety days of instruction out of 365 is the highest average attendance that any county shows. . . .

In the remote districts it is very difficult to get teachers. Even where the school is not given to some of the kinfolk of a trustee, it must usually be given to someone living in the district because there is no suitable boarding place for a stranger. Even if a room were obtainable, an outsider could scarcely afford to apply for the position. The average median salary, at last accounts, was rather less than $250 a year. . .

It was really easier to get teachers when schools ran only three months, July to September, because college and normal school students were available during the summer months. Six-months schools are often taught by ambitious young men or women who can teach through the school term and then return to their studies at Christmas.

The following letter from Miss Potts contains this vivid account of her work in Monmouth County, New Jersey:

I think you may be interested to hear something of my experiences in the recent epidemic of influenza. I had whole families down with it at once. The father and eight children in one home and then the mother came down with it, and labor came on ahead of time. The man got up and almost staggered round the house, just keeping up the fire and giving milk and medicine. One forlorn little tot of three years was around, and she stood by the bed patting her mother's hand, clad in a big sister's sweater that touched the ground. It was one of the careless homes, chairs without seats, panes of glass out of the windows, and doors you could not shut. None of the neighbors would come near—everyone was afraid. I almost begged one of them to do some washing and she did it once or twice, and that was all. The second day the woman's temperature was 105, and I thought we should surely lose her, but she pulled through, and so did all the rest of that family. Across the street was a man who had the "flu" followed by acute nephritis. He had convulsions from 7 a.m. one day until 3 p.m., was unconscious for 60 hours and neither spoke nor swallowed. I stayed with him from 9 a.m. one day until 1 a.m. the following morning—no one would come near except a younger brother of 20. The next day the doctor had ordered hot flaxseed poultices. I stayed from 12 noon to 6 p.m.; went back at 8 p.m., and kept up the poultices until 3 a.m., when he showed the first symptoms of consciousness by grabbing a hot poultice and trying to get it off. He made a quick recovery to our surprise, for there was some pneumonia in one lung as well.

We were not always as fortunate though. One woman nursed her husband and three boys and then came down herself. She was a heavy woman, weighing 195 pounds. All she begged was to be left alone; she was "so tired." The man got up and tried to do his best. I stayed there all night and in the morning telephoned to the woman's sister and she came and tapped on the window. No one would come in, but I went to the door and pulled her in and told her she had to stay. When she heard that her sister's recovery was very doubtful she was ashamed—telephoned to another woman relative and they both helped the man out. I went back at seven, for it was a critical case, and stayed till midnight, when all one could do was to send for the priest.

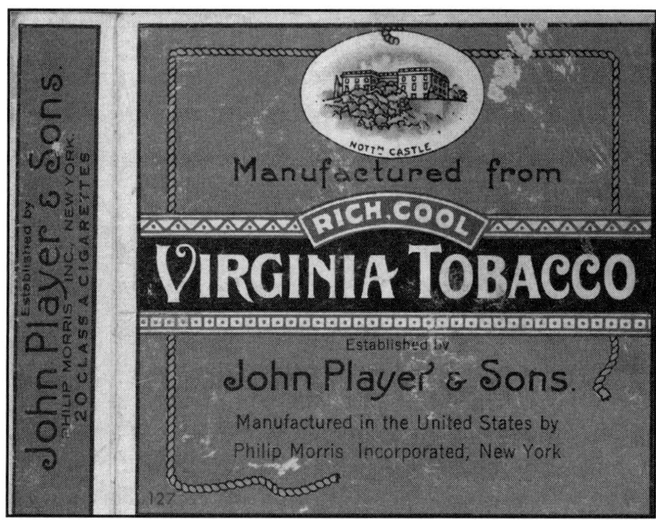

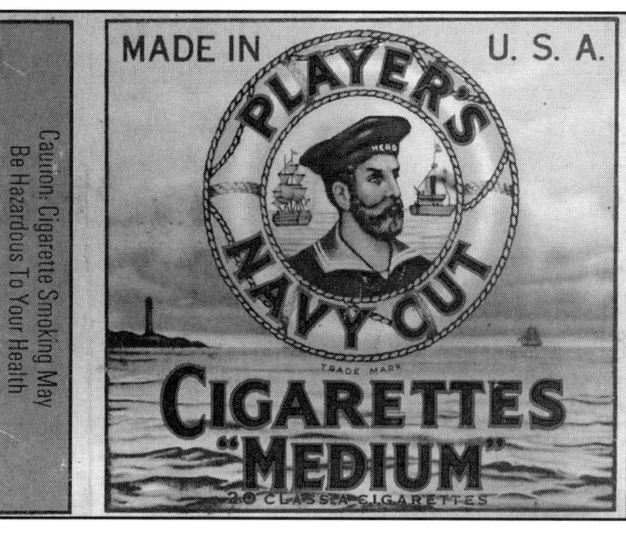

"How to Make a State Be One," by W. O. Saunders, *Collier's*, May 26, 1923:

It hasn't been so many years since a Virginian addressed a threadbare-looking individual loafing on a street corner in Richmond and asked him if he were from North Carolina.

"Nope," drawled the threadbare individual. "I'm sick's the reason I looks so bad."

To-day the press of the South is astounded at the progress of North Carolina, and the eyes of the nation are turning toward this state. This is upsetting all the traditional and common conceptions of a Southern people who are supposed to be full of pellagra, hookworms, malaria, snobbish spirit, and the general inertia that comes from too much corn pone and pot liquor in the kitchen, and too much ancestral pride in the parlor.

A Secret for 47 States

Ten years ago we North Carolinians were just about as inert and backward in education and social legislation as any other Southern state. To-day North Carolina is the most forward of all Southern states in public welfare and social legislation—and everything. (North Carolinians tax themselves more money in a year to spend on education than the proud Empire State of Georgia spends in five.)

A governor of North Carolina once said that if he saw two objects in a field, one of which looked like a farmer and one of which looked like a stump, his only way of determining at a distance which was farmer and which was stump was to wait and see which moved first. The first to move would be the stump. . . .

Fully aware of the storm of pooh-poohs and protests that will arise from the throat of every academician in North Carolina and elsewhere, I am going to say that the secret of the regeneration of North Carolina is the Department of Sociology and Rural Economics at the University of North Carolina. In this university there has grown up robust and strong the most constructive and revolutionary social agency in the South to-day. . .

Raleigh, N. C. Post Office.

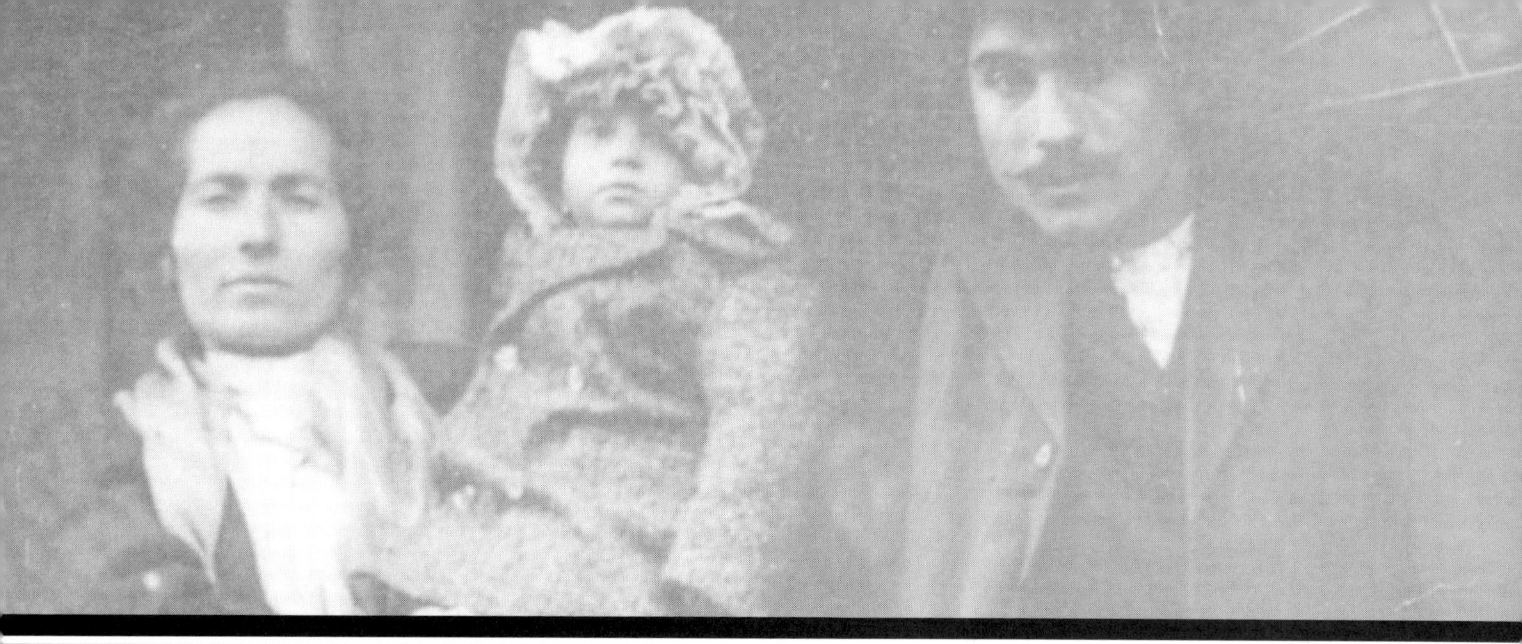

1919 News Feature

Philip Campagne and Theresa Bonacorsi, children of the Lawrence, Massachusetts, strikes of 1912 and 1919, from *The First Generation, In the Words of Twentieth-Century American Immigrants*, by June Namias, 1978:

(Lawrence is one of several once-important mill cities along the Merrimac River. The mill towns, with their growing foreign-born populations, produced the textiles which fed mostly into New York, making the United States a highly productive ready-made clothing producer. The New England mill system as it developed after the Civil War utilized the "family system," in which immigrant men, women and children all worked, and some of the worst child labor abuses in the history of America occurred. Almost everyone in the Campagne and Bonacorsi families worked in the Lawrence mills.—June Namias)

Philip: My father was from Trecastagne, which is a small town near the province of Catania, (Italy). My mother was born in Catania. My father carried merchandise from town to town and then became a middleman. In those days they used to do a lot of bartering. He used to get a commission.

He had some people who were here in this country and he figured it was a better place to come and make a living. Plus, one time my father had beat up the mayor of the town. Some woman was crying that the mayor owed her money for her husband's work and he didn't want to pay, so my father gave him a lickin'. It might have had something to do with it. But he came here because he could make a better living. He had a big family. When he left he had seven children. Then, of course, there were seven more when he came to this country.

Theresa: My mother came from Termini, a small city in the province of Palermo. My father died when I was a little girl, 10 years old. My father came from Leonforte in the province of Syracuse. He was a shoemaker. He had a little shop, but I guess there wasn't enough money. When he used to make a pair of shoes, if they were for a farmer, they'd give him food.

My father came here first. I don't know how he landed in Lawrence—I guess like everyone else. The mills were just starting at that time (1901). The Wood Mill was the biggest mill in the whole world at that time. It must have been a couple of years later or so when my mother came. They had two children. He left them in Italy with the intention, like everyone else, that they were going to make some money and return. But that didn't happen; they never returned. I was born here.

Philip: I started work when I was 11 and a half years old. I was born in 1902. It was about 1913 when I started work. You could work if you were 13 years old and 40 weeks. You were supposed to be 14, but they used to discount vacation time, the summertime. Now when you came from Italy and you've got brothers and sisters working, we used to work with their paper. Like I worked with my older brother's papers. The only one who worked with his own papers was the oldest one. Then there were always 18 months or two years between us.

At the time they used to work 54 hours, so we used to work 48. You think that's much. My father used to work 60 hours when they came to this country. We never used to see him until Saturday afternoon. People congregated together because of the language barrier. They can't go in and buy something. So they go with their own communities.

Theresa: The Naples people and the Sicilian, they kind of stayed by themselves. The Sicilian took the section of Lawrence near the lower end, near the Everett Mills. And the Naples people took over the side near the Common. Then there was this thing that the Naples mothers would say, "Don't go over there! There's all the Sicilians." And the Sicilian mothers, "Don't bother with them, they're Naples people. You know how they are!" Us children, we didn't know any better, so we just stayed together. The rest of Lawrence was all different groups. The Polish people was congregated by themselves, the Lithuanian, the Syrians.

Philip: Everybody lived close. Kids died of diphtheria, measles and tuberculosis. In them days they were poor, but believe me, they understood each other. They were friendly to each other; one had a problem, they all felt it. They were very close, helpin' each other any way they could. Families were pretty good size, of course, but there was always somebody sick, or dying and dead. All you could hear was women cryin' because a child died. I remember one time there was eight of us laid up, but we came out all right. We were pretty lucky; I know whole families who were completely wiped out. . . .

There was a strike in 1912; there was one in 1919 . . . 1912 was the worst. It hit a lot of people. Things were really tough. See, I was 10 years old. I remember I had to read the paper for my father. I remember the bread lines. On Common Street they set up a place for the strikers. They used to give 'em a loaf of bread and some salt pork. That's what you had to eat. Things were pretty damn bad.

Theresa: I remember one woman coming to my mother, not that we were rich, but my father had a store, so it was a little different. Coming to my mother, she says, "How can I just eat this? Bread and salt pork." My mother was always cookin' so she gave her a hot dish of whatever it was.

And that strike was in the winter months. It was terrible. The Polish were used to cold more than the people that came from southern Europe. Half of 'em weren't provided with warm clothes.

I was going to the first grade or second grade at the Walton School. I remember there were the cops there, with the bayonets. When you're a child if there is a soldier or a cop near you, you feel so safe, and they didn't do anything to anybody.

My father had the store. It was a clubroom mostly because he had pool tables and he had a couple of tables to play cards, and then in the front of the store he had this showcase with sweets, candy, chewing gum. On the other side there used to be a shoeshine parlor—this is all in the same store. The store was open till late; but when the strike happened, we had to close very early.

Philip: There was a curfew.

Theresa: In fact, not even two people could be in the same spot. We had to close all the curtains so there wouldn't be no light showing out. We had two large rooms; one was for us, the children, and one was for my father and mother, and always a little one besides, in the same bedroom. At that time my mother was so scared to be alone with just us that she put the two beds together in one room. She locked the outside door and then locked the bedroom door. Even though we had no connections with the strike, we had the effect of it, with all these things going on.

Philip: I don't remember too much, only my older brother was very active. He was one of those guys they used to call, not comrade, socialist. He was a Wobbly. He was 11 years older than I was.

That 1912 strike, the Italians were pretty strong. They were really the spearheads of that strike, but every group—the Polish had their area meetings, the French had their meetings, and the Lithuanians. The Italians were picketing, and going to homes, "Don't go to work or you'll get your head busted in."

Theresa: We were all with the strike. One of the things I remember—of course, this was with the later strike, 1919—they decided not to send the children to school so that (the company) would give in. I don't know what the purpose of that was. I wanted to go to school, but one morning my brother says that we should stay home and we didn't go. Right away the teachers knew why.

One of the incidents I remember very well was when my sister made a dress for me. The material was a khaki dress; it was on the same line as a uniform, only there was a skirt and there was a blouse with a belt. She had all these buttons of the IWW. They used to screw on. So she knew she'd use them, but not with the exposed part, with the IWW—with the other side, the brass.

When I was in school, everyone admired the dress. The teacher sent me from one room to another. "What a beautiful dress!" For some reason, things get unscrewed by themselves. One button unscrewed and the side with the IWW fell on the floor of the school. Somebody picked it up. I think it was the teacher in my room that got hold of it. She wanted to know "Who had that button! Where's the button!" She looked around. She had an idea when she saw my brass buttons on my dress. "Where did you get this?"

I said, "I don't know. My sister made the dress and they were around so we used them."

That sort of made it bad. There was an embarrassment there all the time.

1920–1929

The years following the Great War were marked by a new nationalism symbolized by frenzied consumerism. By 1920, urban Americans had begun to define themselves—for their neighbors and for the world—in terms of what they owned. The car was becoming universal, at least in its appeal. At the dawn of the century, only 4,192 automobiles were registered nationwide; in 1920, the number of cars had reached 1.9 million. Simultaneously, aggressive new advertising methods began appearing, designed to fuel the new consumer needs of the buying public. And buy it did. From 1921 to 1929, Americans bought and America boomed. With expanded wages and buying power came increased leisure time for recreation, travel, or even self-improvement. Advertising reinforced the idea that the conveniences and status symbols of the wealthy were attainable to everyone. The well-to-do and the wage earner began to look a lot more alike, and many of the most feared diseases of the urban ghetto began to disappear.

Following the Great War, America enjoyed a period of great expansion and expectation. The attitude of many Americans was expressed in President Calvin Coolidge's famous remark, "The chief business of the American people is business." The role of the federal government remained small during the period and federal expenditures actually declined following the war effort. Harry Donaldson's song "How Ya Gonna Keep 'Em Down on the Farm after They've Seen Paree?" described another basic shift in American society. The 1920 census reported that more than 50 percent of the population—54 million people—lived in urban areas. The move to the cities was the result of changed expectations, increased industrialization, and the migration of millions of Southern blacks to the urban North.

The availability of electricity expanded the universe of goods that could be manufactured and sold. The expanded use of radios, electric lights, telephones, and powered vacuum cleaners was possible for the first time, and they quickly became essential household items. Construction boomed as—for the first time—half of all Americans now lived in urban areas. Industry, too, benefited from the wider use of electric power. At the turn of the century, electricity ran only five percent of all machinery, and by 1925, 73 percent. Large-scale electric power also made possible electrolytic processes in the rapidly developing heavy chemical industry. With increasing sophistication came higher costs; wages for skilled workers continued to rise during the 1920s, putting further distance between the blue-collar worker and the emerging middle class.

Following the war years, women who had worked men's jobs in the late 'teens usually remained in the work force, although at lower wages. Women, now allowed to vote nationally, were also encouraged to consider college and options other than marriage. Average family earnings increased slightly during the first half of the period, while prices and hours worked actually declined. The 48-hour week became standard, providing more leisure time. At least 40 million people went to the movies each week, and college football became a national obsession.

Unlike previous decades, national prosperity was not fueled by the cheap labor of new immigrants, but by increased factory efficiencies, innovation, and more sophisticated methods of managing time and materials. Starting in the 'teens, the flow of new immigrants began to slow, culminating in the restrictive immigration legislation of 1924 when new workers from Europe were reduced to a trickle. The efforts were largely designed to protect the wages of American workers—many of whom were only one generation from their native land. As a result, wages for unskilled labor remained stable; union membership declined and strikes, on average, decreased. American exports more than doubled during the decade and heavy imports of European goods virtually halted, a reversal of the Progressive Movement's flirtation with free trade.

These national shifts were not without powerful resistance. A bill was proposed in Utah to imprison any woman who wore her skirt higher than three inches above the ankle. Cigarette consumption reached 43 billion annually, despite smoking being illegal in 14 states and the threat of expulsion from college if caught with a cigarette. The Hays Commission, limiting sexual material in silent films, was created to prevent "loose" morals, and the membership of the KKK expanded to repress Catholics, Jews, open immigration, makeup on women, and the prospect of unrelenting change.

The decade ushered in Trojan contraceptives, the Pitney Bowes postage meter, the Baby Ruth candy bar, Wise potato chips, Drano, self-winding watches, State Farm Mutual auto insurance, Kleenex, and the Macy's Thanksgiving Day Parade down Central Park West in New York. Despite a growing middle class, the share of disposable income going to the top five percent of the population continued to increase. Fifty percent of the people, by one estimate, still lived in poverty. Coal and textile workers, Southern farmers, unorganized labor, single women, the elderly, and most blacks were excluded from the economic giddiness of the period.

In 1929, America appeared to be in an era of unending prosperity. U.S. goods and services reached all-time highs. Industrial production rose 50 percent during the decade as the concepts of mass production were refined and broadly applied. The sale of electrical appliances from radios to refrigerators skyrocketed. Consumers were able to purchase newly produced goods through the extended use of credit. Debt accumulated. By 1930, personal debt had increased to one-third of personal wealth. The nightmare on Wall Street in October 1929 brought an end to the economic festivities, setting the stage for a more proactive government and an increasingly cautious worker.

1923 Profile

Middle Class

A native of Seaman, Ohio, Jervey Steffens is a dreamer of big dreams, such as becoming a famous jazz saxophone player or writing a controversial book that will rile the censors, although she may settle for secretarial school or a few years in college.

Jervey Steffens loves to discuss her dreams with her best friend.

Life at Home

- Even though her real name is Eleanor, her father has called her by her middle name, Jervey, since she was a little girl; now everyone does.
- She loves having a name different from everyone else's.
- Now that she is 16 and has read about what Napoleon and Mozart did as teens, Jervey believes it is time to have important thoughts and make big discoveries.
- She feels that greatness is her destiny, too, and that she will make her mark on the world through music or literature.
- To play saxophone with Fletcher Henderson's jazz band, or write a great novel that would make the censors cringe—now that would be grand.
- Last year, when she was much younger, she often spent time wondering about her neighbors' real occupations: Was the debonair man who lived down the street really a desperate criminal, the lady next door a world-famous dancer, or a World War I spy, or both, and did the Wilkersons have countless millions buried in their backyard?
- Now that she is a junior in high school, she has put those fantastic notions behind her, although she still wonders about the true nature of the debonair man down the street.
- The family attends the Methodist church, and her mother is a committed *Epworth* advocate.

The family recently installed a central heating system.

Jervey and classmate Dorothy are fashion rivals.

Her favorite teacher, Miss Patterson, gave Jervey Tales of the Jazz Age *to read.*

- Jervey can tell when *The Epworth Herald* arrives; her mother will either begin to talk about tithing, going to a devotional or helping others—sometimes all at the same time.
- Lately her mother has been devoting her time to the elimination of child labor across America, telling everyone she knows, "Children should have a childhood."
- Jervey and her family live in a turn-of-the-century, Queen Anne-style house that has rooms for dining, living and sitting on the first floor, in addition to a bathroom, pantry and kitchen.
- The front and rear staircases lead to a 790-square-foot second floor with four bedrooms, one of which is Jervey's, and a bath, which she must share with the rest of the family.
- Her father is impossible to figure out; all he ever says to her is, "Turn off the lights when you leave the room; I'm not made of money," yet recently he spent $112 to install a new coal burning central heating system so he won't have to tend to the fire so much.
- For reasons that are beyond her, all of her friends seem to like her mother and come over to the house often, especially now that the Steffens have an electric mixer, which makes cookie and cake baking a breeze.
- The invention of small electric motors has made possible a revolution in household appliances including vacuum cleaners, and reliable refrigerators and washing machines.
- Many appliances can be bought on the installment plan, which allows payments for a new appliance to be spread over 12 months.

Jervey's home is a magnet for her classmates.

- Jervey's mother says her favorite time of the week is when the two of them sit down in the kitchen together and snap string beans, though Jervey is less enamoured with this ritual.
- Recently the entire family took a trip to the cinema to see Cecil B. DeMille's *The Ten Commandments*, which was wonderful.
- Seaman's moving picture theater was created when local businessmen banded together and each bought one or two shares in the Star Moving Picture Company so the village could enjoy the movie boom sweeping America.
- Jervey is just dying to go see *The Pilgrim*, starring Charlie Chaplin, and *The Hunchback of Notre Dame* when they come to town.
- The only time of the year she hates is the Easter season, when "the butterfly story" gets told and retold.
- When she was six, she overheard her mother say that she didn't know if she would have enough money to buy herself new Easter shoes to match her new Easter outfit, so Jervey secretly created and colored a set of paper butterflies that she could sell to her neighbors for $0.10 each.
- At the first stop, she told her next-door neighbor, Mrs. Middleton, that her mother was too poor to buy shoes and she was working to buy them.
- At the second stop, Mrs. Holly was told that Jervey's mother was so poor that she was going to be barefooted at Easter, and at the third house, Mrs. Flowers was told even more stories that included Jervey's mother not having anything to wear at all.
- Each woman expressed delight at the prospect of buying a butterfly from the child and each gave her $0.10.

In high school, Jervey is being encouraged to read current literature by F. Scott Fitzgerald.

- When Jervey arrived home with three dimes, her mother was on the telephone with Mrs. Middleton, who was relaying the sales pitch and the family's recent descent into abject poverty.
- Jervey wrapped her three dimes in the last butterfly and presented them to her mother to buy shoes, which were bought and proudly displayed at Easter.
- It was the last time she was allowed to sell butterflies, but not the last time the story was told; it has become an Easter ritual to retell it.
- Now that the family has a radio, many evenings are spent listening to the glorious sounds of the Rheingold Quartet or the *Lucky Strike Show*.
- Jervey loves listening to jazz and pretending that she is sitting in the midst of the orchestra, wailing away.

Life at School

- In class Jervey is known as a reader and a dreamer.
- On more than one occasion she has been caught reading books other than the assigned text; her favorites are adventure stories with girls as the heroines, as in *The Radio Girls on Station Island* by Margaret Penrose.
- Her favorite teacher, Miss Bertha Patterson, a graduate of Cornell University, understands Jervey's need to read.
- After class, Miss Patterson often challenges her to read current literature, recently giving her F. Scott Fitzgerald's new book, *Tales of the Jazz Age*.
- Jervey absolutely loves the opening sentence of the story, Jelly-Bean: "Jim Powell is a Jelly-bean. Much as I desire to make him an appealing character, I feel that it would be unscrupulous to deceive you on that point. He was a bred-in-the-bone, dyed-in-the-wool, ninety-nine and three-quarters percent Jelly-bean and he grew lazily all during Jelly-bean season, which is every season, down in the land of the Jelly-beans well below the Mason-Dixon line."
- She wants to write just like that someday—loose, free, strong and sure.
- Jervey is on the girls' basketball team and is the only girl in the school's Saxophone Club.
- The basketball team only played five games during the season, because travelling long distances during Ohio winters can be treacherous.

Jervey is the only girl in the Saxophone Club.

- They lost four of the five games, defeated in the first game of the season 23 to 6, but they improved.
- After the boys' game against the Columbus Mutes, the Junior Hi-Y staged a "stag" at the YMCA; they played basketball until two in the morning, then went to the game room until 4:30, slept for an hour and held a breakfast on the basketball court at 5:30 a.m.
- The girls' team was not invited.
- She loves being the only girl playing the saxophone with five guys.
- Some of Jervey's neighbors are concerned that a group composed of five boys and one girl does not look proper, so the club holds most of its practices in the front parlor of Jervey's house, where everyone can be properly supervised.
- When she reads the line in the High School Annual that says the Saxophone Club is "the first organization of its type; it is proving to be a popular organization which has been very acceptable to the public and the pupils of the high school," she snickers.
- Everyone knows that if Jimmy Epting's dad hadn't gone to the superintendent's office and threatened to sue if the group wasn't sanctioned, the club would never have been formed.
- She can't wait to be a senior, when she and her friends will be the oldest and in charge.
- Jervey has always thought she would go to secretarial school, but is now thinking about college.

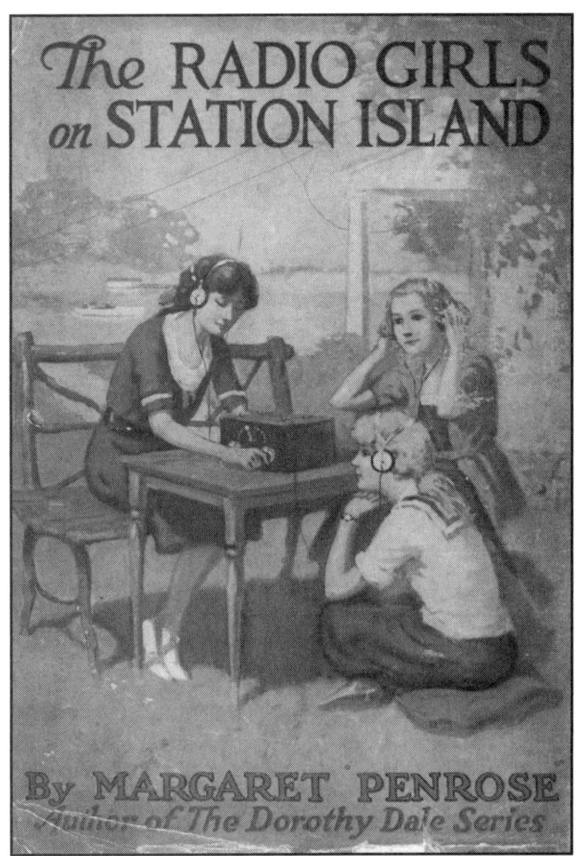

She loves books which feature a resourceful girl.

The basketball team has played five games, winning one.

"Just for the Love of Them," Mansfield (Ohio) High School Annual, 1923:

Breathes there the girl with creative instinct so dead that never to herself has murmured, "I must do something original"? Probably not. At any rate the senior girls progressed beyond that murmur to the realms of accomplishment. Just in the way of proving their originality they set the pace for future classmen by giving a reception to the faculty, if you please.

Seemingly by magic, the third floor had been transformed into an unusually attractive living room. We were "senior-y" throughout the whole, our old cerise and blue having been carried out to a "T." Here our illustrious guests were welcomed. . . .

Our musical ones performed first. Piano solos were given by Naomi Wigton and Naomi Banks, while Louise Emery gave a violin selection. The senior girls' Sextette also gave a group of selections.

Lest this grow monotonous, however, a one-act play was presented. It was one of Oliphant Down's Pierro and Pierette plays, *The Maker of Dreams*. We never dreamed that Louise Booth could make such a handsome Pierro. (Oh, what a Romeo!) And Marion Bradford as Pierrette had us all at her feet. Mirian Rife, the Maker of Dreams was very good, too.

"Code of Conduct for Teachers," Southern Ohio District, W. W. Fuller, Superintendent, 1923:

Some teachers, 1922–3, have failed for the following reasons: (a) lack of knowledge of subject matter and inability to manage children; (b) attention to card playing, dancing, and other social interests to the neglect of their schoolwork; (c) on account of falling in love with high school pupils; (d) on account of keeping company with sorry men; (e) on account of night riding without a chaperon; (f) on account of attendance at rotten vaudeville and sorry moving picture shows; (g) on account of entertaining company until late hours at night, making good schoolwork the next day impossible; (h) on account of failure to take any vital interest in church and Sunday school work and other community activities.

If you think this applicant will and can avoid all the above sources of failure, I shall appreciate your saying so. If you think there is doubt about her having enough sense to avoid these sources of failure, I shall appreciate your frankness. We are after teachers who are in earnest about doing what they are paid to do. We prefer that other kinds go elsewhere.

- Last year nearly half of the class went to college, most to Ohio State and Miami University; a few went to Oberlin and Wooster, but she thinks that going to Cornell would be keen.
- She is very pleased that she now has a school dress that includes a clasp-locker, or what some magazines are calling a zipper.
- Since World War I, the device has become more popular, even in clothing for children and young women.

PLAY THE GAME

With Real Equipment for Baseball, Football and Basketball. Camping Supplies of Quality and Worth.

THE SPORTING GOODS STORE

YUNCKER BROS.

MAIN STREET ADAM 1508

The school annual is graced with student art and section headings.

- Jervey was convinced that her rival, Dorothy Lancaster, would have a dress with a zipper first, but is glad it didn't happen.
- She might even wear the dress to the Isaly's Circus, which is making its third trip around the world and plans a stop near her home in Seaman.
- Featured acts advertised in fliers include John Zellnerino Batistichiski, the Italian knife thrower; Clark Brooks Martinique, the cigarette fiend; Helene Foxe, the graceful rope walker, Clara Beard Evans, the bearded lady, Maurice Bair Valintino, the cowpuncher who courts death and laughs at disaster.

Business in Seaman is booming.

Life in the Community: Seaman, Ohio

- The community of Seaman was named for Frank Seaman, a wealthy farmer who bought a 180-acre farm in 1880 at a sheriff's sale on the courthouse steps to settle the Hamilton estate.
- Much of the village is located on that property today.
- Two years later, Frank Seaman donated two acres to the Cincinnati and Eastern Railway on the condition that they name the station Seaman.

"Amusing Incidents," *A Town in the Makin'*, *History of Seaman, Ohio*, by Frank G. Young, 1929:

At the close of the school year in 1920, there was a lot of excitement in "this man's town," due to the activities of the senior class. One night near the close of the term, the freshmen arranged for a party, but the boys were picked up one by one, as they were going to the party, by the seniors and kidnapped. They were taken to an old house west of the village and kept captive until a late hour, when they escaped, after three or four free-for-all fights in which clothes were torn and faces disfigured. The "freshies" finally got to the party. The next morning the seniors were on the streets in full force, and the freshmen, both boys and girls, were out also looking for a chance to even up for the kidnapping of the night previous. They clashed in front of the mayor's office, and engaged in another free-for-all, the girls joining in the mêlée, but the mayor soon put a stop to the scuffle.

Word had gotten out that the freshmen boys intended to kidnap the seniors as they marched from the home of the superintendent to the Presbyterian church for their graduation exercises, so John Hannah, who was the village marshal, was called upon to escort the seniors to the church, and in the name of the law, made this impossible. After the graduation exercises were over, Mr. Hannah escorted them back to the home of Supt. Fred Lott. With the exception of a wire that was stretched across the street at one point, nothing happened. This is the first thing of its kind that ever happened at graduation time, and the last.

- To encourage the construction of a railway to their land, local farmers donated fine oak logs to the railway company and hauled them to a sawmill to be cut into lumber for the station.
- The current high school, constructed of brick and stone, sits on a five-acre tract west of the village, and includes an auditorium-gymnasium.
- Jervey's grandfather operates the town's biggest produce house, dealing in eggs, poultry, cream and veal calves.
- Business is going so well, he now owns two trucks and takes local produce to Cincinnati twice a week.
- Recently, thanks to considerable lobbying, the streets of Seaman were dramatically improved when the State Highway Department scraped the roads and covered them with crushed rock.
- Seaman prides itself on being a well-mannered town, which extends to its dogs; to keep strays under control, "Stringer" Barnes, the freight conductor on the railway, pays small boys to gather up all the unclaimed dogs and haul them to the station, where the dogs are then transported on the train to the neighboring community of Portsmouth and turned loose.
- Recently, after the Nelson brothers escorted a cow into the office of the cinema, the city fathers attempted to establish a 9:00 p.m. curfew for teenagers, though the matter was dropped after Mr. Nelson gave his two boys a sound whipping and paid for the ledger book and tickets eaten by the cow.

Historical Snapshot
1923

- Even though Prohibition is the law of the land, prescription liquor for those in need remained unrestricted
- Clean Book Leagues formed around the nation to protect America's youth from "smut," while controversy raged about the work of D. H. Lawrence
- Clarence Darrow and William Jennings Bryan debated the issue of evolution versus fundamentalism in the *Chicago Tribune*
- Girls who dressed in the style of flappers in Tennessee were banned from public schools until they rolled their stockings back up over their knees
- The German shepherd Rin Tin Tin captured stardom as a top silent movie star
- Montana and Nevada became the first states to introduce old-age pensions
- The Dow-Jones Average hit a high of 105, a low of 86
- A sign reading HOLLYWOODLAND was erected in Los Angeles; each letter measured 30 by 50 feet
- The rubber diaphragm, Pan American World Airlines, the Milky Way candy bar, Welch's grape jelly, the name Popsicle and the Hertz Drive-Ur-Self all made their first appearance
- President Warren G. Harding died in office and was honored nationwide as his cortège traveled from San Francisco to Washington
- Evangelist Aimee Semple McPherson opened a $1.5 million temple in Los Angeles, which included a "miracle room" where the healed could discard their crutches and wheelchairs
- Music hits included "Yes! We Have No Bananas," "Who's Sorry Now?" and "That Old Gang of Mine"
- Blues singer Bessie Smith's "Downhearted Blues" sold a record two million copies

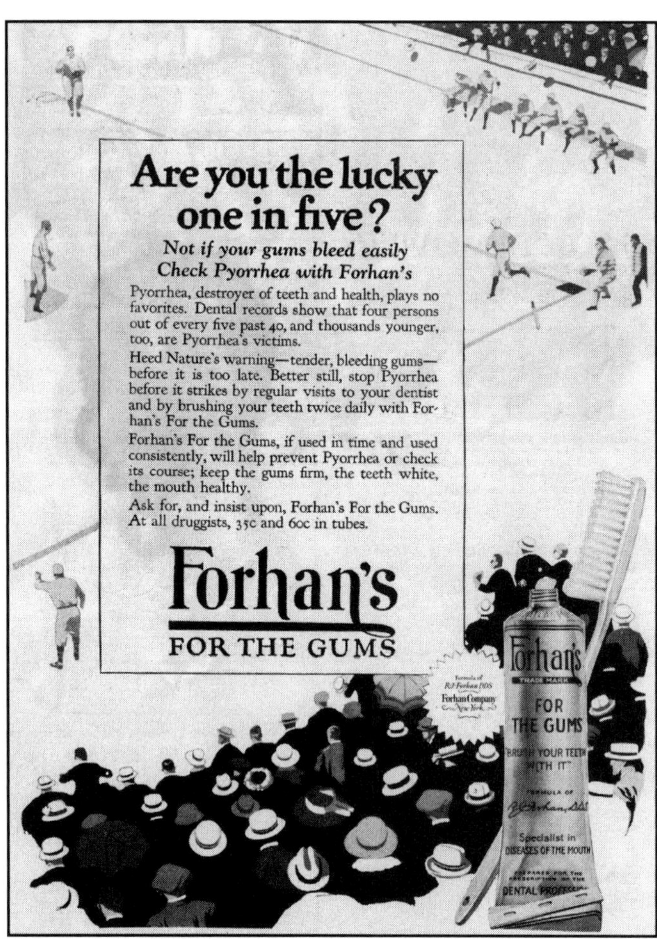

1923 Economic Profile

Selected Prices

Airmail Postage $0.08
Automobile, Buick Standard Six $1,175.00
Cream Separator $69.95
Four-month Around-the-
World Cruise $1,000.00
Grand Piano, Steinway $1,425.00
Instant Coffee $0.10
Magazine, *Life,* One Year $5.00
Mah-jongg Game $22.95
Man's Bathing Suit $5.00
Metal Bed with Mattress/
Box Spring $26.95
Milk of Magnesia Laxative $0.39
Post Card $0.01
Shaving Brush $1.25
Tennis Racquet $10.50
Vacuum Bottle $2.25
Wristwatch, Woman's $20.00

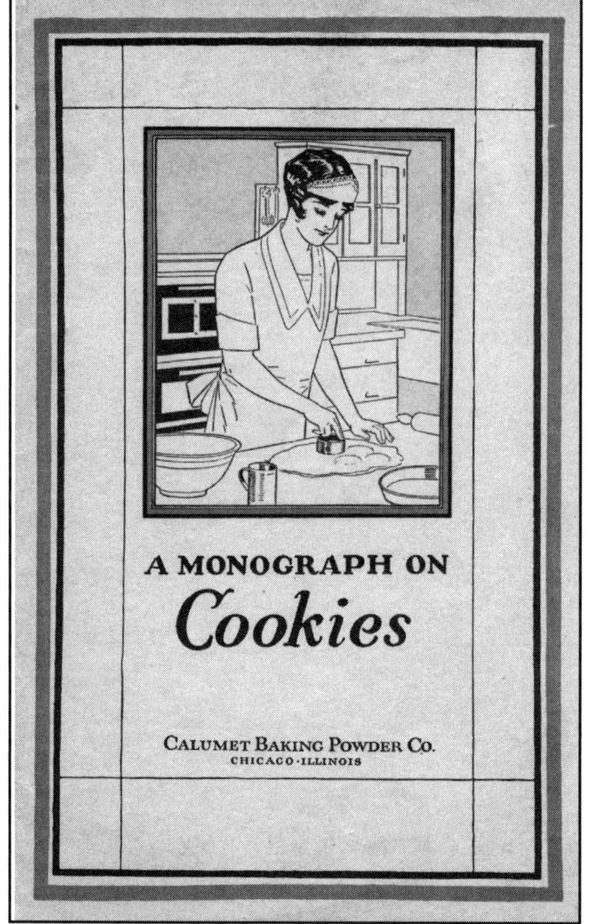

The National Cash Register's "List of Things Not Known" from 1879 to this publishing in 1922:

1 Acetylene	45 Measuring pumps
2 Adding machines	46 Mertens press
3 Addressographs	47 Miners' electric safety lamps
4 Aeroplanes	48 Minimum wage scales
5 Air brushes	49 Monorail
6 Air purifiers	50 Motorcycles
7 Aluminum	51 Moving pictures
8 Antiseptics	52 Offset printing presses
9 Asbestos (coverings)	53 Paper milk bottles
10 Asphalt paving	54 Paper towels
11 Automatic shoe machinery	55 Parcels post
12 Automatic typewriters	56 Pasteurization
13 Automobiles	57 Photoengraving
14 Ball bearings	58 Pianolas
15 Bertillon system	59 Picture post cards
16 Block signals	60 Pneumatic appliances
17 Canning factories	61 Pneumatic mailing tubes
18 Carpet sweepers	62 Pneumatic tires
19 Cash register	63 Power elevators
20 Color photography	64 Radium
21 Department stores	65 Reflectoscopes
22 Dictograph	66 Reinforced concrete
23 Edison storage batteries	67 Rotary printing presses
24 Electric cooking utensils	68 Safety matches
25 Electric furnaces	69 Sanitary drinking fountains
26 Electric heating	70 School gardens
27 Electric lighting	71 Seismograph
28 Electric street railway cars	72 Skyscrapers
29 Electric welding	73 Smoke containers
30 Fireless cookers	74 Smokeless powder
31 Fireless locomotives	75 Stereopticon
32 Gas engines	76 Submarines
33 Gas mantles	77 Telautography
34 Harvesters	78 Telegraph tape printers
35 Hot dining plates	79 Telephotography
36 Hydro-aeroplanes	80 Tube railways
37 Hydroplanes	81 Turbines
38 Industrial hygiene	82 Typecasting machines
39 Janney couplers	83 Vacuum bottles
40 Kinemacolor	84 Vacuum brakes
41 Kinetophone	85 Vacuum cleaners
42 Liquid air	86 Wireless telegraphy
43 Mailometer	87 Wireless telephony
44 Maxim silencer	88 X-rays

"A Vagrant Reader's Evening with the Mail," by Frater Ignotus, *The Epworth Herald*, February 24, 1923:

I have spent an evening looking through some of my favorite printed matter—the stuff, good, bad and worse, which gets into many preachers' letter boxes these days.

Much of it is good. More is bad; not vicious, but plain useless. It is a sheer waste of paper, ink and postage. . . But what I have been reading to-night is not so far astray as some of the third-class mail that comes my way. And I want you to share some of it with me.

Here is my friend Bromley Oxman of Los Angeles, writing in his own brave broadsheet, *In Days to Come*, on Jesus's doctrine of equal rights for all. This is what he says about the right of children to play:

"I have seen little children whose ages ran from six to 10 standing in front of the machine throughout a twelve-and-one-half hour shift, and I have seen little tots dancing around the Maypole in our Los Angeles playgrounds.

Jesus says, 'Equal rights.' The relation of play to growth, to juvenile delinquency, to democracy should be studied by twentieth-century followers of Christ.

A delinquent youngster came to me one day. His nickname was 'Shrimp.' He said: 'Gee, I got pinched again. They took me in just for hooking a lawnmower. Now, what d'ye think of that?'

It was a social attitude born upon the streets. Supervised play was his right. Through it he would have developed a different social attitude, but his right had been denied him."

Changing America

- Belt loops were added to Levi Strauss & Co. blue jeans, although the suspender buttons were retained.
- *The Hunchback of Notre Dame* starring Lon Chaney was released.
- The zipper, first patented in 1893 and refined in 1913 as a fastener for army clothing, came into common use.
- The widespread use of the typewriter in business created standardization of 8.5 by 11-inch paper.
- The nation remained captivated by psychology and self-healing; Emilie Coue's mind-over-matter demonstrations attracted thousands.
- More than 1.5 million sets of the game Mah-jongg were sold as the fad swept the nation.
- In fashion, women's boyish bobbed hair shifted to a shingle cut that was flat and close to the head with a center or side part.
- Nationwide, the number of newspapers totaled 2,038, down from 2,452 two decades earlier.

"Canned Childhood," by Sarah N. Cleghon, *Poems of Child Labor*, National Child Labor Committee, New York, 1924:

Beneath the label "Oysters," "Shrimp,"
Is canned a pound of frolic missed
Upon a summer morn–
Lost fun and frolic, soldered tight
Where no child finds them, morn or night.

A pound of health, a pound of strength
From candles snatched, we find:
A pound of young intelligence
Robbed from a childish mind.
Packed here together, snugly fit
Teresa's eyesight, Tony's wit.

And wasted sunshine here is canned,
With wasted smells of flowers;
The wasted sparkle of green fields
Washed bright by early showers.
And pleasant scampers never run,
And shouts unheard in breeze and sun.

Yea, in the cans are voices hid
Of little sons and daughters,
That should be singing, "London Bridge,"
"I Spy," and "Sally Waters."
"Where oats, peas, beans and barley grows
'Tis you nor I nor nobody knows."

Come buy, my fellow countrymen!
Canned childhood's selling cheap,
And what though little Jack should tire
And fall too fast asleep?
There's work for little Marianne—
Come buy sweet childhood by the can.

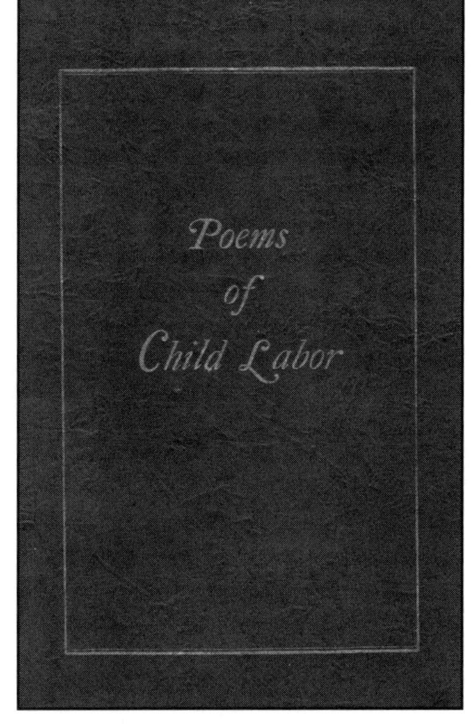

- Lee De Forest devised a method of recording sound directly on film, which he called fonofilm.
- Sociologists calculated that, despite the many new labor-saving devices, full-time housewives were spending 52 hours a week in household chores.
- After years of failure, the U.S. Army reported that it had accomplished the first emergency jump from an airplane without injury, using a chute made of silk.

"The Currents of History in the Making," *The Epworth Herald*, February 24, 1923:

The world's supply of automobiles seems to be quite unequally distributed. While there are so few cars in the desert that many of the nomads live to a ripe old age and die without seeing one, there are so many in Chicago that they caused 517 deaths during the first 11 months of 1922. The significance of these figures is seen when it is remembered that typhoid, smallpox, measles and scarlet fever took only 198 lives during this period. The health department quarantines cases of contagious diseases, but it cannot quarantine reckless drivers.

The Evolutionary Theory is a program of infidelity masquerading under the name of Science.
—William Jennings Bryan

Did you ever look at a map without *learning* something?

As the continents draw closer together, knowledge of geography is increasingly necessary to an understanding of the day's news. The territorial claims of one nation—the commercial expansion of another—a people's demand for self-determination—all are things that can only be followed clearly with a map.

You need RAND MCNALLY Maps to grasp the fundamentals of politics and business. They show the stage on which the drama is played, the entrances and exits, the properties around which the action moves. Without the stage, the plot is meaningless.

Nowadays every home and every business is within the circle of international affairs. As a background for culture and a basis for business judgment, a set of RAND MCNALLY Maps is of paramount importance. Loose notions of geography, leading to loose thinking on foreign relations and trade, is one of the least excusable of faults in view of the genuine interest, as well as information, which a map presents.

RAND MCNALLY Maps, in atlas or other form, are reasonable in cost and invariably accurate. A world-wide organization with a single aim has made this possible.

RAND MCNALLY & COMPANY
Map Headquarters
Dept. F-11

536 S. Clark Street, Chicago — 42 E. 22nd Street, New York

Branches: Philadelphia . Washington . Boston . Pittsburgh
Cleveland . Detroit . St. Louis . San Francisco . Los Angeles

1924 News Feature

"What Is Radio Doing to Us?" by George Humphrey, Professor of Psychology, Wesleyan University, *Collier's*, June 14, 1924:

When MacMillan, the famous polar explorer, arrived home after his last trip, he was asked to go round to a broadcasting station to give an address.

"Radio—talk over the radio—I don't get you," was his puzzled answer.

Radio had happened while he was away! The voyage had lasted about three years, a large part of which he had spent with his companions in the boredom of polar life, waiting on board for the weather to turn.

When he was told that his ship's radio set could be made to bring them music, he refused at first to believe it. The dials had been turned to receive code messages, and no one of the party had the slightest idea that by a half revolution of the pointer, civilization could be brought into the ship's cabin. Hurrying back to his friends, the explorer tried it out, and within 15 minutes he was hearing his first concert out of the air.

What was it that had happened to the world? What is the radio doing to the millions of men and women, small boys and small girls, who now spend hours every night listening in?

The last sentence gives the clue to the peculiar advantage of the new amusement. Radio is an entertainment one hears, an affair of listening to, rather than looking at.

A small girl of my acquaintance was with her mother on a porch, the mother resting, the child skipping around. Suddenly the child stood still and listened.

"That was a train bell, mother, wasn't it? Not a church bell. Just a train bell . . ." and her voice trailed off.

Modern Ears Don't Hear Well

The mother listened. It was a train bell, from the railroad a mile and a half away, but the mother's ears had not caught it. Long years of living in modern cities had almost destroyed for her, as it has for most of us, the universe of sound in which the child was still living and which is the birthright of us all.

We stop our ears almost entirely to the world of sound, for most of the sounds which modern civilization makes are useless noises. Almost all the average man hears during the first hour of his day is the alarm clock and the sound of his wife's voice telling him the coffee

The radio brings a fresh approach to a fast-vanishing world.

is getting cold and he will miss the train. Or, rather, that is all he hears and acts upon. Practically all that he does is directed by his eyes, and so it is until he goes to bed at night.

From the place of great importance which it held in the life of primitive man, who heard the forest almost as much as he saw it, the sense of hearing has shrunk until it has almost no use except as a means of communications with other men. We get our job through our eyes. In golf or reading or the movies, we get our amusement through our eyes. It would indeed be possible to carry on many occupations by the control of this sense without using the ears at all. The kings of Persia used to employ deaf and dumb slaves around the court for certain purposes. In many ways they made perfectly good servants, while a blind house servant would have been an impossibility. A primitive man, could he look into our mind, would pity us for our deafness just as we pity the Persian slave.

But here steps in the radio, with a fresh approach to a fast-vanishing world. What happens is really creation. The man who spends hours every evening on his set, hearing music or the song of the nightingale, is creating his own world of sound where chaos had ruled before. The radio seems a definite step toward the making of a new universe, where people shall listen instead of see, just as our ancestors listened and we ourselves listened as children.

The aim of recreation is amusement without tiring the working parts of the body. Radio is free from this fatigue danger. It has, in fact, a double advantage as a means of relaxation: it uses a part of our nervous system which there is a tendency to neglect, and it rests a part which there is a tendency to overwork. . . .

20 *Collier's*, The National Weekly, *for* June 14, 1924

What Is Radio Doing to Us?

By George Humphrey

Professor of Psychology, Wesleyan University

Sure, Sonny loves his set, for he made it himself

WHEN MacMillan, the famous polar explorer, arrived home after his last trip, he was asked to go round to a broadcasting station and give an address.

"Radio—talk over the radio—I don't get you," was his puzzled answer.

Radio had happened while he was away! The voyage had lasted about three years, a large part of which he had spent with his companions in the boredom of polar life, waiting on board for the weather to turn.

When he was told that his ship's radio set could be made to bring them music, he refused at first to believe it. The dials had been turned to receive code messages, and no one of the party had the slightest idea that by a half revolution of the pointer civilization could be brought into the ship's cabin. Hurrying back to his friends, the explorer tried it out, and within fifteen minutes he was hearing his first concert out of the air.

What was it that had happened to the world? What is the radio doing to the millions of men and women, small boys and small girls, who now spend hours every night listening in?

The last sentence gives the clue to the peculiar advantage of the new amusement. Radio is an entertainment one *hears*, an affair of *listening to*, rather than *looking at*.

A small girl of my acquaintance was with her mother on a porch, the mother resting, the child skipping around. Suddenly the child stood still and listened.

"That was a train bell, mother, wasn't it? Not a church bell. Just a train bell . . ." And her voice trailed off.

Modern Ears Don't Hear Well

THE mother listened. It was a train bell, from the railroad a mile and a half away, but the mother's ears had not caught it. Long years of living in modern cities had almost destroyed for her, as it has for most of us, the universe of sound in which the child was still living and which is the birthright of us all.

We stop our ears almost entirely to the world of sound, for most of the sounds which modern civilization makes are useless noises. Almost all the average man hears during the first hour of his day is the alarm clock and the sound of his wife's voice telling him the coffee is getting cold and he will miss the train. Or, rather, that is all he hears and acts upon. Practically all that he does is directed by his eyes, and so it is until he goes to bed at night.

From the place of great importance which it held in the life of primitive man, who heard the forest almost as much as he saw it, the sense of hearing has shrunk until it has almost no use except as a means of communication with other men. We get our job through our eyes. In golf or reading or the movies we get our amusement through our eyes. It would indeed be possible to carry on many occupations by the control of this sense without using the ears at all. The kings of Persia used to employ deaf and dumb slaves around the court for certain purposes. In many ways they made perfectly good servants, while a blind house servant would have been an impossibility. A primitive man, could he look into our mind, would pity us for our deafness just as we pity the Persian slave.

But here steps in the radio, with a fresh approach to a fast-vanishing world. What happens is really creation. The man who spends hours every evening at his set, hearing music or the song of the nightingale, is creating his own world of sound where chaos had ruled before. The radio seems a definite step toward the *making of a new universe*, where people shall *listen instead of see*, just as our ancestors listened and we ourselves listened as children.

The aim of recreation is amusement without tiring the working parts of the body. Radio is free from this fatigue danger. It has, in fact, a double advantage as a means of relaxation: it uses a part of our nervous system which there is a tendency to neglect, and it rests a part which there is a tendency to overwork.

I call to mind a picture of a friend sitting with his eyes closed listening to the radio concert, and sometimes turning down the light when he had tuned into a particularly pleasing program. Another friend, a press photographer, asks why it is that the men in his office, and virtually all the other photographers he knows, are such unusually devoted radio enthusiasts. The answer seems to be that the photographer makes his living by looking, and it is natural that he should prefer to take his amusement by listening.

"My small boy sits at the radio," writes in effect one father, "and spends his time getting first this station and then that. In the course of half an hour he will hear five minutes of grand opera, part of a bedtime story, the closing bars of a string quartet, and the beginnings of a speech of advice to young mothers. Can this do him much good? Must it not give him a twittery sort of mind? Of course he ought to spend all the time at the string quartet or the grand opera, but, as a matter of fact, he doesn't."

This objection seems at first sight to have considerable force. America is often said to be a nation of intellectual superficiality, where mental cake eaters religiously consume what some obliging person with a knife has cut up into standardized pieces. The radio seems to be of the same baking as the educational cake. In the classroom, French without knowing the French language, civics without knowing society, physiology without knowing the human body; in the air, a lecture on farm accounts, a speech on Browning, a gramophone record played by the navy station, the time signal—a salad instead of a meal, delivered from tin cans with the vitamines carefully extracted. It is surely vicious.

But we must not look at the child with the eyes of a man, and we must not overanalyze. When we argue that a young radio enthusiast is wasting his time, we are committing both these common faults. The boy who sits pushing the bare wire over and back along the worn copper track on his $3.49 set is not "listening to the radio" in adult terms. One should not cut up what he is doing into a bit of a bedtime story, the last part of the "Beautiful Blue Danube," and the peroration of a political speech, any more than one should cut up the action of a dog chasing a cat into so many jerks of the fore and hind legs and so many separate growls.

The dog is chasing the cat; the boy is "getting Philadelphia."

How Radio Trains a Boy

A BOY at the radio is not a man—with a twenty-nine-inch measurement round the trouser tops instead of forty-nine. He is not a ninety-pound copy of dad, and he is not listening to the radio like his dad, to hear the stock reports. He is a *boy working the radio*, and, especially when he has built the set, he is receiving a valuable training in mechanics and in manipulation. As a matter of fact, his evening probably represents a much more highly sustained piece of effort than that of his sister who spends her time playing through a sheaf of popular songs, one verse of each, or that of his father reading the serial stories and the special columns in the evening paper. When we cannot understand our children, we are apt to read our own faults into them.

A friend of mine said of his son's listening-in outfit: "But he really gets some information out of what he hears." That is a piece of luck, which no father has a right to expect.

The value of the radio is, then, that it tends to put us into contact with the great world of sound which we civilized men and women are in great danger of losing. And as scientific seven-league boots, which will go anywhere, radio gives also a uniquely valuable amusement to the boy or girl.

Like a miracle, radio kills the boredom of polar life

"My small boy sits at the radio," writes, in effect, one father, "and spends his time getting first this station and then that. In the course of half an hour he will hear five minutes of grand opera, part of a bedtime story, the closing bars of a string quartet, and the beginnings of a speech of advice to young mothers. Can this do him much good? Must it not give him a twittery sort of mind? Of course, he ought to spend all the time at the string quartet or the grand opera, but, as a matter of fact, he doesn't."

This objection seems at first sight to have considerable force. America is often said to be a nation of intellectual superficiality, where mental cake eaters religiously consume what some obliging person with a knife has cut up into standardized pieces. The radio seems to be the same baking as the educational cake. In the classroom, French without knowing the French language, civics without knowing society, physiology without knowing the human body; in the air, a lecture on farm accounts, a speech on Browning, a gramophone record played by the navy station, the time signal—a salad instead of a meal, delivered from tin cans with the vitamins carefully extracted. It is surely vicious.

But we must not look at the child with the eyes of a man, and we must not overanalyze. When we argue that a young radio enthusiast is wasting his time, we are committing both these common faults. The boy who sits pushing the bare wire over and back along the worn copper track on his $3.49 set is not "listening to the radio" in adult terms. One should not cut up what he is doing into a bit of a bedtime story, the last part of the "Beautiful Blue Danube," and the peroration of a political speech, any more than one should cut up the action of a dog chasing a cat into so many jerks of the fore and hind legs, and so many separate growls.

The dog is chasing the cat; the boy is "getting Philadelphia."

How Radio Trains a Boy

A boy at the radio is not a man—with a 29-inch measurement round the trouser tops instead of 49. He is not a 90-pound copy of dad, and he is not listening to the radio like his dad, to hear the stock reports. He is a boy working the radio, and, especially when he has built the set, he is receiving valuable training in mechanics and in manipulation. As a matter of fact, his evening probably represents a much more highly sustained piece of effort than that of his sister who spends her time playing through a sheaf of popular songs, one verse of each, or that of his father reading the serial stories and the special columns in the evening paper. When we cannot understand our children, we are apt to read our own faults into them.

A friend of mine said of his son's listening-in outfit: "But he really gets some information out of what he hears." That is a piece of luck, which no father has a right to expect.

The value of the radio is, then, that it tends to put us into contact with the great world of sound which we civilized men and women are in great danger of losing. And as scientific seven-league boots, which will go anywhere, radio gives also a uniquely valuable amusement to the boy or girl.

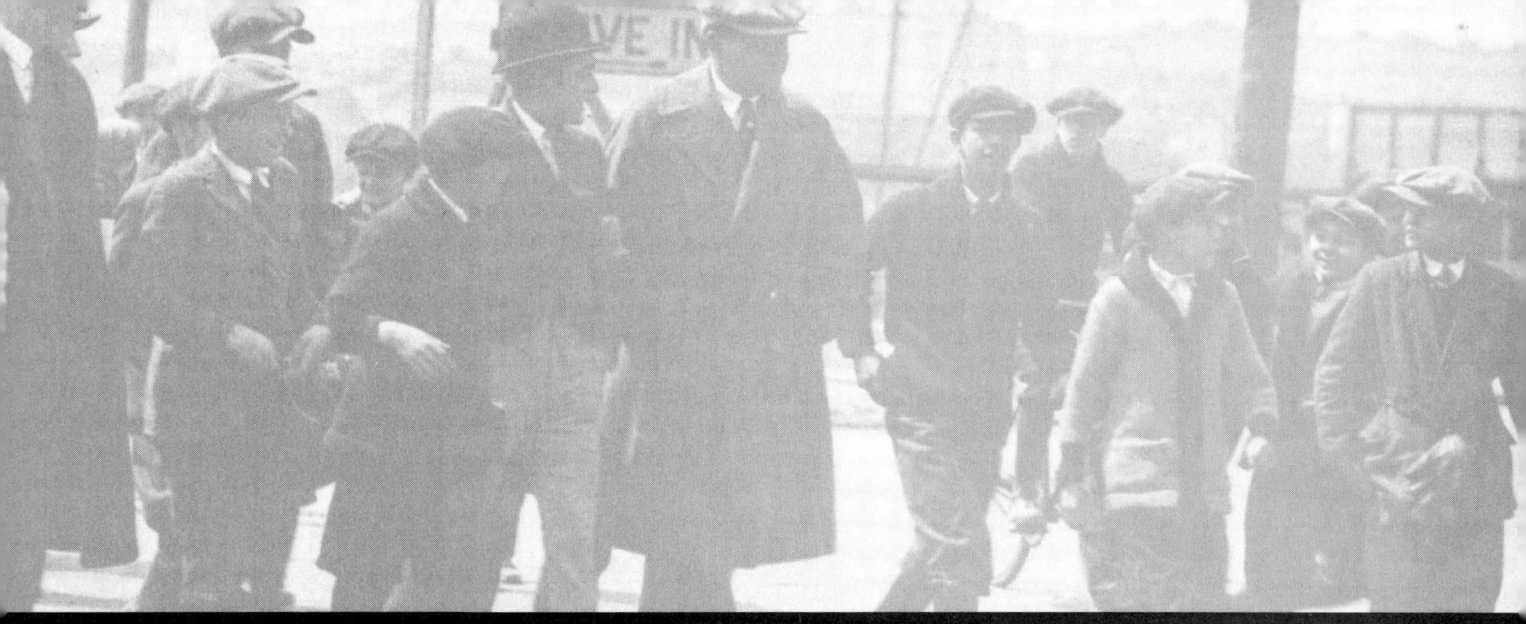

1926 Profile

Working Class

As part of a baseball promotion, the New York Yankees have invited dozens of baseball and stickball teams from across New York City to Yankee Stadium, including nine-year-old Ivo Novajovsky and his champion stickball team from Brooklyn. The invitation gives this boy a chance to fulfill his dream of meeting his hero, Babe Ruth, the Sultan of Swat.

The Novajovsky family came from Croatia nine years ago.

Life at Home

- Ivo Novajovsky loves the New York Yankees, his dog, his mother, his sister, his little brother, and sometimes his father—roughly in that order.
- Now, this son of immigrant parents is getting to live his dream; he will be attending a game between the New York Yankees and the Philadelphia Phillies.
- As part of a baseball promotion, the new Yankees owner, Jacob Ruppert, is taking boys from Ivo's block in Brooklyn, including Ivo's entire champion stickball team, to the game.
- For Ivo and his buddies, following the Yankees' nightly progress on a radio outside the pharmacy just down the street is the number one priority, the second being the chance to drive a rubber ball deep into a brownstone alley—a hit guaranteed to produce at least a double every time.
- The Novajovsky family arrived from Croatia nine years ago, just before Ivo was born.
- Until he was five years old, the family lived on the East Side of New York City, where 200,000 people were packed into a territory measuring less than one square mile.

Enrollment in New York City schools exceeds one million students.

- There, a miniature Europe could be found with dozens of languages spoken, every faith professed, and as many as 15 people living in a four-room flat; 300 people often crowded into tenements originally built to house 50.
- On Ivo's block alone were 27 nationalities; he is proud that he speaks English well and that his father often asks him to help read items in the newspaper.
- Ivo's father, who came to New York nine years ago to work for his uncle as a shopkeeper, now owns a streetfront grocery in the new East Flatbush section of Brooklyn.
- Ivo loves his new home and school, and especially loves helping his father at the grocery, where the entire family works.
- As a third-grader he can now read the magazines at the school, even the ones with long sentences.
- Recently, John Martin's publication, *The Magazine for Young People*, carried a wonderful story called "A Blooded Dog."
- He loves dogs of all kinds, especially his friend Jake, who, like the dog in the story, is "a blooded dog."
- Enrollment in New York City public schools exceeds one million students, of whom 863,232 are in elementary, junior high and truant schools, 131,685 are in high school, and the rest are in training to be teachers or are attending vocational schools.
- The school population of interior New York has begun a shift toward outlying sections; a report in the *New York Sun* reads: "Older sections of the city, not only in Manhattan, but in the Bronx and Brooklyn as well, are losing residents to Queens, Staten Island and to those sections of Brooklyn and the Bronx which a few years ago were sparsely settled."
- According to the report, School District 2 on the Lower East Side lost 11.79 percent of its students in 1925, and more than seven percent in each of the two preceding years.

"A Blooded Dog," by Frances Dickerson Pinder, *The Magazine for Young People*, August 1927:

If one saw him trot round the corner, one knew that there would be a boy right behind him. Pete was that kind of dog. At least, that was what Mrs. Pettis told Jimmie, on his first trip on his new paper route.

"Yes'm, he's an A-1 dog, all right," said Jimmie politely, while Mrs. Pettis hunted in her pocketbook for the change.

Pete wagged his tail and swallowed his tongue and stuck it out again.

"What sort of dog is he?" asked Mrs. Pettis, looking at Pete, very friendly.

Pete cocked his ear and looked at Jimmie.

"Pete?—he's a blooded dog, he is," said Jimmie, dropping the change in his pocket. "All set, Pete."

At the newspaper office, Jimmy had heard a reporter telling about a dog show he had been to, at a place—Jimmie didn't remember the name—but anyway, from all Jimmie had heard, a blooded dog was the cat's cuff and all the rest of it, and the more blood the better.

There were a good many reasons why Jimmie was sure that Pete was a blooded dog. For one thing, he never forgot that business is business. Some dogs, just common dogs—nothing much, that is—run off, all over, nosing into other people's garbage pails and making trouble. And they bark at the wrong thing, without any sense at all. Pete, he could be depended on in all these matters, and in a great many more.

- Areas that are gaining include South Brooklyn, Flatbush, the new East Flatbush section, Midwood and East New York.

Life at Play

- For years, Ivo's secret wish has been to attend a Yankees baseball game and see his hero—Babe Ruth.
- Now that wish has been granted: Thanks to the generosity of Yankees owner and beer king Col. Jacob Ruppert, 50 kids from the neighborhood sat in the bleachers for an afternoon game.
- No one is sure who generated the idea of opening Yankee Stadium up to poor kids, but Ivo is convinced it was the great Babe Ruth himself, because the Babe is the kind of guy who would think of it, even if it meant spending some of his own money.
- After all, wasn't the Babe the man who made three-year-old Ray Kelly his personal mascot, gave him a uniform and lets him sit with him during games? Now that's the life, all right!
- The Yankees planned everything for this big day, including the money that each boy needed to make the round trip by subway.

Ray Kelly served as Babe Ruth's personal mascot, complete with a Yankees uniform.

- All the guys on Ivo's stickball team agreed to take their gloves—in case the Yankees needed some help during the late innings.
- Going to the game was an experience in itself, but emerging from the subway station and seeing Yankee Stadium looming like a skyscraper overhead was breathtaking.
- The stadium opened just three years ago on April 18, 1923, seating 60,000 fans on that first day, while 10,000 more stood outside.
- The Grand Opening music was provided by the Seventh Regiment Band under the baton of John Philip Sousa.
- The structure was hailed as the first true baseball stadium, designed to accommodate massive crowds and make a progressive and confident statement about the future of the game.
- When Ivo's team arrived and sat down, they couldn't believe they were really looking at Babe Ruth himself and not a picture or anything; Ivo couldn't quit smiling—throughout the entire game.
- It was so exciting—the Yankees not only won, beating the Phillies 4-2, but in the very first inning, with his buddies at his side, Ivo saw Lou Gehrig step up to the plate and deliver a two-run homer to put the Yankees ahead.
- Immediately, Ivo knew this was going to be the greatest day of his life.
- Then, in the seventh inning, the Babe, on a count of three and two, drove a line-drive homer into the right field stands, delivering his thirty-eighth homer of the year; the Yankees went up three runs to zero.
- It was a packed house, and all 40,000 fans must have cheered at once: a home run by Babe Ruth himself—wow!

Babe Ruth is known as the Sultan of Swat and a friend to children.

- With his buddies screaming and the popcorn guy shouting, Ivo couldn't believe this was happening to him.
- The newspapers call Babe Ruth the Sultan of Swat, the Behemoth of Swing and the Colossus of Clout, and every word is true, Ivo believes.
- Ruth, a former reform-school boy who rose to riches hitting home runs, has changed baseball from a game based on strategy, base running and surgical bunts into a power game; one swing and the game could be over.
- When he hit 29 home runs for the Boston Red Sox in 1919, historians had to pore over the records to discover that the next-closest man in history was Buck Freeman, who had hit 25 homers in 1899.

Popular Babe Ruth made more than $250,000 a year from his salary and endorsements.

- In 1920, when Ruth hit 54 home runs, the baseball world watched in astonishment, and the Yankees' home attendance soared to a record 1.3 million fans.
- By 1923 the Yankees had won three pennants in a row; Ruth that year batted .393 with 41 home runs.
- In 1924 the Yankees did not win the American league race, although Ruth still led the league with a batting average of .378 and 46 home runs, but last year, 1925, was a disappointment for Ivo and the Yankees.
- With his marriage falling apart, Ruth collapsed during spring training and was out until June.
- But 1926 will be the Yankees' year, Ivo is sure.
- His hero makes more than $250,000 a year; in addition to his $52,000 baseball contract, the Babe will make $75,000 from the movies, $65,000 from a vaudeville tour, $20,000 from post-season barnstorming; $10,000 for a syndicate series of writings on baseball and $10,000 from the endorsement of a variety of products.
- As recently as 1919, when he was sold to the Yankees, Ruth was making $10,000 year but was raised to $22,000; in 1922 he signed a three-year contract that paid him $52,000 a year.
- To stave off hunger, Ivo and his buddies pooled their money and bought three hot dogs among them—everyone got at least one bite.
- When he got home, his mother was eager to hear every word, but, exhausted with excitement, he said little.
- Besides, going to the game was something the guys did together, not something he wanted to talk about with his mother.

Yankee Stadium was designed as a true baseball stadium capable of accommodating massive crowds.

Life in the Community: New York City

- Governor Al Smith, a graduate of New York's tough East Side, is battling the city's poor housing conditions, especially dark, airless apartments.
- He is proposing that loans be provided at low interest rates so more people can buy their own homes, and is also aggressively using property condemnation to open up large parcels of land at reasonable prices for more quality housing, parks and playgrounds in the inner city.
- Smith says, "Someday, the test of a city's merit will be not 'How many inhabitants have you?' but 'How do those inhabitants live?' "
- The average male worker in New York City earns $31.94 a week, while the average female worker makes $19.45.
- The building of the world's largest suspension bridge, and the first of any kind to cross the Hudson River, is now under way.
- It is expected to be two and a half times as large as the Brooklyn Bridge and twice the size of the recently opened Philadelphia-Camden Bridge over the Delaware; the first vehicle is scheduled to cross the structure in 1932.
- An army of 6,000 men is now employed to build a new subway beneath New York City; thanks to more advanced shovels and derricks, the work is going faster and safer than ever before.
- A single steam shovel can now do the work of 12 men, while the Caterpillar tractor, used in the war on uneven, muddy ground, has been adapted for use in expanding the subway system.

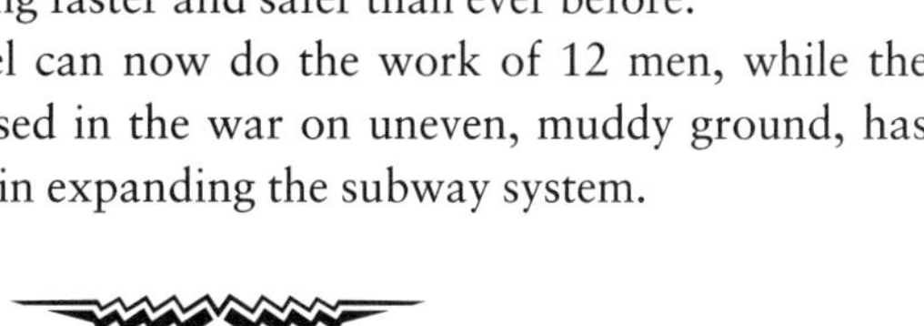

Historical Snapshot
1926

- Congress passed a bill to reduce taxes on income of $1 million or more from 66 percent to 20 percent
- Henry Ford introduced the eight-hour day and five-day work week in the automobile industry
- Walt Disney arrived in Hollywood and produced 10 short features composed of animation and live action
- Oscar Barnack developed the 35mm camera
- The sesquicentennial of the United States was celebrated
- Silent screen actress Greta Garbo was paid $5,000 a week at MGM
- When heartthrob movie star Rudolph Valentino died, 10,000 people attended the funeral
- The national inflation rate was 0.0 percent
- Pop-up electric toasters, the Hotel Carlyle in New York, the Chrysler Imperial, Safeway stores and flavored yogurt all made their first appearance
- The St. Louis Cardinals defeated the New York Yankees four games to three in the World Series; Babe Ruth hit three home runs during one game
- *The Sun Also Rises* by Ernest Hemingway, *The Love Nest* by Ring Lardner, *Abraham Lincoln: The Prairie Years* by Carl Sandburg and *Gentlemen Prefer Blondes* by Anita Loos were all published
- Harry Houdini died from a stomach punch that lead to peritonitis
- Popular songs included "Bye Bye Blackbird," "When the Red, Red Robin Comes Bob, Bob, Bobbin' Along," and Louis Armstrong's "You Made Me Love You"
- The New York Public Library began its Ten Worst Books Contest
- The tabloid publication, *True Story*, reached a circulation of two million with such stories as "The Diamond Bracelet She Thought Her Husband Didn't Know About."
- Nationwide, movies became America's favorite entertainment, with 14,500 movie houses showing 400 movies a year

1926 Economic Profile

Selected Prices

Automobile, Chrysler Imperial $2,995.00
Baseball Bat, Louisville Slugger. $2.00
Book, *Winnie the Pooh* $2.00
Camera, Graflex $80.00
Ceiling Fan, Hunter, 52” $52.00
Funeral Expenses. $935.00
Knife, Boy Scout $1.80
Lincoln Logs, 53 Logs $1.00
Mouthwash $0.79
Scale, Detecto $15.00
Toaster, Pop-up $12.50
Toilet Tissue, Scott. $0.25
Tool Chest, Stanley, w/12 Tools $15.00
Tricycle $3.89

The KoKoMo “Junior”

A keyless and clampless skate for little tots. Can’t slip off and will not damage shoes. Adjustable to sizes from 3 to 6 years. Self-contained ball bearing wheels.

Truss frame construction gives unusual strength and prevents bending in the middle. The “Junior” is a high grade skate distinguished by the *red disc around the hub*, KoKoMoS’ sign of quality.

Further information will be sent promptly on request concerning the “Junior” and the larger model KoKoMoS.

Kokomo Stamped Metal Co.
Kokomo Indiana

KoKoMo

LINCOLN LOGS
"The All American Toy"
For Christmas Gifts
$1—$2—$3—$4
DELIVERED

A new enlarged Design Book containing many novel and original ideas in log construction suggests endless building possibilities with LINCOLN LOGS—*“America’s National Toy.”*

Most Toy Stores Have Ample Stocks of LINCOLN LOGS. Look for the new bright colored boxes—ask for the New Design Book which shows *Blockhouses, Churches, Grain Elevators, Bridges, Railroad Stations, Coal Tipples* and many other forms of log construction which arouse and maintain a keen interest in LINCOLN LOGS after other toys are discarded.

For Girls as Well as Boys
Girls build houses, chairs, tables and beds for their dolls. Boys get the thrill of the old frontier days—they visualize the hardihood of the old pioneers with this *“Building Material of our Forefathers.”*

BIG COMBINATION SET of 234 logs, 2 roofs, and chimney $4
TRIPLE SET of 166 logs, 2 roofs and chimney $3
DOUBLE SET 110 logs, roof, chimney, $2
SINGLE SET of 53 logs & roof . . $1

No Delivery Charges—A Design Book in Each Set

See your Dealer or mail coupon to avoid delay

LINCOLN LOGS
Room 29, 232 E. Erie St., Chicago, Ill.
Please mail at once, postage prepaid:
☐ Big Combination Sets, 234 logs, etc. @ $4
☐ Triple Sets of 166 Logs $3 ☐ Double Sets $2 ☐ Single Sets $1
Enclosed $ . . . for Logs specified. Money refunded if I am not delighted. Send to
Name
Street or R. F. D.
City *State*

The Corn Exchange Bank
NEW YORK
Established 1853
Beaver and William Streets
Various Branches in Greater New York

CAPITAL AND SURPLUS. . . . . $ 22,000,000
NET DEPOSITS. 190,000,000

Accounts Respectfully Solicited

Trust Department to act as Agent, Executor, Trustee, Guardian

Safe Deposit Vaults

Changing America

- The Immigration Act of 1924 dramatically reduced the number of immigrants allowed into the United States.
- Lincoln Logs, named after Abraham Lincoln, had been wildly popular since their introduction in 1920.
- The popular Charleston flare dress sold at Gimbel's for $1.58.
- The film *The Black Pirate* was shown in Technicolor.
- Martha Graham debuted in New York as a choreographer and dancer.
- Alexander Calder held his first exhibition of paintings at the Artist's Gallery in New York
- New scientific discoveries were marketed for commercial use, such as the "new radium permanent wave" for women's hair.
- Wages for bartenders in Detroit during Prohibition were $75 a week, with an extra $50 for each arrest.
- "Yellow Drive-It-Yourself Systems" were becoming popular, costing $0.12 a mile for a Ford.
- Southern blacks continued their migration north as manufacturers toured the South offering good jobs and higher pay.

"Prohibition and New York's Poor," *The Literary Digest*, October 23, 1926:

"The general feeling of our workers," says Miss Stella A. Miner of the Girls' Service League of America, "is that the families with whom we deal in our protective work with girls are in better condition since the Volstead Law has been in effect. Drink and resultant poverty enter less into the home problems. . . ."

As far as she is able to judge, Miss Clara Bassett of the Vanderbilt Clinic believes that "the number of working days among workingmen, the number of families having bank accounts and longer periods of education for their children have greatly increased during the past few years, and that change is due to Prohibition. . . ."

Equally strong statements are made against present conditions under Prohibition. . . Workers in the East Harlem Health Center, representing every type of social work in a specific district, afford, it is said, a definite cross-section of opinion. Workers who have been active in the district for a long time saw little change that could be unqualifiedly attributed to the operation of Prohibition enforcement. Where the pressure has eased at one point, it had increased at another. There might be more money in the homes, but the loosening of parental control over young people and the example to children of law-breaking by the prevalence of the home-brewing, raised new and serious issues. It is a gain that children can no longer be sent to a saloon for a pail of beer, but the most innocent-looking shop in the block may be selling liquor to disreputable customers, with the children observing and commenting cynically on the whole transaction.

- Courtship was beginning to change as the automobile replaced the family parlor as a meeting place.
- Thomas Hunt Morgan's publication *Theory of the Gene* presented his hypotheses on heredity, developed while experimenting with fruit flies.
- Poet E. E. Cummings published "Is 5," and Langston Hughes wrote "The Weary Blues."

White Rock
"The World's Best Table Water"
Executive Offices: 100 BROADWAY, NEW YORK CITY

Interview with German immigrant Hans Bergner concerning Ellis Island in 1924, from *Island of Home, Island of Tears*:

Third-class passengers had to come to Ellis Island, and none of us knew exactly what this would mean. What it meant was that, first of all, the immigration officials would make sure that we knew where we were going when we arrived. We had, of course, been sponsored by someone in the United States in order to be here in the first place, but there had to be some proof shown that someone was going to pick us up or that we had some destination that we were going to go to.

The other thing they wanted to know was whether we had $25, and the third thing they wanted to know was could we read the English language (although literacy in German would have been acceptable) so each of us was asked to read a small paragraph from a book that the official would show us.

And then came the last step and, of course, the most familiar to people who have served in the armed forces, namely that there was a physical inspection awaiting us, the women on one side and the men on the other. Then came the great moment when we stood in front of the immigration official, who was a doctor, who examined us for venereal diseases. And if there was one who had a venereal disease, that particular person would not be allowed to land. There again, I had my peculiar feeling of the strange separation—that venereal diseases among first- and second-class passengers were apparently acceptable, and for third-class passengers, venereal diseases were not. Well, this was one of those introductions one never forgets.

"My Neighborhood," by Edward Corsi, *The Outlook*, September 16, 1925:

Edward Corsi finds in the polyglot boarding-house of New York the makings of the America of to-morrow.

There are 27 nationalities in the neighborhood, including, of course, the Chinese laundrymen, the gypsy phrenologists, and the Greek and Syrian storekeepers. Along the banks of the East River, surrounding Thomas Jefferson Park, are the Italians; on Pleasant Avenue are the Poles, Austrians and Hungarians. West, where Fifth Avenue loses its dignity but not its charm, are the Jews, sons of many lands; near them are the Turks and Spaniards. North, where "Little Italy" makes room for "Little Africa," are the Negroes, gradually moving down, much to the discomfort of the whites. South, resisting the merciless invasion of the Jews and Italians, are the Germans and Irish, remnant of a stock that once ruled this part of town. Scattered throughout the neighborhood, with limits well-defined, are lesser groups—Finns, Russians, French, Swedes, Danes, Rumanians and Jogoslavs. Here and there, like refugees in exile, are a few Americans of old stock, heroically holding their ground.

The cosmopolitan character of the neighborhood is evidenced not only in the signs of the many languages, the chop suey, the rotisseries, and spaghetti houses, the synagogues and Catholic temples, the flags of many colors, the foreign papers on every newsstand, but in the types one meets on the streets—tall, blond Nordics, olive-skinned, dark-haired Mediterraneans, long-bearded Semites and Slavs, massive Africans, East Indians, gypsies, Japs and Chinese.

The Italians and Jews predominate, giving the neighborhood the color of the Roman Ghetto. Few people have less in common than these. They differ in language, religion, custom and temperament. But they get along, even if now and then there is an unpleasant interchange of "kike" and "wop." Under the protecting aegis of the Irish policeman's club or the American flag, even the brotherhood of man is possible. . . .

The Great War itself, with its passions and hatreds, could not disturb the peaceful equilibrium of the neighborhood. Life in that trying hour went on as usual. All fighting was done for America. In the last political campaign the Jews and the Italians joined forces. The result was the election of "the long Progressive Congressman from the East," an American of Italian extraction, and a large vote for LaFollette.

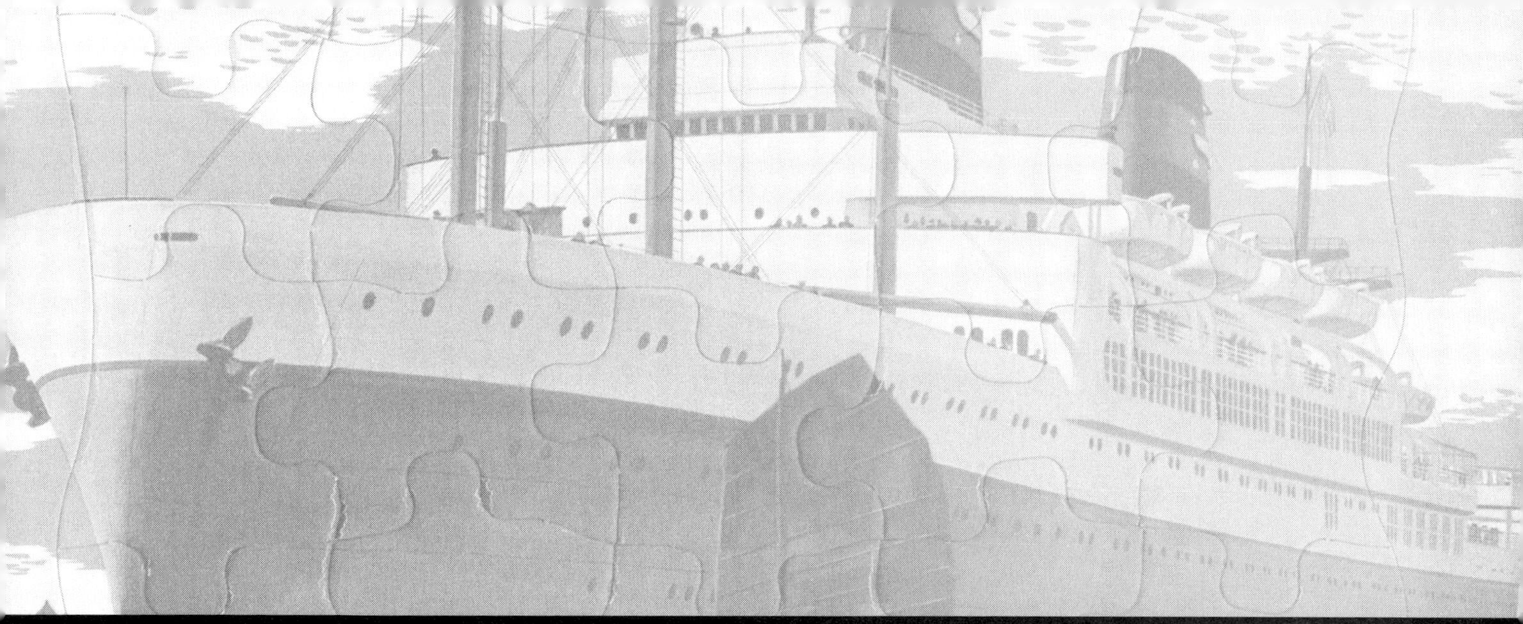

1927 Profile

Upper Class

Grace Ralston, an 18-year-old daughter of old money in Baltimore, has experienced all the joys of the traditional Grand Tour of Europe, as expected of a girl of her age and station.

Grace Ralston's place in Baltimore society has been planned since birth.

Life at Home

- Grace Ralston's family has long been considered "old Baltimore money"; her father, grandfather and great-grandfather all made their fortunes in the shipping business.
- Her place in Baltimore society was carefully planned since she was tiny: attend the right dance school at age six, followed by private school in the city, dinners at the right homes, and then, an invitation to the Bachelor's Cotillion, an event that predates the Civil War.
- When Grace turned 13, her mother marked the date of the cotillion, the first Monday in December—five years hence—on her calendar.
- Even though the hall where the cotillion is held limits the selection of Baltimore 18-year-olds to only 60 to 80 girls each year, she never doubted that Grace would be one of the chosen.
- Once there for the ball and presentation, dressed in the traditional white gown, Grace was overwhelmed by the profusion of flowers sent to each of the debutantes by escorts, relatives and family friends.
- In all, she received 53 bouquets, an outpouring comparable to all of the other girls.
- Her father, older brother and uncle served as her primary escorts for the evening.
- Promptly at 11 p.m., the orchestra stopped, a whistle was blown and the debutante figure, or march, was announced.

- The floor was cleared except for the debutantes and their partners, after which one of the governors led the couples through a simple figure, a tradition that allows everyone to see all the debutantes.
- With everyone staring at her at once, Grace felt like a show horse prancing for a judge—and she loved it.
- But all in all, it was a simple, dignified ceremony that lasted less than 10 minutes, followed by more champagne, more food and more dancing.
- Everyone told her she was a marvelous dancer, but by 3 a.m., when it all ended, she was exhausted.
- Once the cotillion was over, she was able to turn her full attention to the Grand Tour.
- If all went well on the trip, she would find a rich, exotic, exciting husband and live forever in a place where her mother couldn't watch her every move.
- Besides, that way she wouldn't have to attend college, pretending to earn a B.A. in English, when everyone knew her only interest was in getting an MRS.
- Many magazine articles suggest that a trip to the capitals of Europe could be made for $500, but $2,000 had been set aside just for her spending money.
- Her biggest fear was not the trip, but what she would do when she returned; she knows she is supposed to "do something," but is unsure of what it is.
- At least she had Christmas planned: she hoped to receive one of the new phonograph players with an automatic record changer—what a joy when she did!
- Christmas has also been a time to see all her cousins, who grew up in the same area and did everything together as children.
- Now many have moved away, married or gone to college.

Current Joke:

She—I love your eyes.
He—I hate your no's!

New words that entered the English language, thanks to the cartoon efforts of T. A. Dorgan, known as Tad:

Alley tennis: dice
Applesauce: nonsense
Baby carriage jockey: mother
Bonehead: numbskull
Cackle berries: eggs
Centerboard: nose
Chicken fanciers: girl watchers
Flat tire: uninteresting individual
Gay and frisky: whisky
Hire a hall: shut up
Jack: money
Nickel nurser: cheapskate
Rand McNally: face ("map")
Sun dodger: lazy person
Tusk tickler: dentist
Whisper low: speakeasy

Life on the Grand Tour

- For two years, her Grand Tour of Europe was meticulously planned.
- In preparation, she had her long hair cut very short and styled, and was delighted to discover how it horrified her mother.
- She is sure the new look sets off her dimples perfectly; besides, it complemented perfectly the cocktail dresses she had bought for the trip.
- The entire smart set of New England was just mad for the new dresses.
- Soon after the ship was under way, she delighted in using the latest words: rug jumper for dancer; sash weight for doughnut, hog hips for bacon and dogs for feet.
- Her aunt, who years before had agreed to chaperon Grace on the two-month-long trip, hates this new obsession for slang; it sounds so common.
- She also hates the romance novels her niece has been reading; only bad ideas can come from a story entitled *A Rooftop Romance*.
- When her aunt was not around, Grace practiced walking with her hips thrown forward and a cigarette holder between her teeth—a look becoming known as the "debutante slouch."

- On deck she would watch people carefully, torn between being a participant and an observer.
- Her fellow travelers included a bachelor bookkeeper, who spent 10 years' savings on one delirious trip; a German violinist, who seemed to be romancing a drab but very excitable girl; and the college couple, who felt so free about actually kissing in front of people, it made Grace's heart pound.
- She knows it is her turn to get into the flow, but leading an exciting life was much easier when surrounded only by brochures.
- She was also fascinated by several of the older men—professors, she thinks—who often held impromptu talks with flocks of young women eager to hear their every word.
- She wondered if college were like this, and whether she should reconsider her future and follow her mother's wishes after all.
- The first stop on the Grand Tour is, of course, France, where she stepped ashore at Cherbourg and was whisked by rail into Paris.
- She was a bundle of nerves, but loved holding a European train menu, seeing the light on the city at dusk, and reading signs in French: Chocolat Menier, Avenue de l'Opéra.
- She couldn't wait to see Sainte Chapelle when the sun shone through its multicolored windows, or attend a service at Nôtre Dame.
- During the first few days in France, they visited Versailles and Belleau Wood, and shopped for gloves, handkerchiefs, frocks, lingerie and perfume.

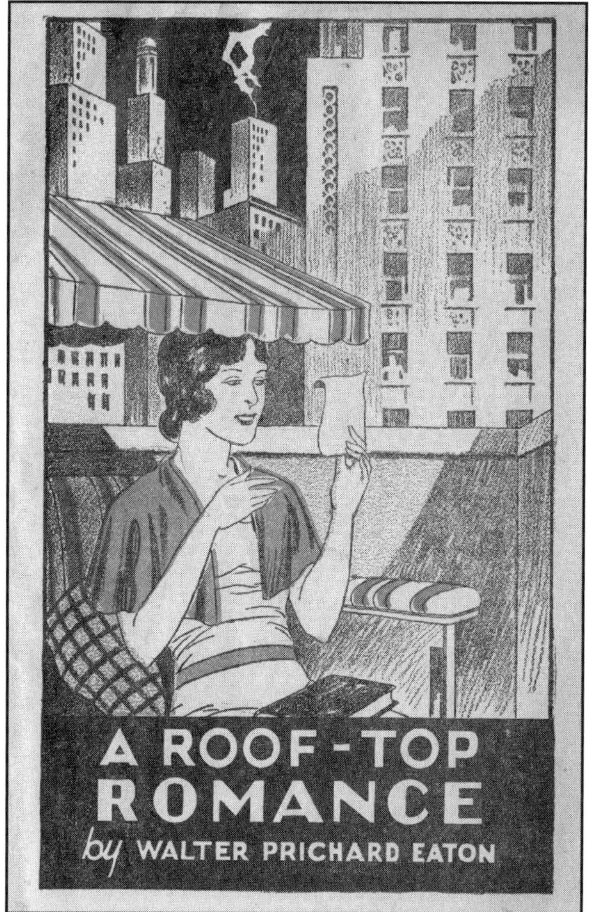

Her aunt hates the romance novels Grace loves to read.

One of the first stops on the Grand Tour is Paris.

Grace has read all about the wickedness of Paris.

- A whole day was set aside to see the Louvre; Grace and her aunt were two eager pilgrims among the 3.5 million who pass through the museum's gates each year.
- Then it was time to see the real France; she desperately wanted to go dancing and meet some French boys.
- Next on the schedule was Marseilles and Nice, with a quick look at Monte Carlo; no gambling, of course, her aunt said repeatedly, just a quick look around.
- Then on to Italy, first Genoa, where the streets are so narrow the houses almost meet across them, then Rome and the Sistine Chapel and Forum Romanum—both disappointments for Grace.
- In Rome, rumors bubbled about problems with the drinking water, so they pressed on to Naples, where the glass-bottomed boats were adorable, and then to Vesuvius, where she and her aunt dined in a scarlet sunset, debating who wrote *The Last Days of Pompeii*.
- Next on the itinerary were Florence, Venice and Milan, after which the two-month cultural adventure was half over.
- In Switzerland, Grace and her aunt collapsed into a deep rest; for two days they did not move except to take long walks in the evenings before meals.
- In Amsterdam, while her aunt was off buying cheese and wooden shoes, Grace was bold enough to take pictures of the men smoking long pipes in the doorways.

- The Hague, home of the World Court, was a bore, although Antwerp was little better.
- She began to dream about going home.
- Then, at last, the white cliffs of Dover and merry, merry England, the last part of the trip.
- The week in London passed like a confusing but pleasant dream, including her delight at hearing the English language again, having eggs for breakfast, and listening to hand organs play jazz tunes in front of their hotel windows.
- There she acquired a pipe for her father and scarves for her mother, and cashed the last of the traveler's checks.
- She couldn't believe she spent $2,000 during the trip; it must have been the dozens and dozens of post cards she purchased and posted home.
- While in London, they attended a performance of *The Merry Wives of Windsor* at the Criterion Theatre, starring James K. Hackett as Sir John Falstaff and Viola Allen as Mistress Ford.
- She was delighted to read in the program that in this age of automobiles, "The curtain will rise promptly at 8 o'clock; carriages may be called at 10:50."
- During a side trip, they visited Kenilworth Castle, and did a bit more shopping before returning home.

THE LATEST GUIDE
OF
VERSAILLES
AND THE
TRIANONS
To visit the Castle the Museum, the Park and the Gardens, with program of the High Waters
ON SELL:
To Mme MOREAU, 10, Rue Hoche, 10
VERSAILLES

The Romance that is France Awaits You!
THESE SERVICES:
New York Plymouth Havre
Express de Luxe Liners
PARIS FRANCE LAFAYETTE
New York Havre Paris
One-Cabin Steamers
DE GRASSE LA SAVOIE CHICAGO SUFFREN ROCHAMBEAU
New York Vigo Bordeaux
LA BOURDONNAIS ROUSSILLON
New Orleans Havre Paris
DE LA SALLE NIAGARA
North African Motor Tours
WHAT really does make France? . . . Not her land and sky and water, but her people. What they have builded . . . what they have lived! A thousand years of daring. Joan of Arc . . . Louis XIV . . . Napoleon . . . the Marne?
And this child of France, the French Line . . . whence comes its amazing differences? Not so many boats on so many seas—so many tours across the sands. But the life that beats in those boats like the heart in the body. The splendor of vision that caught North Africa in the Gallic spell. The art that makes a little poem of a breakfast tray—the gayety that turns a six-day crossing into an adventure!
If you're going to France, walk into France right up the gangplank and land at a covered pier at Havre, which is the port of Paris, only three hours away. Get six days more of France. Begin to understand France before you've dropped Sandy Hook astern . . .
Whether you plan a quick trip on an express liner or a leisurely crossing, the French Line service provides the route idéale.
French Line
Compagnie Générale Transatlantique
19 State Street, New York
Offices and Agencies in Principal Cities of Europe and the United States

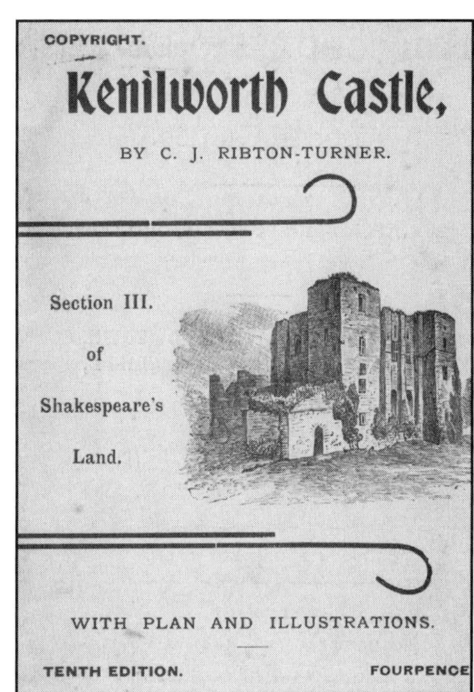

COPYRIGHT.
Kenilworth Castle,
BY C. J. RIBTON-TURNER.
Section III.
of
Shakespeare's
Land.
WITH PLAN AND ILLUSTRATIONS.
TENTH EDITION.
FOURPENCE

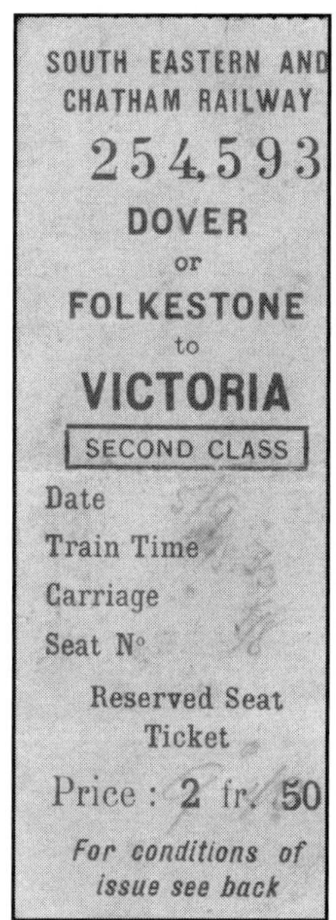

SOUTH EASTERN AND CHATHAM RAILWAY
254,593
DOVER
or
FOLKESTONE
to
VICTORIA
SECOND CLASS
Date
Train Time
Carriage
Seat No
Reserved Seat Ticket
Price: 2 fr. 50
For conditions of issue see back

"Innocence Abroad," by Frances Warfield, *Scribner's Magazine*, October 1928:

Tell me honestly now—do you know a college woman under 30 whose bookshelf does not display the familiar red back of *A Guide to the Louvre*? Do you know a recent sweet-girl graduate who does not, through first-hand knowledge, itch to correct your faltering pronunciation of Magdalen College, threepenny, pain au beurre, St. John Ervine, Exposition Internationale des Arts Decoratifs? Or one who does not look arch at the mention of the Follies Bergères, and who cannot quote the price of her fringed shawl in lire?

To the true college girl the European venture, as soon as possible after commencement, is well-nigh indispensable. It is the accepted thing, the cultured thing. Years ago, on the first day of her freshman year, when she faced the registrar with her health certificate and her father's check for the semester's tuition, the college girl forswore crudity for all time. At that moment she dedicated the future to the conventional, the cultured, and the cultural. During four years of expensive mental hardship, she has learned what every astute bachelor of arts must know—namely, how to separate those cultural things she must do from those she can pretend to have done. The trip abroad falls into the first class. It cannot be faked. The traveled manner gives final shine to that conversational front which is, after all, the beginning and end of culture. And, even for tea-table purposes, the traveled manner must be genuine.

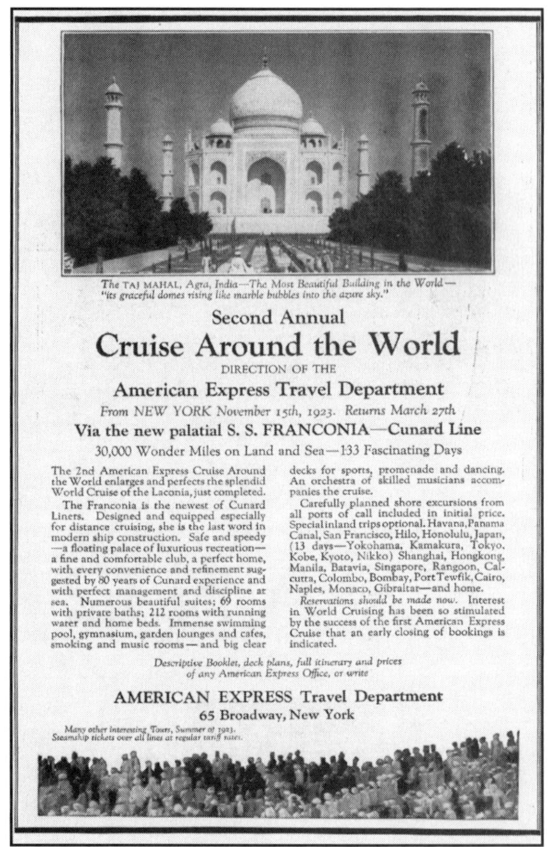

- Even though she can't always keep the dates in her head, and knows she is not really expected to, she loves hearing historical accounts that begin with the phrase, "A thousand years ago. . . ."
- Now that she is fully rested and on the steamship back to the United States, she is determined to be bolder about meeting men, drinking wine and dancing until dawn.

The Grand Tour ended in England.

Life in the Community: Baltimore, Maryland

- The port city of Baltimore has long been a transportation hub, both by water and rail.
- To supplement the area's longstanding dominance as a port, its railroads traveled the Atlantic coast, hauling merchandise and farm produce to the city.
- At the beginning of the Great War, 12 shipping lines, all under foreign flags, operated out of Baltimore.

"Baltimore Asks a Question," by Hamilton Owens, Editor of *Baltimore Evening Sun*, "Review of Reviews," July 1930:

One question more than any other agitates the citizens of Baltimore, metropolis of the Maryland Free State. You may hear it discussed at any local gathering, whether those present be proletarians, Babbitti, or intellectuals. You may follow the pros and cons of the debate in the correspondence columns of the daily newspapers. You may, if you are discerning, hear its complexities thrusting themselves between the resounding periods of His Honor, the Mayor.

That question is, in form, a simple one. It is whether Baltimore is, or is not, a hick town.

The fact that this question remains so live an issue and will not be downed whatever the weight of authority brought forward on one side or the other, is clearly deep-seated in the city's consciousness. In truth, it is comparable to the question which a woman asks herself when she looks in her mirror, or which puzzles a gangling youth when first he aspires to love. The census figures place Baltimore among the elect upper 10. Is the city as generally admirable, as important, as her size indicates, or does she remain merely an overgrown village, like some other American cities? Has Baltimore a flavor, a quality of her own? Is there, perhaps, an overtone of cosmopolitanism about her? Have we arrived, or are we merely standing still? And where do we go from here?

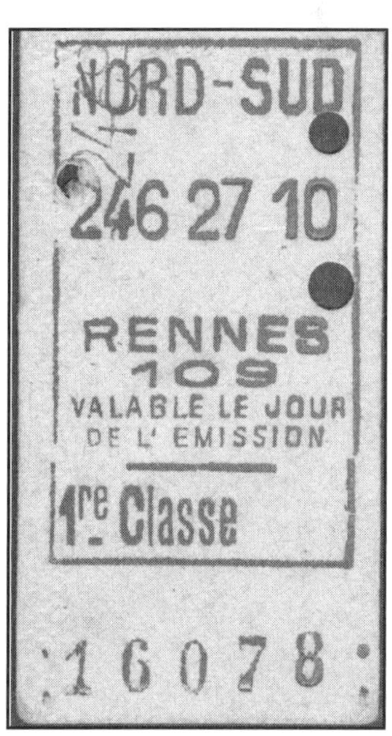

The port city of Baltimore is a transportation hub by water and rail.

- Currently, Bethlehem Steel Company is augmenting the capacity of its plant and hauling ore from Chile and Peru, while tankers are bringing crude oil from the Gulf ports and Mexico to the refineries on the south shore of the Patapsco River.
- New fertilizer and chemical plants are belching smoke and vapors over Curtis Bay.
- Spurred by the excitement generated by the Lindbergh flight, Baltimore's leaders are talking about building the nation's biggest airport.

Historical Snapshot
1927

- The Ford Model A automobile, the successor to the all-black Model T, was manufactured in four colors and included a self-starter, a rumble seat and a shatterproof windshield
- The National Football League was reduced from 32 teams to 12
- Charles Lindbergh captured the world's imagination when he flew solo, nonstop, from New York to Paris, traveling 3,610 miles in 33.3 hours
- The resulting New York ticker tape parade for Lindbergh consumed 1,800 tons of shredded paper; New York City spent $16,000 to sweep up afterward
- Fifteen million Sears & Roebuck catalogs were distributed to American homes
- The gate for the controversial Jack Dempsey-Gene Tunney heavyweight boxing match at Soldier's Field in Chicago was a record $2.65 million, with 104,943 in attendance for the fight featuring the "long count" for Gene Tunney
- The *New York Daily News* initiated the Golden Gloves program to encourage young boxers
- Coney Island introduced the world to the cyclone roller coaster
- Hostess Cakes, the *Literary Guild of America*, Delmonico's, A&W root beer, Lender bagel factory and Gerber baby food all made their first appearance
- Harvard's Philip Drinker devised the iron lung, a respirator for patients who could not breathe on their own
- "I'm Looking Over a Four-Leaf Clover," "Let a Smile Be Your Umbrella," and "Me and My Shadow" were all popular songs
- The average salary nationwide was $1,312; the average pay for teachers was $1,277, and for lawyers, $5,205
- *The Jazz Singer*, the first successful talkie, opened, starring Al Jolson
- Duke Ellington's music radio program premiered from the Cotton Club in New York
- An all-black basketball team, the Harlem Globetrotters, was organized by Abe Saperstein
- Fashion dictated that women's skirts rise again and stop just below the knee, the shortest length of the decade

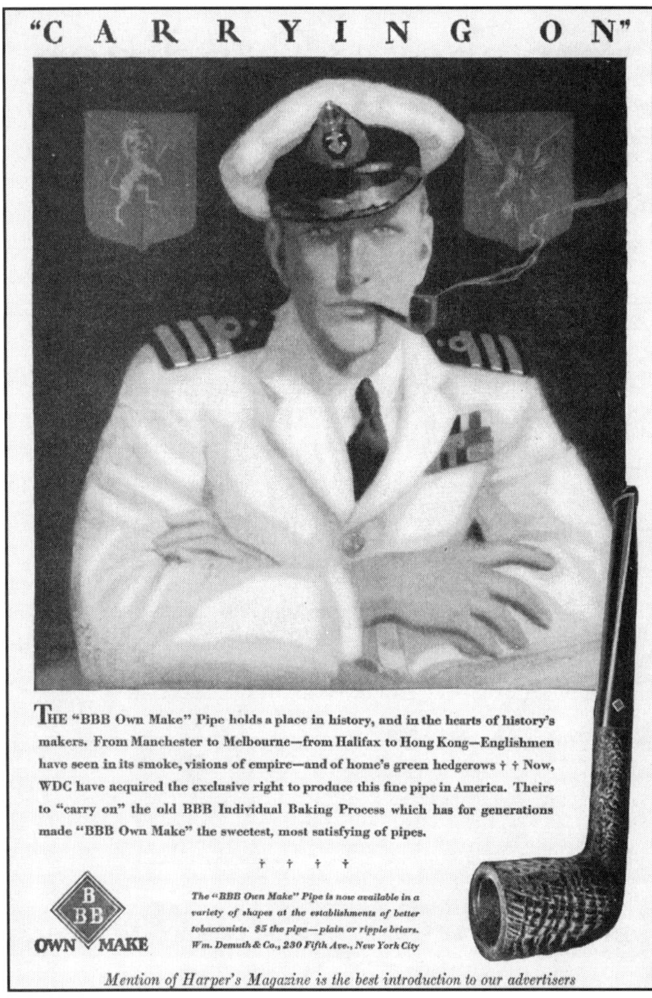

1927 Economic Profile

Selected Prices

Ax, Boy Scout	$1.65
Baby Ruth Candy Bar	$0.05
Blanket, Cotton	$1.72
Board Game, Ouija	$0.98
Cigars, 50 per Box	$3.98
Cloth, All-Wool Flannel, Yard	$1.59
Coat, Woman's Opossum Fur	$129.00
Cruise, New York to Trinidad, 31 Days	$300.00
Desk Fan, Hunter	$30.00
Hair Dryer, Polar Cub, Electric	$4.95
Hunting Coat, Red Head	$3.50
Ironing Table, Daisy	$2.35
Radio, Six-Tube Electric	$65.00
Scooter, All-Steel Roller-bearing	$3.98
Time Magazine, One Year	$5.00

"A Chance for the Rich Man's Son," by William G. Shephard, *Collier's*, June 14, 1924:

The son of Frederick H. Goff, millionaire banker of Cleveland, Ohio, did not sit around twitching nervously when his father's will was read some months ago. Neither did his two sisters.

These heirs had always known they wouldn't get their father's millions. They received by the will incomes less than the salaries of a good many men in the United States. They may build homes for themselves, such as they can maintain on their incomes, but these homes will belong to the estate, cannot be mortgaged and revert to the estate when they die, unless they have children living. When the grandchildren reach the age of 25 years, the estate ceases to pay them any income.

The entire estate then goes into the philanthropic Cleveland Trust Fund. Frederick Goff was against great dynastic family fortunes.

And what do Frederick Goff's children think of this plan? I talked to William Goff, the son, about it. I found him at a clerk's desk in a bank in Cleveland.

He was in his shirtsleeves. The man at the wicket window called him to the front to meet me. I asked him whether he would be willing to tell me how much a son should expect from a rich father.

"Just wait a minute," he said, smiling. He went to the rear of the room, took his coat from a locker and put it on. Then he came out through the gateway in the railing, a brown-eyed, husky six-footer, shook hands, and led me over to a seat in the public gangway.

"Of course I'm willing to talk about what my father did in his will. I'm not married yet, and I haven't many thousands of dollars, but I made a will just like my father's the other day. It's the right kind of will to make. I call it an American will."

He laughed or smiled through all our talk; straight white teeth emphasized the clear brownness of his eyes; behind his evident content with life there was football health. What a smash he, with one of his father's millions, could make—for a while—on Broadway! But he won't—not his kind.

What he says, this boy of less than 25, who might have inherited millions but didn't—and isn't sorry—runs like this:

"I don't think any son these days has a right to be a millionaire just because his father was. If I ever become one, I'll have to make the money myself, if I can, as my father did.

"Here's what my father did with me; he fixed it so that I will never have to go hungry or cold and so that I will be taken care of if I am taken ill. If I get married and have children, I can build a home for them and I will have enough money to care for them and educate them. But when they reach the age that I am now, they must begin to shift for themselves. The same arrangement is made for my sisters. . . ."

"What's the harm of inheriting a million dollars?" I asked.

"Why, it's like wrapping cloths around a fellow's ambition and making a mummy out of it. I know some young fellows who have inherited millions of dollars. They're the unhappiest people I know. They don't know what to do in life. There's no use of doing anything.

"And," he added with a big laugh, "they're the tightest tightwads I know. They're always trying to find out what they can get without using their money—and it's mighty little, let me tell you. They didn't get a square sort of start.

"People don't seem to understand that it's a chance that any boy wants. The son of a rich man needs it just as much as the son of a poor man.

"And that's true about the daughters of rich men, too. It isn't good for a girl to expect a lot of money all her life and then get it. If a girl has an income that keeps her safe from what I call jungle living, or the fight to keep alive, she has as good a chance in life as any other girl. And that's what girls want these days."

Changing America

- Many small-town merchants were hurt by the expanding availability of the automobile, as farmers traveled more often to the nearest city to buy books or take in a movie.
- The National Association of Manufacturers complained that 40 percent of high school graduates could not do simple arithmetic or speak English correctly.
- The average annual medical expense for a family was $80, with 45 percent going for the payment of physicians' services, seven percent for hospitals, 15 percent for dentists, three percent for nurses, and the rest for medicine and incidentals.
- Violinist Yehudi Menuhin debuted at age 10.
- A recent national survey suggested a loosening of manners and morals in America: Mrs. Bertrand Russell publicly defended "free love," while judges openly advocated the concept of trial marriage known as "companionate marriage."
- The Hays list of do's and don'ts for Hollywood films prohibited, "any licentious or suggestive nudity," "ridicule of clergy" and themes such as "the sale of women."
- *Vanity Fair* reported that Harvard, Yale and Princeton men were now wearing gray, sagging Oxford pants, drooping socks over square-toed, barely visible saddle shoes with rubber soles, and a single-breasted, gray Oxford overcoat.
- Forty leading authors formed the Committee for the Suppression of Irresponsible Censorship.
- As ready-made clothing began to dominate the market, Macy's department store declared: "A 94-cent dress is good enough for anyone's child."
- Since the newly imposed U.S. limitations on immigration had left the steerage portion of many ships nearly empty, colleges used the available space for floating fraternity parties organized by each school.

"Play Review: Second Round," by George Jean Nathan, *Judge*, August 29, 1925:

Spring Fever by Vincent Lawrence is another of those plays in which the heroine hates the hero like poison until about quarter to eleven, at which time the hero grabs her and kisses her in such a way that she can resist him no longer and falls into his arms. I have long speculated just what there was about such kisses that make women unable to withstand their impresarios. For years now I have been going to plays and seeing erstwhile adamant women promptly capitulate to men when the latter have kissed them like the hero of the Lawrence play. No sooner has the aforesaid hero glued his lips to those of the heroine than she takes a step backward, gazes at him with an immense admiration and projects herself at once into his loving embrace, where only a minute before she shouted at him that if he so much as touched her she would yell for the police. It is all very mysterious to me. I have asked some of the best and most widely kissed women in America to let me into the secret, but the girls say that they don't know what it is. In real life, if a woman hates a man and he grabs her and kisses her the way the average man drinks a seidel of Pilsner, she hauls off and lands him one. But on the stage, she is his forever. Playwrights must know something about the art of kissing that the rest of us fellows are ignorant of.

"Hints to World Cruisers," *Ship Ahoy!! Nautical Notes for Ocean Travelers, with Charts and Diary*, by Lt. Commander J. G. P. Bisset, R.D., R.N.R., 1926:

SHIP AHOY!!

Nautical Notes for Ocean Travellers, with Charts and Diary.

BY

LIEUT. COMMANDER J. G. P. BISSET, R.D., R.N.R., AUTHOR OF "LIFEBOAT EFFICIENCY."

ILLUSTRATED BY

D. W. SORRELL.

(Copyright.) PRICE TWO DOLLARS.

Made and Printed in England by CHARLES BIRCHALL LTD., 17, JAMES STREET, LIVERPOOL.

Round-the-world cruising has become almost a habit, and in the great 20,000-ton liners that make the cruises to-day, it is also a luxury and a very interesting one, too . . .

Some cruises go round the world east about, that is, through the Mediterranean and the Suez Canal, and return via the Panama Canal. Others go west about, starting out through the Panama Canal and returning via the Mediterranean, or in some cases round South Africa. The only difference is that going east about, the clock is being put up half an hour or so each night as you steam eastward, and going west it is put back correspondingly. To make up for this, when crossing the 180 meridian east about, you will experience an eight-day week, and west about a six-day week . . .

The cruise ships are well-known vessels belonging to the various transatlantic lines, and they are chartered lock, stock and funnel by the travel companies, and manned by the same captain, officers and crew as they carry on their ordinary runs. This is a great factor towards smooth and efficient running. The best ships provide an experienced physician, a tip-top orchestra, gymnastic, swimming and squash instructors, barbers, ladies' hairdressers and manicurists, a well-equipped laundry and valet service, a well-stocked library, indoor and outdoor swimming tanks, garden lounges, deck games, etc., etc. The charters put a staff on board, in the charge of a cruise director, and this usually includes lecturers, clergymen, surgeons, dentists, bankers, host and hostess, photographers and travel experts, and a librarian with an ample stock of travel books, guides, etc., etc. A good supply of clothing, as ordinarily worn in temperate climates, should be taken, and also several Palm Beach suits. There is an impression that these can be best obtained abroad, in places like India or China, but my experience is that they are rarely satisfactory, and you will do well to get them at home. Bring flannels, sweaters and sneakers for deck games, also a gymnastic costume. A swimming costume suitable for the outdoor pool should be brought, as this pool is well in the public eye as it were, and always a great source of attraction. A heavy coat or wrap is required for cool evenings, and a light raincoat or dust-coat is useful for motoring.

Many of the motor drives are very dusty trips, and on occasion, passengers are advised by the "staff" to wear old clothes, so bring along that old suit, and you can get it cleaned up occasionally on board.

(continued)

"Hints to World Cruisers," . . . (*continued*)

Do not bother about a sun helmet; they are a nuisance to pack, and can be obtained better and cheaper in tropical countries.

For gentlemen, a dinner jacket is the usual dress for evenings and should be sufficient, unless you expect to attend any formal functions abroad. For hot weather, a couple of loose dinner jackets made of white alpaca or duck, look and feel cool, and can be laundered on board as required.

For ladies, I am advised by several very charming authorities that amongst other things they should bring dresses of materials that do not crush or wrinkle, and which, upon opening the trunk and being shaken out, will look "perfect." I had no idea such material existed. The same authorities also advised Kayser silk for certain items, but I'm getting into deep water now and guess I'll drop that subject. . . .

By the way, bring a couple of fancy costumes. The masquerade ball is always a fun event, and the first one usually takes place early in the cruise, as it gets folk together.

Should Girls Play Interschool Basketball?

1928 News Feature

"Should Girls Play Interschool Basketball?" by Henry S. Curtis, *Hygenia*, November 1928:

There is a great increase in interest in athletics among girls all over the world. In Germany, France, England and America we find the same enthusiasm. Most women physical directors and school authorities believe that contests for girls should be confined to intramural athletics rather than to interschool competition such as men have. But it is by no means certain that women and girls are going to abide by the decision of school authorities. It is a part of their new feeling for liberty and equality of opportunity that they should be allowed to enter interschool competition if they wish.

Such competition of girls in basketball in the past has often been injurious. It has taken place by boys' rules, under men coaches, with long halves and with inadequate training to bear the strain involved.

In Illinois, the rules permit girls to compete only in volleyball and tennis, while in Maryland they may compete in tennis, playground ball, volleyball and dodge ball.

The Women's Athletic Federation has stood firmly against interschool competition for girls, particularly in basketball, and has insisted that when contests did take place the girls should be in the charge of women physical directors, should play quarters rather than halves, and should always play by girls' rules.

Of the colleges, considerably less than 10 percent allow women to compete in interschool basketball, though such competition is doubtless less objectionable for college women than it is for high school girls. Nearly all women physical directors in colleges are opposed to it.

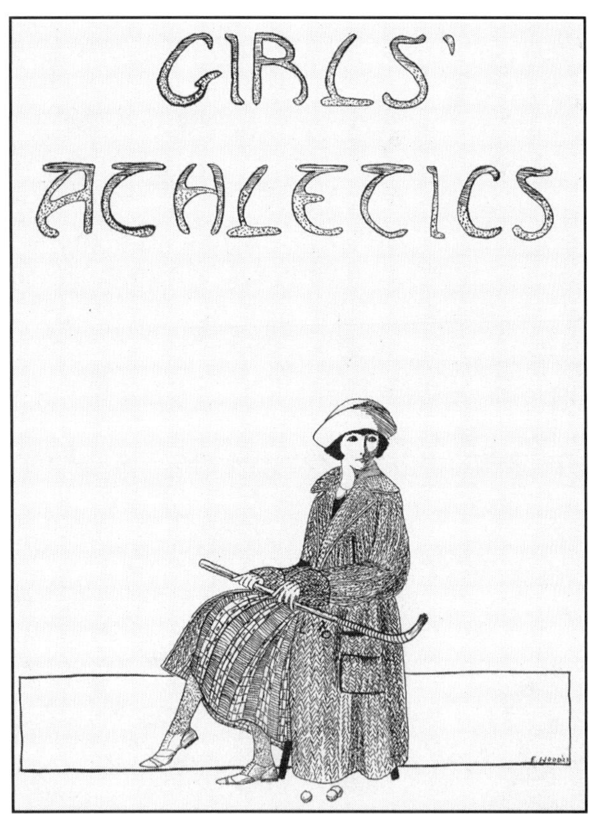

Some of the reasons given are the following: On the social side it is said that women have not been trained for interschool competition and that they do not thus far have the traditions of sportsmanship that have been impressed upon men's teams for generations; they are poor losers and often lose their tempers along with the game. It is further asserted that girls are nervously more unstable than men and are consequently more affected in the way of distraction from their studies, in the loss of sleep before and after games and in general nervous injuries. It is not good social policy to have girls travel about the country for interschool contests. Oft times there is no suitable place for changing their clothes or for taking showers after the game. Remarks by spectators are often discourteous or even insulting, and the publicity in the papers is usually not the kind that emphasizes feminine ideals.

On the physical side it is said that a woman has a much smaller heart than a man and that basketball involves a continual strain which a small heart is not well-qualified to stand, even resulting in the girl's fainting or being unable to stand at the end of the half. Strains of the knee and about the body are more injurious to girls than boys. Bruises on the breast and

HARD TO BEAT

Continuing a heated rivalry, West Durham High School Girls' Basketball Team was defeated only once by the Durham High squad in 1924.

abdomen are likely to be serious. Jumping and falling sometimes result in displacements which may require an operation to prevent sterility.

All these objections are more serious where girls are playing by boys' rules with men coaches. Many former women players believe that these contests are injurious to them.

However, this question is far from settled. Basketball by girls' rules, played in quarters, after adequate training and with a competent woman physical director in charge, is quite different from basketball played in halves, by boys' rules and under a man physical director. It may be that when basketball has been led up to by other, less strenuous games, and when adequate preparation has been given in sportsmanship, we should be ready to hold interschool competitions for girls of which the educational authorities can approve.

1930–1939

Few Americans—especially children—escaped the devastating impact of the most severe depression in the nation's history as banks failed, railroads became insolvent, unemployment rose, factories closed and children left school—many of which operated only five months during the year. Economic paralysis gripped the nation; starvation began to reemerge, and the number of childhood deaths caused by illness began to rise again. By 1932, one in four Americans was jobless. One in every four farms was sold for taxes. Five thousand banks closed their doors, wiping out the lifetime savings of millions of Americans—rich and poor.

The stock market sank into the doldrums. In urban areas, apple sellers appeared on street corners. Bread lines became common sights. The unemployed wandered from city to city seeking work, only to discover the pervasive nature of the economic collapse. In some circles the American Depression was viewed as the fulfillment of Marxist prophecy—the inevitable demise of capitalism.

President Franklin D. Roosevelt thought otherwise. Backed by his New Deal promises and a focus on the "forgotten man," the president produced a swirl of government programs designed to lift the country out of its paralytic gloom.

Roosevelt's early social experiments were characterized by relief, recovery, and reform. Believing that the expansion of the United States economy was temporarily over, Roosevelt paid attention to better distribution of resources and planned production. The Civilian Conservation Corps (CCC), for example, put 250,000 jobless young men to work in the forests for $1.00 a day. By 1935, government deficit spending was spurring economic change. By 1937, total manufacturing output exceeded that of 1929; unfortunately, prices and wages rose too quickly and the economy dipped again in 1937, driven by inflation fears and restrictions on bank lending. Nonetheless, many roads, bridges, public buildings, dams, and trees became part of the landscape thanks to federally employed workers. The Federal Theatre Project, for example, employed 1,300 people during the period, reaching 25 million attendees with more than 1,200 productions. Despite progress, 10 million workers were still unemployed in 1938 and farm prices lagged behind manufacturing progress. Full recovery would not occur until the United States mobilized for World War II.

While the nation suffered from economic blows, the West was being whipped by nature. Gigantic billowing clouds of dust up to 10,000 feet high swept across the parched Western Plains throughout the '30s. Sometimes the blows came with lightning and booming thunder, but often they were described as being "eerily slight, blackening everything in their path." All human activity halted. Planes were grounded. Buses and trains stalled, unable to race clouds that could move at speeds of more than 100 miles per hour. On the morning of May 9, 1934, the wind began to blow up the topsoil of Montana and Wyoming, and soon some 350 million tons were sweeping eastward. By late afternoon, 12 million tons had been deposited in Chicago. By noon the next day, Buffalo, New York, was dark with dust. Even the Atlantic Ocean was no barrier. Ships 300 miles out to sea found dust on their decks. During the remainder of 1935, there were more than 40 dust storms that reduced visibility to less than one mile. There were 68 more storms in 1936, 72 in 1937, and 61 in 1938. On the High Plains, 10,000 houses were simply abandoned, and nine million acres of farm turned back to nature. Banks offered mortgaged properties for as little as $25 for 160 acres and found no takers.

The people of the 1930s excelled in escape. Radio matured as a mass medium, creating stars such as Jack Benny, Bob Hope, and Fibber McGee and Molly. For a time it seemed that every child was copying the catch phrase of radio's Walter Winchell, "Good evening, Mr. and Mrs. America, and all the ships at sea," or pretending to be Jack Benny when shouting, "Now, cut that out!" Soap operas captured large followings and sales of magazines like *Screenland* and *True Story* skyrocketed. Each edition of *True Confessions* sold 7.5 million copies. Nationwide, movie theaters prospered as 90 million Americans attended the "talkies" every week, finding comfort in the uplifting excitement of movies and movie stars. Big bands made swing the king of the decade, while jazz came into its own. And the social experiment known as Prohibition died in December 1933, when the Twenty-first Amendment swept away the restrictions against alcohol ushered in more than a decade earlier.

Attendance at professional athletic events declined during the decade, but softball became more popular than ever and golf began its drive to become a national passion as private courses went public. Millions listened to boxing on radio, especially the exploits of the "Brown Bomber," Joe Louis. As average people coped with the difficult times, they married later, had fewer children, and divorced less. Extended families often lived under one roof; opportunities for women and minorities were particularly limited. Survival, not affluence, was often the practical goal of the family. A disillusioned nation, which had worshipped the power of business, looked instead toward a more caring government.

During the decade, United Airlines hired its first airline stewardess to allay passengers' fears of flying. The circulation of Reader's Digest climbed from 250,000 to eight million before the decade ended and Esquire, the first magazine for men, was launched. The early days of the decade gave birth to Hostess Twinkies, Bird's Eye frozen vegetables, windshield wipers, photoflash bulbs, and pinball machines. By the time the Depression and the 1930s drew to a close, Zippo lighters, Frito's corn chips, talking books for the blind, beer in cans, and the Richter scale for measuring earthquakes had all been introduced. Despite the ever-increasing role of the automobile in the mid-1930s, Americans still spent $1,000 a day on buggy whips.

1930 Profile

Middle Class

The Waltuck family of four is one of the first to take advantage of the "Radburn idea" and move outside New York City to the newly created, fully planned community of Radburn, New Jersey, known as a city designed around children. Nine-year-old Eugene loves the parks, his friends and his secret nickname, Rocko.

Eugene Waltuck's secret nickname is Rocko.

Life at Home

- Limited to 25,000 to 30,000 residents, highly promoted Radburn is widely advertised as "The town for the motor age."
- Currently, about 1,200 people live in the community, which features 24 acres of parkland, sometimes called "green spaces," two swimming pools, four tennis courts, four ball fields, three playgrounds, five basketball courts and an archery plaza.
- During its first year, 202 families comprising 587 people bought homes in the town, prompting *The New York Times* to comment: "If Radburn hasn't already received the Census Bureau's prize for the fastest-growing community, it ought to be awarded it without further delay."
- *Business Week* recently concluded that the town appears to be immune from the Depression, since the dismal state of the economy has "had practically no effect upon" the community's growth.
- The Waltuck family moved from New York City so that Eugene and his younger sister could grow up in a healthy atmosphere.
- Mrs. Waltuck, who is pregnant but insists that only the letters "PG" be mentioned around the children, believes that Radburn provides a type of environment not possible in New York.
- Eugene loves the park near his home; with so few cars around, his mother leaves him alone to run.

Radburn is a city designed around the needs of children.

- His gang of six nine-year-olds has already built a secret fort near the overpass and only allows blood brothers to enter.
- "The Radburn idea," according to one of its planners, "seeks to answer the enigma of how to live with the auto," or more precisely, how to live in spite of it.
- Advertisements for the brand-new community emphasize the role of its parks, saying, "To be complete, and provide fully for family life and growth, a home must be more than four walls. And no matter how attractive a house may be, it will fall short of present-day requirements if its location does not offer recreation and play facilities for children and adults."
- The town was designed with winding cul-de-sacs that follow the contours of the land; in the words of one developer: "At Radburn, everything is planned."
- Eugene's home has all the modern conveniences, including ash chutes, underground garbage containers, accessible coal bins, modern bathrooms, up-to-date kitchens and spacious basements.
- Mrs. Waltuck loves the fact that "everything is new and clean," and that the house is close to the school so that she can help out.
- Appliances in the home include the no-wringer Easy Washer that cuts laundry time in half, and the Hotpoint Electric Cookery, with its high-speed, calrod-element burner.
- General Electric has just introduced an electric waste disposal unit that fits into the sink, but Mrs. Waltuck is uncertain she wants one until she has seen it operate.
- More than 85 percent of the men and 75 percent of the women have attended college, with most of the men holding professional positions.
- Eugene's father, an engineer, walks from their house to catch the 7:52 commuter train to his New York office each morning.
- Seven out of 10 men in Radburn commute to New York City daily.

"The Swing,"
A Child's Garden of Verses,
Robert Louis Stevenson, 1929:

How do you like to go up in a swing,
Up in the air so blue?
Oh, I do think it the pleasantest thing
Ever a child can do!

Up in the air and over the wall,
Till I can see so wide,
Rivers and trees and cattle and all
Over the countryside—

Till I look down on the garden green,
Down on the roof so brown—
Up in the air I go flying again,
Up in the air and down!

"Now We Have a Real Motortown, There Are Automobile Streets and Pedestrian Streets in Radburn, New Jersey, and It's a Safe Paradise for Children," by Harold F. Podhaski, *Motor*, January 1930:

If there exists a paradise on earth for automobile owners, one may find it at Radburn, New Jersey, a dozen miles or so as the crow flies from New York City.

For here indeed has science constructed what may be fittingly described as a model town for this motor age, the only town of its kind, in fact, in the world today.

A town where one may roll the car along at as merry a clip as the heart desires without the fear that some careless youngster may dart suddenly across the way.

A town without street crossings, where traffic boulevards have no sidewalks, where jaywalkers are practically unknown.

In fact, a town where science has done virtually everything that it is possible to do to create a community safe and sane for motorist and pedestrian alike, yet has combined with these elements beauty and charm, and the utmost in modern efficiency.

Two years ago, on the site where now stands the town of Radburn, rolling green fields stretched far and wide, with but an occasional house or farm building here and there in silhouette against the horizon. Since then, ingenuity has transformed this scene into one of the most unique residential communities of the world. Unique for the present at least, though it is hardly likely to remain so because of the popularity the idea has won since the very outset, a popularity that may bring about the development of the motortown idea in other sections adjacent to the more congested metropolitan areas.

As our children are our greatest jewels, and their safety is one of the greatest of our cares, it is perhaps fitting that this story of Radburn and its building should begin with a description of the safety features primarily considered by the owners of this property when they planned their town, designed their houses and inaugurated their building program.

We realize full well in these days when nearly everyone owns an automobile, and many drivers are not as careful as they might be, that the crossing of a street has become a hazardous undertaking for children. The creation of a town where it would not be necessary for children—or anyone else for that matter—to cross the traffic boulevards, was decided upon as one of the main objectives.

At first thought, one might be inclined to consider this virtually a physical impossibility, without the erection of an underpass or overpass at every street crossing, obviously not to be thought of because of the cost involved. But it is possible and has been done at Radburn, which has been so designed and so constructed that there is not a single street crossing for pedestrians, not a traffic boulevard skirted by sidewalks, and only a single underpass. Yet, it is a good-sized town covering some 15 average blocks, or an area of nearly a square mile.

Think of what this means to mothers! In the ordinary town or city, automobile traffic is a never-failing cause of worry to parents, for when the youngster is packed off to school in the morning there are usually streets that must be crossed en route with the ever-present danger of accident. The developers truthfully advertise that, "You can buy safety from traffic accidents for your whole family, and particularly for your children, when you buy a home in Radburn."

If you want to own a lot of spacious private property, then Radburn isn't the answer. But if you like a place which is at the same time busy and safe for children, where you don't have to spend all your time driving around, and where you have beautiful parks and great public amenities, then it's a dandy.

It's a town turned outside in—without any backdoors. A town where roads and parks fit together like the fingers on your right and left hands. A town in which children need never dodge motor trucks on their way to school.

Roads are designed to separate children and cars.

- The Waltucks live on a "superblock," a break from the checkerboard pattern of housing in a traditional residential environment of 200- by 600-foot blocks.
- Radburn blocks are 1,200 by 1,800 feet and are free of automobile traffic.
- Slotted into the edges of the superblocks are cul-de-sacs, each lined with 10 to 18 houses, creating a ratio of seven houses to an acre—nearly twice the density of that in conventional suburban developments.
- By clustering the homes together, the town sets aside 15 percent of the total area for green space that can be shared by the entire community.
- Unlike conventional American houses, the interior design of Radburn's houses evolved from the outside in; rooms for family use and sleeping, which traditionally front the street, face the walkways and parks, while the kitchens overlook the noisier, less aesthetically pleasing cul-de-sacs instead of backyards.
- This interior framework creates a house with two faces, one of which is paved, the other mainly green.
- *The New York Times* editorialized that the Radburn plan was "the first deliberate attempt to harmonize the rights of the pedestrian and of the motorist."

Life at School

- The town's school superintendent believes in promoting good values; every month a new poster from the "Hope of a Nation" poster series is hung in Eugene's classroom.
- The September poster read: "What will your job be out in the great, wide world when school days are over? Make it a BIG job!"
- Three days a week, Eugene's mother takes her children to school and then works in the office all day; she does not want to make any further commitments with a baby on the way.
- Activities for her daughter, a first-grader, include a tot lot (playground for small children) and crafts at the clubhouse.

By clustering the houses, space was created for parks and bike paths.

- A professional athletic director is available to direct activities for all children from ages two to 18.
- After school Eugene plays basketball, baseball and is learning tennis, while his sister is taking ballet.
- During the summer, he attends the town's summer camp, which is managed by a professional staff.
- Summer is a time for learning, not for resting, according to the Teachers' College in New York; as a result, Mrs. Waltuck has encouraged her children to start a hobby during their summer vacation.
- For adults, the community provides courses such as psychology, music appreciation, current events and American literature.
- They also have an amateur theater group, bridge tournaments and craft lessons.
- Mrs. Waltuck is taking a class in conversational French; even though she dropped out of college in her sophomore year to marry, she still dreams of finishing her education and traveling in Europe.
- She would love to spend a week in Paris—if the family could ever afford it.
- For Eugene's birthday, he and three friends were taken to play miniature golf—the current national rage.
- He got a hole-in-one on the ninth hole, and the best score, although there is some disagreement about his math, and afterwards, everyone got to eat ice cream.
- He also got his birthday wish—a game of "Sorry."
- He is driving his parents crazy with his newest saying, which he repeats over and over: "So long . . . until tomorrow," the same words used by radio announcer Lowell Thomas each night.

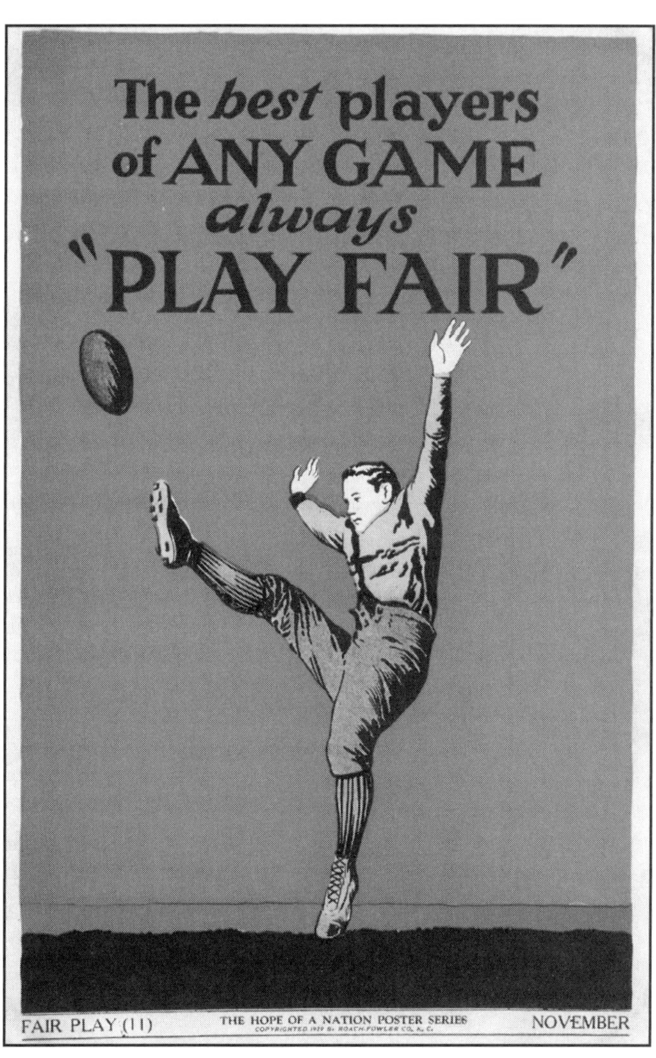

"Among the New Books, A. A. Milne's New Poems, *Now We Are Six*," *Harper's*, November 1927:

The phenomenal popularity of A. A. Milne as a poet of childhood—which is not necessarily the same as a childhood poet—will not be changed by *Now We Are Six*, the latest of the poems supposedly "made up" by Christopher Robin. The decorations are by E. H. Shepard, too. Even the introduction is in Milne's favorite vein, and aptly describes the book: "We have been nearly three years writing this book. We began it when we were very young . . . and now we are six. So, of course, bits of it seem rather babyish to us, almost as if they had slipped out of some other book by mistake. On page whatever-it-is there is a thing which is simply threeish, and when we read to ourselves just now we said, "Well, well, well," and turned over rather quickly. So we want you to know that the name of the book doesn't mean that this is us being six all the time. Some of these poems have been published, and perhaps you have read them in *Harper's Magazine*. There is "Sneezles" and "Busy" and "Furry Bear."

There is the gorgeous story of "The Knight Whose Armour Didn't Squeak." Every now and then there is a reminiscence of "When We Were Very Young." But the book cannot compare with the former for interest and quality, even when allowance is made for the fact that our surprise at discovering these rhymes is over. The first fine, careless rapture seems to have no equal.

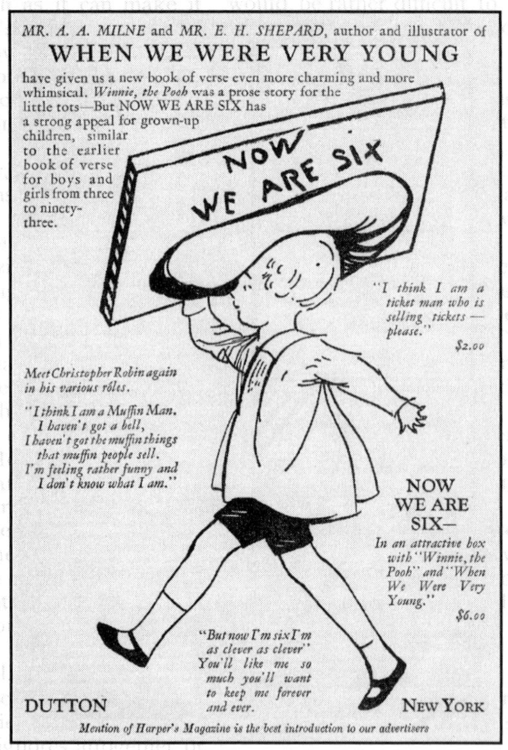

MR. A. A. MILNE and MR. E. H. SHEPARD, author and illustrator of
WHEN WE WERE VERY YOUNG
have given us a new book of verse even more charming and more whimsical. Winnie, the Pooh was a prose story for the little tots—But NOW WE ARE SIX has a strong appeal for grown-up children, similar to the earlier book of verse for boys and girls from three to ninety-three.
NOW WE ARE SIX
"I think I am a ticket man who is selling tickets — please."
$2.00
Meet Christopher Robin again in his various rôles.
"I think I am a Muffin Man. I haven't got a bell, I haven't got the muffin things that muffin people sell. I'm feeling rather funny and I don't know what I am."
NOW WE ARE SIX—
In an attractive box with "Winnie, the Pooh" and "When We Were Very Young."
$6.00
"But now I'm six I'm as clever as clever" You'll like me so much you'll want to keep me forever and ever.
DUTTON
NEW YORK
Mention of Harper's Magazine is the best introduction to our advertisers

- His favorite radio show is "Amos 'n' Andy" followed by "The Lone Ranger," whose opening line he loves and knows by heart: "A fiery horse with the speed of light, a cloud of dust, and a hearty 'Hi-yo, Silver!' The Lone Ranger rides again!"

Life in the Community: Radburn, New Jersey

- When it first opened last year, Radburn, New Jersey, was hailed as a "town for children"; known as America's first garden community, its site plan has captured the imagination of hundreds of families.
- The Radburn idea has five key elements: the superblock, specialized roads, separation of pedestrian and automobile traffic, houses turned to front the parks, and the park as the backbone of the neighborhood.
- Executives of the City Housing Corporation canvassed 27 sites throughout the Northeast before selecting rural land in Fair Lawn, New Jersey, 16 miles from New York.

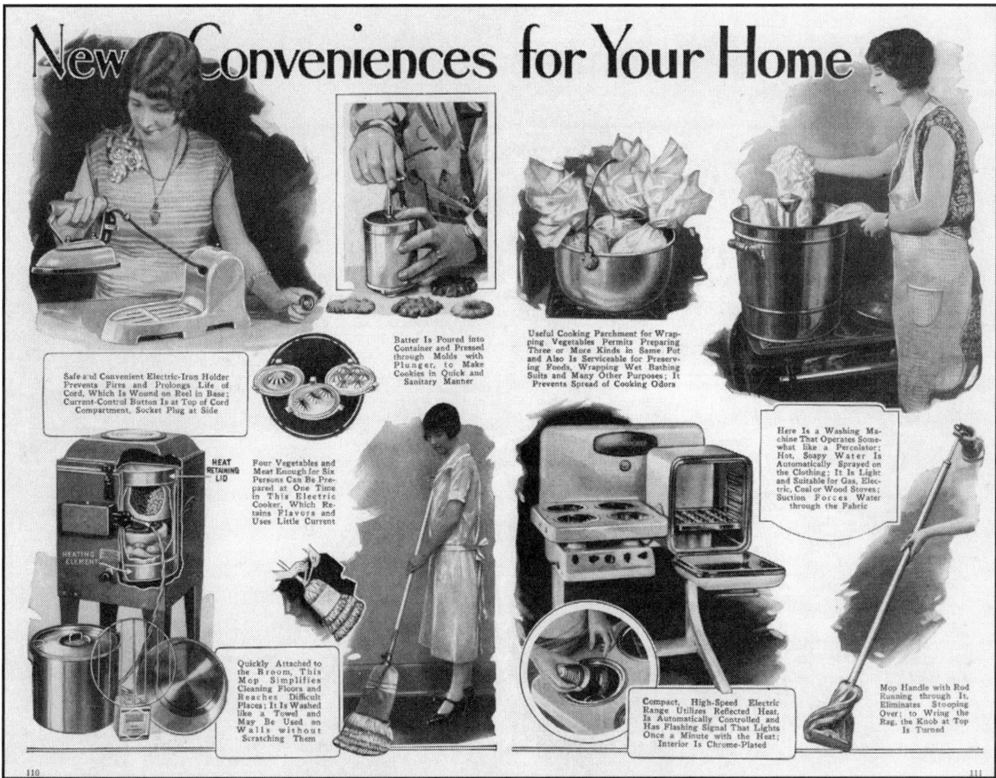

Radburn homes emphasize the latest conveniences.

- In all, 1,300 acres, or two square miles of land, were purchased for $3.4 million; the average price, because of the town's proximity to New York City, was $2,600 per acre, or $0.10 per square foot.
- Because the community was recently created, most of the residents are young married couples with children; most of the families are Protestant, a dozen are Jewish and one practices both Judaism and Catholicism.
- Early plans called for a variety of houses that appealed to all income levels, but as planner Clarence Stein lamented, "If the poorly paid workers were admitted to the garden city, the industry that used them would have to subsidize the workers' houses and advance their wages."
- The typical house built during the past year cost between $7,900 and $18,200, more than twice the average price of an American house in the late 1920s.
- The unique nature of the community is not only attractive, but the clustered housing and expansive parks reduce the cost of building the infrastructure, including roads and water lines, by 25 percent.
- Radburn is the most visible product of the Regional Planning Association of America, an innovative planning group formed in 1923.
- Membership has included social critics such as Lewis Mumford, architects Clarence Stein and Henry Wright, as well as naturalist Benton MacKaye and economist Stuart Chase.
- The first imprint of this group of designers was the Sunnyside Gardens in Queens, New York, which resulted in 1,200 housing units being built from 1924 to 1928.
- The same group, influenced by Benton MacKaye, proposed the creation of the Appalachian Trail as a project in regional planning.

Historical Snapshot
1930

- Unemployment passed four million
- The International Apple Shippers Association gave 6,000 jobless men surplus apples on credit to sell for $0.05 on street corners
- More than 1,352 banks closed in a single year
- The United States had one passenger car for every 5.5 persons; in the wake of the Depression, the car boom was collapsing
- Advertisers spent $60 million on radio commercials
- *The Big Trail*, starring John Wayne, *All Quiet on the Western Front*, *The Blue Angel*, *Monte Carlo*, and *Hell's Angels* all premiered
- Jean Harlow became a blonde for her role in *Hell's Angels*
- Hostess Twinkies, Snickers, sliced Wonder Bread, Jiffy biscuits, windshield wipers, Plexiglas and *Fortune* magazine all made their first appearance
- The University of Southern California polo team refused to play against the University of California at Los Angeles until the latter's one female member was replaced with a male
- Laurette Schimmoler of Ohio became the first woman airport manager
- The movie industry employed 100,000 people
- In fashion, the sophisticated Greta Garbo look was replacing the now passé flapper style of Clara Bow
- *As I Lay Dying* by William Faulkner and *The 42nd Parallel* by John Dos Passos were published; *Lincoln* by Emil Ludwig was a bestseller
- The first all-air commercial New York-to-Los Angeles transport was begun by Transcontinental and West Airlines
- "Georgia on My Mind," "What Is This Thing Called Love?" and "On the Sunny Side of the Street" were all popular songs
- A *Literary Digest* poll showed that 40 percent of the U.S. population favored the repeal of Prohibition, while 29 percent wanted modification
- Tree sitting, contact bridge and knitting were current fads, along with playing backgammon and "Sorry"
- America's illiteracy rate fell to 4.3 percent

1930 Economic Profile

Selected Prices

Borax, Muleteam $0.14
Candy Bar, Hershey's Almond $0.05
Chifforobe $18.95
Cold Cream $0.49
Dress, Ladies' Silk Crepe $2.98
Galoshes, Child's $0.98
Marshmallows, Kraft, 200 Count $0.65
Radio, Philco $20.00
Spark Plug, Champion $0.55
Tent, Boy's Camp $4.95
Thermometer, Fever $0.79
Tulip Bulbs, 20 .... $1.10
Valentines, 16 Cards $0.25
Washing Machine $57.95
Wristwatch, Man's Elgin, Gold $33.25

"The Homemaker's Calendar for October," *Modern Priscilla*, October 1929:

To keep the older children off the street on Halloween, and yet still have them satisfied, takes genius. Last year a neighbor had a particularly happy idea. She cleared a section of her basement and invited the neighborhood children to a basement party. The invitation was for 6:30 and implied that the children were not to dress up. The success of the evening was due to a definite plan of entertainment.

For the first half-hour the usual Halloween games were played, but when the older boys began to push each other's heads into the tub where they were bobbing for apples, the children were invited to sit in a circle and listen to stories of adventure, told by an understanding father. This was followed by a supper of nut-bread, cream cheese and olive sandwiches, individual pumpkin pies, and sweet cider. Milk was provided for the children who did not take cider. That supper might not become too riotous, several guessing games were played; guessing the number of kernels on an ear of corn, beans in a glass jar, and straws in a broom. Inexpensive prizes were given for the nearest guess to the correct number and, all too soon, it was 8:00, time for home.

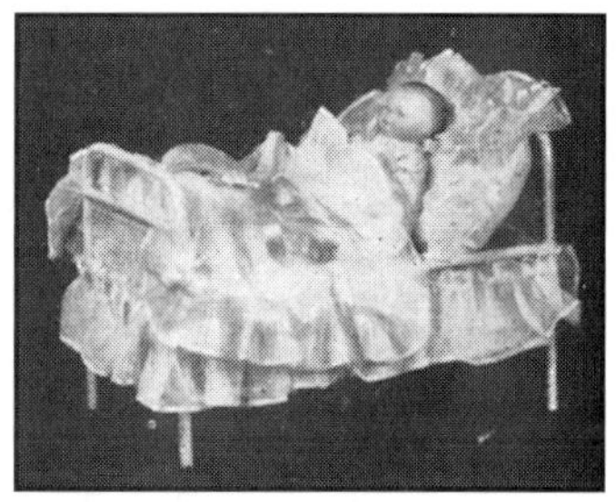

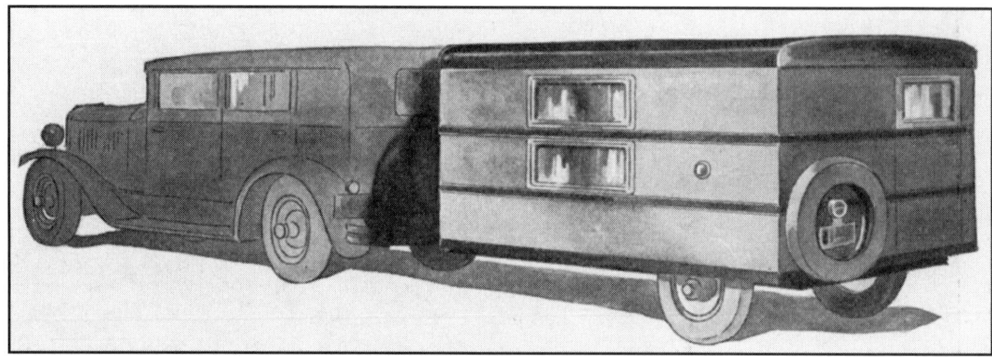

Americans are taking to the road in large numbers to travel and camp.

Changing America

- Automobile registration rose during the decade from eight million in 1920 to 23 million.
- The number of miles of paved roads doubled to 695,000 miles during the past decade.
- Movies began projecting 24 frames per second to accommodate sound, up from 16 frames per second during the silent movie era.

School Again!
Through the Magic Portal of September into the Bright Land of Sport, Fun, Study and Achievement!
EDUCATION (2)
THE HOPE OF A NATION POSTER SERIES
SEPTEMBER

- Movie attendance climbed to 90 million, up from 60 million only three years earlier.
- The proliferation of country clubs in New England, thanks to the automobile, led the well-respected professional journal, *Architectural Record*, to devote regular features to country club styles and influence.
- A clock using the natural vibration of a quartz crystal, subjected to an electrical current, was producing time accuracy within a thousandth of a second for the first time.
- Trousers were becoming acceptable attire for women who played golf and rode horses.
- 3M engineer Richard Drew invented Scotch tape to seal the cellophane used to wrap foods such as bread and candy.
- Presliced bread, introduced just two years earlier by inventor Otto Rohwedder, exceeded 50 percent of all bread sales across America.
- Public school children attended classes an average of 143 days a year; the average length of the school term nationwide was 172.7 days.
- Boeing Airline hired eight nurses to act as flight attendants.
- Alka-Seltzer was introduced by Miles Laboratories, Clairol hair products were invented by U.S. chemists, and Bird's Eye frozen foods were sold nationally for the first time.
- The cyclotron was created as a means of accelerating particles by magnetic resonance for the purpose of splitting atoms.
- The first analog computer was placed in operation by Vannevar Bush.
- WXBS, the CBS pioneer experimental television station, began operation; the first telecast was *Felix the Cat*.
- Rolex began selling the first waterproof watch, calling it the Oyster.

"Bananas for Babies," by L. von Meysenbug, M.D., *Modern Priscilla*, October 1929:

Not so very many years ago, certainly within the memory of most of the mothers who may chance to read this article, it was the universal custom to limit the infant's diet to milk, either from breast or bottle, for the first few years of its life. Most of the bottle-fed babies met a sad fate: those that did not perish from some nutritional disorder were so weakened as to fall easy prey to germ diseases. The fault lay not with the baby or its inheritance but was directly due to lack of knowledge of what to put into the bottle. Those that survived the crude feeding methods of the time did so because of good fortune or an unusually strong constitution.

Chemistry to the Rescue

Most of our modern knowledge of medicine, especially as applied to the science of nutrition, was sired by chemistry and rocked in the cradle of the laboratory. It would be impossible to estimate the number of lives that have been saved by the application of chemistry to medical practice. There is not an organ or tissue in the human body that has not been ground up in the mortar and poured into the test tube. The result is that of empiricism giving way to exact knowledge. The saving of infant life has been the chief concern of all humanity throughout the ages, and it is only within the past decade that this burden has been lightened so that we no longer stagger beneath the weight of our lost babies.

The World War furnished a tremendous impetus to the study of nutrition, for unlike all previous wars the principal problem was not prevention of infection but proper nutrition.

Napoleon's famous dictum that an army advances on its stomach might well be generalized by saying that the health and vigor of a nation depend upon what goes into the stomachs of its babies.

Facts vs. Prejudice

Before telling you how and why to feed bananas to your babies, let me explain why it is that the banana has acquired such a bad reputation.

Most children are extremely fond of bananas, and if they are old enough to toddle, will climb up on the sideboard or table, grab any banana within reach, bite off great chunks and gulp them down. If the banana happens to be ripe they may suffer only moderate discomfort; if it be green, heaven help them, for there will be much weeping and wailing and swallowing of castor oil! What's the reason for this? A very simple chemical reaction! In the semi-ripe or green banana, the bulk of its substance is composed of starch. As ripening takes place this starch is converted or split into a simple sugar, glucose, by the same process that takes place in our digestive tracts when we eat starchy foods, for all starches and sugars that we eat eventually become glucose before we absorb and assimilate them. Therefore, if we allow the banana to ripen properly we will have a food that is already predigested as far as its carbohydrate content is concerned. . . .

***Ultraviolet Mysteries, Sunrays and Health*, by Ronald Millar, 1929:**

It might just as well be confessed right here that nobody knows exactly how ultraviolet rays perform their miracles. On the other hand, there is not the least doubt that the miracles do happen.

These most versatile of all the sun's waves start their work before they ever reach the earth's surface. Fifty to a hundred miles above us they begin by manufacturing ozone out of the rarefied oxygen they encounter. This ozone forms a layer that acts at once as a shield against the sun's excessive violence and as a blanket to keep the lower atmosphere warm.

Lower down, they strike the same moisture and dust particles that scatter the blue and violet rays, and along with them, get partly spread out over the whole sky, so that when they finally reach the earth they are coming down from all sides as well as directly from the sun itself.

Once there, they promptly start doing their special part in helping the green trees and plants build the world's food and fiber supplies. Just what their exact share is in the growth of vegetation has not yet been cleared up, but it has been demonstrated that plants deprived entirely of ultraviolet rays, though they receive all kinds of sunlight, tend to develop all sorts of obscure weaknesses. Probably one of the chief roles of the ultraviolet ray is to stimulate cell division.

1930 News Feature

"What Does Vacation Mean to Your Child?"
by Helen Jackson, *Enlightened Homes*, June 1930:

The last day of school. How the children look forward to it, for it marks the beginning of the long summer vacation!

Unfortunately, many parents do not anticipate the holidays with the same high enthusiasm. They know from experience that after the first carefree weeks, the children become bored and more than a trifle unruly.

Modern educators believe that vacations should be used to supplement the work which school has been doing, and that the child should educate himself during the summer by pursuing his pet hobbies. Instead of disassociating all outside activity from school work, the two should be bound more closely together.

Children who attend the Lincoln School, the model school of Teachers' College in New York, begin to prepare for the summer vacation long before it actually starts, and they talk about it long after it is over. During the last weeks of the school term, the children are encouraged to decide what they will do while they are away from school. Sometimes the decisions are made because of the place the vacation will be spent, sometimes, entirely because of the child's interest in the subject.

This plan of encouraging the children to devote the summer months either to one or to a group of subjects has resulted most interestingly. Some exceedingly fine and well-labeled collections of seashells, of ferns and of flowers have been exhibited in the autumn. There also have been many samples of preserved fruits, delicately made electrical models, and many other fascinating exhibitions of the manner in which the children used the vacation period.

Even though children are tired of the vacation while school is closed, most of them are apt to regret the opening of school after the first few days when the initial novelty has worn off. At the Lincoln School it has been found that the work which has been carried on during the summer months gives the children so much that they want to tell their schoolmates, they return eager to talk about the new things they have discovered and to show what they have done. . . .

For children in the first grade, the vacation activities suggested include the collection of shells, butterflies, stones and the like; while for the fifth grade, more complex activities are

Modern educators believe children should be active in the summertime.

recommended such as the building of a fire-making apparatus, the compilation of a bird book, and the collection of odd coins and stones. But exactly what the child does is not as important as the fact that he does something.

Although the parents are urged not to do any actual work on the child's collection, their interest in the children's activity frequently determines the success of the summer's work. For a child's enthusiasm can be quickly killed by lack of interest on the part of its elders. This summer, instead of worrying about keeping the children amused, encourage them to devote the summer months to a hobby. There are multitudes of interesting things to do in the city as well as in the country. Invite the children to come into the kitchen, the boys as well as the girls, and allow them to make some simple dishes.

Let the boys go fishing if they wish. Encourage instead of scolding them when they bring home curiously colored stones. Vacations never need be dull, nor children bored, just so long as everyone knows they can be interesting. The first few days of vacation are especially important. If no plan has been made beforehand, it is more likely that the children will stay in bed late and then spend the morning lazily. One such lazy morning may be enjoyed, but if three or four of them are allowed, they become a habit.

Urge children to start the summer program in the first week of their vacation. If they are going to collect flowers or stones or shells, a picnic to the spot where the "hunting" is good will give their collections the right start. If the summer work is to consist of building delicate devices, some new tools, materials or blueprints can always be counted on to arouse enthusiasm.

Never worry that the children will need rest. Due to the change of routine and the new interest, the hours that they spend out of doors will provide all the rest they need.

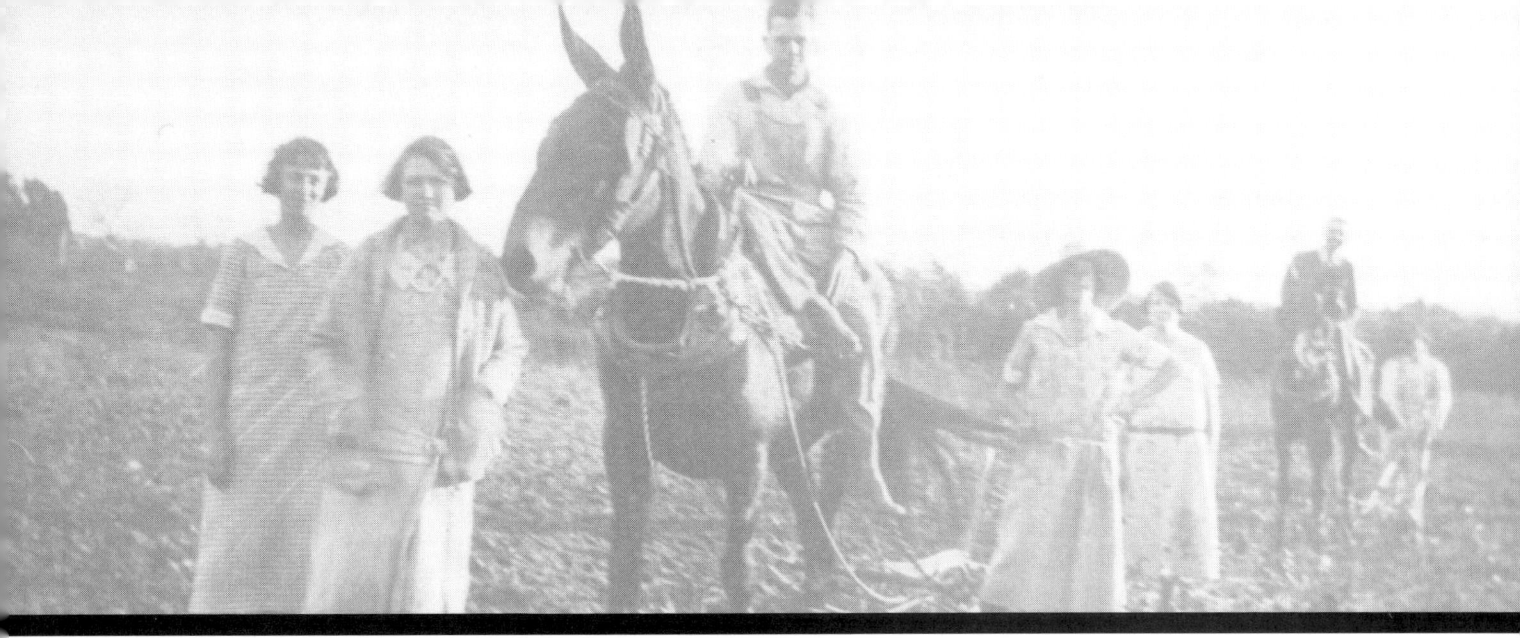

1934 Profile

Working Class

Twelve-year-old Martha Hope and her family are preparing to leave their farm and move into town after her father died and the farm had to be sold; the two children were told he died of pneumonia—a story that disregarded the facts.

Martha Hope is preparing to leave the farm.

Life at Home

- Martha's father's given name was Robert Hope, but everyone called him by his middle name, Meek.
- A farmer like his father before him, Meek raised cotton, but also kept an orchard of apples, grapes and peaches in York, South Carolina; the rest of the family's food was produced by the cows and chickens they raised.
- Meek took great pride in his looks and his farm, but his passion was his hunting dogs.
- Martha loves to tell how her daddy was so smart and his dogs so good, he could tell which dog was closest to catching the quarry based on its howl.
- He often traveled on weekends to demonstrate their hunting prowess in dog shows around the state.
- The dogs loved the trips so much they often waited on the running board of the old Ford truck he drove, eager for the next hunt to begin.
- When he came back from long trips he would bring both children an eight-inch stick of mint candy.
- Since he died all that has changed.
- Martha's mother Edna has been offered a job at a dry cleaner's in town, so she is moving her family to live in one part of her great-uncle's house, where she will pay room and board.

After the move into town, Sonny plans to be a super salesman.

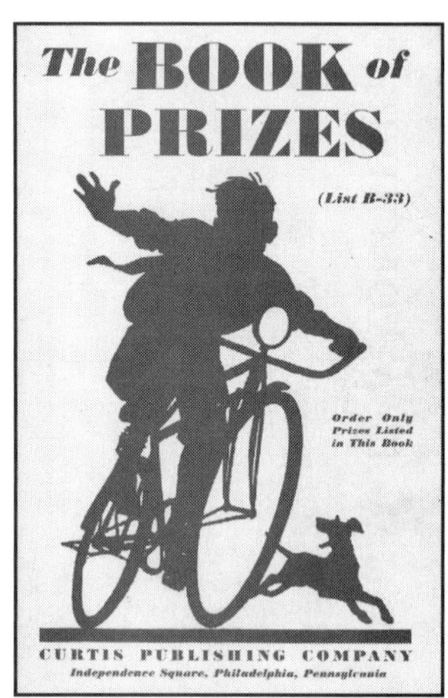

- Times are too tough for anyone to take on additional mouths for free, everyone says over and over.
- Even though the house is big, Martha is worried the yard is too small to grow the vegetables the family needs.
- When she found out the farm was going to be sold, she didn't even cry once—until her little brother Sonny started to.
- Sonny says he is excited about the move to town; he won't talk about his father's death, but instead tells everyone he plans to be a salesman for Curtis Publishing Company and win lots of prizes.
- At night he spends hours going through the book of prizes available to top student salesmen; he knows he can sell enough subscriptions to win a Columbia Motobike by gathering 800 brown vouchers.
- He also thinks he may be the "kick-the-can" champion of the world; every day he practices kicking an Esso oil can from the farm to Uncle Ted's store down the road and back to keep in practice.

- Most of their supplies come from the store, where Uncle Ted keeps lots of food in stock, but doesn't allow credit, especially to relatives.
- Sometimes, though, he gives away little treats, and has been generous with Ritz Crackers, which were introduced in the market last year by National Biscuit Company.
- Since the funeral, Martha has had to take on more responsibility for the family.
- Right after her father died, her aunt came to her and said, "You need to make sure your little brother knows that Santa Claus does not exist and won't be coming this year. There is no use pretending now."
- Martha did as she was told, because an adult said so, even though, until that moment, it had never occurred to her that Santa Claus wasn't real.

Most of the family's supplies come from Uncle Ted's store.

- For her entire life, the family cooked and heated their 900-square-foot house with a wood stove, sometimes sleeping in the kitchen for warmth during the coldest days of winter.
- The wood stove also operated around the clock during the summer months, when the temperature outside often hovered near 100 degrees.
- Wood had to be cut weekly to keep it running; pine made a good hot fire, but oak was needed to keep the stove warm.
- On cold mornings, the dogs fought over the chance to lie by the warm oven door.
- The house has no electricity, although the rural electrical cooperative has now extended lines to 10 miles' distance of the farm, with promises to hook up the rest within the year.
- On top of the wood stove rests a skillet of cornbread; even in bad times, cornbread and honey can be filling.
- They say it will be different in town, but she doesn't know if different is good or bad.
- On the farm, everyone has a role; most fieldwork was done by her father and a sharecropper who has a lifetime of experience with a steel plow pulled by a mule.
- Martha is proud that she can butcher her own meat, cut cane and chop cotton.
- Every year after the weather cooled, her family and one neighbor joined together to butcher three or four hogs.
- During that 18-hour stretch, the hogs were killed and bled, sausage was ground, liver pudding made, lard rendered from the fat and hams hung for curing.
- In the garden, her specialty has been growing turnips and string beans that could be sold at the farmer's market.

Martha cherishes a picture of herself with her parents.

Until recently, most work was done by Martha's father, a sharecropper, and a mule.

- Starting when she was nine, she planted her crop early and gambled that frost would not kill her plants so she would be the first to market with produce—earning a better price.
- This year, right after her father died, she convinced her uncle to take her and her turnip crop to market.
- When she arrived there, she found that refrigerator trucks carrying produce from Florida had beaten her there and forced down the prices; on top of everything in her life, it was a huge disappointment.
- She didn't have enough money to buy any extras, particularly bananas, which she loves.
- She is afraid a similar fate awaits this year's cotton crop; last time her father sold cotton it only brought $0.40 per pound, the lowest cotton had fallen since 1894.
- Times are so hard, a neighbor boy got one gift for Christmas—five shotgun shells costing a nickel a piece—and was told, "Make sure those shells bring food to the table."
- To help bring in the best possible crop, Martha has carefully treated the cotton with a mixture of arsenic and molasses, which she mopped on the cottons stalks to kill the boll weevils that seem to be destroying everyone's crop.
- When applying the arsenic, Martha is always careful not to get any on her hands or in her mouth; her friend Sarah was poisoned and missed several weeks of school—even missing story day when all the children get to read a tale of their own invention.

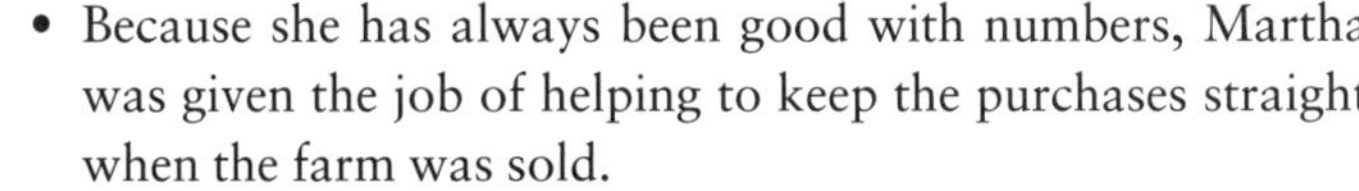

- Because she has always been good with numbers, Martha was given the job of helping to keep the purchases straight when the farm was sold.
- For one whole day she watched her father's entire life being auctioned; the day's total came to $841, after everyone paid like they were supposed to.
- Most of the bidders were from nearby farms, especially aunts and uncles who thought that helping to buy out the farm was a fair thing to do for brother Meek.
- Uncle Neely spent the most, $561, primarily for the mules, but Mr. W. W. Inman only spent $11 because no one wanted him to have anything; Meek's kin folks outbid him whenever he took a shine to anything.

Meek's hunting dogs often wait at the car for the next outing.

Partial listing of the estate of Robert Meek Hope, sold at auction, York, South Carolina, December 22, 1934:

Item	Price	Item	Price
Four Mules	561.00	Grindstone	1.45
Three Cows	72.00	Mailbox	0.50
Wagon	15.00	Farm Bell	1.00
Wagon Harness	9.50	Wheelbarrow	1.50
Horse Collars	1.75	Wagon Wheels	0.60
Disc Harrow	8.50	Hack Saw	0.45
Tractor Harrow	26.00	Pipe Wrench	0.75
Four Side Harrows	8.20	Grain Cradle	0.75
Two Drag Harrows	2.25	Mowing Scythe	1.25
Stalk Cutter	0.60	Pitch Fork	0.50
Mower	1.25	Two Shovels	0.55
Seed Fork and Rake	1.00	Gears	3.80
Five Cotton Planters	14.50	Anvil	2.50
Corn Planter	2.60	Hoses	4.40
Guano Plow	1.00	Manure Spreader	1.00
Single Row Oat Drill	3.60	Crosscut Saw	0.45
Three Row Oat Drills	4.70	Dinner Bell	2.00
Four Plow Sacks	0.70	Icebox	2.50
Four Turn Plows	20.00	Cabinet	3.00
Middle Buster	1.75	Wardrobe	2.80
Three Go-Devils	2.50	Table	2.10
Shop Tools	6.50	Baby Bed	0.25
Bellows	1.25	Two Beds and Springs	3.00
Blower	4.50	Bureau	5.75
Corn Sheller	1.20		

- She thinks it serves him right for talking bad about her daddy after he died; everyone in the family knows he died of pneumonia, but he kept telling them he died from a knife wound he caught in a bar fight down the road.
- The only things the family kept were two beds, one for Martha and her brother and one for Momma, and the portable Victrola Meek bought for his wife; Momma didn't want to give it up for any amount of money.
- Currently, a big argument has erupted concerning the 13-year-old black girl named Lucinda who lives with the family.
- Two years ago, when Lucinda's father tossed her out of the house for talking back, Edna found her crying on the back steps and took her in.
- Shortly thereafter Lucinda's father moved off the farm and has not been heard from since.
- Lucinda has lived with Edna, Meek, Martha and Sonny ever since, sleeping in a cot in the back of the house.
- Martha and Lucinda do everything together—especially if dolls are involved—except go to school.

Martha has been pouring over the Montgomery Ward catalog.

- Even though Lucinda is a year older, she is still on the third-year reader, and Martha helps her with her schoolwork at night.
- All the relatives are urging Edna to turn Lucinda out when they move into the city, saying, "Let the coloreds take care of their own; you've got troubles enough."
- Martha has begged her mother to take Lucinda when moving day comes, reminding her that when Daddy died, Lucinda acted like family, carefully and quietly stopping all the clocks in the house and draping the mirror with a black cloth.
- Momma says she may have to think about what's best for the entire family.

Life at School and Work

- In preparation for the new school year, Martha has been poring over the Montgomery Ward catalog.
- Some people in the neighborhood are Sears fans, but this family has always found Montgomery Ward to be fair.
- In her heart, Martha knows that no money will be available for new dresses this year, but looking at the wonderful pictures keeps her hopes up.
- In the new school year, Sonny will be in the second grade, and hopes there are pictures on the wall like in his old classroom.
- In the first grade he was able to learn how to tie his shoes by looking at a detailed, step-by-step drawing on the wall; some days they even practiced in class.
- Like most farm boys, before starting school, Sonny rarely wore shoes, except for his Sunday shoes, which fastened with a buckle.
- His first-grade teacher, Miss Gaillard, has attended at least two summer sessions at Newberry College, but was not a high school graduate; her formal education ended in the sixth grade, so she was permitted only to teach through the fourth grade.
- When Miss Gaillard is sick or away, Martha teaches Sonny's class because she is the best reader in the school.
- Martha's sixth-grade class program included a commemoration of George Washington's birthday, featuring a program of readings and songs.
- At Easter a pageant was performed in two acts—"At Calvary on the Green Hill Far Away" and "At the Tomb on Sabbath Dawn," followed by an Easter egg hunt.
- Martha was proud to play the role of Martha at the tomb when the stone was rolled away.
- Her father came to both presentations, but didn't say much afterward—he rarely did.
- For her little brother's birthday, Martha and her mother are making a stuffed character from his favorite storybook, *Where's Angus?*
- It has an embroidered nose, mouth and eyes, and a red ribbon with little silver bells around its neck.
- After the farm was sold, Martha's Aunt Cora gave her a gift—a booklet called "How to Make Draperies" by the Singer Sewing Machine Company.
- Since she was a little girl, Martha has enjoyed helping her mother pump the pedal on the family sewing machine, and has been praying she will learn fast enough so she can sew herself a dress to wear to the new school.

Buying Drapery Fabrics, How to Make Draperies, Slip Covers, Cushions and Other Home Furnishings the Modern Singer Way, 1934:

Drapery fabrics rather than dress fabrics are invariably better suited to draperies, especially in texture and color. Fabrics of similar weight and texture often cost less in the drapery department than in the dress fabric department, and the designs are usually more suitable. There are, however, many fabrics obtainable in the dress fabric department that are desirable to use, such as calico, gingham, unbleached muslin and organdie. On the other hand, dotted Swiss, silks for draperies, cretonne and casement cloths should be purchased in the drapery department.

- One of Martha's remaining concerns is the road grader man.
- Ever since she can remember, the man from the county who scrapes the gravel roads three times a year has allowed her to ride in the truck when he cleaned ditches and graded the road.
- At the end of each trip he said, "Thanks for your help; I don't know if I could have done it without you."
- She doesn't even have a way to tell him she can't help him anymore.

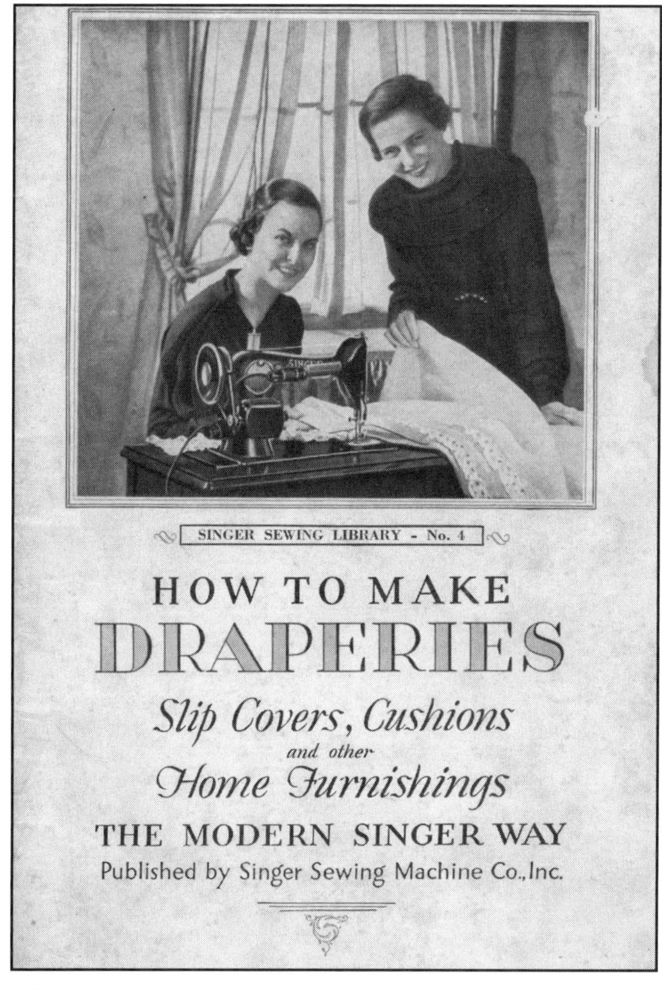

After her father died, Martha was given a book on how to make draperies.

Life in the Community: York, South Carolina

- South Carolina's foreign-born population is only one percent, one of the lowest in the nation; of its 1.8 million citizens, the racial mix is 54.3 percent white and 45.7 percent black.
- Agriculture dominates the state's economy, with two-thirds of the state's 166,000 farms operated by tenants who do not own the land they till.
- South Carolina's 110,000 manufacturing jobs rank sixth among the Southern states; the average annual wage is $615.
- Because the Depression has hit the farm community even worse, the per capita income of South Carolinians has dropped from $261 in 1929 to $150 in five years.
- Only two percent of the state's farms have electricity; with no lights, rural residents of the state tend to go to bed with the chickens.
- To balance the state budget, Gov. Ibra Blackwood reduced state salaries, and employees are paid in state scrip.

"Discipline," *The Tompkins School, 1925 to 1953, A Community Institution*, by T. Felder Dorn, 1994:

The switch and the ruler were prominent implements for administering justice and maintaining order. Standing in the corner with our back to the class or standing in the cloak room during recess (which, recalls one culprit, "broke your heart on a nice day") were also used. The types of devilment that merited punishment often were rather banal—sticking out one's feet to trip a classmate en route to the front of the room, fighting or ugly name-calling, backtalk or sass to a teacher, horsing around on the bus or sailing paper airplanes. Other infractions, such as tipping over the girls' toilet, setting the woods on fire, sneaking off to the creek, or playing on April Fools' Day were a bit more daring. Putting a crayon on a hot stove was a stunt that usually permitted the instigator to escape detection, but it made quite a stink.

One or two teachers acknowledged their prowess with the rod, but others spoke of using the switch sparingly, adding that children minded them. Two teachers, whose tenures at the school were separated by a number of years, were recalled by different pupils with identical words: "She was a lovely lady, but she would tear you up." A punishment for younger pupils recalled most vividly by some who received it began with a teacher grasping the offender's hand and giving it some sound whacks with a sturdy 12-inch ruler.

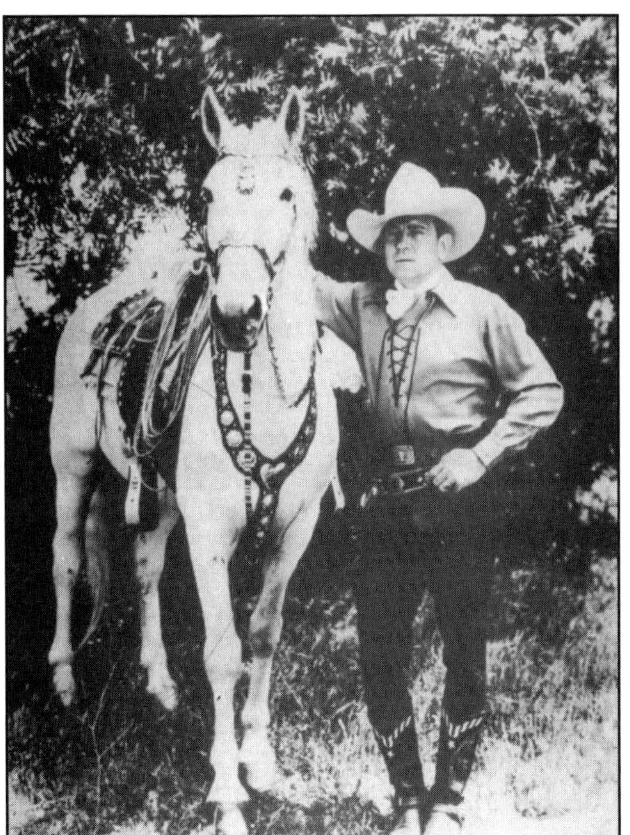

Hop-Along Cassidy is one of Martha's favorites.

- No safety net exists for families.
- The state's constitution permits assistance only for Confederate veterans, their widows and faithful slaves.
- South Carolina is one of six states without old-age pensions, one of 14 without assistance for the blind, and one of two with no aid for dependent children.
- The unemployment rate now exceeds 30 percent, and in some rural parts of the state the elderly are reported to be dying of starvation.
- The Works Progress Administration (WPA), administered by the federal government, is beginning to transform the economic landscape, building roads, schools, bridges and dams.
- Recently, the General Assembly created the Public Service Authority, known as Santee-Cooper, to produce and sell electricity, develop inland navigation along three South Carolina rivers, reclaim swamps and reforest watersheds.

Historical Snapshot
1934

- Leni Riefenstahl directed *Triumph of the Will*, documenting the rise of the Third Reich in Germany
- The Civil Works Administration provided employment for four million people
- Donald Duck, Walgreen's drugstores, Flash Gordon, Seagram's Seven Royal Crown and the term "hi-fi" all made their first appearance
- Ernest and Julio Gallo invested $5,900 in a wine company
- The birth of the Dionne quintuplets in Ontario stirred international interest
- The ongoing drought reduced the national corn crop by nearly one billion bushels
- Edna St. Vincent Millay published *Wine from These Grapes*; F. Scott Fitzgerald completed *Tender Is the Night*
- Dicumarol, an anticoagulant, was developed from clover
- "Tumbling Tumbleweeds," "I Only Have Eyes for You" and "Honeysuckle Rose" were all popular songs
- The Securities and Exchange Commission was created
- The movie *It Happened One Night* won academy awards for Best Picture, Best Director (Frank Capra), Best Actress (Claudette Colbert) and Best Actor (Clark Gable)
- The U.S. Gold Reserve Act authorized the president to devalue the dollar
- Enrico Fermi suggested that neutrons and protons were the same fundamental particles in two different quantum states
- The FBI shot John Dillinger, Public Enemy No. I, generating a hail of publicity
- Greyhound bus lines cut its business fares in half to $8 between New York and Chicago to encourage more traffic

1934 Economic Profile

Selected Prices

Apples, Box of 100 . . . . $3.25
Baby Powder, Johnson & Johnson $0.29
Binoculars $33.48
Cloth, Silk and Cotton Crepe, Yard $0.35
Cook Stove, Cast Iron. $21.50
Croquet Set $3.98
Gum, Wrigley's Spearmint $0.37
Hair Clipper $3.87
Hog Troughs, Steel $0.48
Iron, Electric $1.00
Light Bulbs, Eight, 40-Watt. $1.00
Mattress, 54". $4.65
Phonograph Record $0.29
Saw, 3.5' $1.48
Shampoo, Coconut Oil $0.49

"Sour Milk, Buttermilk and Baking Soda," *Good Things to Eat*, Arm & Hammer Baking Soda, 1933:

Sour milk is best for baking purposes when it has reached the clabbered stage. The curd is thick and heavy, and the whey has not separated to any great extent. It should be clean and in a covered container. If milk is placed in the refrigerator as soon as it reaches the clabbered stage, it will remain in this condition for three or four days and can be used as needed.

Half-teaspoon baking soda with 1 cup clabbered milk will leaven 2 cups flour. Buttermilk can be substituted for clabbered milk.

"From Inner Tubes to Rubber Dollies," by Mabel Dunlap, *Junior Home for Parent and Child*, March 1934:

Do you remember the little girl who sang, "My mother told me that she would buy me a rubber dollie if I'd be good"? Well, you can make these rubber dolls yourself. And you can wash them and dress them as well!

Get a worn-out inner tube and wash it well so that you will not soil your dress while working on it. A light-colored tube makes Suki and Eva; and a black one, Mammy and Topsy. The big picture of Eva, Figure 1. may be used as an idea for each doll. And each doll has a front and back just alike. Fill the inside with cotton or cloth and sew the doll together with a rather large needle and strong thread. The hair and features of Suki and Eva may be drawn with India ink. The lips, of course, are made with red ink. The dotted lines give you an idea for the dress. You can, of course, make changes for the different dolls. Suki's and Mammy's dress will be longer than the other two. Mammy's head kerchief is a triangle of bright cloth, three by five inches. Her shawl collar is a bigger square of white cloth, and her apron is just a rectangle of white cotton. Sew this into a long, narrow strip that serves as the ties. Her dress might be bright red. Make her two little earrings of bright-colored paper and attach them to her kerchief.

For the black faces, cut the eyes and mouths from the light-colored rubber. (Color the mouths red with white centers, and eyes are shown in Figures 4 and 5). Glue them to the black faces. Topsy's pigtails should be cut in one piece with the head, and little red string bows form her ribbons. Her dress might be dark blue, with several bright patches on it. And her belt might be just a string.

Suki, the little Japanese doll, might be dressed in yellow with a bright-colored sash tied at the back. With Crayolas or ink, make a circle on the front and back of her dress, something like the one shown in Figure 3.

In making the dresses for Topsy and Eva, simply cut the sleeves shorter. Highlights on the faces of Topsy and Mammy may be made with white ink, or you can cut small pieces from the light-colored rubber and glue them on.

Make Eva's dress from any pretty material you may have. If you have some narrow lace, you might put that around the neck, sleeves and bottom of the skirt. All the dresses will have openings in order to get them on the dollies!

Changing America

- California physician Francis Townsend's old-age pension plan, which gained wide popular support, proposed levying a two percent tax that would provide $200 a month to all Americans over 60, who would then be required to spend their allotment within a month, thus spurring the economy.
- The average teacher's pay in South Carolina dipped to $683 a year, a decline from the $890 paid during the 1925-6 academic year.
- The massive migration of workers westward continued.
- Coca-Cola sales dropped with the repeal of Prohibition.
- The Sears & Roebuck catalog began listing contraceptive devices.
- Of the 343 golf courses across America, many private courses became public links as the middle class began participating in the rich man's sport.
- A renewed passion for hiking and sunbathing invited briefer sportswear.

- U.S. physicist Isidor Isaac Rabi began his work on the atomic and molecular beam magnetic resonance method for observing spectra in the radio frequency range.
- The A&P grocery store chain now controlled 11 percent of grocery sales.
- The average annual earnings for a physician were $3,382, and $8,663 for a congressman.
- The fan club for Buck Jones, America's number one movie cowboy, had grown to more than three million members.

"Safe Relief from Nervous Tension," ***Dr. Miles New Weather Almanac and Handbook of Valuable information*****, 1934:**

America lives on its nerves. The machine age has lightened physical labor, but has made nerve strain infinitely more severe. As a result, more people than ever before are suffering from diseases caused or made worse by overtaxed nerves. Never before have so many people needed the relief, poise, relaxation and rest that comes from using a good nerve sedative such as Dr. Miles Nervine.

When you feel tense and keyed up; when you are irritable, restless and blue; when you can't sleep, worry over trifles, want to avoid social gatherings; have nervous headaches, nervous indigestion, a bottle of Dr. Miles Nervine will bring about a wonderful change for the better.

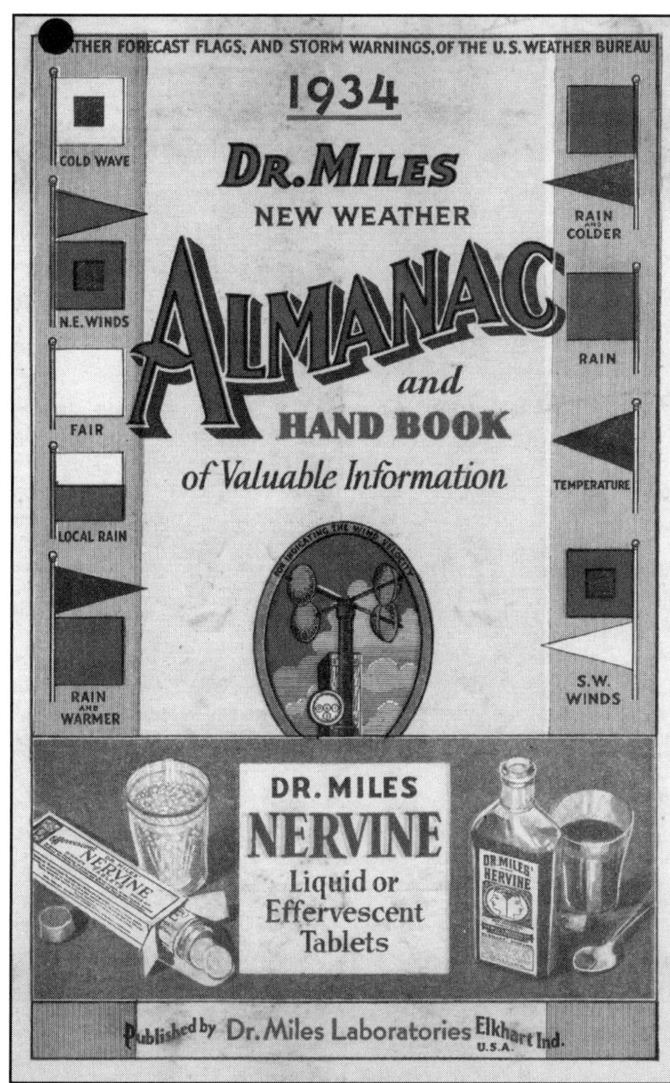

Shirley Temple is a beloved child star in films.

LIFE CAN BE BOUGHT

ISN'T IT WORTH TEN DOLLARS TO KEEP ANY AMERICAN BOY ALIVE?

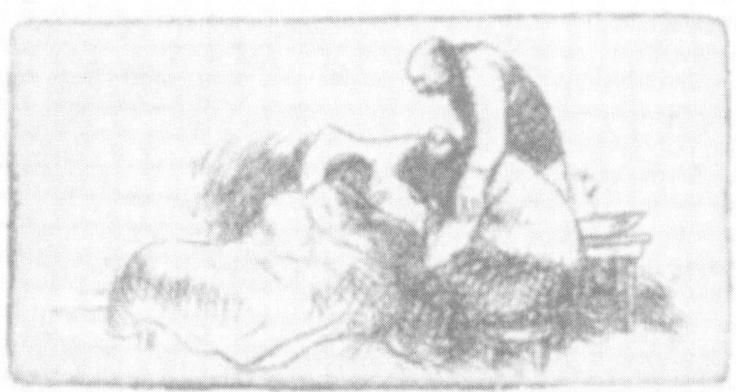

1936 News Feature

"Life Can Be Bought, Isn't It Worth Ten Dollars to Keep Any American Boy Alive?" by Paul De Kruif, *Coronet*, November 1936:

In our wealthy country you can buy life, yes, if you've got plenty of money; and if, on the other hand, you're sunk into the rearguard of those millions who've no longer any shame about swearing the pauper's oath, then if you're properly respectful you can get a dole of life, but God pity you if you're independent and belong to the middle class millions in between. In the last few years I have seen many specific examples of how life can be bought; but what finally drove the infamy, the insult to humanity of this dollar-traffic in life home to me was the way Anthony Scharf and his wife came so near being able to buy life for their four-year-old boy, Anthony, Jr.

There should have been no ifs or buts about Anthony and Elsbeth Scharf buying the best chance of life for the child, frightfully endangered as he was, because, forgetting the merely human end of it, you can prove that an immediate fight to save his life would have been good business for the city of Chicago, and for America. You see, one of the most distinguished authorities on the dollar-value of human life is Doctor Louis I. Dublin, who has figured out that the capital value of a boy baby's life is $9,000, while that of a baby girl is $4,000. There must, therefore, be something rotten in America, since the experience of the Scharf parents proves that the chance to guard the imperiled $9,000 of their Anthony was lost by an argument about $18.75. . . .

The Scharf family's nickname for little Anthony was "Brother," and Brother was a husky boy, living with his younger brother and baby sister, and his grandma, Mrs. Margaret Bircher, in a small house among a row of similar respectable houses under shade trees, on Oakley Avenue, Chicago. Just after seven, Sunday evening of June 14, Elsbeth Scharf—who'd just got out of St. Bernard's Hospital that morning—heard a scream and rushed out her front door, to see Brother being carried toward the house, screaming and bleeding. A Spitz dog had bitten him, and had then run up on a porch and bitten another dog. Brother had been badly slashed across his little face, and bitten on one arm and one leg.

What Elsbeth Scharf now did instantly, automatically, shows her intelligence, and reflects upon the prejudices of those of our prosperous fat boys and girls, and our social workers, too, who feel that working people have their own stupidity and negligence to thank for their misfortunes. Right away Elsbeth called the family doctor. Yes, the dog was foaming at the mouth, she said. And, before you could take time to tell it—sick as she herself still was—Brother was in her arms, only sobbing now, in a neighbor's automobile on the way to St. Bernard's Hospital.

Here the wounds on his arm and leg were cauterized, the bleeding, deep cut under his eye was burned out, and closed with stitches. Should she report the dog to the police or the Health Department? No, the hospital would do that. The next day the police came to take the dog, who since that day had bitten the wife of its owner, away to the pound. Should Brother have the shots that are given for rabies? Elsbeth was anxious. She wanted to know where she was at, she said. The police said no, but to wait for a report from the Health Dept.

That was Monday, June 15, and the next day, Tuesday, sure enough, a Health Department doctor came, round noon, and said, yes, the dog was mad and not to lose any time, but to "take the child down to have the shots." Even last night the family doctor had been anxious to have the rabies vaccine started, and today Elsbeth Scharf didn't have to be told to hurry, knowing face-bites by mad dogs are most dangerous. . . . But now Elsbeth couldn't go—just out of the hospital as she was, and with the doctor's orders to stay in bed.

Well, thank heavens here was her mother, Grandma Bircher, who, as she afterwards told it, grabbed her hat in one hand and Brother with the other, and right away set off downtown to the Health Department in the City Hall . . . Now the youngster would be all right, hardly a doubt of it. Here was Aunty Meisser, and in Grandma Bircher's purse there was a ten dollar bill and a slip that had two men's names on it, if you don't find one of them at the Health Department, the other'll take care of the child, only hurry, you don't monkey round with a baby who's been bit in the face, the Health Department doctor had got that clear in Grandma Bircher's head . . .

They were eager for the guarding of the life of this sturdy, bandaged-faced four-year-old Brother, the protection, the excellent chance of it in spite of the dangerous face wound, made possible by the powerful science discovered by the greatest of all medical scientists, Louis Pasteur. Now Grandma Bircher, though not mind you a learned woman, yet had her share of the almost universal people's faith in Pasteur's treatment, and, loving her little grandson dearly, Grandma was determined Brother must begin his shots, today, right now. . . .

So Grandma Bircher walked into the Health Department this day with confidence, leading bandaged-faced little Anthony. Our municipalities guard us against fire, against murderers, and this protection comes out of our tax-money. Surely protection of our babies against mad dogs—for those running at large the community is absolutely responsible—is also a public service, not to be bought with dollars! So now, if he could have known what now began to happen, wouldn't old Louis Pasteur have turned over in his grave?

Grandma Bircher, and Aunty Meisser, and four-year-old Brother, done up in bandages, came into the Health Department office, and, exactly as she was told, Grandma Bircher asked to see Mr. Chapman, right now, since it was an emergency, since they must hurry, but Mr. Chapman was out, they were sorry and could Grandma please wait, and now Grandma, and Aunty Meisser, and little Brother sat there waiting just about two hours as Grandma and Aunty both remembered it, and you must admit that was a bit tough on all three of them—especially little Brother who'd not yet got over the horrible fright from the mad dog's attack, nor over his pain—but let that pass. At the end of this time Grandma asked had Mr. Chapman come back, and was then told they were sorry, but Mr. Chapman had gone . . .

But there was another official who looked at the slip Grandma Bircher handed him, asked when was the little boy bitten, then said, "this will cost you $18.75."

This was a slight surprise to Grandma Bircher, who doubtless, in a dim way, felt that Brother really had this protection coming from the city, didn't she and the Scharf's pay taxes; and wasn't the city, after all, responsible for the public menace of thousands of dogs unmuzzled, then running at large, with hundreds of them biting people, children, and many of those dogs mad? But Grandma did not at this moment argue; instead she answered all she had with her was $10. Well, sorry, but—for folks who weren't poor—the shots for children who were bitten on the face must have 21 shots instead of 14, 21 shots cost $18.75. So, now, since Grandma Bircher had only $10 with her, she was given another slip of paper, she must go now to Room 1130, County Building, to the Bureau of Public Welfare.

So now Grandma, Aunty Meisser, and Brother who was getting pretty tired and fidgety, had a new experience, new for all three of them. For the first time in their lives they tasted the tender mercy of a social worker. It was Miss Ruth Coleman. . . .

Had Mrs. Bircher ever been on charity and did she own her own home and why hadn't this little boy's mother come down with him? But wait, said Grandma, her daughter, Mrs. Scharf, who was the little boy's mother, was sick, just out of the hospital, still sick in bed, and they weren't on relief. Mr. Scharf was a mail-carrier, and couldn't they have the order for the shots, right now. Grandma had $10 with her, and she had her homeowner's loan, and would come down with the $8.75 in the morning!

No, it was $18.75 or nothing, Miss Coleman said. And then there was another barrage of questions: Did this little boy's mother owe a hospital bill, and how much, and how much did they owe the doctor, and what was the little boy's father's income, and how much did Mr. Scharf make a week? And the now thoroughly confused and puzzled Grandma Bircher said she did not know, she could not answer. . . .

Now Grandma made one last effort, and these are her words, to which she later testified, under oath, "I went over and offered her ten dollars and she refused it." She said, "Eighteen seventy-five or nothing." And I said, "Would you let that little child die of rabies? And she said, "Well, that was our lookout."

So Grandma Bircher left the Public Welfare Office, crying and at 5:30 that evening she got back home with Brother, who was very tired. That was June 16, two days after Brother had been bitten dangerously in the face by a rabid dog, and the next day, starting at 10 the next morning, Grandma went downtown again, with Brother, and Precinct Captain Cramer to help her, and after an elaborate row between Miss Coleman, Precinct Captain Cramer, Grandma, and by telephone, Elsbeth Scharf, who was asked the same snooping questions over, they emerged from the Welfare Office in triumph with orders for free shots of rabies vaccines. . . .

Now there began, in the body of the little Brother Scharf who was a most innocent bystander in this strange fight for buying of the very best chance for life, another kind of battle. It was a mysterious, hidden, unseen fight in Brother's young body, between the subvisible murderous rabies microbes, and the forces of microbe-fighting resistance which must now, finally, be stirred up, mobilized, by the Pasteur treatment.

Now time went on, and now Brother had had all of his 21 shots that the City of Chicago recommends for such dangerous face-bitten cases, and everything was all right, and every day Brother went out to play, and was happy, except that he was terrified of all dogs, any dog would set him running for home, crying, but he was fine, he had never been sick a day in his life, and now it was all of 36 days after the accident, and Brother complained of bad itching in his face where he'd been bitten but of course, said Elsbeth and Grandma, that meant the wound was getting all better.

Now it was 38 days, getting toward the number of days when all danger would be over, and Elsbeth—whose memory is accurate to the point of uncanny—remembers that it was quarter to five in the morning that Brother awakened her, crying, and saying he was so thirsty, and could he have a drink of water, and when Elsbeth gave him the glass, she noticed that his hand was trembling, and then when he tried to drink the water, he - couldn't. . . .

Then Brother screamed, and then he said, “Hold me tight, mommy, I’m so afraid, oh, hold me, mommy!”

By nine o’clock that morning they’d got hold of Dr. Taylor, who’d given the injections, and over the telephone he said it sounded bad, and they should rush little Anthony to St. Bernard’s Hospital. Elsbeth remembered Brother crying and saying he didn’t want to go to the hospital, and then asking: “Mommy, will they give me a baby if I go to the hospital like they did you?” And so he’d stop crying Elsbeth said sure, they would, they’d give him twins if he was a good boy, and that same evening, at 8:40, Brother died, which was very merciful. . . .

You say of course that anything after this is anti-climax, and you say so what, and you say that’s another one of those things, and so it would seem to those who may remember photographs of little Brother, dressed all in white and so beautiful, really peaceful in his white coffin, and pictures, in the newspapers, of that little casket, white, being carried down the church steps by six of Brother’s playmates, all in white, very appropriately. It seemed just another of those sob-stories. So in a couple of days the story was dead.

But a story like this never dies, though I will admit that this will be revealed only by deducing its effect on the heart and brain of Elsbeth Scharf. This never-smiling workingman’s wife, in her day-and-night, bitter retrospect, has swallowed this final insult, that life is for those who can buy it.

Elsbeth knows—and the most sophisticated microbe-hunting savant cannot gainsay her!—that, if her little boy had had the best chance for life, he might still be living—just as that dog is living today, the dog that was bitten by the Spitz dog who bit her Anthony. That dog had shots promptly, and that dog is alive and back home.

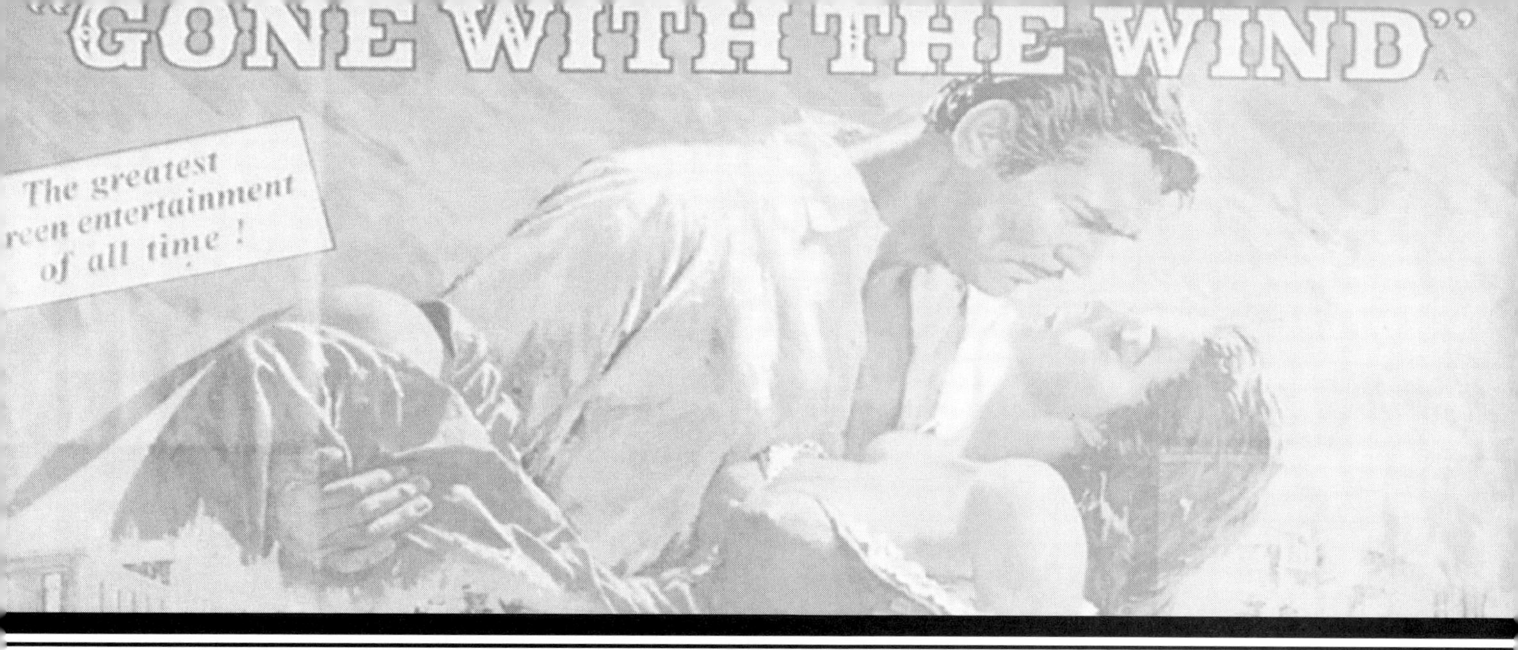
"GONE WITH THE WIND"
The greatest
reen entertainment
of all time!

1937 Profile

Upper Class

Thirteen-year-old Roddy Waggoner and his sisters have recently been allowed to return to their parents' home in Maine after four years of living in seclusion on a remote Georgia barrier island, hiding from potential kidnappers.

Life at Home

- Following the kidnapping of Charles Lindbergh's baby in March 1932, and a subsequent wave of kidnappings—both child and adult—the Waggoner family bought an isolated Southern plantation, where the children could be hidden.
- Their father discovered the island while on a duck hunting trip with fellow businessmen in January 1934, and bought it immediately, knowing it was the safest place in the world for his three children.
- For their protection, Roddy and his sisters have lived with tutors, nannies, and occasionally their mother—who hated the heat of the South.
- Their father, a highly visible, prosperous businessman from Maine, visited his children four times a year, though he, too, struggled with the heat, mosquitoes and humidity of the South and ordered that a pink indoor swimming pool, complete with fountains, be constructed for the children.
- The first year was difficult, especially when Christmas came and went without a hint of snow in southern Georgia.
- At first, Mr. Waggoner allowed no contact between the children and the two dozen African-Americans, all descendents of slaves, who lived on the island, but eventually he relented.
- He insisted, however, that a Maine-trained cook prepare meals, because he did not want his children returning home with a taste for mushy, overcooked vegetables, runny grits and fried meats of unknown origin.

Roddy Waggoner has recently returned home.

On the island, Roddy enjoyed the migration of winter ducks and white pelicans.

- The three-mile-long island, formerly home to a prosperous cotton plantation owner prior to the Civil War, had fallen into disrepair during the previous two decades.
- As no roads lead to the island, only boats traveling through grassy marshes and swamps could reach the plantation; to navigate the tidal creeks and disappearing mudflats from the mainland required extensive experience.
- During the children's first year on the island, they lived almost exclusively in a newly constructed building with bars on all the windows and were guarded 24 hours a day, sleeping and doing schoolwork there while the main house was being reconstructed.
- After the second year, they had the run of the island, except the potentially dangerous section near the tiny boat landing, where kidnappers might be lurking.
- Occasionally, security was tightened, such as when little George Weyerhaeuser was kidnapped in 1935, but largely the island was theirs to roam.
- Last year, their father built a giant wall around their Bangor, Maine, property to maintain a sense of security and hasten the return of his children.
- The sprawling Maine mansion was built in the 1850s by a lumber and ship baron, and purchased by the Waggoner family in the 1920s.
- The children's grandmother refers to the past four years as "your time away," as though they had been visiting an aunt in New York City for the summer.
- Now, as a united family, many evenings are spent playing a long game of Monopoly.
- Roddy became quite experienced at playing this popular board game against his tutors and sisters during his last

Ospreys built huge nests on the island.

year on the island; not only is it competitive, he can get rich by thinking faster and planning better than everyone else.

- When Parker Brothers began selling the game two years ago, it became a national mania almost overnight, played by rich and poor alike.
- Roddy's sister often doesn't play, but sits close by working and reworking her favorite puzzle of a child playing with toys on his bed.
- At her side is her Dangle Dolly, a gift from her best friend when she came back from Georgia.
- One of Roddy's new obsessions is listening to the radio, something he missed in remote Georgia; his favorite programs include quiz shows in which he can match wits with experts such as "Professor Quiz."
- His father, while proud, becomes very vexed when his son shouts out the answers ahead of the radio guests.
- Roddy also wears his Junior G-Man badge everywhere; he sent away for the radio premium right after he returned to Maine.
- Upon returning home, one of the first stops was New York for new clothes, and then a trip to Coney Island.
- While in Georgia, Roddy and his sisters had read extensively about the amusement park and considered themselves experts, even though they had never been there.
- In the car driving to Coney Island, they all insisted that the first stop be Nathan's to buy a hot dog, followed by dessert from Philips.

After returning, one of their first stops was Coney Island.

"Kidnapping: Epidemic of Seizures for Ransom, with More Adults Than Children Abducted, Raises New National Problem, *News-Week*, July 22, 1933:

The sinister word, "Kidnapped," screamed from the front page of the country's newspapers last week. From New York State to the Pacific Coast, aroused communities read of adults snatched from their homes and held for high ransom. In many places guards were thrown around the homes of men of wealth. Defenseless friends and relatives of the victims of what seemed to be organized bands, worked through intermediaries with underworld connections, fearful lest the intervention of police might lead to the killing of the kidnapped.

Definitely a national kidnap fear developed. From city after city came rumors that such and such a prominent resident had received threats. So alarmed by kidnap threats was the Hollywood colony, that many film stars hired special guards. In Chicago, homes of 50 wealthy citizens were being guarded. Baltimore had a bad kidnap scare. Extra guards were assigned to watch the president's grandchildren . . .

PENALTIES: At the present time, the emergence of "Whiskers," as gangsters call Uncle Sam's agents, throws fear into every kidnapper, contemptuous, as a rule, of local police. The Patterson-Cochran bills, passed by Congress in 1932 after the Lindbergh case, impose a maximum penalty of 20 years in prison and a fine of $5,000 "for the use of the mails to convey threats to injure, to kidnap, to accuse of crime, or to demand ransom or reward for the return of an abducted person." Where a kidnapped person is taken across a state line, the judge upon the conviction of the kidnappers may impose any sentence up to life imprisonment. This is the only federal statute with such broad provisions.

C.M. Burd
And all my toys beside me lay
To keep me happy all the day.

Roddy's sister spends hours reworking her favorite puzzle.

- After all he had read, Roddy was surprised that Philips was so small, just a little red-and-white wood candy stand on Surf Avenue, but he was thrilled by the taste of the chocolate jelly bar they bought; his older sister got a cashew cluster.
- The whirl of activity, the breeze and the candy made it a day close to Heaven, all capped off with a fireworks display that danced in his head for weeks.
- After four years of living on the island, he was shocked to see beaches so packed with people he could barely see the sand; it looked like all of America had come to Coney Island to play.
- Slowly, he is learning the pattern of being in Maine, near his parents again and away from the island he grew to love.
- He is still often surprised at the level of urgency everyone feels about time.

- Some days, even his teachers seem more focused on time than on teaching properly; on the island they took as much time as was needed for the children to grasp the subject and then moved on.
- His mother believes he has become far too independent and adventuresome during his time away.
- He is most anxious to learn how to drive his father's Packard, a V12 that oozes power, though his eagerness is not shared by all concerned.
- When possible, he walks the Kenduskeag Stream, which runs through the center of Bangor, to watch the movement of the water and see the light dance on its surface.
- He enjoys knowing that Kenduskeag is an Indian term meaning "eel-catching place," and was the name applied to Bangor until its incorporation in 1791.
- He is finding it difficult to make friends at the small private school he attends in Bangor, because everyone seems to have known everyone else since birth, and he often feels left out of the conversations.
- Besides, most of the boys are captivated by team sports, while he is an excellent tree climber, swimmer and hiker, and understands little about the joy that can be derived from baseball or football.
- Currently, he is in trouble for acting publicly without asking permission; after a trip to the Kenduskeag Stream, he wrote an angry letter to the editor of the Bangor newspaper, protesting the city fire department's habit of rousting migrating birds out of the trees by firing shotguns.
- He said in his letter that the practice was stupid, barbaric and unnecessary, but failed to show anyone in his family the letter before posting it to the paper—causing some embarrassment.
- His mother considers the letter, boldly signed by her only son, an "open invitation to kidnappers" to come and take everything the family has.

Roddy spent hours watching the giant loggerheads come ashore, lay eggs, and return to the sea.

Life at School and the Island

- During the four years away, he had few friends and lots of time.
- He explored the shore, read about nature, watched the movement of the tides and spent considerable time thinking about magic tricks.
- During summer nights, with guards standing watch, he was allowed to spend hours sitting on the beach watching the giant loggerhead turtles lumber ashore to lay their eggs.
- After digging a deep nest in the sand, the turtles laid dozens of Ping-Pong-ball-sized eggs, covered the holes with their hind flippers and returned to the sea, making a distinct mark across the sand.
- Weeks later, the tiny baby loggerheads would break out of the shells and dart across the beachfront for the sea, while hungry herons and ibises tried to snatch an easy meal.
- At first, Roddy tried to keep the birds away from the turtles by standing on the shore and waving his arms, like a policeman directing traffic.

At tide change, the shore is laden with gulls, terns, and sanderling.

- Eventually, though, he understood that both the birds and the turtles were simply in a race for survival, and that neither was better or worse.
- On the island, he watched the mass migration of winter ducks and white pelicans, the nesting of royal terns and the movement of pinfish in the shallows; he came to enjoy the rhythm of the tides on an island that had little interest in clocks.
- At tide change, he often sat on a creek bank and enjoyed watching families of dolphins leisurely feeding on schools of fish.
- He especially enjoyed teaching himself card games, spending hours practicing his deals and double deals in front of a mirror.
- Thanks to his big hands, long fingers, and hours and hours of practice, he perfected dozens of secret ways to palm a deck, deal from the bottom, or deal seconds.
- His mother now refuses to play bridge or gin rummy with him, convinced that she is being cheated somehow.
- He also spent hours casting his own metal toy soldiers and then painting them with exacting detail; his father purchased the Junior Caster Outfit for baseball and football players and army soldiers.

- Molding perfect figures takes practice and patience, skills in which he excels.
- His favorite project involved Continental soldiers; he made dozens of buglers, mounted cavalrymen and infantrymen, and staged elaborate battles for the conquest of the island in 1776.
- School on the island was led by two tutors, both women from New England, who worked with the three children on math, reading, science and writing.
- After moving through the standard lesson plans the first year, the children devised their own curriculum, especially science projects and nature studies that allowed them to take advantage of the island environment.
- To assist in their education, their father purchased all the latest periodicals, including *My Weekly Reader*, so his children "would not return to civilization ignorant of the real world."
- The two girls love to read novels and dream of what life was like with friends and parties, especially Lucy, who went from being age 12 to 17 during the years away, convinced her best years were being wasted.
- Her favorite book is Margaret Mitchell's *Gone with the Wind*, which sold a million copies within six months of publication.

Roddy's sister loves Snow White and the Seven Dwarfs.

"Dangle Dollies," *Needlecraft, The Home Arts Magazine*, March 1935:

Dangle Dollies—Funny little creatures which can be presented to visiting young neighbors, or to juvenile relatives who come to call. "Sick-a-beds" find it amusing to wake up any morning and discover a Dangle Dolly swinging from the bedpost.

To make a Dangle Dolly, buy a powder-puff in a round cellophane container; a pretty colored rubber sponge, oblong in shape; four sticks of candy, paper-wrapped. With a long needle run a stout green thread up through the length of the sponge and then up through the powder puff and out at the top. Run the thread back to the puff and not through it, as it is easier than trying to run it through the puff in the case. Make a loop of the thread at the top of the hanging. Sew the candy sticks to the sponge to make arms and legs. The twists of paper at the ends of the stick give you material to sew through. From black paper cut out pieces to represent eyes, nose and mouth, and three round buttons. Glue the features to cellophane over the puff to make a face, and glue the three buttons down the front of the sponge.

"To the Rescue of Our Sea Birds," *My Weekly Reader, the Junior Newspaper*, November 29-December 3, 1937:

THE STORMY PETREL OF THE SEA
This timid sea bird builds its nest on land, but it spends most of its life on the storm-tossed waves of the ocean.

New England is worried about the sea birds along her coast. The water for miles around is often coated with oil. Sometimes it leaks from passing ships. Sometimes it is dumped into the water when a ship's tanks are cleaned out. This oil is very harmful to sea life of all kinds.

When a sea bird's feathers are covered with oil, the bird cannot swim or dive. He cannot even fly. Often these birds slowly starve to death, because they can no longer dive into the sea for their food. The fish suffer, too, for the oil smothers many of them. It is especially harmful to herring, mackerel, crabs, lobsters and shrimp. The oil in the water kills seaweed and other grasses upon which many deep-sea creatures feed.

So harmful to the sea life has this trail of oil become that bird lovers the world over have taken up the problem. More than 10 years ago, men from 14 countries met to talk about it. They agreed to set up zones extending out from their coasts 50 to 150 miles. No ship would be allowed to discharge any oil within those zones. This rule, however, was never put into force. Nor are there any rules for ships far out at sea.

Ships still dump old oil into the sea or allow leaks to leave trails of oil in their wake. Every year, nearly a thousand tons of oil substance is washed ashore around New York Bay. Along the beaches of Block Island and Nantucket, many kinds of sea birds have been killed by oily water. Nearly 500 bluebills were killed by oil at East Providence, Rhode Island. All along the New England coast, Long Island Sound, Chesapeake Bay, and southward to the Gulf of Mexico and the Pacific Coast, oily waters are killing hundreds of our sea birds.

- When her cousin recently had a baby, the girls got to pick out the presents, including a delicate paper napkin featuring a baby surrounded by flower petals and accompanied by a hobbyhorse.
- Its poem reads "O may the life of you/Full be with singing; Fleet be the woes of you/As of birds winging;/Glad be the soul of you/As Spring returning/All, mother prays for you/Baby of my yearnings!"
- Roddy's younger sister is in love with movies; her father is talking about building his own theater.
- She has seen *Snow White and the Seven Dwarfs* three times and loves to irritate her mother by talking like Betty Boop.

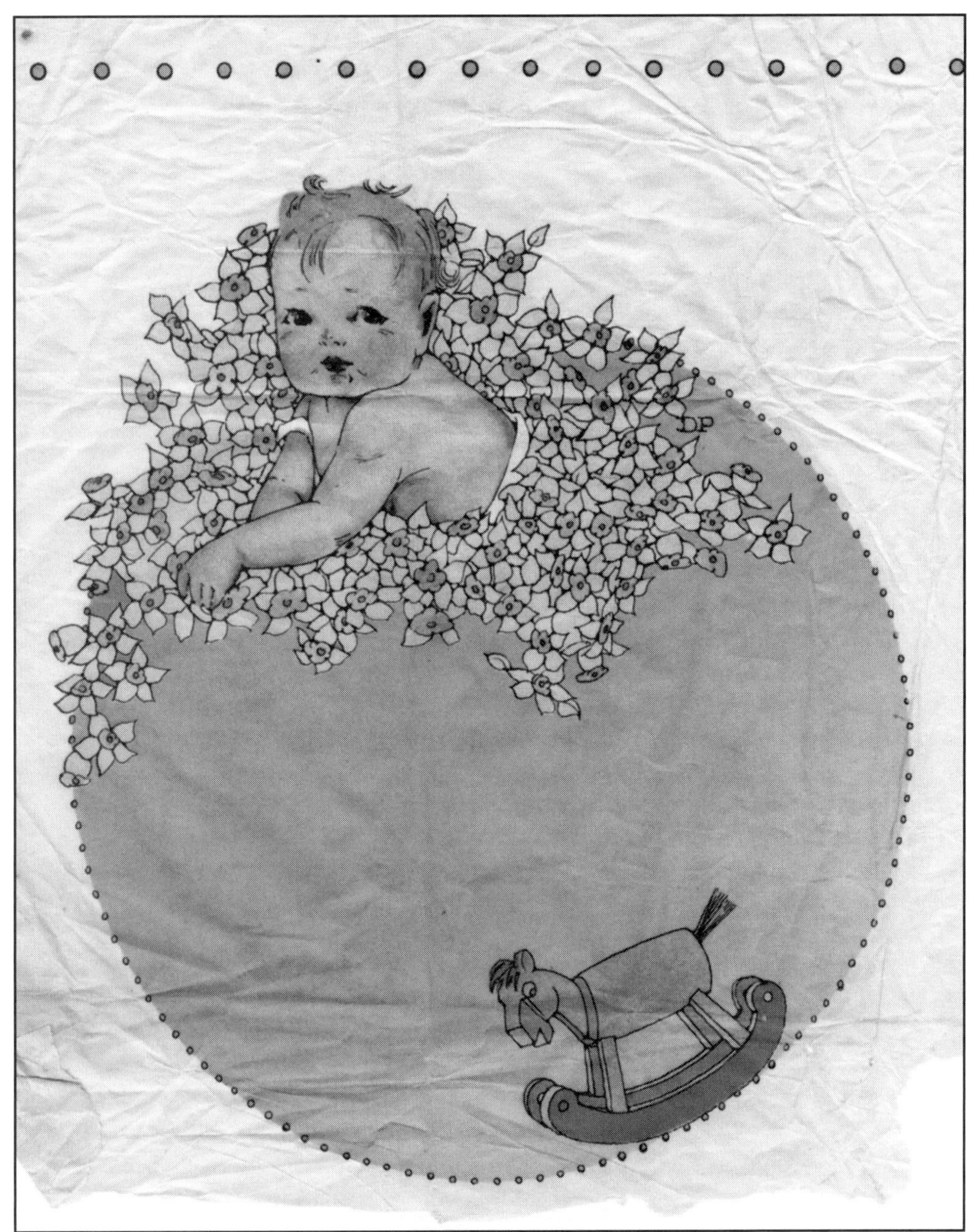

The girls found a paper napkin for the new baby's gift.

Life in the Community: Bangor, Maine

- Settled in 1769, Bangor is the third-largest city in Maine, and the county seat.
- The Kenduskeag Stream enters the city from a northerly direction, running through the central and business districts.
- In the 1850s Bangor was the leading lumber port in the world, and by the 1870s, second only to Chicago.
- Despite a fire in 1911, the city boasts many of Maine's oldest buildings.
- The Bangor House on Main and Union Streets survived from the stagecoach, schooner and steamboat days; guests have included Stephen A. Douglas and Daniel Webster, as well as four presidents—Grant, Arthur, Harrison, and Theodore Roosevelt.

"Suggestions to Teachers," *The Newlon-Hanna Speller, Grade Two*, 1937:

Children's interests: The weekly topics of this speller were also selected on the basis of research in children's interests. To discover these, a survey was made of the school and out-of-school activities of 5,000 children from the age of five through 15. The children participating in this survey were selected with respect to geographic, economic and urban-rural factors. A tabulation showed that certain interests and activities predominated in each grade level. For example, *Playing Ball* was among the first choices of children in Grade III; *Motion Pictures*, in Grade V, and *Aviation*, in Grade VII. For the purposes of this speller, the 20 most frequent interests of each grade were selected. . . .

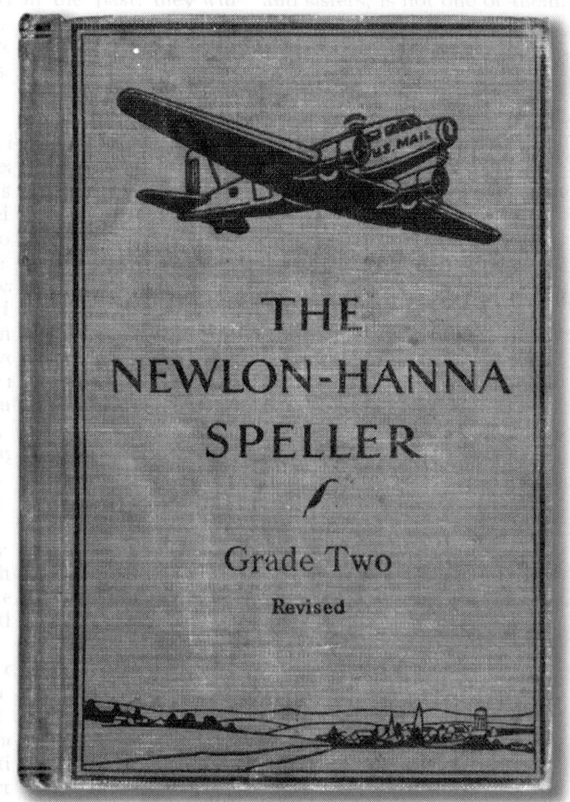

The second step was a comparison of this compilation with three of the best of the recent word lists—the Breed List, the Coleman List, and the Basic English Vocabulary. All words in the Breed, the Coleman and the Basic English lists not already included in the list previously compiled were added to the Hewlon-Hanna Word List. Besides these, approximately 100 words such as television were added, which, in the opinion of the authors, are becoming increasingly essential in our modern world. The Hewlon-Hanna List includes 4,393 words. Of these, the 3,805 basal words were used in the regular weekly lists. In order to provide for varying lengths of school years and varying abilities of pupils, 588 extra words were organized into four additional weekly lessons per grade.

- Oscar Wilde, on his American tour in 1882, made his only stop in Maine at the Bangor House.
- He spoke before an audience in a hall decorated with sunflowers and was booed and hissed "by the vulgarly curious"; no respectable woman, no matter her claim to being one of the intelligentsia, was permitted to attend the gathering.
- The city also features Bangor Salmon Pool, known for its excellent fishing—the only one of its kind in the country within a city's limits.

Historical Snapshot
1937

- Scottsboro defendant Clarence Norris was sentenced to death for the third time on a charge of rape
- The Depression continued, with unemployment reaching 14.3 percent
- Howard Hughes flew from Los Angeles to Newark in a record seven hours, 28 minutes and five seconds
- The crash of the dirigible *Hindenburg* at Lakehurst, New Jersey, killed 38 people and was witnessed by hundreds who had come to see its landing
- Spam was introduced by George A. Hormel & Company
- President Franklin D. Roosevelt called for an investigation of "immoral" tax evasion by the wealthy
- The principle of a minimum wage for women was upheld by the United States Supreme Court
- General Motors introduced the automatic transmission for automobiles
- Radio quiz shows grew in popularity, including "Melody Puzzles," "Professor Quiz," "Spelling Bee" and "Uncle Jim's Question Bee"
- More than 500,000 were left homeless by the Ohio River flood
- "Nice Work If You Can Get It," "Whistle While You Work" and "The Lady Is a Tramp" were all popular songs
- The United Automobile Workers were recognized by General Motors as the sole bargaining agent for its employees
- Nylon, Santa Claus school, the trampoline, Pepperidge Farm and the Lincoln Tunnel all made their first appearance
- Several thousand Americans joined the Abraham Lincoln Brigade to fight with the Loyalists against fascist-supported Franco forces, including authors Dorothy Parker, John Dos Passos, Ernest Hemingway, Malcolm Cowley and Upton Sinclair
- Spinach growers erected a statue to Popeye in Wisconsin
- John D. Rockefeller died, leaving an estate of approximately $1 billion
- *Popular Photography* magazine began publication
- After 70 years of failure, the first successful instant coffee was formulated by the Nestle Company
- Packard Motor Car company sold a record 109,000 cars

1937 ECONOMIC PROFILE

Selected Prices

Bait, Night Crawlers, Quart	$1.00
Camera, Moviematic	$5.95
Charcoal Grill	$1.95
Dental Cream, Colgate Ribbon, Seven Ounces	$0.33
Dog Food, Miller's Kibbles, Eight Pounds	$1.00
Garden Tractor, 4-hp	$242.00
Laxative, Ex-Lax	$0.19
Pressure Cooker	$7.45
Sleeper Berth, Newark to Los Angeles	$150.00
Sofa and Chair	$66.85
Stockings, Silk	$0.21
Sunglasses	$1.98
The Daily Chicago Tribune, Sunday Edition	$0.10
Time, Yearly Subscription	$5.00
Tire, Goodyear	$15.55

PRICE LIST

Order from YOUR DEALER. If he can't supply you, order from us

CHECK ITEMS YOU WANT

JUNIOR CASTER OUTFITS

☐ Continental Soldier Outfit	$2.25	☐ U. S. Machine Gun Outfit	$2.25
☐ Buffalo Bill Outfit	2.25	☐ Football Player Outfit	2.25
☐ U. S. Marine Outfit	2.25	☐ Baseball Player Outfit	2.25
☐ U. S. Soldier Outfit	2.25	☐ Toy Foundry	1.50
		☐ Midget Caster	1.30

EXTRA MOULDS

☐ Continental Soldier Mould	.95	☐ U. S. Soldier Mould	.95
☐ U. S. Sailor Mould	.95	☐ Football Player Mould	.95
☐ U. S. Machine Gun Mould	.95	☐ Baseball Player Mould	.95
☐ Buffalo Bill Mould	.95	☐ Battle Cruiser Mould	.95

EXTRA EQUIPMENT

☐ Metal (36 pigs)	.60	☐ Mould Clamp	.15
☐ 4 Assorted Paints, 2 Brushes	.60	☐ Ladle	.35
☐ Mould Handles, pair	.15	☐ Electric Melting Stove with Asbestos Pad	.60

RAPAPORT BROS.
701 W. Ohio St., Dept. B.
Chicago, Illinois

Please send me the items checked above. Enclosed find money order for $....................

Your Name..

Address...

City...............................State..........

All **Junior Caster $2.25 Outfits** come in a large carton 9¾" x 18¾" (see center spread on opposite side) with an attractive cover in colors. Each of these sets includes 3 moulded figures, as models to show how the finished castings should look. Complete set of Moulds for making these figures, large ladle, strong mould clamp, 4 assorted colors of enamel paint, and two sizes of paint brushes, 2 wooden handles for the Mould halves, and 12 pigs of metal. Each set will make thousands of figures by using the Moulds over and over again.

Continental Soldier Outfit
Complete casting and painting equipment. Makes Buglers, 2¾"; Infantrymen, 3"; Mounted Cavalrymen, 3 x 3". Large, realistic figures in full uniform. **Price $2.25**

Buffalo Bill Outfit
A great action set. Complete casting and painting equipment. Mould makes Buffalo Bill shooting at Indian, 2¾" over-all; Indians on Horseback, 2¼"; Indians on Foot brandishing Tomahawks, 2¼". **Price $2.25**

U. S. Marine Outfit
Handsome group of marching Marines. True to life. Complete equipment for casting and painting. Mould makes Flag-Bearers, 3¼"; Buglers, 2"; Drummers, 2". **Price $2.25**

U. S. Soldier Outfit
Makes a real American Army. Complete casting and painting outfit. Makes Infantrymen 2½"; Flag Bearers, 2¾"; Officers Mounted on Horseback, 2⅝". All large, realistic figures. **Price $2.25**

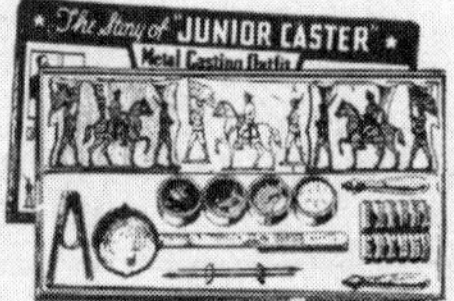

U. S. Machine Gun Outfit
Here's a dandy set for sham battles. Casting and painting outfit complete with mould for making Machine Gunners with Machine Guns, 2¼"; Officers, 2¼"; Soldiers attacking, 2½". **Price $2.25**

Football Player Outfit
Complete outfit for casting and painting football players. Makes Linemen Crouching, 1¾"; Ball Carriers, 2¼"; Kickers, 2¼". **Price $2.25**

Baseball Player Outfit
Just the thing to play baseball games. Complete outfit for casting and painting baseball players. Mould will produce Batters, 2¼"; Pitchers, 2"; Fielders, 1¾". (Fielders serve for infield, outfield, and catcher.) With this outfit a complete set of teams can be made. **Price $2.25**

Toy Foundry
Complete set of Moulds with handles for Moulding large Battleships 3½ x 1¾ x 1". These are real fighting cruisers and they're dandies. Set also includes ladle, 24 pigs of lead, handling and finishing tool, two bottles of paint and brush for coloring. **Price $1.50**

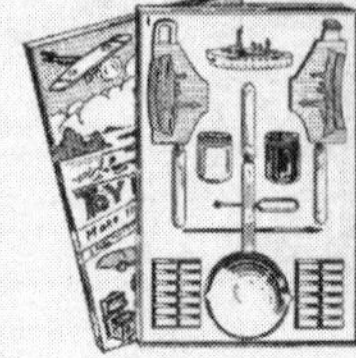

Midget Caster
U. S. Sailors on Parade! Set includes large cake of casting metal, ladle, clamp, mould handles, and Mould for making 3 Sailors. Buglers 2"; Flag Bearers 3¼"; Drummers 2". **Price $1.30**

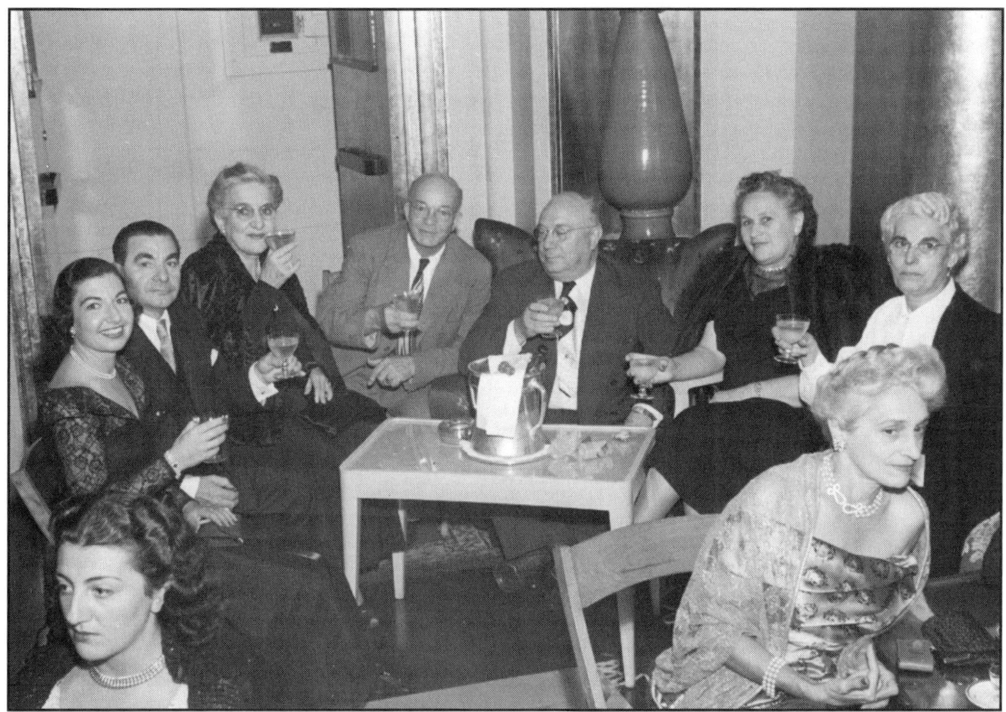

A party was held for the children when they returned to Maine.

Changing America

- A *Harper's Monthly* article concluded that today's young people behaved "without thought of social responsibility."
- An estimated 15,000 cabin camps for travelers, usually having only 10 to 15 rooms at $2 each, had sprouted nationwide to meet the overnight needs of traveling Americans.
- The National Park Service set aside some 600,000 acres for numerous federal parks, as well as fish and game sanctuaries.
- A revolt against progressive education was under way, led by Robert M. Hutchins, president of the University of Chicago.
- German-American pro-Nazi Bund societies were forming, ostensibly devoted to social and athletic pursuits.
- Studies showed that people were spending 4.5 hours daily listening to the radio.
- A *Fortune* magazine story reported, "As for sex . . . the campus takes it more casually than it did 10 years ago. . . . It is news that it is no longer news."
- *Life* magazine reported that one out of 10 Americans had a tattoo.
- In the previous year, the Oklahoma-based Humpty-Dumpty grocery chain introduced shopping carts, setting off a revolution in shopping.
- Several companies, including American Radiator and Sears & Roebuck, attempted to introduce prefabricated housing.
- Icemen continued to make regular deliveries to more than 50 percent of middle-class households.

"Kidnapping: Weyerhaeuser Boy Returned; Police and Federal Agents Begin Grim Manhunt," *The News-Week at Home*, June 8, 1935:

Memorial Day, Edward Anderson, an Associated Press reporter, dozed in a car outside John Phillip Weyerhaeuser's home. For days the AP man and other newspapermen in Tacoma, Washington, had averaged only four hours of sleep.

Down the street a cannon boomed in honor of America's war dead. Instinctively Anderson leaped from the car and fell flat on the pavement; he dreamed he was back in the trenches.

BATTLE: The sudden jolt brought him back into a new kind of warfare waged by local, state and federal police against the kidnappers of George Weyerhaeuser. It was a weary battle, fought with a new strategy—patient waiting, but no attack, lest the nine-year-old boy be killed.

May 27: The child's father, one of the heirs to a $1 billion lumber fortune, paced through his large white house. Feverishly he fingered a mass of letters and telegrams, seeking information of his son, held for $200,000 ransom.

Tight-lipped Department of Justice agents started searching for "at least three men." The Weyerhaeusers pleaded with the federal sleuths: "We most earnestly ask you not to interfere further. If you refuse to do this it will bring all our efforts to naught."

Then the despairing parents inserted an advertisement in *The Seattle Post-Intelligencer*: "Due to publicity beyond our control, please indicate another method of reaching you. Hurry, relieve anguished mother. (signed) Percy Minnie."

May 28: The day before the kidnappers' deadline for ransom payment, the Weyerhaeuser's placed another ad: "We are ready."

Apparently the kidnappers did not reply. Shortly after noon a car with drawn curtains whisked the Weyerhaeusers' three other children away from their home.

May 29: Tacoma was tense. At 6:35 p.m., Pacific Standard Time, the deadline passed. Still no word. Had the kidnappers carried through with their threat to slit the boy's throat?

May 30: Rumors flew that the Weyerhaeusers had assembled a 50-pound package of well-worn Federal Reserve notes.

May 31: Seven days had passed since George Weyerhaeuser vanished on his way home from school, thus permitting federal prosecution of the criminals under the Lindbergh Law.

June 1: Dawn, cold and wet, 25 miles north-east of Tacoma. On a country road a car stopped and let out a small, puzzled boy. After trudging six miles, he knocked on a farmhouse door. To John Bonifas, a chicken rancher, the visitor piped: "I'm the little boy who was kidnapped."

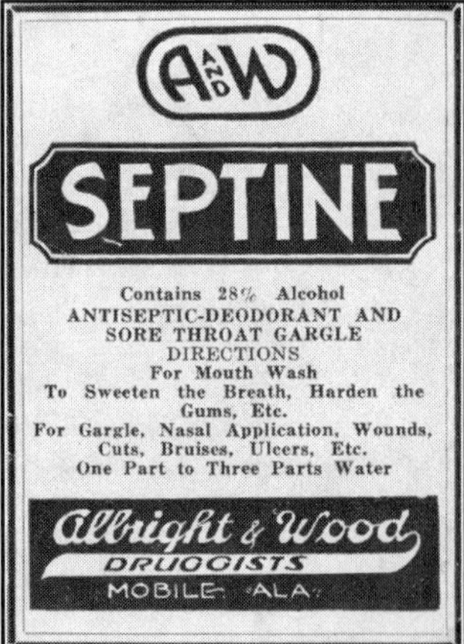

Based on the children's book by L. Frank Baum, the film The Wizard of Oz *becomes an instant classic.*

1940–1949

The dramatic, all-encompassing nature of World War II dominated the lives of all Americans—including children—as brothers and fathers went to war, mothers went to the factories, and shortages of nearly every consumer commodity became a reality. Children joined conservation drives, suffered when tragic telegrams arrived, and learned to eat what the ration tickets made available. America's role quickly shifted from that of passive observer to fierce warrior following the bombing of Pearl Harbor in December 1941.

People from every social stratum either signed up for the military or went to work supplying the military machine. Even children, eager to do their share, collected scrap metal and helped plant the victory gardens that symbolized America's willingness to do anything to defeat the "bullies." In addition, large amounts of money and food were sent abroad as Americans observed meatless Tuesdays, gas rationing and other shortages to help the starving children of Europe.

Business worked in partnership with government; strikes were reduced, but key New Deal labor concessions were expanded, including a 40-hour week and time and a half for overtime. As manufacturing demands increased, the labor pool shrank, and wages and union membership rose. Unemployment, which stood as high as 14 percent in 1940, all but disappeared. By 1944, the U.S. was producing twice the total war output of the Axis powers combined. The wartime demand for production workers rose more rapidly than for skilled workers, reducing the wage gap between the two to the lowest level in the twentieth century.

From 1940 to 1945, the gross national product more than doubled, from $100 billion to $211 billion, despite rationing and the unavailability of many consumer goods such as cars, gasoline, and washing machines. Interest rates remained low, and the upward pressure on prices remained high, yet from 1943 to the end of the war, the cost of living rose less than 1.5 percent. Following the war, as controls were removed, inflation peaked in 1948; union demands for high wages accelerated. Between 1945 and 1952, confident Americans—and their growing families—increased consumer credit by 800 percent.

To fight inflation, government agencies regulated wages, prices, and the kind of jobs people could take. The Office of Price Administration was entrusted with the complicated task of setting price ceilings for almost all consumer goods and distributing ration books for items in short supply. The Selective Service and the War Manpower Commission largely determined who would serve in the military, whose work was vital to the war effort, and when a worker could transfer from one job to another. When the war ended and regulations were lifted, workers demanded higher wages; the relations between labor and management became strained. Massive strikes and inflation followed in the closing days of the decade and many consumer goods were easier to find on the black market than on the store shelves until America retooled for a peacetime economy.

The decade of the 1940s made America a world power and Americans more worldly. Millions served overseas; millions more listened to broadcasts concerning the war in London, Rome, and Tokyo. Newsreels brought the war home to moviegoers, who numbered in the millions. The war effort also redistributed the population and the demand for labor; the Pacific Coast gained wealth and power, and the South was able to supply its people with much-needed war jobs and provide blacks with opportunities previously closed to them. Women entered the work force in unprecedented numbers, reaching 18 million. The net cash income of the American farmer soared 400 percent.

But the Second World War extracted a price. Those who experienced combat entered a nightmarish world. Both sides possessed far greater firepower than ever before, and within those units actually fighting the enemy, the incidence of death was high, sometimes one in three. In all, the United States lost 405,000 men and women to combat deaths; many suffered in the war's final year, when the American army spearheaded the assault against Germany and Japan. The cost in dollars was $350 billion. But the cost was not only in American lives. Following Germany's unconditional surrender on May 4, 1945, Japan continued fighting. To prevent the loss of thousands of American lives defeating the Japanese, President Truman dropped atomic bombs on the Japanese cities of Hiroshima and Nagasaki, ending the war and ushering in the threat of "the bomb" as a key element of the Cold War during the 1950s and 1960s.

Throughout the war, soldiers from all corners of the nation fought side by side and refined nationalism and what it meant to America through this government-imposed mixing process. This newfound identity of American GIs was further cemented by the vivid descriptions of war correspondent Ernie Pyle, who spent a considerable time talking and living with the average soldier to present a "worm's eye view" of war. Yet, despite the closeness many men and women developed toward their fellow soldiers, spawning a wider view of the world, discrimination continued. African-American servicemen were excluded from the marines, the Coast Guard, and the Army Corps. The regular army accepted blacks into the military—700,000 in all—only on a segregated basis. Only in the closing years of the decade would President Harry Truman lead the way toward a more integrated America by integrating the military.

Sports attendance in the 1940s soared beyond the record levels of the 1920s; in football the T-formation moved in prominence; Joe DiMaggio, Ted Williams, and Stan Musial dominated baseball before and after the war, and Jackie Robinson became the first black in organized baseball. In 1946, Dr. Benjamin Spock's work, *Common Sense Baby and Child Care*, was published to guide newcomers in the booming business of raising babies.

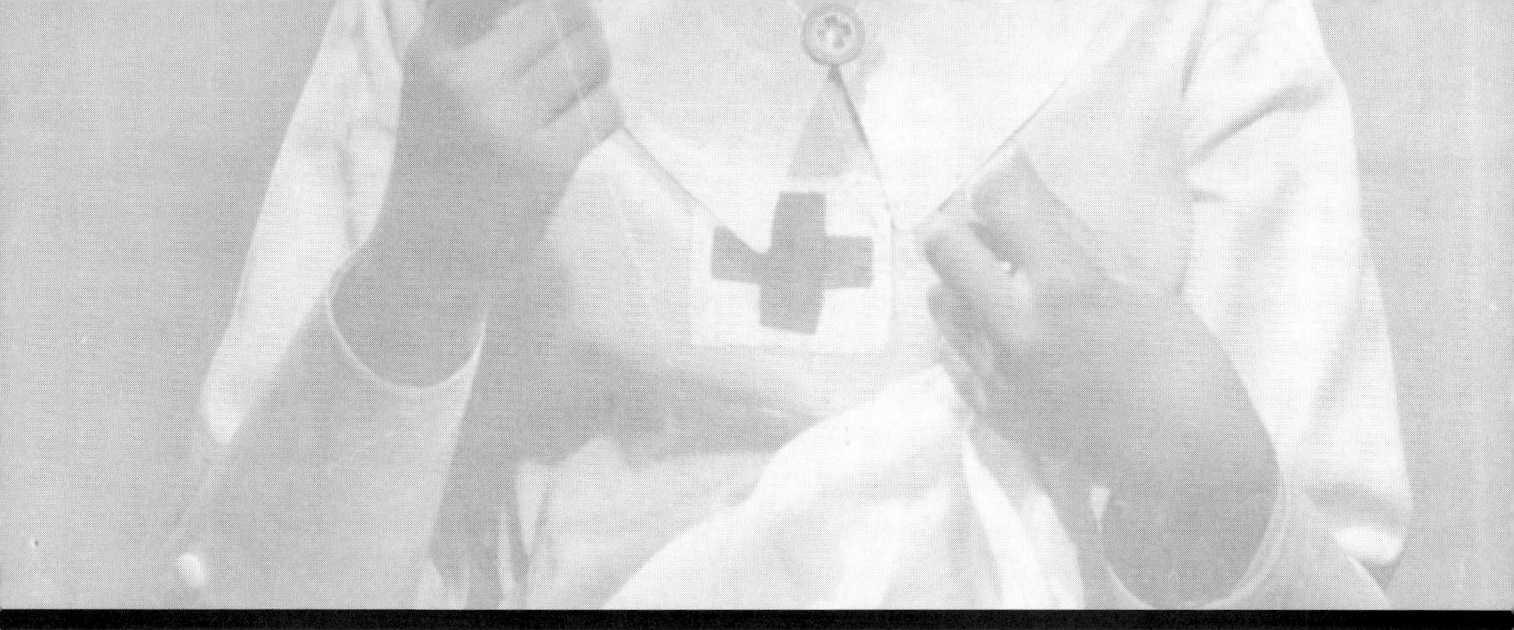

1942 Profile

Working Class

The onset of World War II has provided the Starhawk family with a steady income in Alliance, Nebraska, where this Native American boy was in fights so often at school, he decided to drop out in the sixth grade.

Life at Home

- His name is Michael, but since he was a small boy, his nickname has been Black Mike because of his dark complexion.
- For years his grandfather not only reinforced the name, he ritualized it by giving him first a black chicken, then a black horse and a black goat.
- Black Mike's grandfather, whose Indian name is Long Time Sleep, is a Cheyenne from Wyoming.
- His grandmother is an Oglala Sioux from the Pine Ridge Reservation in South Dakota.
- After Black Mike and his family moved to Alliance, Nebraska, he did not see his grandparents again.
- For many years, the Starhawk family lived in Wood, South Dakota, on the perimeter of the Rosebud Reservation, where approximately 200 people lived.
- They rented a small log house, and his father worked at the federal dam—a job he calls "the best job I've ever had"; he left at 6 a.m. and returned at 6 p.m. most days, earning $1.50 a day.
- The log house included a wood stove, a table, chairs and a bed, but did not have running water, electricity or indoor plumbing.
- At five every morning, Black Mike's mother got up and cooked a large breakfast on the wood stove, including pancakes or hot biscuits, fried eggs and potatoes.
- Black Mike and his brother Joshua were assigned the job of cutting wood every evening and bringing it inside.

Mike Starhawk recently moved to Alliance, Nebraska with his family.

He is one of the few Native American kids enrolled in the school.

- Because their father was not around, Joshua taught Black Mike to ride a horse and a bicycle, and how to fight, impressing upon him that no matter what anyone said, he was better than the white kids in Wood.
- Even though both his mother and father speak the Sioux language at home, their two boys only learned English.
- He tried to get his mother to teach him Sioux, but she was so impatient with his mistakes, he gave up.
- Seven miles outside Wood is Rattlesnake Butte, where so many snakes would congregate, Black Mike could hear them when the wind was right; when he went out to pick up eggs from the hen's nest, he always took great care to make sure no rattlers were in the hay.
- Once after a trip to the creek to get a bucket of water, he returned to the house to find a rattler coiled on his sleeping mother's chest, ready to strike.
- Only with the help of his uncle was Black Mike able to pull the snake away before his mother's face was bitten.
- During summers in Wood, Black Mike and Joshua went to the Bible school at St. Francis, the Indian mission school 30 miles away, where for two weeks they learned about God and the Catholic Church.
- Christmas Eve and Christmas Day were spent at the Catholic church, seven miles from his house, where his father would pitch a tent among dozens of others.

In Alliance, Nebraska, the family lives in a tent city because of the housing shortage.

- Inside the church on Christmas morning, the entire community would open gifts, eat special cakes, drink coffee and celebrate.
- Often, more than 250 Indians would be there for Easter and Christmas; everything was done together.
- One year Santa Claus's gift was a huge box containing a brand-new toy bus.
- For weeks after that, Black Mike and Joshua ignored their dried-bone toys, carved from a horse's hoof, and played with the metal bus.
- When Black Mike started the fifth grade, a neighbor, Mr. Morris, who raises sheep bought him some clothes—cowboy boots, Levi's, shirts, caps and coats.
- The boy is proud that he was able to pay back the rancher almost immediately; late one afternoon he heard a woman screaming for help, and when he ran to the ranch, he found that their ram had pinned the rancher's wife in the outhouse by continually ramming the door.
- Black Mike ran for help and saved the day.
- During the summer of 1941, just before the Starhawks moved, he helped herd 500 sheep into the next town, walking 20 miles a day for three days.
- As a reward, Mr. Morris paid him in cash and took him to a drugstore in town; it was the first time he had ever seen a soda fountain.
- At the same store, he fell in love with comic books, particularly *Batman* and *Superman*, which sold for a dime each.

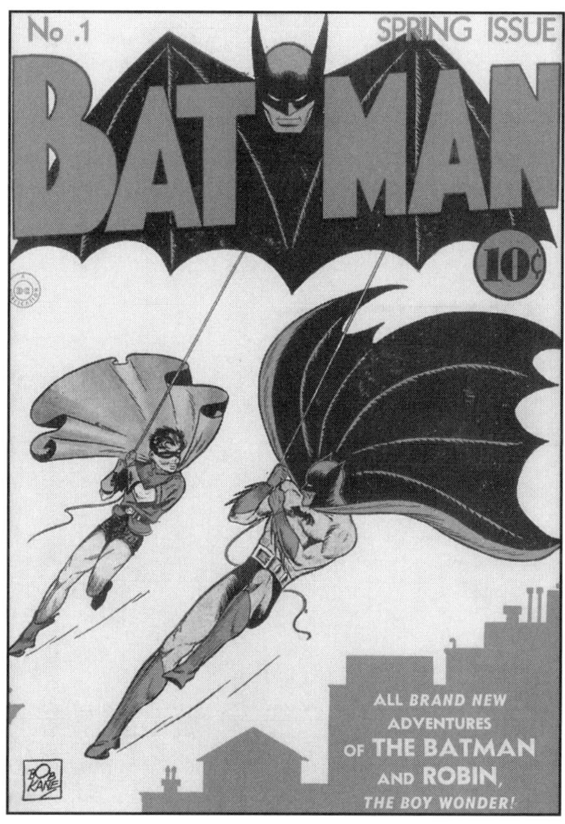

Black Mike has fallen in love with comic books, especially Superman *and* Batman.

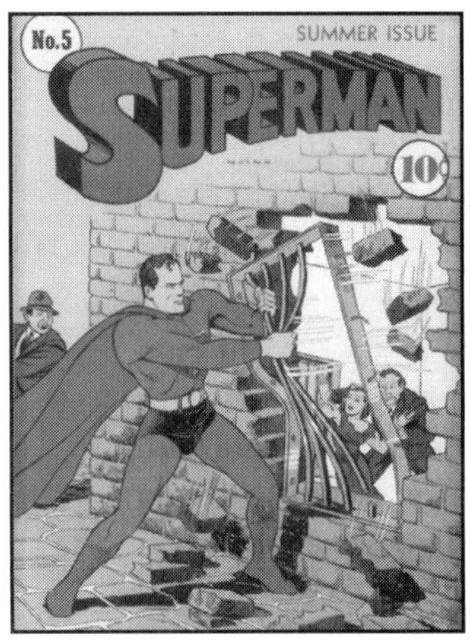

An Indian in White America, by Mark Monroe, Temple University Press, 1994:

When we moved to Alliance, we soon found out there was a ladder of racism. First were the white people, then the Mexicans, then the blacks, and, finally, the Indians. You see, when the American Indian first came to Alliance, the Negro was last on the ladder, but then what happened was the Indian population was discriminated against by blacks, Mexicans, and white alike. When Bill and I started school, the first children we got in trouble with were the Negro kids. I think this was the first time the black people ever felt superior to anybody.

When the Indian people came to Alliance, the businesses in the downtown district put up signs saying, "No Indians or dogs allowed." This meant we couldn't go into restaurants or drugstores, only the grocery and food stores. When we did, we had to go in large numbers for fear of being beaten up.

- After that the family moved to Alliance, where his father could dig potatoes for $50 a week.
- On the potato farm, the family pitched a tent alongside 60 other tents and began work.
- Shortly thereafter, when Pearl Harbor was bombed and the Second World War erupted, Black Mike's dad immediately went to work helping to build a new army air base.
- His job was building latrines and barracks, and scraping roads.
- It was a scary time; every day rumors erupted that Japanese planes would soon attack America.
- Sure, people said, the new base would be a target—the enemy would love to stop it from being built, so everyone took a turn acting as a spotter at night, searching the skies for Japanese airplanes.
- The wide-open Nebraska night skies fill Black Mike with wonder, and he would stay up until midnight protecting the camp against attack.
- With a steady job and good pay, his father was able to buy the family's first car, a 1937 Plymouth.
- The automobile quickly became his father's pride and joy; everyone noticed the green turtle back, named for the long, low, sloping trunk.
- He has even customized the car, removing the running boards, adding a spotlight, yellow and white fog lights, fender flaps, pickup light, trunk light and under-hood light.
- Even with gas and tire rationing they are able to use the car occasionally for pleasure trips.
- They always take the car on Thursdays to see a picture show.

Black Mike's father has customized a 1937 Plymouth, his pride and joy.

Classes in Alliance are harder and more structured.

- One night his father won $100 when his number was selected during a random drawing; he threw his hat in the air and all of his friends came around to offer congratulations.

Life at School

- Black Mike is finding that living in tents winter and summer is tough; no provision has been made for a shower or inside toilet, even as the tent city grows.
- He uses either a bathroom located a block away or an outhouse near the school.
- In the sixth grade, he was one of the few Indian kids enrolled in Grandview Elementary School.

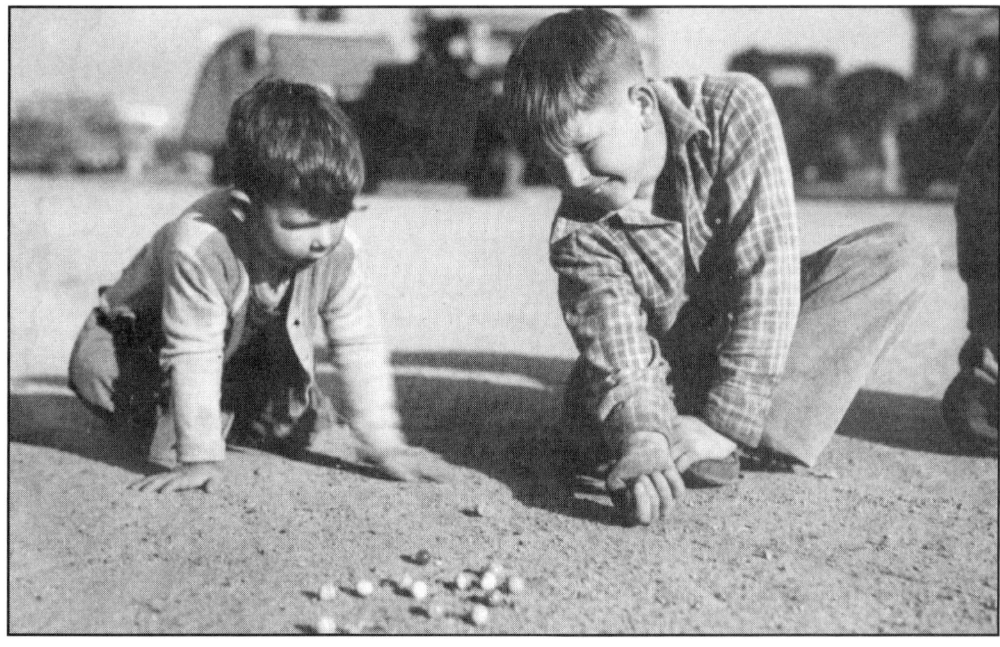

In South Dakota Joshua taught Black Mike to ride, fight and shoot marbles.

On the first day of class, the white kids started fights to prove they were tougher than Indians.

- On his first day, before classes, the white kids looked Black Mike over, talked among themselves, then jumped him from behind, and the fighting has continued ever since.
- Because so many of the white kids wanted to prove they were tougher than an Indian, Black Mike and Joshua sometimes fought in the morning, at lunch and after school.
- Even so, Black Mike felt fortunate that, unlike many Indians in Nebraska, he was not placed in an "opportunity school," where the student's only job seems to be to attend school with other Indians; no lessons are taught, no report cards are given, no advancement provided, and many spend their days drawing pictures on the blackboard.
- Classes in Alliance were different—harder and more structured.
- The teacher was mean, the kids made "Black Mike" sound like a bad name, and he was tired of fighting all the time.
- The teacher called him an "Indian troublemaker" to his face.
- During the dark, snowy days of February, Black Mike quit the sixth grade when the principal's son sat behind him in class, kicking him in the back, over and over and over.
- When he could stand it no longer, he stood up, hit the boy in the eye and broke his glasses, then ran away, not stopping until he got home.
- That night the principal and his son came to the tent village in South Alliance and demanded that Black Mike pay for the glasses or be taken to court.

***Building the New American Army, America, 1941, A Nation at the Crossroads,* by Ross Gregory, 1989:**

The train had pulled in during late afternoon in January 1941, and the engineer had left the passenger cars at a prescribed place on the siding. Inside the coaches, the passengers started to stir without hurrying. They seemed uncertain whether to remain seated or to get up, and, if they were supposed to get off, in what direction they should go. Someone told them to move on, so, wrinkled and sluggish from the trip, they walked through the coach, down the steps to the ground, where they mingled uncomfortably, looking out of place.

The destination they reached could have been any of a number of spots around the country, all of them barren, without color, cheerless, almost hostile, particularly during the gray days of winter. The older establishments at least had paved streets, an occasional tree, and buildings—albeit drab and cold-looking—which appeared to have been standing for some time. The newer ones presented all the disarray and ugliness of a construction site. The ground was bare, and when it rained it was muddy. Off to one side, long rows of tents popped and snapped in the wind. Another section had rows of drab, recently built identical buildings. Nearby, one could see the same type of building still being constructed, and the air smelled of the fresh pine and tarpaper used in their construction. Whether in Georgia, Missouri or Florida, the places showed an unwelcoming aspect to the recent arrivals, and their dismay underscored the knowledge that this was to be their home for at least the next several weeks.

The travelers from the train represented the most profound evidence of the ways the world had begun to affect the nation and people's lives. They were inductees, some of the first people called to be a part of America's new army of 1940-41. . . .

If they resembled soldiers at all, it was stragglers from a lost battle.

- Instead his father shouted, "My son is quitting school, and I'm not going to pay for your son's glasses, so get going before I beat you up!"
- Black Mike now shines shoes at the canteen on the air base.
- At $0.50 a pair, he is making $27 to $30 each night—more than this father.
- He is also learning the rules of the town; only last year he watched the sheriff raise his rifle and shoot an Indian in the middle of the street.
- Nobody ever told Black Mike why it happened.
- Alliance and wartime have proven to be confusing; when it came time for the community celebration of Christmas, arguments broke out in the camp whether Christmas lights should be torn down or turned off now that America was at war.
- All the families in the tent village were given fliers asking them not to make long-distance calls during the holidays so that all lines could be kept open for defense.
- His dad thought the notice was funny: He didn't have a phone, his parents didn't have a phone, his wife's parents didn't have a phone, no one they knew in Wood had a phone; on Christmas day he told everyone he was a patriot because he didn't call anyone.
- Because no money was available for metal trucks or store-bought toys this year, his father repainted an old bike so that Black Mike would get something from Santa Claus.
- Liquor stores in Alliance will not sell alcohol to Indians, so coworkers often buy his father a six-pack of beer and a pint of whiskey on the way home from work.

Black Mike loves the sights and sounds of the County Fair near Alliance.

- On base, when his father's military leaders warn him about talking to the enemy, he laughs and says, "If captured, I'll make them torture me before I reveal the size of the latrines we build."
- Signs are posted everywhere, warning that any stray information could result in the loss of American lives.
- Recently, Black Mike was able to slip away to the County Fair all by himself and join what seemed like millions of people taking in the sights.

"Diet and Destiny, The poor are always with us—and so is the scourge of malnutrition," *Coronet*, February 1939:

Tom is nine years old. So is his pal, Robert. Seeing them together you would never know they were the same age. Tom is small and thin. He is a pretty child, but there are dark rings under his big brown eyes. His skin is sallow, his teeth are irregular, and his shoulders are slightly stooped. Robert is by no means handsome, but he is a good two inches taller than Tom, his eyes are keen, he is quick and walks with a swagger.

Tom is Robert's stooge. He is backward in school, and can't help with the homework. But he stands and holds Robert's coat or baseball mitt when there is a fight to be fought or a race to be run. He submits to Robert's practical jokes. He takes lickings when Robert picks on him to show off before the fellows. In return he is one of the gang. Though he doesn't figure it out, he knows that the price of rebellion is ostracism, because he can't hold his own. So it is better this way.

Why is Tom an underdog and Robert a leader? Is it fate? Has it something to do with "character"? No. The answer is that Tom's father earns $1,000 a year; Robert's father earns $5,000. Tom has two sisters; Robert is an only child. Translated into elementals it means that Tommy does not have, and never has had, enough of the right things to eat. (Yes, there are geniuses who are sick freaks. But how many?)

Although they are so common that you meet them daily on the streets, the Toms and their problem are not uniquely American. They are international. If the world's richest nation has, at conservative estimate, eight million undernourished children, what is the situation elsewhere?

The science of nutrition is new, but its importance increases daily. Why? Because Tom, grown up, will probably be unfit for service in the war for which the world is preparing. He will probably fail the army tests, and as a worker at home, his lack of efficiency will be a liability. Many nations are alarmed at the high percentage of army applicants they must reject because of disabilities traceable to malnutrition. Practically every country is now careful to feed its soldiers according to the best knowledge of nutritional science. . . .

The science of nutrition is so new that every day brings fresh discoveries to kill a set of conclusions only yesterday considered final. But certain facts have withstood all testing. The most fundamental is that the problem of nutrition begins with the mother and the baby. At nine years, little Tommy is already damaged goods; in his small body have been rooted weaknesses that will plague him all his life.

Why, in spite of the medical profession's gloating about progress, do 13,000 mothers die in childbirth every year in the most "advanced" country in the world? Why do 144,000 babies die during birth or in the first month of life? Medical science has failed to answer that question; nutritional science is beginning to furnish answers.

It has been discovered that if the mother was undernourished as a girl, she is likely to have defects of bone structure that will make delivery so difficult as to harm the child or result in puerperal fever—among the commonest causes of death after childbirth. It may have given her anemia or made her receptive to tuberculosis or to other diseases caused by vitamin deficiency. . . .

Tom's diet history in his first few years of life will decide whether he starts school doomed to backwardness or stands a chance of growing into the kind of citizen his country wants—potential cannon fodder. These are the years when Tom and his mother have no assistance from outside agencies, yet they are the most important years of Tom's life. If he does not get the right food, and enough of it, he falls heir to certain physical weaknesses—bad teeth, bent or brittle bones, and low resistance to the serious childhood diseases that may in turn cause new permanent weakness.

The sideshow's greatest act was the Human Blockhead.

- He loved the sideshows—the Monkey Girl and Lobster Boy—but his favorite was the Human Blockhead, a man who could drive giant ten-penny nails up his nose.

Life in the Community: Alliance, Nebraska

- Alliance is near the western border of the Sandhills region of Nebraska.
- When the city was founded in 1887, it was named Grand Lake.
- A year later when the Chicago, Burlington & Quincy Railroad opened a station for business, the name was changed to Alliance by Railroad Superintendent G. W. Holdrege.
- He selected the name because it was a single word, was different from the name of any other town in the state and would be near the top of the alphabetical list of towns.
- Within eight weeks of its founding, 250 buildings were built, mostly of wood and tarpaper which were shipped in by rail.

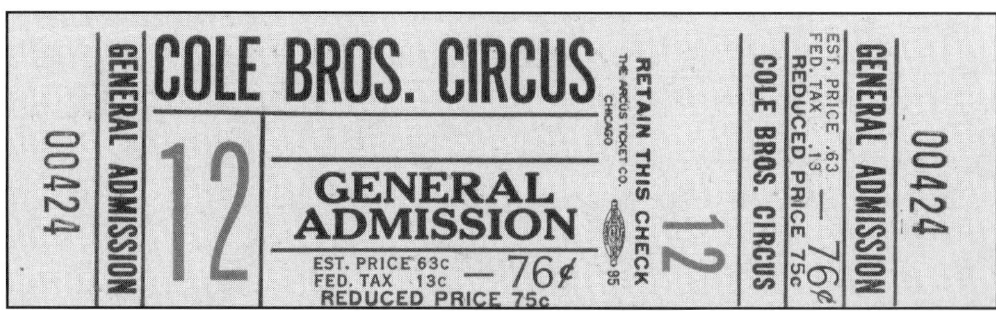

A One Hundred Dollar Bond

WHAT IT MEANS TO THE INJURED SOLDIER

By VINCENT P. MAZZOLA, M.D., *Member of Medical Committee, N. Y. State Education Dept.*

Address delivered at the Grand Bond Rally for Third War Loan, at Manhattan Center, N. Y. C., September 28, 1943. Broadcast over Stations WBNX and WOV.

The deaths resulting from injuries in this war are approximately one per thousand, whereas, the rate for the first World War was approximately five per thousand. The factors affecting this reduction are: (1) Preventing and combating shock, (2) prevention of infection, and (3) speedy hospital care.

I. Preventing and combating shock, by plasma administrated early on the field of battle. The use of morphine to relieve pain and the immediate immobilization of fractures, before transportation, reduced the mortality rate from 85 to 15 per cent in World War 1.

II. Prevention of infection by:

1. Sulfa drugs: Every soldier carries such a drug. It has been reported that in two of our naval hospitals a total of 50 patients with cerebrospinal meningitis were treated with sulfa drugs without a single death. Another report revealed that 300 patients with bacillary dysentery were treated successfully with sulfa drugs. These facts are most encouraging since we should not forget that in the Spanish-American War more soldiers died from disease than from bullets.
2. Immunization: The armed forces are immunized against diseases such as tetanus, typhoid, small-pox, yellow fever, cholera.
3. Proper nourishment: The armed forces of the United States in this World War II are the best fed troops in the world's history.

III. Speedy hospital care: The patients are transported rapidly to the hospital and the hospital facilities are established close to the fighting front. Evacuation of the injured by air to mobile hospital ships, in areas of combat zones, has enabled effectual treatment to be given within a short time after the infliction of injuries.

What a $100.00 Bond Purchases

1. It will purchase sulfa drugs sufficient to treat 200 soldiers suffering from infectious disease or 1,400 wounds, or
2. It will purchase atabrine sufficient to treat 1,400 cases of malaria or afford prophylaxis to 2,000 soldiers, or
3. It will purchase morphine tablets sufficient to relieve 5,000 soldiers of pain, or
4. It will purchase immunization against tetanus for 2,640 soldiers, or
5. It will purchase vitamins sufficient to keep 10,000 soldiers supplied for one day, or
6. It will purchase first aid packs for 675 soldiers, or
7. It will purchase first aid packs for ten medical privates, or
8. It will purchase first aid packs for four medical officers, or
9. It will purchase eight litters to transport the wounded, or
10. It will purchase three splint sets to care for fractures, or
11. It will purchase ten units of plasma sufficient to combat shock in five cases.

In conclusion,

Let us back up our boys who are imperiling their lives for us.

Let us keep our deaths low with proper physical fitness, sulfa drugs, plasma, morphine, modern management and transportation, and unselfish service.

Let us resolve that all men so far as possible will be given proper hospital and medical care so they may come back home.

Let us resolve today that under our institutions men may be permitted to live in health and strength.

Let us all individually do our share

Buy Bonds Now and supply our boys with the necessities to win the war and bring them back home sooner.

FOURTH WAR LOAN — January and February

- Since 1900 the population of Alliance has remained around 1,500, but the town has tripled in size in less than six months, thanks to the influx of workers coming to build the Alliance Army Air Base, bringing new ideas and a lot of change.
- Newcomers have rented every possible living space, from basements and attics to garages.
- The residents of the area are proud to play their part in the war effort and sell their land to the military, but are concerned about all the new people, building and disruption.

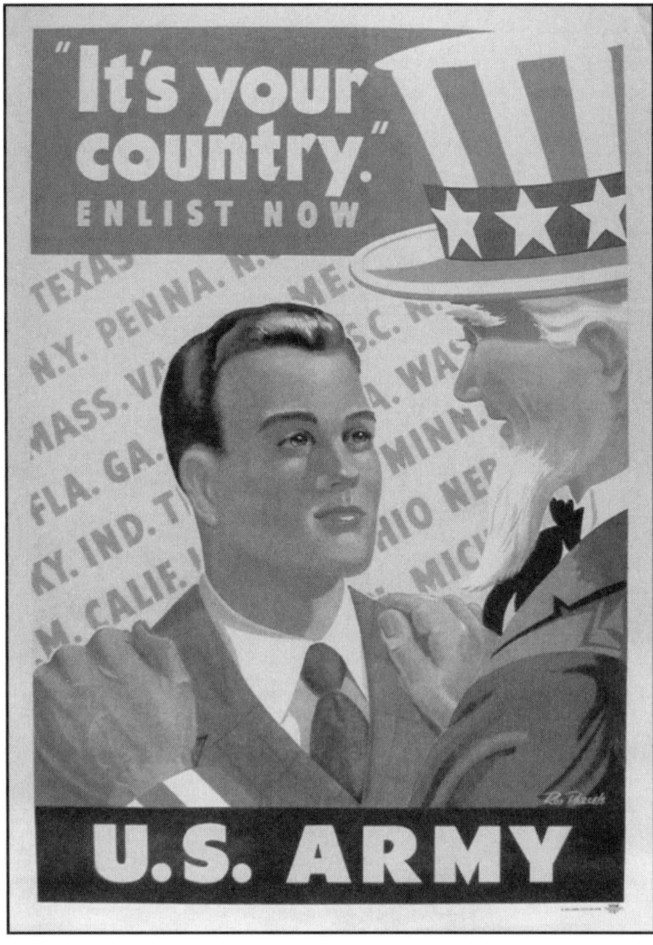

Patriotic posters blanket the Military Command of Alliance.

- This sentiment is especially strong from Sweetwater to Cheyenne avenues, where the community's finest old homes can be found.
- Most of the population still makes its living growing wheat, sugar beets, potatoes or corn.
- A west wind called the chinook blows across the Rockies into northwestern Nebraska, causing that corner of the state to be warmer in winter than are other regions of the same latitude.
- Old-timers claim, "Wherever sunflowers grow, you can raise corn, and most of Nebraska rarely lacks for sunflowers."
- The surge in farming near Alliance was aided by a 1904 Congressional act that gave homesteaders 640 acres in semi-arid regions, up from the 160 acres provided in the 1862 Homestead Act.
- In the center of the town sits the city jail composed of blocks no more than 16 by 20 feet wide and separated in the middle by a wall.
- The boys who play in the streets make a great game of peeking in the windows and yelling at the prisoners before running down the street.

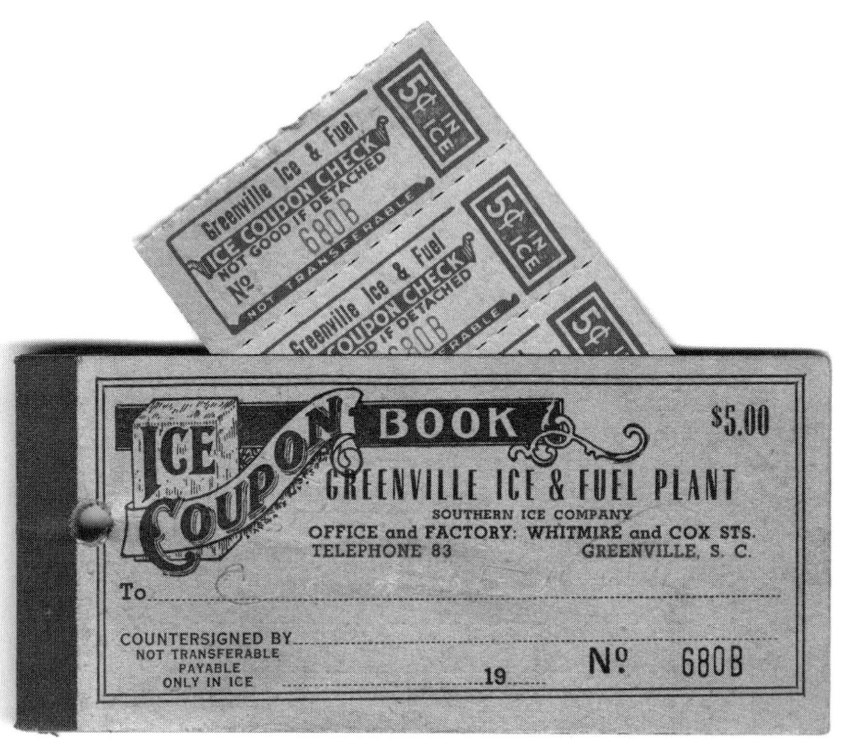

Historical Snapshot
1942

- To support the war effort, the Boy Scouts salvaged 150,000 tons of wastepaper; children receive $0.50 a pound for aluminum foil balls
- America received the first reports of the deportation by the Nazis of Jews from occupied Western Europe
- A tire rationing plan began, followed by gas rationing; U.S. automobile production was halted
- The New York Post Office hired 900 translator-censors to examine foreign mail
- Daylight Saving Time, nylon parachutes, zinc-coated pennies, Paine Webber and Kellogg's Raisin Bran all made their first appearance
- Willow Run, near Detroit, became America's fastest-growing city as thousands moved there for defense work
- *Go Down, Moses* by William Faulkner, *The Just and the Unjust* by James Gould Cozzens and *Men on Bataan* by John Hersey were all published
- A shoulder-held rocket container known as a bazooka, designed to stop a tank, was developed for combat
- The first safe self-sustaining nuclear chain reaction was achieved by Enrico Fermi, Edward Teller and Leo Szilard at the University of Chicago
- By executive order, 110,000 Japanese Americans were sent to relocation centers in America
- In the first attack on the American mainland, a Japanese submarine fired 25 shells at an oil refinery near Santa Barbara, California
- The Office of Price Administration was formed to control prices; a $25,000 salary ceiling was established
- Dannon yogurt was introduced
- The top 10 most popular radio programs were "The Chase and Sanborn Hour," "Jack Benny," "Fibber McGee and Molly," "Lux Radio Theater," "The Aldrich Family," "Bob Hope," "Maxwell House Coffee Time," "Walter Winchell," "The Kate Smith Hour," and "Fitch Bandwagon"
- The space rocket age began with the first successful test of the A-4 as part of the Nazis' Penemunde project
- The heavyweight boxing title was frozen when champion Joe Louis entered the service
- Performer Frances Langford sang tunes requested by U.S. troops throughout the world, and was broadcast via 13 shortwave stations
- LORAN, Long-Range Air Navigation, went into operation, diagramming the air and sea in streetlike fashion
- Lights were dimmed across New York's skyline so that ships at sea were not betrayed to U-boats
- America issued a three-cent "Win the War" postage stamp

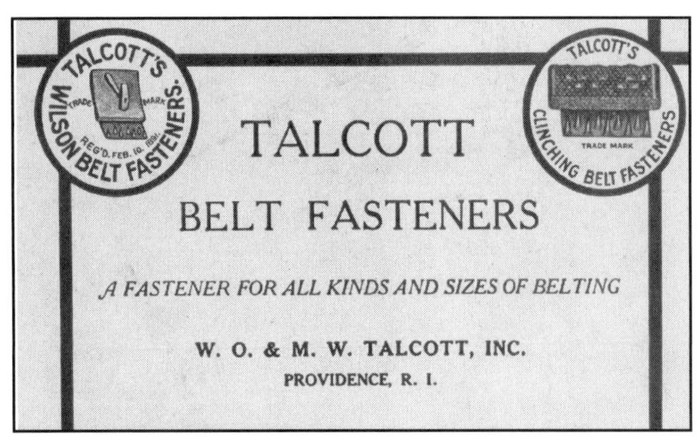

TALCOTT'S
WILSON BELT FASTENERS
TRADE MARK
TALCOTT'S
CLINCHING BELT FASTENERS
TALCOTT
BELT FASTENERS
A FASTENER FOR ALL KINDS AND SIZES OF BELTING
W. O. & M. W. TALCOTT, INC.
PROVIDENCE, R. I.

1942 Economic Profile

Selected Prices

Automobile, Packard Clipper $2,099.00
Bayer Aspirin $0.59
Billfold, Amity Leather $2.50
Blended Whiskey, Fifth $2.70
Bund Bed, Sears & Roebuck $10.98
Brassiere $1.00
Casserole Dish, Pyrex, One Quart $0.50
Chocolates, Whitman's Sampler,
Five Pounds $5.00
Deep Freezer $225.00
Haircut $2.00
Mixer, Sunbeam MixMaster $23.75
Movie Ticket, *Gone with the Wind* $1.10
Shoes, Men's, Thom McAn $4.20
Shotgun, Remington $39.30
Tattoo, Snake Design on Arm $0.25

A SEAL OF SATISFACTION
TOMLINSON QUALITY
CRAFTSMEN OF FINE FURNITURE
SINCE 1900

IN THE COLOR PLATE—LEFT TO RIGHT

The Riddle Fan Chair
W 32 D 28 H 46....$85

The Tazewell Leather Top Table
Top 32x32 H 29....$79.50

The Field Lounge Chair
W 33 D 34 H 33....$75

The Saunders Mirror
Plate 18x30....$18

The Washington Breakfront Bookcase
W 56 D 15 H 88....$295

The Custis Corner Chair
W 31 D 28 H 31....$50

The Monroe Leather Top Refreshment Table
Top 21x35—50....$57.50

The Tazewell Sofa
L 84 D 37 H 32....$258

The Tyler Queen Anne Chair
W 22 D 24 H 42....$55
Matching Arm Chair....$79

The Southall End Tables
45x24—ca. $37.50

SCHROYER

"The Goldbergs," Radio Album, Spring, 1941:

Yoo Hoo, MRS BLOOM! Twelve years ago, that clarion call first boomed over the air waves, and the NBC program director who had taken a 15-minute-a-week chance in launching "The Goldbergs" sat back and hoped he was right. . . . He was. Today, Molly Goldberg and her family—Jake, Sammy and Rosie—are deeply entrenched in the hearts of millions of listeners. Twenty-three CBS stations, 31 NBC stations and Mutual's WOR in New York carry the story of the Goldbergs' struggles and heartaches, defeats and triumphs in a five-times-a-week program that tops all air shows. The saga of the Goldbergs is the saga of radio's most amazing woman, Gertrude Berg, who writes, directs and plays the role of Molly. Like Molly, she's wrapped up in her family—Lewis, her husband, 19-year-old Chernay and 15-year-old Harriet. And like Molly she knows first-hand the urge to "get ahead in the world." As Gertrude Edelstein, she grew up in a modest, four-room apartment in upper Manhattan. An only child, she lived in a make-believe world, peopled by characters of her own imagining. Summers in the Catskills where her father owned a small hotel gave her the first taste of playwriting. Guests liked amateur theatricals like the clever sketches Gertrude wrote for them. . . . Lewis Berg, a Brooklyn Polytechnic Institute student, spent a vacation at the Edelstein hostelry when Gertrude was 16, returned three years later, and they were married that autumn. Came 1929. The sugar refinery, where Lewis was employed as an engineer, burned down, and his job went up in the smoke. Mrs. Berg, who hitherto had been concerned only with homemaking, remembered the sketches she'd written, took them off the shelf, pondered the possibility of getting a skit about two salesgirls on the radio. A program director agreed to air for four weeks, and Gertrude was in seventh heaven. She still doesn't know why the first broadcast was the last. . . But the heady elixir of success, though fleeting, was sweet, and she promised herself one month to prove her mettle. Result: A sketch of a Jewish father and mother in an East Side tenement who wanted to get ahead. A father who said he wanted his son, Sammy, to "have everything money can buy." A mother who said she wanted him to "have everything money cannot buy." You know Jake and Molly. . . Well, in 1931, a sponsor took over the program and scheduled it for five days a week. Mrs. Berg didn't think she could handle that much but said she'd try. She tried—and hasn't stopped since. The paycheck has grown from $7 to a reputed $5,000 per week, and $1,000 for a new show she calls "Kate Hopkins." Her day begins at 6 a.m., when Mrs. Berg tiptoes to the kitchen, brews a cup of tea, carries it back to her study and writes the script that will go on the air three weeks later. After breakfast, she hurries to the NBC studios where, at 10 sharp, she rehearses the 11:30 broadcast. After lunch, she dashes home to knock out the Kate Hopkins sketch. At 4 p.m., she's at CBS, rehearsing the 5:00 show, a recording of which is broadcast the next morning over WOR. At 5:30, the author-director-actress is free to go home to her family. "Jake," says Molly Goldberg to her husband, "the world would be a better place to live in if people only had the courage to act as good as they really are." There you have Gertrude Berg—voicing the all-embracing faith of her generous heart.

Charlie McCarthy is one of America's most popular acts.

Changing America

- Robert Hutchins, president of the University of Chicago, was concerned that, with America on the verge of war, young people did not have the literary or historical background to participate in a democracy.
- Bra-cup sizing, created in 1929, was rapidly gaining in popularity.
- Of all the vegetables being consumed in America, 40 percent were grown in small, localized victory gardens near people's homes.
- As women's fashions shifted toward practical, inconspicuous styles, the sale of trousers for women increased by 10 times over the previous year.
- Florida passed California as the leading United States producer of oranges.
- Tubeless tires were successfully tested.
- "This Is War," performed with extensive sound effects, was broadcast by the four major radio networks.
- As the production of private automobiles was halted, factories converted to the manufacture of war materials.
- Louis Fieser of Harvard developed napalm, a jellylike mixture of gasoline and palm oils that sticks to its target until it burns out.
- African-Americans complained about discrimination in the military, especially in the navy.
- The Nobel Prize ceremonies, discontinued in Stockholm since 1939, took place at a dinner at the Waldorf Astoria in New York.

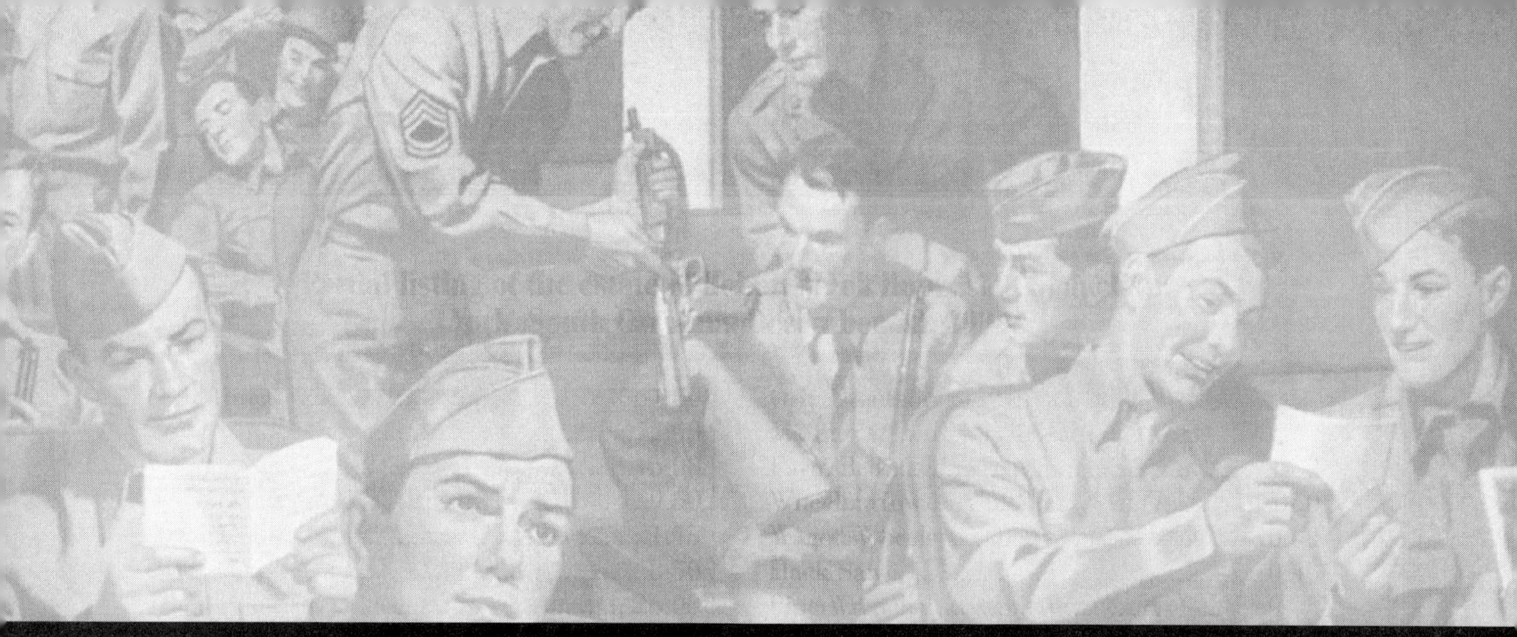

1944 Profile

Upper Class

Jeri Whittaker, a high school sophomore, has joined with her family to support the war effort; her contribution includes teaching bicycle riding lessons and selling war bonds.

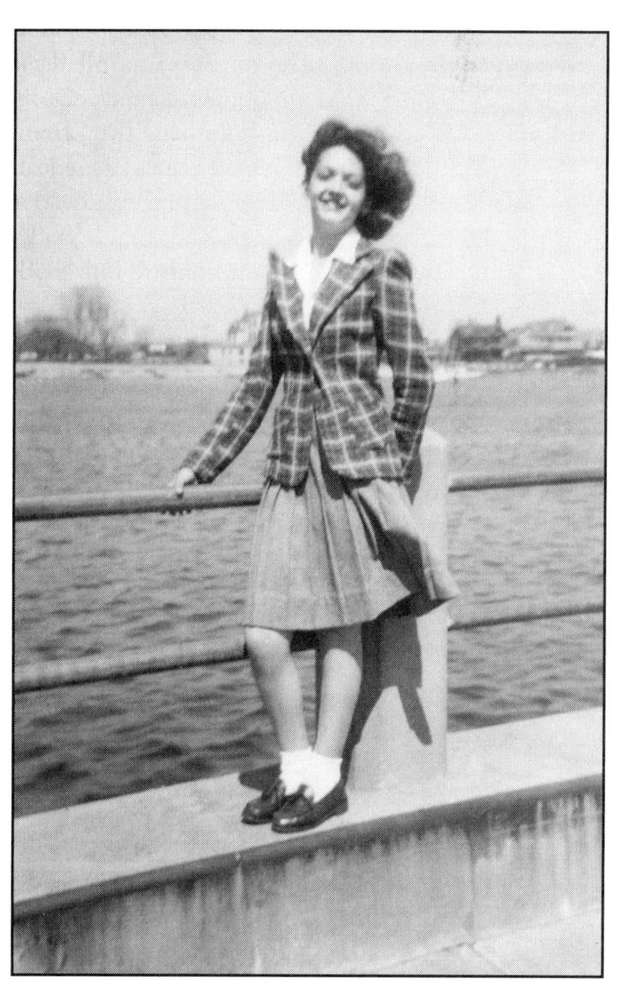

Jeri is determined to sell more war bonds than anyone in school.

Life at Home

- The entire Whittaker family is involved in the war effort, including Jeri, who has a special project.
- The most visible contribution is by her brother Harry, who, after two years at Stanford where he was enrolled in ROTC, quit college to enlist in the navy; he wanted to join up while there was still a war to fight.
- Jeri's father is leading the Civil Defense effort among corporate executives in San Diego, and even her mother, sister and grandmother are doing their part.
- Her little sister has a leading role in the fifth-grade silver foil collection drive; based on her calculations, she and her friends have collected enough foil to build at least three entire airplanes.
- For her part, Jeri and two friends have canvassed the neighborhood, giving personalized bicycle riding lessons at $0.10 an hour to small children, with all the proceeds going to the Red Cross.
- Thus far, they have raised $2.80, counting Mrs. Morris's $0.50 tip.
- In some ways, the family is following in the footsteps of Jeri's grandmother, who put away her role as hostess and neglected her bridge games to march off to war, armed with her shiny black Singer sewing machine; Grandmamma formed a sewing circle among wealthy widows at the country club, and began

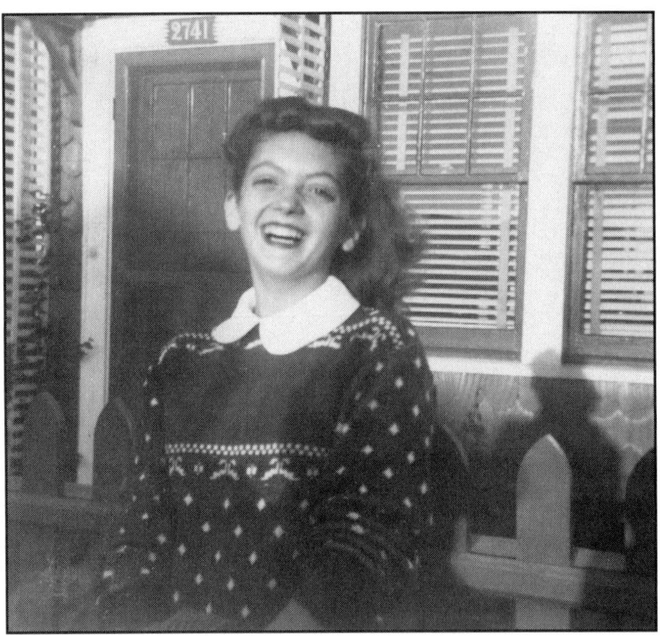

Jeri is tired of eating Jell-O "for the war effort," and dreams of spaghetti with tomato sauce.

sewing slippers for the wounded who are recuperating in local military hospitals.

- She uses a pattern to cut the sole and top portion of the slipper, and though one size fits all, there is a choice of colors—maroon or blue-gray.
- They often meet three days a week, but never on Fridays when most of the ladies have their hair done at the beauty parlor.
- As part of Jeri's sophomore class project, she is selling war bonds and is determined to sell more than anyone in school—especially the snooty eleventh graders, who think they know everything.
- She even has a poster from *House and Garden Magazine* that lists what every bond will buy to support the war effort.
- Being at war can be difficult, though; Jeri is tired of Jell-O as a dessert, and would love to have spaghetti again if tomato sauce weren't so hard to find.
- Besides, every time her mother serves Jell-O and says, "Its for the war effort," she then sings the J-E-L-L-(pause)-O radio commercial, like she's Jack Benny or something.
- But everyone knows that the ration books will only allow you to have so much—no matter how rich you are.
- She likes helping out, but will be happy when her brother Harry comes home and ration books are no longer needed.
- Thanks to the war effort and new construction, sewage has been eliminated from the bay for the first time, and swimming is now safe and sanitary, but the navy has restricted most of the water for its own use.

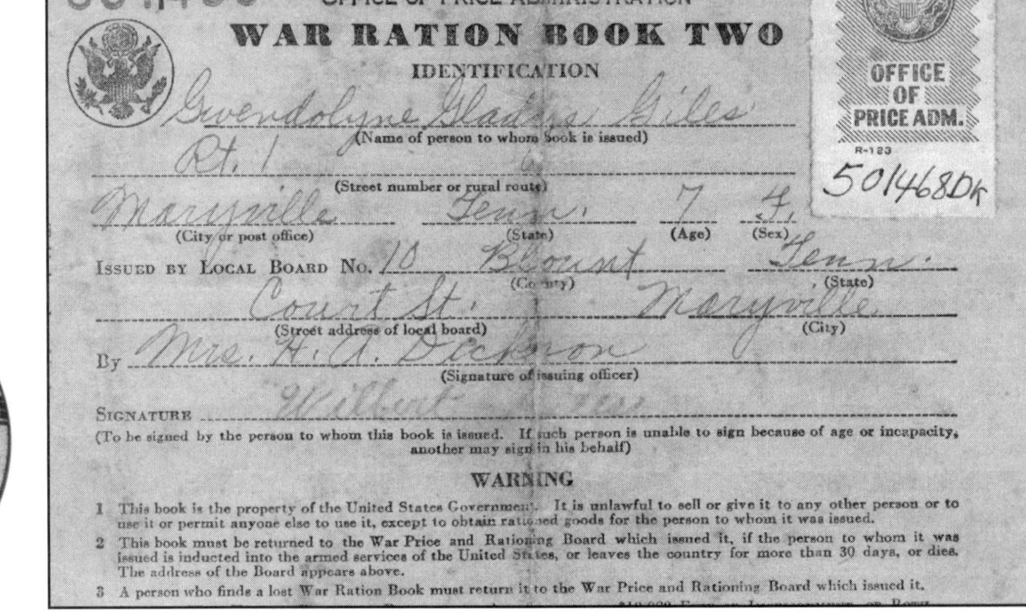

501468 DK

UNITED STATES OF AMERICA
OFFICE OF PRICE ADMINISTRATION

WAR RATION BOOK TWO

IDENTIFICATION

Gwendolyne Gladys Giles
(Name of person to whom book is issued)

Rt. 1
(Street number or rural route)

Maryville — Tenn. — 7 — F.
(City or post office) (State) (Age) (Sex)

Issued by Local Board No. 10 Blount (County) Tenn. (State)

Court St. — Maryville
(Street address of local board) (City)

By Mrs. H. A. Dickson
(Signature of issuing officer)

Signature
(To be signed by the person to whom this book is issued. If such person is unable to sign because of age or incapacity, another may sign in his behalf)

WARNING

1 This book is the property of the United States Government. It is unlawful to sell or give it to any other person or to use it or permit anyone else to use it, except to obtain rationed goods for the person to whom it was issued.

2 This book must be returned to the War Price and Rationing Board which issued it, if the person to whom it was issued is inducted into the armed services of the United States, or leaves the country for more than 30 days, or dies. The address of the Board appears above.

3 A person who finds a lost War Ration Book must return it to the War Price and Rationing Board which issued it.

OFFICE OF PRICE ADM.
R-123
501468DK

Life at School and Work

Jeri leads her class in bond sales, and has been recognized with a letter from California Governor Earl Warren.

- Even though Jeri's tenth-grade class voted to raise war bond money to buy an ambulance, she likes telling her potential customers that three $100 bonds costing just $225 will buy one army submachine gun or 12 antitank shells.
- Customers always look shocked when she talks about machine guns, but her favorite pitch is that $1,000 will provide enough fuel to run three destroyers for 500 miles, because it reminds her of Harry.
- She is leading the class in bond sales, selling in her neighborhood, the country club and at her father's factory.
- She has found that, when asked correctly, everyone has been willing to buy a bond.
- Even her father made a contribution, buying a $1,000 bond from her during the first week of sales.
- During the spring, in recognition of her hard work on behalf of her school, she got a letter from California Governor Earl Warren.
- To show her appreciation, she stayed up and listened to his keynote address on the radio before the Republican National Convention, even though it was boring.
- Her father voted for Governor Warren, and will be voting for Thomas Dewey for president; Franklin Roosevelt should not have run again, he says, because "no man would run for president for four terms unless he really wants to be king."
- Across America, schools and schoolchildren have been the first to respond to President Roosevelt's call to buy Series "E" bonds and defense stamps.
- In August 1941, even before the bombing of Pearl Harbor, Detroit's 400,000 school kids were given leaflets entitled, "What Every School Child Should Know About Defense Savings," prompting many to begin rushing about in an attempt to fill their defense stamp albums.
- By mid-September, 45,000 Michigan stores were selling stamps and bonds; by December, the Michigan plan of involving children was being adopted across America.
- In response to the war, the San Diego city schools have initiated several programs to increase the understanding between the nations of the two Americas.
- As a result, the system's 35,000 students are being advised to enroll in Spanish classes, which now emphasize the culture of Latin America rather than that of Spain.
- In addition, a special series of radio broadcasts based on Latin American music is being presented.
- The requirements for graduation at San Diego High School have been extended to include "Essentials of Effective Living," which teaches first aid, water safety, sports, writing business letters, filling out applications, and budgeting income.
- Girls are expected to be skillful in selecting the right kind of food and preparing it, as well as have the ability to take care of a home and children.
- Boys must know how to use and maintain simple tools, make minor repairs to household plumbing, and fix simple electrical equipment and furniture.

HOW TO CHARGE THE BENJAMIN AUTOMATIC AIR RIFLE
THESE ILLUSTRATIONS SHOW THE EASIEST AND PROPER WAY OF PUMPING THE GUN
Catch knob on end of pump rod under soles of shoes and pull out the pump rod.
Place one hand on breech end of gun, other hand on stock.
Then push DOWN with a Strong, QUICK Movement, pushing the Rod way in every time, by applying weight of body on breech end of gun.
DO NOT pump the Gun as shown above. It is awkward and the weight of the body cannot be used in this way.
About twenty strokes are sufficient for maximum charge. Unless last stroke is completed the pump rod will protrude. After firing several shots put in a few additional strokes to replenish the charge.
DO NOT OIL THIS GUN—Small hole in large barrel near muzzle and is for air intake only—NOT FOR OIL

- Enrollment in high schools has fallen as 17-year-old boys leap from the classroom into the military or high-paying jobs.
- Civilian airplane manufacturers employ more than 50,000 workers.
- To stem the tide, high schools are now quietly discouraging military rallies near school grounds.

Civilian airplane manufacturers employ more than 50,000 workers.

"The World's Biggest Selling Job," by Don Wharton, *Advertising and Selling*, July 1944:

War bonds are the biggest selling job in the world's history. During the first five war loans, more than 750 million bonds were sold to 81 million Americans.

Heading this sales job is 38-year-old Theodore Roosevelt Gamble, national director of the War Finance Division. Gamble owns a chain of movie theaters in Oregon, and had never sold anything except tickets prior to the war. Then he got busy selling war bonds, and was soon breaking records in his state. He was brought to Washington as a dollar-a-year man to build up the war bond organization. . . .

The five million unpaid volunteers who help Gamble in each drive ring the doorbells of half the nation's gainfully employed. They are a determined lot. In Germantown, Pennsylvania, a woman volunteer was notified on the day a drive opened that her son was missing in action. She walked stiff-lipped out of her house and sold $1,000 worth of bonds before the morning was over. . . . A volunteer in Montana was bitten by a prospect's dog—she thinks that may have influenced his sudden decision to buy a $500 bond. On the way home her car stalled in a ditch, and she sold a bond to each of the highway workers who pulled her out.

Among the best buyers of bonds are America's schoolchildren, although the Treasury particularly shields them from any high-pressure salesmanship. The kids' enthusiasm is terrific, and last year they bought more than $660 million worth of bonds. Schools and classes select objectives for "sponsoring." A Jeep at $1,165 is the most popular choice—33,100 were bought by schoolchildren last year. . . . The youngsters of Caribou, Maine, bought bonds for $157,000 worth of ambulances and got a wonderful thrill when letters began to come in from wounded men who had ridden in ambulances bearing their school name. School pupils in Greenville, Michigan, declared a holiday when they learned that their glider was the first to land in France on D-Day. . . .

A touching example of self-sacrifice to further the bond campaign took place in Whiteville, North Carolina. There, a nine-year-old lad put up his beloved cocker spaniel puppy at auction. It brought $50,000 in bonds.

- Administrators believe San Diego already has enough U.S. Navy sailors wandering the streets—many too young yet to have met their first razor.
- At the gaming parlors and shooting galleries on Broadway Street, Jeri and her friends can play the many games alongside the soldiers; her favorite machines allow her to shoot down a Japanese Zero.
- But they don't go downtown on payday, when boatloads of sailors leave the ships and swarms of soldiers from Fort Rosecrans, Camp Callan and Point Loma converge on the city.

Life in the Community: San Diego, California

- Possessing the seventh best harbor in the world, San Diego has come alive since the war began.
- This city, currently the fourth-largest in California, has tripled in size during the past four years.

Roy Rogers was a popular hero to many children of the 1940s.

By 1944, the war brought new words to a popular song from the first feature-length cartoon, Walt Disney's *Snow White*, which had premiered in 1938:

Whistle while you work
Hitler is a twerp
Göring is a jerk
So's his army
Whistle while you work

- Strategically located, the city's highest buildings command a view of Mexico, the Pacific Ocean and backcountry mountains.
- The dramatic level of activity in the Pacific theatre has meant that training and supply bases are needed and West Coast facilities everywhere have been expanded.
- San Diego is the base of the light forces of the U.S. fleet and the nation's largest cantonment of Marines.

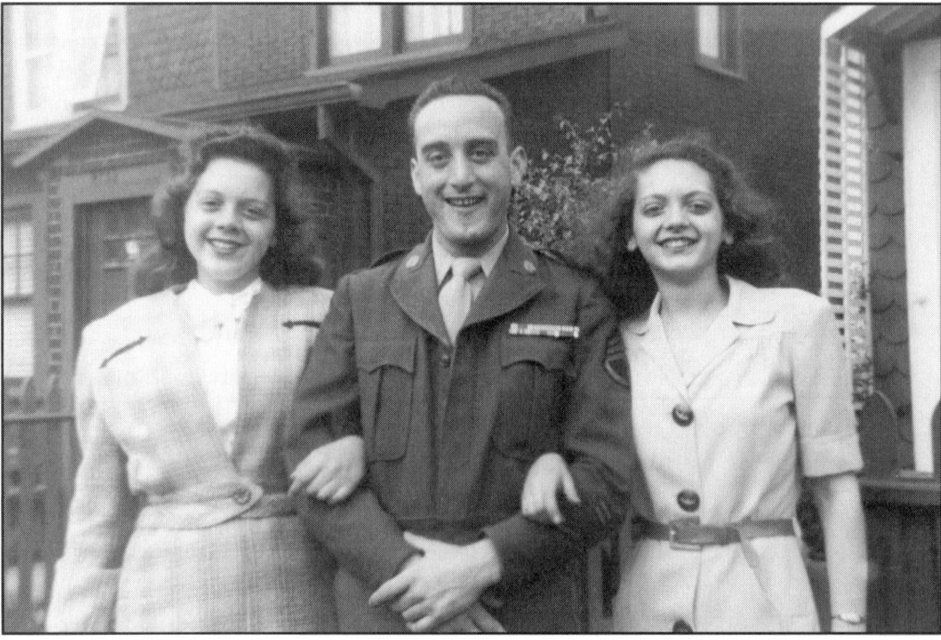

The entire Whittaker family is involved in the war effort.

"What the Blitz-boom Did to San Diego," by Curtis Zahn, *Travel*, September 1944:

San Diego's landscape has been uprooted, excavated, scraped, leveled and rebuilt to suit the specialized needs of the army, the navy, and the aircraft manufacturers. The waterfront has been moved a mile out. Jeeps containing immaculate army officers skid around corners on vague errands. A.W.V.S. station wagons dart everywhere bearing deadly serious Junior Leaguers. More than 12,000 "E" stickers have been placed on windshields, and "B" or "C" ration cards are the rule rather than exception. Everything, everybody, seems to be a priority. It is a turbulent, cockeyed land of deferrables who ask no questions, seek no answers. There is only one answer. This is war.

Yet, beneath San Diego's brisk military buttons and overbearing homage to defense work is an undercurrent of rebellion. The confusion has brought illusion. Patriotism must be prodded with mechanical contrivances, for a kind of sullen apathy is with the people. The various groups—army, navy, small-time merchant and big-time executive, the migratory mass, the culture clique, the sun worshippers—all are divided by growing walls. The military charges civilians with selfish disinterest. The entrenched citizenry says that the Chamber of Commerce wrecked San Diego with its manufacturing schemes. The new masses say they're robbed by landlords and storekeepers. The storekeepers think they are being crushed by the government. All of them think the High Command has been high-handed in its seizures of public buildings, parks, highways and even backcountry. On top of this are the president-haters, the administration-lovers, the college intellectuals and the peaceful church groups which try to hold the heaving, weaving jigsaw puzzle together.

- To accommodate a city on the move, the movie houses run all night and all day, attracting large crowds of swing-shift workers.
- The historic Plaza is still the center of San Diego's life, but life has changed.
- The necktie has been a casualty of war, coats are rare and defense-plant badges are everywhere.
- Due to the combination of wartime shortages and growth, stores are without merchandise, and restaurants are without help.
- Residents of this city, which was first incorporated in 1850, like to say they have plenty of money—but few ways to spend it.
- In addition, liquor sales are up, shooting galleries and penny arcades blossom, the 1,400-acre Balboa Park—twice the scene of World's Fairs—is controlled by the navy, while the Ford bowl, once the home of midsummer night symphonies, is sealed from the public.
- Rationed on food and help, the zoo nevertheless operates and attracts thousands each year.
- To cope with the traffic, dozens of old streetcars have been brought from New York and Philadelphia, but operators—male or female—are hard to find.
- On the plus side, for the first time, well-known bands find it profitable to play the town.

The War Years, 1941-1945, The Stanford Album, A Photographic History, 1885-1945:

Shortly after Pearl Harbor, the Japanese Student Association wrote: "As American citizens of Japanese ancestry, we have been prepared to assume and discharge our duties and responsibilities, yet little did we dream that we would be called upon to prove our loyalty under the circumstances in which we find ourselves. Realizing the necessity of unity in a critical period ahead, we pledge our full support in the present emergency." But by May 1942, fewer than a dozen Japanese American students were still at Stanford. Some had transferred to Midwestern colleges; those who remained were seniors, holding out in their last quarter to receive their diplomas. On May 23, Executive Order 9066, calling for the internment of all Japanese and American citizens of Japanese descent, caught up with the Stanford campus. An evacuation order was unceremoniously tacked on a telephone pole in front of the Japanese clubhouse on Santa Ynez Street. The remaining students were sent by train to the Santa Anita Assembly Center, a converted racetrack in Southern California. . . .

Commencement now would be filled with men in military uniforms, who received their commissions as well as their degrees. Many, called up during the year, received their diplomas in absentia. Male enrollment was dropping fast, and the ratio of men to women fell below two to one for the first time in decades. The normally passive interest in ROTC changed dramatically as men faced the impending draft call. Math and engineering courses were overflowing, language and current affairs courses suddenly popular. Engagement and wedding announcements seemed to appear daily. . . .

Soldiers filled the dormitories and most fraternity houses; the regularly enrolled men—greatly reduced in numbers—lived in the remaining fraternities. The men in khaki became an integral part of Stanford life. "It's a long way from the 'country club' Stanford of a few years ago," reported senior Patricia Clary to alumni readers in the Stanford Alumni Review. "The Stanford of today is a community unmarked by the rah-rah, the Del Monte weekend, the snobbery, and the display of wealth, which, rightly or wrongly, were particularly thought to characterize it."

Jeri and her friends enjoy the gaming parlors on Broadway Street, except on payday when the city is besieged by sailors and soldiers.

- As the newspaper expressed the wartime situation: "There is more crime and less police force; more linen and fewer laundries; more garbage, but few collections."
- The racial mix of the city is also changing; approximately 25,000 African-Americans, many from the American South, have flocked to the city seeking defense contractor jobs, in which the pay is good and the prejudice mild.

Historical Snapshot
1944

- The massive D-Day invasion of Normandy required 156,000 troops; 16,434 soldiers were killed, 7,653 wounded and 19,704 missing
- The War Refugee Board revealed the first details of the mass murder at Birkenau and Auschwitz, estimating that 1.7 million people had been killed
- Half the steel, tin and paper needed for the war was provided by recycled goods
- Paper shortages stimulated publishers' experiments with softcover books
- Franklin Roosevelt was reelected president for a fourth term
- First appearances included Chiquita bananas, quadruplets delivered by cæsarean section, and Seabrook Farms
- The Dow-Jones Industrial Average reached a high of 152 and a low of 135, while unemployment was measured at 1.2 percent
- Popular songs included "Don't Fence Me In," "Irresistible You," "Spring Will Be a Little Late This Year" and Thelonious Monk's "Round Midnight"
- Important museum exhibitions included a reconstruction in Cincinnati of the famous 1913 Armory Show in New York
- The war cost $250 million per day
- The U.S. Army announced the development of a jet-propelled, propless plane
- Lt. John F. Kennedy received the Navy and Marine Corps Medal for "extreme heroism" in rescuing two sailors after a Japanese destroyer cut his PT boat in half
- The GI Bill of Rights was enacted to finance college education for veterans, and to provide four percent home loans with no down payment

1944 Economic Profile

Selected Prices

Chinese Checkers	$0.95
Clog Remover, Drano	$0.25
Corn Remover, Freezone	$0.16
Harmonica, Silvertone	$1.79
Hatchet, Craftsman	$1.45
Hotel Room, Richmond, Virginia, One Night	$3.75
Hot Sauce, Three Ounces	$0.10
Lamp, Brass, 16"	$12.95
Mink Coat	$1,650.00
Motorcycle Goggles	$3.49
Nursers, Evenflo	$0.25
Roaster, Westinghouse	$40.00
Soda Pop, Pepsi-Cola	$0.05
Tie, Hickey Freeman	$3.50
Television, Emerson, 10"	$295.00

BY CONSERVING MEDICAL AND NURSING CARE!

WHO does not want the men in the armed forces to have the best health service possible—the swift and skillful work of medical and nursing units staffed to meet the need? Who cannot think of civilians in his own community whose health is important to the war effort? Who does not hold the welfare of relatives and friends very near his heart? Since most of us do, we need to consider the supply of medical and nursing personnel available to the nation, and make some plans for ourselves.

Medical care is an irreplaceable commodity. We can conserve it by keeping well, by obtaining early treatment if something goes wrong, and working faithfully with the doctor in case we, or those for whom we are in some way responsible, become ill. No one would advocate a neurotic self-protectiveness or *over*-anxiety, but each of us knows or can quickly find out his physician's recommendations for positive health. Whether it is a matter of diet, rest, recreation, or something more deeply technical, conservation of our strength calls for individual self-discipline. Feeling wonderful is the great reward for keeping well.

Obtaining early treatment is easy for those who have been brought up to have confidence in physicians. They cooperate as well with a doctor, forced by the present emergency to carry three practices, as they did with their more leisurely practitioners of a year ago. Others, however, let minor troubles grow into major ones because they fail to overcome a childhood fear of doctors. Some who are on the point of going in to ask about a persistent lump or tired feeling, are held back by know-it-all associates. The net result is likely to be an illness that grows as Hitler did when we failed to stop him in that early stage along the Ruhr.

When calls are coming thick and fast, we can help the doctor by being observant and by keeping records. "Bobby is sick," is less helpful than, "Bobby has a sort of head cold, and seems feverish. This morning when he stepped out of bed he fell. Said his leg hurt." The latter picture makes it easier for the doctor to tell the family what to do right away, and to decide when to fit in that visit. When the doctor arrives, we can be ready to write down his orders, and to ask about the things of which we are not sure: whether a favorite soup, orange ice, or malted milk, may be given, and if "absolute rest" means not even reading, or just staying in bed.

When it comes to carrying out the doctor's orders, the services of a registered nurse may be required. Everywhere in the country there is a shortage of nurses. One way to relieve this is to recruit nurse candidates. Maybe your daughter has always wanted to be a nurse. Parents have sometimes overlooked the potentialities which modern nursing education offers as a vocation and a preparation for life. Or we may help in finding the "hidden nurses": those who have retired or taken up other work, unaware of the urgent need for them in their professional capacity. We can also relieve the shortage by wise use of the service now available.

Physicians and hospitals are assigning special nurses only to those who need them most, and only for the more critical days or nights. The general staff of nurses will give the most urgent care, but the patient will also benefit from constructive use of visiting hours. During convalescence she may be anxious or lonely. Perhaps at this stage it is her happiness rather than her health that is at stake. This is a challenge to relatives and friends. At first, many little attentions of straightened pillows and fresh water may be needed to give a feeling of security—of being cared for. Then, with medical approval, more can be done. Friendly encouragement increases interest in reading, then letter-writing, crocheting, making surgical dressings for the hospital, or mounting recipes for a neighbor. The patient may recover her position in the community and build up her morale while she is recovering her health.

AT HOME, visiting nurse service spreads the care available as far as it will go without sacrificing quality. Once, this was only a means of using charitable funds effectively. However, the demand for part-time service from self-supporting people has extended the program so that now it is offered at cost in most large communities. Working only on doctors' orders and using professional technique, the visiting nurse may in a single day take care of patients having diabetes or heart trouble, arthritis, fracture or burns, of mothers and new babies; she may change surgical dressings or give treatments. The service rendered in a brief visit is effective, but equally important is the help she can give in teaching members of the household how to make a patient comfortable or prepare a formula or do what is necessary during twenty-three hours when she is not there. Knowing how relieves not only the shortage of nurses but the uncertainty into which new duties throw nearly all of us.

31

"Victory, Lasting Peace, Jobs for All," Republican Keynote Address, by Earl Warren, Governor of California, June 26, 1944:

We are here to do a job for the American people. And we mean business. What is your job? Ask any American. Ask the anxious American mother and father. Ask the anxious wives and sweethearts of our fighting men. They will tell you what our job is.

They will give you the keynote for this convention. They will tell you out of their hearts, and what they say will be the same—East and West, North and South—it will be the same. For now the same anxieties are on every American heart—the same hour-to-hour concern for what the day may bring forth, the same steadfast courage to sustain them, the same dreams, the same hope that they will have a chance to make their dreams come true.

This is what is on their heart. This is our job:

To get our boys back home again—victorious and with all speed.

To open the door for all Americans—to open it, not just to jobs but to opportunity!

To make and guard the peace so wisely and so well that this time will be the last time that American homes are called to give their sons and daughters to the agony and tragedy of war.

Isn't that a plain and homely story? But is there any other story which any American would put in place of it? Is there any other thing which, in his heart, any American wants more than these? Is there any American who would not give everything he has to bring these things to pass?

The only good reason I was chosen [to make the keynote speech] was because I come from the great, hopeful, energetic West. Ours is the youngest part of America. My own state of California was a child of four years when the Republican party was born.

Growth and change and adventure are still a part of our daily life.

In the West there is little fear of failure and no fear of trying. That spirit of youth is the spirit of this convention.

Certainly, we are not here to look for a road back to some status quo. There is no status to which we could or should return. The future cannot be overtaken in reverse. Neither are we here to work out some easy-sounding scheme whereby America can stand still. We believe that America wants to get going and keep going. A forward-going America is what we are here for.

Changing America

- College football was becoming the number one sporting event, replacing professional baseball, whose teams had been significantly depleted by the war, though many retired players returned to active play.
- Approximately 350,000 pounds of DDT were shipped monthly to the military to fight typhus and malaria.
- The second atomic pile was built in Clinton, Tennessee, for the manufacture of plutonium for the atomic bomb.
- Women's fashions, though limited by the lack of fabrics, emphasized three-quarter-length box coats and suits with false fronts, while sleeveless dresses exposed the shoulders.
- The city of Boston banned the distribution of *Strange Fruit*, a novel about love between a white man and a black woman.
- Oswald Avery at the Rockefeller Institute isolated DNA, the basic material of heredity.
- U.S. grocers began testing self-service meat markets.

Outdoor activity rarely includes swimming, since the navy put restrictions on water use.

- Adapting to changing tastes, jewelry stores were marketing sterling silver ketchup bottle holders and a mayonnaise bowl and ladle.
- A New York judge ruled that *Lady Chatterley's Lover* was obscene and ordered the publisher, Dial Press, to trial.
- Horse racing was banned during the war.
- Graffiti reading, "Kilroy was here," could be seen on buildings, phone booths and construction fences as a symbol of the valor of America's GIs.
- Howard Aiken and IBM engineers created a mechanical robot at Harvard with a 50-foot panel of knobs, gears and switches.
- The production of soybeans rose as new uses for them were discovered.
- The price of gasoline averaged $0.21 per gallon.

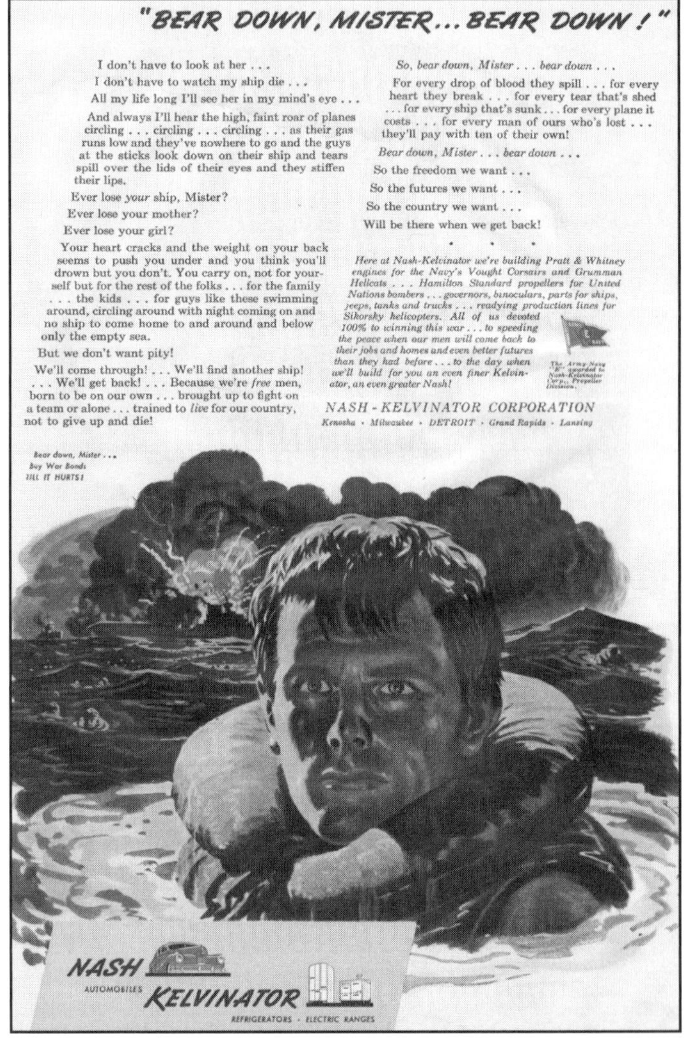

USEFUL GIFTS OF STERLING SILVER
Prices include Federal Excise Tax
8196—Relish dish, glass with silver base, 6½" in dia., $5.50
8197—Relish dish, glass with silver border, 7" in dia., $7.25
8198—Jelly dish, 6½" in dia., including server, $9.00
8199—Mayonnaise bowl and ladle, glass lining, $8.25
8200—Pickle or olive dish, 5½" in dia., $2.75
8201—Ketchup, bottle holder, $10.00
8202—Cheese plate and server, $6.50
8203—Mayonnaise bowl and ladle, $7.75
8204—Sugar basket, blue glass lining, $6.00
8205—Lemon dish and fork, glass with silver border, $4.00
8206—Lemon dish and fork, glass lining, $5.50
8207—Butter dish, glass drainer, 5⅞" in dia., $8.25; pick, $2.00; set, $10.25
AT BROAD · · · PHILADELPHIA
Page UU

"What Your War Bonds Buy: Tag each bond, tuck it away, and watch your house grow dream by dream," *House and Garden*, September 1944:

Today	*Tomorrow*
One $25 Bond (18.75)	**$25**
Field telephone, or	Breakfast set: coffee maker and toaster, or
Complete tropical uniform for a soldier, or	Replace window with French doors, or
Gas mask, steel helmet and first aid kit, or	Electric mixer, or
104 rounds .50 cal ammunition	Waffle iron, sandwich grille, 1 new outlet
One $50 Bond ($37.50)	**$50**
13 life preservers, or	Portable radio, or vacuum cleaner, or
1 marine barometer, or	Electric blanket, bedside electric clock, or
12 navy hammocks, or	Kitchen ventilating fan, auxiliary fan, or
A chemical warfare protection outfit	Cut openings and install 2 new windows
One $100 Bond ($75.00)	**$100**
1 navy chronometer watch, or	Steel cabinets for kitchen unit, or
1 complete rifle range, or	30-gallon automatic water heater, or
.45 automatic pistol, army tent, or	40 electric outlets, or
Bombardier kit, 15 prs. flying gloves	New powder room and lavatory
Three $100 Bonds ($225)	**$300**
1 Coast Guard Lyle gun, or	Game room with pine walls, linoleum floor, or
1 parachute, 1 Garand rifle, or	All hardwood floors in 6-bedroom house, or
1 army mule and 13 tents, or	Television radio set, record changer, or
1 army submachine gun, 12 antitank shells	Garage doors with remote control
Four $100 Bonds ($300)	**$400**
Pilot's flying clothes and equipment, or	Insulate, finish attic room, add dormer, or
Navy calculator and 2 breeches buoys, or	New bathroom 8' x 7' with fixtures, or
1 depth bomb and 3 Coast Guard canisters	Combination heating and hot water system, or
	Tile-drained concrete driveway, 8' by 120'
One $500 Bond ($375)	**$500**
Diving outfit, or	Add new enclosed porch, 7' x 16', or
2 life rafts for 10 people each, or	2-car frame garage, or
10 fragmentation bombs, or	Kitchen range, cabinets, dishwasher, sink, or
Propeller for navy training plane	Erect 1 plane hangar, clear a landing field
One $1,000 Bond ($750)	**$1,000**
3 sextants, or	Prefab guest cottage with bath, or swimming pool, or
Fuel to run 3 destroyers 500 miles, or	
10 miles of barbed wire, or	Air-conditioning, heating for 8-room house
Complete clothing for 9 enlisted men	

> You are about to embark upon the Great Crusade, towards which we have striven these many months. The eyes of the world are upon you. The hopes and prayers of liberty-loving people everywhere march with you. . . . You will bring about the destruction of the German war machine, the elimination of Nazi tyranny over the oppressed peoples of Europe, and security for ourselves in the free world.
>
> —Gen. Dwight D. Eisenhower to the Allied Expeditionary Forces before the Normandy Invasion

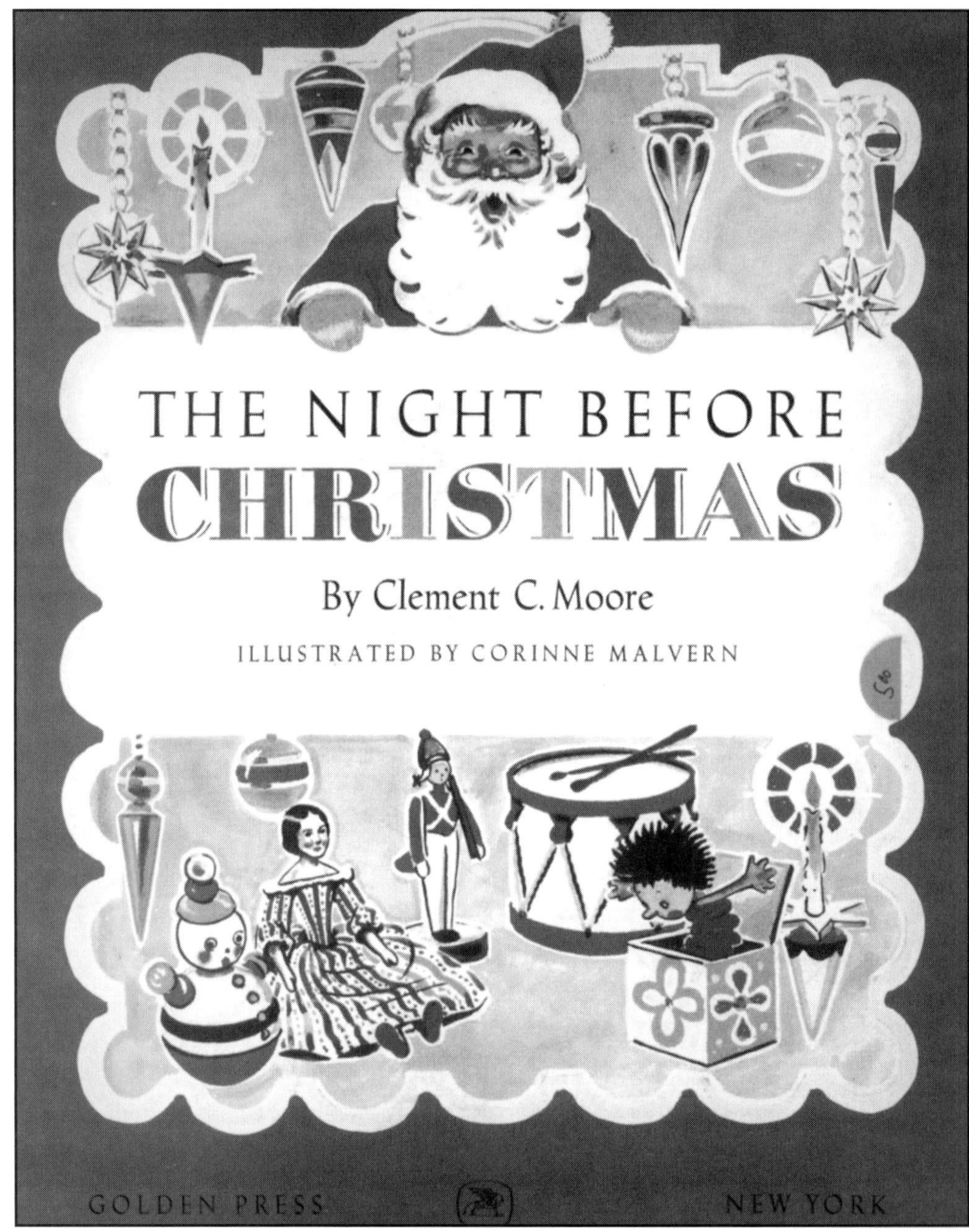

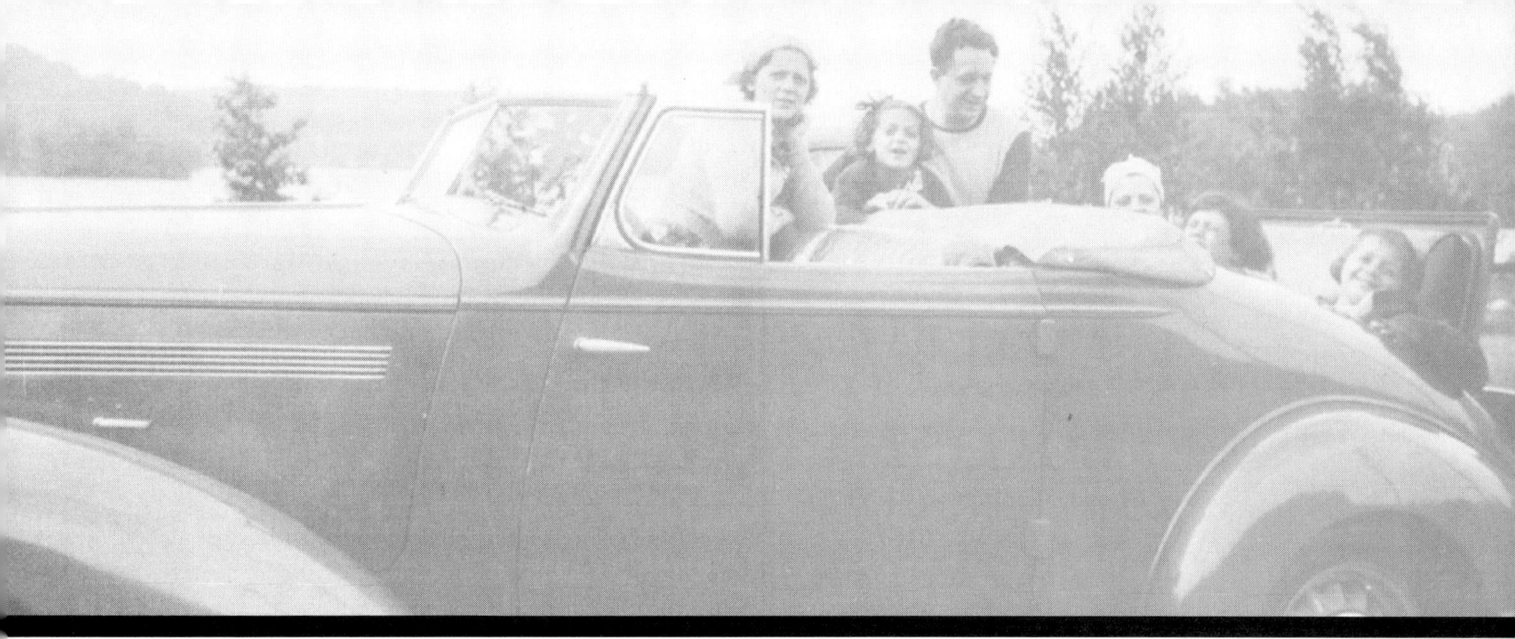

1946 News Feature

"Those Teen-Age Drivers," by Anne Hall, condensed from *Parent's Magazine*, *Pick of the Month's Best Reading*, May 1946:

Parents of 16- and 17-year-olds, here comes the question! "Mums, Johnny is here with his car. Isn't it neat? He wants me to go to the Bite Shoppe with him. Oh, sure, he got his license Friday."

And you have to say, "Yes, my darling daughter." We all have to say "Yes," for if we don't, there's the old cry, "But Mother, everybody does it." They're still using that one, even as you and I did.

What happens is that a boy or girl gets a driver's license, loads up the car with friends, and away they go. Then you stay awake until you hear the crunch of gravel in the driveway and know that this time they are safely home. . . .

You can't refuse to let your child go. Rugged individualist though you may be, you can't make your daughter wait for her father to call for her every time; you can't make your son walk his new girl home from the dance. This is the Machine Age! We thought it up and now we have to control it.

It is not smart to refuse to let your child drive at 16, but it is smart to see that he is a good driver. Every person capable of driving a car should be trained to have the utmost respect for that machine. He should be taught that an automobile is not only an instrument of convenience and pleasure, but also an instrument of destruction.

This does not mean you should scare your child to death or make him fearful and timid. But he must have respect for the power that is under his control. Whether he does or does not, is up to you. You can help promote it if you start early enough to insist on certain rules. Here they are:

Every person in the car should sit down and face the front. I see mothers flying along the road with children standing up on the seats waving pencils or knitting needles or toys. The children of two neighbors of mine use the regular morning ride to the station as a chance to indulge in wrestling bouts. True, the trip is a short one, the road is familiar to the driver, and almost everyone is going to the suburban train.

But such behavior in a moving automobile does not instill in your child the proper respect for the machine itself. He must appreciate that anything can happen, any time. As a driver, you are on the alert and your child as passenger should be trained to be the same.

A friend of mine boasted, "Janey has the most remarkable balance of any four-year-old I ever saw. She can stand on her head in the back seat of our car while I am going 40 miles an hour."

No one should ride on the running board. "Oh, just for the short run up to the station, it won't hurt." But it may hurt. A crash can occur just as unexpectedly outside your own drive as it can 50 miles away.

I am horrified at the carelessness people allow in their cars—loading children on the running boards, fenders, the hood, permitting them to hang out of the windows. Those parents are not laying the groundwork necessary to make good drivers of their boys and girls.

You can't expect your child to assume a businesslike attitude toward driving unless you have instilled it in him. You cannot expect your child, the instant he has 16 or 17 candles on his cake and a license in his pocket, to abandon all childhood habits. Laying down the law the night before he begins to drive will not erase the careless customs of years. . . .

Respect traffic laws and regulations. It is important that your children know that you are aware of the regulations and are observing them. Make your child conscious of them, too. Observe speed limits. Respect areas where the legal speed drops to 25 miles per hour. Ask your child to watch for signs. Encourage his interest by explaining the different signals and their meaning. . . .

The young son of a neighbor shouted as we sped along, "See how fast it'll go. I'll watch for the cops."

Another child spent the summer in a different state where the speed limit seemed to be the miles-per-hour capacity of your individual car. "Mother," he said, "you better not go as fast as these cars. You might get into the habit and they are going faster than our speed law at home allows."

To which of these boys would you like to entrust your daughter's life in a few years?

Let your child know how you feel about drinking and driving. Your attitude on this subject may make your daughter particular about the drivers she finds acceptable to her—or it may not.

A tragedy involving a very young driver occurred near us last spring. At once, parents on all sides were heard to say, "I certainly laid down the law to my Bobby. He can't drive after dark, he can't go over 40, he can't have more than four in the car," and "I told Debby she is not to take any young people in the car unless there's an adult along."

This delayed action is perfectly natural and it may prevent a similar accident. But I firmly believe that it would be much better if we all began to teach our children that it is smart to be good drivers.

Police officers and parents should encourage young drivers to respect traffic rules and regulations.

1947 News Feature

"The Name Game," by Audrey Corn, *Everyday Magazine*, August 1973:
Reading, writing and arithmetic took up much of our school day back in the 1940s when I was growing up in Brooklyn, New York. I liked reading best.

Sometimes we read to ourselves. Other times, Teacher held recitation, which meant that each pupil took a turn reading aloud. The best reading lesson, though, came on Fridays. On Fridays, Teacher read to us.

Teacher's selections were better than the stories in our primers. Her pieces came from real books, and real books didn't need to use short, repetitive sentences and single-syllable words.

One Friday, Teacher read a tale about a little boy named Hezekiah. Hezekiah hated his name. He wanted to be a John, a Joe or a Sam like the other children. After Teacher finished

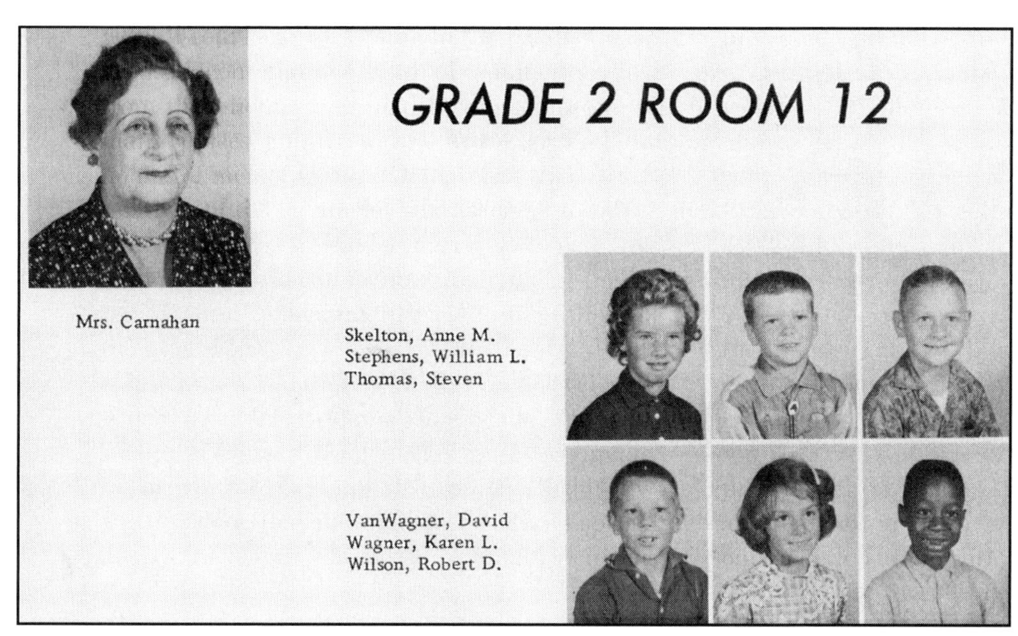

GRADE 2 ROOM 12

Mrs. Carnahan

Skelton, Anne M.
Stephens, William L.
Thomas, Steven

VanWagner, David
Wagner, Karen L.
Wilson, Robert D.

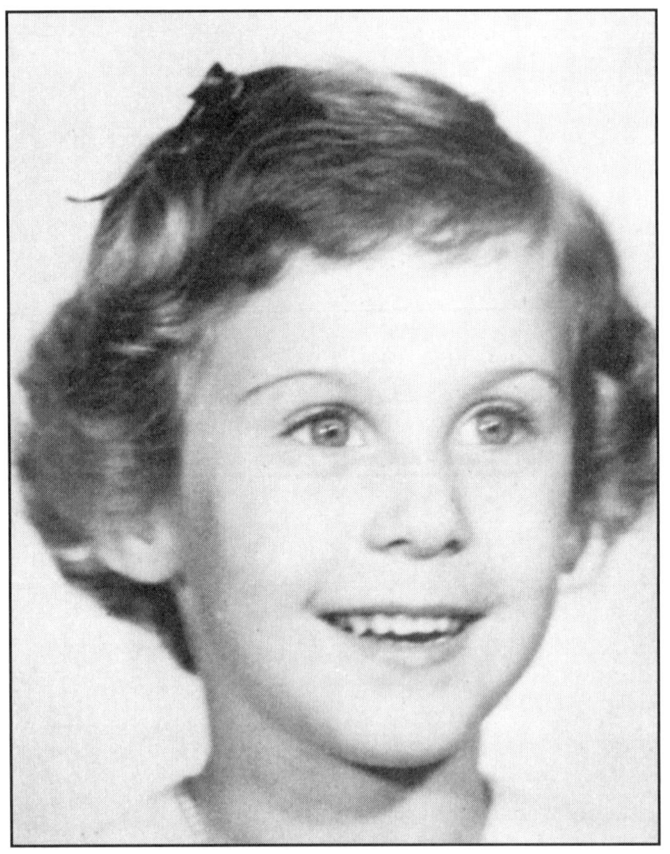

Audrey decided she wanted to be named Elizabeth.

her story, she asked us to raise our hands if we'd ever wished for a different name. Nearly every hand shot up, including mine. My name wasn't as bad as Hezekiah, but I'd often wished for something prettier than Audrey.

Teacher smiled at the sea of waving arms. Our homework, she said, was to choose our favorite name. On Monday we'd print nametags, and all day long we'd address one another by our chosen names. I loved Teacher's plan and I spent much of the weekend pondering the possibilities.

I was particularly partial to flower names like Daisy and Rose.

Names of the months were nice, too. May was only so-so, but April and June were beautiful.

I also liked the more common names. I didn't know a single person named Audrey, but we had three Barbaras, two Davids and two Elizabeths in our class.

The kids with the ordinary names often had nicknames as well. I'd always wanted a nickname. There wasn't much you could do with Audrey. Audie sounded awful, and Aud was 10 times worse. My new name must definitely come with a good nickname.

I finally settled on Elizabeth.

I liked Elizabeth, and Betty was a good nickname. Think Betty Grable! Betty Hutton!

On Monday, after Teacher helped us pin on our nametags, she told us to walk around the room and read each other's selections. Herbert chose Joe after his hero, Yankee baseball great Joe DiMaggio.

Maude's nametag read "Eloise." I'd never heard of an Eloise, but Maude said that a Red Cross volunteer named Eloise had nursed her Papa after the enemy shot down his plane in the war.

Even Teacher had on a nametag! Nobody expected on old lady like Teacher to have a new name. Nevertheless, she fooled us all by penning her choice in bright red letters: "Jewel."

Back when I was a child, we respected our elders. So on that special, long-ago Monday, we called the teacher Miss Jewel.

But Teacher's nametag was nowhere near as surprising as Barbara Elliott's bombshell. Printed on Barbara's card, in bold letters, was the name "Audrey." I couldn't believe my eyes!

Barbara wanted my name! When I questioned her choice, she explained that Audrey sounded classy, like someone who grew up in Manhattan, not Brooklyn.

"Nobody fools around with a name like Audrey. I hate when people call me silly nicknames like Bubbles or Bunny. Would you want to be called Rabbit?" Barbara demanded.

Barbara had even gone to the trouble of walking down to the Brooklyn Public Library to look up my name. "Audrey means 'noble and strong,' " she told me.

I enjoyed my day as Elizabeth, although, truth be told, I felt a little uncomfortable pretending to be a glamorous Bette or a fabled Betty. The following day I was almost content to become Audrey again. It wasn't the most beautiful name in the world. But it wasn't the worst either. It was just a strong, solid name that my thoughtful parents had bestowed upon me back in the good old days.

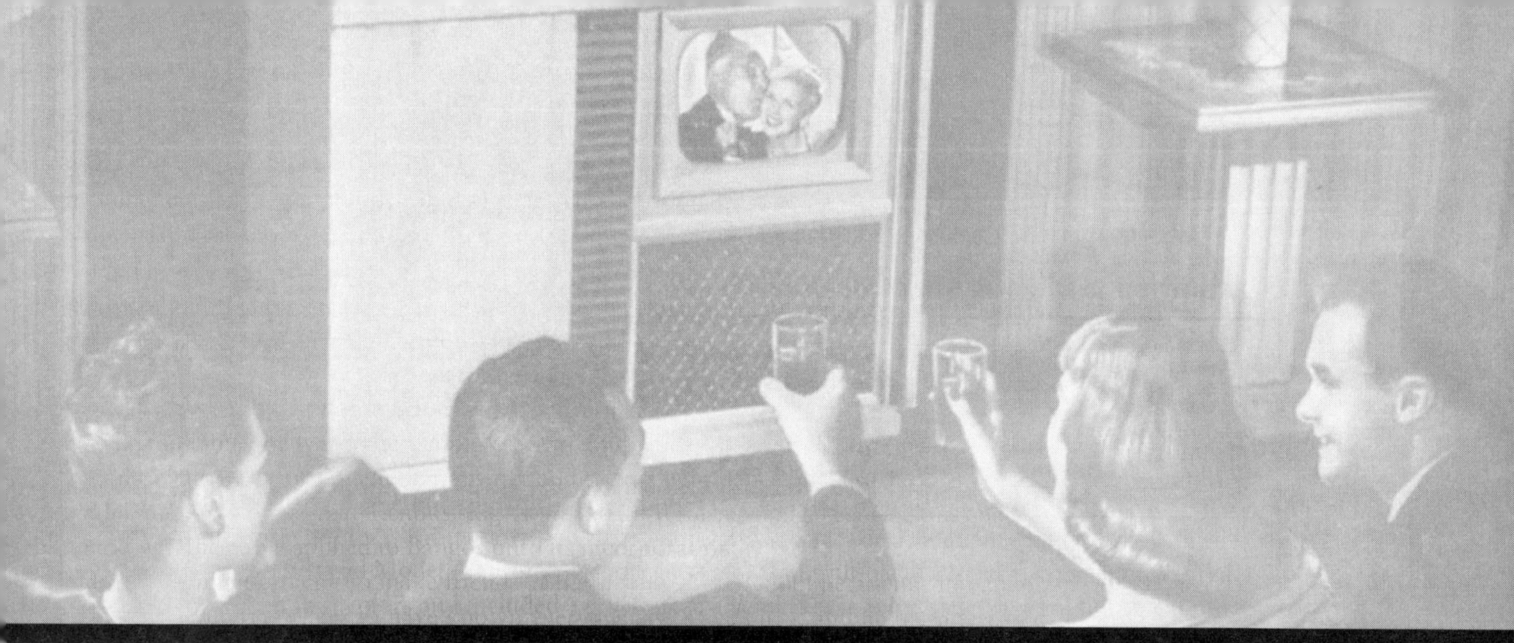

1948 Profile

Middle Class

Mischief, loud noises and screaming sisters seem to follow in the wake of Robin Crenshaw, a science fiction-addicted 17-year-old from Denver, Colorado, who publishes his own sci-fi magazine.

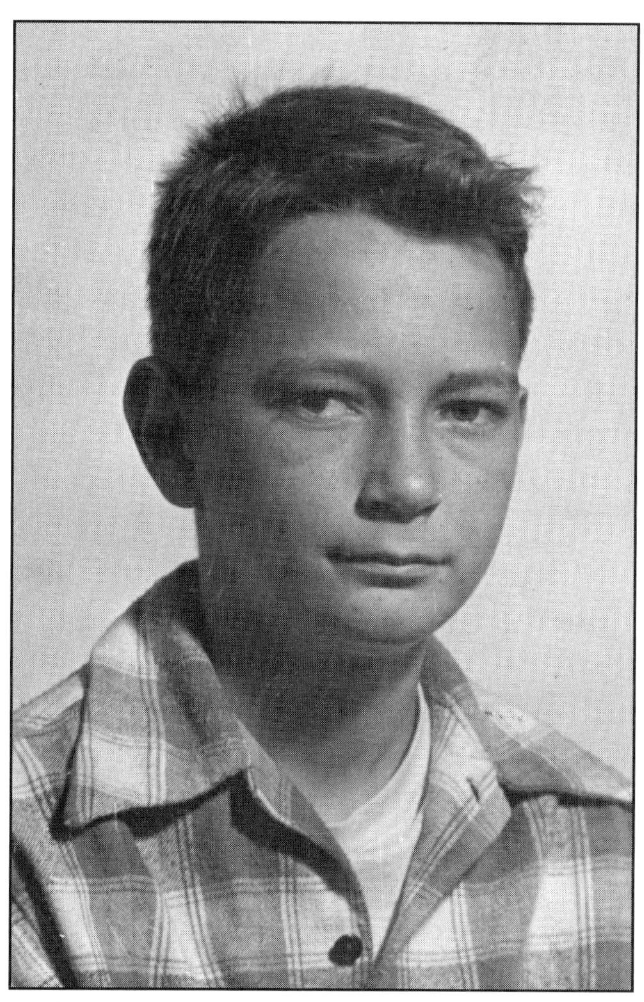

Mischief and loud noises seem to follow Robin Crenshaw.

Life at Home

- Robin is often misunderstood by his mother, even when he is trying to do his best.
- Last year, when a C.O.D. package containing an embalmed cat arrived from a biological supply company, Robin was in a hurry and did not have time to ask permission before putting it in the refrigerator.
- The cat had been ordered so he could dissect it and complete some experiments during Christmas break—a worthy goal, he thought.
- But he forgot to mention the cat's arrival before dinner, causing a huge misunderstanding that got blown all out of proportion.
- Currently, there is much suspicion within the neighborhood, though insufficient evidence, concerning Robin's latest experiment—another noble enterprise gone unappreciated.
- Using sulfur, charcoal and a six-ounce bag of saltpeter purchased from the drugstore for $0.30, he recently tried out an idea he had seen in his Gilbert's Chemistry Set—homemade gunpowder.
- Inserting a baseball bat into a tin can, Robin ground the coarse saltpeter into a fine powder, combined it with the sulfur, and then added charcoal—just as the instructions indicated.

Robin thinks his mother's obsession with designs by Russell Wright is cultural brainwashing.

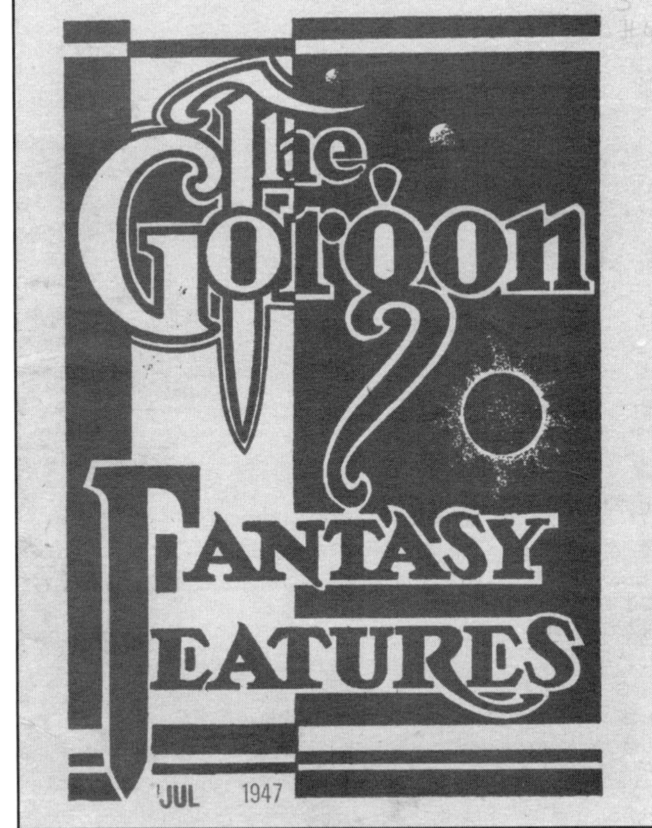

Robin's sci-fi magazine has 188 paid subscribers.

- Then, of course, the only sensible way to test the formula was to create a small rocket and see if the gunpowder worked.
- First, he poured the gunpowder into the open end of several spent .50 mm caliber brass shell casings his uncle had brought home from the war.
- Then, using a piece of string saturated in saltpeter, he created a smoky, smoldering fuse that gave him enough time to flee before the gunpowder-filled shell casing shot off like a rocket.
- It worked wonderfully the first three times.
- No one would have been the wiser had he not decided to use unspent shell casings—with their primer intact—as a potential rocket carrier.
- When the gunpowder-filled shells shot into the air, they erupted in a monstrous, satisfying explosion that brought inquiry from the neighbors and, ultimately, the police.
- He was never caught, but is generally suspected, since most neighborhood disruptions seem to emanate from his house.
- But that is hardly his biggest problem.
- His mother thinks his obsession—her word—for reading, writing and publishing a quarterly booklet on sci-fi is a symptom of cultural brainwashing.
- In response, he thinks that when she rushes out to buy new orange plates made by designer Russell Wright, she is the real victim of excessive brainwashing.
- To avoid the argument, he says as little about his magazine as possible while at home, and no longer asks the family to give up an evening to lick stamps for a mailing.
- The magazine is called *Gorgon Fantasy Features*, and costs his 188 subscribers $0.75 a year.
- He describes *Gorgon* as "an amateur fantasy fan magazine published bimonthly."
- Robin, his friends and a published writer make contributions to *Gorgon*, all in the name of furthering the cause of science fiction, which he considers an emerging art form in America.
- The publication is highly personal; the current issue carries the note: "Beset from all sides by chivalrous dopes who know not women, I am forced to explain (nay, justify) my wild reference in *Gorgon* #11 to Sophia and the Whip. While I am no misogynist (like Hunt), I feel that the ordinary male is at such a disadvantage in dealing with the ordinary (?) female that such an equalizer is necessary. Alas! So far I have been the only casualty. She used it on me, and my shapely calves still bear the scars."
- He writes and lays out the magazine in his bedroom; a teacher helps him mimeograph each edition on the school's A. B. Dick printing press—a violation of school rules that everyone ignores.

"Vanguard of Venus," by Landell Bartlett, *Gorgon Fantasy Features*, July 1947:

In all my experiences in out-of-the-way, God-forsaken places, I have never known fear. I have been shot at by Mexicans, held up by thugs, even bitten by a rattlesnake—but nothing has ever made me afraid. Not even intense shellfire on the Western Front, where I had served the last month of the war as an infantry captain in the 8th Division, ever made me aware of danger. I was cited once by the French Government for bravery, but I take no credit for that. It is simply my make-up—I have no "nerves." But now—this inexplicable rock appearing from nowhere—the very obvious fear it instilled in the horses.

My first impulse was to waken Olin and tell him of this startling phenomenon. The remote possibility that I might be mistaken, and had for some reason failed to notice this rock, due to my absorption in my note-taking, deterred me. How Olin would laugh at me if I roused him because of some foolish fancy about an innocent boulder that had been there all the time. He would never get done guying the life out of me. But I was still positive that it had not been there when we made camp.

I was debating whether to investigate the rock and prove once and for all there was no cause for alarm, or to arouse Olin and get his opinion, when the rock was suddenly thrown back and I could see that it was only a hollow camouflage over a hole in the ground. Before I could cry out, I was seized from behind and strong hands had placed a gag in my mouth and a bandage over my eyes. I attempted to struggle, but my efforts were useless. It was as though my arms and legs were held in a powerful vise. . . .

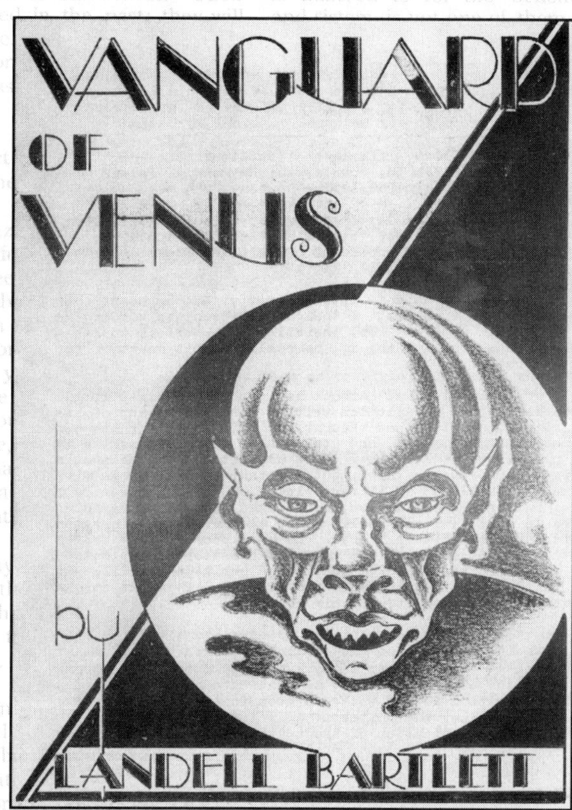

- When problems arise, Robin writes each author a letter, since long-distance calls are expensive and attract unwanted attention.
- The oldest of all science fiction periodicals is *Amazing Stories*, now more than 20 years old; *Astounding Stories* first appeared in 1930, and *Wonder Stories*, renamed *Thrilling Wonder Stories*, began in 1929.
- The sci-fi publication market also includes *Planet Stories*, *Fantastic Adventures* and *Startling Stories*; almost a dozen science fiction pulps, published quarterly or bimonthly, ceased publication following the start of World War II, with its paper shortages and restrictions.
- As the publication has grown beyond his circle of friends, more and more letters have arrived assuming that, since his first name is Robin, he must be a girl.

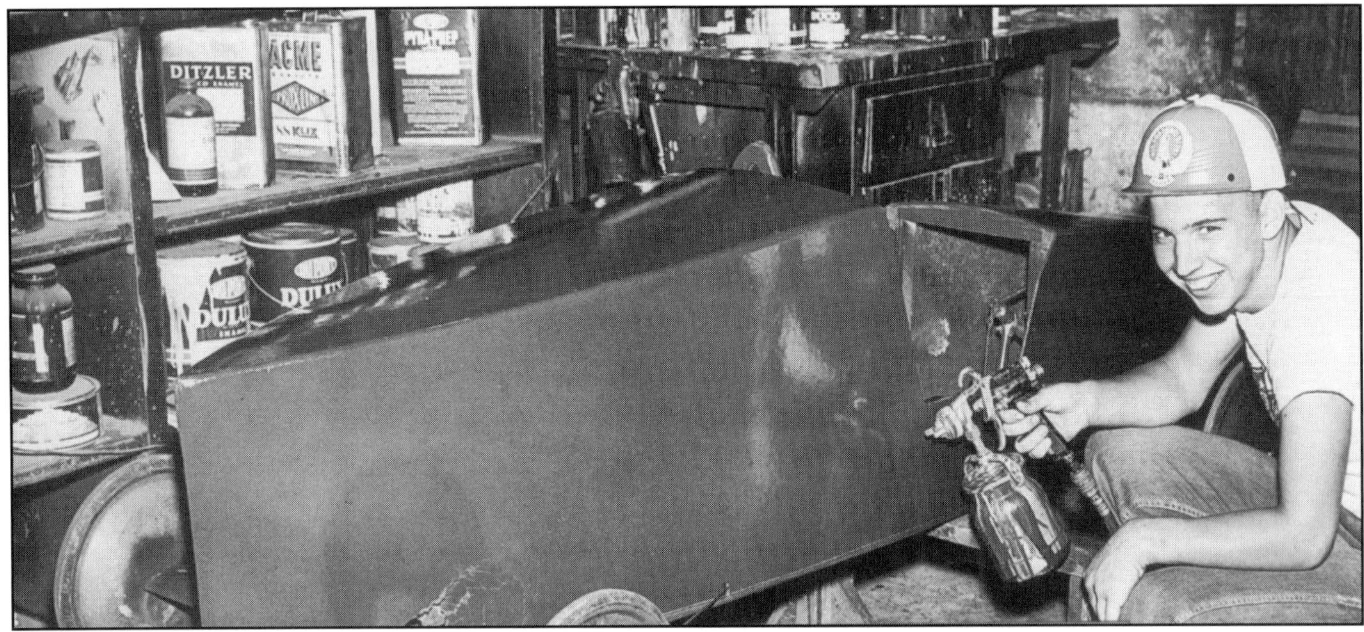

After school he is helping a friend build a racer for an upcoming soap box derby.

- One recent missive went to great lengths to say how pleased the readers were that a girl had taken such a bold step as to create her own publication.
- He wrote back a simple thank you and enclosed his high school picture.

Life at School and the Barbershop

- After school he is helping a friend build a racer for an upcoming soap box derby; making the world's most perfect racer is an exacting science.
- Robin's initial assignment was to sand, oil, grease and push, but his role has expanded to experimenting with a different body material obtained from surplus air gliders, allowing the boys to change the weight structure of the car by creating a ribbed frame over which they can tightly stretch fabric.
- The grand prize is a red and white bicycle with a built-in speedometer.
- His father, who owns a large, 12-chair barbershop in Denver, is sponsoring the race and raising money through his customers.
- Business is particularly good now that the war is over, optimism is up and businesses are expanding.
- To make sure it continues, his father always has something going on at the barbershop, stocking the latest magazines, holding weekly father-son checker contests and bragging that his shop is the best place in the city to catch up on the latest sports gossip.
- Special tables are set aside for the father-son checker matches each Saturday; as custom would have it, nearly every eight-year-old boy in Denver can whip his dad in checkers after a few Saturdays of practice.
- Robin's father takes great pains to entertain his regular customers, too; surprises are common.
- Recently, he and Robin built and installed a mongoose cage in one corner of the barbershop—out of the way, but where everyone could see and admire it.
- Constructed of rustic wood, the faded old box concealed a large sponge rigged to a powerful spring set to explode; then they attached a large sign, "Beware of the Mongoose!"

- For two weeks every customer was warned not to get too close and never open the box, but when the president of the bank couldn't control his curiosity any longer and lifted the lid, the mongoose sponge leaped out at him with a vengeance.
- The elderly, well-groomed gentleman nearly ran over the shoeshine boy in his haste to get away from the leaping mongoose, and now insists he would have killed the critter immediately if only he had had a mongoose-hunting license.
- But not all of the jokes in the barbershop work as planned.
- During the hot summers of Denver, a long sticky fly-catching paper traditionally hangs in the corners of the shop.
- During the course of one day, when the shop is cooled only by a rotating fan, the sticky paper often becomes black with flies.
- One lazy afternoon this summer, Robin was sure that, after the roll had attracted its fill of dead and struggling flies, it would be a great time to attach the sticky roll to his little sister's blond hair.
- He never dreamed she would scream loud enough to get him into that much trouble.
- Recently, the movie theater advertised free admission for anyone who brought a black cat to the Friday the 13th showing of the movie *Abbott and Costello Meet Frankenstein.*
- Robin and his friends formed a cat posse on Thursday night, rounding up 21 neighborhood black cats—domestic and otherwise.

Robin and his friends took 21 neighborhood black cats to the movies as a Friday the 13th prank.

- Few of the cats displayed the patience required to sit silently through the entire movie, and once again everyone suspected Robin as the ringleader; it is unlikely the gimmick will be repeated next Halloween.
- Most of his friends have fallen in love with *Superman* or *Batman* comics but, always the contrarian, Robin is loyal to another.
- For the past five years he has followed the exploits of Plastic Man, a crime-fighting hero who stretches, shrinks and bends at a moment's notice.
- No hero could match Plastic Man's madness, coiling around anything, slinking through everything—plus his ability to shape into any form, from a rug to another human, or any creature he could imagine.

Life in the Community: Denver, Colorado

- Denver sprouted in 1828 when gold was discovered at the confluence of Cherry Creek and the South Platte River.
- The people of Denver are proud of two facts and repeat them often: the city is one mile above sea level and enjoys 300 days of sunshine each year.
- Lush lawns spread before most of the homes and many are watered every day; the average daily per capita consumption of water is 190 gallons—creating a green city in the middle of a brown prairie.

"The Science in Science Fiction," by Groff Conklin, *Science Illustrated*, July 1946:

Until recently, basic science as a subject of lay interest was about as popular as yoga or the theory of marginal utility. But times have changed. In achieving atomic power, radar, television, and rocket propulsion, science has become nearly as popular as politics as a subject for gossip and controversy. . . .

Science has "arrived." And close on its heels in growing popularity comes a venturesome offshoot, stemming from scientific thought but unhampered by rigorous scientific disciplines. It is called "science fiction."

Science fiction is a bizarre and untrammeled byproduct of the amazing forward march of science in the twentieth century. Its very name is a contradiction. By definition, science is "an exact and systematic statement or classification of knowledge," while fiction is "that which is feigned or imagined, as opposed to that which is true." Putting the two together results in: "An exact systematic statement of that which is feigned or imagined." As a matter of fact, that is not a bad definition of the best science fiction.

A story of this genre is based on some scientific premise or principle, which the writer uses as a springboard into the conjectural, the unknown, the sheer imaginary. Nevertheless, good science fiction must have sound scientific foundations. . . .

It is because of this subtle admixture of the scientifically feasible and the purely fanciful that so many scientists are science fiction fans. Knowing so much, they know how little they know, and they are intrigued by the daring speculations of the less scientific and more unhampered writers.

Like serious criminologists who delight in detective stories, hundreds of the nation's top scientists read science fiction for relaxation. It is said that certain experts at the Radiation Laboratory at the Massachusetts Institute of Technology, and equally famous men in the various branches of the Manhattan Project, quietly leave their offices as soon as they hear that the latest issue of *Astounding Science Fiction* is on the newsstands, to buy their copies before the supply is sold. . . .

The true science fiction addict is a fanatic. In no other type of fanship is there so avid and so vocal an audience. The nation is dotted with science fiction fan clubs, whose members are much more loyal to their exotic love than the bobby-soxers are to their matinee idols. Elaborate mimeographed fan magazines are published from Boston to Los Angeles.

- Denver is well-known for its parks system, boasting 24 parks with lakes for swimming, and four golf courses.
- The city's vast water-supply system covers hundreds of square miles on both sides of the mountains, tapping snow-fed mountain creeks and lakes.
- Denver's biggest park lies outside the city; the spectacular Mountain Park System starts at nearby Golden and covers 15,000 acres on the Front Range from the South Platte to Clear Creek.
- The area, within an hour's drive of Denver, is owned by the city and encompasses mountains, canyons, trout streams, lakes, softball diamonds and shelter houses.
- The world-class Colorado Museum of Natural History attracts a million visitors each year, including busloads of schoolchildren on their annual outing.

Historical Snapshot 1948

- The Nikon 33 mm camera was introduced to compete with the immensely popular Leica
- The McDonald brothers began to franchise their name and concept to other fast-food entrepreneurs
- Nationwide, 360,000 soft-coal workers struck, demanding $100 per month in retirement benefits at age 62
- "This is Your Life" with Ralph Edwards and "My Favorite Husband" with Lucille Ball both had their radio premieres
- Mahatma Gandhi was assassinated by a Hindu extremist in India
- Television premieres included "The Milton Berle Show," "The Toast of the Town" with Ed Sullivan, and "Candid Camera" with Allen Funt
- Harry Truman was nominated by the Democrats for the presidency; the Dixiecrats walked out of the Democratic Convention and nominated States Rights advocate Strom Thurmond
- *A Streetcar Named Desire* by Tennessee Williams won a Pulitzer prize
- Captain Charles Yeager broke the sound barrier in a rocket-powered Bell X-1 at 35,000 feet
- General Dwight D. Eisenhower rejected a Democrat effort to draft him for president
- New York began a fluoridation program for 50,000 children
- The garbage disposal, non-glare headlights, Nestlé's Quick, a completely solar-heated house and Scrabble all made their first appearance
- President Harry Truman ordered racial equality in the armed forces and proposed anti-lynching legislation to Congress
- A Gallup poll reported that 94 percent of Americans believed in God
- Dial was introduced as the first deodorant soap
- Kevin Tuohy invented a modern soft-plastic contact lens that covered only the cornea of the eye, not the whites
- Fifty cities banned comic books dealing with crime or sex
- The term cybernetics, the study of information theory, was coined by MIT's Norbert Wiener
- Patents were acquired for the vacuum leaf rake, safety razor, suction earmuff, and the adventure bra with plastic prop-up snap-ins for uplift that wouldn't wash out

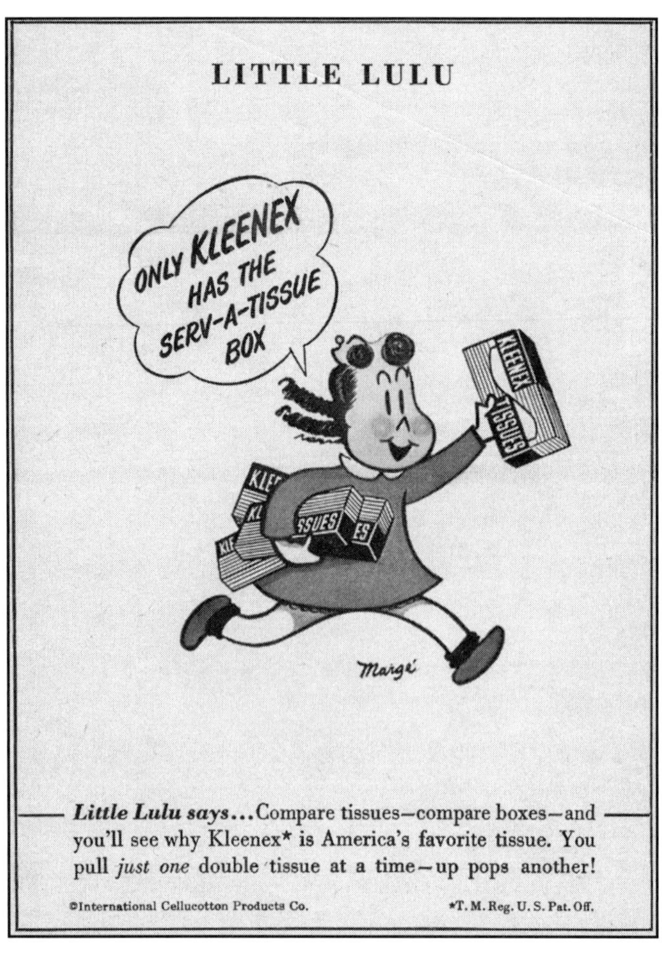

LITTLE LULU
ONLY KLEENEX HAS THE SERV-A-TISSUE BOX
KLEENEX TISSUES
Marge
Little Lulu says...Compare tissues—compare boxes—and you'll see why Kleenex* is America's favorite tissue. You pull just one double tissue at a time—up pops another!
©International Cellucotton Products Co.
*T. M. Reg. U. S. Pat. Off.

1948 Economic Profile

Selected Prices

Automobile, Jaguar Sedan $4,600.00
Bath Towel $0.57
Cereal, Nabisco Honey Grahams $0.27
China, Wedgwood, 20-Piece Set $75.60
Figurine, Meissen $250.00
Flashlight Battery $0.09
Flying Lessons $2.00
Magazine, *Jack and Jill*, 10 Months $1.98
Man's Wedding Ring $8.49
Sprinkler, Sunbeam Rain King $6.95
T-bone Steak, per Pound $0.59
Telescope, 6 Power $1.00
Waffle Iron, Handyhot Twin $12.95

Changing America

- Bernard Baruch coined the phrase "Cold War," saying: "Let us not be deceived. Today we are in the midst of a cold war."
- Gerber Products Company sold two million cans and jars of baby food weekly.
- Seventy-five percent of all corn production was now hybrid.
- The University of Chicago and seven major corporations announced plans for cooperative atomic research for industrial use.
- The transistor was developed by Bell Telephone, allowing the miniaturization of electronic devices such as computers, radios and television sets.
- *Esquire* magazine promoted the "bold look" for the man of "self-confidence and good taste," featuring wide tie

Christmas Gift!

In appreciation of your friendship for Coca-Cola, let us make you a present of this carton of six to enjoy at home

Just present this card (and a carton of empty bottles or usual deposit) to the dealer of your choice and get your full carton with our compliments and best wishes.

This offer Expires Jan. 1

Note to Dealer: Our salesman will redeem this card.

After school and evening radio programming for Mutual Broadcasting Company, August 12, 1948:

3:30 Juke Box Revue
5:00 Mert's Record Session
5:15 Superman
5:30 Adventure Parade
5:45 Tom Mix
6:00 News, Xavier Cugat
6:15 Xavier Cugat
6:30 John Nesbit
6:45 Sports Review
7:00 Kenneth Crawford
7:15 Alvin Keifer News
7:20 Olympic Happening
7:30 Mutual News
7:45 Inside Sports
8:00 Lucky Partners
8:15 Lucky Partners
8:30 Talent Jackpot
8:50 Billy Rose
9:00 Gabriel Heatter
9:15 Mutual Newsreel
9:30 Jan Garber Show
9:45 Jan Garber Show
9:55 Bill Henry
10:00 The Family Theater

clasps, heavy gold key chains, bold-striped ties, big buttons and the coordination of hair color and clothing.

- Bikini swimwear arrived on American beaches to great excitement.
- One million homes now had television sets.
- Five scientists were reported to be going blind as a result of their work with cyclotrons.
- A Nevada court declared prostitution legal in Reno.
- Millions of returning GI veterans took advantage of the GI Bill, and pushed college enrollment to an all-time high, topping six million students.
- Drive-in facilities at banks, introduced two years earlier, were spreading rapidly.

"Current Stuff," ***Gorgon Fantasy Features*****, July 1947:**

Best book news of the moment is contained in a list of new books planned by Arkham House. In reply to a question from me, August Derleth writes: "As for s-f on our lists—we have arranged to publish Leiber's *Gather Darkness*, Van Vogt's *The World of A*, and I think Padgett's *Fairy Chessmen*. I am myself at work on an s-f anthology for another publisher—so far have fine stories by Bradbury, Lovecraft, Bond, Wylie, Hammond, Kuttner, and so forth. I will use 20 in all, one of them a short novel."

- Alabama governor Frank Dixon said during his keynote address to the Dixiecrat convention that the Truman Civil Rights plan "means to reduce us to the status of a mongrel, inferior race, mixed in blood, our Anglo-Saxon heritage a mockery."
- In women's fashion, the squarish straight skirt and flat hip look was replaced by the swirling feminine dress that emphasized the hips and tiny waist.

"Denver, The rough-and-tumble days of its past are gone, but most Denverites wouldn't live anywhere else," by Roger Angell, *Holiday*, August 1949:

There are lots of other stories—the tale about the cannibal mountain guide, Alfred Packer, who reputedly was sentenced by a profane judge who shouted: "There were seven Democrats in this county, and you, you man-eating s.o.b. you ate five of them!; the sad story of Buffalo Bill's alcoholic last years; the story of the Denver tramway horse that used to drag his car uphill and ride it downhill; the story of the baffled Eastern utilities magnate who left Denver, muttering: "There's more sunshine and s.o.b.'s in Colorado than any state in the union"; and the story of the $500,000 jackass. But this is an article about Denver's current history, not its past. The point is clear: Denver talks more about its past than its future; its heroes, its stories and its visions are smaller today than they used to be.

Today Denver's frontier vigor goes into lawn watering; its money into one percent Eastern bonds. Most of the children and grandchildren of the strike-it-rich prospectors are socialites who do their digging in the sand traps of the Denver Country Club and take their liquor watered, in the leather chairs of the somnolent Denver Club. Denver gets, perhaps, its biggest thrill out of basketball; it also goes for stock shows and rodeos. After dark, Denver takes a deep breath and goes to sleep, and the sidewalks are rolled up at 11 p.m. on the heels of the homeward-bound moviegoers. Denver changed overnight from a handsome, exciting, irresponsible and tremendously promising youth into an advanced middle-age—that is, pudgy, comfortable and above all, careful.

This portrait of Denver is not exaggerated, but luckily it is a little out-of-date. Today Denver is being shaken hard by the lapels and shows unmistakable signs of waking up, albeit reluctantly. One of the shaking forces is the town's fast growth. While it is no boomtown in the accepted sense, Denver is approaching a population mark of half a million—nearly a 50 percent growth in two decades—and there is a sizeable number of new Denver residents who want their city to be something more than the Lawn Capital of the Rockies.

Denver is considered a great city for raising children.

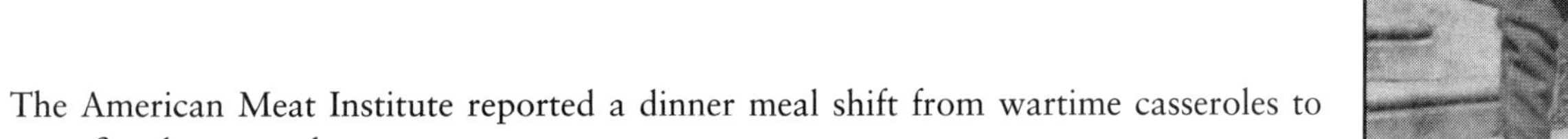

- The American Meat Institute reported a dinner meal shift from wartime casseroles to meat five days a week.
- Congress debated raising the minimum wage from $0.40 per hour to $0.70.
- A house costing $4,440 in 1939 now retailed for $9,060; the price of clothing was up 93 percent over the same period.

"Imagination Runs Wild," by Richard B. Gehman, *New Republic*, January 17, 1949:

Recently, in New York, a man walked into the Argus Book Shop and asked for *The Outsider and Others*, published in 1939 for five dollars. When it was produced he glanced at the price and without blinking, sat down and wrote a check for sixty dollars. He considered this a bargain—the book often had brought a hundred.

The Outsider is a collection of stories by the late H. P. Lovecraft, a writer esteemed by readers of science-and-fantasy fiction. That it sells today at 12 times its published price, and more, is informative.

It is also informative that another New York bookseller has a standing order from a Pittsburgh minister for every science-and-fantasy item that comes in; that a Pasadena manufacturer keeps his collection, which numbers about 2,000 volumes, in a concrete vault with four-foot walls; and that a drugstore in Oak Ridge, Tennessee, sells out 150 copies of *Astounding Science Fiction*, the leading magazine in this field, within three days of its publication each month.

The fact is that science-and-fantasy has come into its own, has been a rapidly expanding literary fad, perhaps even a trend, since shortly before the end of World War II. A foreigner, making a cursory survey of our magazines and bookstores and deducing that the country has gone mad for the subject, might well be correct. Here is some evidence.

- During the past three years, trade publishers have brought out more than 50 anthologies and novels of science-and-fantasy.
- Five new publishing houses devoted entirely to the genre have sprung into existence.
- Twenty-odd magazines in the field are enjoying unprecedented circulation booms.
- Such relatively cautious publications as the *Saturday Evening Post* and *Harper's* have run stories about vampires and interplanetary intrigue.

Readers of science-and-fantasy, like readers of detective fiction, come from all classes and occupations. But unlike the whodunit fans, they seem to be infected with a virus. They read, reread and analyze stories with the zeal of scholars tracking down the key word in a Shakespearean play.

They also publish magazines—fanzines, as someone (someone who reads *Time*, no doubt) has called them. One bibliography of fan magazines recently listed more than a hundred titles, adding apologetically that several more may since have come into being.

1950–1959

As the 1950s began, the average American enjoyed an income 15 times greater than that of the average foreigner, optimism was rampant, and much of America's energy was focused on the potential of its children. Education reform at the elementary, high school and college levels was rabidly debated. Dozens of television programs geared toward children were created. Toys to expand the child's mind were in vogue. Travel was considered a necessity and college a definite possibility for the first time in the history of many families. The vast majority of families considered themselves middle class, and many were enjoying the benefits of health insurance for the first time. America was manufacturing half of the world's products, 57 percent of the steel, 43 percent of the electricity, and 62 percent of the oil. The economies of Europe and Asia lay in ruins, while America's industrial and agricultural structure was untouched and well-oiled to supply the needs of a war-weary world.

In addition, the war years' high employment and optimism spurred the longest sustained period of peacetime prosperity in the nation's history. A decade of full employment and pent-up desire produced demands for all types of consumer goods. Businesses of all sizes prospered. Rapidly swelling families, new suburban homes, televisions, and most of all, big, powerful, shiny automobiles symbolized the hopes of the era. During the 1950s, an average of seven million cars and trucks were sold annually. By 1952, two thirds of all families owned a television set; home freezers and high-fidelity stereo phonographs were considered necessities. Specialized markets developed to meet the demand of consumers such as amateur photographers, pet lovers, and backpackers. At the same time, shopping malls, supermarkets, and credit cards emerged as important economic forces.

This economic prosperity also ushered in conservative politics and social conformity. Tidy lawns, bedrooms that were "neat and trim," and suburban homes that were "proper" were certainly "in" throughout the decade as Americans adjusted to the post-war years. Properly buttoned-down attitudes concerning sexual mores brought stern undergarments for women like bonded girdles and stiff, pointed, or padded bras to confine the body. The planned community of Levittown, New York, mandated that grass be cut at least once a week and laundry washed on specific days. A virtual revival of Victorian respectability and domesticity reigned; divorce rates and female college attendance fell while birth rates and the sale of Bibles rose. Corporate America promoted the benefits of respectable men in gray flannel suits whose wives remained at home to tend house and raise children. Suburban life included ladies' club memberships, chauffeuring children to piano and ballet classes, and lots of a newly marketed product known as tranquilizers, the sales of which were astounding.

The average wage earner benefited more from the booming industrial system than at any time in American history. The 40-hour work week became standard in manufacturing. In offices many workers were becoming accustomed to a 35-hour week. Health benefits for workers became more common and paid vacations were standard in most industries. In 1950, 25 percent of American wives worked outside the home; by the end of the decade the number had risen to 40 percent. Communications technology, expanding roads, inexpensive airline tickets, and a spirit of unboundedness meant that people and commerce were no longer prisoners of distance. Unfortunately, up to one-third of the population lived below the government's poverty level, largely overlooked in the midst of prosperity.

The Civil Rights Movement was propelled by two momentous events in the 1950s. The first was a decree on May 17, 1954, by the U.S. Supreme Court which ruled "that in the field of public education the doctrine of 'separate but equal' has no place. Separate educational facilities are inherently unequal." The message was electric but the pace was slow. Few schools would be integrated for another decade. The second event established the place of the Civil Rights Movement. On December 1, 1955, African-American activist Rosa Parks declined to vacate the white-only front section of the Montgomery, Alabama, bus, leading to her arrest and a citywide bus boycott by blacks. Their spokesman became Martin Luther King, Jr., the 26-year-old pastor of the Dexter Avenue Baptist Church. The year-long boycott was the first step toward the passage of the Civil Rights Act of 1964.

America's youths were enchanted by the TV adventures of *Leave It to Beaver*, westerns, and *Father Knows Best*, allowing them to accumulate more time watching television during the week (at least 27 hours) than attending school. TV dinners were invented; pink ties and felt skirts with sequined poodle appliqués were worn; Elvis Presley was worshipped and the new phenomena of *Playboy* and Mickey Spillane fiction were created only to be read behind closed doors. The ever-glowing eye of television killed the "March of Time" newsreels after 16 years at the movies. Sexual jargon such as "first base" and "home run" entered the language. Learned-When-Sleeping machines appeared, along with Smokey the Bear, Sony tape recorders, adjustable shower heads, *Mad Comics*, newspaper vending machines, Levi's faded blue denims, pocket-size transistor radios, and transparent plastic bags for clothing. Ultimately, the real stars of the era were the Salk and Sabin vaccines, which vanquished the siege of polio.

1954 Profile

Middle Class

Born and raised in Jackson Hole, Wyoming, Walter Perry is now attending Yale on a full scholarship as part of a program to recruit nontraditional students and achieve more diversity in its classes.

Life at Home

- Growing up as the son of a federal park ranger had its advantages, one of which was the opportunity to hunt elk.
- Each fall, a herd of elk comprising about 16,000 to 20,000 head drifted down from the high summer range in the Yellowstone-Teton National Forest area to winter in the lower Jackson Hole Valley.
- Add to elk hunting the opportunity to go mountain climbing and snow skiing, play varsity football, achieve valedictorian status in his high school and receive a full scholarship to college, and Walter Perry's is a nice life.
- During his senior year, Walter was asked to assist one of the world's finest mountain climbers in preparing to scale the cliff-hunt towers of the Middle Teton.
- Walter helped arrange for transportation, located the campsites and participated in the hike, only completing the first half of the climb before turning back—so he could play in his high school football game.
- As the starting right end, he has found football to be lots of fun, but hardly something around which a serious man would build his life.
- He also finds the community's obsession with beating local rivals to be both amusing and annoying; his goal is to attend college and learn the range of his skills.

Walter Perry is attending Yale on a full scholarship.

Walter considers high school football fun, but hardly worthy of a serious man.

- "Your own potential is the greatest burden God gives any person," his father loves to say—over and over again.
- Until he received a personal call from a Yale recruiter offering him a scholarship, he had never considered leaving the area.
- His father called it a sign of things to come, encouraging him to take the challenge, but his mother was less sure.
- Not only is Walter the first in his family to attend college, the invitation included a full scholarship to one of the nation's most prestigious schools.
- "Yep," his father said, "it's a sign."
- Walter's initial excitement soon turned to fear of making a mistake and embarrassing his family and the community.
- He had felt the same thing before his first elk hunt at age 12, his father reminded him, yet Walter made a kill on his first day with his first shot, and hasn't backed away from a challenge since.
- One of his father's duties in Jackson Hole is to monitor the activities of the beavers, whose dams can filter the mountain water and settle the silt, ensuring pure, clean stream water; however, beavers can also be destructive.
- Early on, Walter was taught to "think twice and act once" so he could discover which actions were helpful or harmful; "Not everything is what is seems," his mother reminds him.

His father is a federal park ranger in Jackson Hole, Wyoming.

"Wildlife Adventuring in Jackson Hole," by Frank and John Craighead, *The National Geographic Magazine*, January 1956:

Another old-timer is Mrs. Evelyn M. ("Gran") Dornan.

The patio of Gran's home at Moose commands a superb view over the Snake River and the Teton peaks. Sitting there, we often have watched white-footed mice flick in and out of the shadows. "There goes tomorrow's dinner for your owls," Gran might say.

Though she is a keen naturalist and fond of birds and mammals, she has never been averse to trapping mice for us. She wraps them in foil and keeps them in the refrigerator. Gran's white-footed mice helped feed some of our experimental birds. . . .

Gran claims she's such a font of information because she's a little hard of hearing in one ear. "Everything goes in one ear," she says, "and can't get out the other. . . ."

Often we go to the town of Wilson, just south of the park, to see white-haired Mrs. Nan Budge in her white cottage beside swift-running Fish Creek. Mrs. Budge came into Jackson Hole as a bride in 1896. She and her husband shared with her parents one of the four covered wagons that together clattered into the valley over Teton Pass.

Mrs. Budge has made friends with a school of enormous cutthroat trout in the creek. She has so pampered them that they'll snatch their rations from her fingers. Fetching a bowl of crumbled Spam, Mrs. Budge tossed in a couple of chunks. A streamlined spotted form about two feet long materialized out of the depths and gulped one piece. Two other big trout wrestled briefly for the remaining snack.

Mrs. Budge threw in a whole handful of morsels, and the water boiled with cutthroats up to six and eight pounds in weight. Our hostess beamed, pleased that her pets were behaving so well for visitors.

Walter was taught that clocks were invented by man, not nature.

- He also learned that clocks were invented by man, not by nature.
- Time, he believes, is a sorry way to measure anything, including the length of time a conversation should last or a hunting trip will require.
- At the same time, he recognizes that the region's informal way has its downsides.
- More than once he and his father have made the long drive into town for a necessary tractor part, only to find a sign on Simpson's Hardware Store, reading: "Closed, gone elk hunting. Back Thursday."
- Growing up, he always had plenty of "informal" pets around his cabin home: coyotes, ground squirrels, chipmunks, magpies, ravens, horned owls, sparrow hawks, prairie falcons, Canadian geese, trout and white-footed mice.
- The coyote his father found abandoned as a pup lived near the house, coming and going like the family dog.
- The environment around Jackson Hole also taught him to read danger signals.
- A moose will give warning of its intent to attack by lifting the hair along the back of its neck and spine, then stick out its tongue.
- He is finding that the signs of danger are harder to read in the East at Yale.

Life at School

- Walter was recruited by Yale as part of a program to diversify the Ivy League school.
- Before arriving, he had never been east of the Mississippi River, had never even seen pictures of the campus, and was still unsure of the correct spelling of "Connecticut."
- His first days were intimidating, as though he had arrived in a strange country where everyone spoke a foreign language.
- The specially recruited diversity students, whose fathers and grandfathers had not attended Yale and who had no pedigree, quickly formed their own informal "Public High School Rube Society," where they could make fun of themselves and those around them.

Walter is part of the public school "rube society."

- Walter is the sole representative from his high school in Jackson Hole; Andover, the exclusive private school, has 62 representatives in this Yale class.
- The ratio of private school graduates to those of public schools is 61:34 in favor of private schools.
- Walter has quickly concluded that the Eastern boarding-school students have their own way of dressing, talking and socializing.
- Walter and his "rube society" friends make great sport of imitating the legacy students who often possess long links to Yale and lots of blueblood money.
- Yet, the bluebloods set a tone on campus that is cool, understated and confident; Walter often thinks of himself as a slobbering puppy dog beside these men of class.
- He has found fitting in to be both difficult and easy; when he lets himself go and talks about hunting deer and elk, he gains a lot of attention, though he still finds it hard to relax over a beer while wearing a tweed jacket and a tie.

"At the Roots of Ivy," *Newsweek*, November 15, 1954:

At Yale, Dr. Whitney Griswold informed his undergraduate-school faculty with some asperity that he has not relented on changes recommended to them a year ago. At that time, the report of a committee headed by the university's president suggested the abolition of regular courses for freshmen and sophomores. As a man who feels that the flaws in the present American system have forced colleges into "doing the high schools' job for them," Dr. Griswold thought improvement could be obtained if students were allowed to work semi-independently for two years, attending lectures only when they wished and participating once a week in a discussion group in "areas of concentration." Such freedom might snatch the student from a fate wherein, as the Griswold committee's report put it, he "first loses his interest in and then his respect for the education he's getting." At the end of two years, moreover, the student would have to pass a series of comprehensive tests to stay in school.

Privately, some Yale professors thought such changes would have catastrophic effects. Although they were urged to make the report their "chief academic activity," during the next year, few departments made concrete recommendations. Two weeks ago, Dr. Griswold, head of the university since 1950, made it clear that he still expects action.

- A current rage is Dunkin' Donuts, shipped in weekly from Quincy, Massachusetts, by the father of a Yale sophomore; the sugary donuts seem lighter than air and close to heaven after a long day of arcane English literature.
- Less popular among his classmates is his love of Spam.
- During World War II, his family existed on the canned mixture of pork shoulder, ham, spices and preservatives.
- When homesick, he always resorts to eating Spam, even though his roommate gags at the mere suggestion of a Spam sandwich.
- Movies, when time can be found, are crucial to his existence; anything by Alfred Hitchcock brings him joy.
- Outside his window, he often sees his fellow students endlessly tossing empty pie tins from the Frisbee Baking Company.
- Others take great pride in playing catch using the new Pluto Platter, shaped the same way as the pie tins but made of plastic.
- Although dozens of games of toss take place every day, he cannot imagine this fad ever catching on anywhere else—especially out West.
- Across America, colleges are debating philosophical issues of academic freedom, such as how far it should go and whether a communist should be allowed to teach.

Since arriving at Yale, Walter has printed pictures of his adventures in the West.

Walter still finds it difficult to relax in a sports jacket.

- Academically, Yale is one of the great strongholds of liberal arts education; Walter and his roommates joke that its curriculum is not intended to train anyone to do anything, but instead to be somebody.
- About 630 undergraduate courses are now offered at the school, one quarter of them consisting of small discussion groups and seminars in which students are encouraged to participate.
- Professor Chauncey Tinker no longer teaches his famous course, The Age of Johnson, but his stories live on.
- One famous class comment by Professor Tinker is: "Human progress is like a milk train which can be flagged down by a child, halted by wandering cows, derailed by a twig. But all the while its whistle gives forth little, piercing, hopeful hoots."
- A current educational experiment under way called Directed Studies has students taking only special courses in broad fields of learning for their first two years, along with an integrating philosophy class.
- Yale is aiming its Directed Studies program at 50 extremely precocious 16-year-olds, all lifted out of high schools and preparatory schools, and supported by a Ford Foundation grant, to prove that four years of high school are two years too many.

Growing up in Wyoming was full of adventure.

- In addition, Yale has established a Scholar of the House program in which 13 seniors take no classes, only dropping in on an occasional class suggested by their advisor.
- Instead, they work on lengthy projects in the fields of creative writing, literary criticism, philosophy, mathematics, international relations, city planning, art history, social history, political science and archaeology.

"End of a Tradition," *Time*, April 6, 1953:

In every Yale man's life, there has been one traumatic experience that other people do not have. It is Tap Day—the tense afternoon in May when members of the junior class gather to await the whack on the back that will send 90 of them to the six great Senior societies. William Howard Taft had sweated it out (he went to Skull and Bones); so had his son Robert (Bones), and Robert's political adversary, Dean Acheson (Scroll and Key). Even that fictional stalwart, Dink Stover (Bones), had trembled at the thought of Tap Day; "The morning was interminable, a horror. They did not even joke about the approaching ordeal. No one was so sure of election that the possible rejection of some chum cast its gloom over the day."

But the Dink Stovers who went to Yale after World War II seemed unable to take Tap Day too seriously. Many found it humiliating for the hundreds of juniors rejected; some found the etiquette of the societies ludicrous (in theory, a member hearing his society's name mentioned among outsiders was supposed to leave the room). Finally last week, Yale's Senior societies quietly came to a decision. After 75 years, Tap Day was abolished. Just how the societies will elect members from now on no one yet knew. Said the Yale Daily News: "Tap Day was not a great evil . . but as a tangible symbol it has drawn most of the anti-Society criticism. . . . What remains is for the Societies to justify their existence."

Remembering Denny, by Calvin Trillin, Warner Books, New York, 1994:

Some of our classmates came from the sort of backgrounds we had simply never contemplated. Although I have told the story for years as a joke, one of my roommates—I call him Thatcher Baxter Hatcher in the joke, since a lot of people in our class seemed to have three last names—actually did tell me that after the war his family no longer dressed for dinner, and I actually did think he meant that they were allowed to come to the table in their undershirts. There were people in our class I came to think of as package people: you could go into a store and find their family names on packages, wrapped around candy bars or flour or beer. One of the roommates Denny was assigned to his freshman year was John Mars, whose family produced Mars bars. My boyhood friend from Kansas, who had enrolled in Princeton the same autumn I showed up at Yale, had a roommate I never heard him address as anything but Eberhard Faber, the Pencil King, as in "Could you please pass the salt, Eberhard Faber, the Pencil King?"

- Walter particularly loves the Yale library; he considers it a festival to walk among 2.8 million volumes.
- He calculates that the library back home equates to half of one floor of this 16-story tower.
- Vacuum tubes, elevators and machinery run throughout the imposing, crowded building and permeate the stacks with a faint humming sound.
- It is considered one of the great research libraries in the world and includes a Gutenberg Bible, the manuscripts of Gertrude Stein and the Kanjur, an ancient, 99-volume collection of sacred Buddhist writings.
- In 1947, Yale purchased the first book printed in the American colonies, the Bay Psalm Book, for $151,000.

Life in the Community: New Haven, Connecticut, and Jackson Hole, Wyoming

- Having celebrated two years earlier the 250th anniversary of its founding in 1701, Yale has a firm grip on tradition.
- Scattered around Connecticut, the school was pulled together in New Haven in 1716, thanks to the financial windfall of Elihu Yale, a rich London merchant who gave £562 to the fledgling "collegiate school."
- Following the establishment of a separate science department and autonomous schools of divinity, medicine and law, Yale became a university in 1887.
- This legacy is further reinforced by the occasional presence on campus of Old Blues, as loyal members of the alumni are called.
- Often they are introduced by their professional titles such as president, chairman of the board or Honorable.
- Currently, the school has 4,300 students, up from its traditional 3,800.

Yale recently celebrated the 250th anniversary of its founding in 1701.

- The university is well-known for its graduate school programs, where Paul Hindemith is on the faculty of the Music School, Robert Penn Warren in the Drama School and Filmer S.C. Northrop in the Law School.
- Yale is undergoing considerable new construction to meet the needs of the modern era; many of its clean, modern buildings are in sharp contrast to those in Walter's home town of Jackson Hole, where travelers can look west to the jagged granite skyline of the Teton Range, its tallest summit, clawing the sky at an elevation of nearly 14,000 feet.
- The first white man—a mountain man and trapper named John Colter—set foot in Jackson Hole around 1807.
- In 1829 Capt. William Sublette named the valley for his trapper partner, David E. Jackson, the term "hole" coming from a Western expression for an enclosed mountain valley.
- French-Canadian trappers gave the Tetons their name, dubbing three towering summits the "Trois Tetons" for their fancied resemblance to a woman's breasts.
- By 1897 the Teton National Forest had been created; in 1912 Congress set aside land in the valley for a National Elk Refuge, and in 1929, established Grand Teton National Park.
- Congress in 1950 extended the boundaries of Grand Teton National Park to include some privately owned land and larger areas formerly in Jackson Hole National Monument.
- This more than tripled the size of the park, now over 310,000 acres, with about one-sixth of the new acreage consisting of former private holdings bought by John D. Rockefeller, Jr. and presented to the American people.
- Since World War II, tourism has become king in the Hole, with dude ranching and cattle ranching taking a less important role.
- Most tourists visit because of three emerging avocations: mountain climbing and hiking in the summer, and skiing in the winter.
- Last year more than one million people used the park, making it the sixth most visited national park in America.

Historical Snapshot
1954

- The government reported that 154 Americans had an income of more than $1 million, down from 513 in 1929
- RCA sold the first color TV sets, priced at $1,000 each
- Felt skirts with poodle appliques swept the teenage fashion world
- Panty raids, roller-skating marathons and ducktail haircuts gained popularity
- Disney's TV program *Davy Crockett* ignited a national demand for coonskin hats
- A Gallup poll reported that a family of four could live on $60 a week
- Newspaper vending machines, breath-inhaled alcohol detectors, Miami's Fountainbleu Hotel, the Mercedes 300 SL with fuel injection, Trix, frozen TV dinners and Levi's faded blue denims all made their first appearance
- Elvis Presley made his first commercial recording
- Unemployment rose to 5.5 percent, while inflation was only 0.4 percent and the GNP was five percent
- *On the Waterfront* with Marlon Brando won the Academy Award for Best Picture; *The Teahouse of the August Moon* by John Patrick captured the Pulitzer Prize for best play
- A record $3 billion was spent on new construction
- Disk jockey Alan Freed introduced the "rock 'n' roll" format on radio station WINS, creating a national trend
- The American thermonuclear tests at Bikini Atoll wounded 31 Americans, 236 natives and 23 Japanese fishermen; the U.S. offered an $800,000 indemnity
- Wladziu Valentino Liberace became a TV music sensation with his candelabras, soft lights, wide smiles and outrageous clothes
- "Beat girls" sported heavy eye makeup known as the raccoon look
- Matisse's painting *Odalisque* sold for $75,000, up from $25,000 in 1930
- New words and phrases that entered the language included "do-it-yourself," "greaser," "hip," "bread" (for money) and "windfall profit"
- The Supreme Court ruled that the doctrine of "separate but equal" had no place in public education; separate facilities, the court said, were "inherently unequal."
- Millions of children across America watched *Howdy Doody* and *Buffalo Bob Smith* in the afternoon; *I Love Lucy*'s success moved CBS's rating ahead of NBC's for the first time
- Ernest Hemingway won the Nobel Prize for literature, while the Pulitzer Prize was awarded in fiction to William Faulkner for *A Fable*, and in poetry to Wallace Stevens for *Collected Poems*
- Among the fashionable, a new interest in furs emerged, including coats made of sable, fox, leopard and mink

1954 Economic Profile

Selected Prices

Antacid, Tums $0.10
Automobile, Buick Skylark Convertible. $5,000.00
Board Game, Parker Brothers' Sorry $2.50
Brassiere, Maidenform $2.00
Buffalo Bill Costume $2.98
Candy Bar, Mars $0.06
Card Table and Chairs, Cosco $49.75
Course, "DuBarry Success" $12.95
Doll, Tiny Tears. $7.95
Electric Curling Iron $1.79
Hope Chest, Lane $47.95
Ice Cream Freezer $24.95
Lip Balm, Chapstick $0.39
Smokie Links, Oscar Mayer $0.59
Stapler, Arrow $2.34

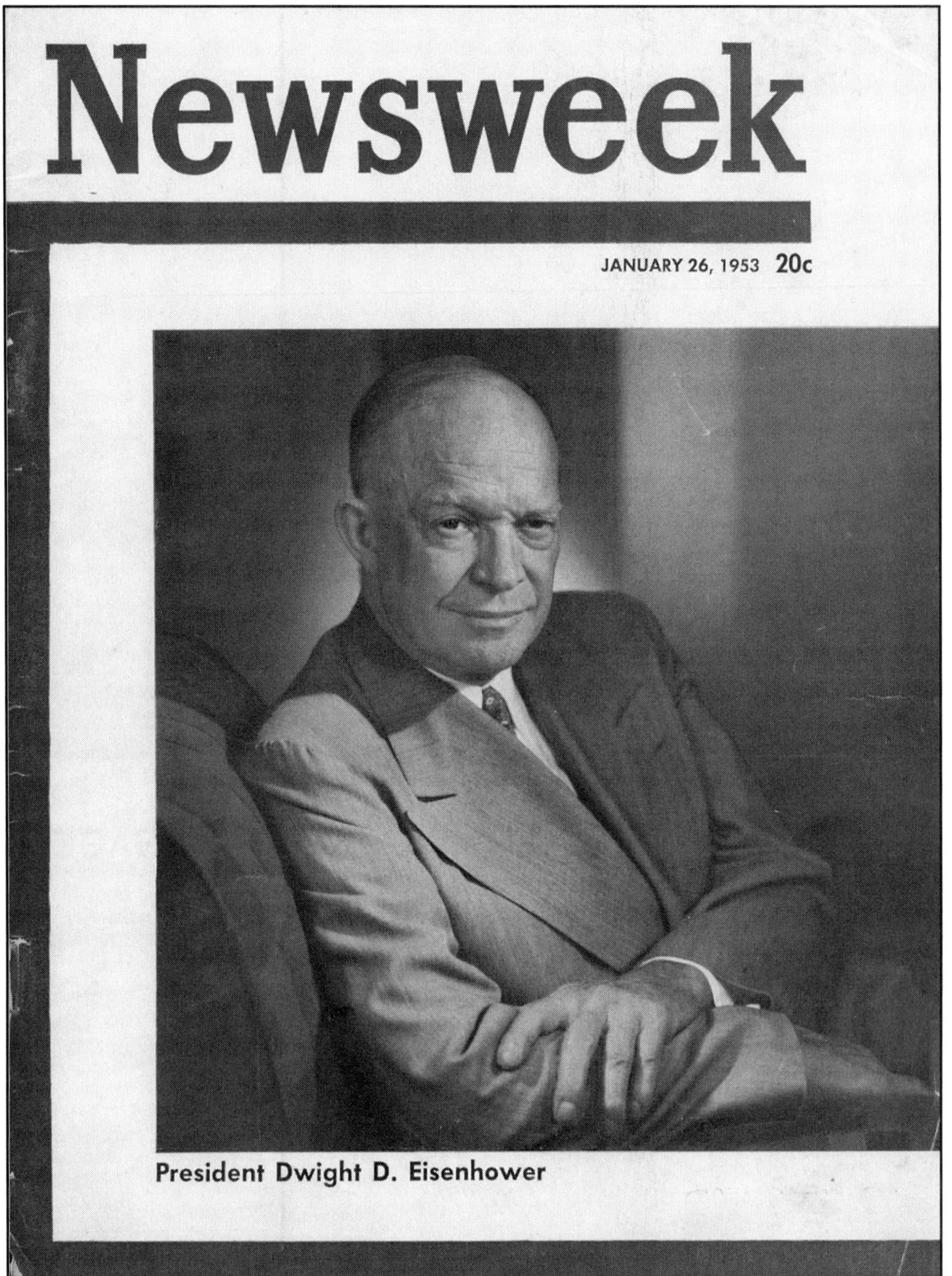

Changing America

- The number of television sets in use was 33 million, up from 10.5 million in 1950; across America, 415 television stations broadcast on the air.
- Ray Kroc began handling franchising for the McDonald's brothers; a working family of four could get a fast, clean meal at McDonald's for $2.50 and no tipping was required.
- President Dwight David Eisenhower modified the Pledge of Allegiance from "one nation indivisible" to "one nation, under God, indivisible."

The success of I Love Lucy *moved CBS ahead of NBC in the ratings.*

- Polls showed that 78 percent of Americans thought it important to report to the FBI relatives or acquaintances suspected of being communists.
- The Toledo Water Commission reported that periodic spikes in water use each night coincided with the evening's TV commercials.
- One in 10 households was headed by a woman; of the nation's 64 million workers, women numbered 21 million.
- City Lights Bookshop became a gathering place for the beat poets such as Allen Ginsberg and Lawrence Ferlinghetti.
- Mississippi voters approved a constitutional amendment to abolish public schools if they were required to racially desegregate their classrooms.
- Large numbers of industrial workers, businessmen and farmers joined civil and fraternal organizations.
- Twenty million horror books were sold monthly.
- The Tobacco Industry Research Committee reported that there was "no proof . . . that cigarette smoking is a cause of lung cancer."

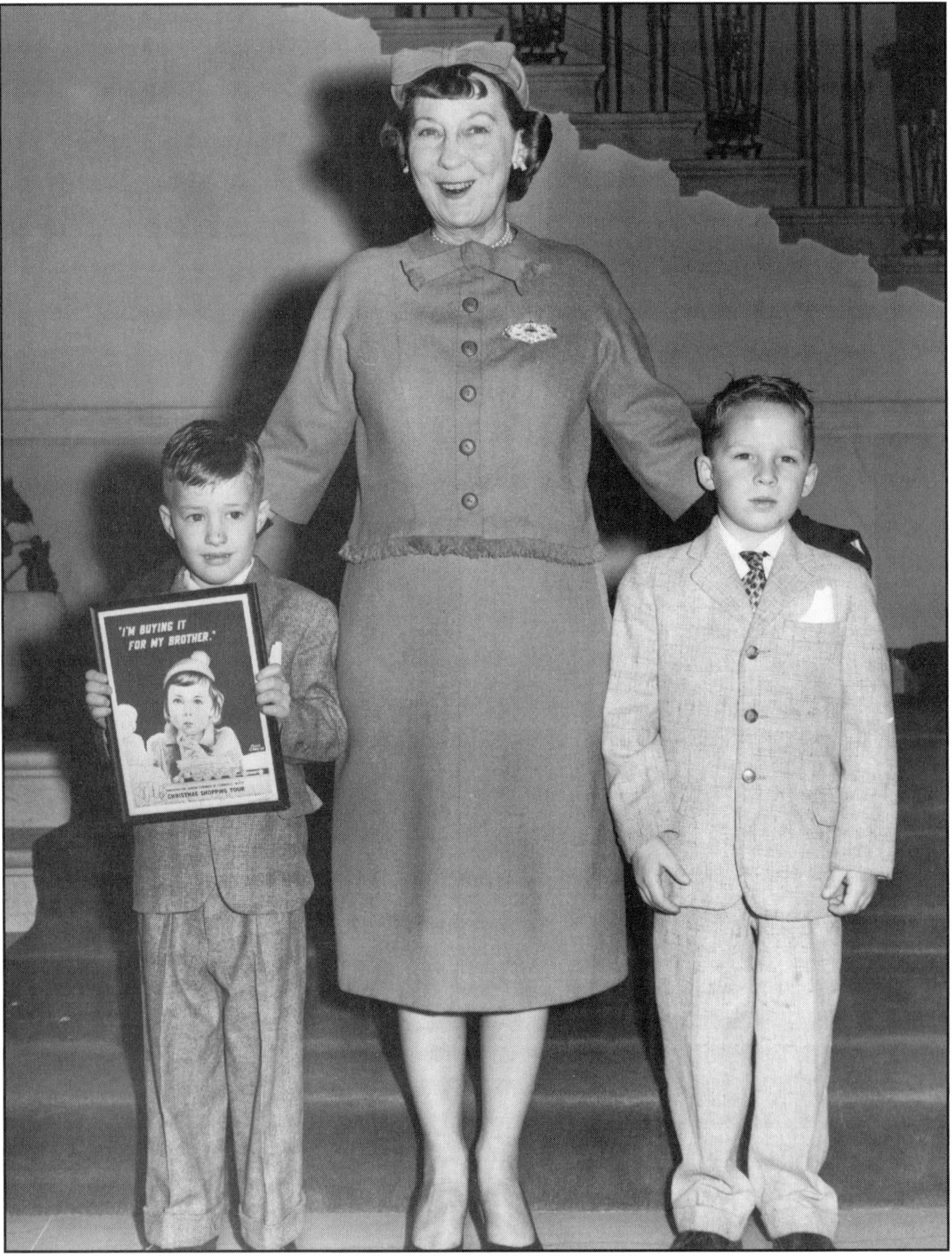

First lady Mamie Eisenhower campaigned for Christmas Seals.

- More deaths were depicted on television than had occurred for Americans in the Korean War.
- Sales were high for the newly introduced tranquilizers Miltown and Equanil.
- The Univac computer had demonstrated its potential by forecasting the outcome of the 1952 presidential election.
- Nationwide, 478 golf courses were in operation.
- Paul Landis wrote in *Your Marriage and Family Living* that, "College women in general have greater difficulty marrying. . . . Men still want wives who will bolster their egos rather than detract from them."
- The British agreed to return the Suez Canal to Egypt in 1956.

"The Yale Man," by John Knowles, *Holiday*, May 1953:

My classmates [in 1946] were busily rehearsing for their careers in a rich variety of other activities, such as the Political Union, which features a three-party system, treacherous parliamentary maneuvering and guest speakers of national renown. Others were trying out for team managerships or the widely traveled glee clubs, or the hoary *Literary Magazine*, where budding writers can consort with the shadows of Sinclair Lewis, Philip Barry, Steven Vincent Benét and other famous alumni. For those less intensely competitive there is an orchestra, a dramatic association, a band, a film-producing club, a debating team, an aviation club, and many other groups.

Meanwhile, like a good Stover (junior grade), I was moving through the labyrinth of Yale society life, in which the first stage is Mory's. As a freshman I was fascinated by this little white Colonial house with its name elegantly inscribed on a brass plate on the door, with its Whiffenproofs and the dear old Temple Bar. Mory's seemed to be the real Yale.

Two friends who were members submitted my name. In due course, I was permitted to pay 18 dollars for a lifetime membership. Inside Mory's I found a crowded little restaurant, the walls almost completely hidden by the pictures of Yale teams, crew oars hanging from the ceiling, the tables everywhere scarred with initials. The food was sometimes mediocre, sometimes awful, always expensive, and the waiters certainly the surliest in New England. The Temple Bar is just another name for Mory's. It is true that the Whiffenproofs sing there Monday nights, waxing loud and careless as they drink their way through a large silver urn, the exotic Green Cup, with its highly secret ingredients of champagne, brandy and crème de menthe. But it wasn't as I had pictured it.

Mory's launches the undergraduate into the social swim at Yale, and the secret societies are presumed to decide, at the end of his junior year, whether he is a winner. To the innocent, uninformed and impressionable freshman, the secret societies are like enormous icebergs glimpsed through the fog, and pondered over because of their immense unknowable beneath the surface. Six of these icebergs float majestically upon the scene at Yale, cold, seemingly lifeless. Their headquarters are forbidding, windowless sepulchers. Skull and Bones occupies an ominous, rust-colored Egyptian pile. Wolf's Head is pure suburban Gothic. I remember, during my first week at Yale, walking past Book and Snake, a small white temple of purest classical Greek, and it seemed entirely useless, an extravagant ornament.

Inexorably, the societies glide into the student's life. The myths about "Bones" usually come first. If you say "Skull and Bones" in the presence of a member he will leave immediately. Three years later we badgered one of them with these words and he only looked embarrassed. "If you get into 'Bones' you're sure of an income of $10,000 a year." Yale is run by 'Bones' men." And new students may be subject to sudden startling encounters, such as the Thursday night I was strolling along a campus walk when out of the obscurity a phalanx of Wolf's Head lock-stepped past, stone-faced.

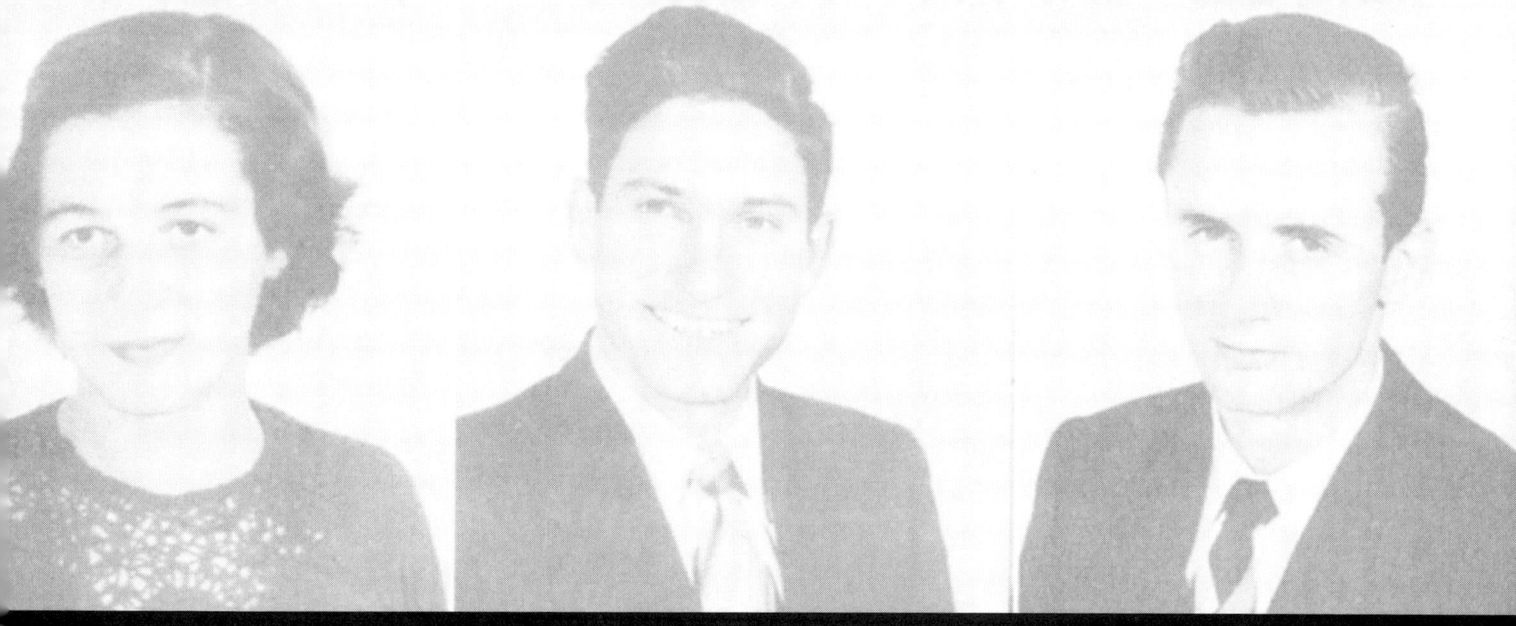

1954 News Feature

"Youth Forum: Youth Is Not Silent," a commentary by Irene Dunne, *Life Today*, April-May 1954:

Silent? No. Confused? Yes. Doomed? Far from it. I sensed in most of the letters an awareness of what the difficulties are, and an inspiring degree of courage and reliance on spiritual values.

The question: "What is your greatest fear for your future and what are you going to do to combat it?" gave writers the option of emphasis on the negative or the positive. With a small percentage of exceptions, youth seemed determined to adjust to the present and hope for the future.

A silent generation! A bunch of crazy mixed-up kids, they say. Sure there are those of us who make the unfavorable headlines, but think of the many more who are ruled by level-headedness. We're individuals—not like boxes that must be packed together and given an overall label.

The silent generation! What human being wouldn't be silent in finding he had inherited a world of corruption and turmoil? It's up to him to find a solution. He makes his way through the hullabaloo in order to stand back and think.

When you of the older generation choose to call us lost, immoral or doomed, think of what you have left for us to finish.

Shirley Haynes
Detroit, Michigan

I was pleased to learn that letters such as the one that follows are in the minority. The editors tell me that the whole idea of the Youth Forum is to provide an opportunity for young people to speak their minds. Naturally, the ideas expressed are the writers', not necessarily those of the editors. In selecting

letters for publication, the editors have chosen those which are representative of classified groups.

Although I never went to high school, I feel that I have as much brains as the average young man of my age. What do the youngsters of today want out of life, and what do they fear most? Young men are confused. What are they confused about? First, they are confused about their future. Will I get drafted? How long will I be in the service? Should I quit school? Should I marry? Will I see action? Why not have fun today and forget tomorrow? All over the United States, young people are so confused and upset that they don't dare have any hope for tomorrow. As a young man myself, I believe that the U.S. people will live in fear forever and ever because they have never seen the worst times like other nations and they fear war with the Russians. We Americans will live in fear for as long as we live no matter even if we have the best war material.

Today, young American boys of 18 to 24 are confused in mind because of war fear. They don't want any part of war, nor any part of politics, and no part of responsibility outside of the home. What they want are love, friends, games, dancing, school, music, and a job. Not a job to be rich, but just to live. We young people will never be able to be rich. Today's prices are up to the sky and wages are down to the ground. Young people get into crime because of the fear of going in the service—and sex-crimes, too, and doing things years ago never heard of. They cannot overcome fear.

Peter Di Biase
Portland, Maine

Somewhat along the same line as the foregoing, but with a calm, almost grim determination to arrive at the "best solution" is this letter—typical of many.

> *Whether or not military service will interrupt my college education is my greatest fear for the future. I am a high school senior and want to enter college upon my graduation. If I should finish several years and then be drafted, those years might be wasted.*
>
> *The insecurity of our age and the animosity existing between nations are serious problems facing every adult, but especially youth, for it is youth that leave their homes and schools and may have to fight on foreign soil.*
>
> *I think the best solution is to attend college anyway, and pray for the best.*
>
> *William G. Poole*
> *Covington, Kentucky*

About 30 percent of the letters indicated what to some will seem to be a surprising amount of interest in social, political and economic affairs on community, national and international levels. In all truth, from these letters I have gained the impression that today's youth are better informed and more thoughtful than the younger generation of which I was a part.

> *My greatest fear is complacency. American youth does not seem disturbed by the anxieties which are so puzzling to the leaders of the world, being preoccupied with atomic weapons. They tell us that they want to preserve peace through armed strength. Since when has peace ever been accomplished by warlike preparation? Is it any concern of mine? Very much so. I must face the fact that it is.*
>
> *Another threat to our future, as I see it, is our materialistic outlook on life. Everybody seems to pursue happiness in nerve-tingling thrills, in sensual indulgence and material success. This has become the prime concern of our life.*
>
> *I see, also, danger in the fact that all the vital affairs affecting our life are left in the hands of professional politicians.*
>
> *I do not believe that all woes and ills of the world can be solved by governments, no matter what social system they represent. I think every individual should accept a responsible share in the task of making the world better. . . .*

> *The potential power of an individual to influence the thinking of our country is much greater than is generally realized.*
> *Herman Mahlerman*
> *Winnipeg, Manitoba*

A surprising number of the letters show insight, reflecting conditions to which their elders should see through the eyes of youth. All of the letter writers expressed fears, which is to be expected because of the topic. Most of the letters indicated that the young people could identify their fears with the draft, the threat of war, economic stress, results of youthful errors, but some—this one in particular—indicated that fear is a contagion.

> *What is my greatest fear? I don't know. Maybe I ought to say—everything. I'm just afraid. The funny thing is, I'm not afraid of anything that's now, like football, or doing a tough job, or girls, or a fight if I have to fight. I guess what I'm afraid of is what comes next. I don't think I'd be afraid to die, but the idea of the draft scares me. We fellows sit around sometimes and bellyache about things. Everyone has got a beef. Girls, too.*
>
> *I used to think it was just me, but now I know that everybody else is scared too. It isn't just us kids, either. I remember my grandfather was afraid all the time, always saying something was liable to happen. I've heard my father tell my mother lots of times how scared he was he would lose his job, and then what would they do? My mother was always afraid for me to go out if it was cold, or wet, and if it was too hot, too. She didn't want me to play games because I might get hurt. Politicians are trying to make us scared of communists and the scientists want us to be scared of the atom bomb and the H-bomb. Even the preacher at my church, where I don't go much, tries to scare us all into religion by talking about hell. I don't know what I fear most so I don't know what to do to combat it except to sit tight and see what happens.*
> *B.J.S.*
> *Chicago, Illinois*

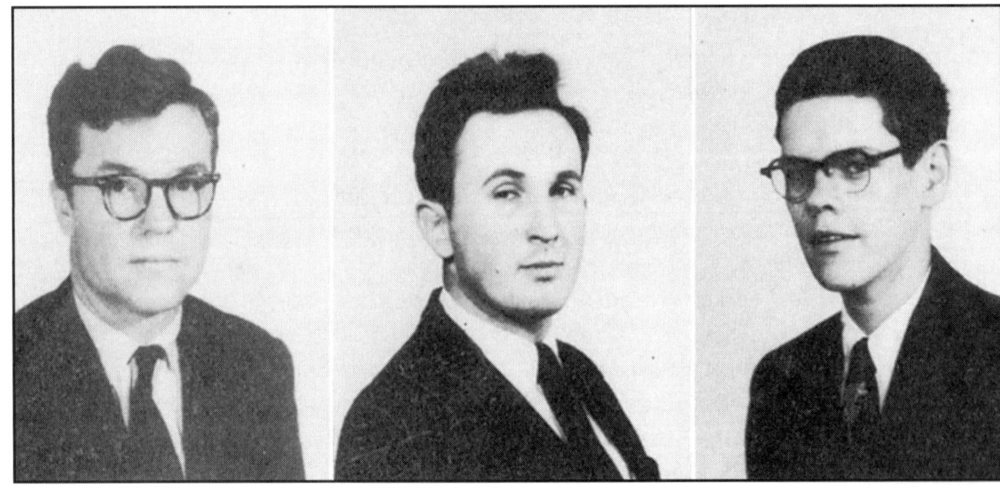

TEEN-AGERS' BIGGEST PROBLEMS IN 1956

MARION NEWMAN, 17, *senior*
Prescott Senior High School
Prescott, Arizona
"What is the ethical thing to do when you do not approve of the behavior of the rest of the crowd? Should you let a boy kiss you on the first date?"

STEPHANIE ADAMS, 16, *senior*
Garden Grove Union High School
Garden Grove, California
"Just how can I get that 'certain someone' interested in me?"

JANE BETTS, 17, *junior*
Central High School
St. Paul, Minnesota
"Popularity—just how important is it? Is the popular teen-ager automatically a happy, well-adjusted teen-ager?"

ANN WOLFE, 16, *senior*
University High School
University, Mississippi
"Ever since the days of Cleopatra the problem of the 'other girl' has plagued women's minds. Today's teen-age girl would like to know how to cope with the dilemma."

1956 News Feature

"Teen-agers' Biggest Problems in 1956—The problems they would like to discuss," *Woman's Home Companion*, January 1956:

Last year the *Companion* started the first magazine column ever conducted for teen-agers, by teen-agers—we present here our new Talk of the Teens Panel and their questions for 1956.

- What is the ethical thing to do when you do not approve of the behavior of the rest of the crowd? Should you let a boy kiss you on the first date?
- Just how can I get that "certain someone" interested in me?
- Future careers and work seem most important to me at the moment. . . . Most teen-agers have many ideas but aren't quite sure which to choose.
- I would like to see discussed the ideas, amusements and activities which keep teen-agers from border to border in continual motion.
- Teen Tact or Teen-plomacy—What do you do when he insists on sounding his horn in front of the house, when your parents insist that he come inside to see you?
- For many parties the country boy or girl is excluded unless he or she has ready transportation. If country teen-agers want jobs, the transportation problem again must be solved.
- Going steady is a problem with which almost every teen-ager comes in contact at least once during high school life.
- Let's have a column to discuss the wallflower—one of the most painful experiences for a boy or girl is to attend a dance and remain in the background because of shyness.
- I would like to know what going to college or getting a job after high school is really like.
- Popularity—just how important is it? Is the popular teen-ager automatically a happy, well-adjusted teen-ager?
- Ever since the days of Cleopatra the problem of the "other girl" has plagued women's minds. Today's teen-age girl would like to know how to cope with the dilemma.
- I know what the teen-agers in Fair Lawn [New Jersey] think of going steady, but I would like to know the opinion of other teen-agers.
- I would like to see discussed boys' and girls' schools versus coeducation, and the value of college fraternities and sororities.

Marianne Fanale, 16, *junior*
Sacred Heart Academy
Springfield, Illinois
"Teen Tact or Teenplomacy—What do you do when he insists on sounding his horn in front of the house, when your parents insist that he come inside to see you?"

Sally Daken, 15, *junior*
Withrow High School
Cincinnati, Ohio
"About the age of 15, girls in Cincinnati get very excited over clothes. I believe articles on fads in other cities and ways to dress for different occasions would be very helpful."

Mary Ellen Clark, 16, *senior*
Lakin Rural High School
Lakin, Kansas
"For many parties the country boy or girl is excluded unless he or she has ready transportation. If country teen-agers want jobs, the transportation problem again must be solved."

Margery Michelmore, 17, *senior*
Foxboro High School
Foxboro, Massachusetts
"I would like to know what going to college or getting a job after high school will be *really* like."

- We wonder what's right and what's wrong, and we wonder about religion.
- About the age of 15, the girls in Cincinnati get very excited over clothes. I believe articles on fads in other cities and ways to dress for different occasions would be very helpful.
- Jobs are on many teen-age minds right now. A breakdown of the main kinds of jobs would be helpful.
- Let's discuss the art of getting along well with other people and of meeting and making new friends.
- How can teen-agers and their parents become better friends?
- All teen-agers are confronted with a serious problem in this day: How can they gain self-confidence?
- What can I do about the fact that my parents and I often disagree on money, clothes and what I should or shouldn't be allowed to do?
- I would very much like to see the problem of interracial dating discussed. . . . I believe that an unprejudiced opinion is needed in discussing both sides.
- There are advantages and disadvantages to going steady. Just what is the general opinion of high school students throughout the country?
- What about manners? Do all teen-agers know which fork to pick up first or how to make proper introductions?
- I would like to see discussed in your column the problem of younger brothers and sisters.
- Should a girl who plans on getting married and does not intend to pursue a career attend college? Is it worth all the time and expense?
- Most teen-agers take greater note of world events, religion and planning their futures than adults often realize. I would like to hear the opinions of teens throughout the nation.

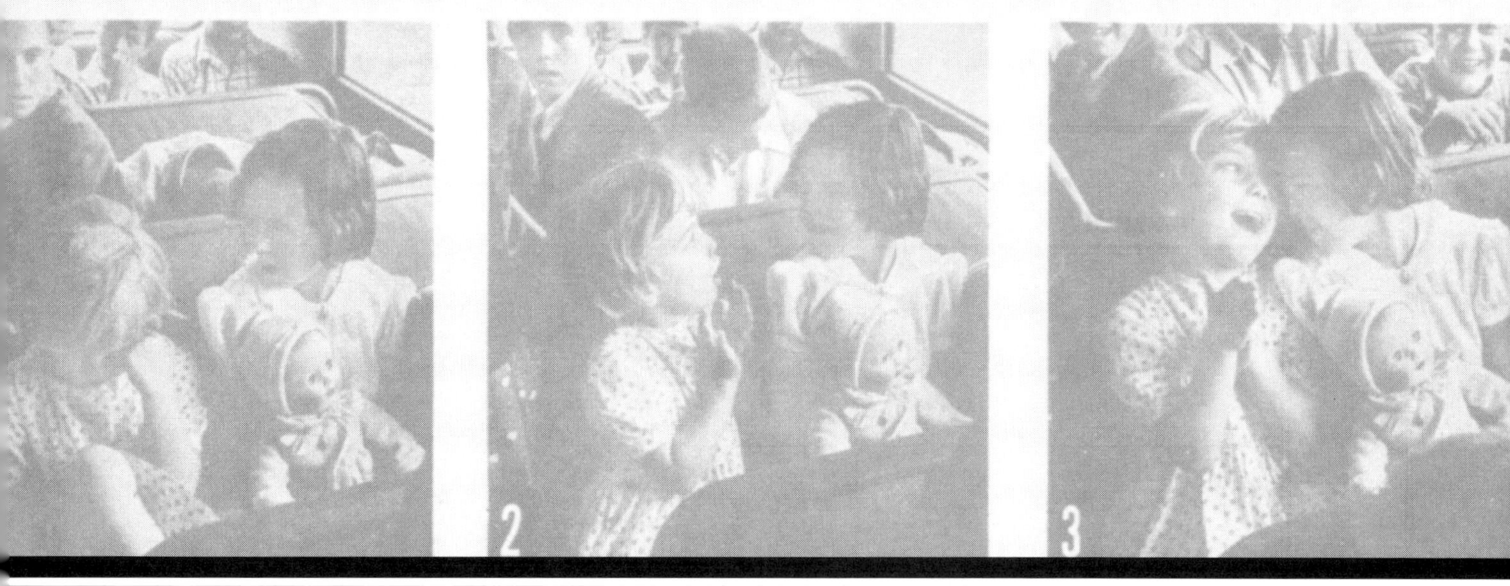

1957 Profile

Upper Class

Even though nine-year-old Evelyn Marsh and her family have recently been ushered into wealth, thanks to her father's decision to become part of the booming travel industry, this television-loving family of eight still works hard at being successful.

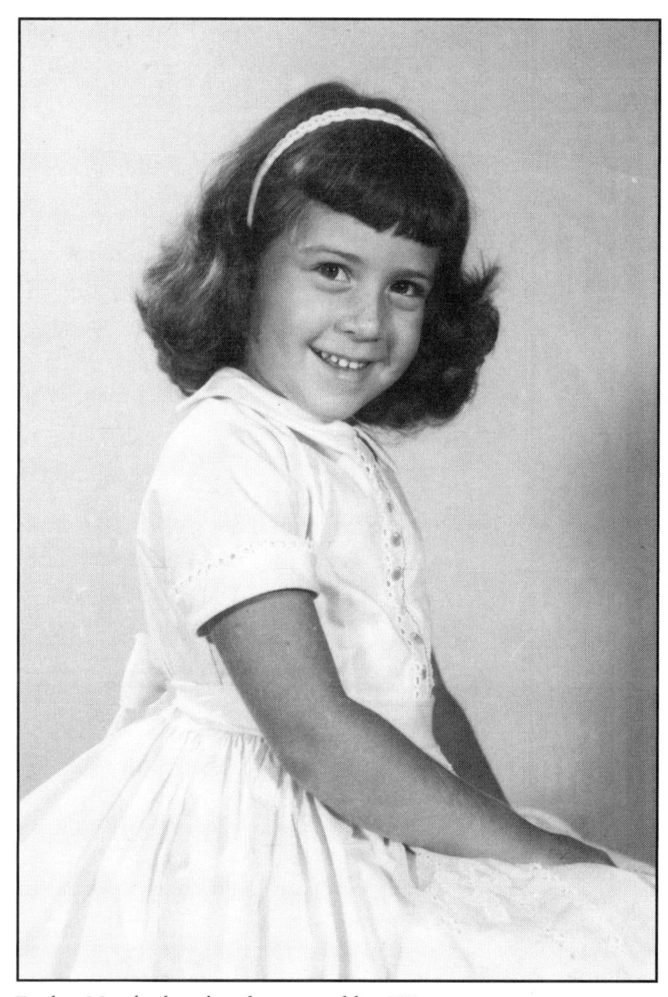
Evelyn Marsh plans her day around her TV programs.

Life at Home

- For the Marsh family, television dictates schedules, helps develop conversations and stops activities.
- Evelyn and her siblings plan their days around their favorite television programs, carefully instructing their mother to call them in when certain shows, especially *The Mickey Mouse Club* or *Howdy Doody*, come on the air.
- This obsession does not end with the children; the parents use the handy *TV Guide* to organize their week.
- Sunday nights at 8 p.m. are reserved for *The Ed Sullivan Show*.
- By that time, dinner is done, baths taken and all in the family take their places in front of the TV.
- Evelyn thinks variety show host Ed Sullivan looks like a cross between her father and the Frankenstein monster.
- She loves the puppets and the circus acts and the singers and everything else, too.
- The fan magazines are reporting that Ed Sullivan makes over $250,000 a year.
- One evening, when there was no school the next day, she even got to stay up and see *The Tonight Show* with Steve Allen, featuring the Muppets; Kermit the frog was so funny.

Evelyn loves to look at the antique dress in which she was christened.

Evelyn and her cousin Betsy love playing with dolls.

- While the family watches television, her father often roams the house looking for lights that have been left on; he seems especially pleased when he can announce that he turned out a light in one of the home's six bathrooms or 14 closets.
- Evelyn is the fourth child and the second girl.
- Thanks to the Silly Putty she got for her birthday, she and her baby sister spend hours lifting comics off the funny pages.
- When they get a perfect image, they can stretch and pull the putty to make the faces change; Evelyn loves to hear her little sister giggle when the funny faces appear.
- To boost sales, Silly Putty commercials are airing on *Howdy Doody* and *Captain Kangaroo*.
- Evelyn also thinks she wants a Mr. Potato Head kit as advertised on television, but she wants a Hula Hoop more.
- This spring, after a baptism at church, she insisted that her mother take out the christening gown Evelyn and her sisters had worn when they were babies.
- Made with Mechlin lace inserts, trim around the bottom, and three tiny mother-of-pearl buttons at the back, the dress was originally worn by her grandmother, who was born in 1889 and christened in the dress in 1890.
- Evelyn is not sure why she wanted to see the dress again, but the girls spent the afternoon talking about clothes with their mother.
- When she is not playing with her baby sister or watching television, she goes to her cousin Betsy's house to play with dolls.
- Betsy has a room full of dolls, doll clothing and furniture—much of it made by her parents.
- Often, the two girls will sew up a dress themselves to make sure their dolls look right for every occasion.
- But Evelyn's greatest joy is playing detective and knowing everything that goes on in the house.
- Recently, the Grand Rapids Police Department brought her older brother home—drunk.
- He had been caught drinking whiskey at a friend's house when their parents were out at their usual Wednesday night bridge game; the police took all the kids home to their respective parents, who could be depended upon to punish them properly.
- She heard her mother say, "At this rate, he may be 90 before he gets his driver's license."
- Nothing was said the next morning, but Evelyn made sure her brother knew that she knew he was in trouble, even though the incident will never be discussed in front of her.
- For Evelyn, knowing that he knows that she knows is enough.

- The next day, her brother and all the people from his class went to a special movie at school.
- They sat in chairs made to look like automobiles and watched a short movie about drinking, sex and cars.
- Recently, all the children were taken to the doctor, even though they were not sick; everyone in town has agreed to have their children vaccinated against polio.
- She did not understand that "vaccinated" meant getting a shot until they arrived there, and was not pleased when she found out.
- To ward off polio, Evelyn's mother insists that the children take afternoon naps when the heat exceeds 90 degrees, because hot days are believed to encourage the outbreak of the debilitating disease.
- On Friday nights her father often takes all the children to a new hamburger place called McDonald's—their favorite place to eat—where the people like kids and the advertising says, "Give Mom a Night Out."
- Wednesday night bridge club is often hosted at Evelyn's house.
- Normally, five other couples will gather at 6:00 for cocktails and snacks, and begin playing bridge promptly at 7:00.
- The game never lasts beyond 10:00.
- Her mother always looks special for bridge club; Evelyn loves sitting in her mother's room while she dresses, combs her hair and applies makeup.
- Sometimes Evelyn is even allowed to use lipstick and rosewater perfume, as long as Daddy doesn't know.
- During these wonderful times, her mother describes her dream that the boys will grow into men, take roles in the family business and be successful; the girls will grow up to be pretty so that they will make good wives.
- Both her parents trace their ancestry back to the 1850s, when approximately 200 Dutch immigrants moved to Grand Rapids.
- They are proud of their heritage but believe their success comes from hard work, not background.
- The Marsh family loves Grand Rapids, and strives to buy and use products made in their city.
- They use a Bissell carpet sweeper, eat Hekman Biscuits, drive an American Motors car and wear Hush Puppies shoes, all made in Grand Rapids.
- Their neighbor is CFO of Wolverine Shoe and Tanning Corporation, the parent company of Hush Puppies, which have become wildly popular.
- Several years ago the company invented a special pig-skinning process that allows the shoes to breathe.
- Recently, during bridge club, their neighbor mentioned that the company is considering a new advertising mascot

Christmas is a special time for the Marsh family.

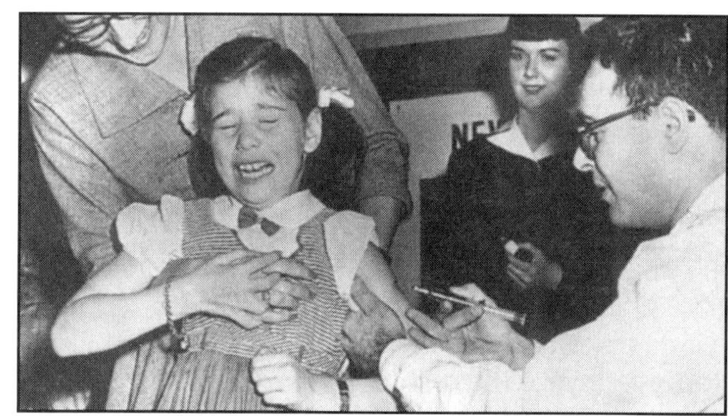

Children across America are getting polio shots.

Sunday nights are reserved for The Ed Sullivan Show.

for Hush Puppies—possibly like the Marsh family's basset hound—and wondered aloud whether a dog could help sell shoes.

Life at School and Summer Vacation

- Evelyn loves to read, but she and her teacher are not always in complete agreement over what should be read—and when.

GIRLS' PAGE

NURSE'S CAP. One white cleansing tissue can be folded into a neat cap to be used when playing nurse. First open the tissue out flat, then crease into a triangle and fold back a "cuff" at the bottom. If you wish, draw a Red Cross symbol on the front of the cap with crayon. Use a bobby pin at each side of this cap to fasten it in place on your hair. —IDA M. PARDUE

COLORED-SPOT PICTURES. You've heard of ink-spot pictures, which are made by placing an ink drop in the fold of a paper, then creasing the paper shut and rubbing over the outside so that the ink spreads out and forms different shapes. The same kind of pictures can be made in pretty colors by using drops of food coloring instead of ink. You can make yellow butterflies, green trees, and various interesting design figures in many different colors. —FAYE HAAS

NEW YEAR'S CONFETTI. At the horn-blowing, whistle-tooting time of a New Year's party, a way of providing more excitement is to provide everyone with a bag of confetti that can be thrown around. Used pieces of Christmas wrapping paper are especially good for making confetti; just cut the papers into long strips and then snip off little pieces. Small cellophane bags that come from the grocery store make attractive containers for the bright bits of confetti. Tie each bag shut with a piece of ribbon so that the confetti will not get spilled before you want to use it. —NANCY K. FORD

"Girl's Page: Colored-Spot Pictures," by Faye Haas, *Jack and Jill*, January 1957:

You've heard of ink-spot pictures, which are made by placing an ink drop on the fold of a paper, then creasing the paper shut and rubbing over the outside so that the ink spreads out and forms different shapes. This same kind of picture can be made in pretty colors by using drops of food coloring instead of ink. You can make yellow butterflies, green trees, and various interesting design figures in many different colors.

Nationwide, schools are expanding rapidly to meet demand.

- Mysteries are good, but math is boring and unnecessary, the little girl thinks.
- *Jack and Jill* magazine is a must-read when it arrives, no matter how much homework has been assigned.
- Her mother also loves to read, endlessly going over articles on child improvement and how to be a better parent; with six children and a husband always on the go, she tries hard to keep everyone happy.
- Lately, she has found that a small tranquilizer pill and a short nap are a better solution to a well-run household than courses in how to parent in a modern age.
- Since the early 1950s, the city has been working on a school construction program costing $12 million.
- Evelyn's class recently took a field trip to the John Ball Zoological Park, where they could visit the animals.
- Her favorite site was Monkey Island, where the monkeys scampered about as though they had organized a game of chase, just for her benefit.

Evelyn's father is part of the Holiday Inn success story.

- The city is known for the development of partnerships that link schools and parks, planning for a park or playground with every school site.
- The park at her new school includes restrooms, swings and recreational facilities, as well as programs built around summer vacations.
- She would like to spend more time at the parks this summer, but her father loves to drive the family around to pick out sites for his new Holiday Inn motels.
- The only way the trips are even bearable is to bring lots of comic books bought just for the trip—five for each child.
- Her older brother, the mean one, is not allowed to touch her comics without her permission or she will tell her mother.
- After 20 years in commercial construction, her father began building and operating Holiday Inns across the Midwest four years ago.
- He has now built 31 motels as part of the company's nationwide march across the country.
- Prior to the creation of the Holiday Inn chain, most travelers stopped at small mom-and-pop motels where the service, cleanliness and amenities varied widely.
- Mr. Marsh's motel-building career began because Kemmons Wilson, a successful home-builder in Memphis, Tennessee, decided to take his five children to see the nation's capital in Washington, DC.
- Unwilling to spend the money required for air travel, they drove a new Oldsmobile without air-conditioning across country, covering only about 300 miles per day, but rarely finding a nice place to stay.
- Most lodgings charged $8 per night, plus extra for his five children, then $1 more to have a TV; rarely was there a place to eat nearby.

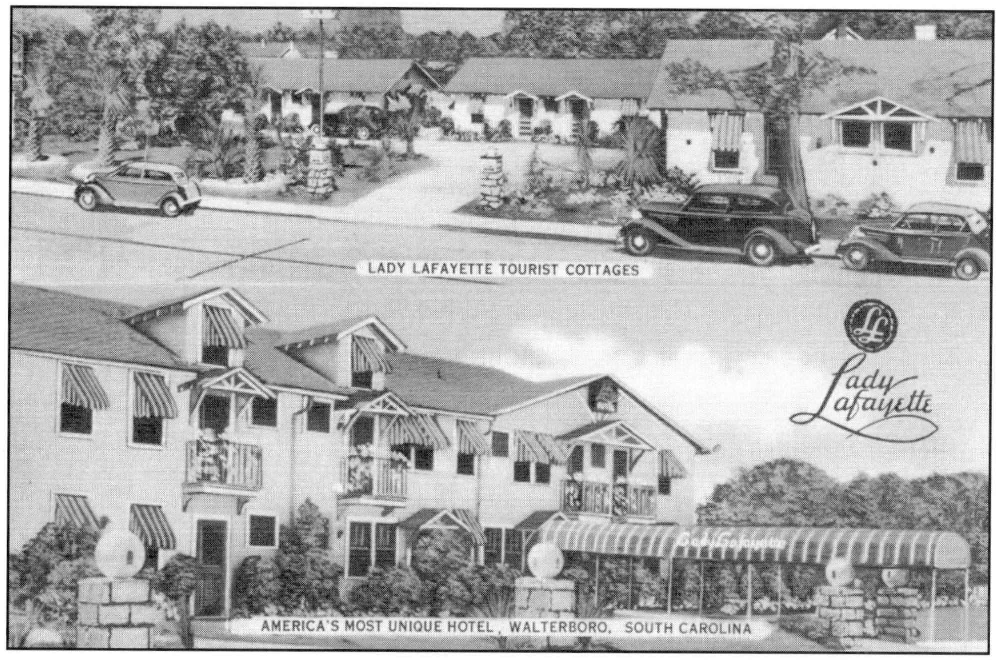

LADY LAFAYETTE TOURIST COTTAGES
Lady Lafayette
AMERICA'S MOST UNIQUE HOTEL, WALTERBORO, SOUTH CAROLINA

- A 38-year-old high school dropout and millionaire, Wilson measured the rooms in the different motels where his family stayed on the way back to Memphis; 12 by 30 feet, plus a bathroom, became the standard.
- Wilson decided to go into the motel business and offered the same opportunity to fellow contractors across America, including Evelyn's father.
- He named his company after a television show special, *Bing Crosby's Holiday Inn.*
- In the beginning, Wilson only charged fellow members of the National Homebuilders' Association $500 for the right to own a Holiday Inn in their city, plus a user fee of $0.05 a night per room.

HIGHWAY 66
PHONE 72
BETHANY,
OKLAHOMA
Lakeview Courts
MAIL ADDRESS
R. 3, BOX 23A
YUKON, OKLA.
FOR THE DISCRIMINATING TOURIST
COOL IN THE SUMMER, FACING ONE OF OKLAHOMA'S LARGEST LAKES
Member United Motor Courts
Telephones - Telegraph - Garages
ELEVEN MILES WEST OF OKLAHOMA CITY ★ FOUR MILES EAST OF YUKON

- Only a few builders joined Marsh and took Wilson up on his offer; many said they didn't want to be in the travel business, while most claimed they didn't see much future in building motels because not enough people took vacations.
- Even though Congress passed a $76 billion federal highway building program last year, few saw the potential.
- Marsh, like Wilson, had grown wealthy building residential homes, generally erecting houses for $10 a square foot.
- Along a city highway, he built the first motel comprising 120 rooms, plus a restaurant, at a cost of $280,000; it took him 90 days to complete the project.
- The newer Holiday Inns now have a gift shop and a swimming pool, and include an air conditioner and free television set in each room.
- The room rates are $4 a night for a single and $6 for a double, while the policy of letting children stay free helps attract traveling families in search of a bargain.
- When Holiday Inn went public, more than 120,000 shares sold at $9.75 the first day.
- For the Marsh family, summers are spent traveling around picking sites for future motels and helping other franchise operators get started.
- Although Evelyn loves to travel, she hates being in the car because her big brother puts his feet on her dress and makes ugly faces at her when no one is looking, but she likes stealing his comics and playing car games, except when she loses.
- Recently, while on a scouting trip, her little brother swallowed too much water while swimming in the Holiday Inn pool and threw up in front of everybody; the pool had to be closed and drained.
- Her father was furious, but Evelyn thought it was funny; her little brother was mortified, though, and stayed quiet for days.
- Her father has copied the work habits of Ray Kroc of McDonald's; every executive's desk must be free of paper at the end of the day, every executive answers his own phone and neatness is an obsession.
- The only typewriters, cash registers and adding machines he will allow in his office are the R.C. Allens, made in Grand Rapids; he often plays golf with the owner at the country club.
- "Be good to those who have been good to you," he says as often as he can.

McDonald's president, Ray Kroc, writing to the wives of his employees about thrift, 1957:

"When beef, steak and chops are extremely high, it certainly seems logical to use more fish, fowl, casserole dishes, and things of that sort that really have more flavor and save a lot of money. The same is true of baked goods. I had some pumpkin bread that Virginia Lea baked that was made with canned pumpkin, orange juice, flour, dates, and nuts that was out of this world. At one time you could bake a month's supply. The same might be said for chicken pot pie when stewing chickens are on sale. One day could be spent processing this and putting it in the freezer. So what I am saying is that the smarter you are, the further your money will go."

Evelyn's mother works hard to make the holidays a happy time.

How to explain the Santa Claus story to younger children.
Careful planning makes champions in any sport.
Strengthen any weak link in a child's character.
A happy child is a healthy child.

Life in the Community: Grand Rapids, Michigan

- Grand Rapids' earliest suburbs began around the turn of the century, arranged along the streetcar routes, making it possible for homes and businesses to spread outward from the city center.
- By the early 1950s, the automobile had clearly established the pattern of city migration, freeing residents from the necessity of living near public transportation.
- Struggling farms, which once ringed the city, became valuable housing developments for people eager to be on the move and part of a modern America.
- The area has long been a center for Dutch life in America, beginning before the American Civil War.

"The School Bus: What Happens in That Period between Home and School?" *This Week*, September 17, 1955:

On the other side of the bus there was some talk about television.

"The bus is always quiet on Thursdays," Leo (the bus driver) told me. "They are tired out from staying up for *Disneyland*. The quietest trip I ever made was the day after *Peter Pan*!"

At one stop, three little girls got on the bus. Their dog, a brown and white spaniel, got on with them. He ran to the rear and crawled under the seat. The children dragged him out, rushed him back down the aisle and pushed him to the ground.

"That dog tries to come to school every morning," Tommy told me. The dog started to bark and chase the bus. The children all rose to their feet and barked back at him.

"Sit down!" yelled the Safety Patrols.

The next stop brought another small boy with an enormous bag of marbles. As the bus lurched, the bag struck against a seat and burst open. A shower of marbles hurtled in all directions. Good-naturedly, the rest of the children helped pick them up.

"That happens nearly every day, too," Leo said, rubbing a marble-sized bruise on the back of his head.

We heard a loud horn honking. A smart brown coupe pulled up in front of us. A lady leaped out, flagged the bus to a halt and jumped aboard, carrying a bundle.

"You forgot your lunch and your arithmetic book and your hat!" she said breathlessly to a child in one of the front seats.

As the mother drove off, the boy opened the lunch box and peered inside. He pulled out a sandwich and ate it. Then he ate an apple. I wondered what he would do at noon.

Some of the children were singing softly, "My Bonnie Lies over the Ocean."

"You should hear the carol-singing on the bus at Christmastime," Leo said. "It brings tears to my eyes."

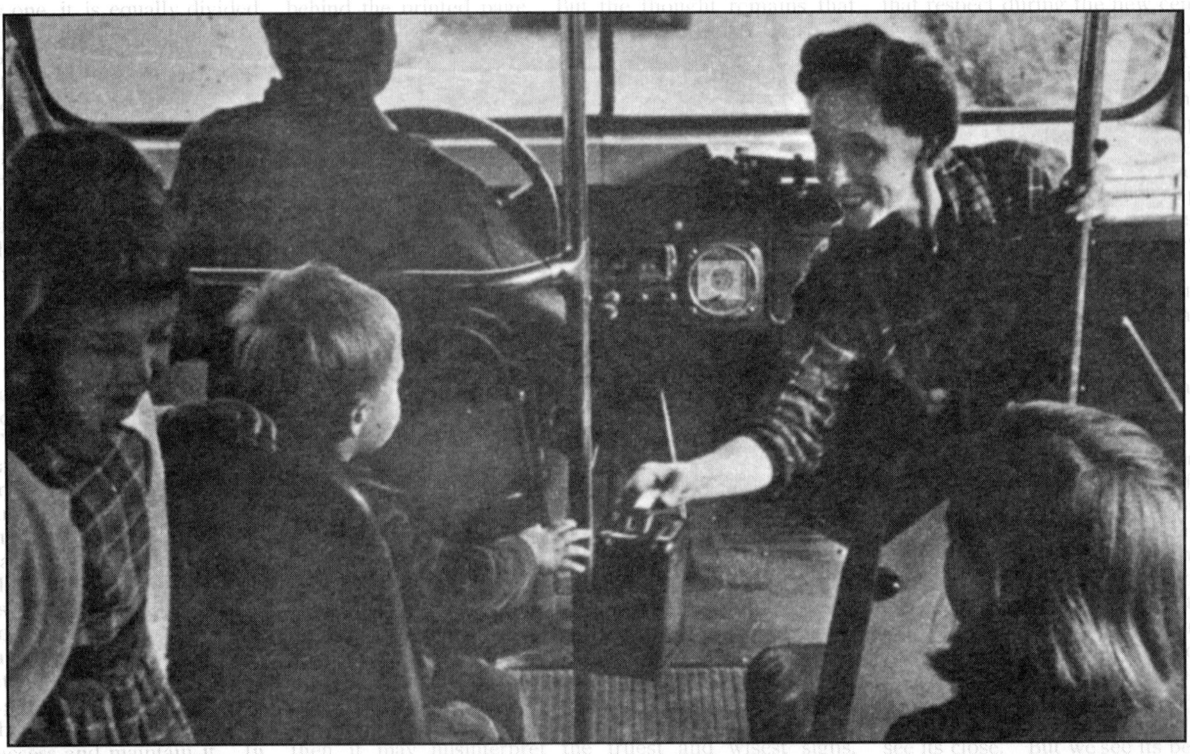

The famous motel chain was named after a television special.

How to develop good sportsmanship.

Keep your child from growing into a "Hot-head."

Don't let your child burden his happiness with grudges.

- Grand Rapids was attractive because of ample job opportunities, the availability of Dutch-language worship services and an existing, accepting Dutch community in the area.
- A second wave of Dutch immigrants arrived in the 1870s, attracted by the city's reputation as the furniture capital of America, welcoming skilled European woodworkers seeking opportunity.
- By 1900 persons of Dutch birth or ancestry made up 40 percent of the city's population—the largest proportion of Dutch in any large American city.
- As a result, Grand Rapids is the headquarters of the Christian Reformed Church, which arose from the beliefs of the first Dutch settlers, who preferred their Dutch-language brand of Calvinism to the Americanized practices of the Reformed Church of America.
- Currently, membership in the Christian Reformed Church and the Reformed Church of America makes up 40 percent of the city's population, while Catholics comprise another 40 percent.
- Grand Rapids retains its distinction as America's furniture manufacturing capital; $100 million in furniture and fixtures are produced in the city for export nationwide.
- Today, the trademark "made in Grand Rapids" affixed to furniture carries a special significance for superiority in design and craft, and is protected by a court ruling.
- Since the end of World War II, the furniture business has been booming as consumers continue their nationwide shopping spree after hard times and the war.
- Grand Rapids is battling a movement of mass-market furniture manufacturers to factories in the South, where labor is cheaper, particularly in North Carolina.
- As a result, many furniture factories have expanded their lines to include furniture for the thousands of new offices and skyscrapers being constructed across America.
- To survive in the traditional, home-based furniture market, many local companies now specialize in limited-production, expensive, handcrafted furniture in a range of classic and modern styles.
- General Motors is the largest employer in Grand Rapids, with thousands employed at a metal-stamping plant built in the Depression, or at the GM Diesel Equipment Plant constructed during the Second World War.
- In addition, the Fisher Body Trim Fabrication Plant, which formerly made fuselages for the F-84 Thunderbird jet fighter, now turns out interior trim for Chevrolets.

Historical Snapshot
1957

- Ford Motor Company's introduction of the Edsel, named after Henry Ford's son, was a major manufacturing and marketing failure
- *The Bridge on the River Kwai, And God Created Woman* and *12 Angry Men* all had their movie premieres
- An intensive study of birth control in pill form was begun in Puerto Rico
- Tennessee Williams's *Orpheus Descending* and Noel Coward's *Nude with Violin* both opened on Broadway
- *Perry Mason*, *To Tell the Truth*, *Leave It to Beaver*, *Maverick* and *American Bandstand* all premiered on television
- Leonard Bernstein became the musical director of the New York Philharmonic
- The Russians launched the first artificial satellite orbiting Earth
- Hit songs included "Jailhouse Rock," "Chances Are," "All Shook Up," "Maria" and "A White Sport Coat and a Pink Carnation"
- An Elvis Presley model record player sold for $17.95; teens could put $1 down and pay only $1 a week
- Anticoagulants were shown to aid stroke victims and reduce permanent damage
- James Agee's *A Death in the Family* won the Pulitzer Prize for fiction; *Promises: Poems 1954–56* by Robert Penn Warren won for poetry
- Sony's pocket-size transistor radio, cars with a retractable hardtop, animal insurance and Gino's all made their first appearance
- The average wage for a factory production worker was $2.08 an hour, or $82 a week
- The arrest of an ex-employee of an electric company ended the 16-year search for the Mad Bomber of New York City, who had planted 32 homemade bombs
- One in three women regularly went to a beauty shop
- Thanks to new medications, the number of long-term patients in psychiatric hospitals decreased
- The Everly Brothers' song "Wake Up, Little Susie" was banned on Boston radio

1957 Economic Profile

Selected Prices

Acne Medicine, Clearasil. $0.59
Airfare, New York to London, Round-Trip $482.00
Automobile, Cadillac Eldorado Brougham. $13,075.00
Chocolate-Covered Cherries, Brach's $0.55
Cigarettes, Pack. $0.24
Crayons, Crayola, Box of 48 . . . . $0.75
Clock, Antique Grandfather $345.00
Girdle, Playtex. $4.95
Home Permanent, Lilt. $1.50
Jeans, Levi's $3.65
Man's Sweater, Pullover $8.98
Newspaper, *Chicago Tribune*, Daily $0.07
Pillow, Goose Down $14.97
Pocket Radio, Emerson. $46.00
Refrigerator, Western Auto Wizard. $259.00
Shaving Cream, Shulton Old Spice $1.00
Silly Putty, per Egg. $2.00
Sweatshirt, Boy Scout $1.95
Toy Truck, Buddy-L, Texaco. $3.50
Whiskey, Seagram's V.O., Fifth. $6.43

The Ed Sullivan Show *captivates America.*

Driver's education class comes complete with make-believe cars.

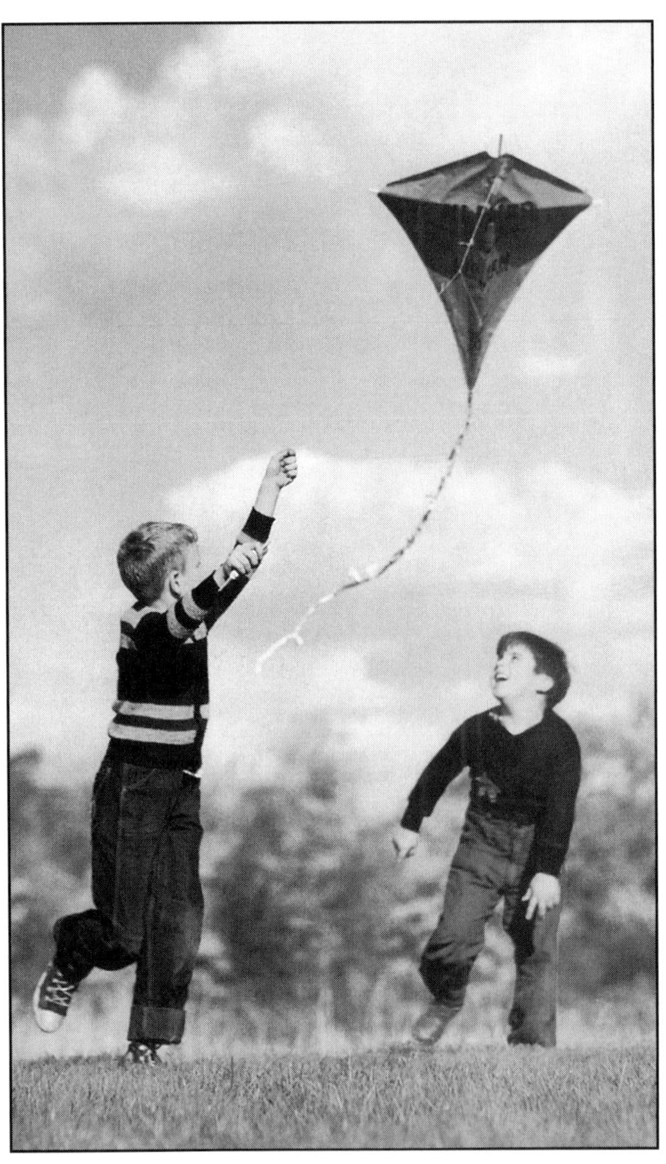

Changing America

- In the previous year, consumers spent more than $1.3 billion buying four million new refrigerators, many of which had large freezers capable of handling the many frozen foods appearing on the market.
- Elvis Presley laid claim to six of RCA's all-time top 25 records; his songs were selling $75,000 worth of records a day.
- Alice Payne Hackett's book, *Sixty Years of Best Sellers*, listed seven Mickey Spillane 50-cent action novels among the 10 best-selling fiction works in American publishing.
- *Scholastic Magazine*'s *Institute of Student Opinion* reported that the nation's 13 million teenagers had an income of $7 billion a year, with each teenager earning an average of $10.55 a week.
- Univac commercially launched the first computer to use transistors—elements that can detect, amplify and switch currents—instead of valves.
- The rate of new cases of venereal disease increased for the first time since 1948.
- Nationwide, 21 million people spent $2 million on recreational fishing.
- Fads included whiskey-flavored toothpaste and radar-like fishing poles.
- Animal lovers throughout the world protested Russia's use of an animal in space flight.
- The Massachusetts governor reversed the 1692 witchcraft conviction of six Salem women.
- The Cadillac Eldorado Brougham sported on its dashboard a lipstick case, vanity case, and four gold cups.

"Eight Mistakes Parents Make and How to Avoid Them," Parents Association, 1958:

MISTAKE No. 5: There's a Secret Trick about the Use of Praise. It's a big mistake not to learn it.

The biggest objection of all to overemphasizing the punishment idea is that it generally means looking into the past with a spirit of fault-finding. This, according to a law of human nature, tends to rub the fur the wrong way. It is far better to use a system that looks forward instead of backward. Then, when a child does something which requires training to avoid a repetition in the future, the matter is put on an EDUCATIONAL basis and the spirit of both parent and child is FRIENDLY, which is the way you want it. When the details of this system come into your hands, you will never even want to try getting along without it.

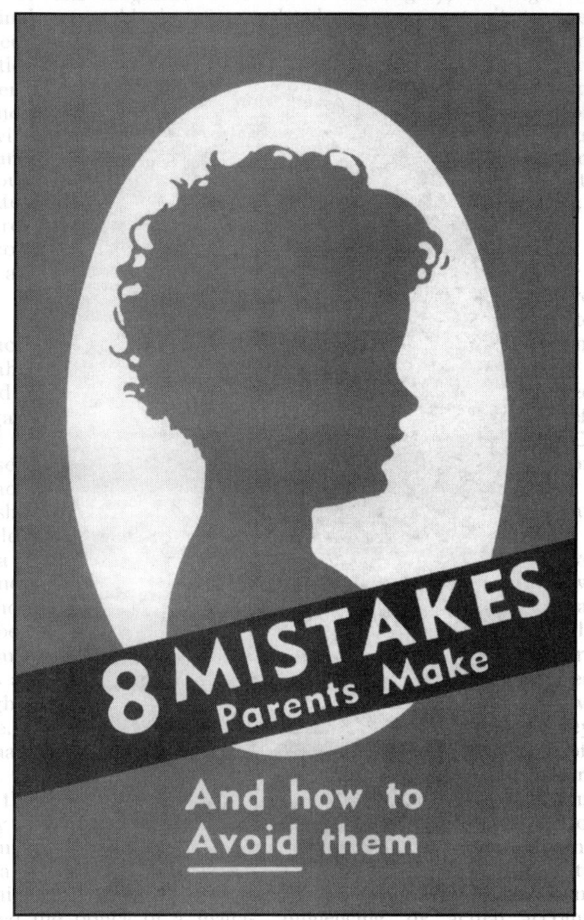

Did you ever stop to think of this? A young child gives very little thought to whether his habits are good or bad. He simply reacts in a natural way to whatever methods his parents happened to use in his training. If the methods are such as to call forth desirable actions, we say the child is "good." But if the methods are not good, we too often think of the child as being "bad."

The first time this thought impressed itself on my mind was when I was riding on a train. My attention was called to a worried mother who was trying desperately to manage two small children. They kept running back and forth from one end to the other of the Pullman car—annoying everyone as they passed. The mother was upset almost to the point of distraction. The children themselves were far from happy because of the mother's continual attempts at correction and punishment.

A Child Reflects His Parental Training—Or LACK of It

It was that incident—perhaps more than any other single one—that led me to devote my life to the study of child training. After watching those untrained children and that untrained mother struggle through unpleasant hours that should have been very happy hours, I had a vision of the happiness I might bring to children and parents all over the world.

Straight across the aisle from me on that same Pullman car was a mother with two nice-looking and well-mannered children. I could not help but admire the quiet way in which this mother talked with her children. I noticed them in the dining car, too. They were all kind and courteous, one to another. It was pleasing to observe such harmony and fine culture. Without any attempt to attract undue attention to themselves, it was evident from their friendly smiles and occasional laughter that they were all really enjoying their trip to the fullest.

(continued)

"Eight Mistakes Parents Make . . ." (*continued*)

Now, since you are to picture clearly in your mind these two mothers I have mentioned with such a wide contrast between their method and corresponding result, let's do a little analyzing. Let's see why one mother failed miserably and why the other succeeded so well.

Why One Parent Fails and Another Succeeds

Of course, for a quick analysis in just a sentence or two, we would say that the mother whose children ran away from her control and were all over the place, disturbing others with their unwelcome noise and antics, had no correction system to help her at all. She was totally lacking in any definite plan, while the other mother was at least doing wonderfully well in practicing ONE of the five basic principles taught in my course—namely, the Principle of Friendship.

But now, let's go a step further in the analysis. The mother whose children gave her such a rough time was constantly scolding them and telling them they were "naughty." That error on her part was in violation of the Principle of Suggestion, and if she had the Course to which you are looking forward, she would know for sure that she cannot violate that principle without suffering a penalty for her violation.

Many parents who are more enlightened than the mother just referred to would know that it is wrong to tell any child that he is naughty. It is the wrong approach entirely. But there is a finer point that is not practiced by most parents until after it is specifically called to their attention.

You Will Soon Learn an Important Secret and How to Apply It

Every parent who thinks clearly has doubtlessly discovered for himself how praise can be used to encourage a child.

After a child has already completed some praiseworthy act, it is common knowledge that to praise him for the act will have the effect of inclining the child toward repeating the act to get further desired praise. But the secret of how to use praise in situations where the child does nothing at all to deserve and justify praise is not common knowledge.

Some of the most outstanding results I ever secured in clinic work were achieved by praising a child for conduct which was the exact opposite of that which he usually displayed. You will be amazed at the simple way in which you can do this yourself.

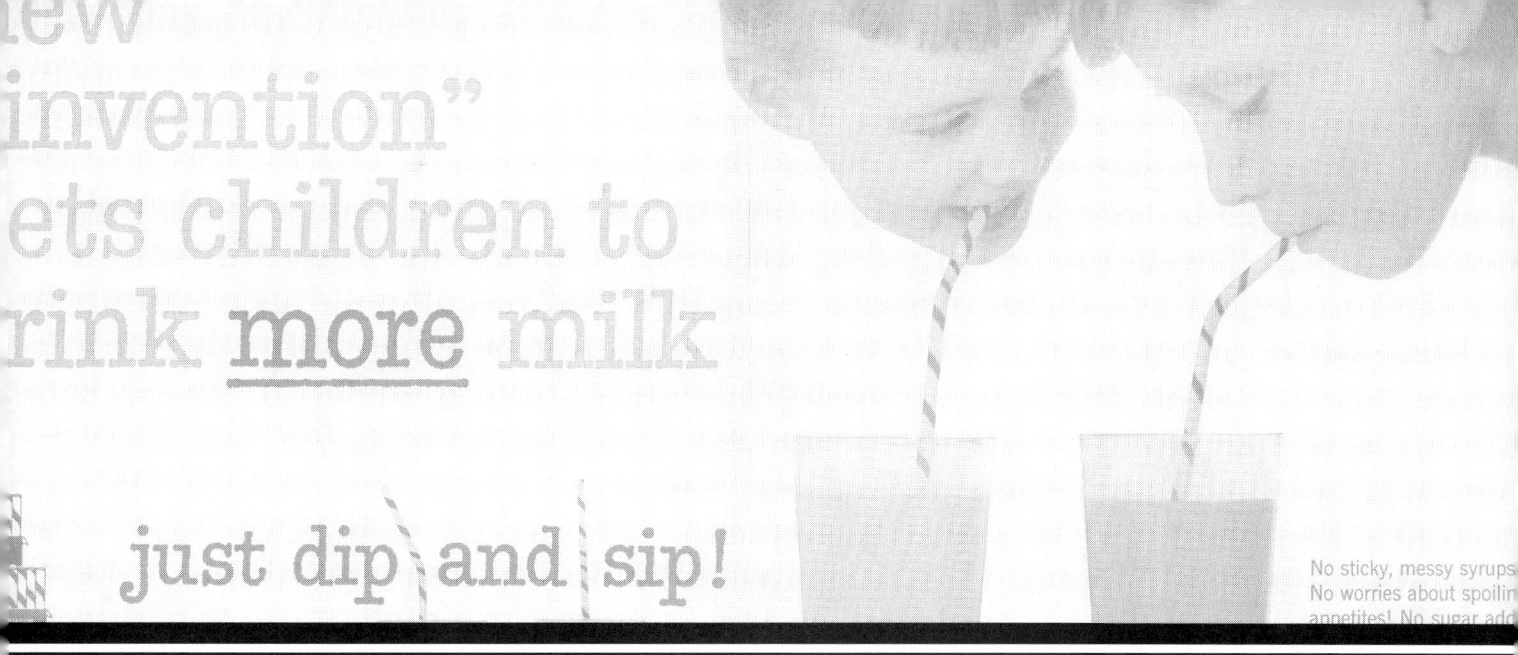

1959 Profile

Working Class

Eighteen months ago, 14-year-old Li-ming Sho moved to Amarillo, Texas, to help his father run a Chinese restaurant along Route 66. Previously, he had lived in Oakland, California, under the watchful eye of his mother.

Life at Home

- When Li-ming Sho turned 12, after a lifetime in Oakland, California, he and his father took over a restaurant in Amarillo, Texas, along Route 66, which stretches like a twisted grin between Santa Monica and Chicago.
- His father signed a contract for the restaurant, sight unseen, and father and son took the train to Texas in the summer of 1957.
- Along the way, Li-ming read a stack of *Mad* magazines, enthralled by the goofiness and anarchy of the stories.
- His father mostly remained silent and worried: The new Chinese restaurant, with its neon signs featuring chop suey and chow mein, is designed to attract American tourists.
- Created in the mid-1800s in San Francisco to feed hungry gold miners, chop suey literally means "bits and pieces"; it is rarely eaten by the Chinese, but loved by traveling Americans looking for "adventure."
- In Oakland, California, Li-ming's father owned and operated a Chinese restaurant for 15 years, until it finally closed.
- Growing up, Li-ming spent most of his time in the rice room at the back of the restaurant, where the soda pop, beer, and boxes of canned water chestnuts and bamboo shoots were stored.
- His earliest memories are of the lively designs printed on the food cans.

Li-ming Sho grew up in Oakland, California.

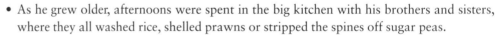

When Li-ming turned 12, he moved to Amarillo, Texas, on Route 66 to run a restaurant with his father.

- As he grew older, afternoons were spent in the big kitchen with his brothers and sisters, where they all washed rice, shelled prawns or stripped the spines off sugar peas.
- Being around food all the time, he enjoys delicious snacks—a favorite is may—salted preserved plums—which invariably sets off explosions in his mouth.
- He loves to eat pickled scallions pulled straight from the jar, and suck on sugar cane fresh from the market.
- The middle child out of five, and the second son, he grew up in a home where his parents always spoke in their native dialect of Cantonese, but he feels little connection to a language and a country he cannot recall.
- The last time his mother and the children were in China was in 1948—when he was three—just as the communists were advancing on Canton; she wanted to see her aging mother for one last time and let her see her grandchildren before it was too late.
- They stayed for five months; a few months later in October, Mao Zedong established the People's Republic of China, known in America as Red China.
- His oldest sister entered the first grade with no knowledge of English and struggled to read until the fourth grade.
- Language is often a problem for Li-ming, also; when his first-grade teacher asked him to name his favorite pie, he wanted to say custard, but didn't know the English word, so instead he said, "egg pie" (the main ingredient), and the classroom was filled with giggles.

The family has travelled to San Francisco for the New Year's celebration.

- Starting when he was just seven, playing with firecrackers has been an important part of his life—even after he nearly blew off his thumb, which throbbed for weeks; hiding the embarrassing wound from his parents, he became even more determined to play with fireworks.
- About that same time, he and his brothers and sisters learned to sing Chinese songs into a record-cutting machine, which etched their words onto plastic-coated metal discs.
- The records were sent to his grandmother in China so she could play them back on a record player.
- Li-ming spends a lot of time alone, thinking.
- He learned that if he sat very still, he could see the minute hand on a clock move, and thus be able to watch time.
- Often, he simply listens to people talk and observes how they move; his sister says he can imitate anyone's walk and talk.
- Until he was eight, Li-ming was convinced that little people lived in the family's Zenith console radio, which stood four feet high.
- Only his introduction to a tabletop radio convinced him otherwise.
- He has distinct memories of the "babysitters" who appeared on the family's tiny black-and-white television: *The Lone Ranger* and *The Great Gildersleeve and the Gangbusters*, known as G-men.
- His first exposure to color television came in the tong, or meeting hall, of the Yin on Benevolent Association, which was above his father's restaurant.
- There, while watching TV amid the smoke from pipes, cigars and cigarettes, he listened to the music of China, played on kotos, flutes and drums.

Weekends are reserved for westerns, especially The Lone Ranger.

- On weekends he'd watch westerns—*Wild Bill Hickok*, *The Range Rider*, *The Cisco Kid* and his favorite, *The Lone Ranger*—while wearing toy cap pistols to help the heroes bring down the bad guys in black hats.

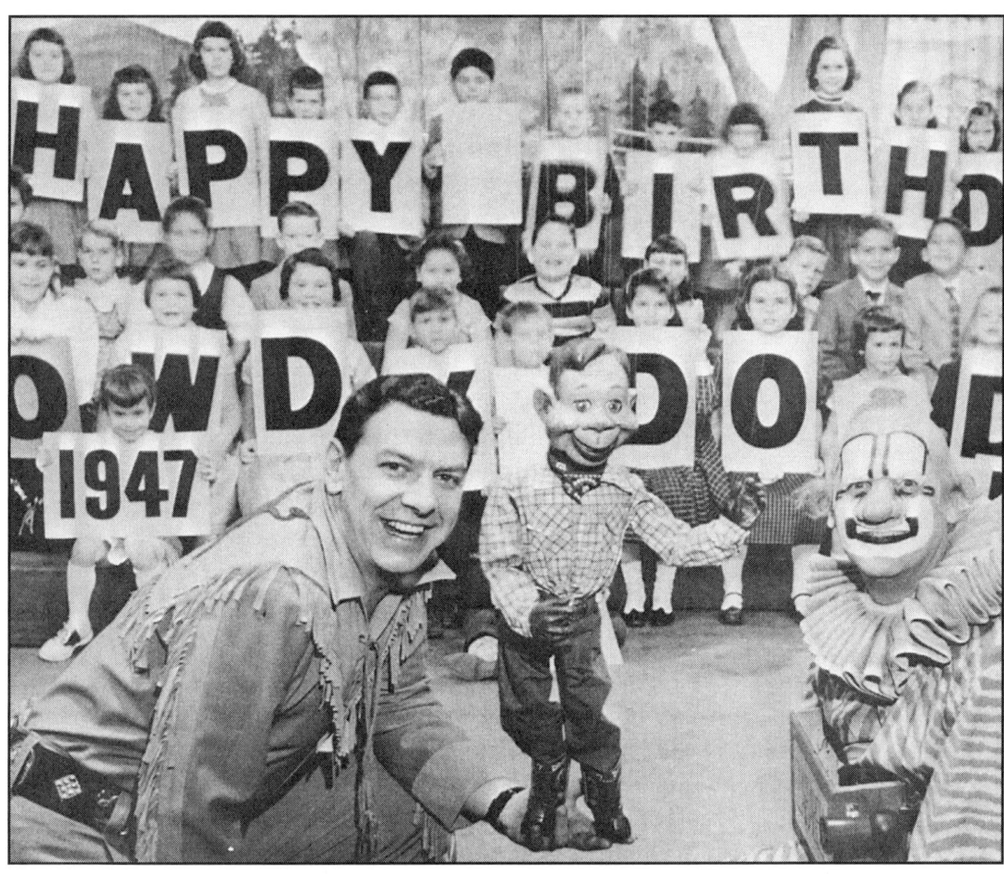

For more than a decade, Howdy Doody *has been a children's-show staple.*

- He and his brother even constructed their own costumes; a yellow kerchief was all it took to be part of the heroic U.S. Cavalry.
- Comedy shows included the *Colgate Comedy Hour* with Dean Martin and Jerry Lewis, Eddie Cantor, Abbott and Costello and Jimmy Durante.
- At the T&D Theater near his home, Li-ming watched *20,000 Leagues under the Sea* and the first experiments with 3-D movie vision.
- On Thursdays, when the family restaurant was closed, they attended Chinese movies in San Francisco.
- Many were anti-communist films, but it didn't matter as long as they contained lots of fighting; the operas were all in Cantonese.
- His parents desperately want their children to have American opportunities within a Chinese cultural mindset.
- Ideally the boys would be doctors, dentists or lawyers, and the girls would become wives of doctors, dentists and lawyers—all Chinese to the core.
- When he entered the third grade, his school day was lengthened by two hours so he could attend the Chinese school held at the Chinese Community Center.
- There he was taught language, calligraphy, culture and manners.

Chinese markets offer a great variety of goods to shoppers.

- His mother required that he split his time between using pencils and Chinese brush pens when doing his homework.
- She often gives his brother long and rattling lectures on marrying the right kind of girl—a Chinese girl, no matter what.
- Growing up, Li-ming found the Chinese calendar confusing, with New Year and his parents' birthdays all falling on different dates every year.
- The Chinese New Year is a two-week-long affair, culminating in each child receiving a little red envelope containing a coin—given to reward them for good manners and to wish them good luck.
- Every year, his parents would put out their round, lacquered wood platter called a tray of togetherness.
- Its compartments held a variety of sweets, each with a meaning: candied melon for health, sugared coconut strips for togetherness, kumquat for prosperity, lichee nuts for strong family ties, melon seeds for happiness, lotus seeds for many children and longan for many good sons.
- After the New Year's Day dinner, they would set off firecrackers outside the house to ward off evil spirits, pretending they were part of the celebrated parade through Chinatown in San Francisco with its block-long golden dragon.
- His most American dinner of the year was served on Thanksgiving, when they enjoyed roast beef, mashed potatoes, apple pie and only a little turkey because, his parents said, it causes gneet-hay, or hot air, in Chinese people.
- As he has gotten older, he wonders if other families use newspaper as tablecloths, wrapping all the bones and other leftovers into a newspaper pouch at the end of a meal.

New Year's Day is marked by a special dinner and celebration.

- All his life he has eaten salted fish or hot egg custard, or roast duck, and even chicken feet, rarely spending much time with lamb, veal, salads, cheese or olives.
- In China, his great-grandfather farmed rice and grew vegetables, and his grandfather sold food, clothing and stationery, traveling on foot from village to village.
- In 1921, Li-ming's father left China at age 18 for the Philippine capital of Manila, where he believed he could make his fortune.
- He insisted to all who would listen that he would not go to America, declaring: "I do not want to lose my Chinese ways."
- After six years in the Philippines, however, he moved to Oakland, California, claiming Philippine birth to circumvent the Exclusion Act of 1882 barring the immigration of all Chinese except for the sons of United States citizens or Chinese merchants.

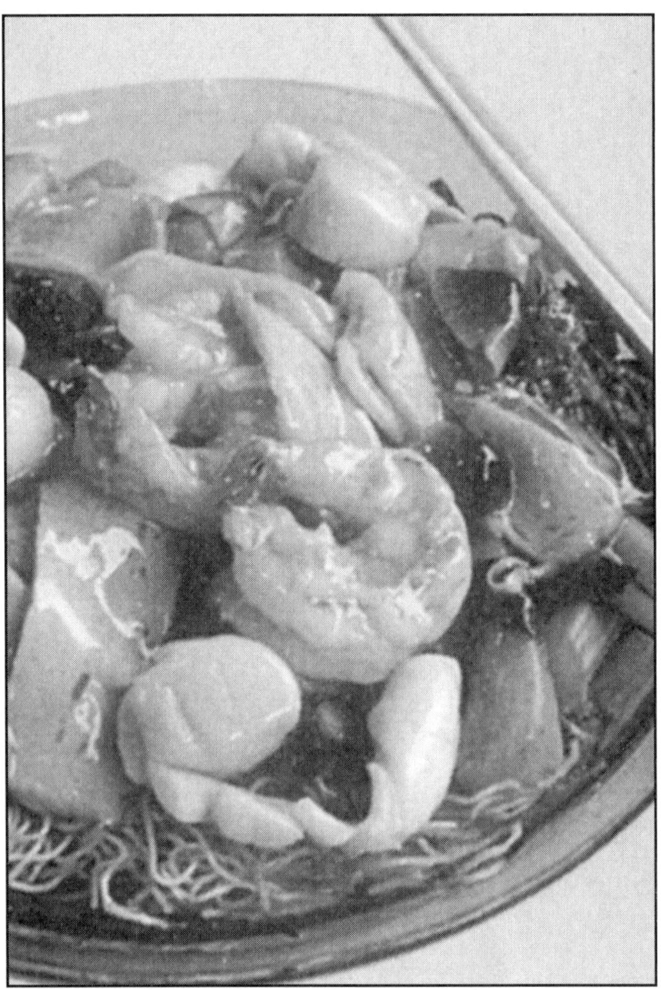

Li-ming has worked in the restaurant his entire life.

- For $1,200 he obtained a birth certificate under the name Ricardo Torres, issued in the Philippines, a colony of the United States.
- Landing in San Francisco in 1927 with only a dollar in his pocket, he took a job in Oakland, first as a dishwasher and then as a cook.
- To earn extra money, he stayed at the restaurant at night, whipping and stretching wheat flour into noodles, which he sold to other restaurants.
- In the 1930s he worked in restaurants, sold Chinese Keno lottery tickets and worked at the racetrack, earning enough to send money back home, help siblings get married, purchase gifts for Spring and Moon festivals, and pay for living expenses.
- Li-ming's mother, too, came to the United States under false papers.
- In 1939, she arrived at the immigration station on Angel Island, the largest island in San Francisco Bay, where she was examined for communicable diseases, questioned about her origin, and detained for 41 days before being allowed entry.
- After her admittance into the U.S., the couple was married in a prearranged ceremony; she was 19 and her husband was 37.
- Shortly after she arrived, she answered the front door to find two children—one dressed as a ghost and the other as a witch; frightened, she slammed the door and ran to the phone to call her sister-in-law, who quickly explained the custom of American Halloween.
- She reluctantly acknowledged it as simply one more aspect of her American education.
- If not for her family and the communists, she would have returned to China years ago.
- About the time Li-ming turned 10 years old, he fell in love with the game of baseball, specifically the Oakland minor league baseball team of the Pacific Coast League.
- While running the cash register in the restaurant at night, he could work and listen at the same time.
- After a few years, his love became a passion, and when the World Series rolled around every year, he developed an amazing array of illnesses to leave school before the games started.
- The restaurant began to decline as many in the Chinese-American community prospered and, for the first time, could move away from Oakland's Chinatown.
- Further cutting into his family's income was the 1954 law prohibiting pak kop piu, a lottery game that was for decades the economic backbone of Chinatown.
- During the 1950s, 40 lotteries had operated in Oakland's Chinatown; Li-ming and his siblings often distributed tickets and took in money for transport to the lottery.
- With the shifting population and loss of these lottery revenues, the restaurant eventually failed; his father was ashamed, out of work and desperate.
- When an offer came for him to run a restaurant in Texas, he grabbed the opportunity.
- To improve his success, he took his second son along for company and as an extra hand, as well as to keep down the fighting in the family.
- In recent years, Li-ming and his mother have had an uneasy relationship.

Language is a growing issue between American-born Li-ming and his mother.

- Increasingly, a language wall has been growing between Li-ming and his mother, mostly because of her refusal to learn English and insistence on speaking only in Cantonese, while her son has grown up speaking English and sees no use for Cantonese except to appease his mother.
- In America, he sees that parents dote on their children, whereas his mother and father preach that children's first obligation is to their parents.

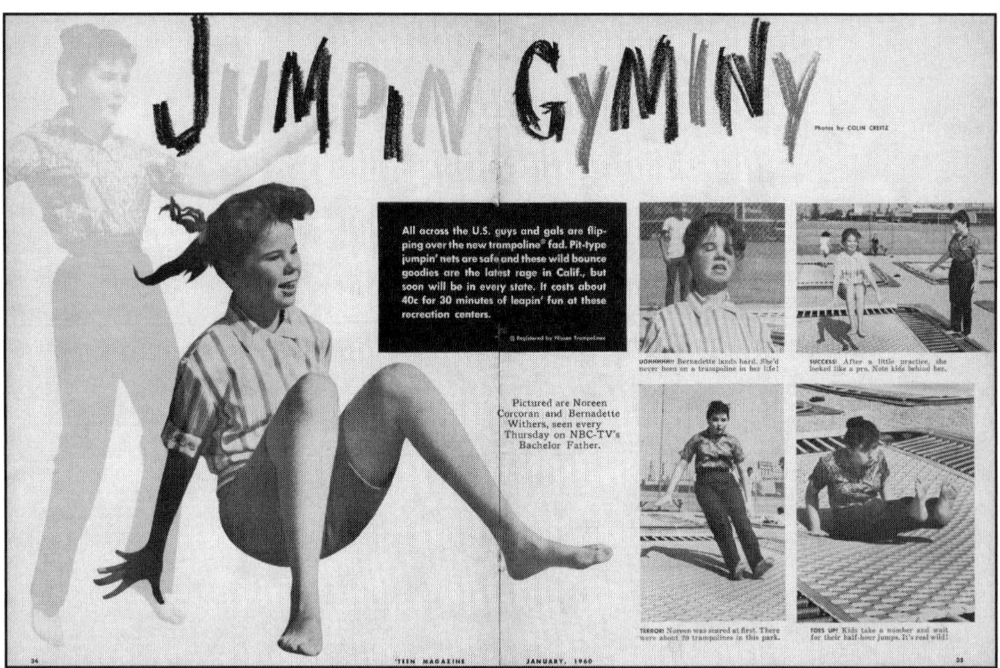

JUMPIN' GYMINY

Photos by COLIN CREITZ

All across the U.S. guys and gals are flipping over the new trampoline® fad. Pit-type jumpin' nets are safe and these wild bounce goodies are the latest rage in Calif., but soon will be in every state. It costs about 40c for 30 minutes of leapin' fun at these recreation centers.

® Registered by Nissen Trampolines

Pictured are Noreen Corcoran and Bernadette Withers, seen every Thursday on NBC-TV's Bachelor Father.

UOHHHHH!! Bernadette lands hard. She'd never been on a trampoline in her life!

SUCCESS! After a little practice, she looked like a pro. Note kids behind her.

TERROR! Noreen was scared at first. There were about 20 trampolines in this park.

TOES UP! Kids take a number and wait for their half-hour jumps. It's real wild!

34 'TEEN MAGAZINE JANUARY, 1960 35

Li-ming's mother is shocked by the activities of American girls.

- When he complains to his mother that other children are not required to work day and night, and even get to go out and socialize, she says, "Americans, they do not care about family."
- His mother is also mystified that his young sister wants to play basketball and listen to rock 'n' roll music; "Girls don't do that," his mother chides.
- Li-ming and his sisters would often sneak off to friends' houses at night to listen to the radio, saying they had homework to complete.
- His mother also discourages all white friends, tagging them all "bok guey," or white demons.
- In the same way, she considers the Japanese to be the vandals of China and, therefore, beyond contempt.

Life at School and Work

- In Amarillo, away from his mother, his world is more open to all kinds of music—especially Elvis Presley.
- He first discovered Elvis in 1956, when the king of rock 'n' roll appeared on *Stage Show*, a half-hour variety show hosted by the Dorsey Brothers on Saturday night.
- As quickly as he could, Li-ming bought every record Elvis made and collected every magazine that featured him on the cover.
- His mother had heard that rock 'n' roll leads directly to juvenile delinquency and banned Elvis and Little Richard records from the house; however, there is little she can do now that Li-ming is struggling to be American in Texas.
- The passport to coolness is rock 'n' roll.
- In school, he is one of a very few Asian students, and the only Chinese person in the school.
- Li-ming quickly developed the nickname of Chop Chop based on the comic book *Blackhawks*, in which a secret military team always fought the Nazis with the help of their mascot, Chop Chop, a Chinese cook who wields a long knife.

In Amarillo, Li-ming discovered Elvis, the "King of rock 'n' roll."

- For years, he had wondered whether his yellow skin stood out as brightly as did the comic book character's.
- In Texas, he found out almost immediately; on the first day of school his physical education class teacher clapped his hands and yelled loudly to him, "Let's go, Chop Chop."
- That year he also learned from a fellow junior high school buddy that sex always happens in the bathroom, although the details were fuzzy.
- From magazines his older brother brought home, he knows that all naked women have big breasts and spend a lot of time playing volleyball.
- Now he knows a little more.
- At his new school, he discovered eighth-grade kids going steady, and exchanging ID bracelets and St. Christopher medals to display their devotion.

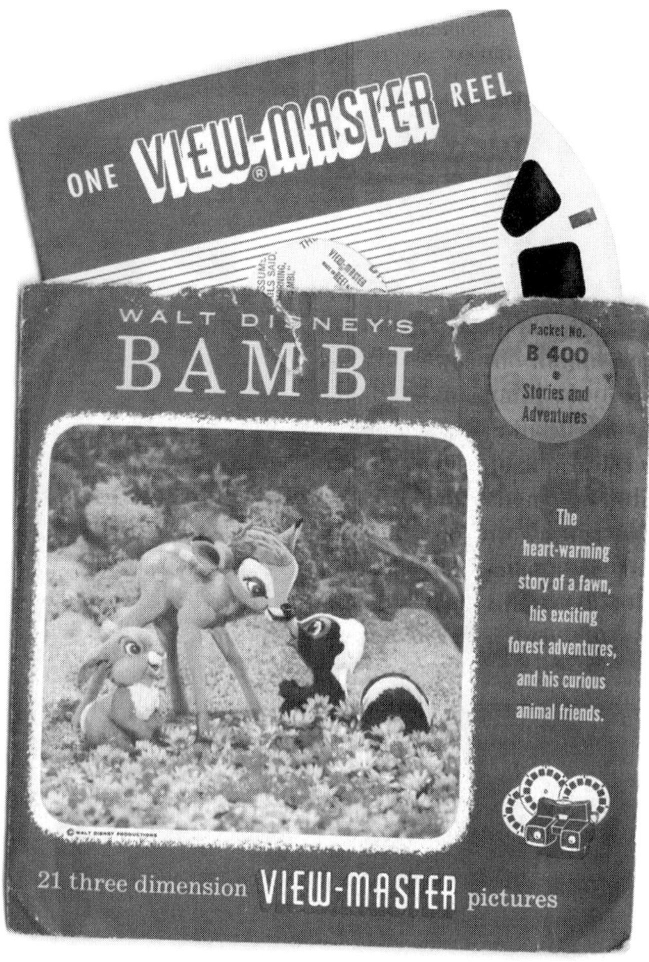

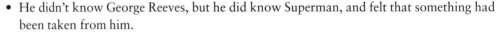

- To think about kissing a girl feels good and bad at the same time.
- Because of his late nights at the restaurant, he rarely attends school parties and dances, often finishing work just as the dances are ending.
- Once or twice he walked a special girl home, but she moved away during the Christmas holidays without a goodbye.
- At lunchtime, when American children line up for lunches of macaroni and cheese or hot dogs, Li-ming's lunch contains sandwiches of chicken, Spam or barbecued pork.
- His lunches attract a lot of attention, but students leave him alone; everyone knows that Chop Chop loves rock 'n' roll and that makes him cool among a small group—even though he does not see them outside of school.
- Recently, to increase his record collection, he shoplifted several 45 rpm records, but a store detective saw him and demanded his name and telephone number.
- They let him go with a warning, but he is banned from the store for life.
- He does not want anyone to know, especially his father, who might send him back to California.
- Deciding that he would fit in better if he were the same size as the other students, Li-ming sets aside time each day to hang from the overhead pipe in the men's bathroom; he is sure it will make him taller.
- Recently, he saw on television that George Reeves, the star of *Superman*, committed suicide; though he was unsure why, the news made him sad and produced a quiet anger he was unable to shake for days.
- He didn't know George Reeves, but he did know Superman, and felt that something had been taken from him.

Life in the Community: Amarillo, Texas

- Amarillo and the Texas Panhandle can be a forbidding place for the uninitiated.
- Locals claim that the winter wind starts at the North Pole and sweeps across the Great Plains with nothing to stop it but a few strands of barbed wire, and say, "It's so wide open, you can see into the middle of next week."
- When the early Spaniards first saw the land, there was not a tree or bush on it, just an apparently infinite sea of grass.
- Li-ming has observed that little has changed since then; when he describes Amarillo to his friends in California, he says it is a town halfway to somewhere else.
- Amarillo was formed at the junction of three railroads in the 1890s.
- As cattle were transported from ranches to packing houses in the Midwest and East, Amarillo became the world's leading cattle shipping market.
- In 1918, natural gas was discovered in the area, petroleum was found in 1921 and zinc smelting started in 1922.
- The town suffered through Black Sunday on April 14, 1935, when dust storms swept through Kansas and the Oklahoma Panhandle, and seemed to boil over into the Texas Panhandle.

For many years a Chinese Benevolent Association was located over Li-ming's father's restaurant.

- In 1942, both the Pantex Army Ordnance Plant and the Amarillo Army Air Field were opened.
- By 1951, a Strategic Air Command base was established to serve the 461st Bombardment Wing, composed of the 764th Bombardment Squadron and the 909th Refueling Squadron.
- Thanks to the base and the activity on Route 66, the population of Amarillo tops 150,000.

Historical Snapshot
1959

- To offset the rising cost of tinplate, Coors beer adopted the use of the aluminum can
- Movie premieres included *Ben-Hur* starring Charlton Heston; *Some Like It Hot* with Tony Curtis, Marilyn Monroe and Jack Lemmon; and *Pillow Talk* featuring Doris Day, Rock Hudson and Tony Randall
- Mary Leakey discovered the skull of the 1.78 million-year-old *Australopithecus* in the Olduvai Gorge, Tanganyika
- Television's top-10 shows were *Gunsmoke*; *Wagon Train*; *Have Gun, Will Travel*; *The Danny Thomas Show*; *The Red Skelton Show*; *Father Knows Best*; *77 Sunset Strip*; *The Price Is Right*; *Wanted: Dead or Alive* and *Perry Mason*
- The Soviet *Lunik II* became the first manmade object to strike the moon
- Rock 'n' roll stars Buddy Holly, Ritchie Valens and the Big Bopper were killed in an airplane crash
- A new law declared modern art to be duty-free
- Weather stations, movies with accompanying scents and a nuclear merchant ship all made their first appearance
- The U.S. Navy successfully orbited a Vanguard satellite, the forerunner of the first weather station in space
- "A Raisin in the Sun," "The Miracle Worker," "The Tenth Man," "Five Finger Exercise," "Sweet Bird of Youth" and "Mark Twain Tonight" all premiered on Broadway
- Fiction bestsellers included *Exodus* by Leon Uris, *Doctor Zhivago* by Boris Pasternak, *Hawaii* by James Michener, *Lady Chatterley's Lover* by D. H. Lawrence, *The Ugly American* by William J. Lederer and Eugene L. Burdick, *Poor No More* by Robert Ruark and *Dear and Glorious Physician* by Taylor Caldwell
- Disc jockeys came under investigation for accepting "payola"
- After rigorous testing, NASA selected the *Mercury* Seven astronauts: John Glenn, Scott Carpenter, Virgil Grissom, Gordon Cooper, Walter Schirra, Donald Slayton and Alan Shepard
- Perry Como signed a $25 million contract with Kraft Foods

1959 Economic Profile

Selected Prices

Accordion	$189.00
Air Freshener, Dazy Spray	$0.49
Automobile, Pontiac Bonneville	$5,782.00
Cat Food, Puss'n'Boots	$0.13
Chop Suey Sauce	$0.19
Eyelash Curler, Maybelline	$1.00
Flashlight Battery	$0.18
Fry Skillet	$15.95
Ironing Board, Met-L-Top	$13.95
Jeans	$1.64
Movie Projector, Argus M-500	$89.95
Outboard Motor, Evinrude	$430.00
Railroad Fare, Chicago to San Francisco	$63.12
Sponge	$4.98
Stereo, Columbia Stereo I	$129.95

THIS NEW HIGHWAY WILL *STAY* NEW. No intersections. No driveways or railroad crossings. Just a safe, swift avenue of traffic—planned for today *and* for tomorrow. Years from now it will still be 100% efficient—thanks to "planned access."

NEW BUT ALREADY OUT OF DATE, this highway was built to speed traffic, is instead a slow, dangerous, expensive waste of money. Cars and trucks pull on and off it constantly. Traffic cuts across it. And congestion grows gradually worse.

BUY A HIGHWAY—NOT A BOTTLENECK

New roads are built for one purpose: to carry a planned number of vehicles from one place to another. The day a new highway begins to fall short of its planned capacity, that day the tax money invested in the new road begins to be wasted. This will not happen with the freeways planned for our nation's essential National System of Interstate and Defense Highways. Here's why.

On conventional highways, traffic can cross or enter or leave wherever there's a driveway. Unplanned access roads soon lead to the highway. Traffic lights go up. The strain of stop-and-go driving gets nastier. In five short years the "new" highway loses 50% of its efficiency. *Half the tax dollars that built it go down the drain.* Losses in lives and property mount.

But Interstate-Defense System Highways will be *"planned access"* roads. That means traffic will enter and leave at specified points only—quickly, safely. No intersections. No clutter of roadside drive-ins. For the through driver, no stops at all.

"Planned access" highways will prevent a million accidents a year. And, they are *insured highways.* Your investment in them is guaranteed, because they will go on carrying their planned capacity indefinitely.

How Every Citizen Can Help

Find out all you can about the Federal-Aid Highway Program. Support careful, farsighted road building. Send today for your free copy of an informative booklet, "The Road Ahead." Write Dept. 15-T, Caterpillar Tractor Co., Peoria, Illinois, U. S. A.

CATERPILLAR

REG. U. S. PAT. OFF.

Diesel Engines • Tractors • Motor Graders • Earthmoving Equipment

THE WORLD'S NO. 1 ROAD BUILDING EQUIPMENT

Changing America

- Dozens of school systems nationwide experimented with 12-month schools to save money; one-fourth of the pupils were on vacation each quarter.
- The introduction of the first credit card by Bank of America was changing the way Americans were buying.
- Police expenditures on the federal, state and local level topped $1.9 billion; 2.6 million people were arrested.
- A Caribbean cruise lasting 15 days and covering seven ports cost $355.
- At $100 per ticket, Maria Callas and Van Cliburn performed to capacity audiences at the Philadelphia Academy of Music.

"The Big Kindergarten," *Time*, March 10, 1958:

"The American school system, from first grade through college, [has become] a huge kindergarten." So, last week, declared self-exiled schoolmaster Philip Marson, who quit famed Boston Latin School last year after teaching English there for 31 years. Marson's reason for walking out: "I could then say what had to be said without gloves."

Marson's bare-knuckle attack on U.S. education made the front page of *The Boston Globe*. "I watched, with increasing alarm, the lack of fundamental information possessed by the pupils who entered the high school, and the disappearance of standards demanded of them by the colleges when they were ready to leave. The elementary schools, by misapplication of the theories of Dewey and Freud, had eliminated unpleasant work and had substituted play." The colleges had so diluted their entrance requirements that they ceased to function as incentive to scholarship.

Those Who Only Breathe? "In terms of numbers and competition," Marson later admitted, "it is, of course, now harder to get into college. But this is a relative thing. Scholarship requirements are much more lax now than they were 20 years ago. In fact, admission criteria have nothing to do with scholarship. They are based on tests that do not test scholarship. In the state universities, it's even worse. All you have to do in most of them is to breathe to gain admission."

By entrance exams that dodge scholarship, school man Marson means "objective" tests that ignore the classics and seldom require an applicant to write a complete sentence. Says he: "The experts may come up with figures which say that the students are better scholars now than they were. But I don't believe them. These figures are based on percentiles—on the student's relative standing."

Is Education Fun? In this generation at Boston Latin, a public high school that has been one of the most respected secondary schools in the U.S., Marson always practiced what he now preaches. His boys knew precisely what they would get from their round-faced, jovial schoolmaster: hard work and solid teaching in the fundamentals of composition and literature. Marson scoffed at curve grading (the clod-coddling marking system that is based on the class average), insisting that his boys measure up to definite levels. One bright boy who measured up: composer Leonard Bernstein, who still talks of Marson's lectures on English poetry. Says a Boston Latin colleague of Marson: "Phil never pretended education was fun or that there was a substitute for hard work. He was the ideal secondary-school teacher."

- Edward Teller, the father of the H-bomb, stated: "It is necessary to provide every person in the U.S. with a shelter."
- Ed Murrow interviewed Fidel Castro, who was wearing pajamas, on *Person to Person*.
- Miles Davis and John Coltrane introduced "free jazz" with their album entitled *Kind of Blue*.
- The American Medical Association sanctioned hypnosis as a medical aid.
- A *Look* magazine poll on moral attitudes reported that one should do whatever he wanted as long as it would be accepted by the neighbors.

"Children Are Not Born Liars," by Dr. Milton J. E. Senn, *McCall's*, February 1958:

"Why is it that many children lie so much more than others? Is lying an inborn personality trait?"

No, it is not. Lying is a method of dealing with a situation—what psychologists call a "coping device." Every child is born with a potential for being both truthful and untruthful, and he will be either, depending on what happens to him as he grows older.

"Our three-year-old has a wild imagination. He's always telling us stories about how he shot a tiger in the bathtub or met a giant in the park. Do you consider this lying?"

No, I don't. A child this age often confuses fact with fantasy. He tells "tall tales" because it entertains him to use his imagination, and because it gives him a pleasant feeling of strength to think he shot a tiger or faced up to a giant. However, the way his parents react to his fantasies can make a great deal of difference in his understanding of truth and untruth later. If parents go along with his stories and if they obviously think them entertaining and cute, the child will not only find it harder to distinguish between what's real and what isn't, but he also will believe that telling these stories is a fine way to attract attention and approval. He can't help but be bewildered when at six or seven his parents begin to apply adult standards to him and label his make-believe "falsehood."

To lay a sound groundwork for truthfulness, parents have to be consistent in their attitude from the beginning and always make it clear to the small child that, though his stories are interesting, they know and he knows they are only make-believe. I don't mean that the three-year-old should be scolded when he claims he can turn into a grizzly bear. Instead you might say, "That sounds like fun. I think I'll pretend I am a mouse."

"Ever since our daughter started first grade last fall she has been telling us how popular she is, how well she is doing in her studies and how much the teacher likes her. We have learned that none of this is true, that she is only average in every respect. What makes her lie to us this way?"

Even though your little girl is now old enough to distinguish between fantasy and reality, she is still clinging to fantasy to satisfy her emotional needs. When reality is too hard to take, some children fall back on fantasy instead of using their own abilities to get what they need. Apparently, your daughter feels it is vital to be outstanding in school, but she doesn't know how to be, and so she takes refuge in this make-believe. Children in this situation need to be helped to find ways of making reality more rewarding—not to be punished or scolded for their fantasies.

- Lamar Hunt organized the American Football League with eight teams.
- To encourage bright students, language studies were introduced in grade school and early college admissions were encouraged.
- Oklahoma finally repealed Prohibition, which had been the law of the land since statehood in 1907.
- Smaller cars such as the Falcon were becoming more popular; the average car cost $1,180 compared with $1,300 in 1939.

Chinese Immigration in the United States

- Chinese began arriving in America in large numbers in 1849 at the height of the gold rush, and within two years, 12,000 Chinese lived in California.
- In 1865, 14,000 Chinese workers were hired to build the railroad, astonishing observers with their work ethic and precision.
- By the 1880s, Chinese became the principal source of migrant farm labor in California; approximately 250,000 had immigrated in 30 years, almost all of them men.
- In 1882 the Federal Exclusion Act forbade the immigration of Chinese laborers for 10 years.
- So many workers returned home that by 1900, only 90,000 Chinese lived in America; by 1920 the census counted less than 60,000 and 80 percent were concentrated in the Chinatown sections of San Francisco, Los Angeles, Portland, Seattle, New York and Chicago.
- Following the San Francisco earthquake and fire of 1906, when Chinatown burned to the ground, the city decided to rebuild it on its original site.
- During the earliest days, Chinese immigrants contributed heavily to support the Chinese-language schools; by 1910 the Chinese goal had become college for their sons.
- During World War II, thousands of American-born Chinese served in the military.
- Following the war, the passage of the "Alien Brides Acts" permitted veterans who had married abroad to bring their wives and children to America, adding 5,000 Chinese women to the population.
- The communist conquest of China's mainland brought another substantial increase in Chinese residents when 6,000 students were stranded in the U.S., unable to return; the majority sought U.S. citizenship.

"The Chinese among Us," by Albert Q. Maisel, *Reader's Digest*, February 1959:

When the two winners of the 1957 Nobel Prize for physics were announced, their youthfulness caused widespread comment. Prof. Chen-Ning Yang of the Institute for Advanced Study at Princeton, New Jersey, was only 34; Prof. Tsung-Dao Lee of Columbia University had barely passed his thirtieth birthday. To historians, however, the recognition that had come to Doctors Lee and Yang had a further significance: It spotlighted the amazingly rapid emergence into the mainstream of American life of an immigrant group which until only a few years ago had seemed almost completely isolated and unassimilated.

BRING
THE TROOPS
HOME NOW

1960–1969

No aspect of American society escaped the tumult of the 1960s. Morality, education, the role of the family, the purpose of college and even the need for parents came into question. Following the placid era of the 1950s, the seventh decade of the twentieth century contained tragic assassinations, momentous social movements, remarkable space achievements, and the longest war in American history. Civil Rights leader Martin Luther King, Jr., would deliver his "I have a dream" speech in 1963, the same year President John F. Kennedy was killed. Five years later in 1968, King, along with John Kennedy's influential brother Bobby, would be killed. Violent protests against American involvement in Vietnam would be led and heavily supported by the educated middle class, which had grown and prospered enormously in the American economy.

From 1960 to 1964, the economy expanded; unemployment was low and disposable income for music, vacations, art or simply having fun grew rapidly. Internationally, the power of the United States was immense. Congress gave the young President John F. Kennedy the defense and space-related programs Americans wanted, but few of the welfare programs he proposed. Then, inflation arrived, along with the Vietnam War. Between 1950 and 1965, inflation soared from an annual average of less than two percent (ranging from six percent to 14 percent a year) to a budget-popping average of 9.5 percent. Upper class investors, once content with the consistency and stability of banks, sought better returns in the stock market and real estate.

The Cold War became hotter during conflicts over Cuba and Berlin in the early 1960s. Fears over the international spread of communism led to America's intervention in a foreign conflict that would become a defining event of the decade: Vietnam. Military involvement in this small Asian country grew from advisory status to full-scale war. By 1968, Vietnam had become a national obsession leading to President Lyndon Johnson's decision not to run for another term and fueling not only debate over our role in Vietnam, but more inflation and division nationally. The antiwar movement grew rapidly. Antiwar marches, which had drawn but a few thousand in 1965, grew in size until millions of marchers filled the streets of New York, San Francisco, and Washington, DC, only a few years later. By spring 1970, students on 448 college campuses made ROTC voluntary or abolished it.

The struggle to bring economic equality to blacks during the period produced massive spending for school integration. By 1963, the peaceful phase of the Civil Rights movement was ending; street violence, assassinations, and bombings defined the period. In 1967, 41 cities experienced major disturbances. At the same time, charismatic labor organizer Cesar Chavez's United Farm Workers led a Civil Rights-style movement for Mexican-Americans, gaining national support which challenged the growers of the West with a five-year agricultural strike.

As a sign of increasing affluence and changing times, American consumers bought 73 percent fewer potatoes and 25 percent more fish, poultry, and meat and 50 percent more citrus products and tomatoes than in 1940. California passed New York as the most populous state. Factory workers earned more than $100 a week, their highest wages in history. From 1960 to 1965, the amount of money spent for prescription drugs to lose weight doubled, while the per capita consumption of processed potato chips rose from 6.3 pounds in 1958 to 14.2 pounds eight years later. In 1960, approximately 40 percent of American adult women had paying jobs; 30 years later, the number would grow to 57.5 percent. Their emergence into the work force would transform marriage, child rearing, and the economy. In 1960, women were also liberated by the FDA's approval of the birth-control pill, giving both women and men a degree of control over their bodies that had never existed before.

During the decade, anti-establishment sentiments grew: men's hair was longer and wilder, beards and mustaches became popular, women's skirts rose to mid-thigh, and bras were discarded. Hippies advocated alternative lifestyles, drug use increased, especially marijuana and LSD; the Beatles, the Rolling Stones, Jimi Hendrix, and Janis Joplin became popular music figures; college campuses became major sites for demonstrations against the war and for Civil Rights. The Supreme Court prohibited school prayer, assured legal counsel to the poor, limited censorship of sexual material, and increased the rights of the accused.

Extraordinary space achievements also marked the decade. Ten years after President Kennedy announced he would place a man on the moon, 600 million people around the world watched as Neil Armstrong gingerly lowered his left foot into the soft dust of the moon's surface. In a tumultuous time of division and conflict, the landing was one of America's greatest triumphs and an exhilarating demonstration of American genius. Its cost was $25 billion and set the stage for 10 other men to walk on the surface of the moon during the next three years.

The 1960s saw the birth of Enovid 10, the first oral contraceptive (cost $0.55 each), the start of Berry Gordy's Motown Records, felt-tip pens, Diet-Rite cola, Polaroid color film, Weight Watchers, and Automated Teller Machines. It's the decade when lyrics began appearing on record albums, Jackie and Aristotle Onassis reportedly spent $20 million during their first year together, and the Gay Liberation Front participated in the Hiroshima Day March—the first homosexual participation as a separate constituency in a peace march.

1960 News Feature

"Are You a Spook, or a Spoke?" by Patience Hartman, *Teen*, January 1960: What's the matter with me? Oh, I know I'm no Miss Universe, but I'm not a beast either. I fix myself up. I go to all the dances. I cheer at all the games. I even hang around the malt shop after school. But the boys never notice me. What am I doing wrong?

This is a complaint of the majority of young teens—the 80 percent who sit out most of the dances in giggling clusters while the "popular girls" cheek-to-cheek it. It's a real problem for that gang of girls who attend all the games together or whisper over Cokes at the soda shop while other gal-type wheels date the school dreamboats. In short, this may very well be your problem. If so, you can change things so that you'll be holding hands with your favorite guy instead of holding cat sessions with the girls.

What's the story? Well, in the first place, take a look around you at the twosomes who go steady, or the gals who dance every dance with a different boy. Sure, a lot of them are strictly Fashion Model stuff, with perfect figures and personalities to match. But what about the others—the ones who would never win a Miss America contest? Betty and Sue aren't any prettier or wittier than you. How did they get their popularity? By following three simple rules: 1) Don't go gangsville; 2) Do go where boys are; 3) Do go where the competition is not.

Newspapers blast with the troubles caused by juvenile gangs. But the gang that can cause trouble for you is never in the headlines. That gang is the bunch of girls you surround yourself with at every public event. Somehow, girls get the idea that by traveling in groups of four or five or more they can get more attention. Often the group even dresses alike and tries to act as much alike as possible. Then, after laughing it up at a dance or screaming like crazy at a game, gals wonder why the boys don't notice them.

Well, guys do notice them. They notice them the way they'd notice a jet formation or a jazz combo at church. But how many jet formations get asked for dates?

Gangsville

The first thing wrong with gangsville is that boys like their girls to be different. They don't want to date a carbon copy or a doll off the assembly line. They want to date somebody who, to them, is special. Of course, you know you're different. You know that you're shorter than Claire and slimmer than Marge. You know you have a better sense of humor than Jane and

It is important to stress your individuality.

better grades than Mary. But know all the likes and dislikes, habits and abilities that make you different from everyone else. But how do you expect any of the fellows to discover the real you when you're doing your darndest to look and act like "one of the gang"?

The second thing wrong with gangsville is that girls in large numbers (anything over one or two) scare the boys off. Put the shoe on the other foot and ask yourself how you would feel about inviting a boy to the club dance when he was surrounded by other members of the football team? Wouldn't you wait until he was alone or with another buddy? Well, most boys feel the same way. If they've been smart enough to single you out at all from the mob of girls you travel with, they'll want to talk to you alone.

The first important step to take, then, is to stress your individuality. This doesn't mean that you have to dress like a beatnik or talk a foreign language. It simply means that you don't follow the other girls right down the line, or imitate your school's Miss Universe. Don't be a slave to the gang's styles and fads if they aren't becoming on you. The sweater that looks good on Claire may look weird on you. Wear your hair and your clothes the way they look best on you; and, most important, be yourself. Boys aren't going to go all ape over a gal who is aping everybody else's personality.

Remember, an evening or afternoon with the girls is fine. But 24 hours a day with them is like crazy! Don't be afraid to break loose a little from the gang. You'll be surprised to find that your friends won't send you to Siberia for being a little different. They may even find you a lot more interesting and a lot more fun than you were before. . . .

Extracurricular Tactics

Amy was short, painfully thin, and talkative. She tried hard to look taller and more glamorous. She wore high heels and high hairdos, she padded herself where she thought she needed it, and tried to slink around quietly like a woman of mystery. It was no use. Boys noticed her no more than they did her kid sister. Amy finally got the message.

Switching her attack completely, Amy stopped trying to be tall and decided to be just what she was—petite and cute. And instead of being a woman of mystery, she decided to use her gift of gab where it would count. All the other girls were going out for dramatics, dancing, singing and cooking activities—clubs that appeal to the female of the species. Only one other girl, however, was on the debate and speech team at high school. Amy decided to make it two, and soon found herself with more than debate partners. Here was an activity where the boys liked to talk and argue just as much as she did. And their arguments and discussions soon extended to evenings and Saturday afternoon dates.

When last heard of, Amy was thinking of becoming a lady congressman; but chances are, with her popularity, she'll be walking up the aisle before running for political office.

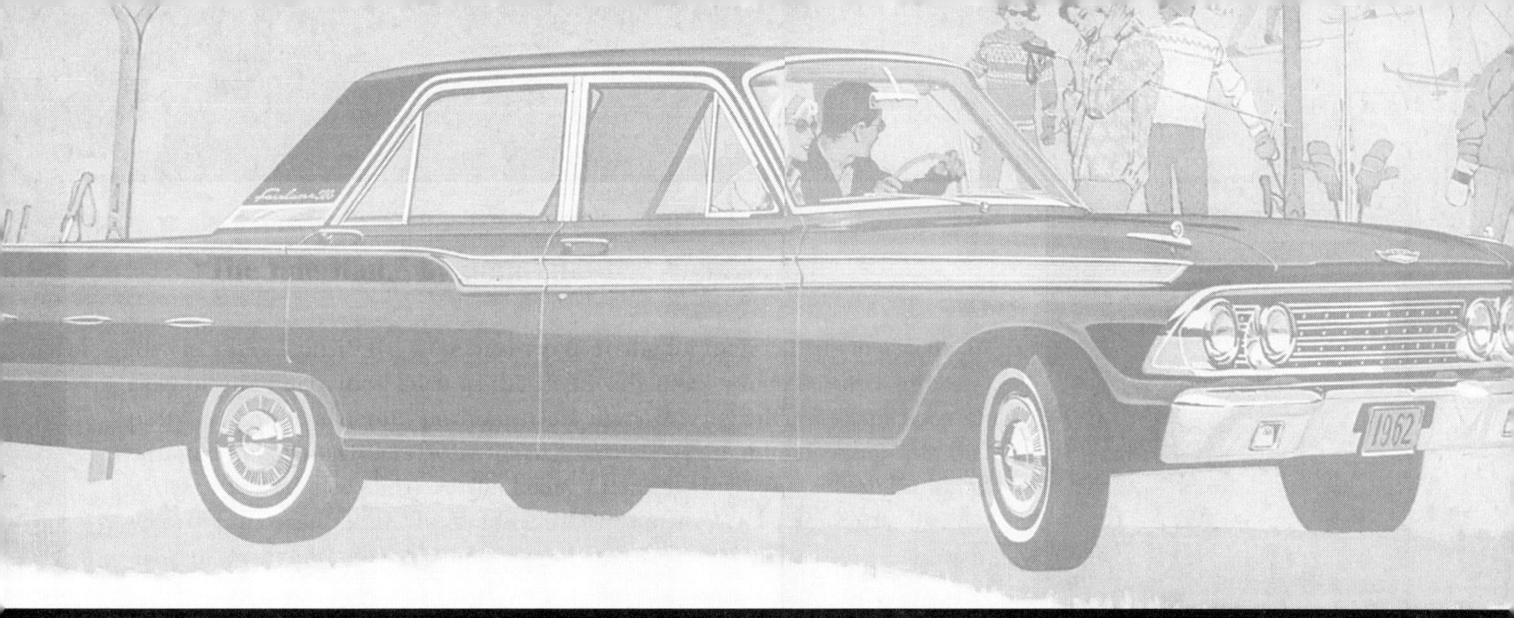

1962 Profile

Working Class

After the tragic death of his parents, Raymond Walker, a 14-year-old African-American, is seeing another part of his city as he steps away from the Cherry Hill public housing project to take a job as a caddie at an exclusive golf club in Baltimore, Maryland.

Life at Home

- Raymond Walker grew up in the Cherry Hill public housing project, which includes a sprinkling of federally subsidized apartments and low-cost, privately owned homes.
- When Raymond was eight years old, his father killed his mother and then himself, leaving behind a suicide note that said he was worried about money and ashamed he would be unable to purchase any Christmas gifts for his children.
- Only two items were found with the note: a $25 money order made out to Raymond's grandmother for the care of the children, and Raymond's newly printed package of school pictures, which he had proudly given to his mother before he went out to play.
- His parents died at 4:30 in the morning in his father's powder-blue 1950 Plymouth station wagon, which they had parked near the construction site of the new colored high school.
- *The Afro-American*, Baltimore's biweekly black newspaper, put the murder-suicide on its front page for two consecutive issues.
- His parents were buried separately, three days apart; Raymond refused to attend either funeral, even though he always believed he was his father's favorite child.

Raymond Walker grew up in a public housing project.

Raymond moved to a public housing unit with his Aunt Etta.

Living conditions were crowded and difficult.

- The children's grandmother, already sick with cancer, died a month later, so three aunts agreed to raise the children, each taking one child.
- Raymond moved to a public housing unit with his Aunt Etta, her husband and six children.
- Nine people shared an apartment with only four rooms: a kitchen, living room and two bedrooms, all with concrete floors.
- The apartment also had a single bathroom with a tub, but no shower, while the kitchen had two sinks: a shallow one for washing dishes and a deeper one for laundry, which was done using a washboard.
- His aunt and uncle slept in one of the two bedrooms, which they shared with their youngest daughter who still slept in a crib, while the two younger children bedded down on the sleeper couch in the living room; the four oldest boys shared the other bedroom, two in each twin bed.
- Meals often included fried salt pork, syrup and bread.
- On Fridays, dinner was usually fried fish; Saturday's dinner was baked beans and hot dogs from the A&P, and on Sundays, the family ate fried chicken.
- When money ran low, supper consisted of a pot of navy beans or pancakes; Spam and potted ham were also staples.
- To make ends meet, Raymond's aunt often sent one of the children to shop at the grocery store where everything could be bought in individual units—one egg for the family that could not afford a dozen, or a couple of cigarettes instead of a pack.
- When Raymond got in trouble, his aunt would holler, "I'm going to give you some medicine you don't want to take!"
- The house was a football field away from the edge of the city dump, and some in the community made ends meet by picking through the mounds of garbage for something to eat—"shopping at the dump," the kids on the street called it.
- Because of its closeness to Baltimore's harbor, the trash dump got most of the fruits and vegetables that failed to clear customs, giving neighbors another reason to "go shopping."
- Sometimes, Raymond and his friend would go to the dump simply for sport—to kill rats by beating them with sticks as they ran for cover.
- When one of his friends got a BB gun, they formed hunting teams; one group of boys would beat the trash pile to make the rats run, while the others would shoot the gun at the fleeing rodents.
- When times were good, Saturdays were spent at the lone movie theater; his aunt would give him a quarter and say, "Don't come home until dark."

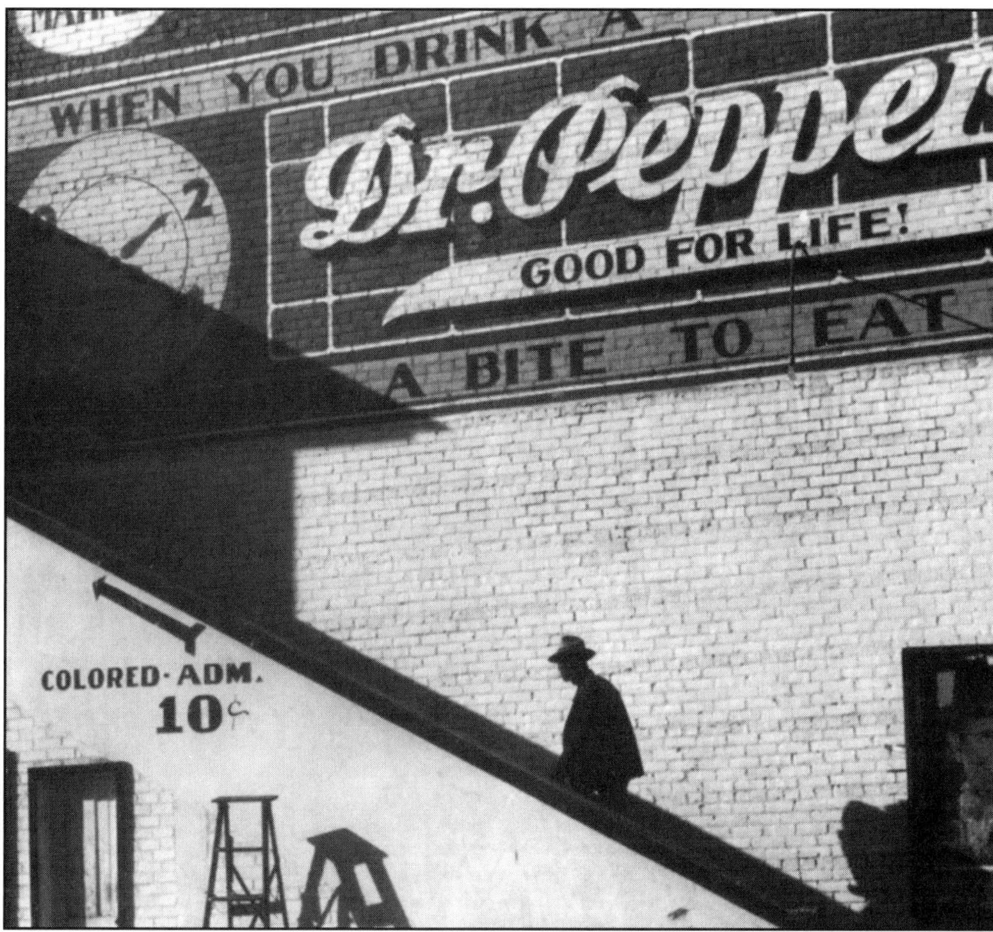

After years of effort, most Jim Crow laws have been eliminated in Baltimore.

- It cost $0.14 for children under the age of 15 to get into the theater, leaving $0.11 for a snack.
- Raymond usually invested a nickel in a box of Jujyfruits, even though he doesn't like the black and green ones.

Life at School and Work

- Raymond's aunt believed in education and would not discuss his dropping out of school; the children's father had forced the girls to leave school in the seventh grade, saying, "All they gonna do anyway is git married and have a bunch of babies."
- All three aunts wanted more for the children.
- While growing up, Raymond's elementary school provided milk and graham crackers during the morning break, and he often was picked to take responsibility for getting the orders right and bringing the food back to the classroom intact—an important job.
- For a class of 32 students, the school provided 16 half-pint cartons of regular milk and 16 of chocolate milk.
- Most mornings, he and a friend would go to the pick-up area and get a half-pint carton of milk and graham crackers for every student in the class.
- Then, he'd return and hand out the milk and crackers; the duty gave him real power, since he decided who got the chocolate milk.

A Black Man's Story of Growing up Alone, by DeWayne Wickham:

Everyone told me that I was my father's favorite child. That's probably true. He used to come home at night with a pocket full of candy—mostly coffee candy—and slip me a piece when others in the family weren't watching. And then there was the time he took the family to Gettysburg to visit the famous Civil War battlefield. I begged my father to buy me a small souvenir from one of the gift shops. He didn't have the money to pay for it, so he just slipped it into his pocket and gave it to me when we got outside.

Once when we were all out in the car together, my father made a quick stop at a tavern. When he came out, he was carrying five hard-boiled eggs—four white and one brown. He gave one white egg to my sister and brothers. "You get white eggs because you were born in white hospitals," he told them. Then he handed me the brown egg, and with a big smile, explained, "This is for you, because you were born in a black hospital." My father always found ways like that to single me out, to make me feel special.

- Anyone who wanted chocolate milk worked hard to be on Raymond's good side—an important shield provided by a teacher aware that children can be cruel to classmates whose parents died tragically.
- The school, like his home, constantly smelled of burning trash; the glow from the garbage trucked in from Baltimore was a local landmark.
- In junior high, he enjoyed a reputation as the class clown; he and his buddy were as much competitors as they were a team.
- Once, his partner in comedy got in trouble for taping a mirror to his shoe so he could look up a classmate's dress.
- For many students, lunch at school was often last night's leftovers, ranging from fried fish heads to potted ham or egg salad sandwiches, which often smelled on a hot day.
- The school had books for the students to read while in class, but not enough for each to take home for homework, so the books were read aloud in class, with each student taking a turn.
- Raymond was aware of his poverty; he wore Converse sneakers to school every day, even during snowstorms.
- When a hole wore through the bottom of the sneakers, he stuffed them with cardboard to keep his feet dry.
- In the eighth grade he wore brogans with steel taps on the first day of school; this later became a school fad.

- He has just completed the ninth grade at an integrated school, having never attended school with whites before.
- At the beginning of the year, his aunt gave him $20.00 to buy clothes and supplies; he got two pairs of khaki pants and a couple of shirts from a surplus store, found shoes at a pawn shop, and still had enough to buy a loose-leaf notebook.
- But money issues remained.
- Following the Christmas break, the teacher asked each child to stand and talk about what they got for Christmas.
- He couldn't tell everyone that he got socks and underwear, so he created a fantasy Christmas for himself, complete with basketballs and his own record player.
- Once during the year he stayed out of school for a week, embarrassed that he could not afford a haircut; when his teacher discovered the reason for his absence, she came to his house, gave him a dollar and took him to a barber.
- As they left the barbershop, she simply said, "I will see you at school tomorrow."
- Based on his test scores, but not his grades, he was selected to attend Baltimore City College, the city's most prestigious public school for boys, next fall.
- As the school year came to a close, though, he and his aunt fought over who had the right to the money sent by the welfare department, and he finally moved out of the house.
- Now, he must carry his own weight.
- Currently, he lives with two friends in Cherry Hill and has begun work at the white country club across town.
- The first time he walked up the long road to the country club, dominated by wealthy Jewish professionals, his stomach did flip-flops.
- Even though he was eager to be a caddie, he had never been on a golf course before, let alone in a fancy country club.
- The club opened in the summer of 1927 as a retreat for the wealthiest of the Eastern European Jews who came to the United States around the turn of the century.
- Many of the newly arrived came to Baltimore, known as the American Jerusalem, but often did not see eye to eye with the German Jews who had emigrated a generation earlier, so the Eastern European Jews set up their own social clubs and eventually established their own country club, starting with 92 members and a nine-hole golf course.
- The club is an important center for Jewish life; every Saturday night, parties for members are held at the club.
- That first day, Raymond arrived a little after 7 a.m., with the morning dew soaking through his Converse sneakers and making his socks cling to his feet.
- The parking lot was filled with Cadillacs, Lincolns, and even a Jaguar and a Rolls Royce.
- Three black men in their early twenties were taking turns chauffeuring cars to the parking lot.
- The senior caddie, who was past 60 years old, knew the rules of the club, including the unwritten rules, which are passed from caddie to caddie and include keeping your mouth shut, staying out of the golfer's way—and totally out of the pro shop.
- On Saturdays, the urgency to "get a bag," is always apparent, even though it means carrying a bag of clubs over nearly four miles of rolling terrain in the heat of summer.

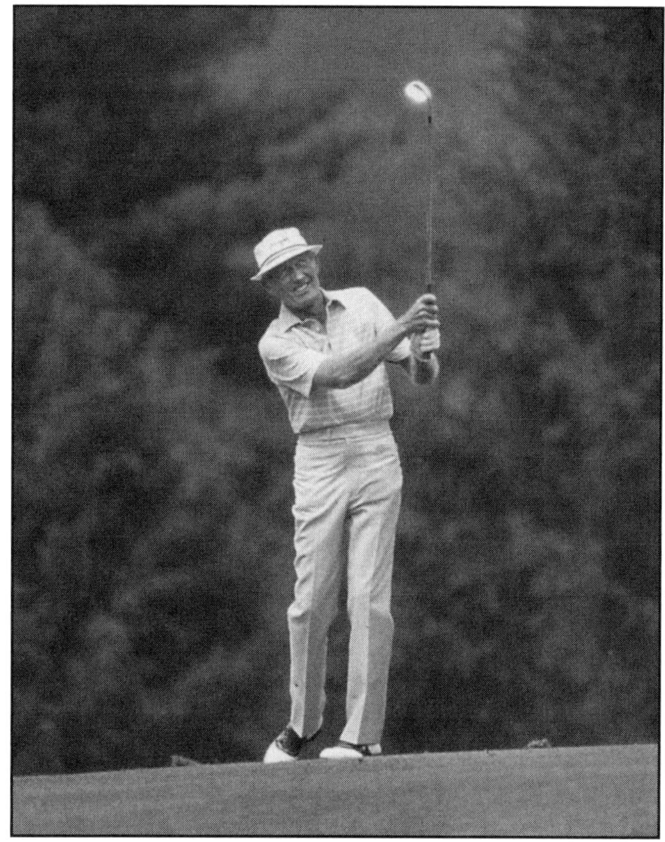

Raymond works as a caddie at the white country club across town.

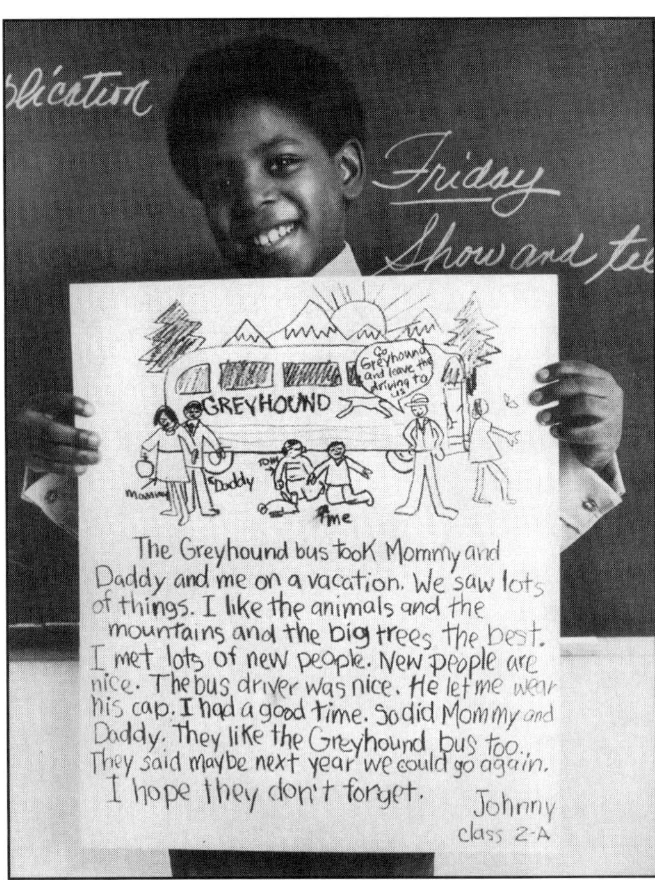

The national media now focuses on the black consumer market.

- Most caddies carry two bags of clubs, one on each shoulder, and are paid $4.00 per bag for a full 18 holes of golf, which normally takes four hours.
- A golf bag's many pockets are not only filled with clubs, but also balls, tees, rain clothes, an umbrella, shoes, sweaters and hats—all combining to push the average weight of a bag to 50 pounds.
- If a caddie does not get any work during an entire day, he is given "caddie welfare"—$2.00 to cover lunch and the bus ride home.
- The club also provides caddie class on Sunday mornings from 6:30 a.m. to 8:30 a.m., so young men from "the Hill" can learn the rules of golf.
- There, Raymond is learning golf protocol, such as who goes first on the second shot, how to replace a divot, when to walk, when to talk and how to keep score.
- He is one of several kids from the Hill who found their way to the country club this summer.
- Like many from his community, his only involvement with white men until then was policemen, mailmen and the milkman.
- Even though he does not know his fellow black caddies very well yet, he feels a brotherhood with anyone who comes from the same public housing project.
- In the caddie shack, where he waits for work, the floor has an uneven roughness that makes the daily crap games a contest of nerves as well as of chance.
- Monday is Ladies' Day at the club; on other days there are restrictions on when women can play, but on Mondays, it belongs solely to them.
- When he caddies on Mondays, he is even more careful about being polite.
- The killing of 14-year-old Emmett Till took place in Mississippi after Till allegedly whistled at a white woman, and the pictures in *Jet* magazine of Till laid out in an open casket still haunt Raymond.
- On most rounds, he has found that he must be invisible; golfers—men and women—discuss extramarital affairs, pass gas and scratch themselves without apology or acknowledgment.
- After work, the caddies often go to a restaurant known as Luigi's, where Raymond invariably orders a plate of fried chicken, collard greens and potato salad.
- From there he catches the number 37 bus back to Cherry Hill.
- Most evenings, he hangs out with two friends at the nearby shopping center, often in their favorite spot between the liquor store and the pool hall.
- Too young to go in either place of business, they occasionally convince someone of legal age to buy them a bottle of Thunderbird, Purple Cow or Richards Wild Irish Rose, though Raymond only watches because he does not like to drink.
- Not far away is the beauty parlor where women go to get their hair "fried, dyed and laid on the side."
- Friday night is also a busy night at the barbershop, where men and boys in need of a clipping sit waiting for their chance in the chair well past the 9 p.m. closing.
- Raymond, like many boys his age, has a Quo Vadis—a hairstyle made popular after the 1951 MGM movie found its way into black theaters; after the hair is cut closely with

clippers, a razor is used to produce a rounded look similar to the hairstyles in the movie.

- The barbershop becomes particularly crowded on the nights that heavyweight fights take place and everyone gathers to listen to the radio.
- When Sonny Liston became the world heavyweight boxing champion by knocking out Floyd Patterson in the first round, men could be heard shouting up and down the street.

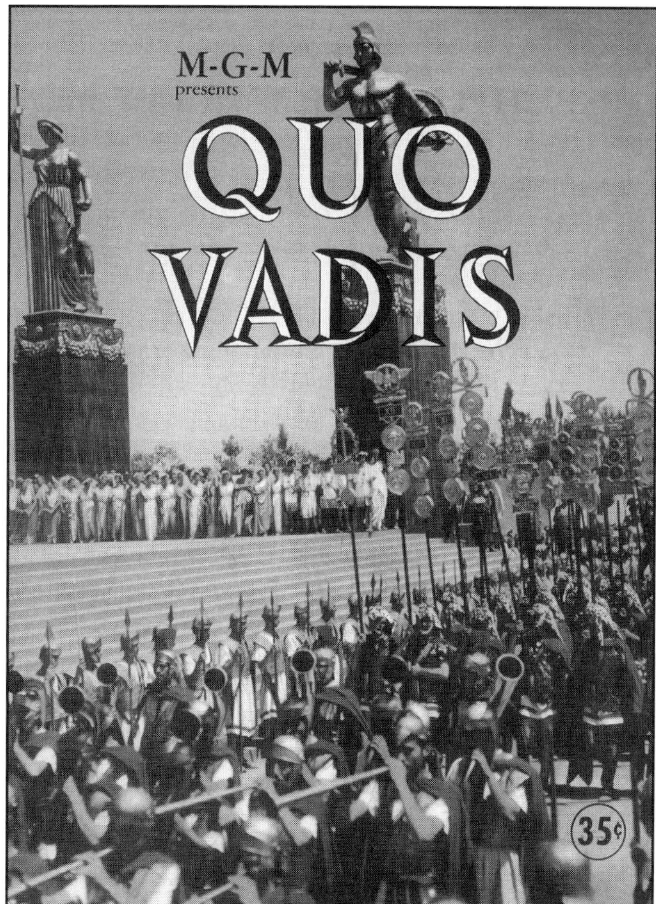

Raymond wears a Quo Vadis hairstyle inspired by the 1951 movie.

Life in the Community: Baltimore, Maryland

- The closeness of the apartments in the public housing project where Raymond lives promotes a strong sense of community.
- The mothers often talk to each other over the backyard clotheslines or across the metal rails that divide the front porches.
- The men, few of whom own a car, often walk together to and from the bus stop or sit side-by-side in the shade of the trees that dot the small hill behind the row houses.
- A husband and wife, plus their children, occupy every apartment in his building; there are few single parents.
- Growing up, Raymond spent most afternoons on the tiny strip of land in back of the row houses, where he and the other boys shot marbles and played catch using a ball with no hide and held together only with tape.
- The girls spent their time jumping rope and playing jacks.
- Sometimes the street in front of the apartments would fill up with kids on skates—which would lead to forming a line, created when a kid skates down the middle of the street as fast as he can with a hand extended out behind him; quickly, other skaters grab hold and offer a hand to someone else.
- The last person is often a daredevil or naïve, because once the lead skater screeches to a stop, the line creates a human slingshot that fires the last person down the street like a rocket.
- Raymond's first experience resulted in a bruised behind and a reputation for toughness that kept a lot of guys off his back.
- The neighborhood is a blend of African-American and Jewish history; some people joke that Baltimore's Pennsylvania Avenue is the longest road in the world because it connects Africa to Israel.
- Before her death, Raymond's mother worked in a clothing store catering to working-class black women.
- The store is located near Pennsylvania Avenue and is owned by the son of a Jewish immigrant who had fled czarist Russia at the turn of the century.
- The owner let Raymond fold boxes used to package the clothes, paying him a nickel, which was immediately converted into a bag of candy corn or jellybeans.
- Baltimore's 1910 land-use ordinances mapped out black and white neighborhoods, designated undeveloped areas to be reserved for blacks or whites, and in some cases converted black neighborhoods to white.

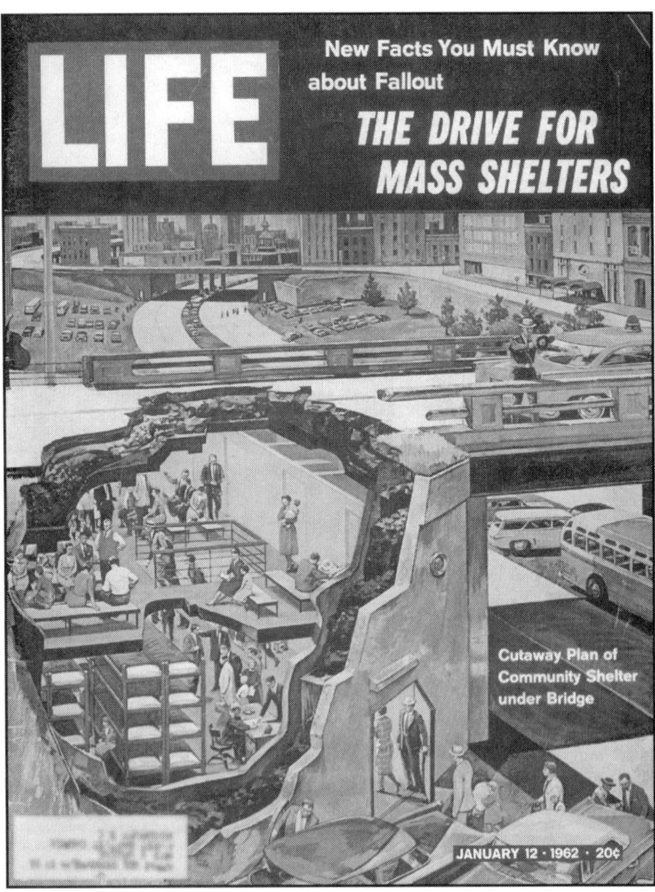

As a major population and industrial center, Baltimore is considered a critical enemy target in the Cold War.

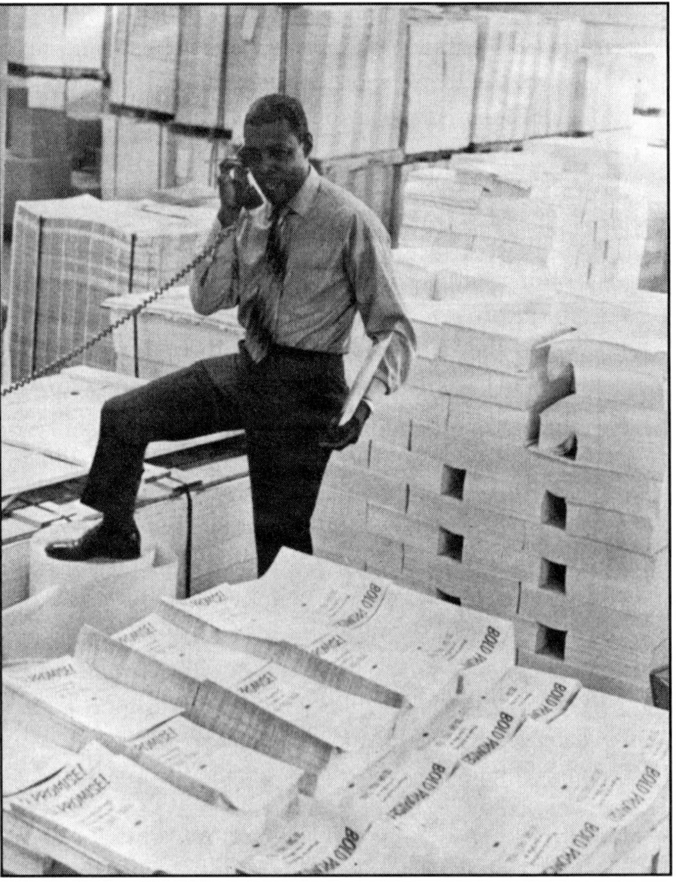

In 1956 the state ended the practice of listing job openings under "white" and "colored."

- These residential segregation ordinances, similar to laws passed in other Southern cities, prompted the founding of the NAACP.
- By the 1930s, segregation was well-organized in the city, with blacks segregated by law into separate schools, hospitals, jobs, parks, restaurants and railroad cars.
- In 1952, Ford's Theater agreed to admit African-Americans after seven years of NAACP picketing.
- That same year, downtown department stores agreed to sell to black customers, although they were not permitted to try on the clothing.
- The next year the municipal parks were desegregated and the first department began hiring black employees.
- In 1956, the city passed an equal employment ordinance, and the state ended the practice of listing separate job openings under "white" and "colored."
- By 1958, most movie theaters and first-class hotels accommodated African-Americans.
- By 1962, many of the most flagrant examples of Jim Crow segregation were being eliminated.

Historical Snapshot
1962

- The late-night television show, *The Tonight Show*, with Johnny Carson, began
- Demonstrations against school segregation occurred throughout the South
- President John F. Kennedy contributed his salary to charity
- The Dow Jones Industrial Average reached a high of 767
- Movie premieres included *To Kill a Mockingbird, Long Day's Journey into Night, The Manchurian Candidate, The Longest Day* and *Lawrence of Arabia*
- The Students' Nonviolent Coordinating Committee (SNCC) organized the freedom ballot in the South, aggressively registering blacks to vote in Mississippi, Alabama and Georgia
- Astronaut John Glenn orbited the earth three times, saying, "It was quite a day. I don't know what you can say about a day when you see four beautiful sunsets."
- Popular songs included "Go Away, Little Girl," "What Kind of Fool Am I?", "I Left My Heart in San Francisco" and "The Sweetest Sounds"
- At nine New York daily newspapers, unions staged a strike that lasted five months
- Walter Cronkite replaced Douglas Edwards on the *CBS Evening News*
- Jackie Robinson was the first African-American inducted into the Baseball Hall of Fame
- *One Flew over the Cuckoo's Nest* by Ken Kesey, *Happiness Is a Warm Puppy* by Charles M. Schulz, *Sex and the Single Girl* by Helen Gurley Brown, and *Pigeon Feathers* by John Updike were all published
- *Mariner II* became the first successful interplanetary probe, confirming that the high temperatures of Venus were inhospitable to life
- Rachel Carson's book *Silent Spring* stated that more than 500 new chemicals were entering our bodies because of widespread insecticide use
- *Who's Afraid of Virginia Woolf?* opened on Broadway
- Inflation was at 0.4 percent, unemployment at 5.5 percent
- Eighty percent of households had a telephone

1962 Economic Profile

Selected Prices

Item	Price
Analgesic Powder, Stanback	$0.98
Automobile Seat Belts, Installed	$5.95
BB Gun, Daisy 1894	$12.98
Bed, Triple-Decker Bunk	$149.95
Can Opener, Electric	$8.44
Doll Clothes, Barbie Negligée	$3.00
Flower Delivery, FTD	$7.50
Ham, K-Mart, One Pound, Cooked	$0.46
Lawnmower	$98.99
Peanut Butter, Jif, 18 Ounces	$0.51
Pen, Scripto Tilt-Tip	$1.98
LP Record, Peter, Paul & Mary	$1.77
Shirt, Ban-Lon Knit	$2.97
Shoes, Classic Saddle	$3.97
Subway Token, New York City	$0.15

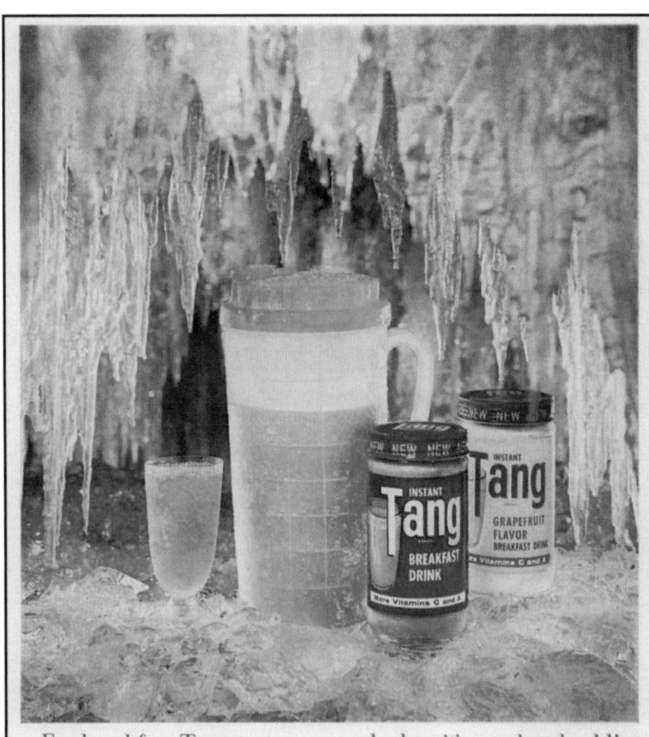

Instant Tang Breakfast Drink
Tang Grapefruit Flavor
For breakfast, Tang tastes so good when it's good and cold!
Tomorrow for breakfast let TANG surprise you. Just mix a decanterful tonight and refrigerate. The cold fact is: one night in your refrigerator makes a new drink out of TANG.
And TANG gives you more vitamin C than orange juice . . . plus vitamin A. So, for breakfast tomorrow wake up to TANG. But make it good and cold.
P.S. Now try new Grapefruit Flavor TANG, too.
more vitamin C than orange juice!

Ask a kid what he wants to be when he grows up, and chances are he won't say an insurance sales manager.

Astronaut. Ball player. Fireman. President. Kids want to be a lot of things, but not too many dream about being life insurance men.

When they grow up it's different. Life insurance offers challenging and expanding careers. Like the openings we now have for sales management people at Ætna Life & Casualty.

If you qualify, we'll enroll you in a two-year program. Two years of preparing you to recruit and train life insurance agents for one of the world's largest insurance organizations selling all lines of coverage. You'll be working in your home area. It's hard work and lots of study, but the opportunities are there, and so is all the training and support you'll need.

An Ætna sales management position is a real opportunity for the college graduate. And it can be an extremely rewarding career.

If you're interested in a bona fide management training offer, we're interested in you. Get in touch with Mr. Fred S. Cox, Manager, Field Management Training, Ætna Life & Casualty, Hartford, Conn. 06115.

JOBS

Ætna LIFE & CASUALTY OUR CONCERN IS PEOPLE

Where America Learns...
Fort Howard Paper Products are there!
Schools learn, too . . . that Fort Howard Paper Towels can cut their maintenance costs. Because Fort Howard makes many grades, folds, and packs, you can choose the quality and price that best suit your needs. And if your purchasing responsibilities include paper towels, remember that the best way to judge them is with wet hands. Your own wet hands will prove the greater drying capacity of Fort Howard Paper Towels. For further information, including economies to be effected with Fort Howard Paper Napkins and Tissue, ask your Fort Howard distributor to call.
AMERICA'S MOST USED PAPER PRODUCTS AWAY FROM HOME
Fort Howard Paper Company
Green Bay, Wisconsin • Sales Offices in New York, Chicago, Los Angeles

Changing America

- Activist Tom Hayden announced the birth of SDS—Students for a Democratic Society—saying, "We may be the last generation in the experiment with living."
- Legislation requiring UHF capabilities on all TV sets was providing a boost to educational and other non-network TV.
- The Broadway musical *My Fair Lady* closed after 2,717 performances, the longest-running musical in history.
- Ralph Ginzberg's conviction for pornography was upheld by the Supreme Court after he applied for bulk mail privileges using names such as Blue Balls, Climax and Intercourse.
- Horror movies like *Premature Burial* and *Tales of Terror* made a comeback.
- The Big Three auto makers in Detroit continued to emphasize the sale of longer, heavier, more powerful cars.
- Former First Lady Eleanor Roosevelt won a Gallup poll as the "Most Admired Woman" for the thirteenth time.
- IBM began selling the "golf ball" Selectric typewriter, which replaced the moving carriage with a rotating ball printer that floated over the paper's surface.
- Of the world's adult population of 1.6 billion, approximately 44 percent were illiterate.
- The Pulitzer prize was awarded to Frank Loesser for *How to Succeed in Business without Really Trying*.

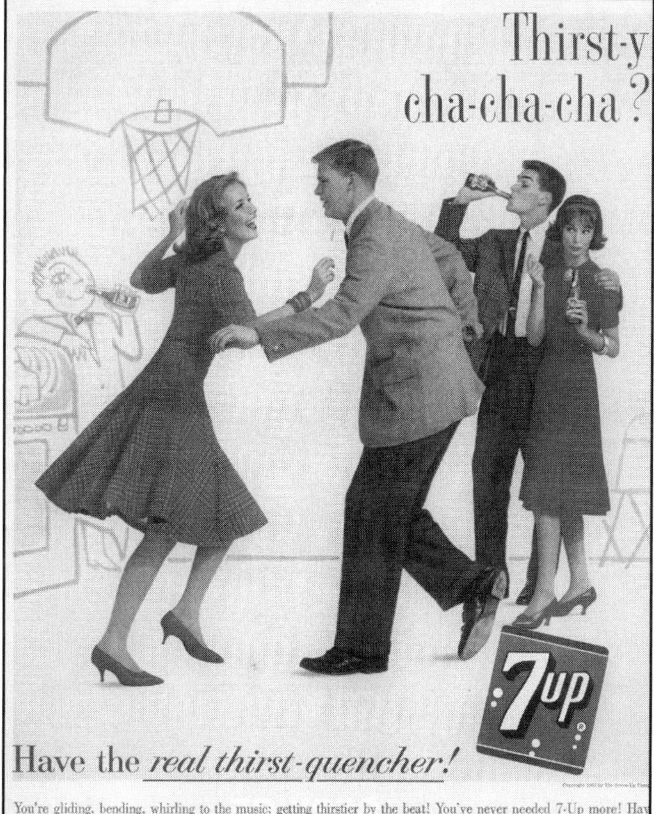

"Your Life Easily May Depend on How Well You Are Prepared, If an ATTACK Comes," by John D. Hacket, *The Evening Sun*, Baltimore, Maryland, August 1961:

Baltimore is a "critical target" for an enemy bomb.

It is the sixth-largest United States city, a principal railroad hub with the fourth-largest ocean port. The largest single steel mill, a major missile factory and a modern jet airport are next-door.

The area is a major production center for steel, copper, aluminum, chemicals, ships, missiles, electronics, automobiles, apparel, food and research.

Some 939,000 people live in Baltimore.

You are one of them. If the enemy dropped an H-bomb in this area right now—could you come out alive . . . ?

CONELRAD May Say: EVACUATE

There are 115 air raid sirens in Baltimore today.

They work.

They are checked out once a month by telephone company technicians.

The entire Baltimore area civil defense communications network, which includes police, fire, military, rescue, hospitals, factory and others, is tested every Monday.

These sirens are a part of the nationwide Civil Defense Warning System. They are set off only in an emergency. (However, these sirens do scream once a year in Baltimore, on "Operation Alert" day. They sounded last April. . .)

Possible Attack

The ALERT signal, the STEADY BLAST for three to five minutes, blares out only when the military and CD people feel planes or missiles are headed for the United States.

It means—PROBABLE ATTACK.

What is the other signal?

Sirens give off a WARBLING sound. It goes up and down, up and down, up and down in tone.

It is the UNDER ATTACK warning.

It screams for three minutes, then stops.

It means the Baltimore area is going to get it, but good—and soon, maybe in minutes.

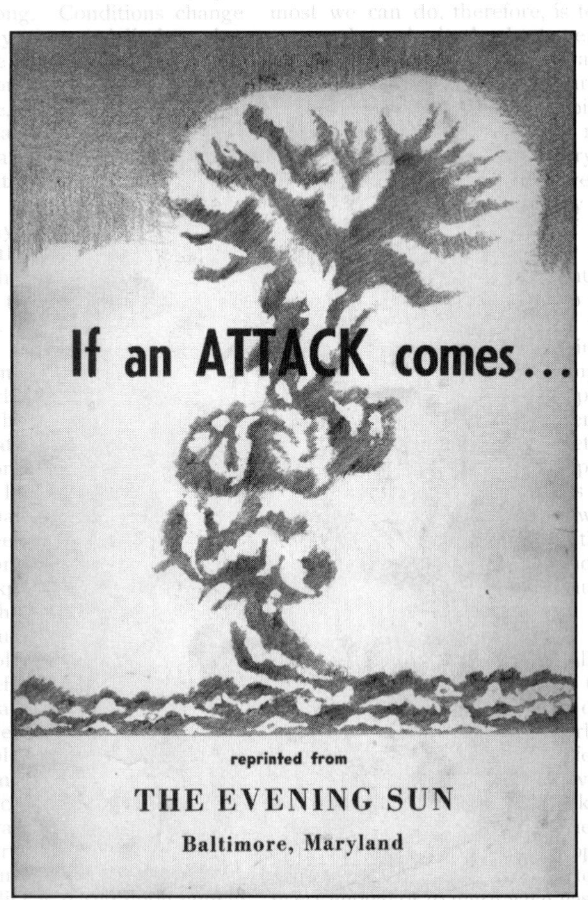

If an ATTACK comes . . .
reprinted from
THE EVENING SUN
Baltimore, Maryland

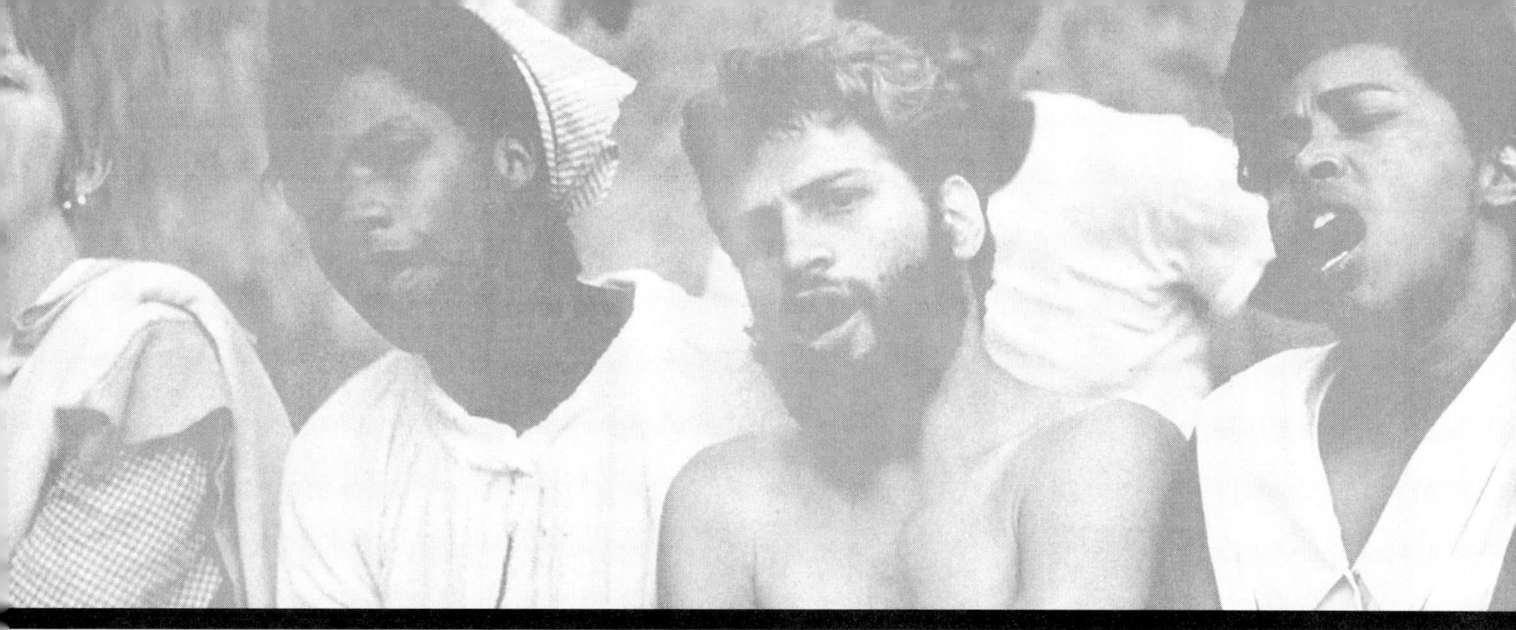

1965 News Feature

"Will SNICK Overcome?" by Richard Armstrong, *Saturday Evening Post*, August 28, 1965:

The freedom songs trailed away in the little brick church in Hattiesburg, Mississippi, and Lawrence Guyot, a veteran organizer for the Student Nonviolent Coordinating Committee, rose to speak. "A few people are going to get killed this summer," Guyot warned. Heads turned as he swung into his oration, prancing back and forth in the front of the church, his heavy frame bouncing. "Not many. Some. But the concept of the Freedom Democratic Party must not be allowed to die! This is the summer we beat Senator Jim Eastland!"

In nearby Poplarville, where a Negro named Mack Parker was lynched six years ago, another SNCC veteran named Charles Glenn explained: "We're going to open up counties all over the fifth congressional district, and that includes some rough ones that have never seen a civil-rights worker before. If there is a mass voter registration, there will be mass reprisals. Me, I've got to go through that same bush I went through last summer. But I don't let that fear conquer me."

The second annual summer pilgrimage to the South was on, bringing civil-rights volunteers from all over the nation. They came in greater numbers than last year and under the sponsorship of a bewildering variety of organizations. For this was the summer that the southern Negro, by means of the voting-rights bill, hoped to move past token progress to tangible political power. And with that power close at hand, civil-rights organizations have begun to struggle over who will control the movement and to what ends.

There are four main groups. At the center of the movement and with influence on every side stands the Nobel Prize winner, Dr. Martin Luther King, who heads the Southern Christian Leadership Conference (S.C.L.C.) and its staff of 170. To his right is the oldest, largest, wealthiest and most conservative of the organizations, the National Association for the Advancement of Colored People (NAACP), with 500,000 members. Somewhere to King's left comes the Congress of Racial Equality (C.O.R.E.), which like the NAACP is mass-based, with 80,000 members, but difficult to assess; some of its chapters around the country are headed by conservatives and some by radicals.

The fourth group, farthest to the left in traditional political terms, is the battered band of student revolutionaries that has sent Charles Glenn "through the bush" again this summer

in Mississippi. It is around the Student Nonviolent Coordinating Committee, or "Snick" as it is called from its initials, that the warmest controversy within the civil-rights movement now swirls. SNCC grew in spontaneous and uncharted fashion out of the student sit-ins of 1960 and has been growing ever since. It has 220 staffers, all but 80 of them Negro. A sprinkling of them hold master's degrees, but a good many were recruited on the spot in the South and have only an eighth-grade education. Their average age is 22; their basic wage is $20 a week. SNCC has 300 volunteers in the field this summer, mostly white students from the North, and they get no pay.

SNCC workers are commonly referred to as the "shock troops" of the civil-rights movement—a particularly tough southern sheriff draws them like a magnet. But for shock troops they are uncommonly gentle. A number of them were studying either philosophy or theology when they joined the movement, and several others are aspiring novelists and poets. Apparently equating motion with progress, they roam about the South in caravans of cars. A reporter may seek them in vain in their ramshackle offices and then find them quite by chance, all in a pack, in some remote Alabama town. For shock troops, too, SNCC workers are astoundingly disorganized—or, rather, unorganized, for a fervent tenet of SNCC's peculiar philosophy is that organization and leaders are superfluous—"people can lead themselves." So deeply runs this mistrust of leadership that Robert Moses, who directed SNCC's summer project in Mississippi last year amid a glare of national publicity, decided he owed it to the movement to change his name (to Robert Parris) and drop temporarily out of sight.

"This place reminds me of a progressive nursery school," said one SNCC staffer, "where the children are encouraged to speak out—all at once."

Yet, these disorganized youngsters have consistently displayed the greatest energies and most fertile imaginations at work in civil rights. In Mississippi they have built a powerful grass-roots movement, the Freedom Democratic Party, organized down to the precinct level all over the state. They helped to form a "Freedom Labor Union" of hoe hands and tractor drivers who went on strike in the Mississippi delta this summer. They worked to organize Selma, Alabama, and brought in much of the northern manpower for the Selma-Montgomery march (which did havoc to Selma but aroused the country to the need for a voting-rights bill). And through northern affiliates called Friends of SNCC, with 150 chapters mostly on campus, SNCC had a hand in radicalizing a sizable minority of today's college generation.

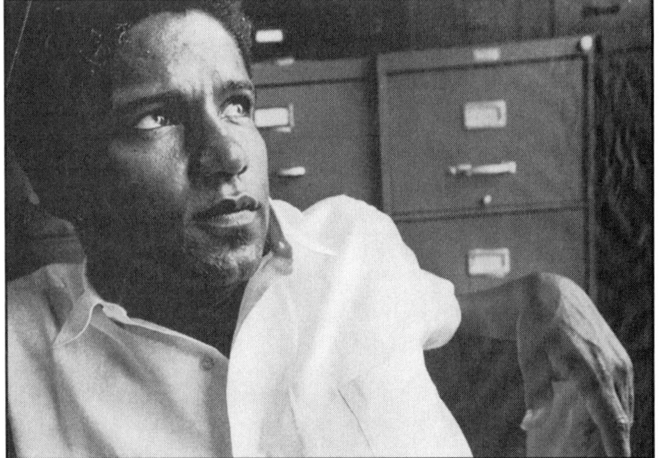

The SNCC has built a powerful grass-roots movement.

1966 Profile

Upper Class

Theresa Blasi, an eight-year-old second-grader, has spent part of the year attending school near her permanent home in Morris-Plains, New Jersey, and four months traveling with her oil executive father, her mother and four-year-old brother in Sardinia.

Life at Home

- In Sardinia, Theresa and her little brother spent their days running up and down the nearly deserted beaches, where seawater was pumped into flats, dried, and the resulting raw salt was piled up and refined into table salt.

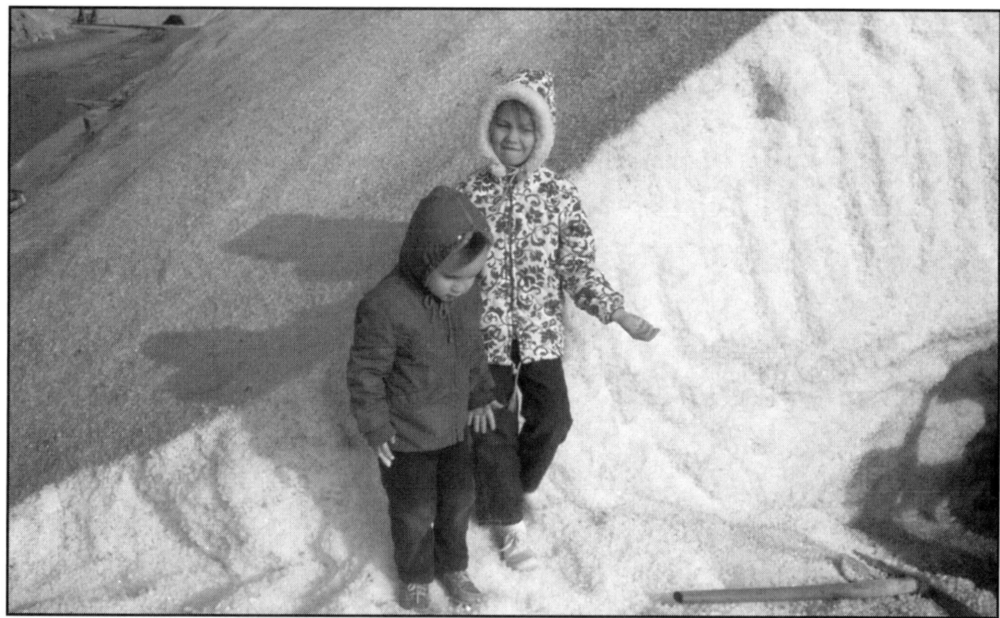

Theresa Blasi is an eight-year-old second-grader with a four-year-old brother.

She soon grew used to the periodic explosions used to dislodge raw salt.

- During her first days on the island, she was disturbed when she heard the periodic explosions used to dislodge the raw salt, but soon she understood and grew accustomed to the noise.
- They lived in a NATO compound, even though her father is an Esso Oil Company executive overseeing the design and construction of an oil refinery in the area.
- Her mother kept her out of school during the trip because she was so far ahead of the rest of the students; a previous assignment in Malaysia included an intensive education in a British army base school that put her well beyond her grade.
- Theresa was told that the Sardinia school had no openings, so instead of attending regular school, she would have a tutor.
- The tutor was a sincere young man who had few skills in controlling a rambunctious eight-year-old intent on constantly showing off.
- Once, to demonstrate her coloring skills to him, she used green chalk to fill in all the white portions of her mother's new oriental rug—to the dismay of all concerned.
- When not with the tutor or playing on the beach, she hung around with the NATO kids, attempting to find friends.
- Some days, she would stand for hours near the entrance to the military Post Exchange, or the commissary where groceries were sold, in hopes that someone would see her and ask if she wanted a green Popsicle.
- Since her family was not military, she didn't think she was allowed in the PX, even though her parents had said it would be okay.
- With no ability to speak Italian, she spent much of her time with Americans and Canadians assigned to the NATO facility.
- Even this was not always safe ground; one day the mother of one of her Canadian friends asked her if she wanted to sit on the Chesterfield, referring to the couch; she froze, petrified of saying or doing the wrong thing.
- The trip opened her eyes to the wider world; while at the market, they visited a butcher shop where dead jackrabbits were hanging on display.
- She also learned to appreciate eating fish, a staple of their diet, even when it was served with head and tail still attached, though she missed the baloney sandwiches she so dearly enjoyed at home in the States.
- She brought her collection of Barbie dolls with her, spending hours playing, talking to and dressing the dolls; one has blond, swirling hair that makes her look elegant, while the other is more conservative, with reddish hair pulled back into a bun.
- Her assortment of Barbie accessories includes a bright pink skirt, fishnet stockings and even a make-up kit.
- If she had not been able to bring her Barbies to Sardinia, she would not have wanted to go at all.
- In addition to her Barbie dolls, she also enjoys dressing several Little Kiddles dolls, which come with their own pink cribs and tiny sandboxes.

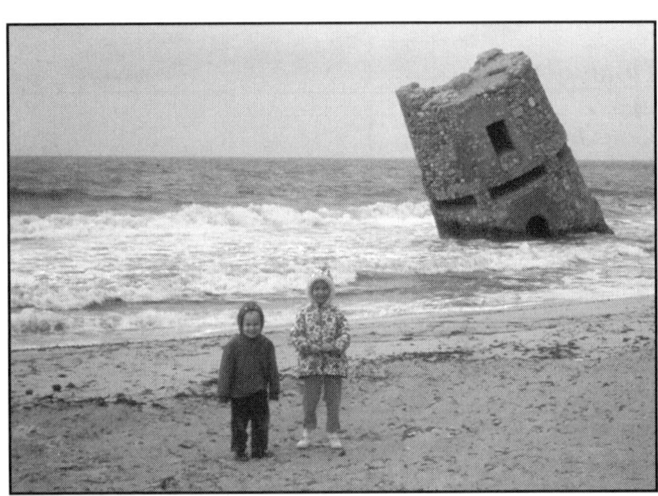

Theresa and her brother played on Sardinian beaches.

The refining of salt is critical to the economy of Sardinia.

- During their stay in Sardinia, her mother decided to take both of the children on a train trip to Venice and Florence.
- The train was crowded with soldiers, many of whom sat on their suitcases because seats were not available.
- During the trip, Theresa bought a salami sandwich from a vendor at one of the train stations; she didn't think to get a drink or ask if the sandwich included any hot peppercorns—which it did, in abundance.
- During the two-week tour, she visited the Murano glassworks factory, rode on lots of trains and took hundreds of black-and-white pictures with her Kodak 126 camera.
- Her brother was a pain the entire time, although she was glad for the company.
- The best part of the trip was the change purse her mother bought for her, made of ornate gold and royal blue Italian leather.
- Although she was born in New Hampshire while her father was completing his ROTC requirement, Theresa has traveled extensively all her life; at four, she was in Germany, at six, in Malaysia, and in between, she was at her home in New Jersey.

Life at School

- When Theresa returned from Sardinia and started the second grade in New Jersey, she found that in some subjects her fellow students were ahead of her, but behind her in others; her education in Malaysia and tutoring in Sardinia resulted in a mismatch.
- Although she is doing well in Miss Post's class, and is delighted to be around her friends again, she finds the transition hard at times.
- Everyone sits in neat rows and does their work as told.
- Theresa does not like to go into the hallways without her friends; walking down the hall all by herself produces an echo when her shoes touch the floor, so she always tries to leave class with a group.
- Since she learned to read, she has enjoyed the Little Golden Books, especially *Dumbo,* the elephant with the biggest, floppiest ears ever.

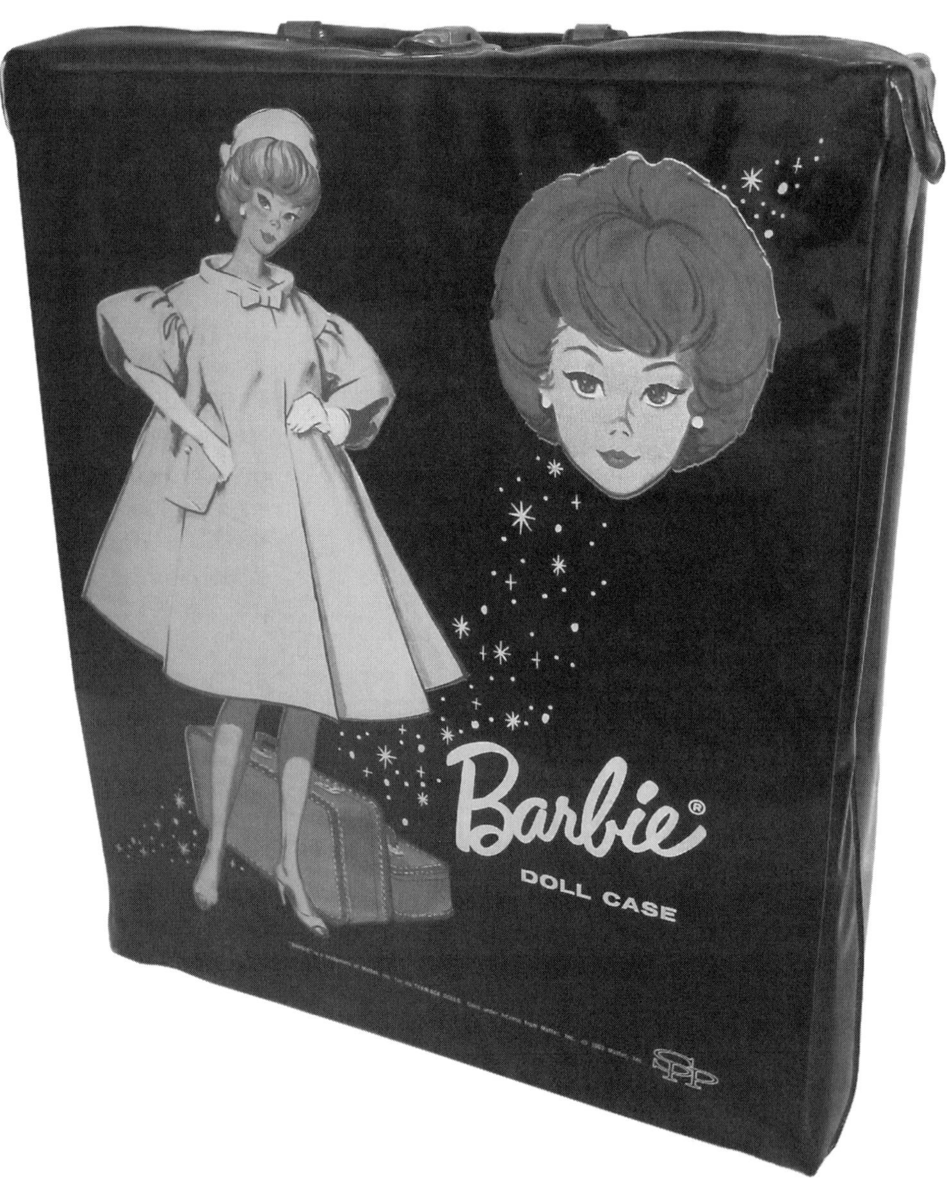

Theresa spends hours playing with, talking to and dressing her Barbie dolls.

- Recently, she has been captivated by the movie *Born Free* and the idea of raising lions.
- Shot in Kenya, the movie won two Oscars—and Theresa's heart; she begged and begged to be allowed to see it a second time.
- Although her mother is careful to limit Theresa's television viewing, she does approve of *The Andy Griffith Show*.
- Her mother likes Andy and Opie, but thinks Aunt Bea is like a member of her own family.
- Another favorite is *Batman*, which airs twice a week; at least once a week, the family gathers around the black-and-white television set and watches the show together.
- Every house in the area has its specialty: one house is the "strawberry milk" house; in another, there are always blue lollipops; the neighborhood twins have a classroom in their basement; the Bennett boys have a fort.
- Theresa's specialty is Kool-Aid; everyone knows that her mom always keeps Kool-Aid for the kids, no matter how many arrive or when.

Theresa's mother approves of The Andy Griffith Show.

- One father loves to load his tiny Triumph Spitfire convertible with as many children as possible for the short trip to the gas station; recently, Theresa was one of the lucky ones to get a ride.
- At the end of the housing development, the kids have discovered a huge vineyard, where the grapevines are perfect for swinging.
- With vines this long, a role in the next Tarzan movie cannot be far away, although several broken arms have resulted over the years.
- Some afternoons are spent playing army; the boys all have guns and shoot each other, while Theresa and her friend serve as the nurses.
- At night, especially on weekends, Theresa and her friends go into a nearby pasture where they can secretly watch movies playing at the drive-in theater.

Batman is one of Theresa's favorites.

- Recently, her entire family went to the drive-in; the two children were dressed in their pajamas before they left the house in case they fell asleep during the movie.
- Theresa loved being able to play there on the jungle gym in her pajamas.
- For school, she always dresses well, as dictated by her mother.
- Many of the shirts her mother buys are ribbed or have stripes.
- Theresa loves wearing the flowered corduroy outfit her mother found, but is distressed by her recent birthday present.
- After telling her mother that she likes the color chartreuse, because it's fun to say the word, Theresa was given a pair of electric green polyester pants that practically glow in the dark.
- She wore her birthday present to school only once, and was teased for an entire day; the pants are now buried in the farthest, darkest corner of her dresser drawer.
- She also hates the red coat her mother makes her wear; she is sure she is the only child in the entire school who has a coat with fake fur, or any fur at all.

- Besides, the fake fur on the collar always goes up her nose—it's just not fair.
- She does like the red plaid school lunch box her mother bought for her, which goes with many of her outfits.
- Recently, when she discovered that her mother had failed to wash her favorite jeans one Saturday and only dresses were available to wear, she immediately vowed to run away.
- When she announced her intentions, her mother offered to help her pack; Theresa then burst into tears and decided not to leave home.
- Right now, she is nursing a bruised lip; while attempting to play telephone with a friend, using the long pole running atop her swing set, she got her lower lip stuck in the metal.
- When she could not get unstuck, her father had to rescue her from the pole, which had severely pinched her lip.
- When she misbehaves, she knows what will happen; a spanking paddle painted with the words "For the Cute Little Deer with the Bear Behind" hangs prominently in the kitchen.
- For years, her mother has been threatening to flush her down the toilet when she was bad, but Theresa did sufficient measurements to determine that this would be impossible.

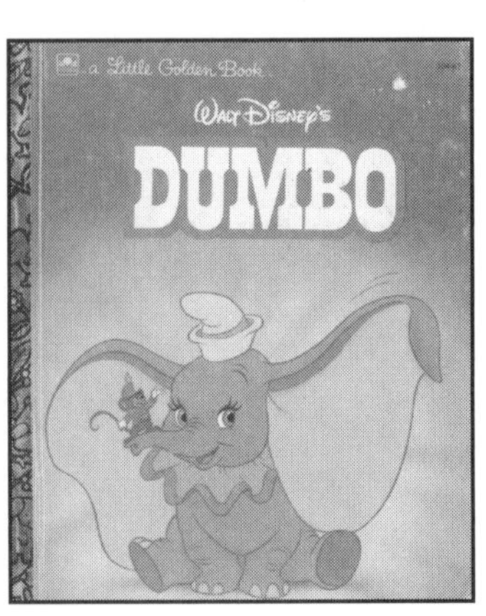

Life in the Community: New Jersey and Sardinia

- New Jersey is known for its factories and industrial output, ranking first in the United States in chemical products, thanks to its large number of pharmaceutical, basic chemical and paint industries.
- In addition, New Jersey is known for food processing, as well as the manufacture of apparel, electrical machinery and stone, clay and glass products.
- One of the state's most prominent special events is the annual Miss America Pageant, which takes place in Atlantic City—a very different environment from that of Sardinia, an ancient island with a deeply embedded culture from many lands, including nearby Italy.

"Pleasures and Places: Sardinia," by Philip Dallas, *Atlantic Monthly*, March 1966:

The foreigners who are now moving into Sardinia are Milanese, Parisians, Swiss, Germans, English and Romans. They are setting up highly automated factories and luxurious hotels; but they are moving in by proxy and behind a smoke screen of lawyers, engineers and architects, who fly in and out continually on brief visits, meeting their Sardinian opposite number who are overseeing the practicalities of the various enterprises. Simultaneously, hundreds of Sardinians are moving out, bringing their already small number to less than a million and a half on an island the size of West Virginia. . .

Each of Sardinia's two principal cities—Cagliari in the south and Sassari in the north—has its sphere of influence and a youthful sense of rivalry. If Cagliari puts up a high-rise building, Sassari must have one too, no matter how little it needs one. However, Cagliari is a historic, if not a prehistoric, city, while Sassari is only eighteenth century, though not without a considerable provincial charm.

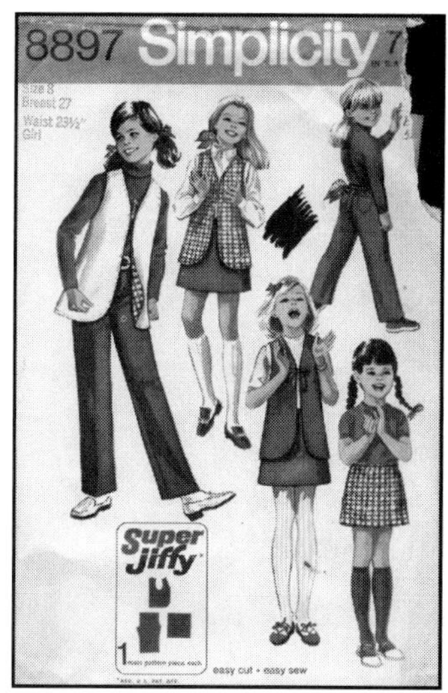

- More than a billion dollars are being invested in dams, public works, communications, subsidies for agriculture and the building of luxury hotels and tourist facilities.
- Sardinia already supports two universities, graduating doctors, engineers, architects, lawyers and academics.
- The first invaders were the Phoenicians, followed by the Carthaginians, Romans, Arabs, Pisans, Genoese and Spaniards.
- In Rome's Etruscan Museum and the museums of Cagliari and Sassari can be found hundreds of tiny, exquisite Sardinian bronzes from the eighth century B.C.
- Throughout the island remain 3,000 little fortresses dating from prehistoric time to about the third century B.C.
- With the Treaty of London in 1720, the house of Savoy was forced to swap Sicily for Sardinia, which Austria had picked up after the War of Spanish Succession.
- So little did the Savoyards value the island, they tried to give it to Napoleon in exchange for Milan and Parma; Napoleon simply ignored the offer, took all of Italy, and left the Savoyards on the island.
- Scattered throughout the island are hundreds of fierce shepherds, who continue to tend their flocks and speak a dialect that resembles Latin.
- It is said that the shepherds must always be tough and vigilant; sheep rustling is an activity of long tradition there.
- Also an important tradition in Sardinia are handicrafts, including hand-woven carpets, tapestries, coverlets, unusual baskets, and carved wood chests.

Historical Snapshot
1966

- *Time* named the "Twenty-five and Under Generation" its "Man of the Year"
- Blanket student deferments were abolished; draft calls for the Vietnam War reached 50,000 a month
- Strobe lights, liquid color blobs, glow paint, and psychedelic posters began appearing in new-style dance clubs
- A study showed that food prices were higher in poor neighborhoods than in affluent areas, where more choice was available
- In a decision to end the chaos of touring, the Beatles played their last live concert on August 29 at Candlestick Park, San Francisco
- The per capita consumption of processed potato chips rose from 6.3 pounds a year in 1958 to 14.2 pounds
- Jimi Hendrix popularized the electric guitar
- The top music hits of the year were "The Ballad of the Green Berets," "Born Free," "Good Vibrations," "The Impossible Dream," "Sunny," "What Now, My Love?", "Winchester Cathedral," "Alfie," "The Sounds of Silence" and "Georgy Girl"
- *Batman*, which aired twice weekly on television, became a national fad; villains included Art Carney as the Archer, Burgess Meredith as the Penguin and Cesar Romero as the Joker
- The words abort, big bang theory, cable TV, flashcube, flower children, miniskirt, Third World and psychedelic entered the language
- To combat the smog, California imposed car exhaust standards, to take effect in 1969
- Bestsellers included *In Cold Blood* by Truman Capote, *A Thousand Days* by Arthur M. Schlesinger, Jr., *Valley of the Dolls* by Jacqueline Susann, *Capable of Honor* by Allen Drury and *All in the Family* by Edwin O'Connor
- Heavyweight boxing champion Cassius Clay became a Muslim and changed his name to Muhammed Ali
- Television premieres included *The Newlywed Game*, *Mission: Impossible*, *Batman*, *Star Trek*, *The Monkees*, *That Girl*, *The Dating Game* and *The Smothers Brothers Comedy Hour*
- Stokely Carmichael was elected head of the Student Nonviolent Coordinating Committee

1966 Economic Profile

Selected Prices

Beer, Schlitz, Six-Pack	$0.99
Calculator, Electronic	$1,950.00
Camera, Kodak Instamatic S-10	$35.00
Coffee, Folger's Two-Pound Can	$1.27
Doll, Mattel Teenage Barbie	$2.29
Electric Scissors, Dritz	$7.45
Electric Shaver, Lady Kenmore	$13.97
Flight Bag	$39.47
Lawn Flamingo	$3.69
Magazine, *Life*, Weekly	$0.40
Pool Table, Imperial	$334.50
Shirt, Man's Arrow	$7.50
Recliner, King-Size, Plastic	$59.95
Slide Projector, Kodak Carousel	$80.00
Water Skis, Wizard	$19.95

"Being a Tomboy," *The Hite Report on the Family, Growing up under Patriarchy*, Sherry Hite, 1994:

Two memories:

"I was a tomboy in grade school. Until second grade (when we moved into a regular neighborhood with lots of kids), I played mostly by myself, exploring fields, streams and woods, making up stories and plays. After second grade I played with both girls and boys in the neighborhood, but mostly girls. We played 'Muffy' dolls a lot, rode bikes, married our cats, played Red-Rover, Red-Rover, played on the school playground equipment a half-block away, played in the woods, went bob-sledding in the winter (a great big sled—the neighborhood kids all piled on and were pulled behind a car), played with the whole neighborhood (there must have been 10 or 12 regulars) on an amazing truck inner-tube, bouncing on and off, went sledding down a giant hill. I was never warned against acting too rough or being a tomboy. My dad played catch with me (baseball and mitts); I picked up snakes and loved to dangle them in front of my thoroughly disgusted mother (that may be the only example I can think of where she showed a 'feminine' trait)."

"Was I a tomboy! Man, there wasn't a tree within a 50-mile radius that I didn't at least try at climbing. I loved the power of sitting up there, being able to see far, far. On the other hand, I spent a good bit of my childhood in casts, and, of course, incurred the wrath of both parents for these exploits. Mother devoted her life to trying to make a proper lady of me. I think her greatest woe is her miserable failure in this."

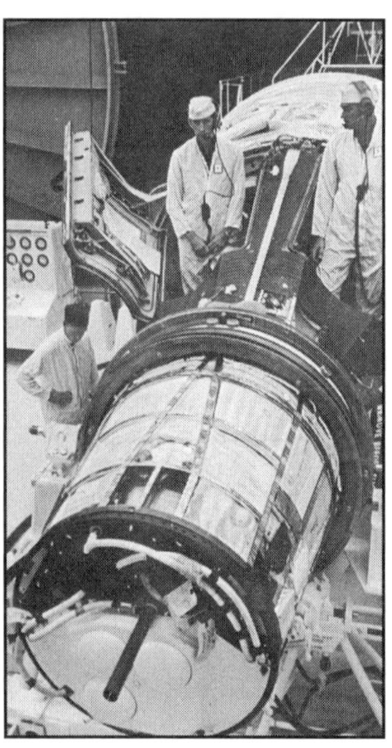

Changing America

- Sears introduced the Allstate radial tire with steel-cord tread plies for $30.80 to replace the unpopular two-ply tire.
- The approximately 80 million Americans born between 1946 and 1964 came to be called the Baby Boomer Generation
- Fully fledged computer programming languages were in use: FORTRAN for scientific and engineering applications, COBOL and ALGOL for business use and BASIC for novices.
- Procter & Gamble researchers Robert Duncan and Norma Baker came up with the wholly disposable diaper, test-launched as Pampers.
- Total U.S. car registrations reached 78 million passenger cars and 16 million trucks and buses.
- Consumer expenditures for alcoholic beverages totaled $17.4 million for the year.
- Black Power was introduced into the civil rights movement, differentiated from the pacifist followers of Martin Luther King, SNCC and CORE.
- After years of debate, Congress passed the Traffic Safety Act to provide for auto safety standards and recalls.
- The National Association of Broadcasters instructed all disc jockeys to screen records for hidden drug or sexual messages.

"The Talent for Listening, Help your child learn to love good music," by André Previn, *American Home*, October 1966:

I've never met a child who couldn't be interested in music—good music. That doesn't mean he must play an instrument. More often his innate talent is in the area of intensive listening pleasure. But to develop that talent, he needs exposure—and of all the art forms, good music is the most neglected in this matter of exposure. Some music pursues us everywhere—in elevators, airplanes, even supermarkets—but this is music designed for inattentive listening. How then can we expose our children to a real listening experience?

The Bernstein Young People's Concerts have proved that even very young children can be held by great music, especially when they hear it with other young people, accompanied by information given with authority and charm. In quite a few cities where I have conducted, I throw open the last rehearsal to young people only. They can come dressed as they like as long as they're quiet. (I occasionally mention they are enjoying the same program their elders will hear later at $7.50 a seat.) It is wonderful to see the astounding number of kids who come to these rehearsals, and even more thrilling to hear their intelligent, searching comments and questions afterward.

An important word about children's tastes belongs right here. From experience I have learned some startling facts. The old standard fare for "beginning musical appreciation" doesn't interest most young people today. What we adults consider easily assimilated melodies and harmonies are apt to be more difficult for them to grasp than complicated, contemporary dissonances. They are very likely to fall in love at first hearing with a lot of what we may have deemed to be "difficult" classical music. I have heard marvelous, instinctively knowledgeable comments from 12-year-olds after performances of Stravinsky and Bartok—and conversely, admissions of boredom after Mozart and Haydn. To think that the purity and elegance of eighteenth-century music is easier than the complexities of today's output is to misunderstand today's children. They identify more thoroughly and quickly with a musical mirror of their time than with a remembrance.

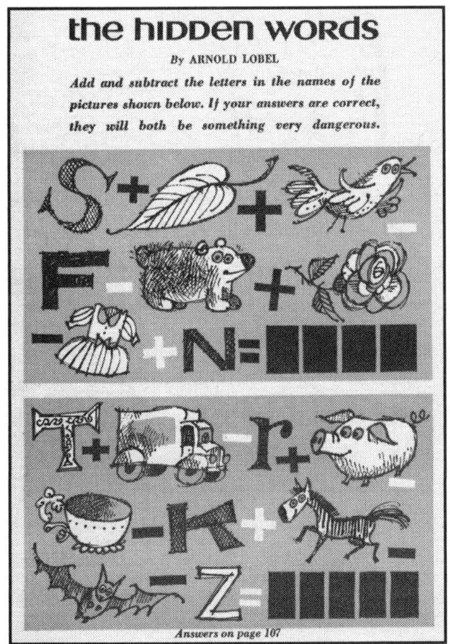

"The Secret Heart of Hayley Mills," *Hollywood Life Stories*, July 1964:

She was a movie actress at 12, a star at 13 and an Oscar-winner at 15—and that's only the beginning. Hayley Mills, dubbed by Walt Disney "the greatest movie find in 15 years" is, at 18, at the most exciting point in her exciting young life. Standing on the threshold of womanhood, she can look back on a childhood brimming with fun and loaded with love, and a career as phenomenal as the comet which bears her name.

At seven, Hayley was enrolled in the Elmhurst Ballet School, where she became skilled in the art of dance and slightly less proficient in academic subjects. "I enjoyed the ballet part," she admits. "But I was never very keen on things like math." Her bubbly, outgoing personality won her friends by the score, but she was actually close to very few of them. Her sister has always been her closest confidante, and she found the acquaintances of her parents twice as much fun as a group of girls her own age. The Mills house was always bustling with witty, sophisticated people like Laurence Olivier and Noel Coward, and by the time she was 12, Hayley was already a devout Shakespeare and Dickens reader. And, having observed the miracle of birth among the animals on the farm she loved so much, there was little she didn't know about the so-called "facts of life." "Childhood is virtually finished at 12," she explains simply. "By that time I had had all I wanted of dolls and cowboys and Indians. I was ready to find something new," and lucky for her, that "something new" was just around the corner.

She was playing in the garden one day, when movie director J. Lee Thompson came to the house to visit her father. Thompson was in the process of conducting a search for a small boy to co-star in his new production, *Tiger Bay*, but when his eye fell on Hayley, he suddenly had a new thought—he would change the role to that of a girl and sign Mills's 12-year-old charmer to play it! Hayley's parents were dubious, but they believed in letting their children have a hand in deciding their own destinies. They explained the pros and cons of a movie career to their younger daughter and told her she could accept the offer or not. Confronted with the chance to turn her "playacting" into the real acting, Hayley accepted at once, and *Tiger Bay* became the first real milestone in her life. In her first professional appearance, she astounded critics, and even overshadowed her own father, who was also in the film. The latter truth caused her so much anxiety, she hid the rave newspaper notices so as to avoid any hurt feelings. But she needn't have worried; John Mills didn't mind a bit.

1968 Profile

Middle Class

Popular, seventeen-year-old Carl Cochrane is wrestling with the impact of the Vietnam War, the murder of Martin Luther King, Jr., and whether his girlfriend will kiss him.

Life at Home

- Carl Cochrane is not only president of the student body, he heads the National Honor Society, the beta club, drama club and gets invited to all the best parties, even though he often doesn't go.
- He just got back his SATs, scoring 1180, split fairly evenly between math and verbal.
- With his scores and an all A average, he has been assured of acceptance into almost any college he chooses.
- He wants to attend William and Mary College in Virginia in prelaw, although he is unsure of exactly what that entails.
- He loves the challenge of math, the memorization of history, and his biology teacher.
- His father is a college theatre professor, his mother a high school drama teacher, so someone always has a play, rehearsal or other activity going on; up and out in the morning, free in the afternoons and back to the theatre for rehearsals at night is a schedule Carl has experienced his entire life.
- Meals, prepared by his father, are often hurried, and it is not unusual for dishes to be stacked up in the sink after dinner until the next morning when breakfast is prepared.
- If it were not for Daisy Douglas, the black maid who comes each morning, the household might not run at all.
- She is paid $35 a week.

Carl Cochrane hopes to attend William and Mary College as a prelaw student.

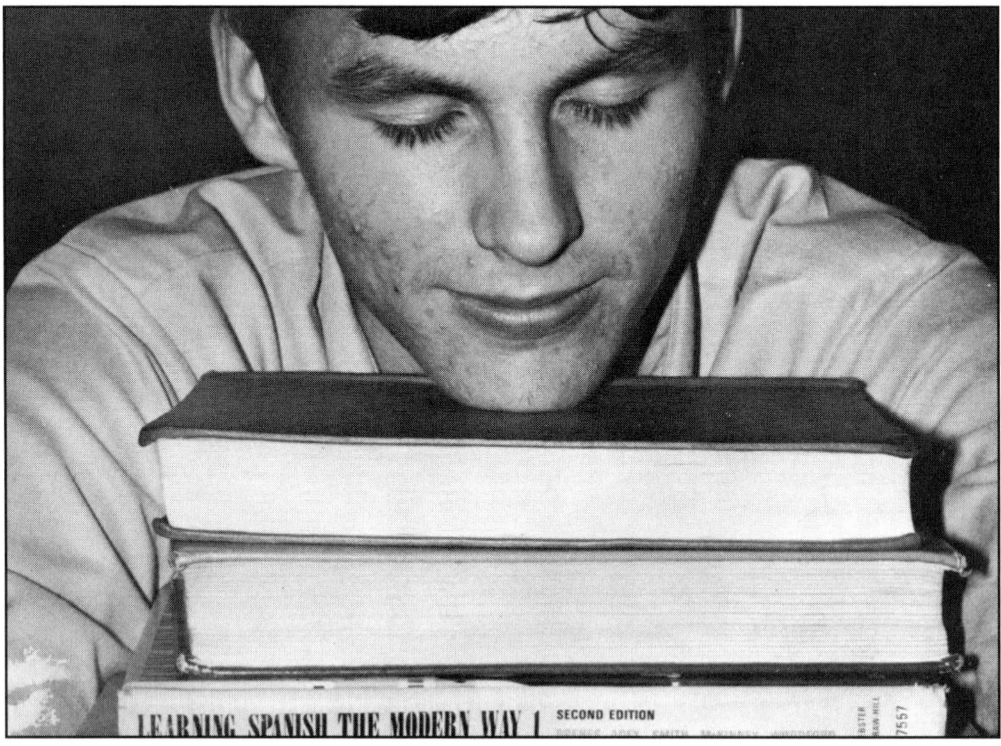

His high school is considered one of the best in the area.

He is skilled in the technical aspects of running a play.

- A typical dinner might include fried chicken and well-cooked vegetables, rice, gravy and a salad.
- The only seasonings allowed in the house are salt, pepper and barbecue sauce; his father says his stomach was ruined in graduate school and in the military, and can only tolerate blandness.
- Currently, Carl has the house to himself; his brilliant, flamboyant and dominating brother Greg has left for Yale, while his younger sister is at Whitten Village, a home for retarded children.
- It's wonderfully liberating to be out from under the shadow of his big brother, but lonely, also; when Greg is around something is always happening—good, bad or wild.
- Until he left for college three years ago, Greg selected and laid out the clothes Carl would wear to school the next morning.
- Although college is expensive, the Cochranes believe in education; learning is good—money will take care of itself.
- Most afternoons for Carl are spent working at the high school as a janitor two to three hours each day for $1.25 an hour; his paycheck is used to support his music habit, particularly to upgrade his drum kit.

Carl is the popular student body president and head of several school clubs.

- His band, The Claystone Blues, practices often and loudly; paying gigs are rare, most often consisting of junior high parties and small dances in the neighboring towns of Fort Mill or Chester.
- Carl loves the role of entertainer, especially drummer, but is learning to enjoy stepping upstage to be lead singer.
- His songs often track from the greatest hits list of the Tams, Drifters, Billy Stewart, the Swinging Medallions and Otis Redding.
- The group rarely does Motown, preferring Southern soul to the overproduced sounds of Detroit.
- The music world is still buzzing about the Beatles' 1967 groundbreaking album, *Sgt. Pepper's Lonely Hearts Club Band*, featuring experimental sounds, nontraditional instruments, enigmatic songs, and a psychedelic ambience that seems to express a new direction in art and music; it is also the first album ever to include printed lyrics on its cover.
- When Carl steps into the theatre world of his parents, he immediately moves backstage; over the years he has developed considerable expertise in the technical aspects of running a play.
- He loves being known as the "lighting guy," because so few can compete for the role.
- Both his mother and father take great pride in their heritage and have collected all of the furniture left behind by previous generations.
- Their collection includes an Elizabethan chest with "1670" carved on its lid, a three-legged carved Jacobean chair, 200-year-old Chippendale chairs, original paintings

"What Those Draft Classifications Mean," *Good Housekeeping*, June 1968:

Current draft policy calls for the drafting first of oldest eligible men in the age group of 19 through 25, although under the law deferred men are liable for military induction until age 35.

All young men are required to register with the local draft board within five days after their 18th birthdays. This local board will retain jurisdiction, even if the man moves. The board places him in one of 18 classifications on the basis of information about his dependents and from such sources as his employer, high school or college. The young man is required to report changes in his address and status, such as marriage, fatherhood or education, to his local board within 10 days of their occurrence. . . .

Draft boards have been selecting single men from 19 through 25, or those married after August 26, 1965, first, with a priority given to delinquents, volunteers and oldest members of this group. . . . The average age of current draftees is about 20.5 years. . . .

Starting in June, students graduating from college, who expected to attend graduate school, and those in their first year of graduate school, will no longer be deferred from the draft except for students in medicine and related fields such as dentistry.

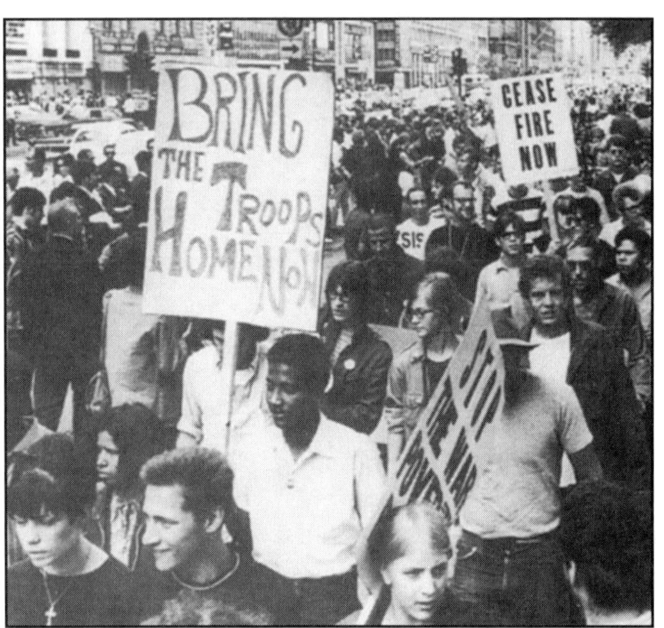

Protests against the war are common nationwide.

by some of America's most renowned illustrators and, in the dining room, 12 sets of china.

- Even though the family has collected all the china from their ancestral lines, his father still brings home the dinner plates given away at the grocery store as premiums.
- Mrs. Cochrane's bedroom features an impressive 200-year-old, four-poster English canopy bed made of exquisite mahogany veneers, held together with the original handmade 14-inch removable screws, each constructed for its intended hole or connection.
- In Carl's open, high-ceilinged bedroom are an oak rolltop desk found in North Carolina, the bed in which his father and 10 uncles and aunts were born, and a collection of statues, including a figure of David and a WWI Uncle Sam with only one arm.
- The house is chilly, generally due to the high ceilings, poor insulation and a retrofitted heating system.
- The two-story, colonial-style house, purchased when Carl was in the fourth grade, cost $8,000.

- His parents had borrowed $10,000 from the bank, investing the extra $2,000 in a heating system that never quite met the task of warming the rambling, 6,000-square-foot home.
- But hot or cold, people are always welcome; its door is always open to students, former students, actors, friends, great-aunts, friends of great-aunts, and the lonely.
- Some stay for days, camping on the floor, most finding a way to help out before they leave.
- Carl's mother loves to entertain with grand gestures, as though she is performing a role never quite relinquished.
- As a result, everyone feels welcome at almost any time of the day or night.
- This is especially true at Christmas, when the entire family erects an all-white Christmas tree in the front hall.
- Following a longstanding tradition, the boys cut a 10-foot sweet gum tree growing near the railroad tracks that has lost all of its leaves.
- Then, each and every limb is carefully wrapped in cotton ticking to create the image of a multilimbed tree just after a snowstorm.
- To enhance the effect, each limb is trimmed with individually placed silver icicle tinsel, placed one at a time on the tree at a precise distance from the last.
- The display, when seen through the front door, is impressive enough to stop traffic on the street, once even attracting a photographer from *Southern Living Magazine*.
- The house also attracts stray animals indiscriminately; cats, dogs and mice all find a place here.
- Recently, Carl discovered that three adult mice are at least one too many after dozens and dozens of baby white mice were born.
- To cope with the population explosion, he sold many of the mice to a local pet store that needed food for its snakes.
- But to keep the house running takes work; after returning from his job as school janitor, Carl often assists his father in physical work around the house—hauling furniture, constructing theatrical sets, digging roots out of the sewer lines or cutting trees.
- Undertaken, but soon abandoned, were efforts to rid the old home of honeybees nesting in the top section of the 35-foot-tall fluted Corinthian columns flanking the front porch.
- Because the family has only one car, Carl often cuts his Friday night dates short so he can be back to take Aunt Katie home before it gets too late.
- He leads a split life; nine months in his hometown and the three summer months in Manteo, North Carolina, at the Lost Colony, an outdoor theatre production company.
- There, night after night, the story of the arrival of English settlers in the New World and the birth of young Virginia

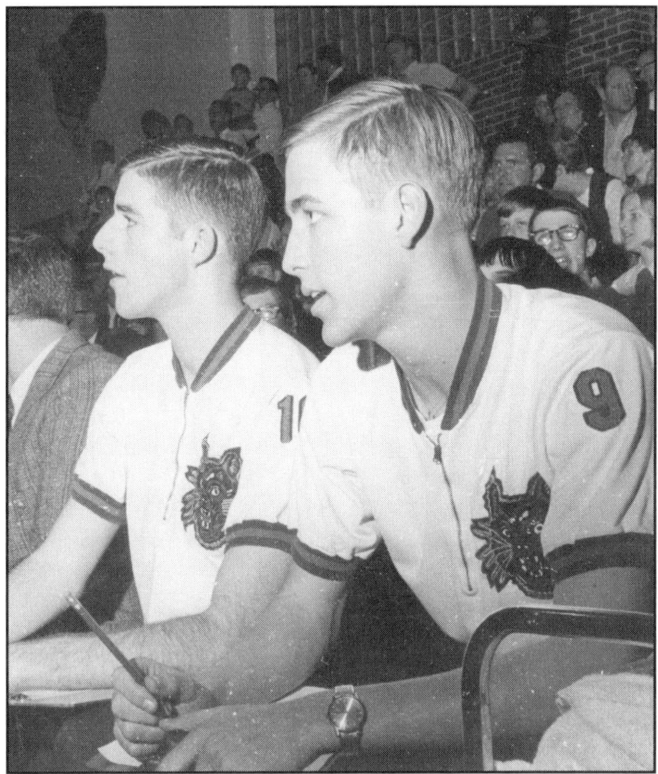

Carl loves the excitement of athletic events.

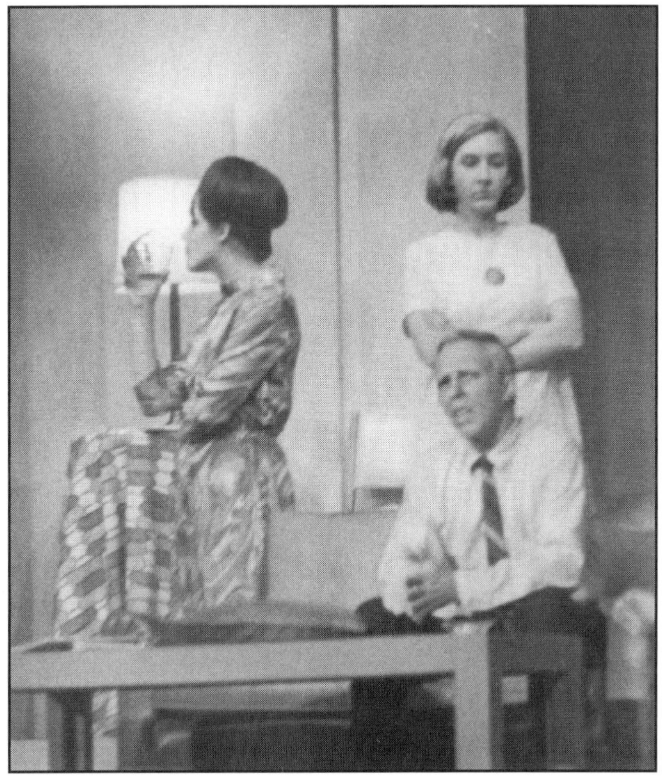

Carl's family is immersed in the theatre world.

Carl enjoys the controlled chaos and teamwork of the theatre.

Dare is performed for tourists, who are invariably mesmerized both by the drama itself and the energy that accompanies outdoor theatre.

- When Carl was small, his mother played the glamorous role of Queen Elizabeth II, directed by his father; in his earliest days, Carl was the newborn baby featured in the play.

In the summer, he spends hours rehearsing with college girls.

- In the mid-1950s, their pictures appeared prominently in *National Geographic* in a feature on the outer banks of North Carolina; his mother was shown in costume, while Carl and his father were featured eating watermelon.
- Growing up at the theatre, he enjoys the rhythms of the work, the controlled chaos and the teamwork.
- It was on the back deck of the Lost Colony, overlooking the bay, that he saw an American-launched satellite sail across the sky; for a moment everyone stopped backstage to stare before plunging back into their tasks.
- Carl appears onstage in a changing array of costumes during numerous crowd scenes so that scenery and props can be moved inconspicuously.
- Better yet, he spends hours rehearsing with the college girls who arrive annually to learn acting or dancing.
- He French kissed for the first time during a rainstorm while taking refuge in a white station wagon with an older girl named Dela, who used the idle time to tutor him in the fine art of kissing.

- During the school year, his constant love is Jill Clarke, an energetic, beautiful pixie with a Mona Lisa smile.
- They spend hours talking and thinking and dreaming about the future; one day, she will be a missionary in Africa.
- Her governing rule is: both of her feet stay on the ground at all times during dates.
- They have been dating for two years, ever since their first cotillion dance held annually at the town's Moose Lodge.
- During his summers away, he finds that some of the young women who are attracted by the summertime bliss of being professional actors have less strict governing rules.
- But a lifetime of going to Manteo year after year has its penalties.
- Every fall when he returns to school, he hears about the First Week at the Beach exploits of his friends.
- Traditionally, when school ends, nearly every high school student in the state will journey en masse to Myrtle Beach to live and party in houses arranged along the shore.
- By the end of each summer, when Carl returns to town, the level of revelry reputed to have taken place during First Week—after being told and retold numerous times—has reached epic proportions and makes him jealous.
- In addition, his time away working at the Lost Colony means he cannot be part of the late summer football practices that are a ritual of high school life; as a result he has

Carl has been dating Jill Clarke for two years.

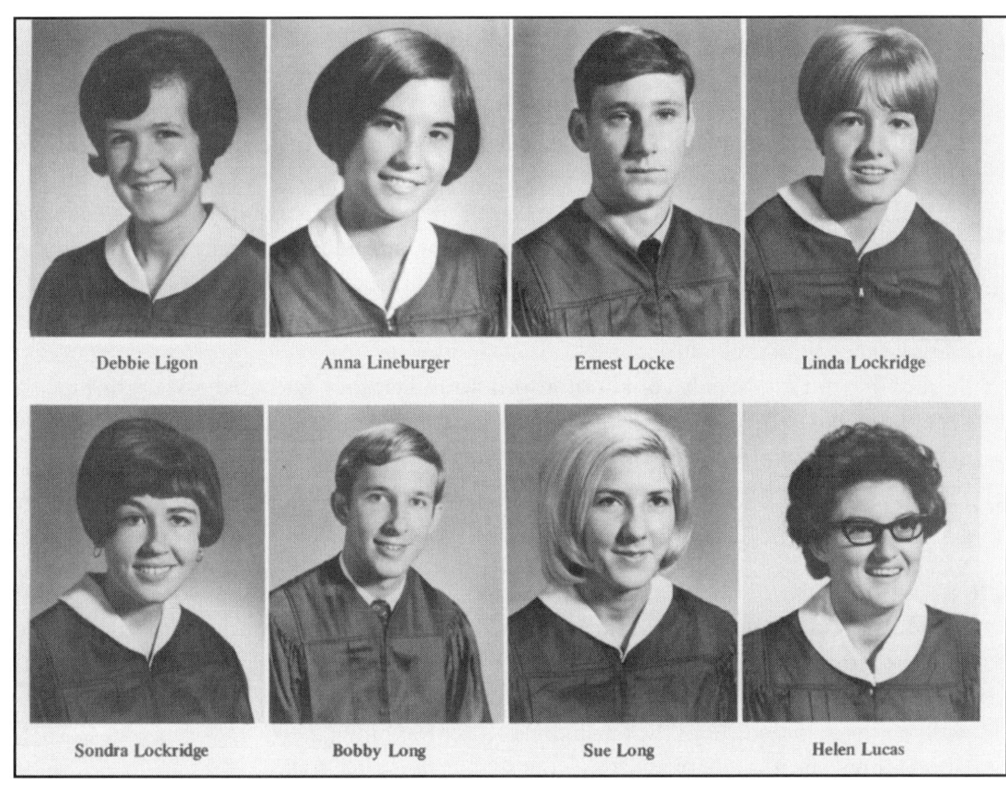

Debbie Ligon | Anna Lineburger | Ernest Locke | Linda Lockridge

Sondra Lockridge | Bobby Long | Sue Long | Helen Lucas

Summers are spent along the North Carolina shore at Manteo.

never gone out for the team or earned any stories about throwing up on the first day of practice in the 100-degree heat.

- Recently, he and several of his buddies completed work on repairing a 1957 Triumph TR3 given to him by his friend Leon.
- For nearly a year, he and his friends have been installing a plywood floor to replace the rusted metal, finding a hood, tinkering with the engine and installing seats by nailing the seat belts to the floor.
- When the moment of victory arrived, the engine roared to life and he took his first exhilarating ride—until the police arrived.
- Because he and his friends could not afford a muffler, they had used a straight pipe to vent the exhaust, producing a highly pleasing roaring sound that attracted both the neighbors and the police to view their hard work.
- Carl got a stern warning from the local police, but little else took place.

Life at School

- As student body president, Carl starts every day making the announcements school-wide over the intercom.
- Trips by the 4-H Club, victories by the boys' basketball team and requests that no one walk on the gym floor until the finish dries all get top billing.
- Good school spirit is important to Carl; it signals that all is well.

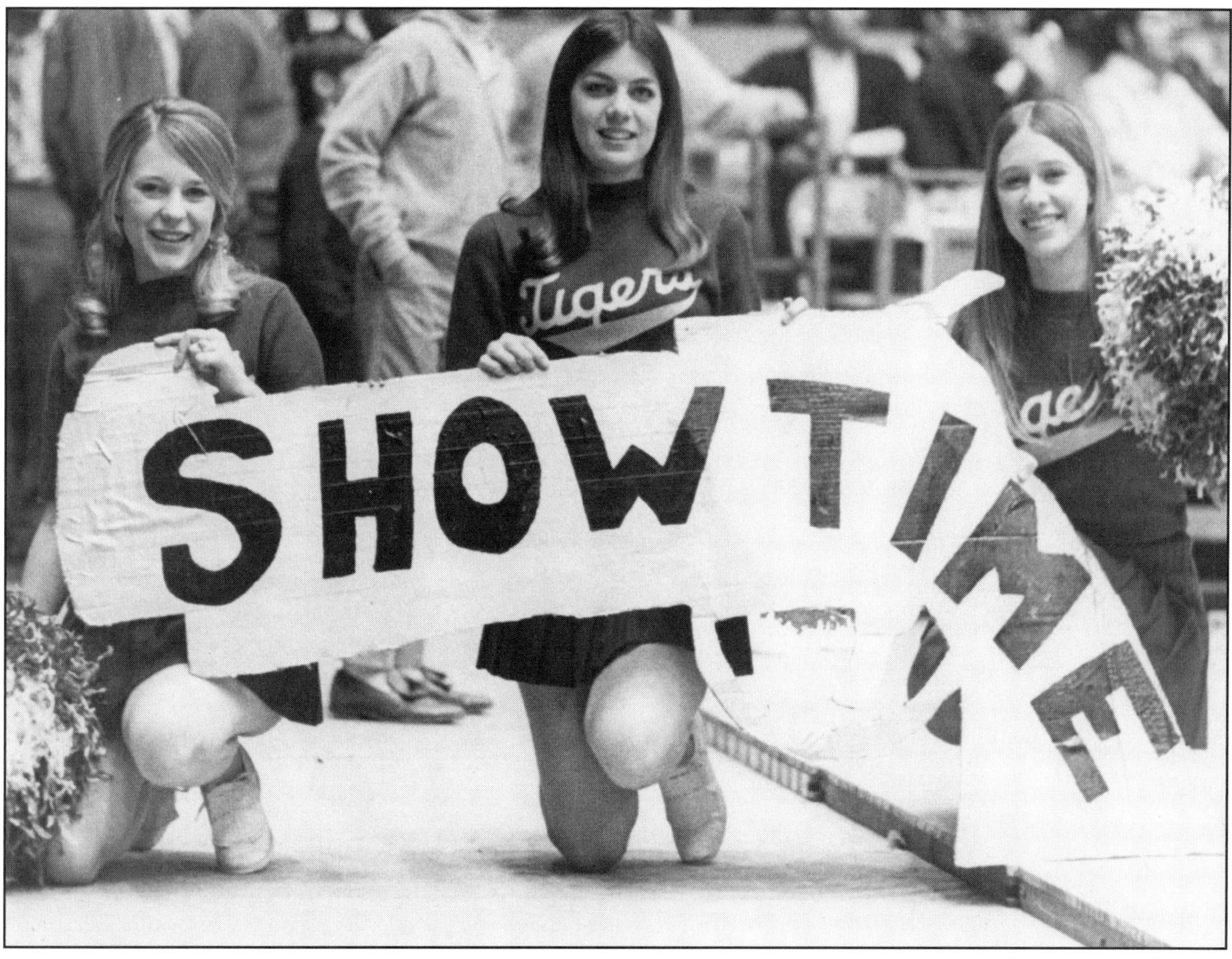

Football is an exciting high school pastime.

- Although he is not athletic, he loves the excitement of the football games and holding his girlfriend close when the team does well.
- Everyone knows him, both because of his active student role and because his mother is one of the school's most popular teachers.
- Her drama classroom is always alive with motion and sound, including exaggerated arm waving and loud, dramatic speeches—activities not permitted elsewhere.
- This year the fall production of *The Man Who Came to Dinner* attracted 150 student actors and technicians; the show ran three consecutive nights in the 1,200-seat school auditorium and was sold out for each performance.
- This is the second year that students from the nearby black high school were allowed to attend the all-white school through the "freedom of choice" plan.
- The ninth, tenth, eleventh and twelfth grades achieved a racial mix of approximately five percent.
- Many of the African-Americans who chose to attend the white school were the children of black professionals and teachers.
- Carl believes the freedom of choice plan gives everyone an equal opportunity, although he is concerned that many of the black students were placed in the less challenging tracks along with the kids from the textile mills.

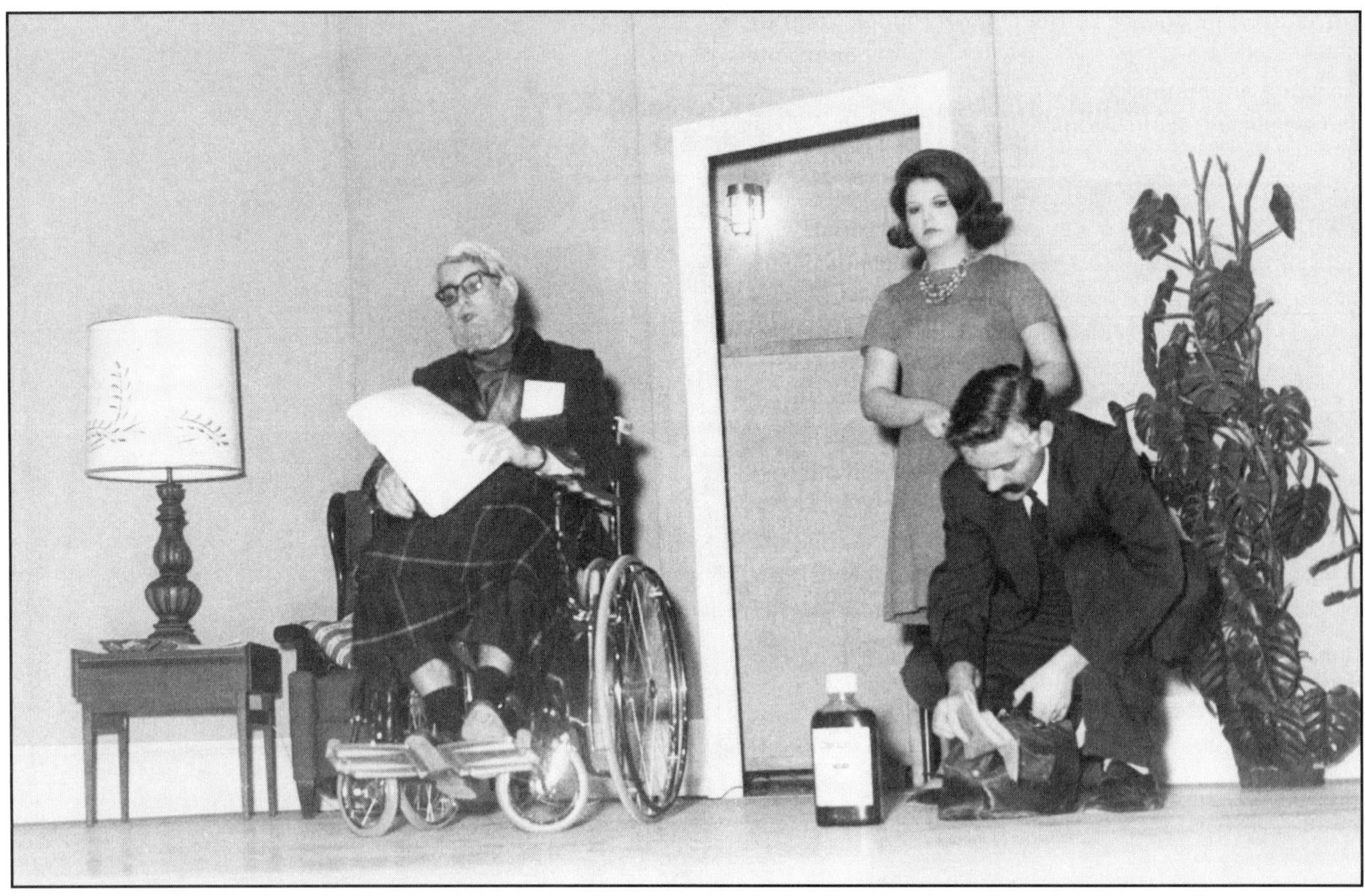

Students enjoy Carl's mother's drama class.

- Few of the freedom of choice kids are in his college preparatory classes, although several are doing well on the football and basketball teams.
- To cope with the new sensitivity expressed by the black students, the marching band has learned to play the song "Dixie" more slowly and somberly so it will not be as offensive.
- Recently, when his mother invited the entire high school drama club—including the three black members—to the Cochrane home for a celebration party, there were whispers that this socially integrated gathering could attract members of the Ku Klux Klan, but to everyone's relief, none appeared.
- However, when Carl was giving everyone a tour of the house he included a visit to his room, where a framed Confederate flag hangs that was carried by a relative in the Civil War.
- At least one of the black students was shocked and privately complained to his mother.
- It was during a school journalism trip to Washington and Lee College in Lexington, Virginia, that Carl learned Martin Luther King, Jr. had been shot in Memphis, Tennessee.
- Traveling with a group of eight from the high school newspaper, the leaders decided to stick with the prearranged schedule, including a trip to the Natural Bridge and then a tour of the college.

> We've got some difficult days ahead. But it really doesn't matter with me now because I've been to the mountaintop. Like anybody, I would like to live a long life, [but] I've seen the Promised Land. I may not get there with you, [but] we as a people will get there . . . so I'm happy tonight. I'm not fearing any man. Mine eyes have seen the glory of the coming of the Lord.
>
> —Martin Luther King, Jr. in Memphis, shortly before his assassination

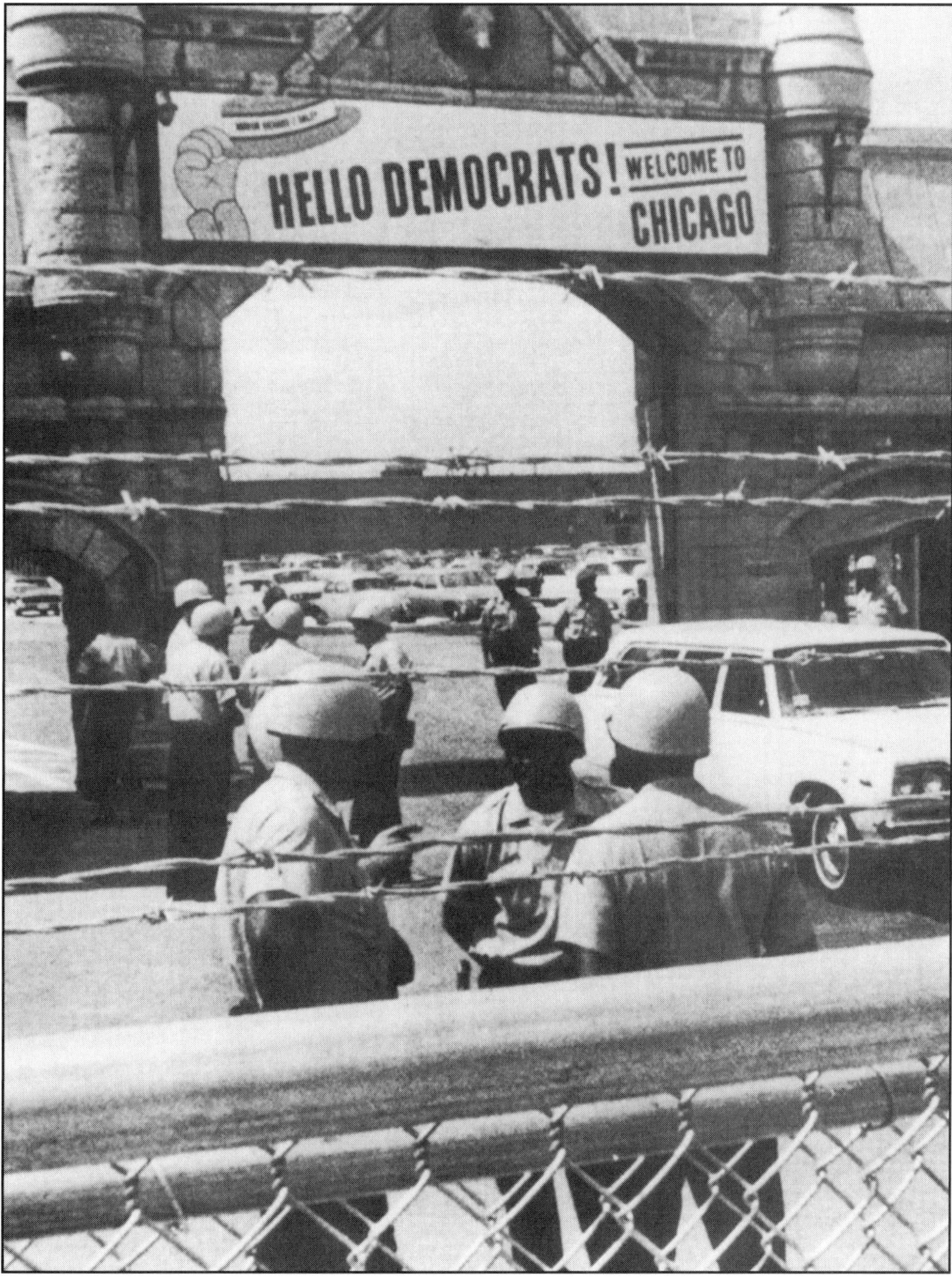

The Democratic Convention in Chicago spawned riots.

- Silently, Carl spent considerable time sorting out what the shooting would mean, while looking for an appropriate gift to take back to his girlfriend as a memento of the journey.
- That night several members of the group were positive they could see Washington, DC, burning when the riots broke out, but Carl was unsure of where his eyes ended and his imagination began.
- When Carl returned home, the school principal called the student leaders together to discuss the situation and set a direction for controlling violence at the school.
- Carl is trying hard to understand the Vietnam War, the protests and his role.

After the riots, Carl bought a bumper sticker reading, "America: Love It or Leave It."

- After the riots at the Democratic Convention in Chicago, he bought a bumper sticker reading, "America: Love It or Leave It," but has yet to put it on the family car, because he does not know whether these words truly reflect his opinion now.
- Although many young men from the local textile mill village, particularly those who dropped out of school to work, have been drafted into the army, Carl knows no one who has actually died in the conflict.
- He is aware that under current law, his entry into college next year will provide an exemption—but for how long?
- No one truly believes the war will push on for two more years; even if the U.S. is wrong, North Vietnam is a tiny country with too few people and resources to resist the power of American weaponry.
- Carl has begun making an inventory; despite his many successes, he realizes that he is almost a legally drinking adult and has yet to fly on an airplane, travel north of Baltimore, south of Orangeburg, South Carolina, and west of Knoxville, Tennessee.

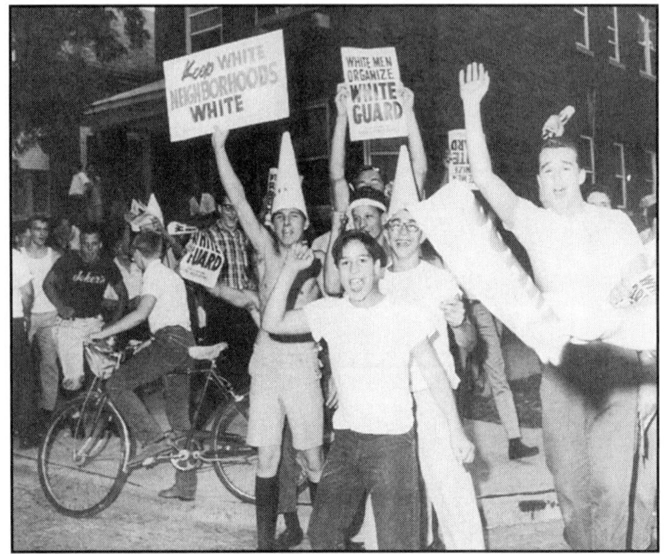

School integration has sparked protests.

Life in the Community: Rock Hill, South Carolina

- Compared to the neighboring town of Fort Mill, Rock Hill, South Carolina, seems big and cosmopolitan, thanks to the presence of Winthrop College in the center of the town.
- Historically, the town has been dominated by a handful of textile companies around which villages comprising hundreds of small homes grew up.

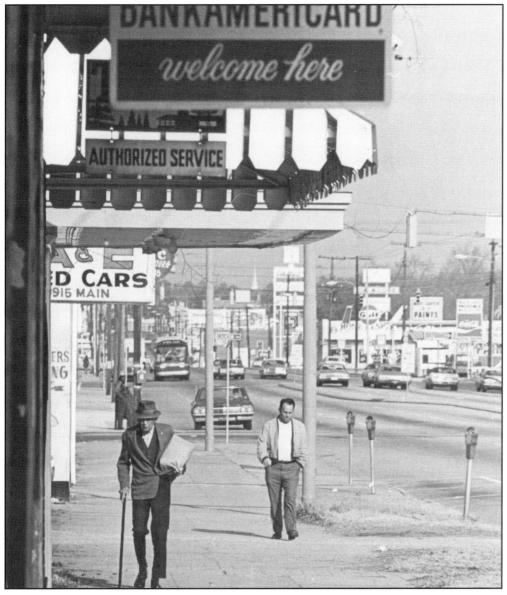

Historically, the town has been dominated by the textile industry.

- Winthrop, the local college, has been a fully accredited member of the Southern Association of Colleges and Secondary Schools since 1923.
- The all-women college currently has 115 faculty members, six large dormitories, five classroom buildings and a library with more than 150,000 volumes.
- The largest garden is the six-acre Glencairn Garden, opened by its owner and then donated to the city so the public could enjoy the hundreds of azaleas, camellias and other Southern favorites planted there.
- For entertainment, though, high-schoolers consistently travel to the South Park section of Charlotte, North Carolina, to listen to musical acts like the Temptations or Dionne Warwick.

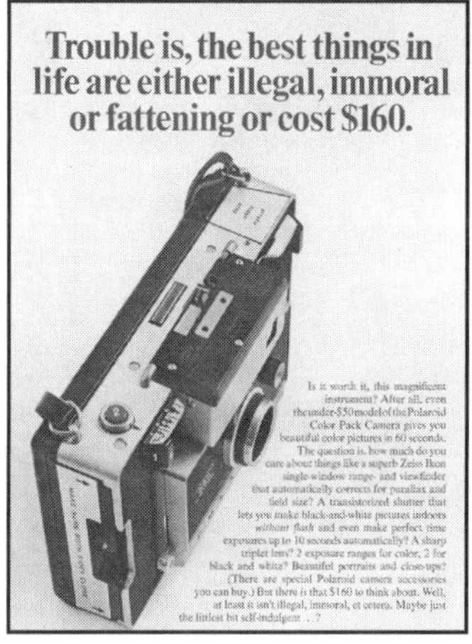

Historical Snapshot 1968

- Following the assassination of Martin Luther King, Jr. and Robert Kennedy, Sears & Roebuck removed toy guns from its Christmas catalog
- Yale College admitted women
- The Vietnam War became the longest war in U.S. history, with American casualties exceeding the total for the entire Korean War
- Riots erupted in more than 100 cities following the King assassination; 46 people died, and 21,000 federal and 34,000 state troopers were called out—the largest military civil emergency force in modern times
- Mobile coronary care ambulances, waterbed filtration systems, Redwood National Park, Zero Population Growth Inc., and Zap comic books all made their first appearance
- The off-Broadway play *Hair*, which featured on-stage nudity, was billed as the first tribal-love-rock musical
- *The Great White Hope*; *Promises, Promises*; *A Day in the Death of Joe Egg*; *The Prime of Miss Jean Brodie* and *I Never Sang for My Father* opened on Broadway
- The National Democratic Convention was disrupted by antiwar protestors, whose arrest and beatings by Chicago police created a national uproar
- Dr. Christiaan Barnard performed a heart transplant on Philip Blaiberg, who survived 18 months
- Bestsellers included *Airport* by Arthur Hailey, *Couples* by John Updike, *Testimony of Two Men* by Taylor Caldwell and *Myra Breckenridge* by Gore Vidal, while critics praised *Soul on Ice* by Eldridge Cleaver, and *The Electric Kool-Aid Acid Test* by Tom Wolfe
- Former vice president Richard M. Nixon was elected president with a 43.4 percent margin of victory, the lowest percentage since 1912
- *2001: A Space Odyssey*, *Rosemary's Baby*, *Yellow Submarine*, *Planet of the Apes* and *Oliver!* opened in movie theatres
- Americans were witnesses, via the TV nightly news, as the Saigon chief of police calmly shot a prisoner in the head
- Jackie Kennedy's wedding gift from her new husband Aristotle Onassis—a ruby ring surrounded by large diamonds, plus a pair of matching earrings—was valued at $1.2 million
- On television, *60 Minutes*, *The Dick Cavett Show*, *Rowan and Martin's Laugh-in*, *Hawaii Five-O* and *The Mod Squad* premiered
- The Summer Olympic Games were held in Mexico City, where two athletes gave the Black Power salute on the winner's stand
- Norman Mailer's book *Armies of the Night* received the Pulitzer prize for nonfiction
- The largest reservoir of petroleum in North America was discovered on Alaska's North Slope
- To protest the Vietnam War, Jesuit priest Daniel Berrigan, his brother Phil and seven other priests entered the Maryland Selective Service offices and burned hundreds of 1-A classification records
- *Apollo VI* astronauts circled the moon 10 times

1968 Economic Profile

Selected Prices

Artificial Fingernails, Nu-Nails	$0.49
Automobile, Toyota	$1,666.00
Baseball Glove	$15.95
Boots, Cowboy	$26.80
Clothes Dryer, Speed Queen	$178.00
Coat, Suede	$38.90
Color TV, Zenith 20-Inch	$399.95
Dancing Shoes, Tap	$5.77
Necklace, Cultured Pearl	$29.95
Socket Set, Wizard	$56.95
Tent, Eagle 5' x 7'	$17.75
Toy Truck, Tonka	$1.69
Trumpet, Student	$79.50
Walker-Stroller	$18.95
Whole Wheat Doughnut	$0.10

Changing America

- TV sets numbered 78 million in the U.S., 25 million in the U.S.S.R., 20.5 million in Japan and 19 million in Great Britain.
- Crimes of violence had increased in the United States by 57 percent since 1960.
- Ralph Abernathy led the Poor People's Campaign in Washington, DC, where a 15-acre tent community known as Resurrection City was created to protest racial discrimination and economic conditions in America.

"A Shaky Start," *Time*, October 27, 1967:

Washington's scruffy Ambassador Theatre, normally a pad for psychedelic frolics, was the scene of an unscheduled scatological solo last week in support of the peace demonstrations. Its anti-star was author Norman Mailer, who proved even less prepared to explain Why Are We in Vietnam? than his current novel bearing that title.

Slurping liquor from a coffee mug, Mailer faced an audience of 600, most of them students, who had kicked in $1,900 for a bail fund against Saturday's capers. "I don't want to grandstand unduly," he said, grandly but barely standing. It was one of his most coherent sentences. Mumbling and spewing obscenities as he staggered about the stage—which he commandeered by threatening to beat up the previous M.C.—Mailer described in detail his search for a usable privy on the premises. Excretion, in fact, was his preoccupation of the night. "I'm here because I'm like L.B.J.," was one of Mailer's milder observations. "He's as full of crap as I am." When hecklers mustered the temerity to shout, "Publicity hound!" at him, Mailer managed to pronounce flawlessly his all-purpose noun, verb and expletive: "**** you!"

Thirty-five thousand anti-war protesters converged on the Pentagon.

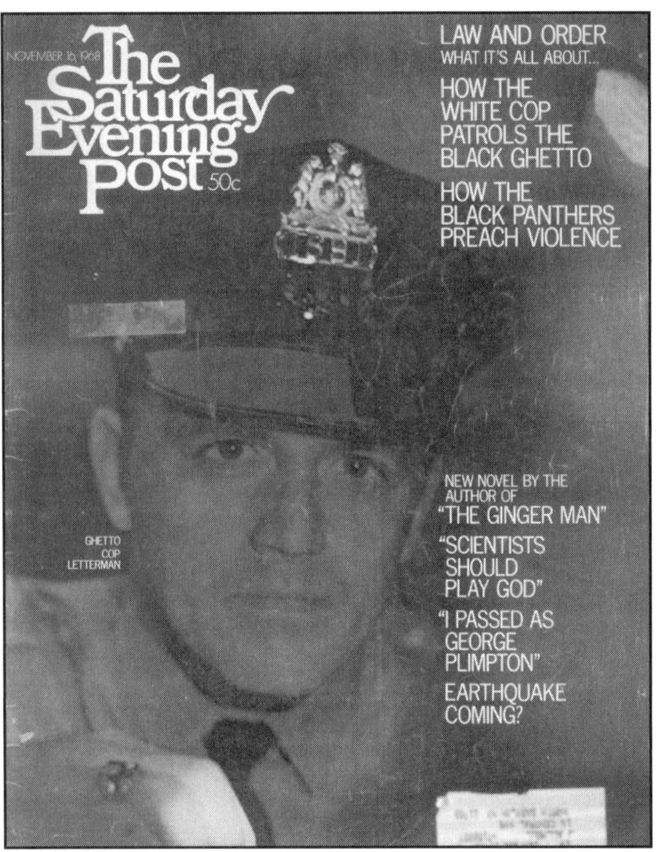

- Electronic composition was used to set an entire book of type for the first time.
- Ruth Eisemann-Schier became the first woman named to the FBI's "Ten Most Wanted" list.
- A professional school exclusively for training circus clowns opened in Venice, Florida.
- The offering of college courses in Eastern theology, religion, sorcery, witchcraft and Zen dramatically increased.
- Celibacy of the priesthood became an issue in the Catholic Church, and Pope Paul VI's ban on contraception was challenged by 800 U.S. theologians.
- Black militancy increased on campuses; numerous black studies programs were developed at universities across America.
- One hundred shares of IBM stock purchased in 1914 for $2,750 were now worth, after numerous stock splits, $20 million.
- Rock ballrooms included the Fillmore in San Francisco, the Fillmore East in New York, the Boston Tea Party in Boston and Kinetic Playground in Chicago.
- John Lennon and Yoko Ono's cover for their record album *Two Virgins*, which featured a photograph of them naked, was banned.
- Twenty thousand people were added monthly to New York City's welfare rolls; one-fourth of the city's budget was allocated to welfare payments.

"PROTEST: The Banners of Dissent," *Time*, October 27, 1967:

The Pentagon is the most formidable redoubt in official Washington. Squat and solid as a feudal fortress, it hunkers in a remote reclaimed Virginia swamp that used to be called Hell's Bottom, across the Potomac River from the spires, colonnades and domes of the federal city. Through its two tiers of sub-basements and five aboveground stories, windowless corridors weave like badger warrens. The bastion of America's military establishment not only houses the secretary of defense, the Joint Chiefs of Staff and a mint of high brass, but is also a beehive of bureaucracy where some 10,800 civilians shuffle routinely through the daily load of paperwork. It is actually five giant buildings, concentrically interconnected and braced one upon another.

Against that physically and functionally immovable object last week surged a self-proclaimed irresistible force of 35,000 ranting, chanting protestors who are immutably opposed to the U.S. commitment in Vietnam. By the time the demonstration had ended, more than 425 irresistibles had been arrested, 13 more had been injured, and the Pentagon had remained immobile. Within the tide of dissenters swarmed all the elements of dissent in 1967: hard-eyed revolutionaries and skylarking hippies; ersatz motorcycle gangs and all-too-real college professors; housewives, ministers and authors; black nationalists in African garb—but no real African nationalists; nonviolent pacifists and nonpacifist advocates of violence—some of them anti-anti-warriors and American Nazis spoiling for a fight.

Acid & Acrimony. The demonstration began under a crystalline noonday sky at the Lincoln Memorial. It took on special impact by climaxing a week of antiwar protests across the nation. Beneath the marbled gaze of Lincoln's statue, red and blue Viet Cong flags mingled with signs affirming that "Che Guevara Lives," posters proclaiming "Dump Johnson" and asking "Where is Oswald When We Need Him?" The meeting had hardly begun before three Nazis were arrested for jumping a British trade-union orator who criticized U.S. involvement in Vietnam.

Speakers caterwauled in competition with blues and rock bands as the demonstrators jostled across the lawns. "The enemy is Lyndon Johnson; the war is disastrous in every way," cried baby doctor Benjamin Spock. Aroused by acrimony and acid-rock, the crowd moved exuberantly out across the Arlington Memorial Bridge toward the Pentagon. Inside the Pentagon, a siege mood prevailed. Defense Secretary Robert McNamara had entered his third-floor office at 8:15 a.m. and immersed himself in his customary workload. The skeleton staff of 3,000 that usually mans the Pentagon on Saturdays had been sharply pared by orders to all personnel to stay home unless their presence was absolutely necessary. . .

Abortive Assault. When the main force arrived, its good humor had begun to fray. An assault squad wielding clubs and ax handles probed the rope barrier in front of the Pentagon entrances, taunting and testing white-hatted federal marshals who stood in close ranks along the line. After 90-odd minutes of steadily rising invective and roiling around in the north parking lot of the Pentagon, flying wedges of demonstrators surged toward the less heavily defended press entrance.

A barrage of pop bottles and clubs failed to budge the outer ring of marshals, and military police were summoned from the bowels of the bastion to form a brace of backup rings. A final desperate charge actually breached the security lines, and carried a handful of demonstrators whirling into the rifle butts and truncheons of the rearmost guards at the Pentagon gate. At least 10 invaders managed to penetrate the building before they were hurled out—ahead of a counterattacking wave of soldiers vigorously wielding their weapons from port-arms. Handcuffs clicked as marshals corralled their captives, left behind in the abortive assault on the doors. Bloodstains clotted in rusty trails into the Pentagon, where prisoners had been dragged. Among them, uninjured, was Novelist Norman Mailer, who had tried to breach the police line after a wild build-up of booze and obscenity.

"Take Everything You Need, Baby," *Newsweek*, April 15, 1968:

It was Pandora's box flung open—an apocalyptic act that loosed the furies brooding in the shadows of America's sullen ghettos. From Washington to Oakland, Tallahassee to Denver, the murder of Martin Luther King, Jr. in Memphis last week touched off a black rampage that subjected the U.S. to the most widespread spasm of racial disorder in its violent history.

The fire this time made Washington look like the besieged capital of a banana republic with helmeted combat troops, bayoneted rifles at the ready, guarding the White House and a light machine gun post defending the steps of the Capitol. Huge sections of Chicago's West Side ghetto were put to the torch. The National Guard was called out there and in Detroit, Pittsburgh, Baltimore and in four Southern cities, and put on alert in Philadelphia and Boston. In New York, Mayor John V. Lindsay was heckled from a Harlem street by an angry crowd. In Minneapolis, a Negro vowed to kill the first honky he saw—and promptly shot his white neighbor to death. "My King is dead," he sobbed, after pumping half a dozen bullets into his victim. . . .

Washington, which is 66 percent Negro but which had been almost untouched by the last four riotous summers, was the hardest hit this time. Minutes after the news of King's death was broadcast, crowds began to gather on the edges of the capital's sprawling ghettos. They did not have to wait long for a leader. Into the volatile mix swept Black Power-monger Stokely Carmichael spouting incendiary rhetoric. "Go home and get your guns," cried Carmichael. "When the white man comes he is going to kill you. I don't want any Black blood on the street. Go home and get you a gun and then come back because I got me a gun"—and he brandished what looked like a small pistol.

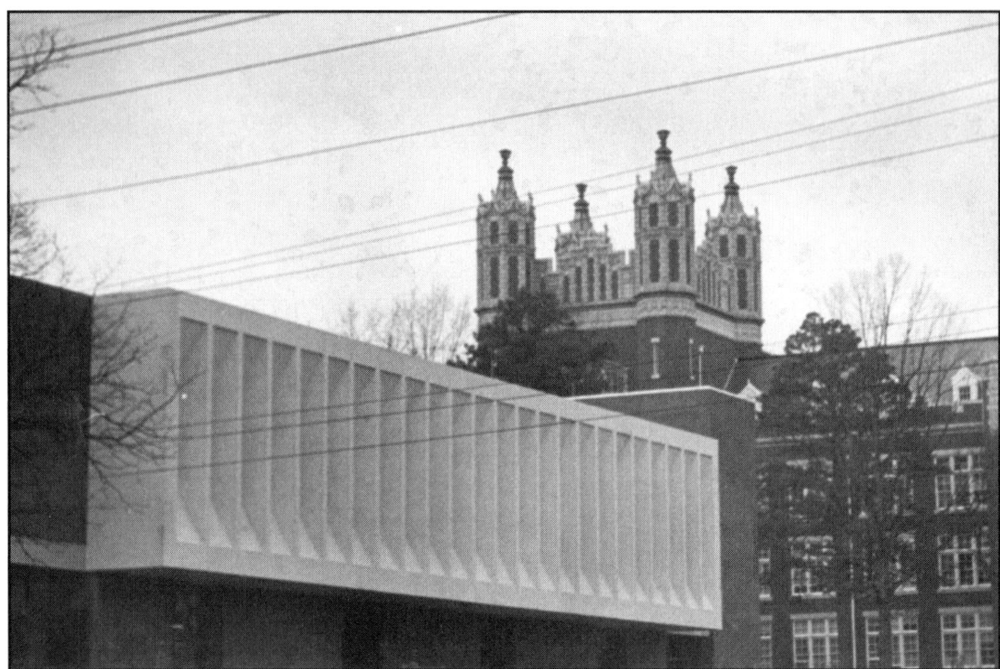

Winthrop College now has 115 faculty members and a library with 150,000 volumes.

35
23
30

1970–1979

The turbulent legacy of the 1960s spilled into the 1970s, igniting racial unrest in the schools, rapidly shifting musical tastes and a movie industry determined to challenge the status quo. Social unrest was only one reminder of the 1960s and the Vietnam war; another was the spiraling cost of living set off by several waves of inflation. The result was an America stripped of its ability to dominate the world economy and a nation on the defensive. In 1971, President Richard Nixon was forced to devalue the U.S. dollar against foreign currencies and allow its previously fixed value to "float" according to changing economic conditions. By year's end, the money paid for foreign goods exceeded that spent on U.S. exports for the first time in the century. Two years later, during the "Yom Kippur" War between Israel and its Arab neighbors, Arab oil producers declared an oil embargo on oil shipments to the United States, setting off gas shortages, a dramatic rise in the price of oil, and rationing for the first time in 30 years. The sale of automobiles plummeted, unemployment and inflation nearly doubled, and the buying power of Americans fell dramatically.

The economy, handicapped by the devaluation of the dollar and inflation, did not fully recover for more than a decade, while the fast-growing economies of Japan and western Europe, especially West Germany, mounted direct competitive challenges to American manufacturers. The value of imported manufactured goods skyrocketed from 14 percent of U.S. domestic production in 1970 to 40 percent in 1979. The inflationary cycle and recession returned in 1979 to disrupt markets, throw thousands out of work, and prompt massive downsizing of companies—awakening many once-secure workers to the reality of the changing economic market. A symbol of the era was the pending bankruptcy of Chrysler Corporation, whose cars were so outmoded and plants so inefficient they could not compete against Japanese imports. The federal government was forced to extend loan guarantees to the company to prevent bankruptcy and the loss of thousands of jobs.

The appointment of Paul Volcker as the chairman of the Federal Reserve Board late in the decade gave the economy the distasteful medicine it needed. To cope with inflation, Volcker slammed on the economic brakes, restricted the growth of the money supply, and curbed inflation. As a result, he pushed interest rates to nearly 20 percent—their highest level since the Civil War. Almost immediately the sale of automobiles and expensive items stopped.

The decade also was marred by the deep divisions caused by the Vietnam War. For more than 10 years the war had been fought on two fronts: at home and abroad. As a result, U.S. policy makers conducted the war with one eye always focused on national opinion. When it ended, the Vietnam War had been the longest war in American history, having cost $118 billion and resulted in 56,000 dead, 300,000 wounded, and the loss of American prestige abroad.

The decade was a time not only of movements, but of moving. In the 1970s, the shift of manufacturing facilities to the South from New England and the Midwest accelerated. The Sunbelt became the new darling of corporate America. By the late 1970s, the South, including Texas, had gained more than a million manufacturing jobs, while the Northeast and the Midwest lost nearly two million. Rural North Carolina had the highest percentage of manufacturing of any state in the nation, along with the lowest blue-collar wages and the lowest unionization rate in the country. The Northeast lost more than traditional manufacturing jobs.

The largest and most striking of all the social actions of the early 1970s was the Women's Liberation Movement; it fundamentally reshaped American society. Since the late 1950s, a small group of well-placed American women had attempted to convince Congress and the courts to bring about equality between the sexes. By the 1970s, the National Organization for Women (NOW) multiplied in size, the first issue of *Ms.* magazine sold out in a week, and women began demanding economic equality, the legalization of abortion, and the improvement of women's role in society. "All authority in our society is being challenged," said a Department of Health, Education, and Welfare report. "Professional athletes challenge owners, journalists challenge editors, consumers challenge manufacturers . . . and young blue-collar workers, who have grown up in an environment in which equality is called for in all institutions, are demanding the same rights and expressing the same values as university graduates."

The decade also included the flowering of the National Welfare Rights Organization (NWRO), founded in 1966, which resulted in millions of urban poor demanding additional rights. The environmental movement gained recognition and momentum during the decade starting with the first Earth Day celebration in 1970 and the subsequent passage of the federal Clean Air and Clean Water acts. And the growing opposition to the use of nuclear power peaked after the near calamity at Three Mile Island in Pennsylvania in 1979. As the formal barriers to racial equality came down, racist attitudes became unacceptable and the black middle class began to grow. By 1972, half of all Southern black children sat in integrated classrooms, and about one-third of all black families had risen economically into the ranks of the middle class.

The changes recorded for the decade included a doubling in the amount of garbage created per capita from 2.5 pounds in 1920 to five pounds. California created a no-fault divorce law, Massachusetts introduced no-fault insurance, and health food sales reached $3 billion. By mid-decade, the so-called typical nuclear family, with working father, housewife, and two children, represented only seven percent of the population and the family size was falling. The average family size was 3.4 persons compared with 4.3 in 1920.

1971 News Feature

"The Family Is out of Fashion," by Ann Richardson Roiphe, *The New York Times Magazine*, August 15, 1971:

> *"Blood is thicker than water only in the sense of being the vitalizing stream of certain social stupidity,"* The Death of the Family, *by David Cooper.*

In a silent room on West 79th Street in New York City, 10 women rub their hands rhythmically over their large, pregnant bellies while their husbands stare at stopwatches, encouragingly giving hand signals. The couples are in training for natural childbirth with Mrs. Elizabeth Bing, who has spread the gospel in this country that male and female should share in the dramatic event of the birth of their child. Fifty to 60 new couples sign up for this course each month. What are they all doing? What are they doing several months later, walking around in their nursing bras, buying mobiles that swing from crib tops and potties with musical boxes and on and on to a future radically different from that of their childless past? Don't they know, this army of young people pushing strollers through the park, that they are behaving in a reactionary way? The nuclear family is not now a thing of fashion.

Weary from long discussion on economic theory and wasted by years of futile peace marches, bored by campaigns for compromise candidates and stunned by pollution and ecological reports, the intellectual community has turned with primal fury against a newly discovered evil: the family. Women's Liberation points out again and again how burdened, minimal and trivial is the life of the woman who tends the family. Books are appearing that attack the nuclear unit as the source of the alienated, bomb-throwing society we have come to know all too well. The call is out for new structures, babies brought up in daycare centers, new communes—or perhaps, as Germaine Greer proposes, let us do away with connected permanent relationships entirely. Let each man, woman and child shift for himself. Like the insects that fly singly throughout the ephemeral summer days.

One night my teenaged stepdaughter tearfully accused her father of being interested in her only if she was accepted into a good college so he could enjoy a little reflected status. My God, I thought, she's talking about the man who burped her, carried her to the zoo, played endless games of Monopoly and Clue, and stood in 100-degree heat to watch her ride dumb beasts in meaningless circles around a dusty ring. She's talking about the man who carried 10 bottles of ketchup all through Europe because she wouldn't eat anything without it. How did she miss the tenderness, despair, passion, pride and fear he feels for her? Of course, I knew the facts. She has to grow away, to tear apart the first love and start again—but how painful the ripping of the sinews, how wretched we all become in the process.

I looked at our new baby. "Da da," she says with joy, pulling off her father's glasses. He kisses her on the stomach. She laughs, comic, total, beautiful pleasure—but where is it going? Is it worth it? Sometimes it seems as if the tensions, the angers we have accumulated against each other will get together and flood out this family, each of us floating apart on a river of nightmares, to drown eventually.

The other day I looked at my 10-year-old. "Fix your hair," I said, "wash your face. You look like an orphan. Why won't you wear any of the dresses that hang neglected, wasted, in the closet?" Then I listened. It wasn't my voice speaking at all. It was my dead mother, out of my own body, screeching from the grave the very words I had so loathed. Within me the ghost of values past was possessing, displacing the present. Family of origin, family of procreation, tied together, despite my heroic efforts to separate them, to create a pure and different life. Patterns of the past, rejected or accepted, have a way of imposing themselves on the present. We all live with the dark designs of our early loves; our hates and our attractions are colored by the intense experience of family life. We cannot easily be freed. It is true as David Cooper in *The Death of the Family* says, "A thousand ghosts roam within us." They depersonalize, limit and bind us. We are like natives with large disks protruding from distorted lips, or like primitive tribes with earlobes stretched to elephantine proportions.

Most people suffer from anxieties, are neurosis-ridden, limited, uncreative, socially normal, but inwardly cut off from feelings of self. That is the usual result of our family system. No one I have ever known has made it through without scars on the psyche that became open wounds on the backs of the next generation, and yet I feel as I struggle over the bikes, sled and carriage that block access to our stairway that I and my contemporaries, male and female, are truly engaged in a revolutionary drama. We who live in families are the frontiersmen of a new world. That this was equally true of the generation before, and will apply to the generation after, is not discouraging, but from a certain distance, merely the stuff of history.

Margaret Mead, in writing a text to a photography book on the family, has said that "no society anywhere has ever sanctioned illegitimacy." This means that every society from Aborigine to Maoist China has structured some form of family life to raise, socialize and protect the children—to guarantee institutionally the social, sexual needs of the adults. Some of these systems have worked better than others; all of them have demanded a price from the participants—some personal freedoms and institutional pleasures must be abandoned when human groups are formed, and it is these very restrictions that enemies of the family are now calling abominations.

Germaine Greer would have us set no limit on sexual pleasure. Submit to no discipline of nursing schedules or possessive needs. She would have us abandon ugly security for free flight. David Cooper and R.D. Laing incriminate the family unit as the originator of all pathology, personal and political. They envision a utopia of people truly separate from one another, each self-realized and alive in his own present. David Cooper suggests that mothers should learn not to pick up babies when they wail in the first year of life, but allow them to experience the desolation and aloneness of their position. If we do this, he promises, we will create people who are not tied to others, not destroyed by family romance.

His method seems extreme, but the goals are unarguable. We all want better human beings. We want to create a society in which each man can live creatively and experience self-love and love of others. We want fewer divorces, fewer psychotics, no Lee Harvey Oswalds, and finally, in a wonderful new world, no Lyndon Johnsons, no George Wallaces, no bigots, no liars, no destroyers—the Pentagon turned into a botanical garden. But the question is,

The tradition of family has come under attack by the intellectual community.

how do we make better people, how will we perfect, tame, simultaneously harness and free the conflicting forces of aggression and love that are an absolute part of every human child that opens its new eyes on the jaded world of its parents?

I cannot believe that further disconnection of child from parent, an atomization of each human unit into a single orbiting star, will achieve anything more than the certain death of the species. It seems self-evident that we are now stuck with one another, parent and child, male and female, and that the changes that must be made need to take into account the necessary balances we have to find in order to assume the separate dignity of each living soul. It is my baby's right to take her first steps away from me and my obligation to follow, not too

The nuclear family is blamed for today's alienated society.

close but not too far, for the next moment when she needs to be restrained from pulling the boiling soup down on her head.

As my husband and I go about our day, we are trying to form between us the shape of a family that will enable our children better to integrate the pressures on them from without and within, and to make them freer, their ghosts more benign than ours, their limitations less paralyzing. We try not to let our time go dead with security and wooden with known experiences. We attempt to do better than our parents—some days we succeed. Too often, we definitely don't.

s the BLACK Public College DYING?

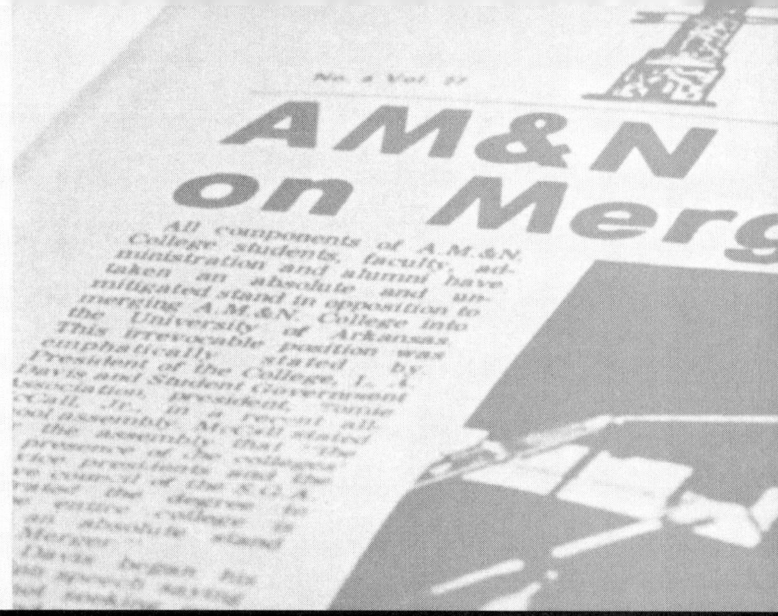
AM&N on Merg

All components of A.M.&N. College students, faculty, administration and alumni have taken an absolute and unmitigated stand in opposition to merging A.M.&N. College into the University of Arkansas. This irrevocable position was emphatically stated by President of the College, L. A. Davis and Student Government Association president,

1972 News Feature

"Is the Black Public College Dying? State Schools Fight for Life Amid Integration and Merger," by Jack Slater, *Ebony*, October 1972:

Before the "separate but equal" farce, before 1954 and Brown vs. Board of Education, before the current fabricated agony over busing—before any of it, there was the black-supported college. And now, after nearly a century of providing higher education for tens of thousands of black youths denied access to white universities, after opening faculty positions and administrative posts to thousands of blacks who could not find similar employment in white institutions, after supplying much of the human ammunition for the sit-ins and the civil rights movement of the sixties—after all of these things, the black public college is now in danger of losing its identity and, in some cases, is being dismantled at a rate faster than our sluggish sense of priorities can grasp. Soon only the memory of some of these colleges will exist. And soon that, too, like yesterday's newspaper, will be put aside.

Merger with larger white universities, integration, new competition from nearby white public colleges or outright abolishment are among the causes of the black colleges' threatened demise. And with that demise, black faculty members and administrators are in danger of losing their posts and black youths may lose one more access to a college education.

Maryland State College was recently annexed to become a part of the largely white University of Maryland—Eastern Shore branch. Several formerly black colleges such as West Virginia State, Bluefield (West Virginia) State and Lincoln (Missouri) University are now enrolling a majority of white students. (These schools' white enrollment is 75 percent, 80 percent and more than 51 percent, respectively.) Delaware State, Bowie (Maryland) State and Kentucky State currently have white enrollment of 30 to 40 percent and appear likely to have a white majority in a few years. And during this past summer, against the will of many black citizens, Arkansas AM&N College vanished forever into the folds of a merger and became a part of the largely white University of Arkansas.

The root of the present crisis can be found in Title VI of the Civil Rights Act of 1962. The Act forbids any institution that receives federal aid to discriminate on the basis of race, creed, color or national origin. Since 1964, all black institutions have complied with that ruling and have managed (some only minimally) to integrate both their student bodies and their faculties. Yet, it isn't integration per se which troubles the institutions; it is the use or misuse

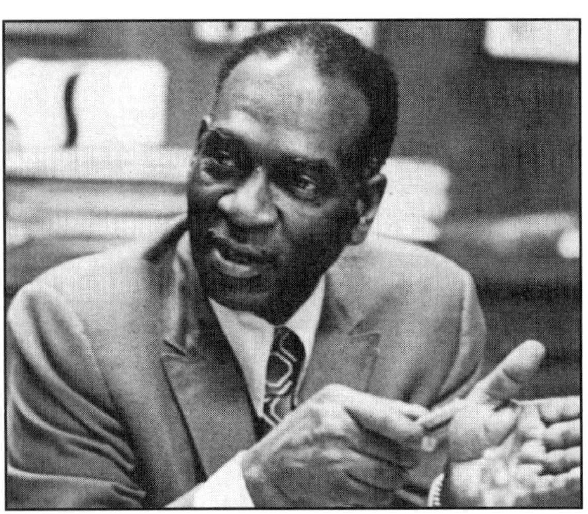

Mergers are eliminating many jobs for black administrators and presidents.

of integration to destroy them. Merger, for example, unrelated to any existing federal guideline, is a state tool which some legislatures are wielding, or attempting to wield, in a scramble to tighten state budgets—not to enforce greater compliance with the Title VI ruling. And the creation of new white competition to drive neighboring black colleges into decline (a device which is also unrelated to any federal guidelines) is a "political tool, a comment on the racist mentality surrounding black colleges," says Dr. Herman B. Smith, Jr., director of the Atlanta-based Office for Advancement of Public Negro Colleges.

In all fairness, however, it should be noted that all of the nation's 35 black public colleges are not in trouble—or, at least, do not view integration or merger as trouble. The offices at some schools (Kentucky State, Bowie State and Delaware State) maintain they welcome integration as a means of assuring their colleges' survival, while the administration at Maryland State believes that the institution has become financially and academically stronger since it became annexed two years ago by the University of Maryland. . . .

It should be noted that a few of the less integrated colleges—unchallenged for the moment—are not in trouble, either. In fact, such schools as Cheyney (Pennsylvania) State, Grambling (Louisiana) College, Alcorn (Mississippi) A&M and Norfolk (Virginia) State have been improving academically in recent months by substantial grants from federal or private sources to develop new curricula. Despite such encouraging examples, however, many other colleges do feel themselves seriously menaced, and there are enough "white clouds on the horizon," as one punster put it, to justify the current alarm about the future of the black public college. . . .

A case in point:

Florida A&M University. For the past five years, Florida's state educators and public officials have been attempting in a variety of ways to dissolve or change Florida A&M University, which has some 5,000 students. When segregation was the order of the day, white state officials evidenced little or no public concern about the wasteful duplication of having two state universities situated virtually side-by-side in Tallahassee. But now that desegregation has arrived, legislators have "discovered" that it is economically impractical to support both FAMU and the largely white Florida State University. Since 1967, unsuccessful attempts have been made to 1) abolish FAMU altogether, 2) make it into a semi-autonomous satellite of FSU, 3) merge it with FSU, and 4) change it into an undergraduate institution concentrating on specialties not offered by FSU. To date, none of these proposals has been acted upon. Yet, the issue of FAMU's liquidation still hangs in the air, in spite of the fact that "the legislature and the board of regents have now assured FAMU of autonomy in the nine-institution state system," says Dr. Benjamin L. Perry, president of FAMU. Although Dr. Perry is obviously pleased to have such assurances, he nevertheless remains skeptical. "We'll continue to maintain vigilance," he says.

The role of historically black colleges is changing.

"I can't point to a single example of hope in the record," a high-ranking black educator was quoted as saying in John Egeron's *The Black Public Colleges: Integration or Disintegration.* "Here is a blueprint to get rid of the black institutions. We're not talking about integration but disintegration, not about merger but submerger, not about equality but inequality."

1973 Profile

Upper Class

After an enjoyable but taxing year at Woodberry Forest School, Charles Ethridge has been instructed that he must return home and work in the family coal business, while his friends and family spend the summer at the shore.

Charles Ethridge is not looking forward to working in his family's coal business this summer.

Life at Home

- Charles Ethridge is not happy.
- As school at Woodberry Forest in Virginia draws to a close, Charles has been told him he will be returning to Jasper, Alabama, despite his plans to visit friends this summer.
- After all his hard work at school, his father wants him to learn the family coal business, while the rest of the family vacations at Gulf Shores for three months.
- Not only that, classmate Punky Arthur has invited him to spend a couple of weeks with his family in Maine, but his father is firm: This summer will be spent in Jasper working for the Cathcart Coal Company as the low man, assigned to work in the field.
- Worse yet, even the few people he still knows in Jasper will be gone to the beach or the mountains.
- His father insists that even if the family decides to sell the coal company, the Jasper community will continue to thrive on coal, and Charles needs to know coal.
- The only thing Charles knows is that Jasper is the last place he plans to settle when he finishes prep school and college—the absolute last place.
- He believes his future is in Atlanta, Washington or New York; he has no desire to be a big fish in a pond of 12,000 people nestled in the Appalachian foothills northwest of Birmingham.

The Ethridges' two-story home is located on the finest street in town.

- But as the only son of Edward Ethridge and the heir apparent to the Cathcart fortune, he has little choice right now.
- After all, the Cathcarts *are* Jasper, having first arrived in 1893.
- Ancestors include several men who have served in the United States Congress and Senate.
- Charles's great-grandfather was majority leader of the Senate, while his great-great-uncle was Speaker of the House of Representatives.
- Over the years, thanks to hard work, good politics and well-timed capital, the family has acquired major financial interests in Jasper's largest bank, the coal company, a land development company and Jasper's only radio station.
- Throughout history, Cathcart men have been raised to run one or another of the family businesses.
- Unfortunately for the family fortune, Charles's grandfather and grandmother produced only daughters.
- Marion, the eldest daughter, married Edward Ethridge, son of a local doctor and an honors graduate of the University of Alabama Law School; thus, the torch was passed to Edward, who now handles most of the family's affairs and was recently elected to the Board of Trustees of his alma mater.
- Charles loves and admires his family, but he simply wishes to chart his own course.
- Since leaving Jasper to attend school in Virginia two years ago, his eyes have been opened to the possibilities of the wider world, leaving him little patience for the small, backward ideas of his former high school mates.
- Surrounded by bright students from throughout the South and Midwest, Charles was just beginning to grasp his potential when he was summoned home.
- Now, with the Arab oil embargo just under way and gas queues forming across the nation, a worldwide call has arisen for alternatives to foreign oil—including coal.
- Charles's father thinks this could be a good—no, make that a great—year for domestic coal.
- After all, now that a cloud has formed around that darling of science, nuclear energy, and the Arabs have cut off America from its precious oil supplies, new life is being pumped into an old product—a great year indeed.
- The Ethridges' two-story home is about 110 years old, located on the finest street in town, and has six bedrooms, a large kitchen area, living room, den, a sewing room for Charles's mother and a small office for his father.

Growing up, the Ethridge family has been close.

"The 1973 Cars: Year of the Bumper," *Newsweek*, September 18, 1972:

Just a few years ago, the auto industry's annual new model showings were the high point of the year in Detroit—and the stylists' fins and furbelows stirred passionate cravings in auto buffs across the U.S. But Ralph Nader and the spreading smog over the cities have changed all that; this week, as the industry finishes its autumn round of press parties and sneak previews of the 1973 models, the stress is on unglamorous safety improvements and exhaust/emission controls. With hordes of government regulators constantly at their shoulders, some Detroit executives are grumbling that their industry is becoming no more independent than the public utilities. Significantly, this week's ballyhoo will be overshadowed by hearings in Washington pitting the industry's top brass against the Price Commission. All in all, it is a transformed industry—and Newsweek's Detroit bureau chief, James C. Jones, in his 23rd rites of autumn filed this report on the metamorphosis:

"The usual barrels of booze have been poured, tens of thousands of shrimp iced and tons of beef Wellington carved, and the moguls have trotted out their standard superlatives. It's a pattern four decades old, but this year there were major variations.

For one thing, 'planned obsolescence' is out. Nobody can afford the old three-year styling cycle of an all-new car one year, a minor face-lift next year, a major facelift the third year and then scrap the dies and start over. Most of the industry is going to a six-year cycle, and the result is a good deal less emphasis on cosmetic changes.

There are a few tidbits for the diehard styling fans. Pontiac, for instance, has a spectacular entry in its new Grand Am, a love-it-or-hate-it machine that is being compared to the abortive Tucker Torpedo of 1946. And there are minor frills as options in ludicrous profusion: swiveling bucket seats on Chevrolets, a sling-like spare-tire extractor on Ford station wagons, a 'panic button' alarm system on Chryslers and an outside thermometer built into the rear-view mirror of Cadillacs. American Motors' Gremlin comes in a 'Levi's' series with genuine denim upholstery, complete with denim stitches and copper rivets. Hot diggety!

For the most part, however, the significant changes this year are in safety features and the intricate engine modifications needed to meet federal rules on what can come out of the tailpipe. The devices may have been made in Detroit, but they were mandated in Washington, and they join a formidable list of items forced on Detroit in the past few years: head restraints, shoulder belts, engine blow-by devices, side marker lights, locking steering columns, fire-resistant fabrics, impact-resistant fuel tanks and even coat hooks and glove-compartment latches designed for safety.

Up to now, the stress has been mainly on standardizing features that were already available as options. But from here on, the safety and emissions standards are going to create pure invention, which means large amounts of money. And the first such major innovation comes in the lowly bumper. For the 1973 cars, federal standards require bumpers capable of sustaining without damage a 5-mile-per-hour crash from the front and half as much from the rear."

- The household is normally managed by a full-time maid/cook, who goes to the Gulf Shores each summer with Charles's mother Anne, and his 16-year-old, wheelchair-bound sister Elizabeth, who was in a serious automobile accident a year ago while returning from a school sporting event, where she was a cheerleader.
- She is now a paraplegic and requires around-the-clock care.
- Now, the family insists on only the safest vehicles for their children and often wonders what it would have taken to keep Elizabeth safe.

Expenses for a boarding student are $3,600 a year.

Life at Work and Prep School

- The 1,000-acre Woodberry Forest School, located in the foothills of central Virginia, is bounded on one side by the Rapidan River.
- The campus includes hundreds of acres of woodlands, a working farm, a nine-hole golf course, and ample space for outdoor recreation such as hunting and fishing.
- Established in 1889, the school is well-known for offering the latest technology and superior athletic fields and facilities such as the Dick Gym.
- Currently, enrollment is 350 with 45 faculty members.
- Tuition for boarding students is $3,600 a year, with day students paying $1,800 annually.
- Charles lives in the Walker Building, the central school building and residential home to sophomores, juniors and seniors.
- He likes the rhythm of the school, including attending chapel services every Sunday after advisee dinner.
- A typical Monday, Wednesday or Thursday includes breakfast from 7:15 to 7:50 a.m., morning classes, lunch at 1 p.m., athletics and extracurricular activities from 3:40 to 5:30 p.m., seated dinner with faculty from 7:45 to 8:45 p.m., followed by study periods running until 10 p.m.
- Woodberry has mandatory lights out for all students, generally at 10:30 p.m. during the week, 11 p.m. on Fridays and 1 a.m. on Saturday nights.
- The curriculum, the school likes to say, prepares students for not only the University of Virginia and the University of North Carolina, but also for colleges such as Davidson, Washington and Lee, Princeton and Yale.
- He has known since he was small that once he reached high school age he would be attending prep school at Woodberry.
- After school desegregation began and the violence in schools rose, Charles was pleased that he had a place to which he could escape.
- The public high school he would have attended is integrated, but still self-segregated, with black and white students rarely mixing during classes or lunch breaks.
- On some days tensions are so high that changing classes in the hall can be dangerous if someone says the wrong thing at the wrong time.
- Woodberry is experiencing little of this trauma.

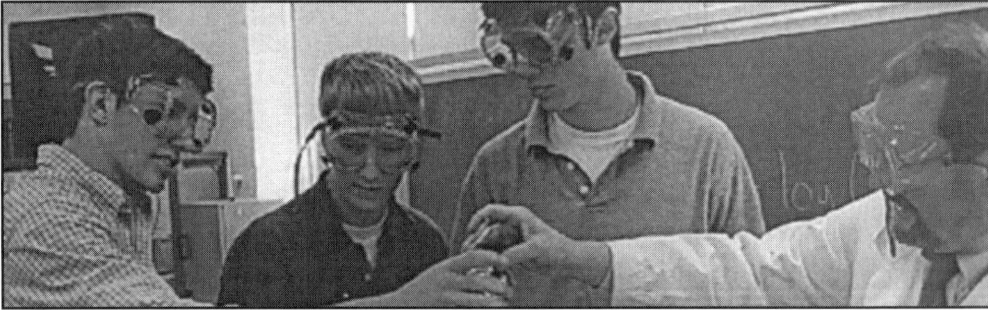

The Woodberry curriculum prepares students for the nation's finest colleges.

"The Failures of Educational Reform," *Crisis in the Classroom*, by Charles E. Silberman, 1970:

"The decade which began in 1955, and through which we are still churning," Professor Robert H. Anderson of Harvard predicted in the early '60s, "may come to be regarded as one of the major turning points in American public education." Anderson's optimism was widely shared: 1950s and '60s saw one of the largest and most sustained educational reform movements in American history, an effort that many observers, this writer included, thought would transform the schools.

Nothing of the sort happened; the reform movement has produced innumerable changes, and yet the schools themselves are largely unchanged. In one study, John I. Goodlad, dean of the UCLA Graduate School of Education, along with several colleagues, visited some 260 kindergarten-through-first grade classrooms in 100 schools in 13 states to determine the extent to which the reform movement had changed the schools. He found what this writer and his colleagues found: that things are much the same as they had been 20 years ago, and in some respects, not as good as they were 40 years ago, when the last great school reform movement was at its peak. "We were unable to discern much attention to pupil needs, attainments, or problems as a basis for individual opportunities to learn," he reports. "Teaching was predominantly telling and questioning by the teacher, with children responding one by one or occasionally in chorus. In all of this, the textbook was the most highly visible instrument of learning and teaching. . . . Rarely did we find small groups intensely in pursuit of knowledge; rarely did we find individual pupils at work in self-sustaining inquiry . . . we are forced to conclude that much of the so-called educational reform movement has been blunted on the classroom door."

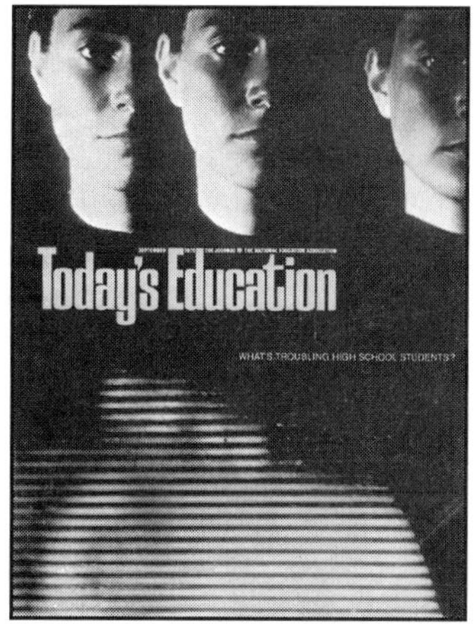

Life in the Community: Jasper, Alabama

- The city was named in honor of Sergeant William Jasper, a Revolutionary War soldier.
- Coal propelled its growth from a hamlet of only 200 people in 1886 to a town of more than 3,000 people just four years later.
- Most of the coal was shipped to Birmingham, 45 miles to the southeast, for the production of iron and steel.
- Today, with a population of 12,000, Jasper's major customer for coal is the power industry.
- Alabama Power is the largest single buyer, replacing coal's traditional markets which formerly included the railroads and commercial heating.
- U.S. reliance on coal declined from nearly 50 percent of U.S. primary energy consumption at the end of World War II to about 18 percent today.
- Through the years, the industry has changed, too; with increased mechanization came fewer workers, most of whom at Cathcart Coal are over 40, with many of those approaching retirement.

Charles has known he would attend Woodberry Forest since he was a small boy.

Outlook for U.S. Coal, Energy Information Administration, U.S. Department of Energy, August 1982:

U.S. reliance on coal declined from nearly 50 percent of U.S. primary energy consumption at the end of World War II to about 18 percent by the 1973-1974 oil embargo. Oil and natural gas consumption grew in relative importance during the same period. The share of energy provided by cheap natural gas supplies doubled. The decline in coal demand was due largely to the loss of the transportation, residential and commercial markets. The railroad systems turned from coal to diesel fuel and reduced their consumption of coal from approximately 62 million tons in 1950 to 10.1 million tons in 1973. The residential and commercial sectors turned to oil and natural gas, decreasing coal consumption from 115 million tons in 1950 to 11 million tons in 1973. The industrial sector's demand for coal also gradually declined as manufacturing firms switched to cheaper oil and natural gas supplies. During the latter half of this period, the electric utility sector was virtually the only growing market for steam coal. Electricity demand in the United States increased almost sixfold from 1950 to 1973, and coal consumption in this sector increased fourfold from 92 million tons to 389 million tons.

After World War II, the coal industry's labor productivity increased steadily as mechanization of mines continued. This caused the work force to shrink and be composed of mostly older, experienced miners. Productivity in the coal industry began to decrease in the late 1960s, especially in underground mines, due in part to the added procedures required by the Coal Mine Health and Safety Act of 1969. To make up for the decline in labor productivity, the work force expanded again: young, inexperienced workers were added, resulting in a still further decline in productivity.

In the mid- to late 1960s, environmental issues began to surface, affecting both coal supply and coal consumption. On the supply side, reclamation became a factor as many surface mines were abandoned and the land left unusable and unrestored. . . .

Just before the 1973-74 oil embargo, the abundance of cheap residual fuel oil (domestic and imported) and the growing availability of nuclear power made coal's future for use other than as metallurgical coal (in steelmaking) highly uncertain. Investment in coal mining was low and the industry was struggling to improve productivity within the framework of the new regulations. Many industrial, residential and East Coast utility consumers had converted to oil following the removal of the oil import quotas and the establishment of pollution control requirements. Due to the availability of oil imports, the decline in oil and natural gas reserves seemed to go unnoticed. The coal industry appeared to have entered a long period of decline. Environmental concerns and the air quality standards of the Clear Air Act accelerated this trend. It was generally believed by the energy community that nuclear power would continue to provide an ever-increasing share of the U.S. electric power generation. The prospect of the coal industry's eventual demise caused little concern outside the coal and railroad industries.

Against this background, the 1973-74 oil embargo caused a major reappraisal of coal's contribution to domestic energy production. In addition, growing uncertainty began to cloud the nuclear industry.

- Cathcart Coal extracts the mineral from surface mines, using 100-foot-tall draglines to scoop up 15 cubic yards of topsoil at a time.
- Fifty years after the end of Prohibition, Jasper remains dry, with only private clubs such as the Walker County Country Club allowed to serve alcohol.

Historical Snapshot
1973

- The last of the federal price controls were lifted; 25 percent of Americans said they had participated in various boycotts against the inflation of food prices
- The Nobel Peace Prize was awarded to Henry Kissinger and North Vietnamese Le Duc Tho, who refused the honor
- Television premieres included *Barnaby Jones*, *Police Story*, *The Young and the Restless* and *The Six-Million-Dollar Man*
- Space-exploring *Pioneer X* produced significant detail of Jupiter and its great red spot
- *The Sting* with Paul Newman and Robert Redford captured the Academy Award for Best Picture
- Popular movies included *The Paper Chase*, *Scenes from a Marriage*, *The Last Detail*, *The Exorcist* and *American Graffiti*
- A computerized brain scanner known as CAT was marketed
- Hit songs for the year were "Tie a Yellow Ribbon," "Delta Dawn," "Let's Get It On," "Me and Mrs. Jones," "Rocky Mountain High," "Could It Be I'm Falling in Love?"; Roberta Flack received the Grammy Award for Best Record with "Killing Me Softly with His Song"
- Richard Nixon resigned the presidency of the United States; vice president Gerald Ford became president
- The OPEC oil embargo raised the price of crude oil by 300 percent, causing shortages and long lines at the nation's gasoline pumps
- Bestsellers included *Jonathan Livingston Seagull* by Richard Bach, *Once Is Not Enough* by Jacqueline Susann, *Breakfast of Champions* by Kurt Vonnegut, Jr. and *I'm O.K., You're O.K.* by Thomas Harris
- Words and phrases entering popular usage were Skylab, juggernaut, biofeedback, ego trip, let it all hang out, and nouvelle cuisine
- The "pet rock" fad captured the imagination of America

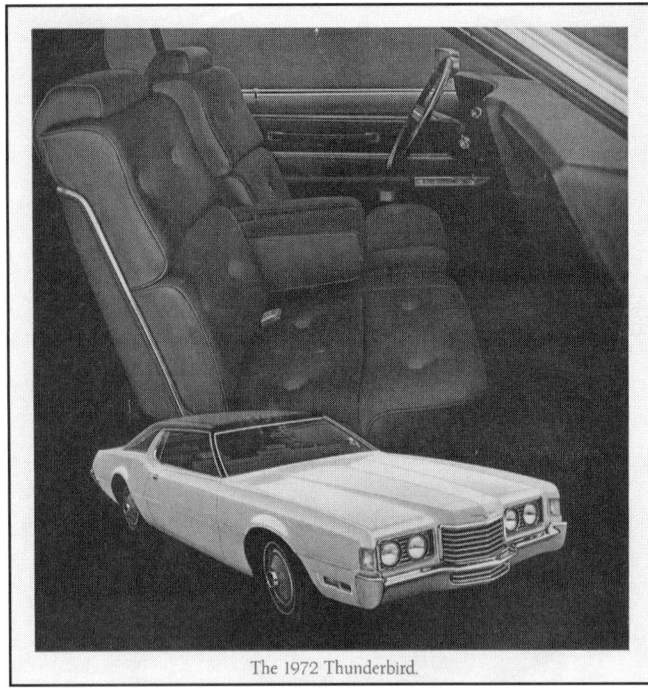

The 1972 Thunderbird.

1973 Economic Profile

Selected Prices

Bicycle $56.00
Biofeedback Monitoring Kit. $125.50
Book, *Breakfast of Champions*. $7.95
Cassette Tapes, Three-Pack. $1.99
Cigarettes. $0.42
Crayola Crayons, Box of 48 . . . . $3.09
Excedrin, 100 Count. $0.89
Levi's Jeans $11.25
Hairspray, Adorn. $1.09
Life Vest. $20.59
Metal Detector $19.95
Safari, East Africa $1,519.00
The Chicago Tribune, Daily $0.10
Time, Yearly Subscription. $16.00
Wig, Valmor High Fashion $29.99

You Receive

2 GIANT BATTLEFIELDS a total size of 3 square feet. (Six Islands in the Pacific Ocean beautifully colored.)

88 PIECE TASK FORCE IN GRAY & GREEN

4 AIRCRAFT CARRIERS 24 PLANES
4 DESTROYERS 8 LANDING BARGES
4 BATTLESHIPS 4 HEADQUARTERS
16 TANKS WITH MOVEABLE TURRETS
24 PILL BOXES

These unbreakable 3-D metallic plastic toys are authentically scaled and each is realistically proportioned to the giant battlefields.

375 RED MARKERS—enough to record the massive bombings and shellings.

Simple directions for a tense battle on land, sea and air. The general best able to strategically place his forces and direct his firing will be the only survivor of this terrific battle.

There is no imagination necessary here!! You get the equipment, the battlefield and the rules on how to Locate, Occupy and Destroy the enemy. This is not just another juvenile game, it is actually played and tremendously enjoyed by over 200,000 people including members of our real Armed Forces.

TASK FORCE

$1.89 ea. PLUS POSTAGE

NOW! ALL FULL SCALE BATTLE GAMES PROCESSED IN 48 HOURS & SHIPPED IN HANDSOME SIMULATED BOOK FORM-ONLY!

EXPLODING BRIDGES ACTUALLY BLOW APART RIGHT OFF THE RIVER

YOU RECEIVE

A COMPLETE GAME

• A GIANT 3 SQUARE FOOT PLASTIC BATTLEFIELD in color, depicting Chickamauga "the river of death" appropriately named by Indians as 34,400 troops were killed or wounded there..
• 1 HUGE REALISTIC CONFEDERATE STOCKADE FORT
• 4 STOCKADE GATES — open to attack — close for defense.
• 1 HUGE REALISTIC UNION STOCKADE FORT
• 4 SHELTERED OBSERVATION TOWERS* • 2 FORT FLAGS with masts
• 6 FIELD CANNONS* — 12 spoked wheels
• 2 ARMIES* 64 Troops in Blue and Grey, fully equipped and in all battle positions
• 25 RED TNT BOXES • FORT COMMANDER • 6 EXPLODING BRIDGES*
• SIMPLE DIRECTIONS for fighting your way across the battlefield with enough men and equipment to attack and capture the enemy fort.

*3-D plastic-safe and reusable.

2 FORTS

TASK FORCE sells in stores for $5.00. We offer it to you for the amazingly low price of $1.49. We omitted the bulky box, wholesaler and retailer. ACT NOW to save $3.51.

CANNON BALL

THIS GAME IS DEDICATED TO FIGHTING HEROES OF CHICKAMAUGA.

BLUE & GREY

HELEN OF TOY, CO.
Commack, New York 11725

NO C.O.D.'s
DEPT. 254-C1

Please RUSH me the item(s) I have checked. I have added the proper postage & price and enclosed the correct total. I may return each item in 10 days for a refund if they don't beat games costing 3x as much!!

☐ TASK FORCE COMPLETE GAME ______ $1.89
☐ SPECIAL!! Complete game and 88 extra toys (total of 176 toys) ______ $2.69
☐ CANNON BALL COMPLETE GAME ______ $2.39
☐ SPECIAL!! Complete game plus 6 cannon 4 sentry posts—6 exploding bridges ______ $2.89

U.S.A.: add [illegible] postage to each item checked above.
Canada-Foreign: add [illegible]—International M.O. or cash

NAME ______
ADDRESS ______
CITY ______ STATE ______ ZIP ______
N.Y. ADD TAX

ORDER TODAY TO RECEIVE FREE! A "CHESS" GAME PLUS A CATALOG WITH EACH ORDER - Please don't delay your order(s) by forgetting to ADD POSTAGE to price on EACH of the items ordered!

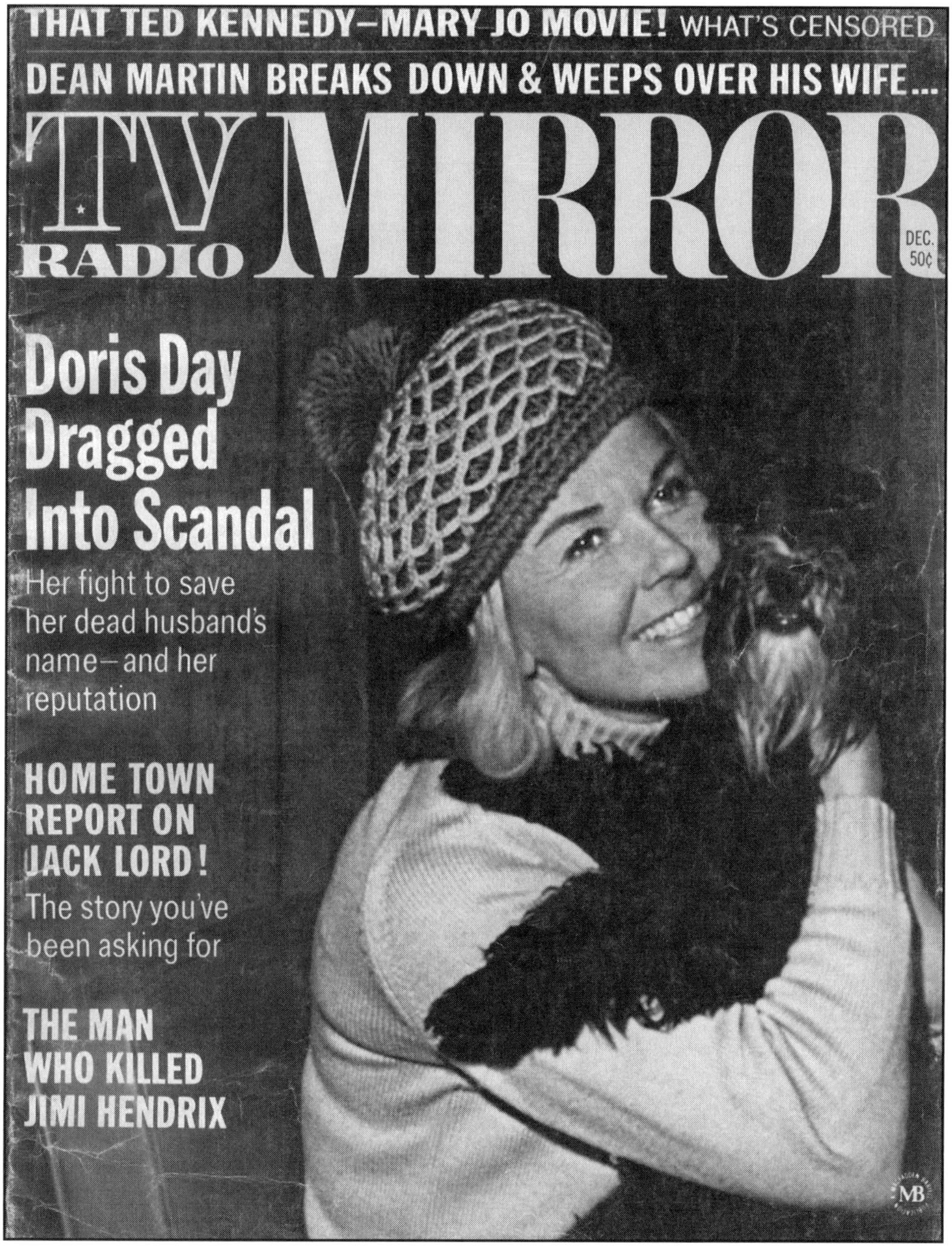

THAT TED KENNEDY–MARY JO MOVIE! WHAT'S CENSORED

DEAN MARTIN BREAKS DOWN & WEEPS OVER HIS WIFE...

TV RADIO MIRROR

DEC. 50¢

Doris Day Dragged Into Scandal

Her fight to save her dead husband's name—and her reputation

HOME TOWN REPORT ON JACK LORD!

The story you've been asking for

THE MAN WHO KILLED JIMI HENDRIX

CHRISTMAS
CLUB
TIME
JOIN NOW!
we pay
4½%

Changing America

- Heinz Kohut's book, *Analysis of the Self*, emphasized self-worth rather than instinctual drives, a challenge to current psychoanalytic theory.
- The United States Supreme Court ruled that employment advertisements could no longer specify gender.
- A cigarette-pack-size electronic brain-wave reader was developed that could detect and signal lapses in concentration.
- The median sales price of a single-family house was $28,900, up from $20,000 in 1968.
- Oregon became the first state to decriminalize marijuana.

"The 'Weaker Sex' Comes on Strong," *Life*, May 19, 1972:

"Women," declares University of California physiologist Jack Wilmore, "have been pampered too long. Most of them would like to be stronger than they are." Wilmore, who teaches physical education at the Davis campus, believes there is no reason why women cannot be, pound for pound, just as strong as men. Nor need they fear any unsightly bulges. All they need to do is work out regularly with barbells, and depend on their naturally low level of the hormone testosterone to keep them from looking like Mr. America.

It wasn't all that easy getting girls to sign up for Weight Lifting I, so that Wilmore could test his theories. In fact, only four showed up for his first class last fall. But when he changed the name of the course to "Weight Training for Figure Control" and began spreading the word about how nicely his students were shaping up, candidates began flocking in. This term he has 200 co-eds grunting and groaning in the Davis Gym. Some of them have found that they doubled their strength in a single quarter. Meanwhile, Wilmore is keeping a close watch with his tape measures and calipers on the general distribution of adipose tissue and muscle.

Students choose Wilmore's weightlifting class for a variety of reasons. Some of the recruits obviously want to shed fat. A few say that their boyfriends urged them to try it. Others, like Natalie Nickerson, think, "It's neat to do something that girls aren't supposed to do."

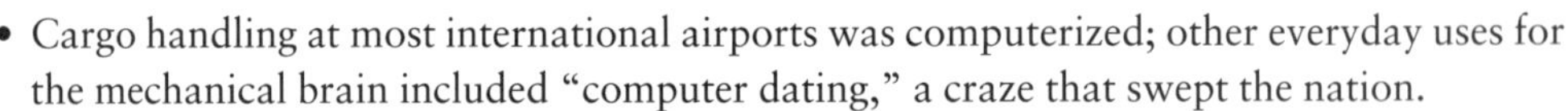

- Cargo handling at most international airports was computerized; other everyday uses for the mechanical brain included "computer dating," a craze that swept the nation.
- More than 80 percent of General Motors cars were equipped with radial tires, up from 11 percent two years earlier.
- The percentage of foreign-born Americans fell to 4.7 percent.
- With one out of three meals eaten away from home, approximately one-quarter of the family food budget was spent in restaurants.
- Frederick Smith, son of the founder of Dixie Greyhound, invested $72 million in a mail service to deliver international packages within 24 hours; for $5 a package customers could buy Federal Express service.
- Fifty rock stars earned from $2 to $6 million a year.
- An estimated 600,000 people attended the Watkins Glen Rock Music Festival to hear the Grateful Dead and the Allman Brothers.
- The American Psychiatric Association revised its categorization of homosexuality, saying it was no longer considered a mental disorder.
- The Supreme Court allowed the use of local, not national standards to define when pornography is obscene.
- The University of Miami provided an athletic scholarship to a woman.
- Interest grew in Pentecostal and charismatic religions, as well as Eastern movements such as Hare Krishna, Zen and *I Ching*.

"What's Troubling High School Students?" *Today's Education*, September 1970:

Last spring, the editors of *Today's Education* invited seven secondary school students—six juniors and one senior—to come to our offices and discuss topics that trouble high school students today. The group—a cross-section of American youth—includes representatives from various racial groups, and urban, suburban and rural areas.

The seven are Jim Anderson, Falls Church, Virginia; Sue Arshack, Silver Spring, Maryland; Marsha Babcock, Omaha, Nebraska; Bob Dieterle, Nutley, New Jersey; Sandi Garcia, Nogales, Arizona; Tonya Kneece, Batesburg, South Carolina; and Eric Ward, Philadelphia, Pennsylvania.

Eric Ward: Basically, my school has the same problems that exist in all of our schools. There has to be a change in the traditional ways of education, and it has to come soon.

Students are being turned off. Young people today are not going to sit around and wait. They're going to make people pay attention even if it means tearing up books or setting buildings on fire.

Jim Anderson: Are you advocating violence to make the change?

Eric: No. I'm saying that this is what many of today's young cats have been doing in order to get what they want and that society must find some answers and listen to these cats, because things are not going to get any easier.

Bob Dieterle: You stress the need for change. That seems to be the trend today, that everything has to be changed, that everything has to be new. I don't quite understand why things have to be changed.

Eric: Well, probably if you came from a school like mine, you'd understand. If you went to school every morning and you walked into a dark building—I mean, totally dark—and you walked down a long hallway that looks like a subway, you'd understand. There's an atmosphere of unrest, dissent. Students are disgusted. They're frustrated.

When you're in a classroom with 50 other students, your teacher just cannot work with you individually. Then, at lunchtime, you go down to a lunchroom which is not a lunchroom. It's just some dingy place where they serve you food.

Is this fair to today's young people? I don't feel that students should have to come into what I call a subway system every morning. They should be able to come into a decent building.

But a new building isn't the answer to all educational problems. Teachers should be the kind of people who want to teach kids and really try to motivate them. And I think that teachers like that would turn the kids on.

Tonya Kneece: As Eric was saying, teachers have to try to relate to their students—and not only in class. If a teacher cares about his students, cares about their personal problems, kids go into his classroom knowing this and wanting to study under him.

But I think the bigger problem is the curriculum. We have teachers in my school who have been teaching the same thing for years and years.

Jim: High school prepares you for college. Right? Now, what type of course do you want?

Eric: I agree with you. The courses today do prepare you for college, but we need courses to teach you how to get along with each other. That's something that's got to be done, because people are not getting along. Let's face it. The conditions in this country are coming to a point where pretty soon things are going to blow. So, teaching people how to work with each other is important.

Not every kid in school is going to college. What about the kid who cannot read and cannot make it to college? We cannot forget them. I feel courses should be geared to relate to what all students need.

Sue Arshack: Saying that school is to prepare us for college is the biggest mistake we can possibly make. I think schools should also prepare

(continued)

"What's Troubling High School Students?" (*continued*)

us to live in the world rather than just prepare us for college.

Marsha Babcock: That's why I think the schools should offer more vocational courses than they do.

Jim: Do your schools have vocational courses?

Eric: Yeah. We have five vocational schools where students can go.

Marsha: In our city, they offer an electronics course. It's small; very few kids are in it. But I've gone down there and it's really neat.

Jim: Do you all know what an EFFE program is? EFFE means Experiment in Free Form Education. We're going to have one of these programs at my school. We'll drop all our old classes and set up experimental classes in anything we want.

Bob: We have something like that called May courses. Students suggest things they would like to study. Like, say, you wanted a subject on the stock market. You'd suggest it. Then, the subjects that get the most votes are put into the curriculum. Classes meet once a week. Kids can come out of the study halls or free periods and go to these classes. There's no homework, and kids get a pass or fail grade.

Jim: Are EFFE and May courses what you have in mind?

Eric: No. I think maybe you're missing what we're saying. We're not saying that we want to just drop everything that's been traditionally taught in school. But what we're saying—history, for example. We're taught what was done in the Civil War, what was done in the time of Columbus.

This is fine. We have to have a background. But what we're saying is: Why don't schools teach people what's happening in Vietnam? I mean, like why?

Sue: That kind of discussion makes people think, and who knows—?

Eric: Amen.

Jim: Do you think schools are trying to be repressive? Stop you from thinking?

Sue: I don't know that they're trying to be repressive, but I think the whole system is set up in a way that leads to repression. Schools too often are not places for creative, expanded thinking, and one week of an EFFE program is tokenism—that's not what the whole year is about.

Sandi Garcia: I'm just noting the differences in our schools. Like my school is really bad. Have you ever seen army barracks? That's what we have for some of our classes. We don't have anything like some of the classes you've been talking about. We'll have four years of English and we'll have algebra, geometry, and that's it.

We don't have any protests or anything. But we're situated right on the border of Mexico, and we have a really big problem in drugs. Probably because of the big flow from Mexico. Parents don't even let their kids out anymore because of the drug scare.

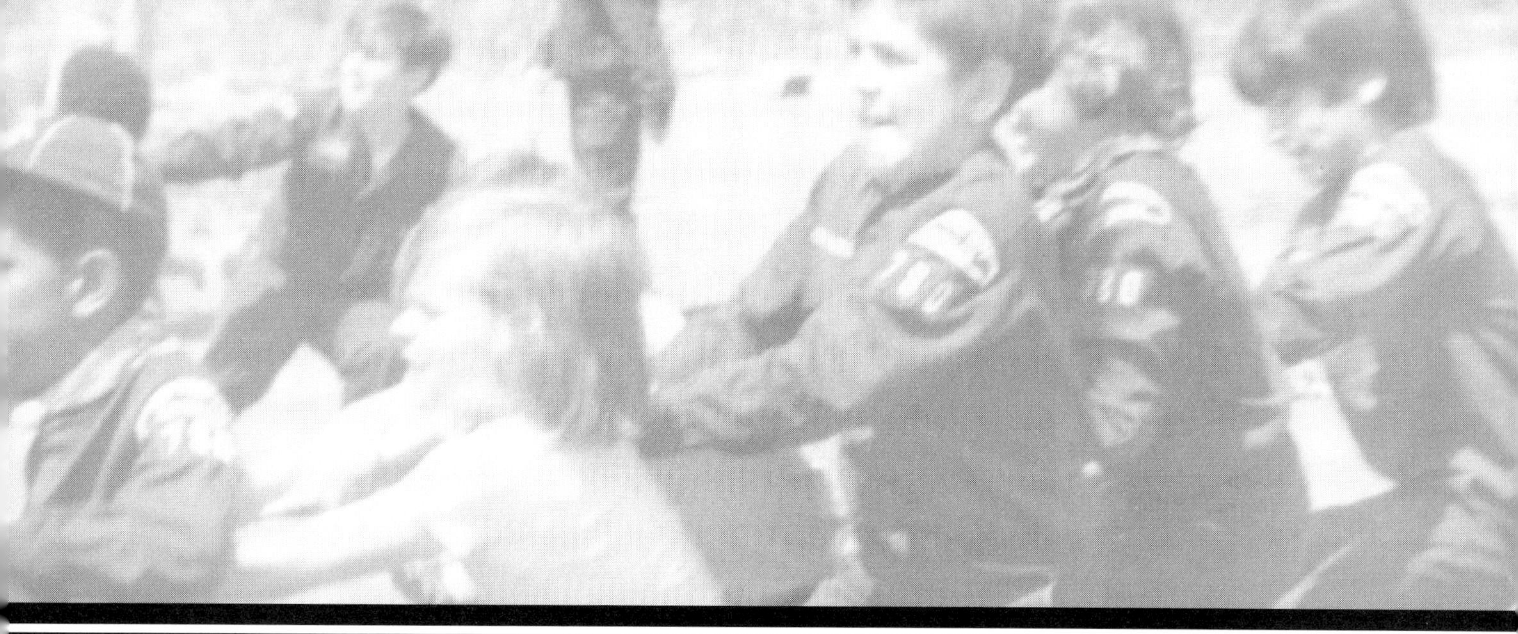

1977 Profile

Middle Class

Raised by a single mother, eight-year-old Maria Genovese is learning to fly kites, wash dishes and gossip with her best friend Barbara in Buffalo, New York.

Life at Home

- Eight-year-old Maria Genovese and her mother Anne live in an urban renewal housing project on the shores of Lake Erie, on the lower west side of Buffalo, New York.
- Maria attends a nearby elementary school and spends most afternoons at a daycare center organized by her mother, who is now in her second year as an attorney for the Erie County Department of Social Services.
- Her specialty is child welfare; one of her most demanding tasks is determining which children should be removed from their homes because of abuse, neglect, or inadequate food.
- Maria has never met her father, who is rarely mentioned, and she has learned not to ask too many questions.
- Shortly after they moved to the area, Maria's mother led a committee of parents to form an after-school daycare program at the housing complex.
- When school is over at 2 p.m., children from throughout the area are brought to the facility to study, play, watch TV or wrestle until their parents arrive.
- Like Maria, several of the children live with only their mothers; most see their fathers occasionally, some as often as weekly.
- Maria likes the center, especially since her mother is always busy and nearly always late getting home from court.
- She has dozens of friends at the center, and often they construct intricate games or work on art projects together.

Maria Genovese lives with her mother in Buffalo, New York.

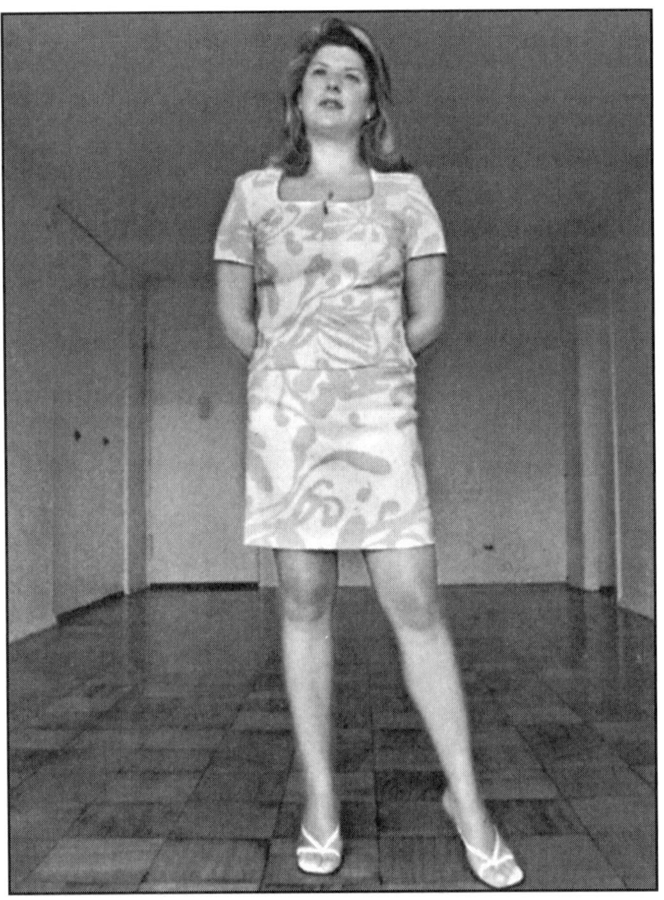
Maria's mother worked her way through school.

- Occasionally, with her mother's written permission, they have gone on field trips, which are tremendous fun as long as everyone behaves, holds hands crossing the street and keeps quiet when the leader is talking.
- Maria hates for adults to get mad and scold the children.
- Maria's mother Anne grew up in a strong Catholic household in Queens.
- She attended parochial school, lived to watch *American Bandstand* with her friends, talked endlessly about guys and argued about what a boy was actually doing when he reached "second base"—and whether or not she would like that.
- In college she confronted a much wider—and wilder—world away from the protection of her home.
- She realized how sheltered she had been and concluded that she was letting down her country by not speaking out concerning the war in Vietnam.
- With some encouragement from her new friends, she felt it her duty to protest, often and loud.
- Quickly, she absorbed literature she had never seen in her home, regularly reading radical newspapers such as *The Great Speckled Bird* and discussing concepts of war and sacrifice well into the night—occasionally to the detriment of her studies.
- She also fell in love with her soul mate, a man who shared her views and took her seriously.
- During the last days of her sophomore year, her boyfriend left the United States for Canada to escape the draft.

Maria has a wide range of friends.

- Two weeks later she discovered she was pregnant with Maria.
- She wrote to her boyfriend repeatedly with the news, but never received a response.
- An abortion was unthinkable; her own father disowned her and forbade anyone in the family from speaking to her ever again.
- After the baby was born, Anne and little Maria attended college together, living on welfare, school loans, part-time jobs and a small trust fund set up two decades earlier by Anne's grandfather.
- Anne finished college with a degree in social work, a badly bruised ego, lots of student debt and a two-year-old child.
- Somehow, law school seemed the logical next step, so Anne and Maria went through it together, studying every minute of the day.
- Now Anne thinks she can make a difference and make up for lost time with Maria.
- Poverty, unemployment, underemployment, rage and frustration are among the many issues Anne confronts each day on the job.
- Often after saving Buffalo's children, Anne has little time for her own, but pushes on.
- She worries a lot about whether she is a good parent, even while in the midst of organizing another project for the community.
- As a special treat, she and Maria recently stayed up night after night to watch every episode of the television miniseries *Roots*.
- Though Anne kept telling her what each scene meant, Maria didn't care about the history or who was wronged; she just loved the story and watching TV with her mom.

"Dilemma for Working Mothers: Not Enough Daycare Centers," *U.S. News & World Report*, April 12, 1976:

From small towns to big cities across the U.S., there's increasing need for facilities to look after the children of the multitude of mothers who work outside the home. This need, it turns out, is not being adequately met.

One of the big reasons is spiraling costs.

In the last five years, the number of commercially operated daycare centers has quadrupled, but profits remain low and some centers now are being squeezed out by rising costs. Others are shelving expansion plans. Government regulations are piling up.

Many others are finding that, after paying for the care of their children while they work, there's little profit in holding a job. . . .

All told, according to a trade group known as the National Association for Child Development and Education, there are about 13,000 commercial daycare centers in the United States.

These range from large chains run by well-known corporations to tiny "mom and pop" places quartered in the owners' living rooms.

These enterprises share one goal—to meet the growing demand for dependable child care and to profit from it.

"There's no question the market is out there, and it is substantial because there is a tremendous need," says Richard J. Grassgreen, executive vice president of Kinder-Care Learning Centers, Inc., of Montgomery, Alabama. His firm, which operates 124 centers in 17 states, is still expanding, with plans for 19 new centers in May.

According to the New York-based Child Welfare League of America, about 33 million children up to age 18 need some form of daycare while their mothers work. An estimated seven million are under school age.

Yet, the league estimates, only about 4.3 million spaces now exist in daycare facilities, with something like one million available to preschool children.

Despite this gap, daycare has not proved to be the easy road to riches that some operators hoped it would be.

For one thing, the ability of working women to pay for child care is limited. Women's pay averages only $7,124 per year, while high-quality daycare can cost $2,000 a year or more.

Another problem: Federal subsidies for daycare—although already in the billions of dollars—have not expanded as quickly as anticipated. And Congress has imposed stiff quality-control standards that operators are finding expensive to meet.

Life at School

- Most mornings, Maria walks to her second-grade class, only five blocks away.
- Even though the newspapers have been filled with stories about the integration of schools, she has seen little change; everyone in her class is white.
- Her mother says that will change soon; a judicial order recently handed down will require that black children from the east side of Main Street be bussed into her school this fall when she starts the third grade.
- Maria has heard several of the mothers talk about moving to the suburbs where there are few blacks.
- Anne, on the other hand, is excited that the black children will have an opportunity to get a better education, and has talked endlessly about what a great learning experience Maria will have going to school with black children.

There is plenty of snow in Buffalo.

- Maria doesn't care as long as she gets to attend school; she loves learning and reading and being with her friends.
- Going to school is simply heaven, particularly her handwriting class, where the teacher consistently says her work is among the best.
- At night, when alone, Maria endlessly practices her cursive strokes and prepares entire pages of script, simply for her own satisfaction.
- She also loves owning a calculator—a gift from her mother on her birthday in February.
- She is not allowed to use it at school, because calculators are banned there, and considered an inappropriate shortcut.
- But she uses it at home to add up everything; last week she added up every telephone number on one page of the phone book, just for fun.
- When asked by her mother's friends, "Are you going to be a lawyer like your mother when you grow up?" she says she wants to be a mathematician, which always draws praise.
- She is not really sure what a mathematician does all day except play with a calculator.
- Maria also loves to talk, especially with her friend Barbara who lives next door and is a year older.
- Barbara knows everything, even things about boys, because she has brothers.

Maria loves school and being with her friends.

"It's 1986 and Every Student Has a Calculator," by George Immerzeel, *Instructor*, April 1976:

(Pretend) The year is 1986. I have been using calculators in my classroom for some time now. I have had a few difficulties, but as I look back on my experiences, it has been fun and certainly worthwhile. All of my students are prepared for today's world because everyone in 1986 is using a calculator. Let me share some of these experiences with you.

Years ago I started with one calculator in the fifth- and sixth-grade math learning center. The students liked to play with the machine and soon learned to add, subtract, multiply and divide on it without help from me. Once in a while I took a few minutes to have the students share what they were learning using the calculator. When one of the students asked me how to find the square root of two, I knew it was time to use the machine in my teaching. I found if I gave the class a calculator problem-of-the-week, I stimulated a great deal of interest.

The students themselves began to bring in their own problems. One student asked how high the 17 billion hamburgers sold by a hamburger chain would be if they were piled on top of one another. Still another asked how many steers were required to provide the hamburgers. The students really took an interest in developing their own problems, and each problem had a way of leading to others.

I soon found that having one student at the calculator was an asset during our class discussions. That "machine student" could easily generate many examples when we wanted to learn to multiply by 10 or 100. The students soon learned that they could multiply by a power of 10 and it was easier to do without the calculator. . . .

When I was correcting papers I found that using the calculator provided a handy answer key. It also helped me when students gave me fractional answers that were not in the lowest terms. The calculator made it easier for me to analyze student mistakes. I could quickly generate partial products for multiplication and compare them with the student computation. The calculator was also very useful to me when I was making up new worksheets for student activities with the calculator.

It must have been right after Christmas of 1975 when many students started bringing their own calculators to class. We found lots of new ways to use them. It was about then, too, that the PTA became interested in our "real" mathematics and bought us six more calculators, so we had one for each team of four students. These were a big help in extending our classroom activities.

- She also knows which songs are cool and has her own record player in her room.
- Thanks to Barbara, Maria learned that continuing to wear Mickey Mouse panties was baby stuff and should stop immediately.
- Just being around Barbara makes Maria feel grown up.
- When they are together, Anne calls them the "giggle girls."
- Several days this winter, school has been cancelled because of snow.
- Buffalo has experienced 47 consecutive days of snow, and not only was school cancelled, it was too cold even to go outside.
- For the past several months, Anne has been dating Joe Notvitski, a sociology professor who lives nearby.
- A native of Michigan and a Vietnam War veteran, he is attending college on the G.I. Bill, and will eventually earn a Ph.D.

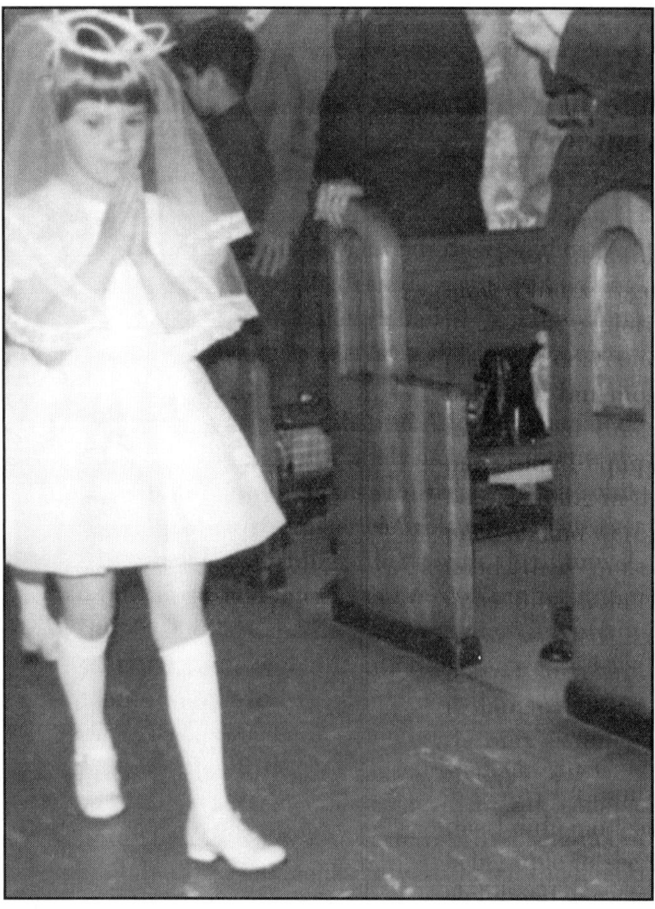

Christmas is a special time for Maria.

- Maria loves having him around.
- Because of his flexible class schedule, he occasionally comes by the daycare center around 4 p.m. and takes Maria to the park and other places.
- With Anne's permission, the two have explored the Buffalo Museum of Science, the Albright-Knox Art Gallery and her favorite, the Buffalo Zoo.
- Mr. Notvitski has even promised to rent a boat and take her sailing on Lake Erie.
- Twice they have flown kites together; Mr. Notvitski can make his kite dive like a rocket and then jump back into the sky at just the right moment.
- They also wash dishes together—Mr. Notvitski says he doesn't need a dishwashing machine as long as Maria is around—and sometimes they fix meals.
- Without being asked, he has taken her to her favorite movie, *Rocky*, three times—more than any of her friends—and she is hoping for a fourth showing.
- Maria is especially pleased that he ignores all the warnings from her mother about eating healthy, and sneaks her a taco on the field trips and a pop tart for breakfast.
- It feels so deliciously wicked to eat a taco behind her mother's back.
- Recently, Maria has been spending even more time with Mr. Notvitski; her mother seems to be called away almost nightly to handle emergencies, but she did not miss Maria's birthday party, which began at their apartment, but then shifted to his house.
- There she opened her presents, including a Bionic Woman doll, from her favorite television show, and a Beauty Salon and Repair Station.
- At Mr. Notvitski's, she also found a sign posted on the door of the spare bedroom where she often sleeps when her mother is away at night.
- Printed in green and white letters on computer paper were the words "Maria's Other Room."
- When she opened the door, she found that he had painted the room pink and hung frilly floral curtains just like in the magazines.

Life in the Community: Buffalo, New York

- Currently, the economic base of Buffalo is drying up due to the opening of the St. Lawrence Seaway, which ended the city's long run as a transportation center.
- The steel and automotive industries, which were a mainstay of the economy, have begun to contract.
- Today, Buffalo's population is shrinking, its unemployment is rising, and the general age of the citizenry is getting older.

"Down and Out in America, In anger and sadness, people in Buffalo tell the story of unemployment," by members of the American Studies Program, SUNY at Buffalo, *The New York Times Magazine*, February 9, 1975:

"I didn't realize it was this bad . . ."

"Poor people are people that you didn't know . . ."

"The government don't give a damn . . ."

"Just a vicious circle of nothing . . ."

"I had seven different jobs . . . every plant closed . . . that's it . . ."

"And this country thinks it's so damn great . . ."

The voices of those of the unemployed in Buffalo, NY. With the national unemployment rate at 7.1 percent, this city on Lake Erie epitomizes the special problems of the country's industrial urban areas. Buffalo's official unemployment in December was 10.3 percent, third-highest in the East.

Even 10.3 percent fails to suggest the full measure of unemployment. The official figure does not include many who, for bureaucratic reasons, are not counted in the eligible workforce. Nor does it include the great number of underemployed who work full-time but need another job to rise above the poverty level.

Further, the official figure is for the entire Standard Metropolitan Statistical Area—in Buffalo's case, a huge two-county tract that includes suburban, ex-urban and even rural areas. The overall figure thus hides the true rate of the heavily populated central city, with its many working class neighborhoods, including those of blacks, whose unemployment rate is double that of whites.

When these dimensions are added, one begins to see the extent of the problem. According to some government statistics, in the urban areas most heavily affected, actual unemployment and underemployment may total well over 60 percent of the labor force, broadly defined. Such a figure is probably closer to Buffalo's reality than the official 10.3 percent.

Buffalo's past prosperity stemmed from transportation advantages—the lake, the Erie Canal, the railroads—and the heavy industry they generated, especially grain milling, steel and automobiles. In recent years, however, these locational advantages have more or less evaporated, and many companies have moved. Buffalo's business leaders have sought to shift the city's base away from factories, but the decline in manufacturing has left a large pool of industrial workers whose skills are unsuited to what new jobs can be generated.

- At the same time, well-intentioned urban renewal projects and threats of desegregation are breaking apart many once-stable ethnic neighborhoods.
- Those who can afford to move into the suburbs are fleeing the city.
- Attempts to stem the tide with a new campus of the University of Buffalo on the lakefront ended with investments going to Amherst instead, making that community the fastest-growing in the state.

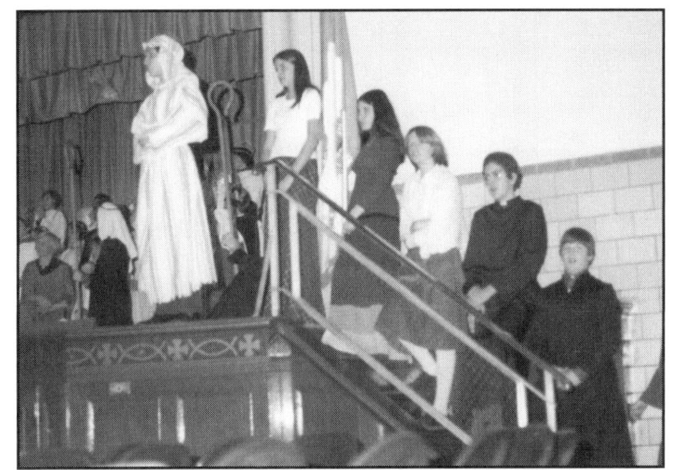

Historical Snapshot
1977

- The United States Supreme Court ruled that the spanking of school children by teachers was constitutional
- Elvis Presley died; two million records were sold within a day of his death
- Grammy Awards were presented to the Eagles for "Hotel California" and to Fleetwood Mac for "Rumours"
- Freddie Prinze, the 22-year-old star of the television hit *Chico and the Man*, committed suicide
- Consumers boycotted coffee because of rising prices
- Movie openings included *Annie Hall*, *The Goodbye Girl*, *Looking for Mr. Goodbar*, *Saturday Night Fever*, *Oh, God!*, and *Pumping Iron*
- Pocket television, a woman referee for a heavyweight championship fight and the use of lethal drugs for capital punishment all made their first appearance
- Hit songs for the year included "Tonight's the Night," "Nobody Does It Better," "Don't Leave Me This Way," the "Theme from Rocky," "Torn between Two Lovers" and the title song of *Star Wars*
- The Dow-Jones Industrial Average peaked at 999 for the year, closing at 800 at year's end
- The television miniseries *Roots* drew 130 million viewers, the largest audience in TV history
- Emmy Awards went to *The Rockford Files* for drama, *All in the Family* for comedy, *The Muppet Show* for variety and *Hollywood Is Grinch Night* for children
- Toni Morrison's *Song of Solomon*, Joan Didion's *A Book of Common Prayer*, John Cheever's *Falconer* and *True Confessions* by John Gregory Dunne were all published
- The first fusion reactions by laser were achieved
- Former president Richard Nixon's appearance for an interview on David Frost's program drew an audience of 45 million viewers
- The Supreme Court ruled that states do not have to use Medicaid funds for elective abortion
- More than 400,000 teenage abortions were performed, comprising one-third of all abortions in the United States
- CB radios achieved cult status as 25 million Americans installed the devices in their cars

1977 Economic Profile

Selected Prices

Bean Bag, Vinyl	$37.95
Bikini Swimsuit	$13.00
Calculator, Cannon Electric, 16 Functions	$29.95
CB Radio	$39.88
Coffee, per Pound	$3.58
Fruit Cake	$6.00
Makeup, Revlon Ultima II	$8.50
Massage Shower Head	$26.95
Maternity Top	$9.00
Movie Ticket	$1.00
Seal-N-Save Food Sealer	$16.49
Stereo Cassette System, Sony	$400.00
Storm Window, Triple Track	$32.95
Viewmaster 3-D	$17.44
Weebles, Horse and Wagon Toy	$2.97

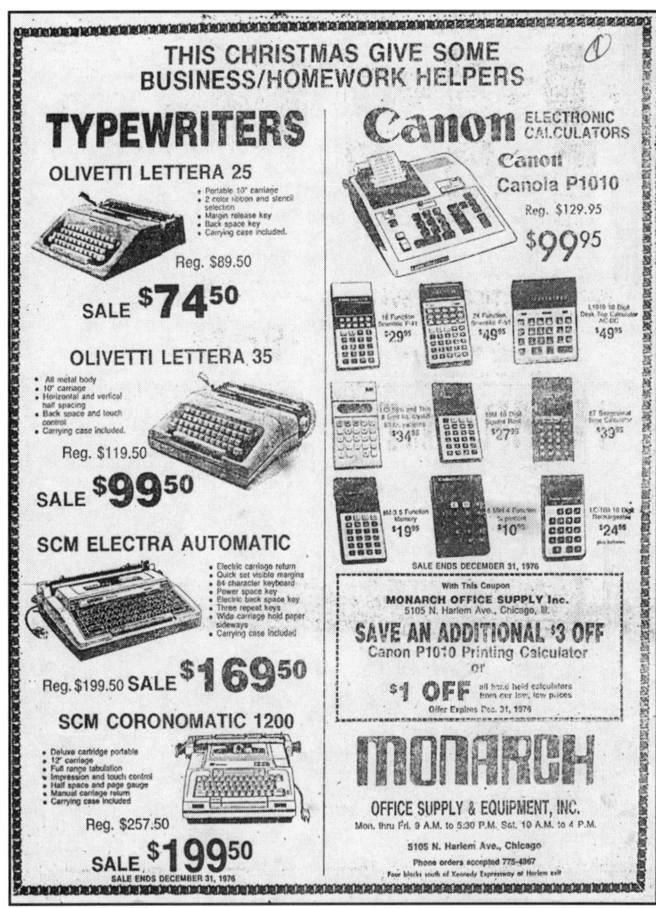

Changing America

- A Princeton University study showed that 6.8 million married couples had elected surgical contraception.
- The FDA banned Red Dye No. 2 as an additive in foods, drugs and cosmetics.
- The Supreme Court reversed a New York law that prohibited the distribution of contraceptives to minors.
- The *Li'l Abner* comic strip ceased publication.
- International tourism broke all records; popular destinations were Venice, London and Paris.
- America's infant mortality was 16.1 per 1,000 births; maternal mortality was 12.8 per 10,000 births.
- Fred M. Hechinger, editor of *The New York Times*, wrote, "The massive failure in basic skills—particularly reading and writing—is nothing short of scandalous."
- Charleston, South Carolina, hosted the new Spoleto Festival U.S.A., which opened with Tchaikovsky's *Pique Dame*.
- Van Gogh's painting *La Fin de la Journée* sold for $880,000.
- A study reported that alcohol consumed during pregnancy may injure the fetus.
- The Japanese car industry employed 7,000 robots for painting, welding and assembly.
- A study showed that only 21 percent of pregnant, unmarried teens chose to give birth, of whom 87 percent decided to keep their children.
- America imported 1.5 million foreign cars, breaking all previous records.
- The popularity of smoke detectors soared, with more than eight million sold.

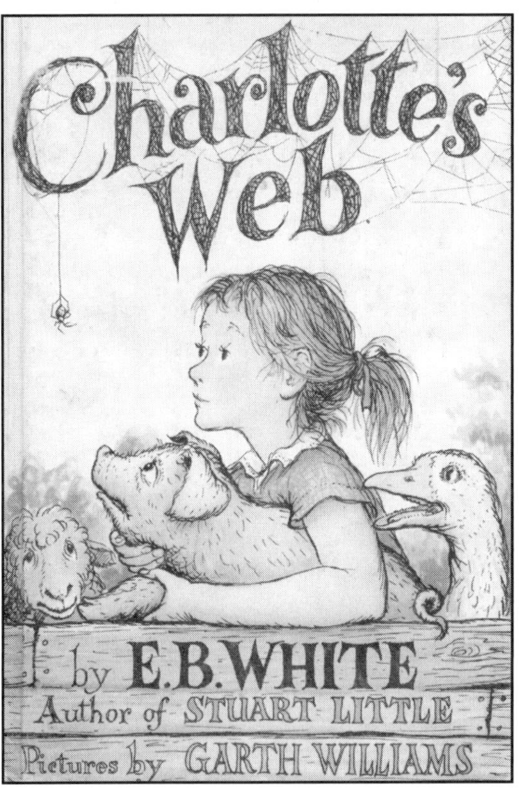

Charlotte's Web *is a favorite children's book.*

"What It's Like—Living in a City Drowning in Snow, Buffalo, New York," *U.S. News & World Report*, February 14, 1977:

Here in this city of 450,000, you face the shattering reality of what it's like to live in the full fury of the worst winter in memory.

Snow of epic proportions has governed the lives of Buffalo's citizens since late November. It determines whether you go to work or not. It decides whether offices, stores, factories and schools are open or closed. And, sometimes, it determines whether you live or die.

The travail started with the worst early-season snowstorm in Buffalo's history, a storm that dumped four feet of snow on some areas. During December, January and into February, the snow continued—for 47 consecutive days.

By February 4, Buffalo had been hit by more than 160 inches of snow—more than 13 feet. Broken were city records for the most snow in one day, most in a week, and most in a month.

Residents, accustomed to gibes from other parts of the country about the "deep-freeze city," took the pummeling in stride, even joking about it. The laughter stopped January 28, when the snow turned into a killer.

Driven by wind gusts of more than 69 miles an hour, more than a foot of snow fell in a blizzard that paralyzed the Buffalo metropolitan area of 1.3 million people. The temperature, measuring the wind-chill factor, dipped to 50 degrees below zero.

Cars, buses and trucks were abandoned on streets by the thousands. Motorists took refuge in office buildings, churches, and fire and police stations. About 13,000 were marooned.

Some of those stranded were not so fortunate. When the winds subsided, police on borrowed snowmobiles toured the streets, checking the abandoned cars, and found the frozen bodies of eight men.

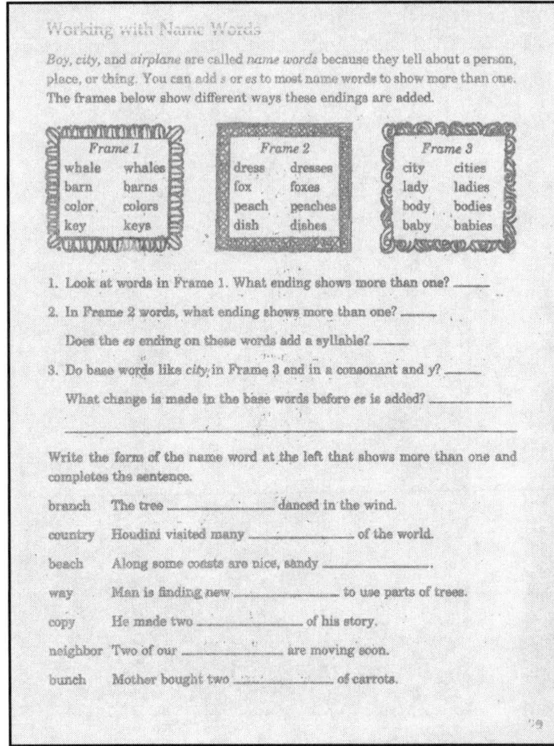

Working with Name Words

Boy, city, and *airplane* are called *name words* because they tell about a person, place, or thing. You can add *s* or *es* to most name words to show more than one. The frames below show different ways these endings are added.

Frame 1	
whale	whales
barn	barns
color	colors
key	keys

Frame 2	
dress	dresses
fox	foxes
peach	peaches
dish	dishes

Frame 3	
city	cities
lady	ladies
body	bodies
baby	babies

1. Look at words in Frame 1. What ending shows more than one? ______
2. In Frame 2 words, what ending shows more than one? ______
   Does the *es* ending on these words add a syllable? ______
3. Do base words like *city*, in Frame 3 end in a consonant and *y*? ______
   What change is made in the base words before *es* is added? ____________

Write the form of the name word at the left that shows more than one and completes the sentence.

branch	The tree ____________ danced in the wind.
country	Houdini visited many ____________ of the world.
beach	Along some coasts are nice, sandy ____________.
way	Man is finding new ____________ to use parts of trees.
copy	He made two ____________ of his story.
neighbor	Two of our ____________ are moving soon.
bunch	Mother bought two ____________ of carrots.

We were smart enough to know we were dumb.

A calculator is not enough. A calculator is not enough. A calculator is not enough. A calculator is not enough. A calculator is not enough A ca

When it comes to making calculators, nobody can touch us.

But helping teachers to teach? That takes a different kind of know-how. And lots of it.

We wanted to give classroom teachers more support than just task cards and wall charts.

So we joined forces with the Encyclopaedia Britannica Educational Corporation and together we sponsored the development of a unique program of teaching aids and student learning aids.

Our software package contains all the tools that nobody else even bothered to think about. Everything from teacher films to student films to a complete multi-media kit with calculators.

The program is designed for grades 4 through 8 and basic high school math classes.

It shows how calculators can be used in the classroom to stimulate a student's interest and understanding of math—without developing a dependency on the calculator.

Every word was written and approved by educators. And it all started with Novus, the people who make more hand-held calculators than anybody else.

For more information, contact Jay Hemming, Educational Services, Novus, 1177 Kern Ave., Sunnyvale, California 94086.

Then decide for yourself how smart we were.

NOVUS // NATIONAL SEMICONDUCTOR

See Materials/Information Listings 141 and 148

1979 Profile

Working Class

Vang Ghia and his Hmong family escaped from Laos into Thailand after the fall of Vietnam and emigrated to Fresno, California, where basketball has become this 12-year-old's greatest obsession.

Life at Home

- Vang Ghia is a 12-year-old Hmong boy living with his family in Fresno, California.
- He is the oldest child of the Vang family, a clan that follows a tradition of using the family name first, the given name second.

Vang Ghia escaped from Laos with his family.

In Fresno, a growing Hmong community is forming.

- His mother, who believes herself to be 37, has had eight other children, six of whom are still living.
- Ghia, his family and another family from the same subclan live together in a two-bedroom apartment on the west side of Fresno.
- The eight members of the Vang family live in one room, sleeping on pallets on the floor.
- The younger children, including their new-born brother, sleep near the adults.
- The new baby is the first child in the family born in the United States, and the first born in a hospital.
- When he was born, the Vangs asked, through a cousin who could speak English, for the baby's placenta.
- The nurse relayed the request to the doctor, who, remembering stories he had heard of rural Asians eating their children's placentas, turned it down immediately.
- The Vangs are very upset at his refusal; in Hmong culture, the placenta of a newborn child is buried with the expectation that, after the child grows up and dies, it will retrace its life steps and then don the placenta—the baby's first jacket—in preparation for rejoining his ancestors and eventually being born again.
- Ghia's parents are afraid that because the placenta was sent away, their child will be forced to wander naked for all of eternity after his death.

Changing Lives of Refugee Hmong Women, by Nancy D. Donnelly, 1994:

Almost the first thing many people told me was of their tragedies (recorded in February 1981, a conversation with Ker):

" 'We walk 32 days from Laos to the river. All is trees. I carry one boy and one boy walk. Chue Neng carry rice. We carry one pan and knife and clothes. We carry silver, also seeds. Little Neng have four years that time, Ly more than two years. Food is not too much.'

I looked at Ker squinting into the warm spring sun, Chue Neng beside her, walking from the garden through the neighborhood of small neat houses. There was a wall of unmortared rocks beside us, well grown with cascades of alyssum. Ker pulled off a bit of green, glancing at me.

'We eat like this. What you call this? Leaves.

'We eat leaves. Everybody eat leaves. There is one leaves, I give to the younger boy and he die. Many people die from that leaves, maybe more than two hundred. We just keep going.' "

- On the third day after the birth, the family held a soul-calling ceremony to name the child; friends were invited to the house and a pig was slaughtered—an invitation for an ancestor to inhabit the child's body.
- Eventually, the name Ger was bestowed upon the child; two chickens were then sacrificed, plucked, eviscerated and boiled.
- All in attendance were delighted to see that the chicken skulls were translucent and the tongues curled backward—signs that the soul of the ancestor is happy to reside in Ger's body and pleased with the name—even though the family has moved far away from its traditional territory and village in Laos.
- Ghia was born in the mountains of Laos where his family farmed, growing beans, melons, yams, corn and vegetables.
- Their most important cash crop was opium poppies.
- Forced to abandon their farm in 1976 because of the Hmong people's historic support of the United States during the Vietnam War, Ghia and his family fled Laos, crossing the Mekong River into Thailand to escape the wrath of the new communist government.
- Two of Ghia's siblings and several other family members died during the arduous trek.
- In Thailand, they lived in a refugee camp, barely able to survive on the meager food supplies, but grateful to be alive.

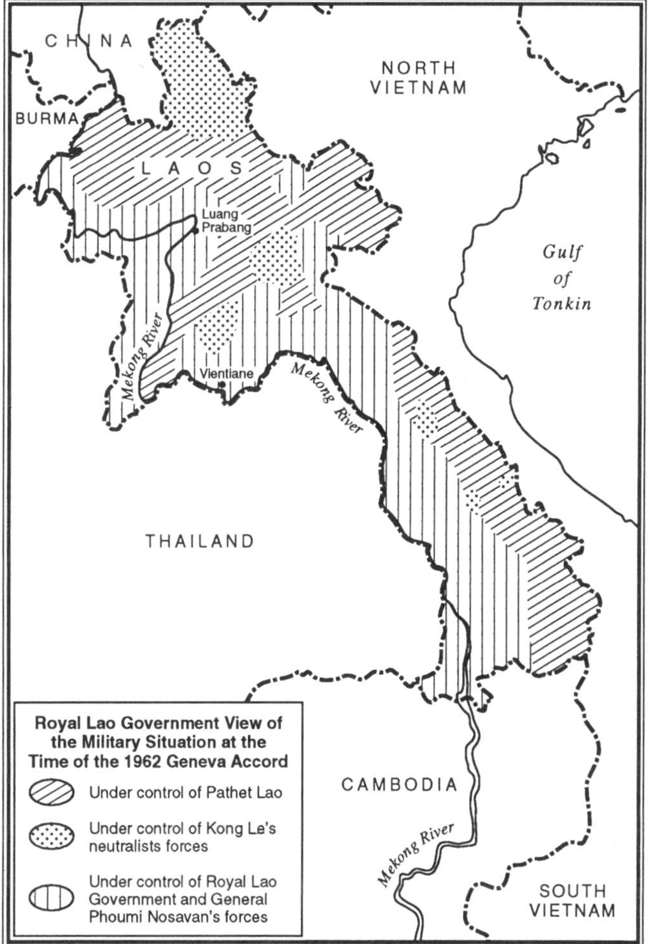

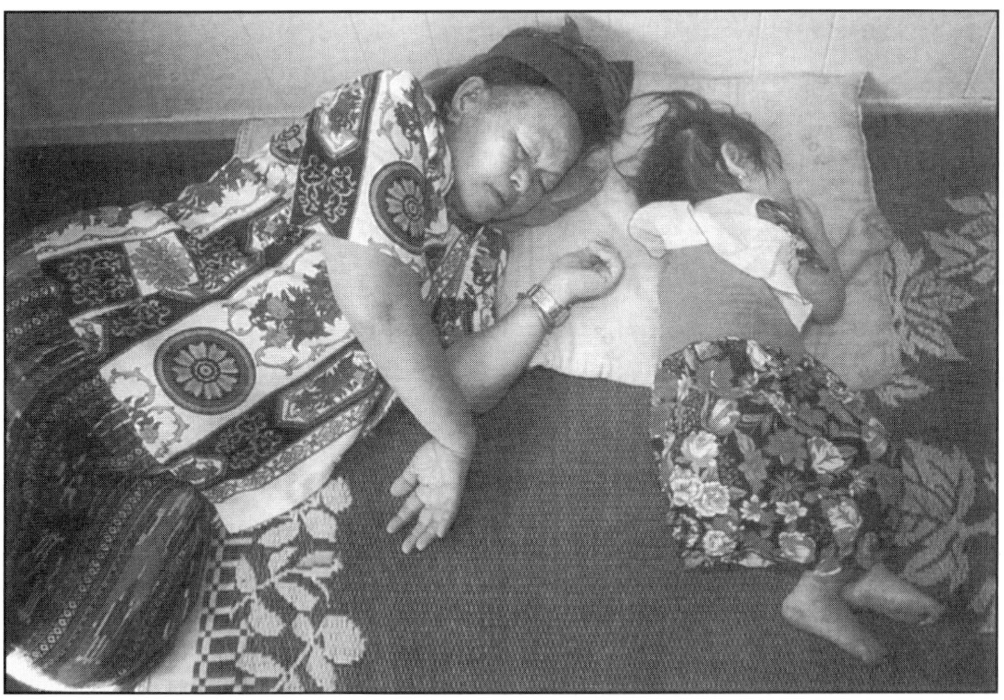

The family sleeps on pallets on the floor.

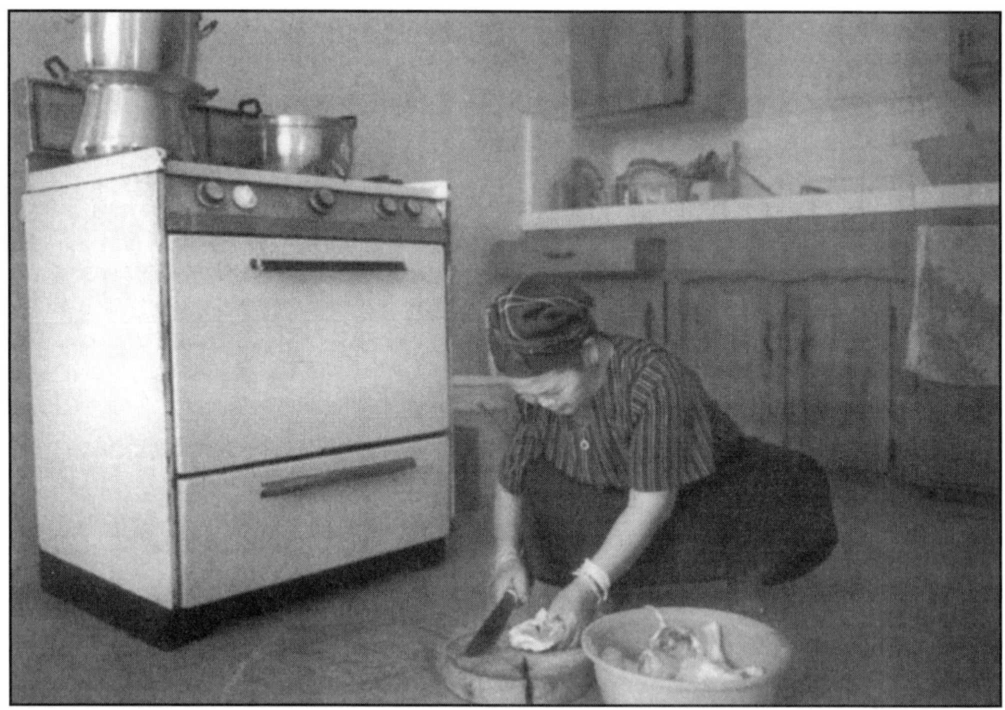

Approximately 40,000 Hmong refugees have emigrated in the past four years.

- There, they met American missionaries who taught Ghia and his other brothers and sisters to speak English.
- In appreciation for their support during the war, Laos Highland refugees, 90 percent of whom are Hmong, have been coming to the United States since 1975.
- Approximately 40,000 Hmong refugees have emigrated in the past four years.
- Earlier this year, three years after they left Laos, the family received permission to enter the United States.
- Their host family found them a place to live on the west side of Fresno, California, where a growing Hmong community is forming, including many members of the Vang clan.
- When they arrived in Fresno, Ghia's parents were not only unable to speak English, but were also labeled illiterate in their own language; the Hmong did not have an alphabet until the 1950s.
- Thanks to the missionaries in the refugee camps and hard work, the older children can read and write in English, and often served as translators for their parents during the early days in the United States.
- The family initially survived with the help of public assistance checks after Ghia's father was unable to find work.
- Recently, Ghia's mother joined with several of the other local Hmong women in sewing intricate story cloths, which tell of life in their village and the exodus to Thailand.
- The ready market for story cloths is helping the family meet its needs, but finding work for Ghia's father has been more difficult.
- His skills as an Asian farmer do not transfer well into the highly mechanized agribusiness world of Fresno, where a good knowledge of machinery, chemicals and English is a necessity.
- He and several of the other Hmong men in the apartment complex have started a large garden on nearby vacant land, growing a variety of fruits and vegetables for their families to eat.

The Hmong women sew intricate story cloths, which tell of village life in Laos.

- No one is certain to whom the land belongs; it was not a consideration, since the concept of private land ownership is rarely practiced by the Hmong people.

Life at School

- Ghia is attending the seventh grade at a public school.
- When he first arrived, his skills, especially in conversational English, were far behind those of his American classmates.
- The two children from his American host family provide regular tutoring, and he has worked hard to catch up.

Ghia has worked hard to learn English so he can do well in school.

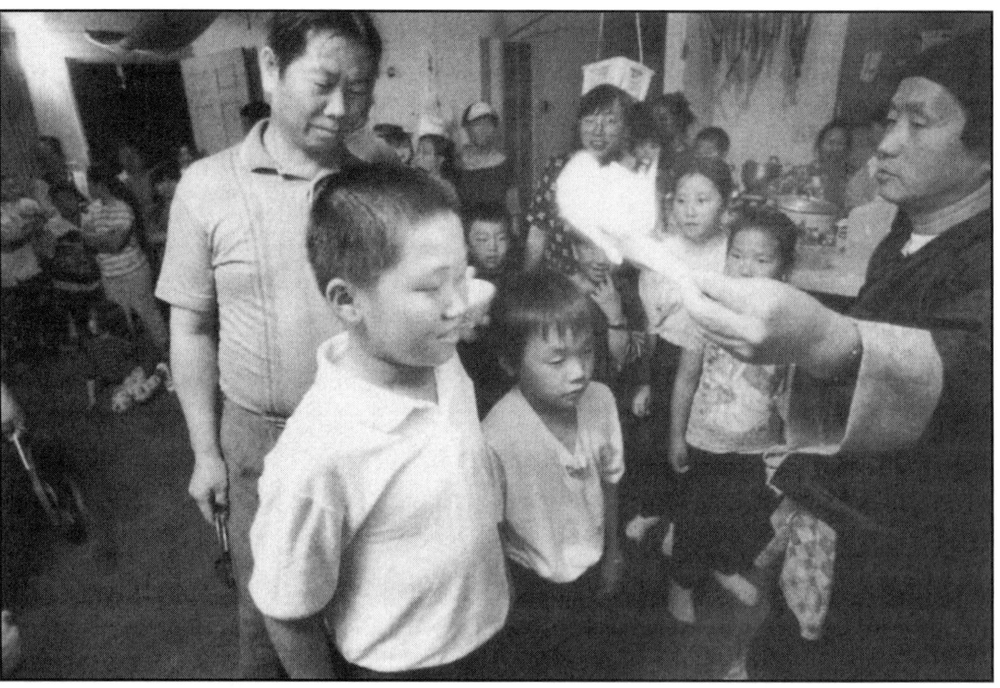

Most of his time is spent with other Hmong children.

- He understands most of what is said in class, but confusion still arises.
- At first, when his new friends said things like, "See you later," he thought it was an invitation for another meeting.
- Some days, he hung around after school for several anxious hours attempting to fulfill his obligation to "see you later."
- His fellow classmates are a diverse group, including African-Americans, Mexicans, Chinese and a few whites.
- He has encountered few problems and less prejudice than he had expected, although the majority of his time is spent with the other Hmong kids, who share his language, problems and background.
- While still in Thailand, he learned about many aspects of American culture, including basketball, with which he has become obsessed.
- Currently, he plays for the middle school B team.
- Even though he rarely gets to play in a game, his family comes to every home game and cheers wildly when he is on the court.
- The coach says he has natural talent and that with practice, he will catch up with the boys who have been playing the game their entire lives.
- Though Ghia has adapted rapidly to American life, the transition for his parents continues to be more difficult.
- Issues such as cars, paved streets, neon signs, traffic lights and airplanes continually upset them.
- In Laos, his father possessed great instincts of where he was in the jungle and how to return home, no matter how dense the vegetation.
- In Fresno, he rarely goes more than a few blocks from home without taking a child to guide him back.
- Once, the police brought him home after he had gotten lost and wandered the streets for hours.

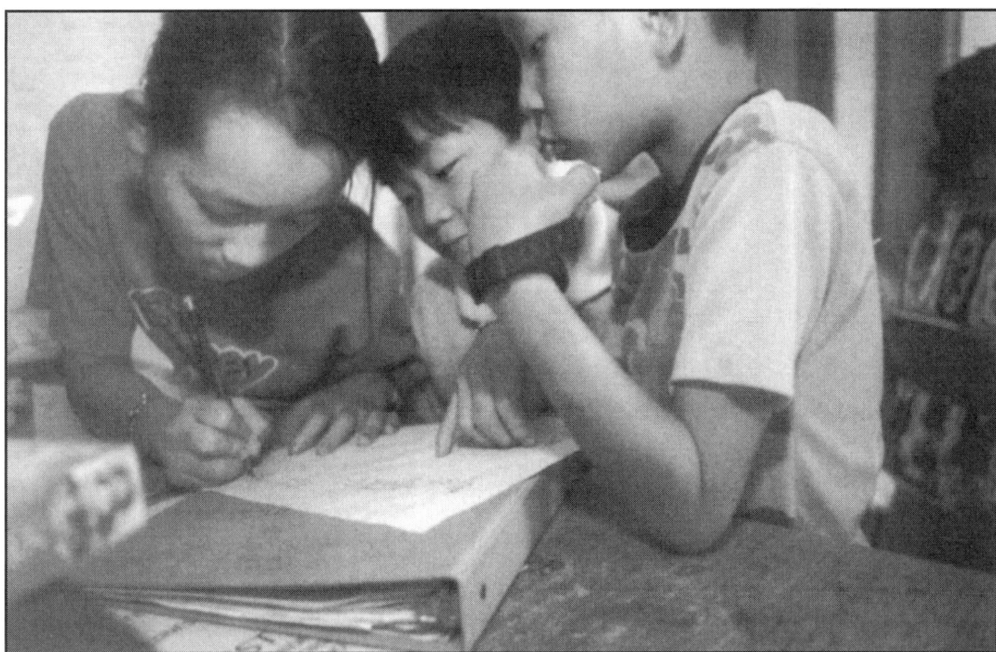

The transition to American life can be difficult.

- Afraid and unable to communicate with the policeman, Ghia's father showed the police the telephone number for their host family, who helped in the rescue mission.
- Afterward, he was withdrawn and declined to talk with his family for days.
- He often sits in the community garden for hours, staring at the horizon; in Hmong culture, the man is always the leader, working and providing for his family.
- The Vang family has contacted a local shaman to assist in the job search; thus far, several animals have been sacrificed, with no result.
- The host family is concerned that he might be considering suicide.
- At Thanksgiving, when the host family held a traditional American dinner for the new Asian immigrants, everyone except Ghia's father piled into the host family's station wagon and headed across town.
- Upon entering the home, they were struck by the strange smells of turkey, cranberry sauce and cornbread, unknown in Laos.
- The highlight of the meal was when Ghia's mother, who is taking English classes and gaining confidence in her skills, told a story—all in English.
- She modestly described her latest sewing creation and the woman who bought it, and ended by saying how grateful she is to be in America and that the future will be bright.
- When she finished speaking, the host family was in tears.
- Ghia loves eating American food and asked for seconds of everything, especially the yams, which remind him of home.
- To accommodate both families, the adults and smallest children were seated at the dining room table, while Ghia and the other teens dined by themselves at fold-up card tables covered by a cloth.
- Ghia got so excited telling stories about his basketball team and his new friends that he knocked a small bowl of cranberry sauce off the table, embarrassing his mother.
- Afterward he apologized to his mother and to the host family for both his manners and his father's inability to attend this important family function.

American food is easy to get used to.

- Before leaving, Ghia noticed that the house was filled with paintings of faraway cities or mountain ranges, or even drawings that had no point at all.
- His apartment is decorated by a line of 8"x10" photographs hung high on the living room wall of family members in Hmong costume and old images from Laos and the camps; pictures of parents and grandparents, enlarged from old snapshots, gaze out at their descendants all day long.
- In addition to practicing basketball, Ghia spends his spare time focused on learning to dance in time for his middle school's end-of-semester dance.
- Ghia had thought little about the event until Rosita, a cute Mexican girl in his class, asked him to go with her.
- Since then he has thought of little else.
- He has asked numerous friends to teach him how to dance, got advice about what to wear, and even asked his sisters what girls like to talk about.
- His family has neither a radio nor a television, so he goes to another friend's house just to know what music is popular.
- His mother is so excited about the dance she has set aside money to buy him a new shirt to wear.
- His father's concern is that his Hmong son is going out in public with a Mexican girl.

Life in the Community: Thailand and Fresno, California

- By the late 1970s in Thailand, 21 refugee camps had been established to receive hundreds of thousands of people fleeing Vietnam, Cambodia and Laos.
- The camps are supported by the United Nations High Commissioner for Refugees and staffed by volunteers, including many missionaries.
- The Thai government was instrumental in determining official and unofficial refugee camp policies; as a result, camps are opened and closed by Thai authorities, and refugees are shifted about abruptly.
- Ban Vinai has become the largest Hmong settlement, both in Thailand and in the world, containing 40,000 people in an area of less than one square mile.
- There, many are taught English and Christianity by the missionaries.
- Fresno County is one of the largest counties in California, extending across the San Joaquin Valley from the Central Coast Ranges to the crest of the Sierra Nevada.
- With a population of more than 175,000, Fresno, which means "ash tree" in Spanish, is the ninth largest city in California; when the entire county is included, the population totals nearly 500,000.
- Ninety percent of the west side housing in Fresno is occupied by Hispanics, blacks and Asians; because of recent immigration patterns, Fresno is considered the American Hmong capital.
- Canned, frozen and dehydrated fruit and vegetable processing leads all other industrial sectors in employment, accounting for one-third of all manufacturing activity.

Historical Snapshot
1979

- The Broadway play *Grease* had presented 3,243 performances, passing *Fiddler on the Roof* as the longest-playing show
- The rate of inflation reached 13.3 percent; the prime rate was 15.75 percent
- Seven states raised the legal drinking age from 18 to 20
- The United States established diplomatic relations with China, while ties with Taiwan were severed
- An industrial accident at Three Mile Island, Pennsylvania dramatically increased fears concerning the use of nuclear power-generated energy
- Movie openings included *Kramer vs. Kramer*, *Apocalypse Now*, *Norma Rae*, *The China Syndrome*, *Star Trek—The Motion Picture* and *10*
- The federal government approved a $1.5 billion bailout loan guarantee program for the Chrysler Corporation
- *The Dukes of Hazzard*, *Archie Bunker's Place*, *Knot's Landing* and *Hart to Hart* premiered on television
- Hit songs included "I Will Survive," "Reunited," "Hot Stuff," "Too Much Heaven," "Money Can't Buy You Love"
- Eleven people were trampled to death while rushing for seats at a Cincinnati concert by the Who
- Norman Mailer's *The Executioner's Song* received the Pulitzer Prize for fiction; Edmund Morris won the biography award for *The Rise of Theodore Roosevelt*
- Judith Krantz received a record $3.2 million advance for the paperback rights to *Princess Daisy*
- The popularity of electronic games such as Chess Challenger, Microvision, Speak and Spell and Little Professor swept the nation
- Marvel Comic, No. 1 was purchased for a record price of $43,000
- Video digital sound discs, electronic blackboards, throwaway toothbrushes, *Drabble* cartoons and Cracker Jack ice cream bars all made their first appearance

We know vitamin C does a lot for them. What new discoveries lie ahead?

Like you, these youngsters can be susceptible to infection that overwhelms the body's natural immunities. Vitamin C, along with other essential nutrients, optimizes your body's natural capacity to resist illness and helps keep your tissues healthy.

Tripping and falling means cuts, scrapes, bruises or a fracture. None of these will heal properly without adequate vitamin C, along with other essential nutrients.

Vitamin C also increases the body's ability to absorb iron from foods. Iron, the most common deficiency in the diet, may be related to a loss of energy.

What about the future? A great deal of research is being directed at possible relationships of vitamin C to infections, diseases, cholesterol levels, stress, and air and chemical pollution.

The role of vitamin C is still being evaluated, but in the meantime it's still important to get enough. So eat foods rich in this essential nutrient. To be sure, you can take a vitamin C supplement. A wide selection of formulations is available. Read the label to make sure you get your vitamin C in the amount you want.

Vitamin Communications, Hoffmann-La Roche Inc., Nutley, N.J. 07110.

Vitamins. Something you can do for your health. RCD 3389

1979 ECONOMIC PROFILE

Selected Prices

Airplane Fare, Los Angeles to Boston $230.00
Baby Carrier, Pak-a-Poose $14.00
Bandages, Curad $0.69
Calculator, Texas Instruments, Pocket Size $74.95
Charcoal Starter, Gulf Lite $0.57
Collector's Case, Matchbox $6.97
Diapers, Dozen $4.86
Figurine, Steuben $160.00
Microwave Oven $168.00
Perfume, Chanel No. 19 . . . . . $9.50
Pressure Cooker, Presto $10.88
Shirt, Tie-dyed $5.99
Sunglasses $7.99
Ticket, Radio City Music Hall . . . . . $7.50 to $10.50
Tricycle $16.99

"Agriculture," *California Yearbook, Bicentennial Edition*, 1975:

Fresno County in 1974 was a leader in agricultural production in California and the nation, with an annual gross value of $967,350,000. It has been a leading county in the state for over 20 years. Field crops were the most important commodities with a gross value of $347,460,000. Cotton lint was valued at $165,456,000; cotton seed—$46,926,000; alfalfa hay—$4,250,000; barley—$28,619,000; sugar beets—$22,845,000; rice—$10,992,000. Other important field crops were wheat, corn, sorghum grain, safflower and pasture.

Translating languages is just the beginning.
The revolutionary Craig M100.
We introduced the Craig M100 as an electronic language translator; an amazing hand-held interpreter that could translate as many as three languages simultaneously. But that was just the beginning. Because of advanced new technology the M100 opens the door to instant information on an incredible variety of subjects far beyond language translations. The key to this revolution is the amazing Ami Memory System, the heart of the Craig M100. This system is the latest in micro-memory technology, making it possible to store in one tiny capsule an amount of information that yesterday required a large computer.
Today, there are language capsules in French, German, Spanish, Italian and Japanese, even a new phonetic language pronunciation capsule. Next will be fascinating new capsules featuring Memory Improvement, First Aid, a Tax Guide and word games.
The Craig M100, with the exclusive Ami Memory System is the recognized standard for hand-held computers. There are virtually unlimited possibilities for storage of knowledge.
You must see a demonstration of the Craig M100 to believe it. It's the first revolution you can hold in the palm of your hand.
CRAIG
M100

Letters to the Editor: "Boat People," *Life*, November 1979:

I am sick and tired of hearing about the homeless boat people ("Island of Hope," September). As a veteran of 18 months in Vietnam, I will never forget that we couldn't trust most Vietnamese. The farmer by day was a fighter by night. How can the American, Australian, French and Canadian governments ascertain whether the people being accepted are communist sympathizers or not? Articles like yours are a disgrace to the millions of GIs who served in that terrible conflict. How about 11 pages on the Vietnam vet?

Harvey Gobin
Gainesville, Fla.

I was particularly struck by your account of the American official screening boat people. insisting that a young man must be older than 14 because he had a large Adam's apple. I could just picture my own 14-year-old son in that young man's place, trying to convince an opinionated official that he was really 14, for his voice is deeper than his father's, his Adam's apple so prominent that it looks as if he has a chicken thighbone stuck in his throat, and he is taller and more muscular than friends a year or two older than he. My son is a Sansei, a third-generation American of Japanese descent.

Perhaps it is more difficult to tell the ages of Asians. It may not matter greatly in the long run: perhaps this young man was not destined to be an American. To have to "play God" is an awesome responsibility when we do not have God's ability to discern the truth when it is presented.

Marie Honmyo
Seattle, Washington

Changing America

- Polls reported that 55 percent of the population, up from 23 percent in 1969, saw nothing wrong with premarital sex.
- The price of gold reached $524 per ounce, up from $223 in 1978.
- A current public service advertisement read, "If 2,225,000 Americans were starving to death, this ad would be a lot bigger. Feed Cambodia."
- The tour of the Moscow Philharmonic in the United States was canceled after several Bolshoi Ballet stars defected.
- More than 100,000 attended a memorial concert in Boston for conductor Arthur Fiedler.
- *Pioneer 11* reached Saturn and reported that its rings were composed of ice-covered rocks.
- Americans purchased 315,000 microcomputers, up from 172,000 in 1978.
- California was the first state to initiate gas rationing using a method of alternate-day purchasing.

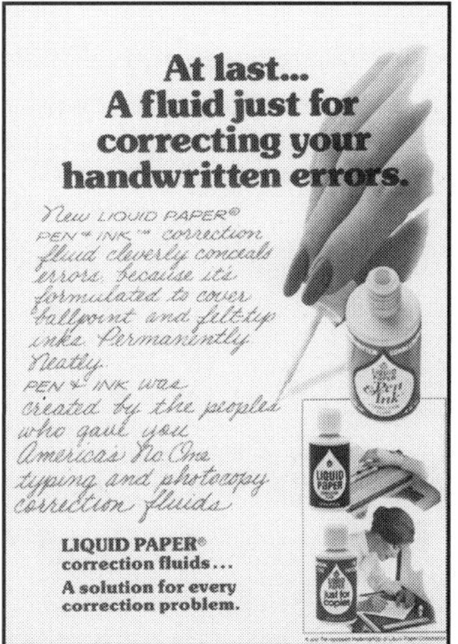

At last...
A fluid just for correcting your handwritten errors.
New LIQUID PAPER® PEN & INK™ correction fluid cleverly conceals errors because it's formulated to cover ballpoint and felt-tip inks. Permanently. Neatly.
PEN & INK was created by the people who gave you America's No. One typing and photocopy correction fluids
LIQUID PAPER® correction fluids...
A solution for every correction problem.

- A study reported that T-shirts carrying slogans or mottoes expressed a wish for a connection with others.
- The sale of health foods topped $1.6 billion, up from $140 million in 1970.
- The U.S. Trust reported that 520,000 Americans were millionaires, or one in every 424.
- The federal government ordered the recall of numerous brands of hair dryers because of harmful amounts of asbestos.
- The divorce rate increased 69 percent in the past decade; the median duration of marriage stood at 6.6 years.

"The Spirit Catches You and You Fall Down," *A Hmong Child, Her American Doctors and the Collision of Two Cultures*, by Anne Fadiman, 1997:

If Lia Lee had been born in the highlands of northwest Laos, where her parents and 12 of her brothers and sisters were born, her mother would have squatted on the floor of the house that her father had built with ax-hewn planks thatched with bamboo and grass. The floor was dirt, but it was clean. Her mother, Foua, sprinkled it regularly with water to keep the dust down and swept it every morning and evening with a broom she had made of grass and bark. . . Even if Foua had been a less fastidious housekeeper, her newborn babies would not have gotten dirty, since she never let them actually touch the floor. She remains proud to this day she delivered each of them into her own hands, reaching between her legs to ease out the head and then letting the rest of the body slip out into her bent forearms. . . . Because Foua believed that moaning and screaming would thwart the birth, she labored in silence, with the exception of an occasional prayer to her ancestors. She was so quiet that although most of her babies were born at night, her older children slept undisturbed on a communal pallet a few feet away, and woke only when they heard the cry of their new brother or sister. . . .

When Lia was born, at 7:09 p.m. on July 19, 1982, Foua was lying on her back on a steel table, her body covered with sterile drapes, her genital area painted with a brown betaine solution, with a high wattage lamp trained on her perineum. There were no family members in the room. Gary Thueson, a family practice resident who did the delivery, noted in the chart that in order to speed the labor, he had artificially ruptured Foua's amniotic sac by poking it with a foot-long plastic "amni-hook"; that no anesthesia was used; that no episiotomy, an incision to enlarge the vaginal opening, was necessary; and that after the birth, Foua received a standard dose of Pitocin to constrict her uterus . . . Lia was shown briefly to her mother. Then she was placed in a steel and Plexiglas warmer, where a nurse fastened a plastic identification band around her wrist and recorded her footprints by inking the soles of her feet with a stamp pad and pressing them against a Newborn Identification form. . . .

Some Hmong parents have given their children American names. In addition to many standard ones, these have included Kennedy, Nixon, Pajama, Guitar, and, until a nurse counseled otherwise, Baby Boy, which one mother, seeing it written on her son's hospital papers, assumed was the name the doctor had already chosen for him.

It's gonna be a great day.
We've been making great days for more people, for more years, with more cereals than anyone. Trust your morning to us. We'll make it a great day for you too.
Kellogg's
FROSTED FLAKES
RICE

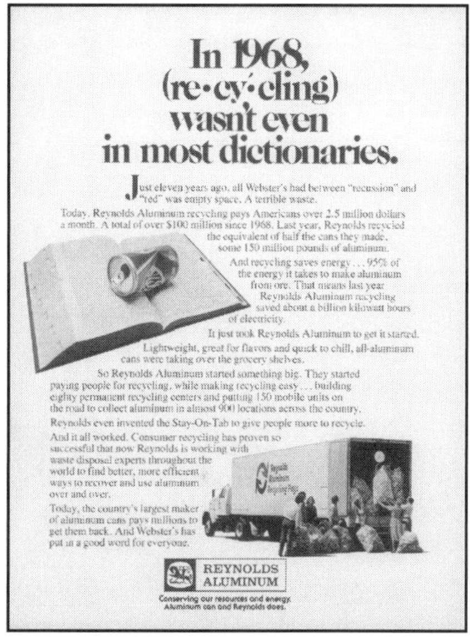
In 1968, (re•cy'cling) wasn't even in most dictionaries.
Just eleven years ago, all Webster's had between "recussion" and "red" was empty space. A terrible waste.
Today, Reynolds Aluminum recycling pays Americans over 2.5 million dollars a month. A total of over $100 million since 1968. Last year, Reynolds recycled the equivalent of half the cans they made, some 150 million pounds of aluminum.
And recycling saves energy . . . 95% of the energy it takes to make aluminum from ore. That means last year Reynolds Aluminum recycling saved about a billion kilowatt hours of electricity.
It just took Reynolds Aluminum to get it started.
Lightweight, great for flavors and quick to chill, all-aluminum cans were taking over the grocery shelves.
So Reynolds Aluminum started something big. They started paying people for recycling, while making recycling easy . . . building eighty permanent recycling centers and putting 150 mobile units on the road to collect aluminum in almost 900 locations across the country.
Reynolds even invented the Stay-On-Tab to give people more to recycle.
And it all worked. Consumer recycling has proven so successful that now Reynolds is working with waste disposal experts throughout the world to find better, more efficient ways to recover and use aluminum over and over.
Today, the country's largest maker of aluminum cans pays millions to get them back. And Webster's has put in a good word for everyone.
REYNOLDS ALUMINUM
Conserving our resources and energy. Aluminum can and Reynolds does.

VOL. 160, NO. 3
SEPTEMBER 1981
TROUBLED ODYSSEY OF VIETNAMESE FISHERMEN
SILVER
A MINERAL OF EXCELLENT NATURE
MANHATTAN—IMAGES OF THE CITY
OMAN: GUARDIAN OF THE GULF
NAHANNI: CANADA'S WILDERNESS PARK
OFFICIAL JOURNAL OF THE NATIONAL GEOGRAPHIC SOCIETY WASHINGTON, D.C.

1980–1989

The economic turbulence of the 1970s continued during the early years of the 1980s. Rates for both interest and inflation were at a staggering 18 percent. With the economy at a standstill, unemployment was rising. By 1982, America was in its deepest depression since the Great Depression of the 1930s. One in 10 Americans was out of work. Yet, by the end of the decade, thanks in part to the productivity gains provided by computers and new technology, more and more Americans were entering the ranks of the millionaire and feeling better off than they had in a decade.

Convinced that inflation was the primary enemy of long-term economic growth, the Federal Reserve Board brought the economy to a standstill in the early days of the decade. It was a shock treatment that worked. By 1984, the tight money policies of the government, stabilizing world oil prices, and labor's declining bargaining power brought inflation to four percent, the lowest level since 1967. Despite the pain it caused, the plan to strangle inflation succeeded; Americans not only prospered, but many believed it was their right to be successful. The decade came to be symbolized by self-indulgence.

At the same time, defense and deficit spending roared into high gear, the economy continued to grow, and the stock market rocketed to record levels (the Dow Jones Industrial Average tripled from 1,000 in 1980 to nearly 3,000 a decade later). In the center of recovery was Mr. Optimism, President Ronald Reagan. During his presidential campaign he promised a "morning in America" and during eight years, his good nature helped transform the national mood. The Reagan era, which spanned most of the 1980s, fostered a new conservative agenda of good feeling. During the presidential election against incumbent President Jimmy Carter, Reagan joked, "A recession is when your neighbor loses his job. A depression is when you lose yours. And recovery is when Jimmy Carter loses his."

The economic wave of the 1980s was also driven by globalization, improvements in technology, and willingness of consumers to assume higher and higher levels of personal debt. By the 1980s, the two-career family became the norm. Forty-two percent of all American workers were female, and more than half of all married women and 90 percent of female college graduates worked outside the home. Yet, their median wage was 60 percent of that of men. The rapid rise of women in the labor force, which had been accelerating since the 1960s, brought great social change, affecting married life, child rearing, family income, office culture, and the growth of the national economy.

The rising economy brought greater control of personal lives; homeownership accelerated, choices seemed limitless, debt grew, and divorce became commonplace. The collapse of communism at the end of the 1980s brought an end to the old world order and set the stage for a realignment of power. America was regarded as the strongest nation in the world and the only real superpower, thanks to its economic strength. As democracy swept across eastern Europe, the U.S. economy began to feel the impact of a "peace dividend" generated by a reduced military budget and a desire by corporations to participate in global markets—including Russia and China. Globalization was having another impact. At the end of World War II, the U.S. economy accounted for almost 50 percent of the global economic product; by 1987, the U.S. share was less than 25 percent as American companies moved plants offshore and countries such as Japan emerged as major competitors. This need for a global reach inspired several rounds of corporate mergers as companies searched for efficiency, market share, new products, or emerging technology to survive in the rapidly shifting business environment.

The 1980s were the age of the conservative Yuppie. Business schools, investment banks, and Wall Street firms overflowed with eager baby boomers who placed gourmet cuisine, health clubs, supersneakers, suspenders, wine spritzers, high-performance autos, and sushi high on their agendas. Low-fat and fiber cereals and Jane Fonda workout books symbolized much of the decade. As self-indulgence rose, concerns about the environment, including nuclear waste, acid rain, and the greenhouse effect declined. Homelessness increased and racial tensions fostered a renewed call for a more caring government. During the decade, genetic engineering came of age, including early attempts at transplantation and gene mapping. Personal computers, which were transforming America, were still in their infancy.

The sexual revolution, undaunted by a conservative prescription of chastity, ran head-on into a powerful adversary during the 1980s with the discovery and spread of AIDS, a frequently fatal, sexually transmitted disease. The right of women to have an abortion, confirmed by the Supreme Court in 1973, was hotly contested during the decade as politicians fought over both the actual moment of conception and the right of a woman to control her body. Cocaine also made its reappearance, bringing drug addiction and a rapid increase in violent crime. The Center on Addiction and Substance Abuse at Columbia University found alcohol and drug abuse implicated in three-fourths of all murders, rapes, child molestations, and deaths of babies suffering from parental neglect.

For the first time in history, the Naval Academy's graduating class included women, digital clocks and cordless telephones appeared, and 24-hour-a-day news coverage captivated television viewers. Compact disks began replacing records, and Smurf and E.T. paraphernalia were everywhere, New York became the first state to require seat belts, Pillsbury introduced microwave pizza, and Playtex used live lingerie models in its ads for the "Cross Your Heart" bra. The Supreme Court ruled that states may require all-male private clubs to admit women, and 50,000 gathered at Graceland on the tenth anniversary of Elvis Presley's death.

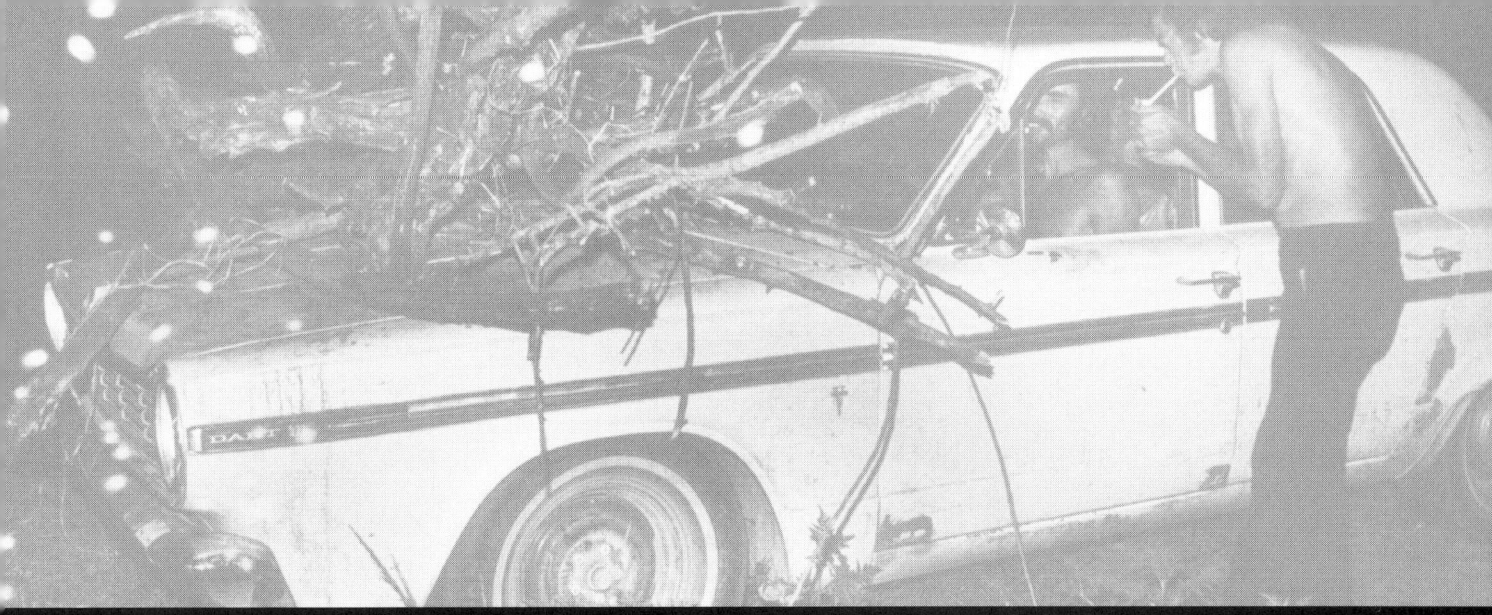

1981 PROFILE

Working Class

Fruit tramp Betty Elizabeth Putnam is desperately seeking a way out of her migrant life and a chance to stay in one school so she can one day become an English teacher.

Life at Home

- Fifteen-year-old Betty Elizabeth Putnam hates her name and hates moving around all the time.
- She wants to live in one house, in one town, and know one group of kids; meeting new people is hard.
- She was named after her grandmother and her mother's favorite actress, Elizabeth Taylor, whom Betty has seen in several old movie magazines.
- Betty doesn't think she looks like her grandmother or Elizabeth Taylor, and doesn't want a used name anymore.
- Sometimes she tells her new friends to call her Sugar or Peaches—depending on which school she's attending.
- But at home she is Betty Elizabeth, and in the community she is simply called "a fruit tramp" because her parents are migrant workers and follow the crops.
- Even her parents call themselves fruit tramps, much to her embarrassment.
- Each year, they travel up the East Coast from Florida to New York picking crops: citrus in Florida; peaches in Georgia; tomatoes, cucumbers and beans in South Carolina; apples, squash and beans in North Carolina; and apples, pears, cherries and cabbage in New York.
- As quickly as one job is finished, the family will pack themselves into their ancient Plymouth—with duct tape and paper covering the rear window—and head up the road looking for more work.

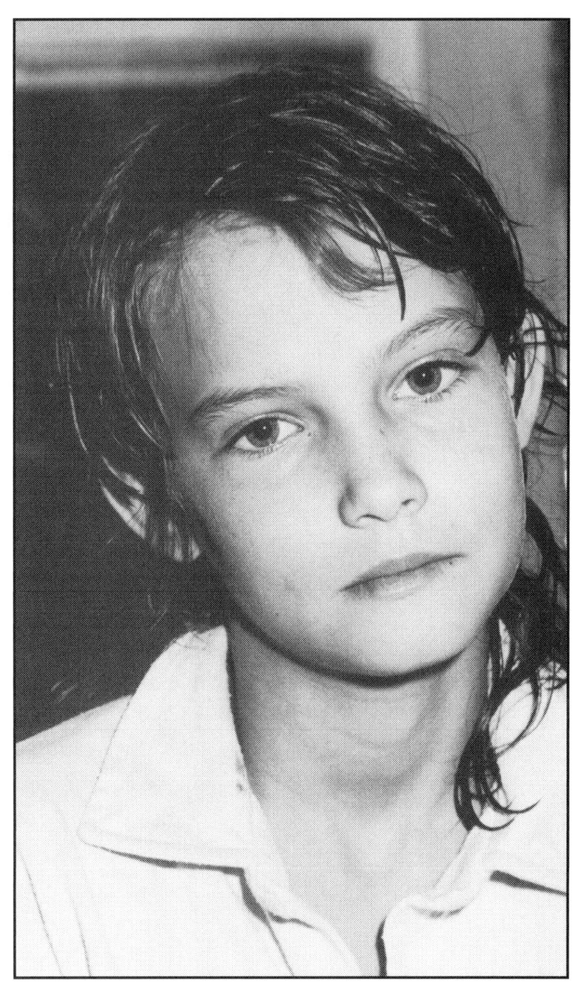

Betty Elizabeth Putnam wants to escape her life as a fruit tramp.

Each year, the family travels from Florida to New York picking crops.

- When the job is big enough and scheduled to take more than a few weeks, the children are enrolled in school.
- The little ones are placed in daycare or the older children are given the job of staying home to baby-sit.
- Even the children who attend school must help in the fields; it takes the entire family to make ends meet.
- Betty Elizabeth's oldest sister, Lurken, dropped out of school four years ago when she was 14.
- Last year Lurken married another fruit tramp and now has a baby girl who sleeps in a makeshift tent during the day while the picking is going on.
- Lurken and her husband often follow the Putnams from place to place seeking work, acting as an extended family work team.
- Betty Elizabeth is determined to graduate from high school, even though she is already at least a year behind her age group.
- Since she was a little girl, she has loved language and literature, and dreams of being a teacher one day.
- Currently, the family is picking cherries in Olcott, New York, on the shores of Lake Ontario, where they have been since the beginning of this school year.

"One Percent Right," *Fruit Tramps, A Family of Migrant Farmworkers,* by Herman LeRoy Emmet, University of New Mexico Press, 1979:

The irrigation canal stretched straight as a rule for miles down through the citrus, bringing water in from the Everglades. Tina Michelle skipped along the top of the levee to a point where the water deepened and looked cleaner. Linda followed, hugging her baby son, Shannon Dewayne, to her hip with that very maternal sway, and every so often would pause and peer down into the canal. Stopping at Tina's spot, she sat down on the bank, laying Shannon in her lap, and then looked up and down the canal for alligators.

She told Tina to run back and fetch a towel, took her son's diaper off, slid down the embankment, and lowered him into the water. As she lathered him up, he cried and reached out to her to end this chilling bath. Waiting for the right moment, Tina handed her the towel.

Later in the day, Linda came down to the canal to wash her hair. It was not easy for her to find a clean spot in the water; an oily residue covered the surface, possibly run-off from spraying the fruit. She poked around with her hand, making a hole in the thick scum, bent over, lowering her hair into the water, and massaged shampoo into her hair. Foam spread out and bubbles merged with the iridescent chemical film, reflecting its silky hues of blue-green, magenta and purple. . .

That night Linda made a stew with two cans of Dolores California Jack mackerel, two cans of Thrifty Maid Spanish-style tomato sauce, rutabaga, onions and carrots. (Her husband) L. H. cut open the cans with his long pocketknife, so sharpened and used that all the writing on the steel was worn away. He sawed up and down and around the tops as if through butter. Linda did the rest.

She cooked the contents in a blackened pot next to a campfire that L.H., Calvin and Ray had built from wood foraged off the land. She used a small, two-burner Sears gas stove I'd brought with me. Before I'd arrived, she worked off the corner of the evening fire to cook the family meal, a long and dangerous process because of the heat and shooting sparks. She already had burns on her skin, and singes and holes in her clothes. . .

L. H. dug his elbows into his sides and stretched out his hands. "All I want is a little respect for me, my family and people like us, our kind of people. People treat us like dogs. They just want the sweat off our backs and to hell with us.

"We fill up the supermarkets of these United States every day with food. . . . You ever go into one of them places and see all of them fat-assed people? Pathetic! They got the money to buy all that food and drive all them fancy cars. But what do we get? We got a jalopy, right? And we ain't hardly got enough money to buy grits, for chrissakes, let alone get fat. I'm skinny as a rail; my wife and kids is skinny."

- The family lives on the beach because, even though they have saved up their money, they can't find anyone in the area who will rent to them.
- Betty Elizabeth's father, C. O. Putnam, has gained a reputation for heavy drinking, rowdy behavior and a casual attitude toward his financial obligations.
- When it rains, the family huddles under picnic tables in a nearby public park, which also provides them with a bathhouse complete with showers and toilets—if they are not caught trespassing by the police.

Fruit tramps follow the crops, moving from place to place.

- Now that the weather is turning colder and the Florida citrus season will be starting, C. O. is talking about taking the family back down South.
- Besides, more than once the police have hinted to him that vagrancy charges are just around the corner.

- He says it doesn't matter where they live anymore because foreigners have moved in and taken over America; loud and often, he says they are "driving down wages and harming real Americans who are trying to make a living."
- In Florida, the compensation for picking oranges two years ago was $0.80 a bushel, but the presence of Latin and Caribbean immigrants has driven the wages down to nearly $0.40 a bushel.
- A young, fast picker can gather about 100 bushels a day for about $40 in earnings.
- When the weather is bad, the crops late, or the family is traveling, they earn nothing.
- Last year, C. O. and his wife Alfeda earned about $2,800.
- Betty Elizabeth loves her school in Olcott and does not want to leave, but arguing with her father can be dangerous.
- C. O. thinks that "Queen Liz," as he calls his high-minded daughter when he is drinking, has enough education and should not only move to Florida, but drop out of school and earn her keep in the fields.
- Besides, he knows that Skeeter Matuse, a 26-year-old divorced fruit tramp who often travels the same route as the Putnams, would be happy to take her off his hands.
- Betty Elizabeth's mother, who can sign her name and read street signs, wants her daughter to chase dreams and get an education, but is not willing to cross her husband.

Life at School

- By Betty Elizabeth's count, this is the fourth time in the past 10 years she has attended a school in Olcott.
- Her English teacher, Mrs. Agardy, is very excited about teaching English and enjoys the girl's enthusiasm, loaning her books and creating a reading list of library books for her, knowing she may leave abruptly.
- After class, they read poems together and discuss what makes a good novel.

Education, A Case of Despair, by Ronald L. Goldfarb, The Iowa State University Press, 1981:

Education is the classic route out of poverty. A painful reality is that the very migrancy of these farm workers often forecloses this route to their children. Inherent in the migrant life is the special problem of educating the young. When always on the move, there can be no stable school life for children; their children are constantly in and out of different schools. When they are attending, they are strangers, often marked by language and cultural differences. They usually are without friends and meaningful associations. Migrant children are hungry and without necessary books and supplies; they usually can be found in the worst facilities, in places not conducive to a good educational experience. They have no assistance at home because their parents are away all day and often are without means and abilities to be helpful when they return. These children are strangers in a hard and puzzling world.

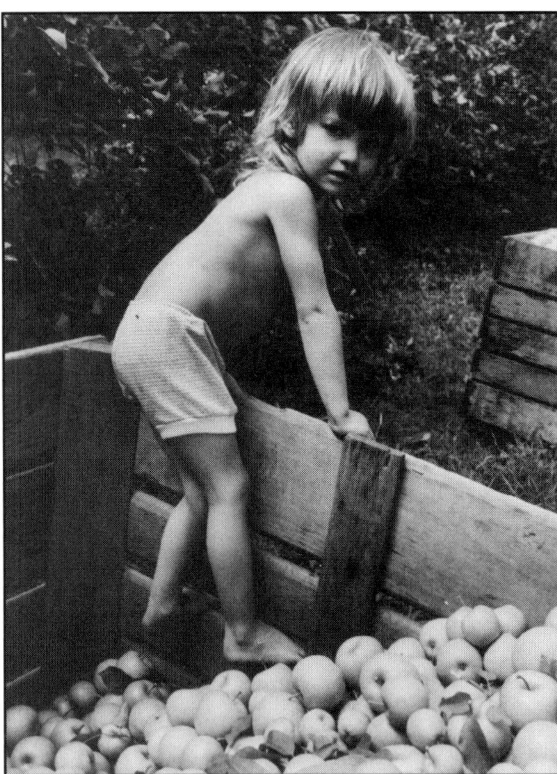

Betty Elizabeth's sisters have grown up on the road.

- Betty Elizabeth loves her family, but if they go to Florida when the winter weather arrives, she wants to stay in New York.
- With the encouragement of Mrs. Agardy, she is spending more time in front of the mirror at the bathhouse, combing her hair and pressing her clothes so she will look like the other children.
- Her teacher has even bought her some outfits from the local thrift store, and shown her how to do alterations.
- Even though they know she is a fruit tramp and will be gone soon, several girls in the class have been nice to her lately, sharing their makeup and chatting with her during lunch.
- A cute boy has even spoken to her several days in a row and wants to see her outside of school, but she is terrified that he will come to the migrant camp looking for her and see how she lives.
- She first realized she didn't want to be a fruit tramp when she was nine years old and the family was spending Christmas at a large migrant camp where the local people staged a large Christmas Party, complete with food and someone playing Santa Claus.
- During the gift-giving, Betty Elizabeth was given a doll with long, blond hair, rosy-red cheeks and an innocent expression on her face.
- She fell in love with the plastic doll, even though it was missing a leg.
- She got her mother to show her how to make a doll's dress from a piece of light purple cloth, a lilac color that made the doll beautiful and covered the missing leg.
- Then, she tied a cord around the doll's neck and hung it on the wall to make sure everyone knew it was hers alone, and that no one should mess with it.
- Having the one-legged doll made her wonder why her family worked so hard and had so little; she kept thinking, "Is this all there is to life?"
- Almost immediately, she and her doll began to take imaginary journeys together to faraway places where children had bedrooms and friends, and received Christmas presents that didn't include hand-me-down dolls with one leg.

Life in the Community: Olcott, New York

- Olcott's year-round population of about 1,000 swells significantly in the summer when the community becomes a center for boating and fishing on Lake Ontario.
- New York is unique in that it is the only state which touches both the Atlantic Ocean and the Great Lakes.
- The coastline meanders 127 miles along the ocean, and borders 371 miles of Lake Ontario and Lake Erie.
- Although only about four percent of New York's 18 million-plus people are engaged in farming, it is a leading source of the state's revenues.
- Primary crops include clover, timothy grass, apples and grapes, while secondary crops comprise corn, oats, wheat, peas, peaches, cherries, melons, beans, beets, onions, cauliflower and potatoes.
- Much of this harvest goes directly into the state's canneries and freezing plants; New York is where Clarence Birdseye, of frozen-food fame, developed his technology.

Historical Snapshot 1981

- Picasso's self portrait *Yo*, painted in 1901, sold for $5.3 million, the highest price ever paid for a twentieth-century work
- Cave paintings of sacred Mayan ball games, circa A.D. 800, were found in Guatemala
- Sandra Day O'Connor of the Arizona State Court of Appeals was named to the United States Supreme Court
- Hit records included "Lady," "Starting Over," "9 to 5," "Slow Hand" and "Take It on the Run"
- Moments after Ronald Reagan was inaugurated president, Iran released 52 hostages who had been held for 444 days
- The United States Supreme Court ruled that radio and television coverage of criminal trials was constitutional
- The Rolling Stones earned a record $25 million from their U.S. tour of 40 American cities
- The movies *Chariots of Fire*, *Raiders of the Lost Ark*, *On Golden Pond* and *The French Lieutenant's Woman* premiered
- VCR sales increased 72 percent over the previous year; 34 million units were in use
- NutraSweet, a test-tube baby and the Guardian Angels made their first appearance
- The $7.9 billion merger of DuPont and Conoco was the largest in U.S. history
- Baseball fans suffered through a seven-week strike, the longest in sports history
- The national unemployment rate topped eight percent for the nation, 16.8 percent for blacks and 40 percent for black teenagers
- *Dallas*, *60 Minutes*, *M*A*S*H*, *The Dukes of Hazzard* and *Three's Company* were Nielsen's top five television programs of the year
- An estimated 750 million people watched the marriage of Prince Charles to kindergarten teacher Lady Diana Spencer
- Walter Cronkite retired as the CBS news anchor and was replaced by Dan Rather
- *Hill Street Blues* won an Emmy for best drama and *Barney Miller* won for best comedy
- A furor erupted when the federal government attempted to count ketchup as a vegetable in subsidized school lunches
- Fads included books about cats (*Garfield*, *101 Uses for a Dead Cat*) and Rubik's Cube; the book, *The Solution to Rubik's Cube*, sold four million copies

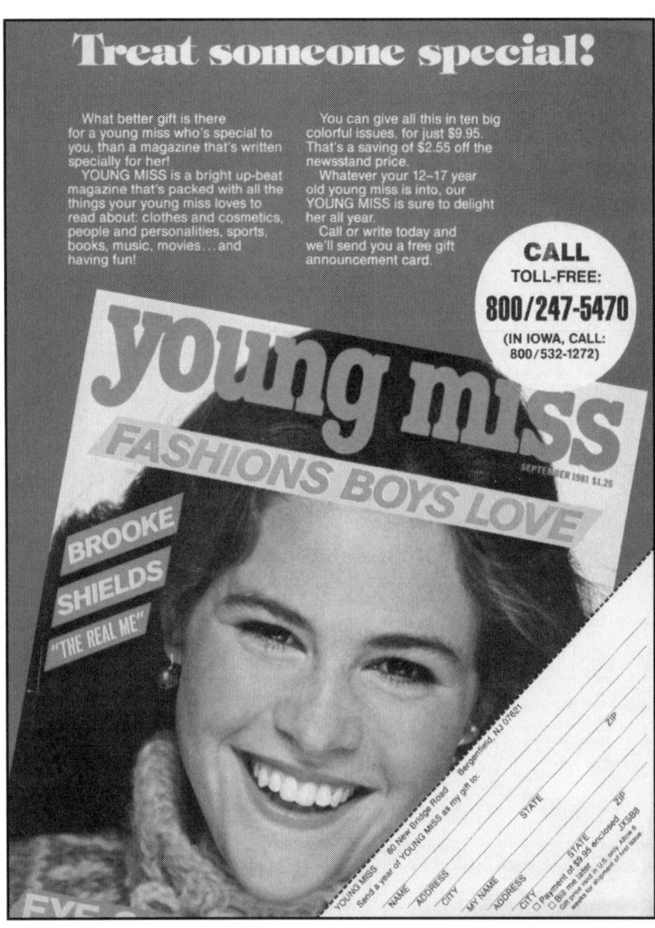

1981 Economic Profile

Selected Prices

Automobile, Cadillac Eldorado. . . . $19,700.00
Beef Roast, Sirloin Top Round, per Pound $1.89
Beer, Pabst 12-Pack $3.19
Boat, Bass Tracker1 . . . . $3,795.00
Golf Clubs, Wilson $219.99
Heater, Kerosene $289.95
Hotel Room, Juneau, Alaska, per Night $48.50
Knife, Six-Inch Chef's $10.00
Pants, Men's U.S. Marine Camouflage $39.00
Paper Shredder, Destroyit $474.95
Screwdriver, Stanley $14.95
Work Shirt, Man's $9.95
Washing Machine, Kenmore. $529.95
Window Fan, Two-Speed $34.99
Yogurt, Breyer's, Two 8-Ounce Containers $0.89

The royal wedding drew worldwide attention.

Changing America

- Stephen Jay Gould published *The Mismeasure of Man.*
- Andy Warhol, who began his career with shoe advertisements, designed ads for Halston.
- Surgeons were able to relieve coronary artery obstruction with a stretchable, balloon-tipped catheter.
- Lucy, a four-foot humanoid fossil found in 1974 by Donald Johanson and Maitland Edey, was named after "Lucy in the Sky with Diamonds" by the Beatles.
- A 10-year study correlated fatal heart disease to the saturated-unsaturated fat ratio in the diet.
- The combination of First Lady Nancy Reagan's elegance and the wedding of Lady Diana to Prince Charles stimulated a return to opulent styles.
- Supply-side economics proposed that government increase incentives such as tax reform to stimulate production.
- The 1980 census reported the smallest rate of population growth in America since the Depression.
- An eight-year Veteran's Administration study stated that Vietnam veterans suffered more emotional, social, educational and job-related problems than did veterans of other recent wars.
- The Stop Handguns Before They Stop You Committee ran an advertisement reading, "Last year handguns killed 48 people in Japan, 8 in Great Britain, 34 in Switzerland, 52 in Canada, 58 in Israel, 21 in Sweden, 42 in West Germany, 10,720 in the U.S. God Bless America."

With These Hands, The Hidden World of Migrant Farmworkers Today, by Daniel Rothenberg, Harcourt Brace & Company, 1998:

Dora Medina, Faison, North Carolina

Dora Medina is the oldest daughter and second-oldest child of a family of 12 children. Each of her brothers and sisters was born about a year apart. Medina grew up migrating with her family, traveling back and forth between Texas and Ohio in a large truck. Her father never went to school and her mother only studied up to the third grade. Beginning at a very young age, Medina took on the responsibility of caring for her younger brothers and sisters. In addition to working in the fields, she cooked, cleaned, washed and helped raise her siblings. Her parents were stern, disciplined and traditional.

"I was six years old when I first remember helping out in the fields.

We'd go out early in the morning while it was still cool. Sometimes there would be a fog, and you could only see the rows a couple of feet away from you. We had a little stretch of field that we worked. When it was getting hot, we'd quit for a little while, and in the afternoons we'd go back for another round. There were times that we needed to get the field picked and so at night Mom would park the car at the end of the field and turn on the headlights so we could see the cucumbers we were picking. It's not like we were good workers, but we helped. That's the way we grew up. We were all in it together.

As far back as I can remember, I always had a little baby in my arms. I was like the second little mother. While I worked, the babies would be at the end of the field inside a car or a truck. They'd be crying and they'd be dirty. They were always hungry and always thirsty. Once in a while, the little children would come out to where we were in the fields and we'd have to carry them back. Sometimes they'd get so cranky that Dad would say, 'I'll take your row. You go out there and stay with them for a while.'

Some days we tied a bedsheet to a tree and made a little tent. We'd lay the baby in the middle and cover it up so it could breathe and the mosquitoes wouldn't get to it. Then we'd work for a few minutes and go back to check if the baby was fine and then run back to the field. Other times, we'd have the other little children take care of the smallest ones.

As a child, all I knew was fieldwork. In school, I would think, 'I don't know how to count, multiply, or do division. All I know is that I can fill up a hamper with tomatoes and cucumbers.' There were times we didn't even go to school. Mom would say, 'Let's not even send them to school, we're only here for a couple of weeks.' Then we'd see the school bus passing by. Being in the hot sun, we'd think how good it would feel to be on the bus, in a cool place.

We were always leaving one place and going off to another where a farmer promised us more. There was always a different farmer, always a different house. If we had a bad day today, we'd hope that tomorrow would be better. In the migrant stream, tomorrow is as far as you look ahead. Tomorrow . . . tomorrow.

Christmas in a migrant camp is the saddest type of Christmas. I remember one time we were stranded on a labor camp in late December. We asked our parents what we were going to do for Christmas. Mom said, 'We don't have nothing.' We were really torn up about that. Then one of my sisters went outside and found a small tree. She pulled that little tree inside our room and wrapped a ribbon around it."

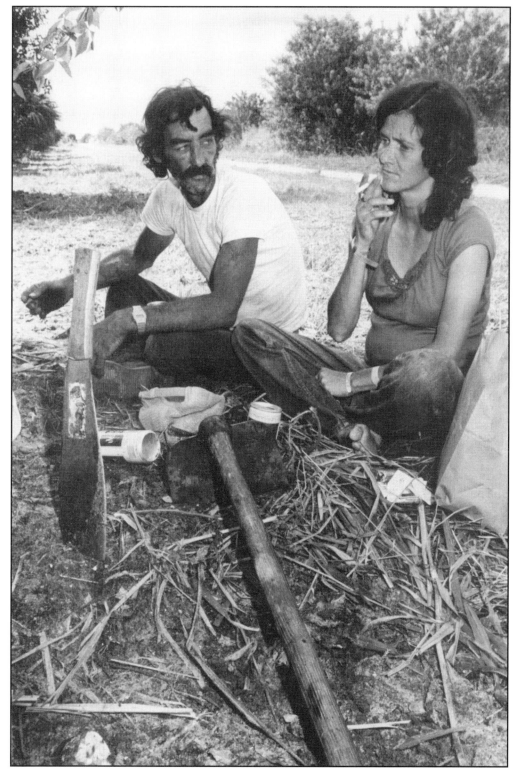

Work in the fields is a tough, tiring, difficult life.

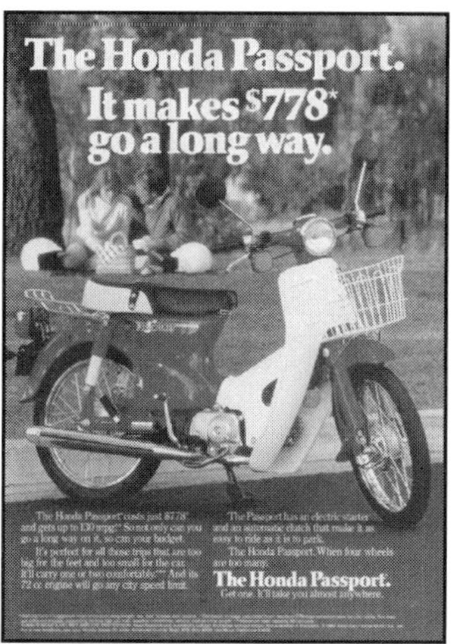

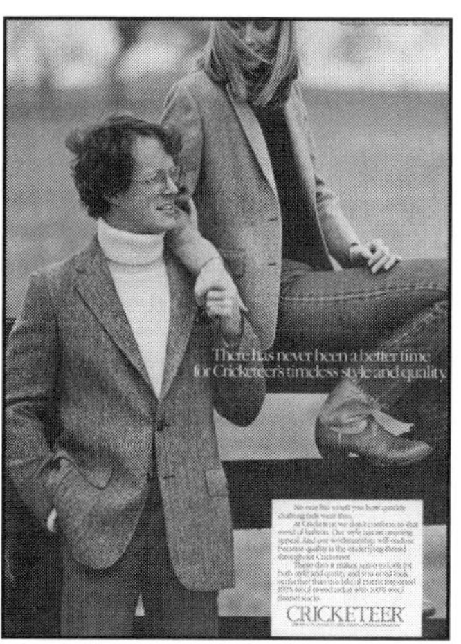

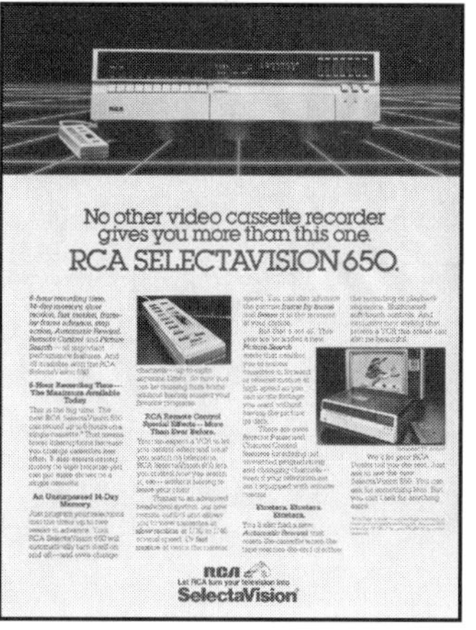

"The Pantry Raid, Sneaking sugar from Grandmother's pantry was sweet fun," by Sylvia Roberts, 2001:

I was raised solely by my grandparents, whom I called Mama Lady and Papa Man, in their home in San Antonio, Texas. Though we were by no means wealthy, we were not nearly as bad off as I was led to believe.

To hear Mama Lady tell it, we were going over the hill to the poorhouse at just about any moment. She was always pointing out that things were hard to come by. She often hinted that my new crayons may have been just the purchase that would send us to our financial dooms.

By the age of five, I had come to equate quality with quantity. So when Papa Man brought home an entire bushel basket of grapefruit he received as payment for a favor, I was very nearly overwhelmed by the extravagance.

I was allowed to share this bounty with Ginny, my friend next door. Ginny was unfamiliar with the tartness of grapefruit and convinced me the flavor could be improved with sugar.

I knew sugar was a precious commodity to my grandmother, and that she would never allow us to use any. So, without asking permission I knew we wouldn't get, I took a cup from my toy tea set, and Ginny and I tiptoed into the dark, cool pantry.

The sugar sack sat on a high shelf, along with the jars of beets, tomatoes and peaches that Mama Lady had pickled, canned and preserved. It was out of the reach of two five-year-olds, so we dragged in a heavy wooden chair from the kitchen.

I climbed onto the chair, and with one knee on a shelf, reached over my head and scooped out a cup of sugar. I handed the cup down to my waiting partner in crime and climbed off my precarious perch.

We slid the chair back to its place, then giggled our way back to the porch steps and our waiting grapefruit.

The success of our adventure was exhilarating as well as tasty. So much so that after the grapefruit was gone, we raided the pantry again, this time wetting our fingers, sticking them in the teacup, then licking the sugar off our hands.

We managed to avoid Mama Lady all that afternoon as we sneaked in and out of the pantry. We were almost caught once when she came out to take her wash off the line. After that we began to hide—under my bed, in a wardrobe and even in the bathroom—as we repeated our sticky raids.

It never occurred to us that the sugar sack had been full when we began our raids. Nor did we realize the trails of evidence the overloaded cup had been leaving to our hiding places. . .

Mama Lady knew what had happened as soon as she walked into the pantry, crunching with every step, and saw the ants, the sugar all over the shelves and the nearly empty sack. We knew when she followed the trails to our hideouts, and when I came moaning to her side, begging for something for my tummyache.

And as if my miserable tummy weren't punishment enough, I had to suffer the added indignity of going out to the backyard and cutting my own switch from a peach tree.

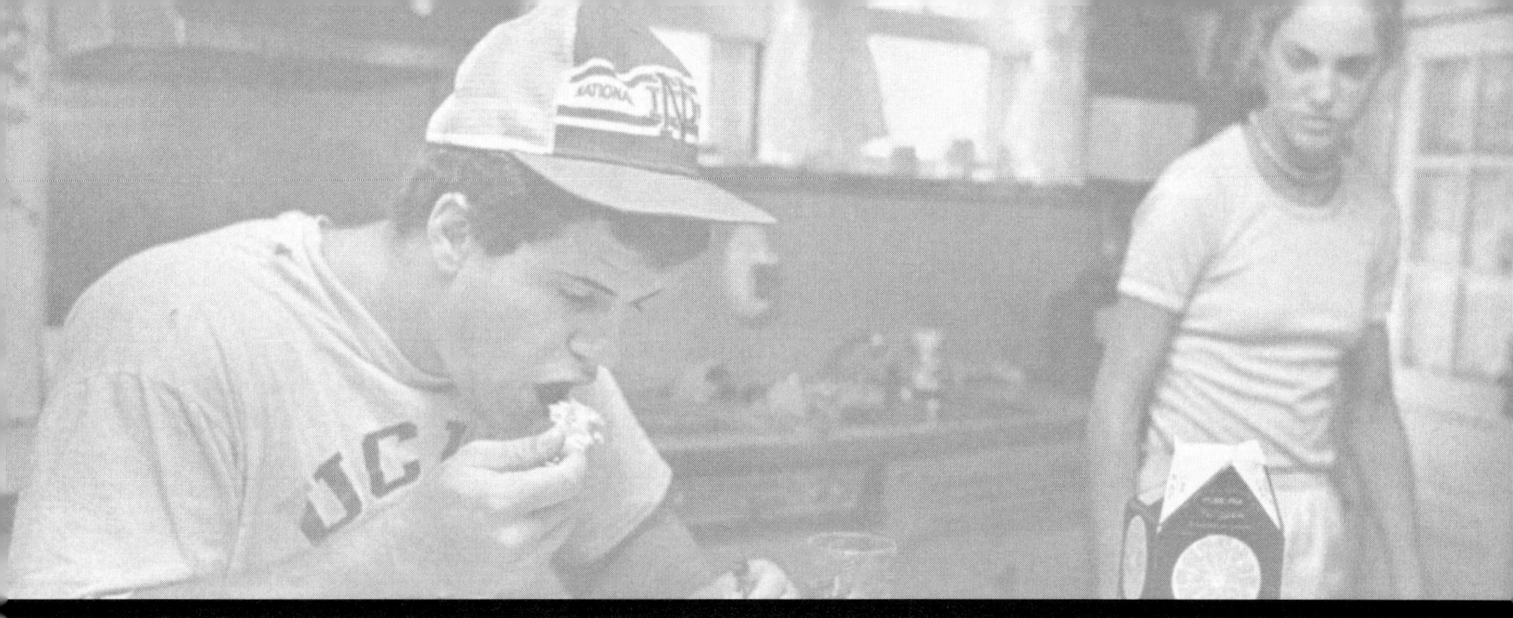

1982 News Feature

"A Case Study of Anorexia Nervosa, The Skeleton at the Feast," by Anne Fadiman, *Life*, February 1982:

In the spring of 1980, a 16-year-old girl named Jane Daly lay in bed in the second floor of her family's large brick house in New Rochelle, NY, and drew in her sketchbook. It was difficult for her to see what she was drawing, since she insisted on having the lights off, the windows closed and the curtains drawn 24 hours a day. At first her sketches were uniformly gray and depicted such subjects as an empty chair, an empty bed, an empty garden and a leafless tree. When her parents gave her some colored pencils, telling her that her pictures looked gloomy, she drew several interiors in pastel colors, but when she drew a stove, a plate, a glass, a teakettle or any other object that pertained to food, she colored in gray. Jane also drew three self-portraits. In all of them her eyes were averted and her face was redrawn many times, as if she was unsure what she really looked like. The other feature the portraits had in common was that in all of them, Jane was fat.

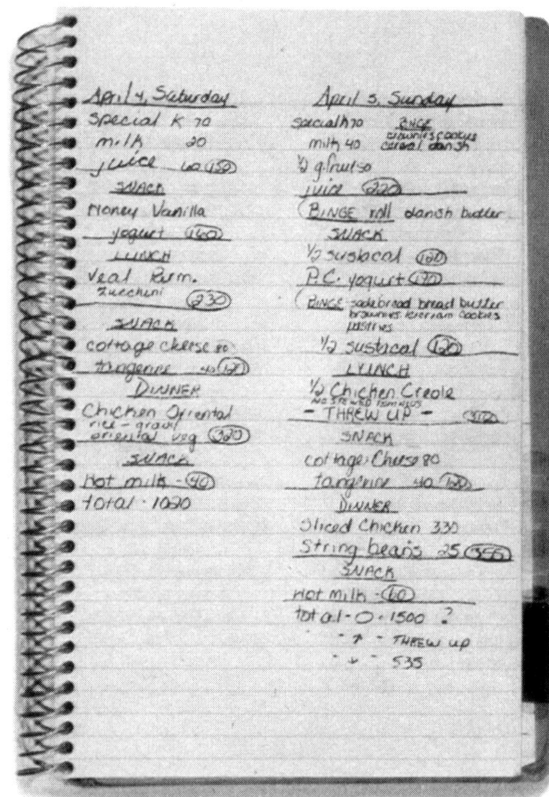

At the time, Jane Daly, who is five feet eight inches tall, weighed 90 pounds—45 pounds less than she had eight months before and nine pounds more than she would weigh six months later. Her hair, which had once (as they used to tell her in the beauty parlor) been "enough for four people," was thin, her nails were brittle, her skin was dry, her lips were blue, her hands and feet were cold (the result of a lowered metabolic rate, appropriate for a starving organism), and on her arms, stomach, lower back and buttocks she had grown a layer of fine black hair called lanugo, also found on fetuses, and thought, in the case of malnourished adults, to be a primitive response to the problems of heat conservation caused by the loss of subcutaneous fat. Jane considered the lanugo to be a double cross, since she associated thinness with refinement and delicacy and had hardly expected the diet she began the previous autumn to produce black hairs all over her body. . . .

Almost two years have passed since then. Jane now weighs 115 pounds, and though she must still push back the panic each time she charts a quarter-pound gain on her medical scale, she realizes that she is still too thin. The surrender of her illusions was a process to which more than 50 doctors and therapists contributed. Foremost among them was an idiosyncratic psychotherapist named Steven Levenkron, under whose care Jane will remain for at least two years. Though he has pronounced her almost completely recovered, she is still shaky from the 18 months she spent as a voluntary exile from the real world, embracing a disease that began with her attitude toward food and eventually took over all her thoughts, her actions, her conversations and her dreams: for anorexia nervosa is not just an eating disorder but a disorder of the whole person.

The rest of the family, though their faces shine when they speak of the glossy-haired, clear-eyed creature who has been restored to them, are still shaky too. Her parents say they would have dealt better with cancer, which at one time they feared might be the cause of their daughter's emaciation. Cancer would have been a common enemy against which the family could have united; instead, anorexia became a wedge between them, as they tried to threaten, bribe and cajole Jane into recovering from a disease of which she did not wish to be cured.

The remedy for anorexia is simple. All the patient must do is eat. That, unfortunately, is the one thing she will not do, and in order to avoid it, she will use every tool at her disposal, including deceit, manipulation and an intensity of stubbornness that seems incredible in one so frail and weak. While her family watched, Jane Daly became a starveling in the midst of plenty, a skeleton at the feast. . . .

A generation ago psychiatrists ran across it once in a lifetime. Now there are 100,000 anorexics in the United States alone, more than 10 times as many as there were a decade ago. Between 10 and 15 percent of them will die (of heart failure, infections, irreversible hypoglycemia and simple starvation), a higher mortality rate than for any other psychiatric disorder.

Anorexia nervosa has been called a glamorous cross between Victorian favorites, consumption and hysteria, but updated for the modern audience. Not surprising, it is unheard of in Third World countries: People who might be forced to starve are unlikely to practice starvation by choice. Just as obesity (according to one classic New York study) is seven times as frequent among the very poor as among the very rich, so anorexia is almost exclusively a disease of the upper middle and upper classes. In public schools, one out of every 3,000 girls is anorexic; in the private schools, one out of 200. But like other fashionable disorders, this one is gaining popularity among the upwardly mobile. Montefiore Hospital in the Bronx reports that it has started to receive its first blue collar, rural and black anorexic patients.

1985 Profile

Upper Class

Talented, musically gifted 12-year-old Valerie Jaffen is anxiously waiting to celebrate her Bas Mitzvah in a new home in Stamford, Connecticut.

Life at Home

- Valerie Jaffen is only a few weeks away from her twelfth birthday and her long-awaited Bas Mitzvah.
- For the past several months, she has been learning the passage of the Torah assigned to the week of her birthday and working closely with Rabbi Edelman on her speech.
- Each week she and the Rabbi meet at the Reformed Temple not far from her home in Stamford, Connecticut.
- The memorization is not difficult—Valerie prides herself on learning passages quickly—but preparing her talk has been a challenge because it must be perfect and accurately reflect the impact on her of becoming an adult and being a Jew.
- True to her meticulous nature and depth of religious feeling, she has struggled through draft after draft.
- Rabbi Edelman believes that her parents are less devoted than she and that her speech will help guide them into a deeper faith.
- He keeps telling her how impressed he is with her effort, which makes her work even harder.
- For Valerie, order is important.
- She brings the same dedication to playing the cello, doing her homework, or arranging her complex schedule.
- Over her parents' heated objections, she is currently involved in sailing, horseback riding, tennis and dance.
- Her mother has repeatedly said she must give up something, but Valerie insists that as long as her grades are good, she has earned the right to stay busy.
- She keeps a calendar on her bedroom door so everyone in the house knows her daily schedule: Monday, horseback riding and cello; Tuesday, sailing and

Valerie Jaffen is looking forward to her Bas Mitzvah.

Tennis is one of Valerie's many interests.

allergy shot; Wednesday, tennis and cello; Thursday, dance and orchestra; Friday, Hebrew School and Bas Mitzvah preparation.

- From sundown Friday until sundown Saturday, she keeps free for Temple, reflection, and work on her Bas Mitzvah speech.
- Sailing and tennis she finds hard and unnatural, but when she is on horseback, especially a quarter horse named Perry, she feels totally alive.
- Her other passion, when she is alone and playing her cello, is talking with her cat Greyboy, who has been her best friend since she was three.
- Her father likes for her to play the Romantics and more modern works on the cello, but she prefers Baroque, particularly Bach, because of its order and precision.
- She has few friends, since her family only moved to Stamford last summer from her childhood home in Mount Kisco, New York, where her grandparents still live.
- Her sprawling new house has 10,000 square feet, encompassing six bedrooms, six full baths and an artist's studio, which is being used as a music room.
- Sitting on two acres, the house was built in 1914 on the tip of a point extending into Long Island Sound.
- The compound includes a pool, tennis court and four-car garage.

"Bas Mitzvah," by Sandra Gerstein, *Issues Magazine*, May 1985:

At last! The Sabbath eve of my long anticipated Bas Mitzvah! More than the culmination of months of study, it was a step toward maturity. As I waited on the bimah during the Friday evening service, I savored the exciting thought that in just a few short moments I would officially enter into Jewish adulthood in the tradition of my forefathers.

From my seat next to the Rabbi, I gazed down at the faces of my family and friends. How proud my parents looked—proud that their daughter was about to make a public commitment to the God of Israel.

I was filled with a combined sense of devotion and nervous expectation. My heart began to beat faster as the time drew near, until finally I was called! I walked over to the lectern, took a deep breath and slowly began with the brachah that is chanted before the Haftorah reading.

My Rabbi had patiently taught me the Haftorah portion of Scripture for that week. It was Yithro, taken from Isaiah 6:1-13, which describes the call of the prophet Isaiah to his ministry. Isaiah had a vision of God in the Temple. When the Lord asked who would go forth in His name, Isaiah answered, "Hineni; shelachani!"—"Here am I; send me!" His willingness to serve God greatly impressed me as a powerful example that I, also, should follow.

After chanting the Haftorah, I was ready to begin my Bas Mitzvah speech. The Rabbi and I had carefully written and rewritten this special message. Through it I desired to communicate my deep feelings of dedication to God and Judaism.

Honored Rabbi, dear parents, relatives and friends: This Sabbath eve I am ready to take my place in the world as a Jew. In the sense that Isaiah was willing to serve God, so, too, am I willing to accept any obligation that I as a Jew may meet.

I pray that the spirit of dedication which fills my soul tonight will remain with me in the years that lie ahead, and that I might live in a manner which will bring pride and honor to my family and my people. To them and to God I say, Hineni; here am I.

Her sprawling 10,000 square foot home was built in 1914.

- Valerie's mother, Ruth, is completely redecorating the interior of the home; this is her dream project.
- For two years she has been lobbying for a new home, ever since her husband Richard took several companies public and earned millions of dollars in bonuses.

Valerie's busy schedule includes sailing.

Club Mitzvah, Atrium Bar & Bas Mitzvah Reception Menu, Mediterranean Manor Caterers, Patchogue, New York:

(Served throughout your reception by white-gloved attendants):
Filet of Sole, Scampi Style
Stuffed Cabbage
Sirloin Tips Bourguignonne
Tempura Chicken Polynesian
Eggplant Rollatine
Breast of Chicken Champagne
Seasoned Rice Pilaf

- After all, as Ruth has said repeatedly, she quit college to support Richard through the Wharton School of Business; now that their hard work and investments have paid off, this house is her diploma.
- Valerie's Bas Mitzvah reception will be her mother's first opportunity to unveil the new home, a way of greeting her new community in style.
- She is currently splitting her time between supervising the renovations and planning the reception.
- Valerie wants to keep the reception simple, but feels no one is listening to her.
- She is saving her excitement for the arrival of both sets of grandparents, who will be coming from Mount Kisco for her birthday, the Bas Mitzvah and the reception.

Life at School

- The move from Mount Kisco to Stamford has been difficult.
- In contrast to her old school, Greenwich Academy, which she now attends, is private, all-female, and has fewer Jewish students.
- The teachers are very nice, the classes hard, and the girls very cliquish; she is finding it hard to make the kind of friends she enjoyed in her old school.
- Some girls have even made remarks about her hair, which she has always considered one of her best features.
- Valerie is self-conscious that she must take an allergy shot once a week; no one at the school knows about her allergy except her friend Amy.
- For her birthday, Valerie's mother says she is getting contact lenses to replace her glasses, and though Valerie is not sure she wants contacts, her mother insists it will help her fit in better at the new school.
- The one major change she likes at Greenwich Academy is the school uniform of a plaid skirt, white blouse and blazer; it suits her sense of order.
- Since arriving at the school, she has auditioned and been accepted by the Young Artists Philharmonic, which is known throughout the state.
- The audition in front of dozens of people she had never seen scared her to death; to block them out of her mind, she concentrated on playing her audition piece perfectly.
- She has been disappointed by the lack of Baroque music on the orchestra program, but is glad to have found her friend Amy McAdam, who is one year older and plays the violin with the orchestra, and loves Bach and cats as much as Valerie does.

"Statement of Goals & Purpose," Greenwich Academy Catalog, 1986:

Greenwich Academy is an independent college preparatory day school for girls and young women. Its mission is to provide a challenging, comprehensive educational experience grounded in a rigorous liberal arts curriculum with the objective of developing independent women of courage, integrity and compassion.

- They practice together frequently and have devised plans to invite two other girls to join them so they can form a string quartet.
- But Valerie knows that might mean giving up something, like sailing or horseback riding, or tennis, or dance.
- Naomi, the au pair from Israel, who is a distant cousin of her mother, makes meeting the hectic schedule possible.
- Naomi came to America to perfect her English, meet boys and have adventures; getting up at 6:30 a.m. to coddle two children is not her favorite part of the plan.
- Even though she thinks keeping up with two kids is a chore, she knows better than to complain out loud.
- Most mornings Valerie gets up, feeds Greyboy, changes his litter box and is in the shower by the time Naomi comes upstairs to wake up six-year-old David.
- After breakfast, Naomi piles Valerie and David into the family station wagon and drives them to their respective schools.
- After school, she picks them up and begins the seemingly endless procession to lessons and appointments.
- Valerie normally sees her mother at dinner and sometimes before bed, but seldom sees her father since their move to Connecticut.
- When they lived in Mount Kisco, he worked hard but always came home at night, no matter how late.
- Now, he has an apartment in the city, coming to Stamford only on Sundays.
- When home, he delights in hearing Valerie play the cello; sometimes entire Sunday afternoons are spent showing her father all she has done during the past week.
- Recently, she even dressed up for a Sunday concert for one, as though it were a formal orchestra recital, wearing her long black skirt, white blouse and black dress pumps.
- While her father enjoys her performances, Valerie knows that he likes her brother best.
- David's boisterous recitations and antics have her father roaring with laughter; he never laughs that hard at her stories.

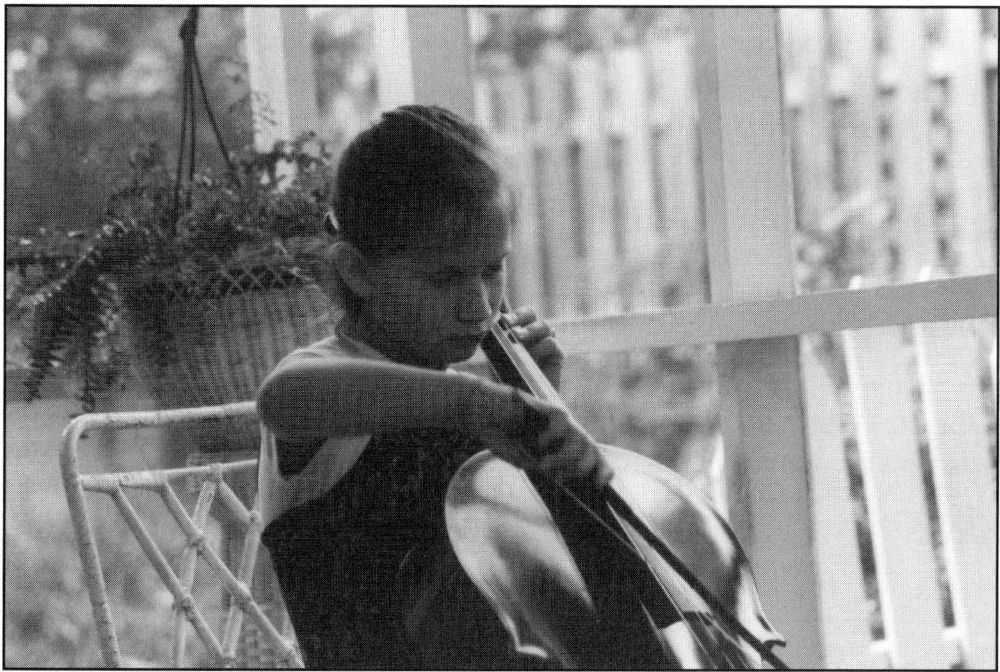

Growing up, she learned to play the Romantics, but now prefers Baroque.

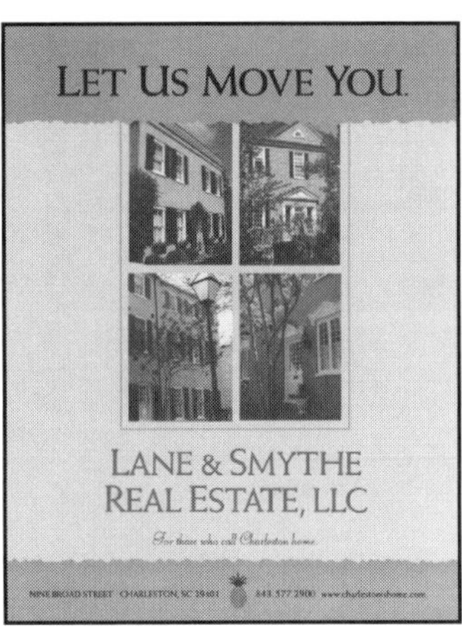

- Late at night, after Valerie goes to bed, she sometimes hears her mother and father arguing; one night her father called for a driver and left in the middle of the night.
- The next night at dinner, her mother said terrible things and even blurted out that Valerie's music teacher thinks that she is very technically competent, but will never be a great artist.
- That night Valerie cried herself to sleep, afraid her father might never come back, and equally afraid her music teacher was right in his assessment of her talent.

Life in the Community: Stamford, Connecticut

- Located in southwestern Connecticut, Stamford is located on Long Island Sound, at the New York border; its population is approximately 103,000.
- Because of its location, the city serves as the headquarters of numerous Fortune 500 corporations.

"Stamford, Connecticut Weathers Reaganomics," by Donald Ferree, Jr., W. Wayne Shannon and Everett Carll Ladd, *Public Opinion*, February/March 1983:

Stamford is different from many central cities in the Northeast: It is not economically troubled and declining. It has a highly educated population, a substantial but smaller proportion of the poor and minorities, and an expanding economy.

In many ways, Stamford resembles a "sunbelt city." Its modern population experience has been one of growth rather than decline. In 1940, when Hartford had 166,000 people and New Haven 160,000, Stamford was a very small city of 48,000 residents. After 1940, the population of Connecticut's larger cities declined, but Stamford's grew steadily until the 1970s when a modest decline occurred. This population profile is much like that of many newer cities of the South and West, and quite different from that of most older northeastern urban places. . . .

While most of the older northeastern cities are poorer than the states where they are located, Stamford residents continue to be better off than the entire Connecticut populace. In 1970, when the state's median family income was $11,811, Stamford's was $13,571. In 1980, even with the substantial influx of lower income minority residents, the Stamford median income was $26,692, against a state figure of $23,151. Similarly, Stamford is an anomaly among northeastern cities in its education base: a higher proportion of its residents than of the state as a whole are college graduates—this even though Connecticut itself ranks high in educational attainment. Property values and property costs are far higher in Stamford than in any other Connecticut city and far surpass the state averages. Unemployment is lower than in other central cities.

The Young Artists Philharmonic, Admission:

Admission to the orchestra is by closed auditions which are held in September and May of each year. Students should come prepared to play any short piece or étude of their choice which best reflects their abilities. Older students will be asked to sight-read. Students are auditioned on an individual basis by the conductors, who have the sole determination as to group placement. Students are placed by ability, not age, although some students find it beneficial to be placed relative to their peer group. Students, with the exception of the flute players, are informed of their placement at the time of their audition.

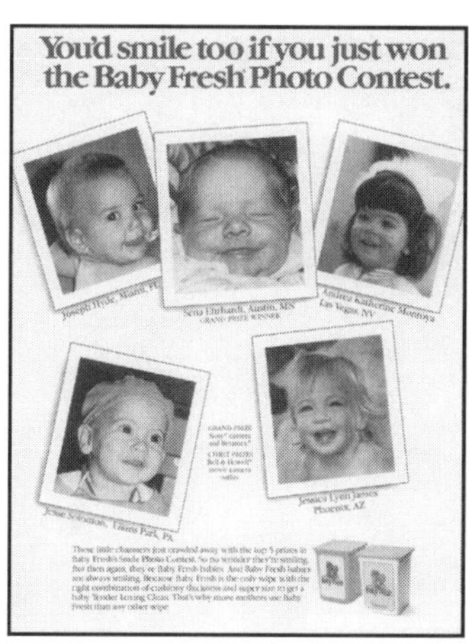

- Ruth Jaffen felt that living closer to New York City would provide the children with the many advantages they deserve.
- Stamford boasts a branch of the University of Connecticut, a branch of the Whitney Museum of American Art, and the Stamford Museum and Nature Center.
- In music, the city is known for the Stamford Symphony Orchestra, the Young Artists Philharmonic, and the Connecticut Grand Opera.
- The Young Artists Philharmonic was organized in 1960 to give talented young musicians a chance to play challenging music and participate in concerts.
- Through the years, it has been invited to perform for national, state and special events; quartets and quintets from the orchestra often perform at local functions.
- The Stamford Marriott Crossword Puzzle Tournament is an annual event in the city, attracting thousands.
- Since incorporation in 1893, city officials have bestowed a variety of nicknames and mottoes on Stamford: City of Research, City in Step with Tomorrow, and Lock City.

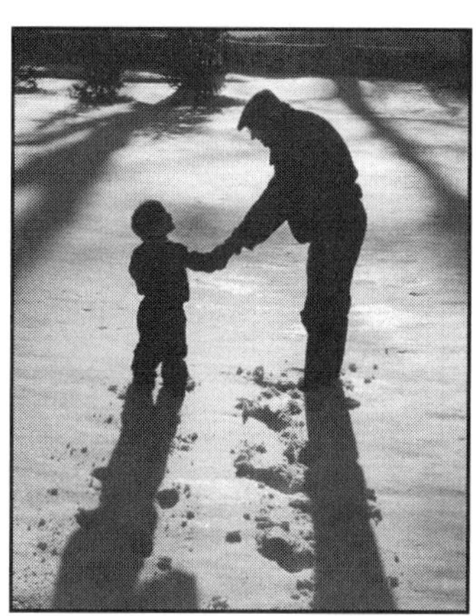

Historical Snapshot
1985

- Nintendo introduced its game system
- "Born in the U.S.A." by Bruce Springsteen, "Like a Virgin" by Madonna and "Private Dancer" by Tina Turner were among the top albums of the year
- The Dow-Jones Industrial Average topped 1,300 for the first time, peaking at 1,553 for the year; the low was 1,184
- Television premieres included *The Equalizer*, *Spenser for Hire*, *The Oprah Winfrey Show* and *Golden Girls*
- ABC was acquired by Capital Cities Communications for $3.43 billion
- Hit songs included Madonna's "Material Girl"
- Average salaries in the National Football League reached $163,145, up from $90,102 in 1982
- Hollywood movie premieres included *Out of Africa*, *The Color Purple*, *Back to the Future*, *Rambo: First Blood Part II*, *Desperately Seeking Susan* and *Kiss of the Spider Woman*
- Bach, Handel and Scarlatti tercentenaries were celebrated throughout the world; at Yale, 33 recently discovered Bach chorale preludes were performed
- Food fads included wafer-thin pizza with toppings like duck and lamb sausage, whole grain pita bread and ice cream substitutes like tofu and yogurt
- The "Live Aid" concerts in Philadelphia and London were viewed by 1.6 billion people on television and grossed $70 million for famine-stricken Africa
- Corporate takeovers reached a record high of $120 billion
- Coca-Cola began marketing "New Coke"; three months later, after a consumer uprising, the company reinstated its original product under the name "Coca-Cola Classic"
- Missing children's photos on milk cartons, the Ford Taurus, a female Harlem Globetrotter, a congressman in space and the Rock and Roll Hall of Fame all made their first appearance
- Young children watched 27 hours and 21 minutes of television a week
- The phrase "Where's the Beef?" became a national slogan of exasperation, thanks to a Wendy's Hamburgers television advertisement

1985 Economic Profile

Selected Prices

Ballet Ticket, *The Nutcracker*	$18.00
Briefcase, Lladro, Leather	$565.00
Car Phone, Metrocom	$995.00
Computer Chess Game	$149.00
Compact Disc Player	$229.95
Disposable Diapers	$16.46
Floppy Disks, Fuji	$9.95
Liqueur, Kahlua, Bottle	$9.97
Movie Ticket	$2.00
Pen & Pencil Set, Cross	$30.00
Potato Chips, Ruffles, 6.5-Ounce Bag	$1.19
Television Satellite Dish	$1,995.00
Shirt, Man's Velour	$14.92
Silk Spider Plant	$54.99
Tuna, 6.5-Ounce Can	$0.59

food

TERRIFIC SOUP—IN 20 MINUTES!

Try our yummy homemade family pleasers—from broccoli-cheddar to tortellini-vegetable

by Lori Longbotham

A chicken classic updated

Think soup has to boil in a big pot for hours to taste really good? We're about to change your mind about that! By taking some shortcuts (such as using frozen veggies), you can easily create a tasty, comforting meal for your clan in mere minutes. Try these four tempting recipes and see for yourself how no-fuss soup can be.

Chicken Soup With Sugar Snap Peas

PREP TIME: 5 minutes
COOKING TIME: 8 minutes

3 cups chicken broth
1 9-oz package frozen sugar snap peas, sweet peas, and carrots in lemon pepper sauce
6 to 8 oz thinly sliced, uncooked chicken cutlets, cut diagonally into

Changing America

- The rapid development of computers included the creation of the Cray 2, which could perform a billion calculations—one gigaflop—a second.
- America had 476,000 physicians, 132,000 dentists and 1.3 million hospital beds.
- Disposable lighters and watches were flooding the market.
- Television specials for the year included *Death of a Salesman* with Dustin Hoffman, *The Statue of Liberty* and *Vietnam: The Real Story*.
- The RP Foundation for Fighting Blindness ran an advertisement reading, "Put a dog out of work."
- New York City restricted the erection of new high-rise buildings on residential streets of the Upper East Side to protect its architectural character.
- *Art News* pressured the Austrian government to return to their rightful owners 3,900 works of art seized by the Nazis.
- The superstrings theory proposed that the most elementary particles were one-dimensional, and that the universe is 10-, not four-dimensional.
- School boards across the nation battled over whether AIDS-afflicted children should be allowed at school.
- Medical malpractice suits skyrocketed, up threefold since 1975; the average award reached $333,000.
- The number of Barbie dolls sold since their inception surpassed the entire current population of the United States.
- An estimated 27 million adults were functionally illiterate.

"The Lucrative Little LBO Shops: Who needs mega-mergers? Some small firms are profiting from buyouts of emerging growth companies," by Solveig Jansson, *Institutional Investor*, August 22, 1985:

Canny investors have long sought out shares of emerging companies for their potentially dazzling returns, of course. But why just buy the stock of such promising enterprises, reasons a small group of merger and acquisition specialists, when you can reap far greater rewards by buying the companies themselves?

By doing precisely that—acting as principals in leveraged buyouts of small companies with sparkling prospects, nurturing their growth and then taking them public—these little LBO shops have achieved some spectacular payoffs. Small to mid-sized companies—those with sales of less than $100 million—offer higher growth potential, higher return on assets and higher gross margins than 500-list behemoths, points out Theodore Stolberg of the investment counseling firm of Weiss, Peck and Greer.

So enticing is this little LBO business, in fact, that Carl Marks & Co., the maverick market maker of foreign securities, has committed more capital to it—some $150 million—through its CM Capital Corp. subsidiary than it has to its regular trading activities. . .

In contrast to the headline-grabbing mega-mergers, small buyouts tend to be conducted in relative obscurity—which suits the dealmakers just fine. "Large transactions add no real value," contends Weiss. "They tend to be overpriced and shopped all over the country." Because little LBO's never appear on the national auction block, they don't get bid up excessively. "When you buy small private companies, you typically get them for discounts of 20 to 40 percent vis-à-vis equivalent public companies."

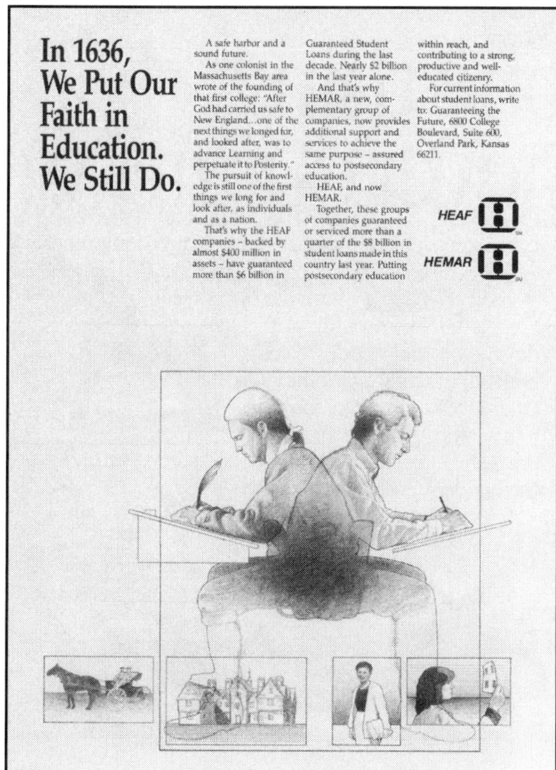

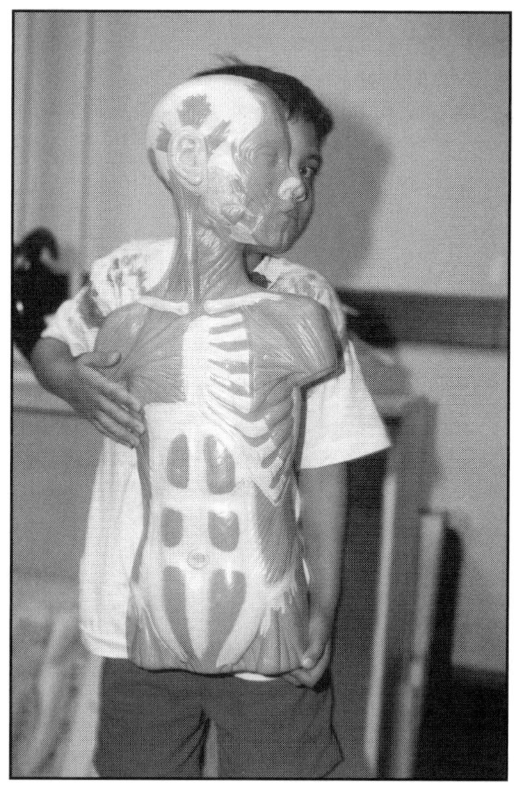

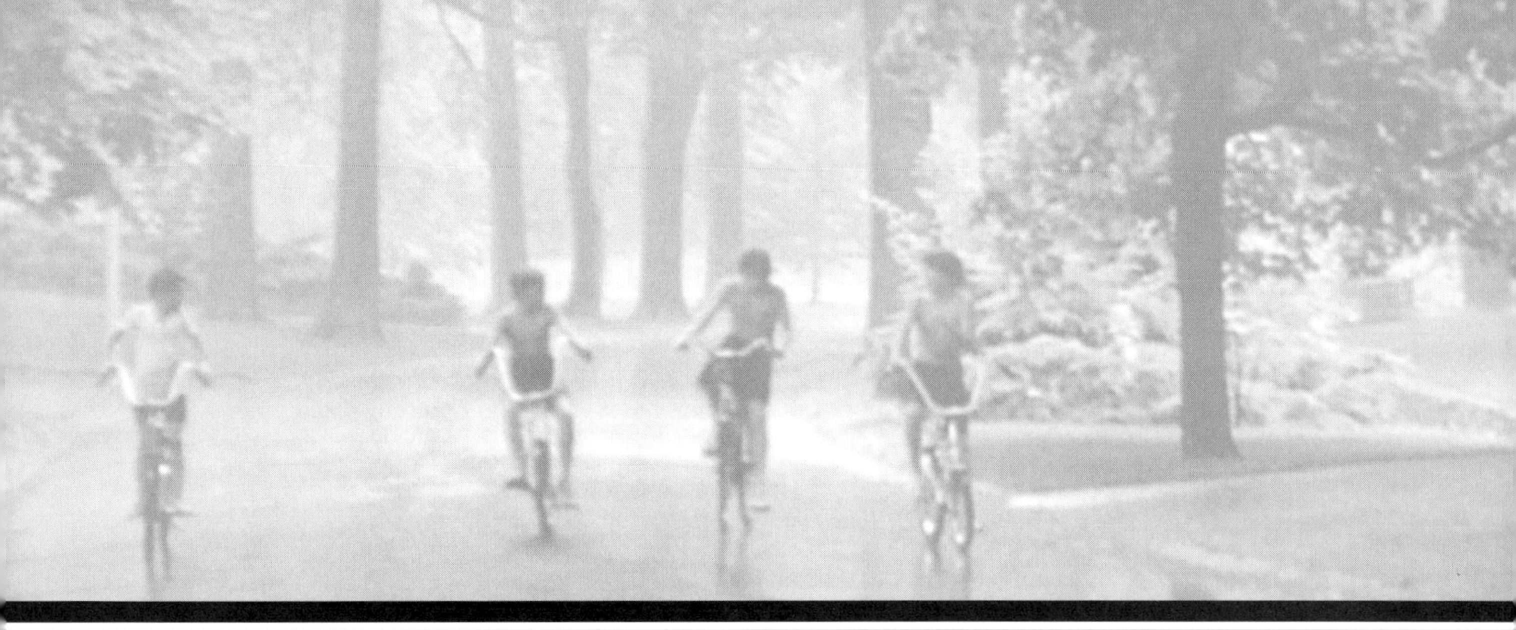

1989 Profile

Middle Class

Six-foot, six-inch Irby Hipp of Charleston, West Virginia, hates basketball but loves to play video games, listen to Nirvana, dream about surfing and memorize facts to help him excel at a schoolyard version of Trivial Pursuit.

Irby Hipp's interests include video games, Nirvana and surfing.

Life at Home

- Everyone—his father, his brother, the coach and kids at school—wants Irby to be a basketball player.
- Irby wants to play video games and one day, like Douglas Smith, become a developer himself.
- After all, Smith wrote Lode Runner on a VAX 11780 computer while he was a student at the University of Washington; who better to develop America's next video-game sensation than a video-head?
- Besides, now that Nintendo's Game Boy has been introduced, the field is expanding, more competition is opening up and your own skills are your only limitation.
- While others in his hometown spend their time incessantly dribbling a basketball, Irby and his friends have contests to see who can imitate the most video-game sounds: The descending arpeggio that signals "Game Over" for Pitfall Harry, the sounds of dragons crashing into the walls in Adventure, or the sound of Mario jumping over a barrel in Donkey Kong.
- When bored with a lecture at school or at home, he loves to quietly make the "wakka-wakka" dot-eating noise of Pac-Man.

"Here Come the Super Mario Bros., Don't know who they are? You probably will by Christmas," *Business Week*, November 9, 1987:

When you jump up and get a magic mushroom or fire flower, press 'A' when the transformation is over, and you'll do a midair jump. *Nintendo Fan Club News*

If this tip from a recent video-game magazine sounds like gibberish, ask any kid to explain it. It's a hint for players of Super Mario Bros., a video game played on a pint-size Japanese machine called a family computer, or "fami-com." For two years, Super Mario Brothers has raged across Japan, helping to push fami-coms into a quarter of all Japanese households—about 10 million homes. The fami-com, a graphics computer that turns a TV set into a game machine, was brought to the U.S. in 1985 and is now one of America's hottest toys. Its creator, Kyoto-based Nintendo Co., hopes to sell three million fami-coms in the U.S. this year.

Jaded American consumers who recall the collapse of the video-game craze in 1983 may not believe it. But the folks who brought Asteroids and Donkey Kong into your living room are back. During the boom from 1979 to 1982, industry leader Atari doubled revenues three years running, and the industry's annual sales of hardware and games topped $2 billion. When kids wearied of the shoot-'em-up software, the industry crashed.

Now, a fresh crop of game-hungry kids is reviving demand for game machines. Even Atari, which fired a president and 4,500 employees and lost $539 million when the game market went bust, is back. With home computer pioneer Jack Tramiel in charge, Atari hopes to move two million machines worldwide this year. Hasbro, Mattel, and Japan's SEGA Enterprises are getting back in the business, too.

So far, Nintendo is leading the comeback. A century-old toymaker that earned $177 million on sales of $1 billion in the year ended last August, Nintendo made arcade games before crafting the family computer in 1983. It quickly overtook such domestic rivals as Sony Corp. and Matsushita, which were pushing a standardized home computer called MSX.

Nintendo grabbed more than 90 percent of its home turf and now has a 70 percent share of the $500 million U.S. market. Its formula is good graphics at an affordable price and tight control on software quality. The result is "a newly developing video-game market," says Peter L. Harris, president and CEO of New York toy emporium F.A.O. Schwarz. "Nintendo is the most important line." The new wave won't be as big as the first, Harris believes, but it may be more enlightening. "The games have much more depth, more learning value, and more play value," he says.

The key to Nintendo's success is its policy on software. Instead of encouraging developers to crank out as many games as possible, Nintendo commits them to rigid contracts. Each of them is limited to half a dozen new titles a year. Nintendo manufactures the game cartridges, then forces the developers to buy the cartridges in batches of 10,000, which they are then responsible for selling. The arrangement can soak up 50 percent of the developer's profits. And it means that each game has to be a winner. But the payoff is a chance to sell into Nintendo's huge fami-com owner base, where a megahit like Super Mario Bros. can sell five million copies. . . .

Nintendo machines are now available at some 12,000 U.S. retail outlets, including such chains as Toys 'R' Us, Crazy Eddie, and K-Mart. The strategy is working. Last Christmas retailers exhausted their stock of Nintendo systems, which range in price from $89 for a simple console to $149 for a set with a robot, light-gun, and two cassettes. Some K-Mart outlets already are reporting shortages.

- Irby cut his video teeth on Pac-Man and Defender, stealing quarters from his father's dresser top so he could compete at the arcade.
- If his father suspected where his spare change was going, he never said anything.
- Then came Zonk, the world's first commercially distributed interactive adventure game, and Irby was hooked.
- The key to Zonk was its puzzles, requiring the players to think their way through the Great Underground Empire, past lakes and grottoes and trolls.
- Irby was fascinated by the possibilities, returning to the game week after week to see what lay around the corner this time.
- Indifferent to subjects such as who won the basketball game on Friday night or who is going out with whom, Irby and his friends joust for respect by talking about their progress through various video games.
- It's great to belong to something that doesn't require you to strain yourself and ache all the time.
- Recently, his father attempted to get Irby more involved in the city's annual Sternwheel Regatta festival; this year, Irby's father is chairing one of the major committees.

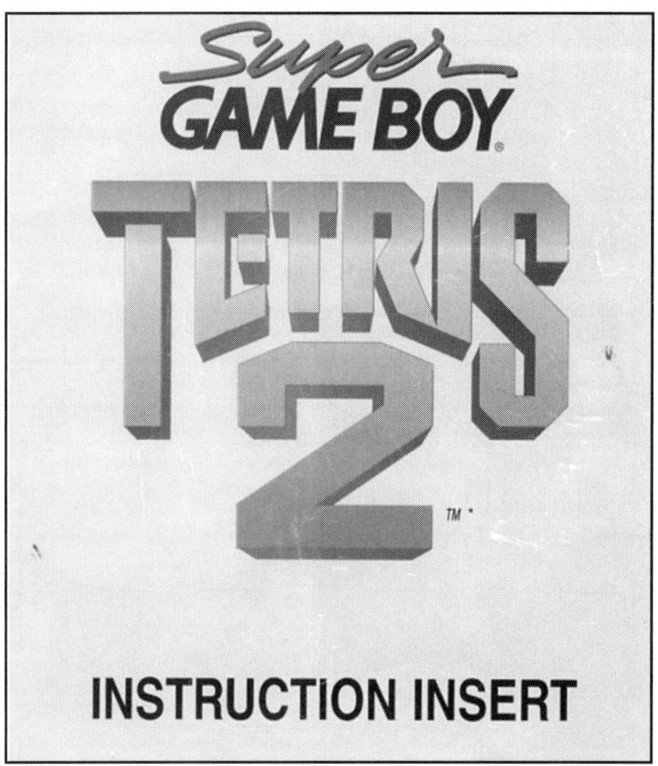

"Where All the Quarters Go, NARC to Bad Girls, the latest in coin-fed fun,"
***Newsweek*, December 5, 1988:**

There are a couple of ways to gauge the health of the coin-operated amusement-machine business. The first is to examine the numbers, which show an industry on the upswing. Revenues for 1987: Up a billion dollars over 1986, to almost $7 billion. Video games on top ($2.9 billion), pinball close behind ($2.6 billion). CD jukeboxes making inroads: 36 percent of operators reported buying them last year. That's one way. Another is to visit the annual trade show of the Amusement & Music Operator's Association in early November and see how long it takes until you go deaf as a post. Imagine the biggest arcade in the universe. Imagine sirens, bells, buzzers, klaxons, racketing bumpers and CD jukeboxes, every last one of them playing "Also Sprach Zarathustra" at peak decibels. Imagine the din of one million hellhounds. This is what a healthy coin-operated amusement-machine business sounds like. . . .

Video games and pinball are strong nationally, although video tends to be stronger in the West than in the Midwest. Basketball shoot-out games are going well on the East Coast and in the Midwest, where electronic darts have also taken off sharply in the last few years. . . . The dark days of 1982 and '83 and '84, when the video glut led to a sharp drop in revenues and a shakeout among manufacturers, are behind the industry now. . . .

Consider the industry leaders in pinball and video games. Gottlieb rolled out a battery of 33 Bad Girls in Chicago, a dizzyingly fast new pinball machine whose hot-pink bumpers read "Kiss Me!"—which, if nothing else, would seem to confirm several generations of parental concern that there is some terrible, unfathomable connection between pinball and sex.

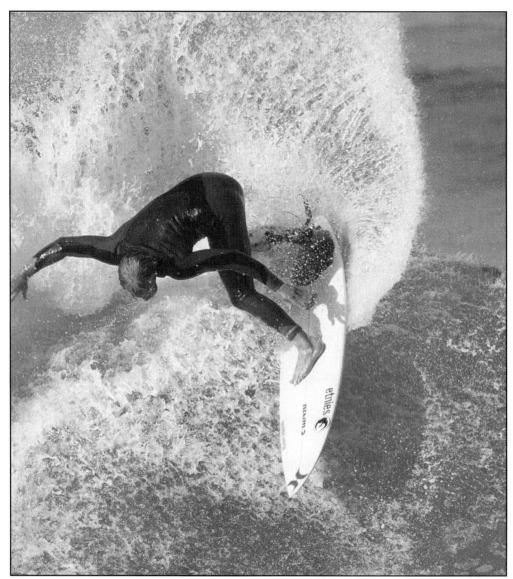

Irby has surfing posters on his bedroom wall.

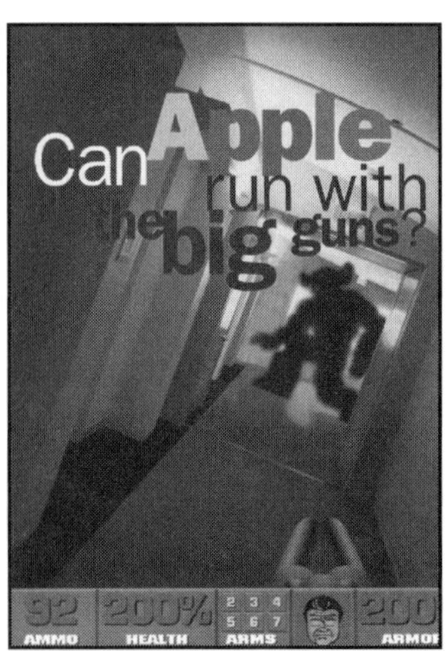

- Every five minutes, it seems, Irby is being asked to drop the controls on his game and look something up on his computer.
- He thinks it is a plot to lure him away from his games because his father thinks all this computer/video time serves no purpose.
- Currently, Irby is exploring Populous and the ability to rotate and alter the scale of the game's isometric world.
- His room is the universe he controls; on one wall is a huge picture of a surfer high and tight in the inner realm of a wave—cool and powerful.
- Irby has never learned to surf and rarely swims, but the poster epitomizes all the skills and control he would like to have.
- On his other wall is a picture of Nirvana's Kurt Cobain sprawled on a drum kit in total abandon.
- The rest of his room is cluttered with pictures of people like Clint Eastwood and old dinosaur models he created from wooden kits as a child.

His room is cluttered with pictures of Clint Eastwood and old dinosaur models made of wood.

- The only thing that will lure him out of his room is a chance to see another segment of a new cartoon program, *The Simpsons*.

Life at School

- High school, in a word, sucks.
- When he was a freshman, everyone talked about how he was going to help the basketball team and which college he could attend.
- During his sophomore year, he was caught smoking dope and got kicked out for a semester.
- Now he is back and behind the rest of his class.

Nirvana's Kurt Cobain symbolizes the freedom Irby desires.

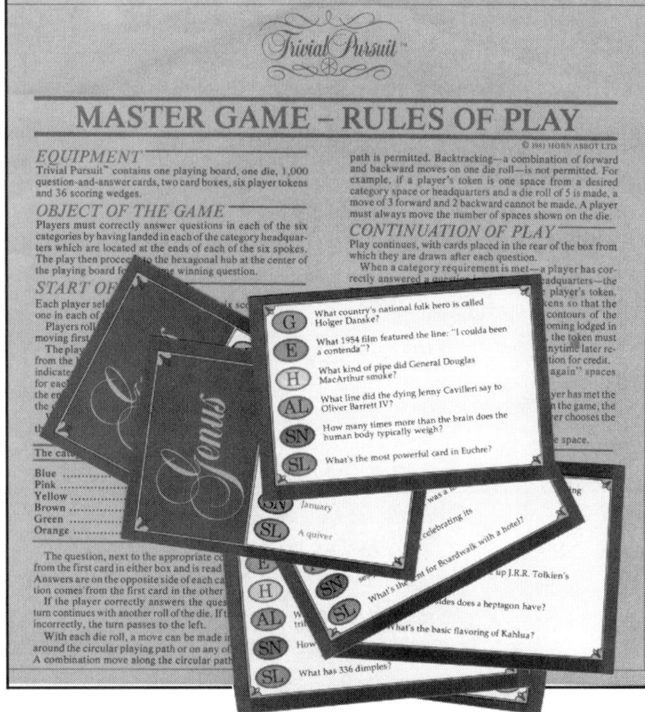

- The teachers think he is a slacker and watch him like a hawk, while the popular girls think he is a dopehead, and the athletes don't talk to him because he won't go out for the basketball team.
- Who cares?
- The teachers never consult each other about assigning homework, so they always give out loads to do on the same day.
- It's not fair—how is anyone supposed to read a chapter in a boring English novel, do chemistry and algebra, and still be in a good mood?
- His mother says he doesn't handle pressure well.
- He is sure he handles it just fine; he just doesn't think that all of his time should be consumed by useless, stupid facts.
- After all, no one—but no one—talks about people named Heathcliff when class is over.
- If only they taught real stuff, or let him show everyone his best game moves, everything would be different.
- His school is an amalgamation of three schools brought together in redistricting, creating a huge campus with sparkling new buildings.
- The School Board believes that changing district lines will draw the community together.
- Irby just feels hostile.
- His only school activity, besides organizing video-game tournaments, is playing Trivial Pursuit.
- At lunchtime, teams form on each side of a picnic table and call out questions; the other team must answer eight of the 10 questions to gain the right to call out questions in the second round.
- Irby especially likes questions such as, "What part of the body gets cut during a bunionectomy?" or "Which of Jean-Paul Sartre's novels has the sickest title?"
- He hates TV trivia questions such as "Which of TV's Cartwright boys wears the biggest hat?"

Life in the Community: Charleston, West Virginia

- Charleston is West Virginia's capital and its second-largest city.
- Started as a frontier fort, the city is now a major center for the chemical industry, as well as glass-fabricated metals and synthetic fabrics.
- Charleston's Italian Renaissance-style Capitol, built on the banks of the Kanawha River, is considered one of the most beautiful buildings in the state.
- The city is now experiencing an economic boom, thanks to new industry moving into the area.

Historical Snapshot 1989

- The longest peacetime period of economic expansion reached its eighty-fifth month in December; per capita income was up 19 percent since 1982
- Television's top programs included *Roseanne*, *The Cosby Show*, *Cheers*, *A Different World*, *Dear John*, *The Wonder Years* and *Golden Girls*
- Congress passed $166 billion legislation to bail out the savings and loan industry
- Cocaine and crack cocaine use was up 35 percent over 1985
- Sony of Japan purchased Columbia Pictures, sparking comments of Japan invading Hollywood
- Demonstrators at Tiananmen Square carried a Styrofoam Statue of Liberty as part of the protest against the Chinese government
- A private U.S. satellite, comedy cable TV, the pregaphone to talk to a fetus, and a girl in the Little League World Series first appeared
- Scientists speculated that the New World Peruvian architecture could be as old as the Egyptian pyramids
- The movie *Batman* grossed $250 million, the fifth-highest in movie history
- *Field of Dreams*; *When Harry Met Sally*; *Glory*; *Driving Miss Daisy*; *Sex, Lies and Videotape*; and *Roger and Me* premiered at movie theaters
- In women's fashion, Calvin Klein's lean and refined look included soft fabrics with little or no jewelry
- *The Heidi Chronicles* by Wendy Wasserstein won both the Tony Award and the Pulitzer Prize
- Baseball Commissioner Bart Giamatti banned ballplayer Pete Rose for life from the game for allegedly betting on games
- *The Joy Luck Club* by Amy Tan, *The Satanic Verses* by Salman Rushdie, *The Temple of My Familiar* by Alice Walker, *The Oldest Living Confederate Widow Tells All* by Allan Gurganus and *A Brief History of Time* by Stephen Hawking were bestsellers
- In Chicago, U.S. veterans protested at the Art Institute where the American flag was draped on the floor
- "Wind Beneath My Wings" by Bette Midler won a Grammy Award for best song
- Top singles for the year included "Every Rose Has Its Thorn" by Poison, "Miss You Much" by Janet Jackson, "Girl, You Know Its True" by Milli Vanilli and "Love Shack" by the B-52's

1989 Economic Profile

Selected Prices

Audio Tapes, Sony, Three-Pack $7.99
Bed Pillow, Hermes $75.00
Book Club Membership,
Literary Guild $1.00
Computer, Apple IIGS $795.00
Easter Lily $4.99
Glue Gun, Craftsman $24.99
Ground Beef, per Pound $1.71
Ice Cream, Dove Bar $1.45
Hosiery, Ladies', Three Pairs $8.07
Lawn Chair, Adirondack $129.00
Necklace, 16" Herringbone
Chain, 14-Karat Gold $79.00
Socks, Boys' Crew-Length,
Six-Pack $4.99
Synthesizer, Yamaha $188.88
Water Heater, Kenmore $89.99
Wine, Bolla Soave $3.13

INTRODUCING NCAA CHAMPION

WANNA GO

Tonight's Game

64 NCAA DIVISION I TEAMS AND ARENAS. Home court floor graphics, team colors and fans-in-the-stands signage give you the whole flavor of the NCAA college hoops experience.

ADVANCED ARTIFICIAL INTELLIGENCE. Wild student sections bring built-in home court advantage to life. Players improve over four years. Performance varies with game pressure, age and skill ratings.

4,500 FRAMES OF PLAYER ANIMATION. Over 100 player moves include alley-oops, slam dunks and behind-the-back dribbling. All with real-time SGI motion-capture graphics. If it were any more realistic, you'd see it on the 11 o'clock news.

First Seen in the 1980s

1980
- Post-It Notes
- Space Shuttle
- Prime-time soap operas—first *Dallas*, then *Dynasty*

1981
- IBM sells first personal computer
- MTV
- Test-tube baby
- AIDS symptoms

1982
- Michael Jackson's *Thriller* becomes biggest-selling album ever
- Liposuction
- Vietnam Memorial erected in Washington, DC
- Human artificial heart transplant

1983
- Cabbage Patch Kids
- Camcorders
- Sally Ride is first American woman in space
- Compact discs

1984
- Infomercials
- The term "cyberspace" is coined

1985
- Crack cocaine
- *Titanic* wreckage found
- Nintendo game system
- Rock and Roll Hall of Fame

1986
- Fox Network
- *Oprah Winfrey Show* goes national

1987
- U.S. budget reaches trillion-dollar mark
- Last California condor taken into captivity
- World population hits five billion
- Prince Charles and Princess Diana separate

1988
- CDs outsell vinyl
- Prozac
- McDonald's opens in Russia
- Human genome project begins

1989
- Berlin Wall falls
- Chinese student protest in Tiananmen Square
- Dalai Lama wins Nobel Peace Prize
- *The Simpsons* premieres

Changing America

- Harvard studies indicated that 30 to 45 minutes of brisk walking five times a week reduced heart attack mortality by more than 50 percent.
- Duke Ellington's ninetieth birthday was celebrated throughout the United States.
- A report by the National Research Council stated: "If all racial discrimination were abolished today, the life prospects facing many poor blacks would still constitute a major challenge for public policy."
- Americans watched live news coverage of the Chinese and Eastern European revolutions, and the San Francisco earthquake.
- Across America, 57 percent of households had cable TV, while 66 percent owned a VCR.
- A piece of the fallen Berlin Wall could be purchased at Bloomingdale's for $12.50.
- Van Cliburn made a successful comeback after 11 years, playing the Liszt and Tchaikovsky piano concertos in Philadelphia and Dallas.
- Physicists agreed on three basic types of matter: up and down, charmed and strange, and top and bottom quarks.
- AZT was shown to delay the onset of AIDS, and to be valuable in treating HIV-positive individuals.
- The Civil Rights Memorial in Montgomery, Alabama, was designed by Maya Lin.

"Not Altogether Done Yet, Appalachia," *The Economist*, November 22, 1986:

It is 25 years since the extraordinary poverty of Appalachia—the Southern mountain region centered in eastern Kentucky, West Virginia and eastern Tennessee—was brought to national attention. The anniversary was marked on November 1 with a quiet symposium in Lexington, Kentucky, to honor Mr. Harry Caudill, the author whose writings played a large part in persuading Presidents Kennedy and Johnson to set up the Appalachian Regional Commission. It was also marked in Washington by yet another brush with death for the ARC itself. Mr. Reagan asked for its money to be eliminated from the budget for fiscal 1987. Its work, he said, was done.

The tall, fiery-tongued Mr. Caudill originally agreed with the president; he thought a "Southern Mountain Authority," as he called it, ought to be able to bring Appalachia up to the national standard of living within two or three decades. The Tennessee Valley Authority had, after all, done as much for the neighboring Tennessee Valley, inspiring an industrial boom by bringing them cheap power. Appalachia had perhaps been ravaged too long by the combined efforts of careless mountain farmers and the lumber and coal companies, but if federal officers provide the encouragement and much of the money, the local authorities might eagerly improve matters.

Over the past 21 years, the ARC has poured $5 billion into a wide "Appalachian" region, with another $10 billion coming in from other sources. The governors of the 13 states covered by the commission fervently support it, and each year they are careful to draw up a current Appalachian development plan. There has been notable success, in patches. The area encompassing Bristol, Kingsport and Johnson City, in Tennessee, has prospered on chemicals and electronics; it grew up 11.1 percent between 1979 and 1985, the second-fastest growth in the state. Beckley, West Virginia, once just another dusty coal town, has become a regional medical center; Charleston, the state capital, has attracted numbers of computer firms. . . .

Other statistics cast doubt on what the ARC has accomplished. Barely half the children in the area finish high school. Unemployment, which for years has been two to three percentage points higher than the national average, was twice as high last March in a quarter of the mountain counties. Three-quarters of these unemployed are thought to be functionally illiterate, meaning that they are virtually unable to apply for work even if the jobs are there. In West Virginia, the only state entirely within the ARC's remit, a third of the mining and manufacturing jobs have disappeared since 1979. A journey through central Appalachia turns up great numbers of people still living in trailers on hillsides, collecting discolored drinking water in buckets, and throwing their rubbish and sewage in the creeks, as if the commission had never happened.

"Relode, Douglas Smith and Lode Runner," *Next Generation*, August 1989:

Anyone who owned a personal computer in the early '80s will likely recall a clever puzzle and action game titled Lode Runner. Few know, however, that this was the debut game from a University of Washington student named Douglas Smith.

In the summer of 1982, Smith wrote Lode Runner on a mainframe VAX 11780 computer while working in the University's computer center. In lieu of graphics, Smith used the available character set, casting the dollar sign as the protagonist and the paragraph mark as enemies. He had no intention of marketing the project, which he created just for the fun of it.

When his nephew expressed an interest in playing the game at home, however, Smith spent three days rewriting the game for the Apple II. And on a whim, Smith submitted the game, under the name Miner, to software publisher Broderbund. The response was as prompt as it was hopeless: He received a one-line rejection letter that same week. Little did Smith know that Broderbund's president, Doug Carlson, was out of the office with a broken leg. His secretary, in an effort to keep his desk clear, was summarily rejecting all submissions.

Smith's hopes were bruised, but at the urging of a local Computerland employee who loved and believed in the game, he persevered. His next step was to borrow a thousand bucks to purchase a color monitor, a joystick, and some development software that enabled him to add color graphics and joystick support to the game.

He then resubmitted the game to Broderbund, as well as three other Apple II software publishers: Sierra, Synergistic, and Sirrus. Within three days, he had eager offers from all four companies.

Since Broderbund was more of a known entity to Smith than the other companies were, he chose it as the game's publisher. Broderbund's major suggestion for the game was a name change. Because the name Miner was so similar to another computer game, Miner 2049ers, Broderbund renamed the game Lode Runner.

From December to June, Smith created the final Apple II version of Lode Runner. The first copy of Lode Runner shipped June 23, 1983. Since that time, Lode Runner and its sequels have been ported to 15 computer and game platforms, and sold more than three million copies worldwide.

"Coal Country's War with Itself, Families get caught in the middle as union traditions clash with a mine operator's need to compete globally," *U.S. News & World Report*, July 24, 1989:

In the land of Hatfields and McCoys, another generation-spanning feud is unfolding. With a bluster worthy of legendary labor organizer John L. Lewis, the miners of southwest Virginia. West Virginia and Kentucky have been battling their coal-company bosses like their daddies did before them. These days, however, homespun grit is colliding with the coal field's new economic imperative: Remaining competitive in global markets.

So far, the four-month-old conflict between the Pittston Coal Group and 1,700 United Mine Workers has left both sides bleeding. Coal production is down 35 percent, and the firm, which sells 65 percent of its 10.6 million-ton output abroad, is considering layoffs.

"August Races to an End in Charleston," *Southern Living*, August 1985:

Paddle-wheelers hold a fascination for most of us. They are, after all, the stuff of rich legend. Mark Twain felt the romance of them and wrote about them in his sharp-cut style. And even today, nothing draws a crowd so quickly as the sight of a steamboat gliding downstream. The wide wheels churn up visions of river life a century past, of pilots and packet boats and the heyday of steamboating.

Charleston. West Virginia, proved again last August that nothing has dimmed the allure of the stern-wheelers. They can still turn out a town in grand style, even when their port of call is a modern state capital. The evidence? The annual Charleston Sternwheel Regatta Festival.

For 10 days last summer, 300,000 people amassed down by the Kanawha River and around town to celebrate Charleston's paddle-wheeling heritage. They joined in tennis and soccer tournaments and a 15-mile distance run. They watched films and reviewed parades. They gathered for concerts on the levee, and they lined the banks of the river to cheer as more than 20 stern-wheelers and tugboats raced down-river with a flourish. Charlestonian festival-goers explain the whole extravaganza this way: "Ya' gotta regatta."

Charleston's 15-year-old festival grew out of the dream of a 12-year-old boy who wanted to see these grand boats at their paddling best. . . . "There are two things that draw a crowd: parades and fireworks," says W. T. Brotherton, Jr., president of the Charleston Festival Commission. "And we emphasize both parades and fireworks."

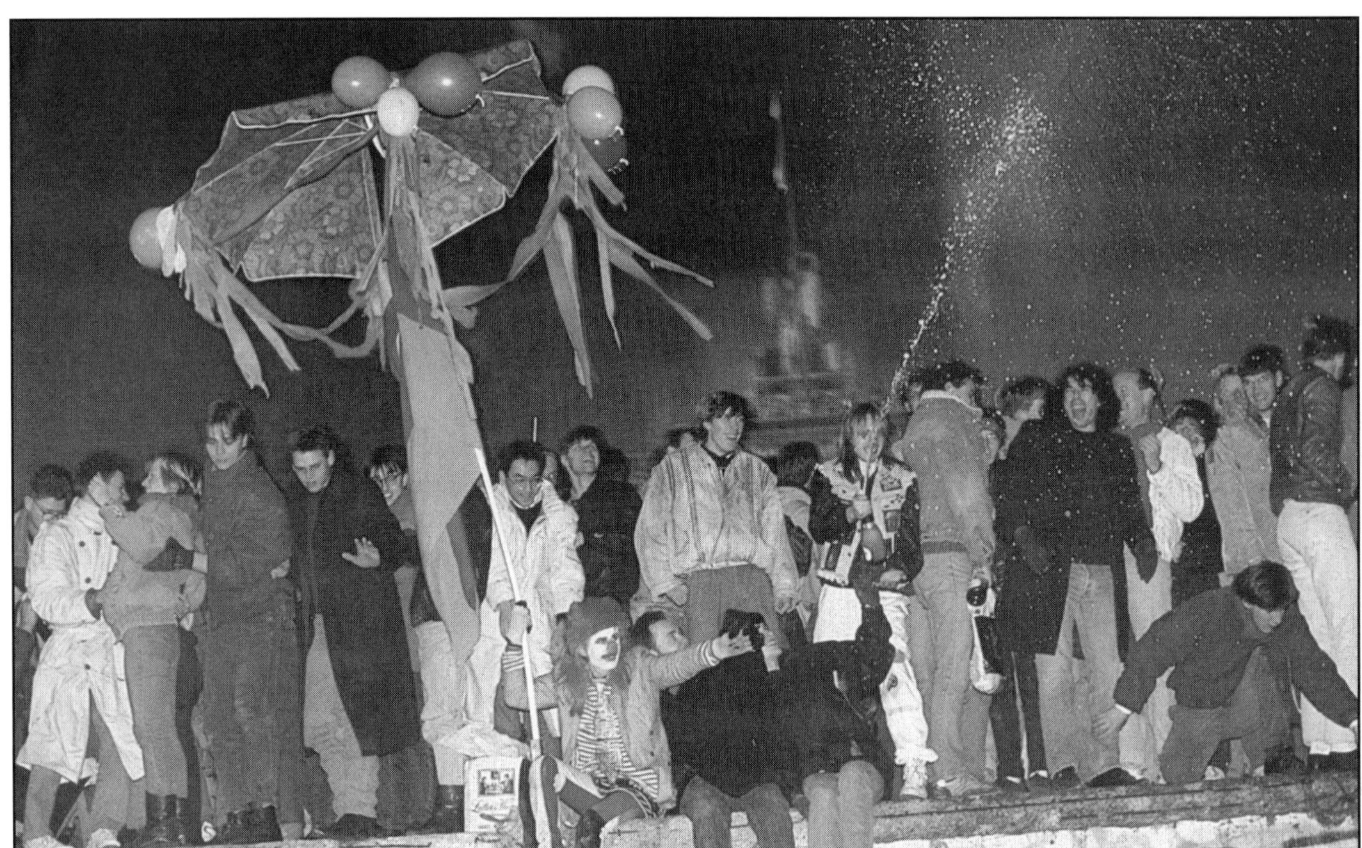

The fall of the Berlin Wall resulted in spontaneous celebration in Germany.

Blue Print

her High School, 701 Adger Rd., Columbia, S.C. 29205 September, 20

tudents' SAT Scores Improve, Remain bove State and National Averages

By Carrie Givens

Dreher High School SAT es increased 29 points from

Last year, Dreher's SAT team, coached by **Dr. Cliff Barrineau**, won the 3-A state championship

Guy Boudreaux, Mary Kathryn Keane, and a student from Riverside High tied for runner-up in the individual

Kudos to..

The Varsity Footba Team and **Coach Bill Baco** for their thrilling wins ov C.A. Johnson High ar Columbia High Schools.

Katherine Warden f

1989 News Feature

"Student Journalists Fight for Free Expression," *Scholastic Update*, September 8, 1989:

Each time Nicci Millington sits down at her computer, a wave of anxiety washes over her. "I feel like I should be watching over my shoulder," says Millington, 17, editor-in-chief of her high school newspaper in St. Charles, Illinois. "I've gotten away from thinking 'I should be writing to inform the public.' Now it's 'I think if I write this I could get in a lot of trouble.'"

Millington has good reason to worry. Ever since January 1988, when the Supreme Court handed down its decision in the case of Hazelwood v. Kuhlmeier, high school principals have held broad authority to censor student newspapers. According to young journalists like Millington, that decision has cast a dark shadow over the student newsroom.

Nearly all of the 16,748 public high schools in the U.S. publish a student newspaper or magazine, usually through a journalism class or after-school club. In many schools, the principal plays the role of publisher, or "owner," overseeing the final product from afar. Just how much power the principal can wield in that role became the central issue in Hazelwood.

The case began in the spring of 1983, at Hazelwood East High School in St. Louis, Missouri. Student editors were preparing the final issue of their paper, "The Spectrum." As usual, just before the paper was due at the press, Hazelwood's principal, Robert Reynolds, took a look at the final pages.

He didn't like what he saw. One story, about the effects of divorce on teenagers, quoted a student who criticized her father for not spending enough time at home before the divorce. Reynolds found the article biased because it gave the father no chance to defend himself.

A second story dealt with teenage pregnancy. It quoted three students who had been pregnant, but it changed their names. Reynolds worried that Spectrum readers would still be able to identify the pregnant students. And he thought the discussion of sex was inappropriate for readers in younger grades. Reynolds cut the two stories—plus four others that happened to share the same pages.

Cathy Kuhlmeier and two other Spectrum staff members claimed their rights had been violated. The students pointed to the First Amendment, which guarantees that "congress shall make no law . . .abridging the freedom of speech, or of the press." The students took their complaint to the American Civil Liberties Union, which helped them file against the

school district. Eventually they appealed the case of Hazelwood School District v. Cathy Kuhlmeier all the way to the Supreme Court.

The students had good reason to believe the Court would back them up. Ever since the 1969 landmark decision in Tinker v. Des Moines—which involved a student protest against the Vietnam War—courts have held that as long as students don't substantially disrupt school, they hold First Amendment rights much like those of adults.

But lawyers for the school district argued that the case had nothing to do with First Amendment freedoms. The Spectrum was part of the school curriculum they said, not a public forum. Administrators should be free to regulate the curriculum in their schools.

In a 5–4 decision, the Supreme Court sided with the school district. "A school need not tolerate student speech that is inconsistent with its basic educational mission," wrote Justice Bryon White in his majority opinion. As long as a principal can show his decision is "reasonably related" to educational concerns, White ruled, he or she is free to censor the student paper.

Administrators and conservative political groups applauded the ruling. But Supreme Court Justice William Brennan, in his sharply worded dissent, warned that the decision could convert public schools into "enclaves of totalitarianism that strangle the free mind at its source."

Less than three hours after the decision was made public, on January 13, 1988, a principal in Cupertino, California, first used Hazelwood to cancel a student story.

When reporter Kathryn Pallakoff agreed to profile a student at Homestead High who had tested positive for AIDS, she and the other staff members of the school newspaper, "The Epitaph," approached the topic with care.

First, their advisor told the principal about the story. Then, the students put off running the story for an extra month while they double-checked all the facts.

Once satisfied that the reporting was complete and accurate, the student-run board of The Epitaph voted to run the story. But the next morning, Hazelwood was announced.

The news reached Homestead High just before third period. Saying he needed "time to learn if the decision had substantially changed his responsibilities," Homestead principal Jim Warren announced he was "shelving" the story on AIDS.

Features

Senior Welcomes Freshmen and Offers Sound Advice

By Jessica Jordan

As I jauntily stroll down the corridors of Dreher High School, my senior status enables me to walk confidently, caring very little about my appearance or demeanor. My thoughts are focused on getting through the day, and eventually to graduation day.

As 450 new freshman faces joined the turmoil of Dreher on August 8, I was flooded with memories of my freshman year. On my first day of high school, I was terrified I wouldn't be able to find my classroom or would be harassed in the canteen, or possibly even the victim of flying jello in the courtyard at lunch. As my first day at Dreher melted away into a jumble of three years, I only recollect a haze of parties, good-looking upperclassmen, some parental troubles, and a whole lot of fun.

The school year is now well underway, and freshmen now know where their classes are and are beginning to make themselves known to upperclassmen. Soon they will find themselves comfortably in place with their social circles, and consequently they will find their niche in the courtyard at lunch.

Slowly, trepidation will surely fade into a hum of excitement amongst the class of 2006. Freshmen will find out for themselves if high school is really all it is cracked up to be. For ninth graders, now is a tumultuous time: decisions are made this year that may dramatically affect the rest of their high school careers.

Should I join a social club? Should I skip first period tomorrow? Should I compromise my morals to fit in? These are crucial decisions freshmen, as well as all high school students, are frequently forced to make. The decisions we make these four years define our character and will ultimately shape the adults we will soon become.

I was once a freshman, and so was everyone else. We all know what it is like to scurry timidly around Dreher with apprehension. I wish I had known then what I know now. In an attempt to make freshman life a little easier, I'll share my wisdom: Always respect seniors; respect yourself; be a good friend; don't skip school (it only promotes bad habits and creates more make-up work, and you'll probably get caught anyway); and finally, stay cool with your parents.

I know from experience that trust is easily broken but hard to regain, and in the meantime, your life will not be a happy one. Heed these rules, and your freshman year will be an unforgettable experience. Enjoy your time as underclassmen.

Thoughts of college applications and times of stress are far in the future for you. As freshmen, take part in Dreher activities and indulge in the Dreher social life. Each freshman possesses unique qualities, adding needed spice to Dreher life. We welcome you, class of 2006.

Dreher Welcomes Several New Faculty Members

Dreher welcomes several new staff members for the current school year.

Julie Anderson, who taught math at Dreher several years ago, will serve as the Curriculum Resource Teacher. She recently published a book entitled *The Answers*.

Karen Brown comes to Dreher from Dent Middle School, where she taught for the past nine years. A social studies teacher, she grew up in Omaha, Nebraska.

Jose Caamano, originally from Spain, has taught at St. Andrews, Gibbes , and W.A. Perry Middle Schools. He is teaching Spanish at Dreher.

Joyce Fortune commuted to Camden and Lower Richland High Schools before joining the Dreher English faculty. She grew up in Bishopville.

Maria Hood was a music teacher in South America before teaching Spanish at Keenan High and A.C. Moore Elementary Schools. She is teaching Spanish at Dreher.

Janet Kenney will work as a media specialist this year. Before coming to Dreher, she taught social studies and English. For three years she taught English at the Department of Juvenile Justice.

David Kleinfelder returns to Dreher after 12 years at Lexington High. This year he will teach physical education and biology and serve as a tennis and soccer coach.

Kathleen Lee is the new dance teacher. She has taught dance with several companies, including USC, Columbia Ballet School, and the Governor's School.

Heather Parker is a first-year English teacher at Dreher, where she did her student teaching last semester. She graduated from Lugoff-Elgin and USC.

Amari Paulovic has taught at C.A. Johnson and Gilbert High Schools. From West Columbia, she is currently teaching ninth grade English at Dreher.

Richard Rowell will teach English and journalism and will serve as the boys' soccer coach. Originally from Charlotte, he taught at Hand Middle School last year.

Cindy Ryan served as chair of the English Department at Keenan High before joining the faculty at Dreher. She grew up in Greenwood.

Barbara Warren taught in Florida and California, as well as Lexington District 5 and W.A. Perry Middle School. At Dreher she will teach mathematics.

7

Features

Decorative Doors

By Carrie Givens

Many of you have seen the decorative doors lining the streets of Columbia. Indeed, there is one across the street from Dreher. The doors are the sequel to the painted Palmetto trees.

Formally called Connecting the Past to the Future, the doors are the Cultural Council of Richland and Lexington Counties' newest art project. These decorative doors are not just any doors either: they were taken out of trash pile in the 50-year-old Saxon Homes community.

The doors are part art and part history. Out of 129 submissions, 50 designs were chosen. The doors do vary in design. One of the doors at the SouthTrust Plaza entitled Time Warp has working clocks on it.

Another entitled Arc Waves is constructed out of colored stained glass.Some doors are standing straight up and others are lying on their sides.

The doors will be lining the streets of Columbia until the end of September. They will then be moved to the South Carolina State Fair before being auctioned off. Don't miss them; they are a sight to be seen.

*For more information and a complete list of doors, go to http//www.get cultured.org/NCR.ASP.

Suspense 'Til The End

By Carrie Givens

When the television preview says "Don't see it alone," they meant it. *Signs* is one of the most frightening movies I have ever seen. Judging by the audience's gasps and screams at certain moments in the movie, I would discern that they felt the same way.

What makes *Signs* frightening is not gore and violence. It is pure suspense.

The movie is shot in such a way that you catch glimpses of objects, but you don't see the whole picture. Throughout the movie there are hints to the end of the world and to existence of extra-terrestrial being. The thriller culminates in a scene that will simply steal your breath.

Signs, directed by M. Night Shymulan, is definitely Shymalan's best movie so far and is definitely one of the best movies of the summer. As senior **Melissa Discepolo** says, "*Signs* is a suspenseful thriller with great acting. It was one of the best movies I've seen."

"I was really surprised that a movie as scary as *Signs* could be so funny," senior **Marie Sudduth** adds. The truth is that *Signs* is a masterpiece that should not be missed.

Support-Monitor Cynthia Jackson and student body president Sylvia Sanchez enjoy an early-morning chat. (Photo by Richard Rowell)

4

When It's Time

By Michael A. DuBard

When the summer sun is seething
And some shade is all you seek,
The beach's call grows fainter
As do memories of first week.

When sleeping late becomes tiring
And lying around has worn you out,
It's time for some motivation
To find out what life's about.

When television no longer fascinates
And watching it wastes your day,
It's time to go back to work
And stop idling your time away.

When vacation days become mundane,
Turning from merely dull to boring,
You need to find new activities
That are worthy of exploring.

When things in your life become routine,
The law of change must rule.
Your mind needs rejuvenation.
It's time to go back to school.

Blakeney to Direct Student Activities

By Rebecca Givens

There are many new faces at Dreher, and **Roy Blakeney**, our assistant principal, is one of them.

Blakeney says he likes being assistant principal because he "enjoys the chance to work with young people and teachers, and help them accomplish their goals." Blakeney says he has been in the school system before, but not in Richland District One. He has taught at Irmo Middle School and been an administrator at Irmo High School.

Blakeney adds that he wants to see Dreher improve on the successes we already have with winning awards. Furthermore, he wants us to improve on the 3 A's: arts, academics, and athletics.

When asked about his children, he replied, "I have a son who is going to Lander University, who just graduated from Irmo High School. And I have a daughter who is starting in the ninth grade at Irmo." Laughingly Blakeney said, "I tried to bring her with me, but she wanted to stay with her friends."

An interesting fact about Blakeney is that he rides his bicycle from Camden to Myrtle Beach, which is a total of 150 miles in two days, for the Muscular Sclerosis Society. This is the ninth year biking the trek.

Blakeney oversees activities and facilities at Dreher and can be found in his office on the first floor front hall.

"We were probably the first paper in the country censored after Hazelwood," says Epitaph advisor Nick Ferentinos. But it was also the first to fight back. Mike Calcagno, editor-in-chief of the paper, pounded out a resignation letter. Then he discovered a more effective way to overturn the "hold" order.

The Hazelwood decision turns the question of school censorship over to the individual states. And under an obscure section of the California Educational Code, California students were already guaranteed broad freedom of the press. Once Calcagno and his staff learned that the state law overruled Hazelwood, they voted unanimously to run the AIDS story. The Epitaph came out complete as planned—with an additional editorial condemning censorship.

1990–1999

The 1990s, called the "Era of Possibilities" by *Fortune* magazine, were dominated by an economic expansion that impacted every segment of society, especially children. During the decade the influence, buying power and media attention paid to youth exploded. Advertising programs once aimed at the youthful 18- to 24-year-old market began aiming for the highly affluent 12- to 18-year-old segment. As wealth grew, possibilities flourished. Colleges became overcrowded, while the mini-baby boom of the 1980s swelled the ranks of elementary schools. Characterized by steady growth, low inflation, low unemployment and dramatic gains in technology-based productivity, the resulting expansion was particularly meaningful to computer companies and the emerging concept known as the Internet. This economy swelled the ranks of the upper class as Americans of all backgrounds invested in the soaring stock market and dreamed of capturing a dot-com fortune.

The decade opened in an economic recession, a ballooning national debt, and the economic hangover of the collapse of much of the savings and loan industry. The automobile industry produced record losses; household names like Bloomingdale's and Pan Am declared bankruptcy. Housing values plummeted and factory orders fell. Media headlines were dominated by issues such as rising drug use, crime in the cities, racial tensions, and the rise of personal bankruptcies. Family values ranked high on the conservative agenda, and despite efforts to limit Democrat Bill Clinton to one term as president, the strength of the economy played a critical role in his re-election in 1996.

Guided by Federal Reserve Chair Alan Greenspan's focus on inflation control and Clinton's early efforts to control the federal budget, the U.S. economy soared, producing its best economic indicators in three decades. By 1999, the stock market produced record returns, job creation was at a 10-year high, and the federal deficit was falling. Businesses nationwide hung "Help Wanted" signs outside their doors and even paid signing bonuses to acquire new workers. Crime rates, especially in urban areas, plummeted to levels unseen in three decades, illegitimacy rates fell, and every year business magazines marvelled at the length of the recovery, asking, "Can it last another year?"

The stock market set a succession of records throughout the period, attracting thousands of investors to stocks for the first time, including the so-called glamour offerings of high-technology companies. From 1990 to the dawn of the twenty-first century, the Dow Jones Industrial Average rose 318 percent. Growth stocks were the rage; of Standard and Poor's 500 tracked stocks, almost 100 did not pay dividends. This market boom eventually spawned unprecedented new wealth, encouraging early retirement to legions of aging baby boomers. The dramatic change in the cultural structure of corporations continued to threaten the job security of American workers, who had to be more willing to learn new skills, try new jobs, and move from project to project. Profit sharing, which allowed workers to benefit from increased productivity, become more common. Retirement programs and pension plans became more flexible and transferable, serving the needs of a highly mobile work force. The emerging gap of the 1990s was not always between the rich and the poor, but the computer literate and the technically deficient. To symbolize the changing role of women in the work force, cartoon character Blondie, wife of Dagwood Bumstead, opened her own catering business which, like so many small businesses in the 1990s, did extremely well. For the first time, a study of family household income concluded that 55 percent of women provided half or more of the household income.

During the decade, America debated limiting abortion, strengthening punishment for criminals, replacing welfare for work, ending Affirmative Action, dissolving bilingual education, elevating educational standards, curtailing the rights of legal immigrants, and imposing warnings on unsuitable material for children on the Internet. Nationwide, an estimated 15 million people, including smokers, cross-dressers, alcoholics, sexual compulsives, and gamblers, attended weekly self-help support groups; dieting became a $33 billion industry as Americans struggled with obesity.

The impact of the GI Bill's focus on education, rooted in the decade following World War II, flowered in the generation that followed. The number of adult Americans with a four-year college education rose from 6.2 percent in 1950 to 24 percent in 1997. Despite this impressive rise, the need for a more educated population, and the rapidly rising expectations of the technology sector, the century ended with a perception that the decline in public education was one of the most pressing problems of the decade. Throughout the decade, school violence escalated, capturing headlines year after year in widely dispersed locations across the nation.

The '90s gave birth to $150 tennis shoes, condom boutiques, pre-ripped jeans, Motorola 7.7-ounce cellular telephones, rollerblading, TV home shopping, the Java computer language, digital cameras, DVD players, and Internet shopping. And in fashion, a revival of the 1960s' style brought back miniskirts, pop art prints, pants suits, and the A-line. Black became a color worn at any time of day and for every purpose. The increasing role of consumer debt in driving the American economy also produced an increase in personal bankruptcy and a reduction in the overall savings rate. At the same time, mortgage interest rates hit 30-year lows during the decade, creating refinancing booms that pumped millions of dollars into the economy, further fueling a decade of consumerism.

On the open road
th my favorite guy.
I like where
this is headed.

1992 Profile

Upper Class

Fourth-grader Cordelia Dorffman lives a dream life on her family's Texas ranch, always aware she is the rich kid whose lifestyle is now under attack by a changing world.

Life at Home

- Cordelia Dorffman and her family are close.
- She even likes her older sister, who attends a prep school in Houston; both girls favor stuffed animals and frilly dresses.
- Her brothers are the most handsome men in the world, and surely will break many hearts before they marry.
- Her oldest brother has already attended college and graduate school, and has taken his place among the corporate management of the increasingly diversified Two Crowns Ranch, Inc., in Houston.
- Her second brother is still in college; unlike his older brother, he is taking his time and enjoying every minute of his college experience, much to the frustration of their father.
- She also loves being with her mother and looking at pictures of her mother growing up, especially a picture taken years ago when she was a teen, dancing with Cordelia's grandfather.
- They are all dressed up in white gloves and enjoying themselves tremendously.
- But most of all, she loves going out to tour the ranch with her father.
- The ranch, which is literally about the size of Rhode Island, is always a gumbo of activity.

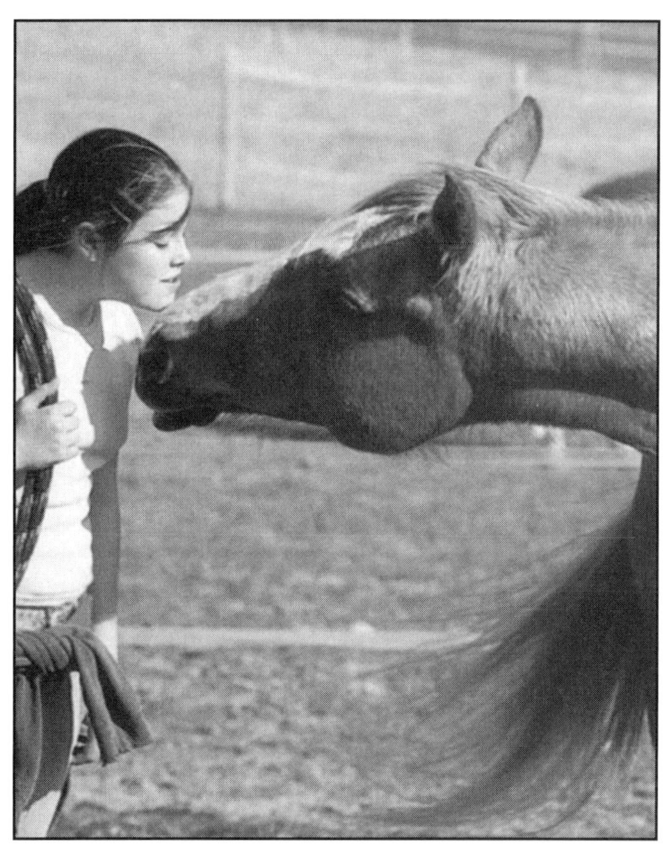

Cordelia Dorffman loves life on a Texas cattle ranch.

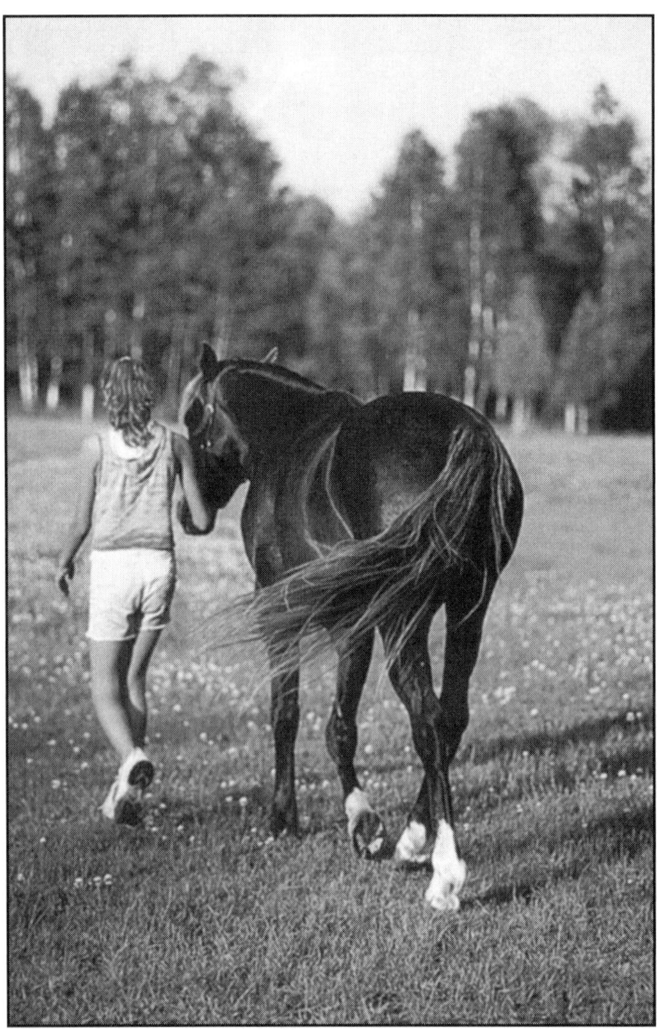

Every day something new is happening on the ranch.

- Every day, something new is happening—breaking new horses, castrating bulls or branding cows.
- Cordelia is convinced that there is no greater place to be in the entire world.
- The family lives in a modern split-level house, large enough to require a full-time maid and a live-in cook.
- Cordelia dreads the cook's day off, since cooking is not among her mother's finest talents.
- Her father may feel the same way; often on those nights, he takes the family to a restaurant in Kingsville or brings home barbecue.
- Her mother absolutely refuses to ride in the Ram Charger pickup truck her husband loves so dearly, so when they go out, they ride in her Suburban.
- In a large clearing near Cordelia's house stands the ranch hacienda, a 25-room Spanish-style manor with a bell tower, which served as the owner's house for the first half of the twentieth century.
- Now, it is carefully preserved in a museum-like state and used only by family members for very special occasions, such as the annual weeklong meeting of the Two Crowns Ranch, Inc., shareholders.
- All 60 stockholders are descendents of Julius and Cordelia Dorffman, although some kin are closer to the trunk of the family tree than others are.
- Over the years, many branches of the family have moved away from the hot, heavy work of Texas ranch life, and today only a few direct descendents are still involved with any agricultural pursuits at all.
- That's only one of the reasons her father, as vice president for agriculture, dreads the annual gathering of what he calls "the sorta-clan."
- On more than one occasion, he has explained to Cordelia that his title means he "runs the ranches"—the 13 million acres of agricultural property owned around the world by Two Crowns, including cattle ranches in Brazil, Venezuela and Australia; citrus groves in Florida; and a large horse farm in Kentucky.
- For the past several years, the other stockholders have been critical of the agricultural division's performance.
- This group of non-ranchers, who can't ride to save their necks, are city folk who always know more about how to manage the ranches than he does.
- A handful even bring in articles from *The New York Times* (of all things!) on how to make money in ranching in the 1990s.
- Currently, there is growing sentiment that the corporation needs a Harvard M.B.A. type who knows the "value of a dollar" to run this far-flung empire.
- The shareholders are convinced that the employee benefits are too generous, the return too small, and ranching, overall, too much trouble in this modern age.
- Last year, he was accused of being too sentimental because he allowed retired employees with 40 years of service to live out their lives in the company-provided homes built on the ranch.

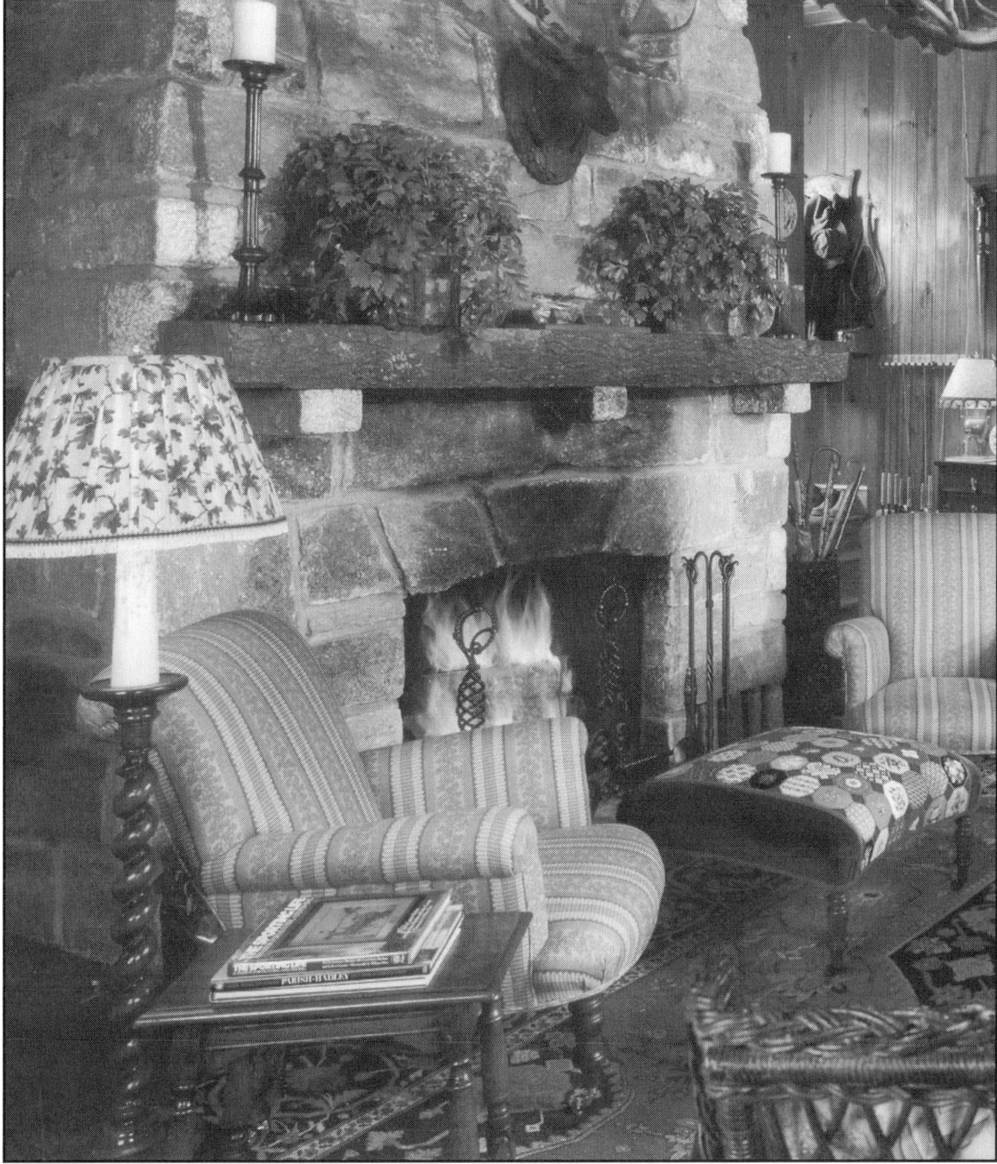

Cordelia's friends say she is rich; her father says they are comfortable.

- He is not about to change that, no matter what the absentee stockholders have to say; loyalty got Two Crowns where it is today.
- Cordelia finds little to like about the cousins who show up each summer; although a few have grown up around horses, most are city kids looking for a country adventure and ready—oh, so ready—to make fun of everything.
- Even cousin Lavinia, who is an excellent rider, looks down her nose at Two Crowns' horses because they don't measure up to her standards.
- Lavinia, as she likes to mention in every other sentence, is a champion dressage rider.
- Cordelia's favorite visitors each summer are Davie and Daniel, whose father manages the Australian operations.
- They promised that if she would return with them to Australia one year she could see kangaroos and even pet a koala.

Exploring the cattle ranch is always a joy.

- They even worked out a secret code all their own so they could send messages back and forth.
- Most of the kids are from places like San Antonio, Houston or Dallas or, worse, "back East," where their parents buy them brand-new jeans and boots each year for their "ranching adventure."
- When the shareholder meetings get too bad or long or theatrical, Cordelia's father seeks her out and they jump into his pickup for a long ride around the ranch.
- Typically, they will pass herds of grazing cattle and miles of cotton, sorghum and sugar cane; often, they will run up on small parties of cowboys working the range as they have for hundreds of years.
- These days, he tells his daughter, "It's good to get out in the open air with you, Cordelia."
- She hates stockholders and corporations and ranches that end in "Inc."
- After the stockholders go home each year, her sister and mother immediately head to the family beach house, where there are tons of boys, and that means Cordelia and her dad can enjoy time together.
- The two often get up early, fix a campfire breakfast, and then ride around the ranch supervising operations.
- At night, she tends to her filly, Heidi, and has dinner with her father and a few of her father's oldest friends—men who work for him on the ranch.

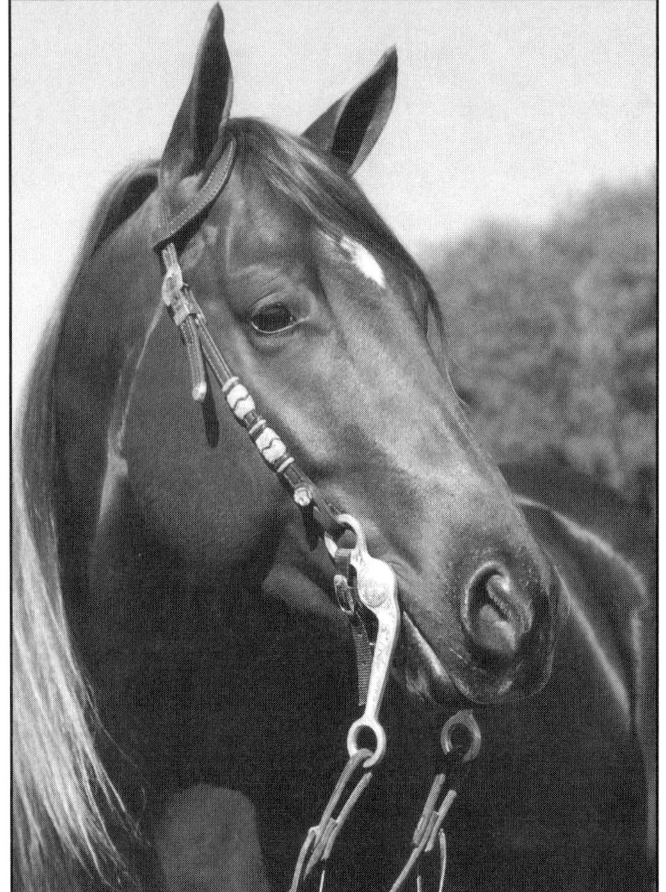
She has loved horses as long as she can remember.

Life at School

- The fourth grade is a mixed bag of joy and disappointment.
- First of all, lots of what she is being taught feels like a review of the third grade and is not challenging at all.
- Second, it is sometimes hard to make friends because her name is Dorffman: Everyone says she is rich, even though

"Codemaster, The Ruler Code," *Boy's Life*, June 1994:

The Ruler Code is a speedy way to send secret messages to friends. And it offers a way to have fun with numbers.

To begin, lay a 12-inch rule on a blank sheet of paper. Make a small dot above the 0 (the first mark on the rule) and the 12 (the last mark). Then write a letter of the alphabet at every half-inch.

Since there are only 25 half-inch markings and 26 letters, squeeze together the Y and Z.

There! You have a secret code for sending information in Ruler Code. By now you may have guessed the Ruler Code secret. The numbers on the rule replace the letters above them.

To disguise the secret code sheet, just take away the ruler.

All that is left is a simple line of letters! NO one will suspect that you used a rule to make up the code. Even if someone finds your code sheet, he won't know what it means.

To write a hidden message in Ruler Code, position the ruler so the 0 is below one dot and the 12 is below the other. Then substitute the ruler numbers for each letter in your message.

For example, a K is coded as 5, since that is the rule number below it. An L is coded as 5½. The code number 0 stands for A and the number 12 means Y or Z.

See how easy it is? Here is how the warning DO NOT TRUST BARRY looks in Ruler Code:

1½–7 6½–7–9½ 9½–8½–10–9–9½ ½–0–8½–8½–12.

her father insists they are simply a comfortable family that worked for what they have and will have to work hard to keep it.

- Cordelia wants to have friends because she is just "Cordelia."
- Sometimes, the girls will whisper about her and the size of her house, and then not talk with her at lunch, as though it is her fault her father works hard.
- Cordelia loves the nuns because they are like her parents—strict but fair—and she is often shocked by what the other children do when the nuns' backs are turned, even imitating the walk of one of the older nuns when she is right there in the room.
- Some girls even make ugly remarks about Cordelia's name.
- She loves having a unique name, shared by both the good daughter of Shakespeare's play, *King Lear*, and the first white woman—her ancestor—to come to this semi-desert of the South Texas Coast 140 years earlier.
- The first Cordelia survived a harsh land of thorn bushes and tidal flats to raise 10 children on what was to become the largest ranch in the country.
- The favorite activity of her namesake is reading, especially about horses.
- Her father's sprawling library is packed with great books about horses of every type.

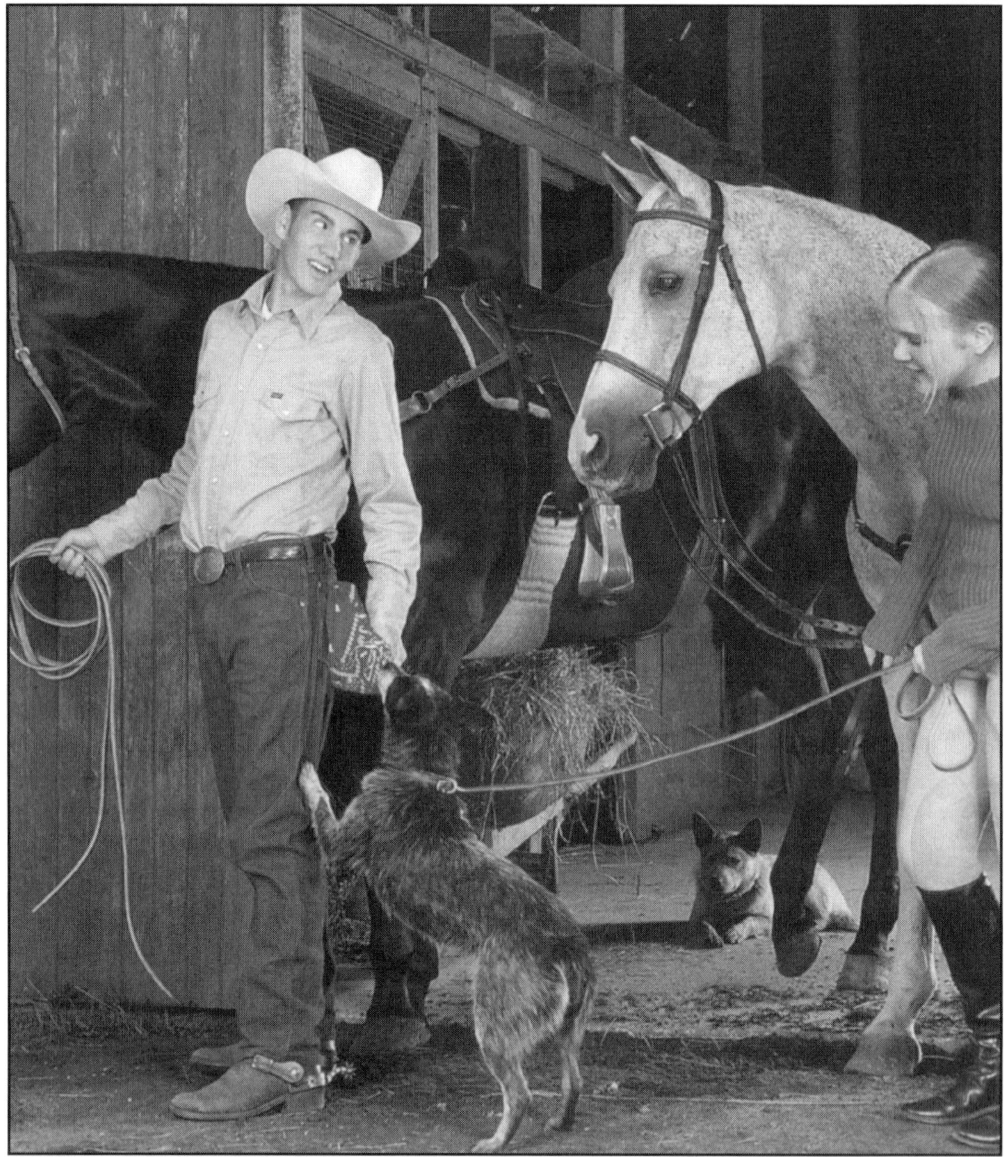

Before she could walk, she could ride.

- He even takes the time to find unique books which Cordelia is allowed to keep in her room on a special bookshelf of her own.
- She has loved horses for as long as she can remember.
- Before she could walk, she would ride with her father on his big stallion, Anthracite; when she was four, she frequently rode Pepe, an old and gentle pony which she regularly fed and looked after.
- Recently, Heidi, the most beautiful filly in the world, was born—predestined to be Cordelia's very own horse.
- When Heidi gets old enough, Cordelia is sure the two of them will be inseparable; at night, she dreams of riding Heidi like the wind into the broad fields of the ranch.
- Even though she likes many of the girls at school, her real best friends are the children who live in neat frame bungalows with shady yards on the ranch and go to the school on ranch property.

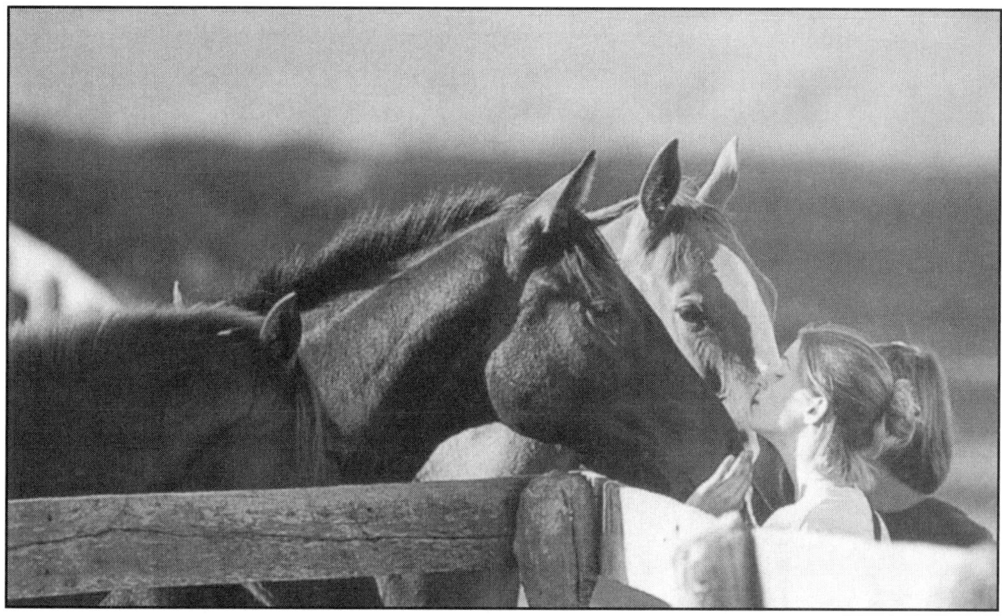

Heidi, the most beautiful filly in the world, is predestined to be Cordelia's very own horse.

- Most are descendents of an entire Mexican village who were recruited years ago by Julius Dorffman to work for him on Two Crowns.
- Cordelia's father and Two Crowns, Inc., handle all their pay, health care and retirement.

Life in the Community: Houston, Texas

- The ranch covers 825,000 acres, or 1,289 square miles, and is crossed with so many fences that, if stretched end to end, they would run from the ranch headquarters in South Texas to Boston.
- The fences hold 65,000 head of cattle managed by riders using 550 quarter horses, a breed developed on the ranch.
- The dominant breed of cattle is the cherry-red Santa Gertrudis, a disease-resistant breed created to withstand the region's hot, arid conditions.
- It was the first breed of cattle produced in America.
- The ranch's diversified corporation includes among its assets 630 oil and gas wells.
- Spanish colonists called this land El Desierto de los Muertos—the Desert of the Dead.

Historical Snapshot
1992

- Unemployment topped 7.1 percent, the highest in five years
- U.S. bombed Iraq for its failure to comply with United Nations-sponsored inspections
- The 10 most popular television shows were *60 Minutes*; *Roseanne*; *Murphy Brown*; *Cheers*; *Home Improvement*; *Designing Women*; *Coach*; *Full House*; *Murder, She Wrote*; and *Unsolved Mysteries*
- David Letterman was offered $16 million to move to CBS opposite late-night host Jay Leno; Johnny Carson's last night as host of *The Tonight Show* drew a record 55 million viewers
- Bestsellers included Rush Limbaugh's *The Way Things Ought to Be*, H. Norman Schwarzkopf's *It Doesn't Take a Hero*, John Grisham's *The Pelican Brief* and Anne Rice's *The Tale of the Body Thief*
- The Supreme Court ruled that cross-burning is protected under the First Amendment, and that prayer at public school graduations is unconstitutional
- Royalties for Barbara and George Bush's dog's autobiography, *Millie's Book*, earned them $890,000
- In Kenya, Meave Leakey discovered the oldest hominid fossil to date, estimated to be 25 million years old and believed to be from the period of the ape-human divergence
- Movie openings included *Unforgiven*, *The Crying Game*, *Scent of a Woman*, *Malcolm X*, *Aladdin*, *Sister Act*, *Basic Instinct*, *The Last of the Mohicans*, *A River Runs Through It* and *White Men Can't Jump*
- Rudolph Marcus won the Nobel Prize in chemistry for his theory of electron-transfer reactions
- Eric Clapton won a Grammy award for his record "Tears in Heaven" and his album, "Unplugged"
- Poverty rose to 14.2 percent, the highest level since 1983
- At the Olympic Summer Games in Barcelona, the U.S. basketball team included Larry Bird, Magic Johnson and Michael Jordan
- More than 20,000 people in California bought guns after the Los Angeles riots, which erupted when the men accused of beating Rodney King were acquitted
- In Washington, DC, more than 500,000 people marched for abortion rights
- New-age clear beverages, mega CD video games, The Mall of America and the Intel 486 chip made their first appearance
- Research indicated that the level of HDL, or good cholesterol, may be more important than the overall blood cholesterol score
- The FDA restricted the use of silicone-gel breast implants for reconstructive purposes
- In competitive voting, more than 1.1 million people selected the picture of a young Elvis Presley over the older one to appear on a postage stamp

1992 Economic Profile

Selected Prices

Automobile, 1992 Miata $14.978.00
Bath Towel, J.C. Penney $4.90
Bed, Cherrywood, Full-Size $399.88
Christmas Tree, 7' Artificial $124.99
Crackers, Nabisco Ritz-Bits $1.69
Cruise Ticket, Alaska, per Person. $2,395.00
Dishwasher, Whirlpool $299.00
Fax Machine $353.43
Festival Ticket, New Orleans Jazz $25.00
Flashlight, First Alert, Rechargeable $7.99
Hose, 3-Gauge Sprinkler, 50' $7.99
Shirt, Man's Spalding Golf Shirt $14.98
Turkey, per Pound $0.69
Weed Killer, Monsanto Round-Up, 24 Ounces $16.99
Vodka, Absolut, 750 ml $12.29

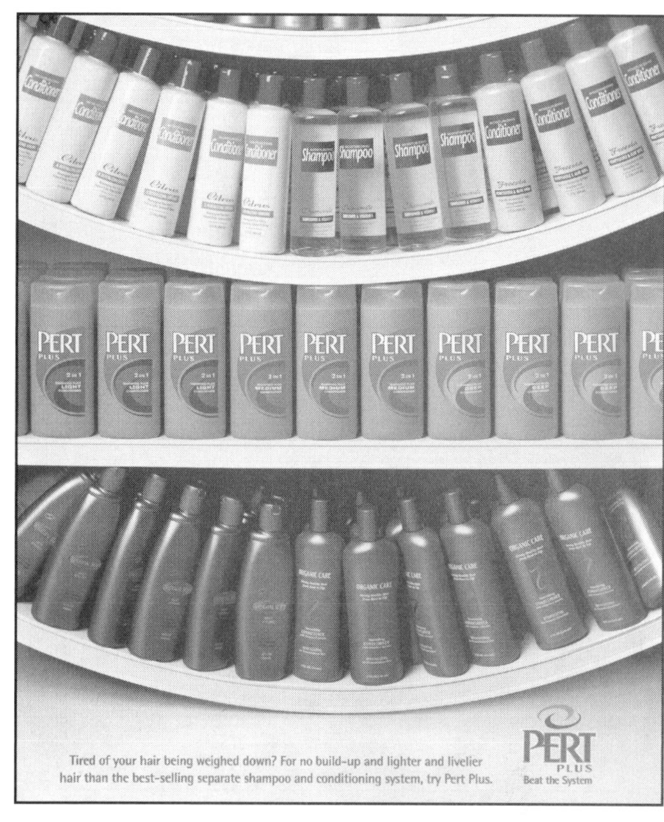

Tired of your hair being weighed down? For no build-up and lighter and livelier hair than the best-selling separate shampoo and conditioning system, try Pert Plus.
PERT PLUS
Beat the System

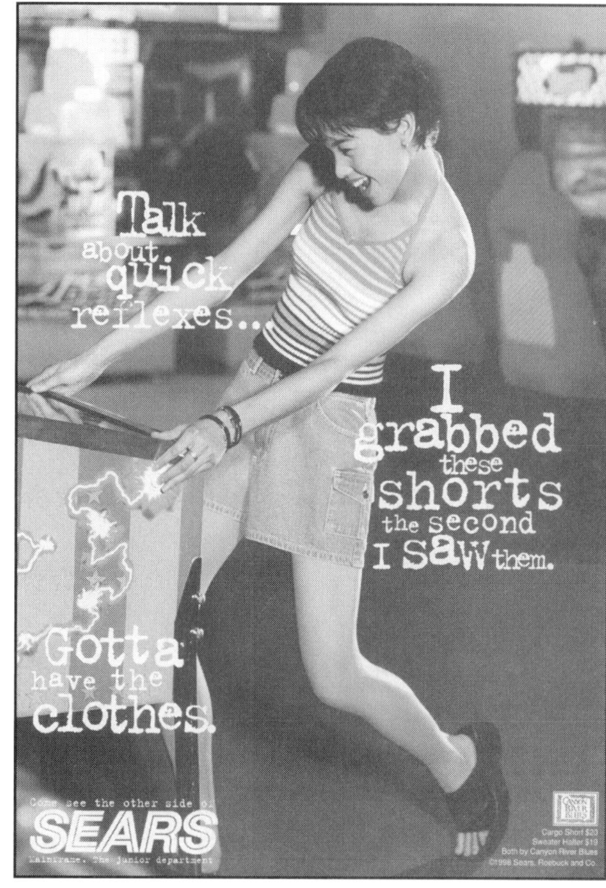

Changing America

- An Apple Powerbook laptop computer cost between $2,299 and $4,599.
- Vice President Dan Quayle attacked the television show *Murphy Brown*, saying it mocked "the importance of fathers by bearing a child alone and calling it just another 'lifestyle choice.' "
- A copy of the first *Superman* comic, published in 1938, sold for $82,500.
- The one hundredth anniversary of *The Nutcracker* was celebrated with performances staged throughout the country.
- Studies reported that the U.S. had the highest incarceration rate in the world: 455 per 100,000 citizens—double the rate of 1980.
- Marvel comic book hero Northstar revealed that he was gay.
- Fewer Americans took wedding vows, the lowest rate since 1965.
- A total of 52,000 books were published during the year.
- A record 46 women ran for Congress; four women were elected to the U.S. Senate.
- Singer Sinead O'Connor created a storm of controversy on the *Saturday Night Live* show by tearing up a photograph of the pope.
- The grunge look moved into the mainstream and college students began sporting (often temporary) tattoos.
- Barney the purple dinosaur was a major fad.

Cordelia enjoys looking at pictures of her mother growing up, especially when she was a teen.

"A Fistful of Dollars, the King Ranch of Texas rides into a profitable new business era," *U.S. News & World Report*, July 24, 1995:

It's scorching hot out in the South Texas mesquite brush, and the dust kicked up by several hundred skittish calves leaves a stifling haze over the cattle pens where the ranch hands poke and prod the 400-pound babies through the weathered wooden chutes. The work is hard and dirty and smelly, but it's what King Ranch cowboys have been doing for more than a century: separating the crying three-month-olds from the mother cows, branding them with the famed "Running W" and making the necessary slices of the knife that turn young bulls into steers.

In some respects, time has stood still on these 825,000 acres once known by Spanish explorers as the "Desert of the Dead," and for many years, the most famous cattle ranch in the world. The smell of burning cowhide, the bulging eyes of the calves and the bloody bucket full of bluish-white ovals have been part of the ranch's work since steamboat Capt. Richard King first set up a cow camp on this forbidding land in 1853. But times change. Today, the Kinenos (King's Men) keep cellular phones next to their lassos as they watch over the ranch's 60,000 head of cattle, which are penned in by 2,000 miles of fencing; the branding iron is plugged into an electrical outlet instead of being heated in a pile of hot coals, and, in addition to riding and roping, cowboys attach transponders to a calf's ear to track genetic makeup, feed schedules and health records from birth through slaughter.

Many elements of the modern American cattle industry were invented on this arid savanna at America's southern tip. Through the years, the King Ranch has fought for survival against Union and Mexican soldiers, drought and pestilence, land-appropriating dictators, and militant vegetarians. But more recently, the fight for survival has involved issues that are more corporate than cowboy. In an era of downsizing and technological efficiency, the ranch has confronted these latest adversaries and positioned itself for a third century of growth. The major change is that "we no longer see ourselves in the cattle business, as such," explains Stephen J. "Tio" Kleberg, a fifth-generation descendant of Captain King and the ranch's vice president in charge of agribusiness. "We are in the resource-management business. And we all feel we have a lot of resources to manage."

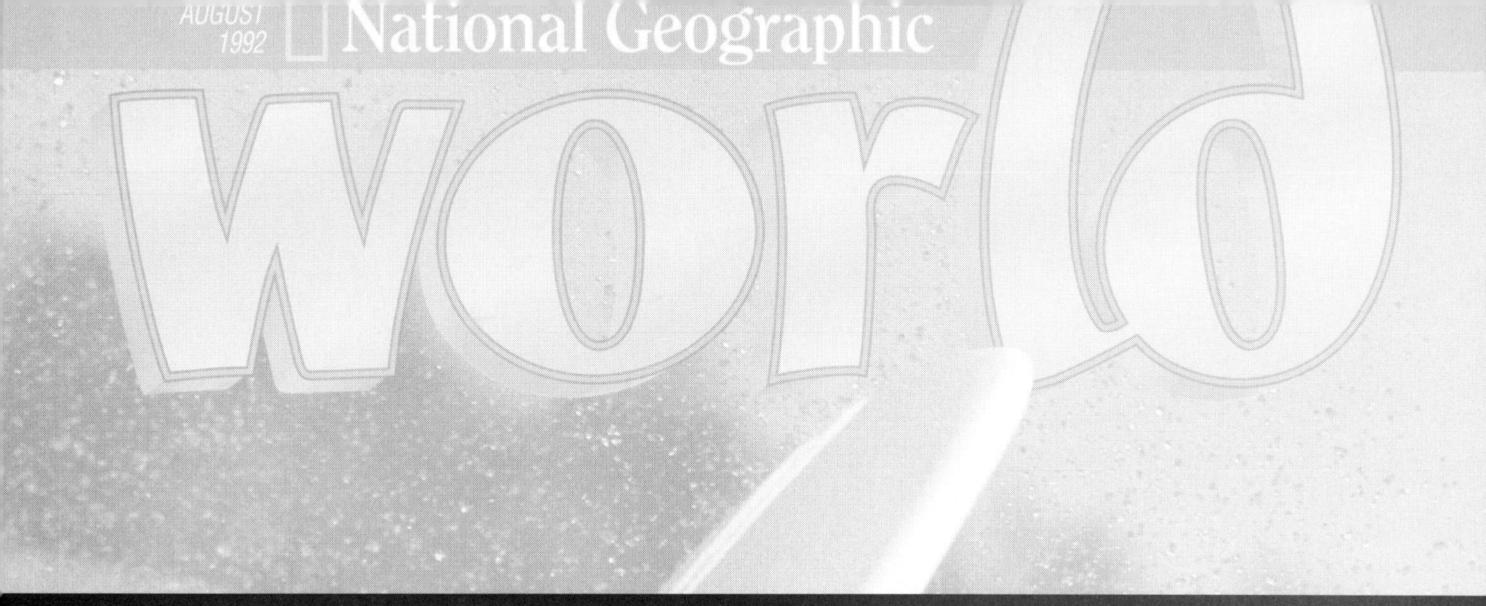

1992 News Feature

"Kneeboarding," *National Geographic World*, August 1992:
Bank out, mule kick, or flare . . . whatever you call it, this jump makes a splash. So does Zachary Rohner whenever he hits the water. Zack, who lives in Davie, Florida, set records in the junior boys' division for kneeboarding for four years. He graduated from that 12-and-under group as Number One. Now at 14 he hopes to spin and flip his way to the top of the 18-and-under boys' division. . . .

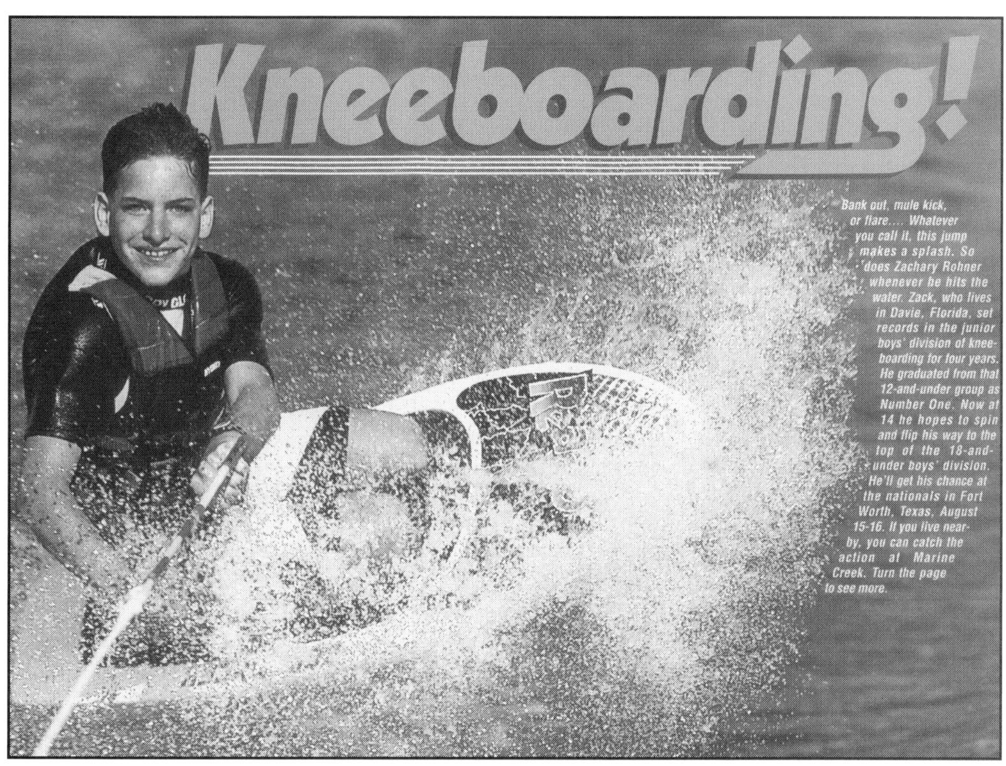

Kneeboarding!

Bank out, mule kick, or flare.... Whatever you call it, this jump makes a splash. So does Zachary Rohner whenever he hits the water. Zack, who lives in Davie, Florida, set records in the junior boys' division of kneeboarding for four years. He graduated from that 12-and-under group as Number One. Now at 14 he hopes to spin and flip his way to the top of the 18-and-under boys' division. He'll get his chance at the nationals in Fort Worth, Texas, August 15-16. If you live nearby, you can catch the action at Marine Creek. Turn the page to see more.

Kneeboarding started in California in 1975.

"You have to love to compete and love to crash." That's Zack's prescription for kneeboarding success. He's a veteran of more than 30 competitions with a long string of titles—and a long string of practice crashes (falls) that helped him earn those titles.

"If you can't do something at first, just keep trying," says Zack. He practices every weekend on Lake Red Water in Florida, near his home.

Kneeboarding behind a motorboat started in California in 1975 as a spin-off from surfing. Zack discovered the sport when he was eight. "A neighbor showed me how to do it," he says. "I liked it right away so I just kept going."

"It's so easy to learn; 95 percent of the people who try it slide right off the beach and get a good ride the first time," says Mario Fassa, the reigning world champion.

Once you get beyond the first ride, what keeps you coming back for more? Zack, Mario, and others say it's the variety (you can do more tricks than you can on water skis) and the fun of flipping the board into the air. There's even a competition category called flip-out. The goal is to do 10 flips as fast as possible.

Kneeboarders also compete in slalom and trick events. Each trick earns a set number of points. Two of Zack's favorites are the wake O front (a complete turn while jumping the boat's wake) and the barrel roll.

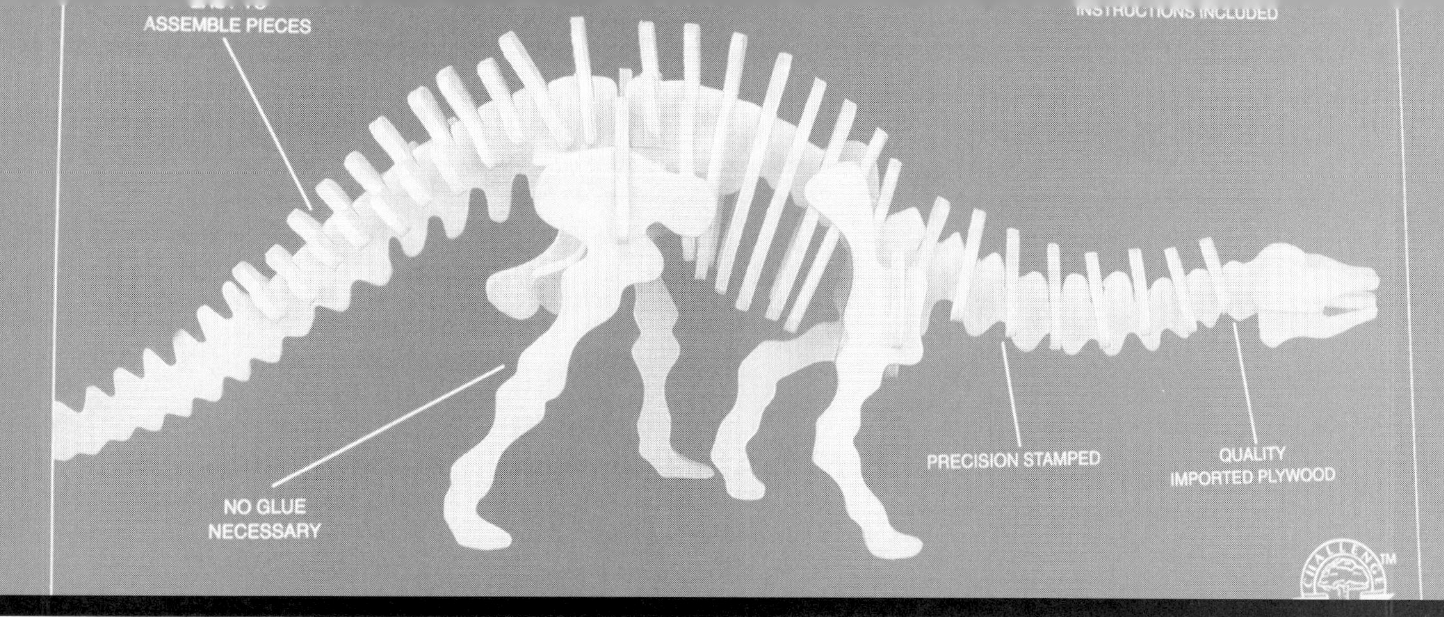

1995 Profile

Working Class

Fifteen-year-old John Pritich is the fifth of nine children; he attends a Jesuit high school in Cleveland, Ohio, where he ponders the value of playing college football, maintains a paper route and helps his father paint houses on weekends.

Life at Home

- John Pritich is a 240-pound 15-year-old who attracts attention wherever he goes because of his size and gentle nature.
- The fifth of nine children in a family that proudly identifies itself with Croatia, John attends an all-male Jesuit high school in Cleveland, Ohio.
- The school has a reputation for being strict and academically challenging—just what his parents, Peter and Elizabeth, want for their son.
- He lives with his family in a neat bungalow in Eastlake, a suburb 20 miles east of downtown Cleveland.
- His entire family, on both sides, came from Croatia to Cleveland between 1880 and 1925.
- Croatia, formerly a district of Yugoslavia, is situated to the east of Italy across the narrow Adriatic Sea.
- Like most early Croatian male immigrants, they originally worked in the iron and steel industry, where big-boned, hardworking men are an asset.
- John's father, a member of the United Steel Workers of America, is now foreman in a plant that makes industrial hoses.
- His previous union, the United Rubber, Cork, Linoleum and Plastic Workers of America, merged with the Steel Workers earlier in the year.

John Pritich attracts attention wherever he goes.

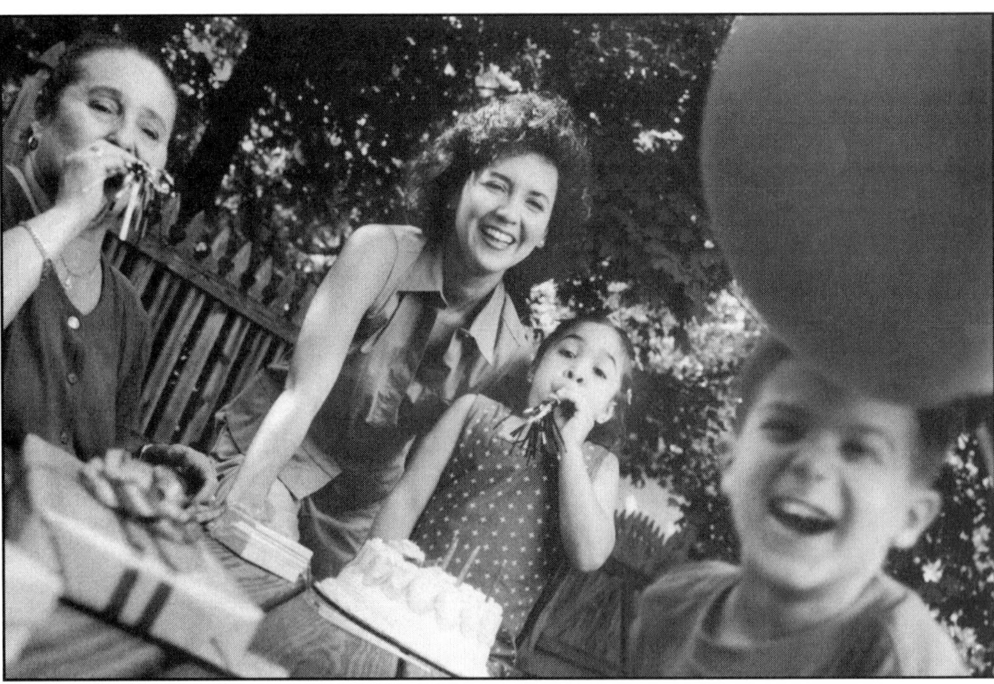

The Pritich family is large and close.

- He knows he will always be part of a union, but is unsure whether that is the way for his children to go, especially if they can get a college education.
- On weeknights and weekends, John's father paints houses to earn extra money, while his mother manages the books, buys the paints and handles the customers.
- During the week, John has little time to assist his father, but most Saturdays are spent on a ladder swinging a paintbrush at someone's house.
- After three years of practice, he thinks he is very good at doing outdoor trim work and is proud of his skills.
- John's day begins at 5:00 each morning, when he picks up the *Cleveland Plain Dealer* for house-to-house delivery in his own neighborhood and the surrounding area.
- Grounded in family history, he is allowed to keep all the extra money he makes—if he is willing to save half of every paycheck.
- He usually makes $75 to $85 a week on his route.
- Collecting payment from all his customers is still the hardest part of the job, but as he has grown bigger and more confident, the task has become easier.
- When the snow is especially deep or the winds stronger than 30 miles an hour, his father will help him peddle his papers.
- John can't wait until he is 16 and can drive one of the family cars; then he will be eligible for a larger, more lucrative paper route.
- After his delivery is complete at 7 a.m., John changes into school clothes and has breakfast with the entire family.
- Then, everyone piles into the station wagon for school; the four youngest children—aged seven, nine, 11 and 13—are dropped off at a Catholic grammar and middle school a few miles from their home.
- John is then taken to the Jesuit school in downtown Cleveland.
- Many Croatians are Roman Catholic, but John's family is Eastern Catholic and uses the Byzantine Rite based on the Rite of St. James of Jerusalem.

Union Membership Declines: Competing Theories and Economic Implications, by Gail McCallion, Congressional Research Service, Library of Congress, August 20, 1993:

In 1992, union members comprised only 15.8 percent of the workforce. Union membership, as a percent of the workforce, peaked at 34.7 percent in 1954, and has been declining since. Until 1978, the number of union members was continuing to grow, but was outpaced by the growth of the labor force. Since 1978, the absolute number of union members has been falling. In 1978, there were 20.2 million union members; by 1992, there were 16.4 million union members. These figures reflect the decline in total union membership (private and public sector). However, the decline in private sector union membership has been even more dramatic. If current trends continue, some experts estimate that the private sector union membership could decline to as low as 10 percent of the labor force by 1995, and then continue to decline until it levels out at three percent of the labor force.

The decline in union membership can be examined by looking at changes in the demand for and supply of union services (the quantity of union membership). In the late 1970s, the absolute number of union members began to fall. This is a period marked by recession, increased foreign competition and the deregulation of many major industries such as trucking and aviation. The appreciation of the dollar between 1979 and 1985, which hurt U.S. exports, also resulted in employment losses in unionized manufacturing industries. These factors operated to make workers more vulnerable to the threat of job loss, thereby lowering the demand for union services. Other demand factors linked to the decline of union membership include a reduced need for union representation due to labor-management cooperation, and increased government regulation and statutory protection of individual worker rights, thus reducing the benefits of unions to potential members.

- The Byzantine Rite is proper to the Church of Constantinople, and has a large following in Croatia.
- The Pritich family is extremely proud that John's oldest brother, Peter, is in his second year at a seminary in Pittsburgh, training to become a Byzantine Catholic priest.
- Many of the family's activities center around the American Croatian Lodge near the family home.
- This complex houses the Croatian Museum, a large library, and a banquet hall for community dances and gatherings, plus an outdoor sports field for boccie and soccer.
- The building is also home to the Dubrovnik Garden Restaurant, which is open to the public and often used for special occasions such as confirmations and graduations.
- The hall has become the central gathering place to discuss the progress of the war in the Balkans and the recently concluded Dayton peace talks.

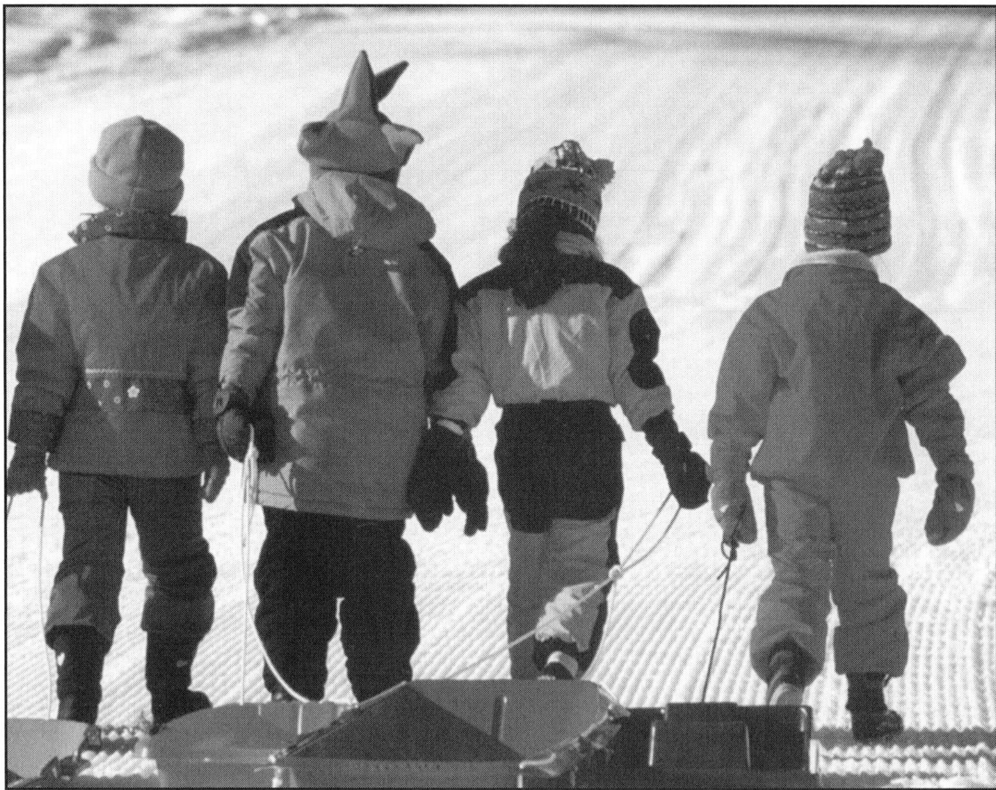

Winter sports are part of growing up in Cleveland, Ohio.

- Since the country's break with Yugoslavia in May 1991, the lodge has been the best place in town to get the real inside story of what is happening, because the evening news is not always correct.
- For its part, the lodge is sponsoring an 18-year-old Croatian student named Mislava, whose home in Bosnia was destroyed and several members of her family killed.
- Lodge members contributed cash to pay for her immediate return from the war-torn country, while others are raising money to provide her with tuition to the State University in Cleveland.
- Since arriving in America, she has stayed with the Pritich family, sharing a bedroom with the two oldest girls, Mary and Anne.
- The four younger girls share another bedroom; John and his 13-year-old brother Mike occupy a third bedroom.
- Mislava is grateful to be in America with a chance to attend college; she does chores around the house and has gotten a job as a waitress in a restaurant to help with expenses.
- Twice a week she hangs out with the more than five dozen kids, many still in high school, who left the Balkans and are now living in Cleveland's "Little Croatia."
- North High School at Eastlake has now added classes teaching English as a second language because of the sudden influx of new foreign students.
- According to the Croatian Consulate at Eastlake, the Croatian population in northeast Ohio now tops 35,000, up from 20,000 in 1980.
- Twenty years ago, when the family moved into their one-story home, built in 1960, it included three bedrooms, two baths, a kitchen, living room and dining room.
- When the seventh child was born, they added an extra bedroom, bath and small office, which now serve as the family's part-time painting company.

"A Debt Repaid: Rescuing the Future, A Chance for Bosnian Students," by Harvey Fireside, *Commonwealth*, September 23, 1994:

For me, what is happening now in Bosnia brings to mind memories of a time—54 years ago—when my parents and I waited in Vienna for relatives in the United States to rescue us from the Nazis. Because there was no way for Jews to earn a living, we relied on American soup kitchens for our one hot meal of the day. Finally, after 18 months, the treasured invitation came. But there were still anxious moments at the U.S. consulate, where we had to prove that we were in good health and could support ourselves. Because of childhood polio, my father walked with a pronounced limp. Fortunately, the doctors who examined us were interested in photography, my father's profession, so, in fluent English, my father explained to the doctor the features of a new camera, thereby demonstrating his ability to make a living. Finally, with tickets supplied by HIAS, an American relief organization, we three boarded the Italian ship that brought us to New York harbor and the welcoming torch of the Statue of Liberty.

Now, seeing something very close to a new holocaust taking place in Bosnia, it is frustrating to realize that the official U.S. reaction has been as grudging and skeptical as it was 50 years ago. Once more, I'm learning that bureaucracies lack empathy and respond poorly to crises; one must look to individuals and private groups to keep us human. In my own case it was the New School for Social Research in Manhattan where I took my Ph.D. In 1933 it had set up a "University in Exile" that saved some 100 European scholars from the Nazis.

A few months ago, I was offered a chance to repay my moral debt. I learned that there were nearly 600 Bosnian students hoping to continue their education in the United States. Stranded in Croatia, Slovenia, or Serbia, out of contact with their families, they were indubitably refugees, but U.S. embassies routinely denied them immigrant status. They could, however, obtain student visas, a chance to survive and study, if an American college or university would admit them, and if they could show they would not be dependent.

A rescue operation was organized by the Fellowship of Reconciliation (FOR), an ecumenical antiwar group in Nyack, New York, and by the Jerrahi Order of America, a Sufi Muslim organization. In response to an appeal from FOR, I called friends who contacted others; each of us jumped at the chance to approach colleges in the area. One friend, a professor at Tompkins-Cortland Community College in Dryden, New York, was sure the college president would offer a scholarship. FOR had sent us the papers on Jasmina Burdzovic, a 22-year-old woman who had completed a year of university work before her family was forced to flee by Serbian soldiers. They had taken her Muslim father to a concentration camp.

Sure enough, Eduardo Marti, the college president, immediately offered a tuition waiver. He had himself fled Cuba in 1960 as part of the "Peter Pan Brigade" that brought children to the United States. Catholic Charities had responded to his parents' call for help in getting an education; he became a biology teacher, then a college administrator. "Now it's my turn to help," he said.

Jasmina would still need a place to stay, expense money, a network in the community. In less than a week, 20 people—from Jewish, Catholic, Protestant, and Muslim backgrounds—gelled into a cohesive support group: the Bosnian Student Project of Ithaca. Jerrahi supplied the airfare for Jasmina. One of our friends, a linguist fluent in Serbo-Croatian, offered temporary housing and an Affidavit of Support required by the U.S. consulate in Istanbul, where Jasmina's family had found refuge.

(continued)

A Debt Repaid: . . . (continued)

Six weeks later, on February 4, about 20 of us, including Dr. Marti, welcomed Jasmina at the Ithaca bus station. We knew her story: the confiscation of her family's house and possessions, the arrest and torture of her father, threats to abduct her and her sister, their hair's-breadth escape to Turkey. But what was most memorable was her refusal to fit the stereotype of a victim.

"I am only part Muslim," she said. "My father is Bosnian, but my mother is a Christian Serb." She had no desire for revenge against all Serbs. Indeed, she said, it was a highly placed Serb officer, a friend of the family, who had gone the rounds of the concentration camps until he found Jasmina's father, whose breath rasped through crushed ribs. The officer brazened the father's release from his captors to his own custody, so that he could spirit him to a hospital in Belgrade.

Jasmina confirmed that Bosnians had constituted one of Europe's most cosmopolitan societies. Jews, Christians and Muslims had lived close to one another for generations; something like a quarter of them had intermarried. Yet, the fanatic nationalists, mostly Serbian, had been able to whip up religious hatred against the Muslims, even those who were thoroughly secularized. Jasmina's home had been taken over by the family's Serbian maid, who just moved in because her family needed more room.

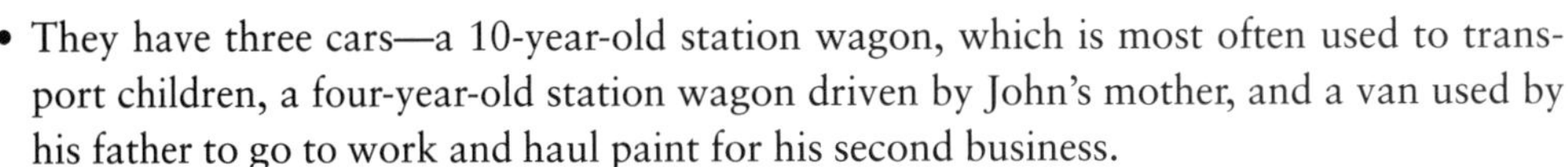

- They have three cars—a 10-year-old station wagon, which is most often used to transport children, a four-year-old station wagon driven by John's mother, and a van used by his father to go to work and haul paint for his second business.
- When he was younger, John spent many a spring or summer day waiting for night to fall so all the guys in the neighborhood could play hide-and-go-seek.
- Although he made jokes about his little sisters running willy-nilly about the grounds, he enjoyed watching them compete to see who could collect the most fireflies in a Mason jar.
- He loves being from a big family, and playing big brother to the little ones.
- Rarely a day goes by that he doesn't tease someone; his current victim is his young brother.
- In a loud voice, John tells how his brother was too embarrassed to go to the bathroom around strangers; while attending his first summer camp at age nine, he got constipated and had to return to Cleveland homesick, humiliated and in great pain.
- Once he got home, he was fine—until the teasing began.
- His sisters are fascinated by the trial of actor and former football player O.J. Simpson, who is accused of brutally killing his estranged wife Nicole Brown Simpson and her friend Ronald Goldman.
- Day after day, they stay glued to the TV set; for his part, John has been convinced that Simpson is guilty since the day he ran away in his white Bronco to avoid being arrested.
- The youngest children are more interested in *The Lion King*; it seems to John that everywhere he looks, something—whether it is a book, a record or a lunch box—has a *Lion King* character; even the thirty-fifth anniversary of the Barbie doll last year didn't get that kind of play.

Life at School

- In school, regular classes have been set aside while everyone talks about the bombing of a federal office building in Oklahoma City.
- Students wonder, if it could happen in Oklahoma, could it happen here?
- John wants to know how someone could hate enough to kill that many people; it doesn't make sense, and he feels revenge is justified in this case.
- He is proud of the fact that he makes good grades, thanks to hard work and solid organization; others are smarter, but few work harder.
- This is especially true on the football field, where his coach has said repeatedly that John has the skills, dedication and size to win a scholarship to a Big Ten School—even Notre Dame.
- He is unsure whether he wants to play college football; he is not sure what he wants to do.
- A football scholarship would give him access to many fine schools, but the priests at school have convinced him that he should set his sights on Georgetown, the Jesuit University in Washington.
- The many family discussions around the dinner table concerning the Balkan War have convinced him that a career in the foreign service is more important than playing football.

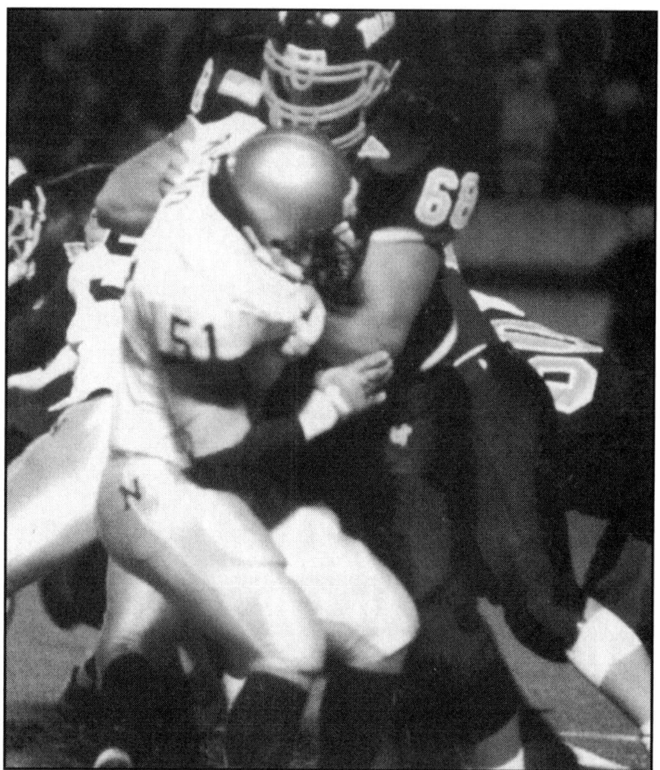

John's football skills have the coach talking about a college scholarship.

Current Kids' Dumb Jokes:

Q. What word upsets a baseball player, but makes a bowler smile?
A. Strike
Q. How long is a pair of shoes?
A. Two feet
Q. What did the zero say to the eight?
A. "Nice belt"
Q. What goes fast and is spelled the same forward and backward?
A. Race car
Q. What do you call Oreos that cut class?
A. Cookie cutters
Q. What did the ruler say to the pencil?
A. You must draw the line somewhere
Q. Where do politicians learn to be candidates?
A. Primary school
Q. What's a bird's favorite gadget?
A. A seedy ROM

"Make Way for the Baltimore Browns," *U.S. News & World Report*, November 20, 1995:

He had just landed one of sports' juicier sweetheart deals. Fans chanted, "Art! Art! Art!" One waved a WE LOVE YOU, MAN poster. But Art Modell, sitting on a rostrum in Baltimore, was not smiling. He sensed what people back home, back in Cleveland, would say about his decision to make their Cleveland Browns—correction: his Cleveland Browns—the Baltimore Browns. "A death in the family," Otto Graham, the great Browns quarterback of the 1950s, called it. "A chop block to the heart," moaned the *Cleveland Plain Dealer*. Disgust was voiced even in Baltimore, which lost its beloved Colts to Indianapolis in 1984. "The Browns name belongs in Cleveland, just as the Colts' name belongs in Baltimore," wrote the *Baltimore Sun*'s Ken Rosenthal. "It's not much to offer when you've stolen a franchise. But any sign of decency would be welcome now."

In this dollar-driven decade, it's no surprise that free-agency franchises are all the rage in the National Football League. But few fans imagined movers coming for Modell's Browns who, even in losing years and sleet and snow, drew crowds of 70,000 to Cleveland Stadium. Only months ago, Modell said this about the Los Angeles Rams becoming the St. Louis Rams: "You can't have clubs jumping for the big bucks and deserting a marketplace at a whim."

The 70-year-old, whom many Ohioans knew as "Mr. Cleveland," grew up in Brooklyn. After his father, a radio retailer, went bankrupt and died in the Depression, 15-year-old Art went to work in a shipyard. At 22, he took a television course. Before long, he was a pioneer producer of daytime TV programs. After a Madison Avenue stint, he bought the Browns in 1961 for $4 million—then the most ever for an NFL team. The league made him its TV chairman for 31 years and thrived on his expertise. He helped cut deals that produced $8.4 billion and made pro football television's No. 1 sport.

Modell advocated "leaguethink"—what's good for the NFL is good for all its revenue-sharing owners. But leaguethink has taken a drubbing. The big bucks generated by the luxury suites, parking and concessions at new stadiums are now shared. . . .Bitter fans complained that Modell signed his Baltimore pact—including a posh stadium to be built with lottery dollars—without waiting for the outcome of a referendum. (It passed a day after his announcement.) But the 64-year-old stadium, he argued, could not be improved enough to allow him to compete in the changing NFL. . .

To bring back the NFL, Cleveland will need a new stadium, as attractive as its new baseball, basketball and rock-and-roll museum facilities. But it dare not hope for an expansion team: The NFL says its next new club probably won't be born until the next century. Cleveland, as Baltimore did, will have to tempt a vagabond.

- His father hopes his son will become a certified public accountant, where the money is good and steady, and that he will then settle down in Cleveland and still come over to the house every Sunday.
- John has grown up in a family obsessed with the Cleveland Browns professional football team.
- During football season, Sunday afternoons after church and dinner are spent watching the Browns play.
- Once or twice a year, John's father snags enough tickets to take the entire family to a home game.
- The Browns' recent decision to leave Cleveland for Baltimore has caused their loyal fans to mourn.

- John knows that when his entire extended family—grandparents, uncles, aunts and cousins—all gather for the traditional Thanksgiving meal, the subject of owner Art Modell taking their beloved Browns away will come up again and again.
- At the community center, where he sometimes hangs out to meet girls, the most popular theme seems to be the song, "Shut Up and Kiss Me"; shy by nature, he is not sure how to take the laughter when the song is played.
- Another hot topic is whether the Grateful Dead will get back together now that Jerry Garcia has died, though John is not really interested one way or the other.
- Many of his friends are wild about the Rock and Roll Hall of Fame and Museum opening in their city; since it cost $92 million, he figures he should go, but hasn't gotten up the energy yet.

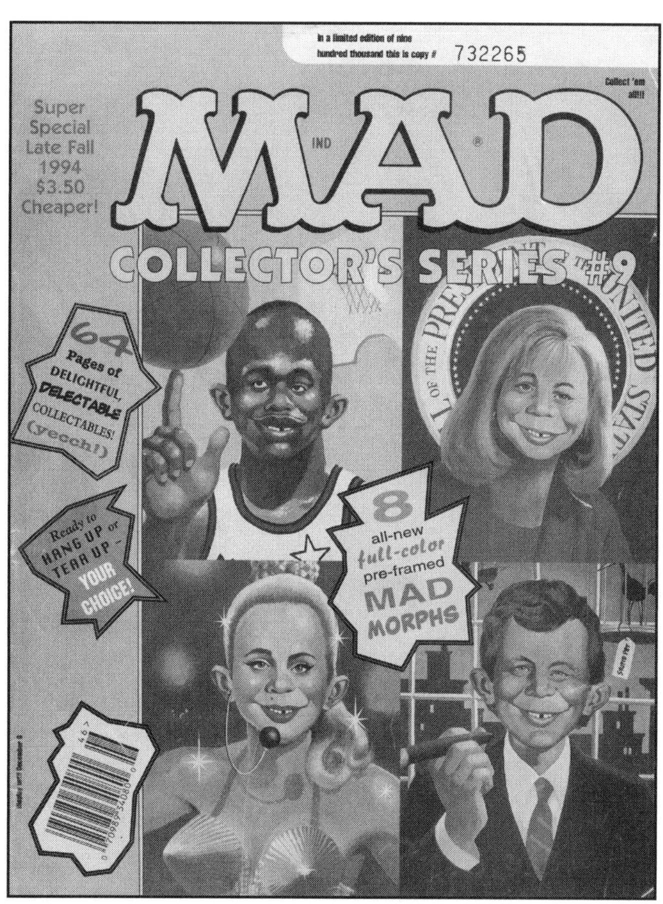

Life in the Community: Cleveland, Ohio

- The people of Cleveland believe they have plenty to brag about.
- The Cleveland Museum of Art is second only to the Metropolitan in New York in the value of its collection.
- The city's 18,000-acre park system is considered one of the nations finest, and the Cleveland Playhouse is the oldest professional resident theater company in the United States.
- Cleveland is considered the melting pot for the Midwest and enjoys a long history of attracting immigrants eager for work.
- The city currently accounts for more than a third of all Croatians in the state.
- Ohio's first residents were the mysterious, prehistoric Indians known as the Mound Builders who left behind burial and effigy mounds.
- When white people arrived in Ohio in the seventeenth century, the land was populated by Shawnee, Miami, Wyandot and Delaware Indians.
- By 1788, settlers from the East were discovering a land said to be so fertile, a farmer only needed to "tickle the soil with a hoe to laugh with the harvest."
- In fits of "Ohio Fever," entire New England villages pulled up stakes to move west, followed by immigrants from Germany and Switzerland, who headed for Ohio right off the boat.
- So many Swiss came to the state that parts of Tuscarawas and Monroe counties, where they settled, were referred to as "little Switzerland."
- The factories of Cleveland, Toledo, Youngstown and Dayton brought even more diversity to the state.
- At the turn of the twentieth century, 63 different ethnicities and nationalities settled in Cleveland, giving the city a cosmopolitan character.
- After World War I, when stricter immigration laws slowed European movement, Ohio's factories began recruiting blacks from the South.
- From 1870 to 1970, the black population of Cleveland grew from 62,000 to 970,000.
- The need for manufacturing labor has been a magnet for immigrant groups ever since.

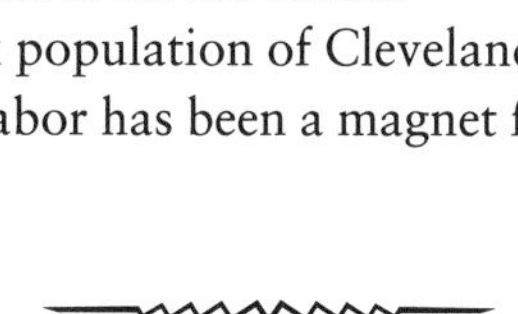

Historical Snapshot
1995

- On television, *ER*, *Seinfeld*, *Friends*, *Caroline in the City*, *NFL Monday Night Football*, *Single Guy*, *Home Improvement*, *Boston Common*, *60 Minutes* and *NYPD Blue* led in the Nielsen ratings
- The Dow-Jones Industrial Average reached 5,216; the low for the year was 3,832
- The movies *Braveheart* with Mel Gibson, *Apollo 13* with Tom Hanks, *Leaving Las Vegas* with Nicolas Cage and *Dead Man Walking* with Susan Sarandon premiered
- America boasted 720,000 physicians and 190,000 dentists
- Fifty-seven million viewers watched the murder trial of O.J. Simpson, accused of killing his estranged wife Nicole Brown Simpson and her friend Ronald Goldman
- Top record singles for the year included "Can You Feel the Love Tonight" by Elton John, "Gangsta's Paradise" by Coolio and "Dear Mama" by Tupac Shakur
- The frozen body of a 500-year-old Inca girl was found bundled in fine wool in the Peruvian Andes
- Research showed that three ounces of salmon a week reduced the risk of fatal heart arrhythmias by 50 percent
- Two Americans were arrested for the Oklahoma City bombing, which killed 169 people and left 614 injured
- The all-male college, The Citadel, finally admitted its first female cadet, who withdrew after only a few days
- Louis Farrakan led a "Million Man March" on Washington, attracting 400,000 men who pledged greater social and family responsibility
- Hollywood's most expensive film, *Waterworld*, which cost $200 million to make, was a flop
- More than seven million people subscribed to online computer services such as America Online, CompuServe and Prodigy
- Blue M&Ms, custom-made coffins, Pepcid AC and the computer language Java made their first appearance
- The Centers for Disease Control reported a leveling-off of teen sexual activity; reportedly, 52.8 percent used condoms
- Businesses nationwide introduced casual Fridays, allowing employees to wear less formal attire

1995 Economic Profile

Selected Prices

Airline Ticket, Los Angeles to Chicago	$198.00
Bathtub Reglazing	$170.00
Bra, Maidenform	$12.99
Carpet Deodorizer, Arm & Hammer	$0.99
Cat Food, Purina Cat Chow, 20 Pounds	$7.99
Computer, Compaq Presario 1235	$1,199.00
Dental Extraction, per Tooth	$25.00
Krazy Glue	$1.00
Luggage, Samsonite 750 Jumbo Hardside Cart	$399.99
Organizer, Electronic Palm III	$369.00
Piano, Yamaha, Digital	$997.00
Roasting Pan, Calphalon	$99.99
Rollerblades	$34.97
Soccer Cleats	$129.95
Tire, Bridgestone High-Performance HR15	$85.00

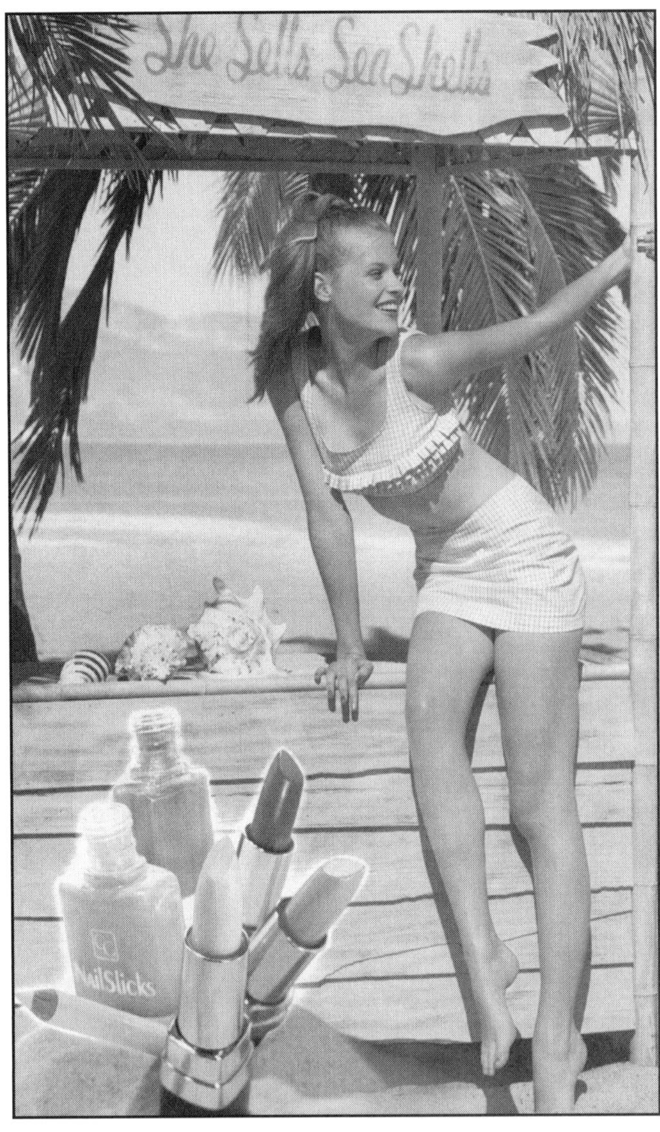

Changing America

- The San Francisco Bay area overtook New York City as the nation's jazz center.
- Controversies grew concerning the impact of TV sex and violence, particularly on teenagers.
- Television talk shows such as *Ricki Lake* and *The Jerry Springer Show* premiered to discuss the intimate lives of their guests.
- C. DeLores Tucker launched an attack against gangsta rap for its effect on African-American children.
- To attract younger classical music audiences, interactive concerts were created; during a Philadelphia Orchestra program, the audience e-mailed their requests during intermission.
- Physicists discovered the megaparticle consisting of a few thousand atoms, predicted by Einstein.
- After 139 years, Mississippi lawmakers ratified the Thirteenth Amendment abolishing slavery.
- In the face of a media storm, Calvin Klein withdrew his advertisements featuring very young teenage models in sultry poses.
- For the first time in its history, Ford sold more trucks than cars.
- Coffee bars such as Starbucks spread rapidly, providing an inexpensive, safe dating haven.
- Singer Kurt Cobain's bloodstained guitar sold for $17,000 after his death by suicide.
- Nearly 180 years after her death, author Jane Austen gained new popularity through the major motion pictures *Persuasion*, *Emma*, and *Sense and Sensibility*.
- Approximately 55 percent of women provided half or more of household income.

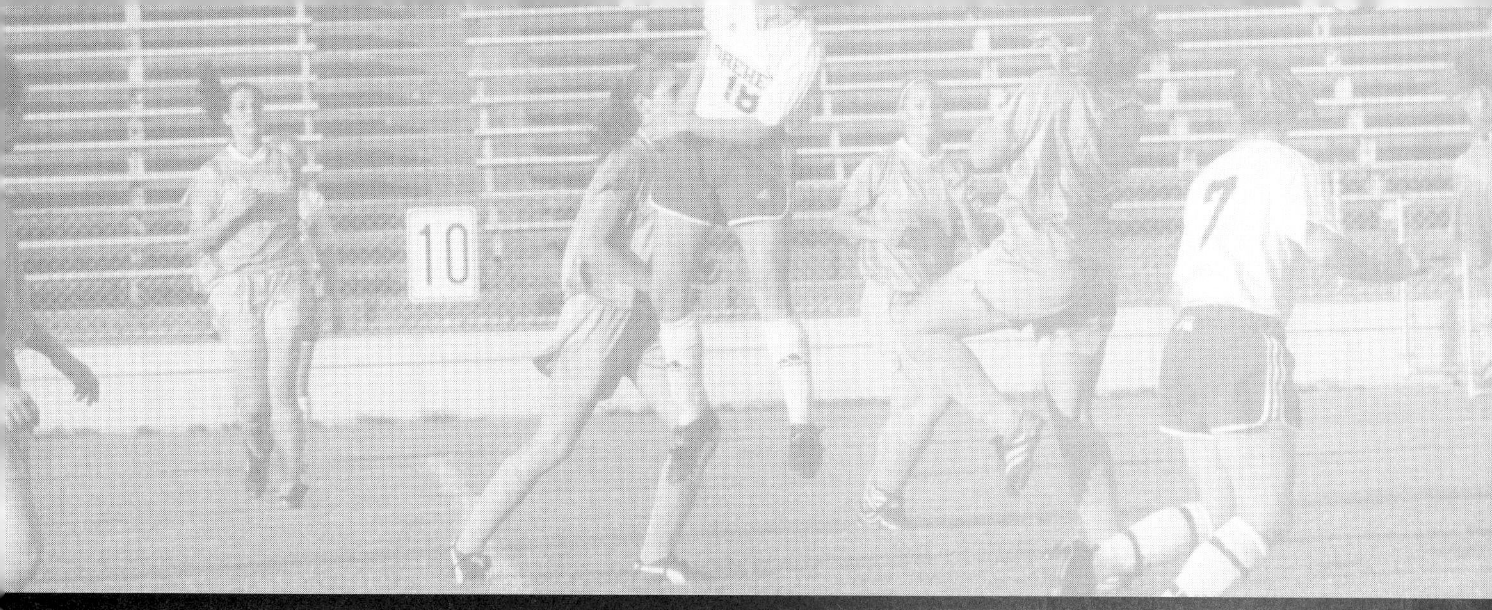

1998 Profile

Middle Class

It's been quite a year for Robin Lye. As a high school sophomore, she played on a basketball team that emerged second in the state, a soccer team that was state champion, and she was named player of the year; best yet, she is making all A's in advanced classes and has a boyfriend.

Robin Lye is having a great year.

Life at Home

- The past year has been rewarding.
- It began with the high school cross-county season last fall, when Robin finished eighth in the state of Georgia and fifth in Atlanta.
- But soccer is her real passion.
- During the same season, Robin played "club" soccer with girls aged 17 years and under, many actively recruited for the team from seven other high schools in the area.
- Each weekend they would travel to locations as distant as Jacksonville, Florida; Columbia, South Carolina; Washington, DC; or Raleigh, North Carolina, to play soccer against the region's best teams.
- They won more than half their games and were seen by a wide range of college recruiting coaches; because Robin is a sophomore, no coach was allowed to talk with her, but many asked questions of her coach.
- When basketball season arrived, the high school coach asked her if she would try out, and she became the only white girl on the squad.
- Her school, which is 50 percent African-American, generally observes clear dividing lines—black girls play basketball and white girls play soccer.

Robin travels throughout the South playing soccer on weekends.

- Most of the teams they play reflect the same racial makeup; at most basketball games, 90 percent of the fans are African-American, while at the soccer games, less than five percent are black.
- Her primary job on the basketball team was playing defense, and she was only occasionally called upon for her skills.
- Her jump shot is awkward and the source of great amusement for her more experienced teammates.
- Before one important game, when the other members of the team decided to fashion their hair in cornrows, Robin wove her hair into French braids in a show of unity.
- Spanning two seasons, the team won 40 games in a row before losing in the state finals.
- Because she never left the bench in the final game, she is unsure whether she will rejoin the basketball team next year or simply concentrate her junior year on visiting colleges, rock climbing, water sports and soccer.
- Rock climbing is a particular attraction because her fellow athletes are so laid-back and supportive.
- She believes she can be less self-conscious while rock climbing than in any of the team sports she plays.
- She especially enjoys the fact that many of the indoor climbing walls in the area provide both physical and mental challenges.
- Several times, her athletic skills allowed her to reach places that turned into dead ends, but now she is learning to combine her strength with excellent planning.
- The highlight of the year has been high school soccer, where she played with many of her best friends.
- Entering the season, she and her teammates knew the coach would be leaving in the fall to attend law school, so they wanted the year to be special.

The fans were enthusiastic at the championship game.

- He delayed his entry into law school for one year so he could coach the team; he, too, wanted the year to be special.
- Robin plays center forward and is the leading scorer on the team.
- She believes her greatest skill is passing and creating good ball movement, and dreams of taking a leadership role in life.
- The two-week buildup to the game was exciting and agonizingly slow as they worked their way through the playoffs.
- On the day of the championship, played at her high school's highly manicured, natural-grass stadium, the student body arrived in force.
- For the first time all season, all seats were filled an hour before the game, and many of the fans had brought giant banners and horns.
- Having lived with the embarrassment of the basketball team's loss of its state championship game, Robin was focused on winning.
- The first half ended in a scoreless tie, and then the other team scored first to break the deadlock, 1-0.
- Late in the game, Robin sprinted past two defenders and drove the tying goal into the upper corner of the net, forcing the game into overtime.
- During the extra time period, with the crowd screaming, she contributed two additional assists, resulting in a 3-1 victory; it was the school's first state championship in women's soccer.
- Pandemonium reigned afterward.
- Following the game, a panel of coaches named her player of the year, even though she was only a sophomore, and the local sportswriters then bestowed on her the same honor, earning her a picture in the newspaper.

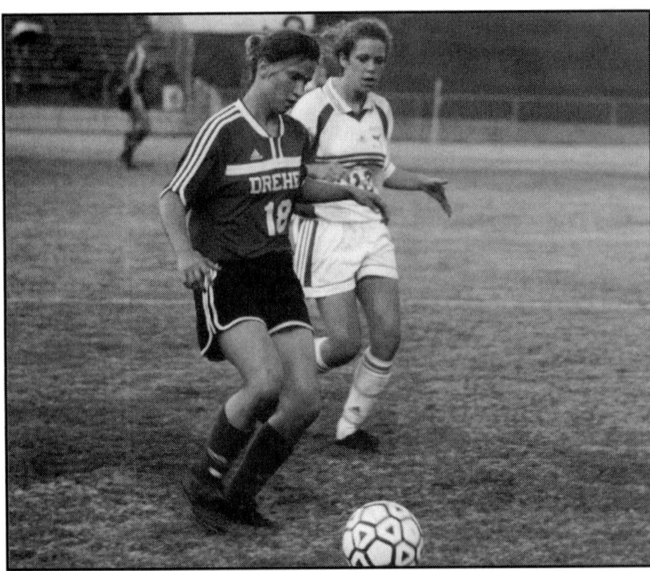

Robin scored during the championship game.

- The three local television stations showed her goal and assists over and over.
- She realizes that the quality of her coaches, uniforms, fields and referees are a direct result of the 1972 Title IX law that required schools to provide equal opportunities for men and women.
- In 1972, females represented seven percent of high school varsity athletes, while today, they represent 42 percent.
- At the college level, the number of women athletes has risen from 15 percent to 42 percent during the same period.
- Now that school is over, Robin is working at a summer camp in the mountains of North Carolina as a junior counselor.
- Her cabin is populated with nine-year-olds who have a fascination with her personal life, especially her boyfriend.
- Even the slightest tidbit of information will keep them up for hours giggling with each other.
- When the year began, she was dating a senior from a neighboring school, whom she could only see after school and on weekends.
- The relationship ended when she caught him with another girl.
- Within two months, she met a guy at a local gym, a college sophomore who is working his way through school.
- Her parents, who divorced eight years ago, are unsettled by the four-year age difference.
- Robin's mother, in particular, is concerned about the relationship, but her father makes very few negative comments, and even invites her boyfriend to the house for meals and conversation.
- Since the divorce, Robin has lived with her mother, even though her parents have joint custody.
- Her parents live only a few miles apart; she spends Wednesdays, Thursdays and every other weekend with her father, who remarried several years ago.
- Recently, as part of the divorce settlement, her mother sold the home in which Robin had grown up to help pay college tuition for her older brother.
- Robin still does not think it's fair that her mother and father waited six years until her brother graduated from high school to sell the family house, but could not wait three more years for her graduation.
- One of the hardest parts of living between two houses is telling friends where to find her on any given day.
- She also worries that if she leaves schoolbooks and notes she needs for homework at one house, someone will get mad.
- When she was in middle school, she felt different from other kids because of the divorce; everyone else's parents were married and many had stay-at-home moms who could help with school projects.

Atlanta is known for its innovative educational programs.

Following the championship victory, pandemonium reigned.

- Now, though, it bothers her less, especially since she has a car and can drive where she needs to be.

Life at School

- Last year, in an attempt to raise standards and test scores, Robin's school adopted block scheduling, in which all classes are 93 minutes long and last for only one semester.
- Robin takes four classes per semester, 2 of which are AAP, or Advanced Academic Placement classes for college.
- She is also taking two AP, or advanced placement, classes, allowing her to earn college credit if she passes a nationally sanctioned exam at the end of the semester.
- She thinks the longer classes are stupid, believing that the absorption rate of high school students—even smart ones—ends long before the 93 minutes are up.
- Besides, most of the teachers gear their lesson plans to 50-minute classes, and most have had difficulty shifting to the longer format, resulting in wasted time.
- Last semester, she took Spanish 4, U.S. history, chemistry, and business computer applications.
- Her favorite was chemistry, because of both the subject and the entertaining way the teacher presented the material.
- This semester, she is taking anatomy and physiology, precalculus, history and English.
- Her English class, which includes an intensive unit on writing, is taught by her favorite teacher.
- Unlike many of her other teachers, Ms. Haggett provides the freedom to learn; if you know the material and don't want to pay attention all the time, it's okay.
- Robin is currently preparing to take the SAT exam; her PSAT came in at 1260, but she wants to break 1400 to ensure a good choice of colleges.

Atlanta was the home of the 1996 Olympics.

- Friends have repeatedly said she is a shoo-in to get a college soccer scholarship, but, having heard that college soccer is all-consuming and will dominate her life, she is unsure if she wants to play in college.
- She has too many interests for that, she thinks.
- Besides, she dreams of attending a college that will prepare her for a career in medicine, and though she has not yet chosen a school, her criteria include an out-of-state location and a premed course.
- A current favorite is Wake Forest University in Winston-Salem, North Carolina, even though she has never been on the campus.
- In class rank, she is now number five overall in a class of 350, having moved from the number eight slot as a freshman; in her high school career she has made one B out of all A's.
- She is also trying to decide how active she would like to be in her high school sorority.
- As a freshman, she was honored to be invited by the popular girls into the social club, which is banned by the school because of its exclusivity, but she is now wondering how much time she wants to devote to it.
- Athletics and schoolwork allowed her only occasionally to attend the parties thrown by the group most of the year.
- Currently, the newspapers are replete with stories about high school drug use; when her father asks about marijuana, she readily admits that a lot of people "smoke up" in the mornings.
- Acid and cocaine, she believes, are used primarily by the rich kids in school who can afford a more expensive high.
- Alcohol, especially beer, is the drug of choice at her school; it's readily available at parties, especially those that form almost spontaneously at homes where parents have left for a weekend, trusting their children to do the right thing.

The dynamics of the Atlanta economy electrify the state.

Life in the Community: Atlanta, Georgia

- The city of Atlanta, where the 1996 Olympics were held, is struggling with what to do with the Olympic caldron, the symbol of the summer games.
- Atlanta media mogul and billionaire Ted Turner, who recently pledged $1 billion to the United Nations, is being criticized because his foundation has only given $2.7 million to Atlanta-based charities.
- Atlanta ranks fifth among major American cities in the percentage of people living in poverty.
- The latest FBI statistics show that the city's murder rate plunged to 36 murders per 100,000 residents, the lowest level in a decade.
- An intensive manhunt continues for Eric Rudolph, accused of three bombings in Atlanta, including a blast at Centennial Olympic Park during the Olympics.

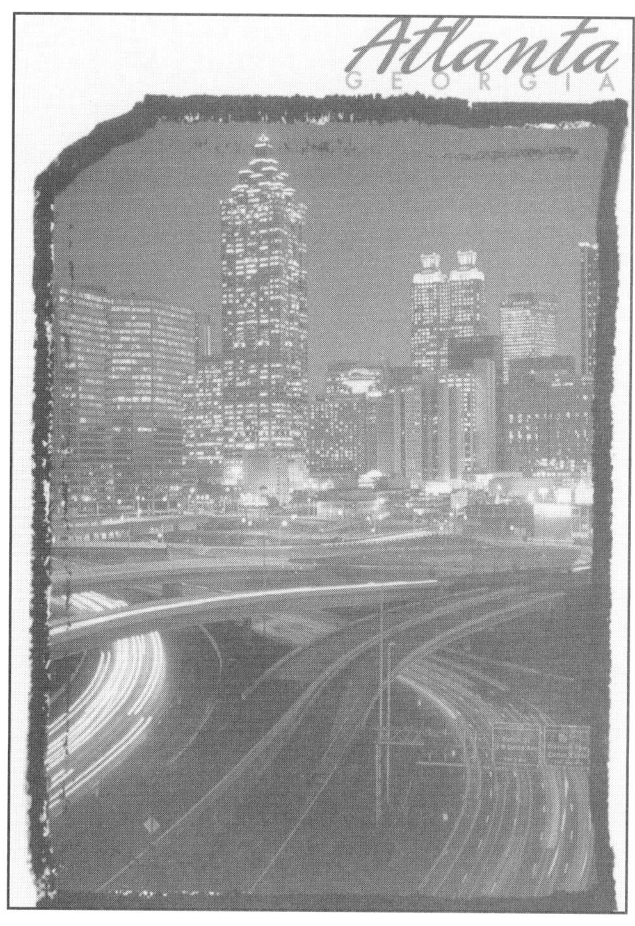

Historical Snapshot
1998

- The movie *Titanic* became the highest-grossing film in history at $850 million
- Studies indicated that 50 percent of all Americans were overweight
- Seventeen major newspapers called for President Bill Clinton's resignation following his admission to a grand jury that he had engaged in an extramarital affair and lied about the relationship
- Online birth, surgical glue, vaccines for Lyme disease, drive-through cigar stores, nanotubes, iris-scanning ID systems and a quantum computer network made their first appearance
- Georgia Governor Zell Miller proposed that newborns be sent home with a recording of Mozart and Bach to stimulate brain development
- Births to unwed mothers and infant mortality fell to 25-year lows
- Popular books included *Confederates in the Attic* by Tony Horwitz, *Pillar of Fire: America in the King Years* by Taylor Branch, *Slaves in the Family* by Edward Ball, *A Man in Full* by Tom Wolfe, *The Street Lawyer* by John Grisham, *Rainbow Six* by Tom Clancy, and *Tuesdays with Morrie* by Mitch Albom
- The Pulitzer Prize for U.S. history went to Edwin G. Burrows and Mike Wallace for *Gotham: A History of New York City to 1898*
- Nineteen students were killed as a result of several small-town shootings by teenagers at their schools
- A New Jersey fertility clinic doubled its stipend to egg donors to $5,000 for a month's supply, igniting fears of a bidding war for human eggs
- Fads for the year included the use of ginkgo, Internet shopping, "Teletubbies" and techno
- The Dow-Jones Industrial Average peaked at 9,374, while unemployment was at its lowest since 1970
- The undergraduate tuition at Princeton reached $22,820 a year, plus $6,711 for room and board
- U.S. rockets were fired at Osama Bin Laden's terrorist network in Afghanistan and Sudan
- President Clinton ordered air attacks against Iraq's Saddam Hussein for obstructing the work of UN inspectors
- The United States budget showed a $70 billion surplus, the first time it had been positive since 1969
- On television, *Sports Night*, *Jesse*, *That '70s Show* and *Felicity* premiered
- Geraldo Rivera signed a six-year, $30 million contract with CNBC
- Dr. Jack Kevorkian demonstrated patient-assisted death on the television program *60 Minutes* and was arrested for first-degree murder
- *Shakespeare in Love*, *Saving Private Ryan*, *Life Is Beautiful*, *A Bug's Life* and *Out of Sight* opened at movie theaters
- Top albums of the year included the soundtrack from *Titanic*, Celine Dion's "Let's Talk about Love," "Come On Over" by Shania Twain and "The Backstreet Boys" by the Backstreet Boys

1998 Economic Profile

Selected Prices

Book, Mediterranean Cooking Kitchen Library $14.95
Bulbs, 100 Tulips. $43.00
Breadmaker, Welbilt $129.99
Chair, La-Z-Boy $332.99
Comforter, Quallowarm II, King Size $160.00
Cookware, All-Clad Soup Pot $230.00
Envelopes, 100 9 x 12 Brown Kraft $4.65
Jacket, Adidas Polar Fleece $69.95
Museum Admission, New York, Museum for African Art $8.00
Purse, Kenneth Cole, Leather $148.50
Soccer Ball $69.95
Soccer Cleats $129.95
Suit, Man's Hickey-Freeman. $760.00
Tea, Tetley Ice Tea Mix, 42 Servings $0.99
Videotape, Disney's *The Lion King* $29.99

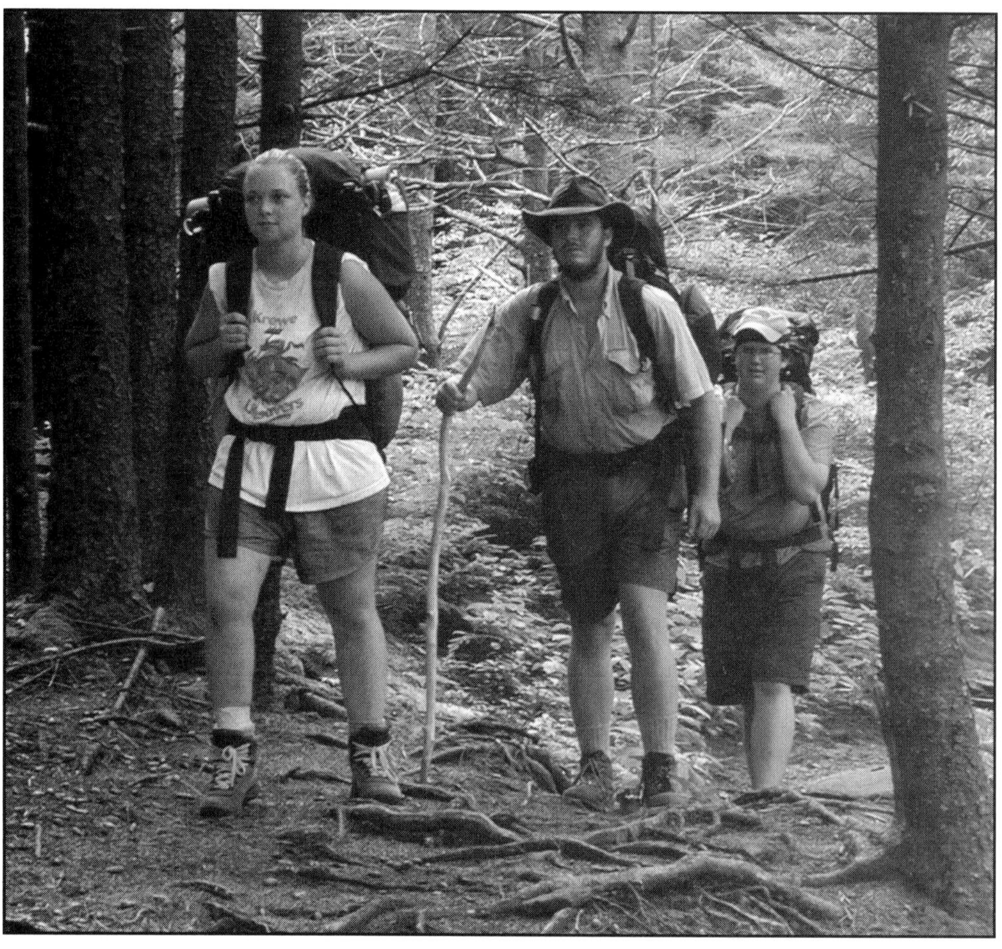

Robin often hikes with friends in the Appalachian Mountains.

Changing America

- The typical tire for a large automobile weighed 25 pounds, down from 32 pounds in the late 1960s.
- America's Hispanic population jumped by 58 percent during the past decade to 35.3 million people.
- The number of corporate pension plans fell from 112,200 in 1985 to 42,300.
- Viagra, for male erectile dysfunction, captured national attention and sold at a record rate, despite its cost of $10 a pill.
- The per capita consumption of food by Americans had increased eight percent during the past decade, or approximately 140 pounds of food a year per person.
- Roughly one-half of the average household food budget was spent outside the home, up from one-quarter in 1970.
- Ku Klux Klan leader Samuel Bowers was convicted in Mississippi for the 1966 murder of civil rights leader Vernon Dahmer.
- AIDS deaths fell nearly 50 percent from the previous year.
- DNA evidence proved that Thomas Jefferson fathered a child with his slave/mistress Sally Hemings.
- The number of welfare recipients dropped below four percent, the lowest in 25 years.
- A study reported that PMS was a biological, not a psychological, syndrome.
- The New York Philharmonic toured Asia, performing in Beijing for the first time.

"Practice Makes Perfect (and Poorer Parents)," by James Schembari, *The New York Times*, January 27, 2002:

Has so little changed since Allan Sherman, the late comedic songwriter, recorded these lyrics in 1966 (sung to "Makin' Whoopee")?

"My daughter, Linda, she takes ballet.
Her first recital was yesterday.
She dropped her tutu, her left shoe, too.
She needs more lessons.
Then there's my daughter, Dottie,
She takes guitar, that's true.
Junior, he takes karate.
Smashed her guitar in two.
For all these lessons, I have to pay.
I must raise money. I found a way.
Read my brochure folks, learn how to be poor, folks.
I'm giving lessons."

Parents seem to have been as crazed then about training their children as baby boomers are now.

My three sons, ages seven to 11, play on community baseball and T-ball teams, and once played organized soccer and basketball. They have taken trumpet lessons and chess lessons.

My daughter, Marian, 14, has been a member of the Brownies, has played the violin and is now taking piano lessons. She has also joined the drama department and the choir at her high school, a step that means buying costumes and show tickets. This spring, the choir is taking a $400 field trip to Virginia. Before Thanksgiving, she announced that she wanted to try out for the highly competitive regional chorus. I encouraged her.

"But if I'm going to make it, I need to take voice lessons," she said.

That was $40 a week for several weeks, but she made the cut, and her concert this month was a delight.

That explains, of course, why we say yes to our children. We want them to find their passion—and what if they are really talented and just need a bit of coaching? So even before they go off to college, we've spent a fortune on them.

Actually, we may be a bit more obsessed about this than our parents were. According to figures from the Agriculture Department, which tracks family expenditures, parents with incomes of $38,000 to $64,000 spent $18,510 on miscellaneous items for the average child from birth through age 18. That is up from $17,600 in 1960, adjusted for inflation. The category includes entertainment, reading material, VCRs, summer camp, and lessons. A study by Child Trends, a nonpartisan research group in Washington, found that about 82 percent of American children had participated in at least one extracurricular activity in 1998.

One? How about five or six? Bugs Peterschmidt, 44, of Plymouth, Minnesota, said her two children were involved in piano, trumpet, soccer, scouting, after-school math classes, swimming and summer enrichment programs. She said she was spending about $3,000 a year on all the activities.

"I was working part-time, and once one of my paychecks went to all of this stuff," she said. "The thing is, I was bummed."

Susan Kakuk, 42, also of Plymouth, said she was also spending about $3,000 a year on her two children. Barbara Carlson, 53, of Greenfield, Minnesota, put the total for her four children at a few thousand dollars. Mark Lino, an economist for the Agriculture Department, said parents found ways to pay for all of this.

"People seem to be purchasing more of this for their children since 1960," he said. "I think it is one of the reasons more women have joined the workforce. Parents are also cutting back expenditures on themselves. They are not cutting back on their children; they are spending more on their children."

Kristin A. Moore, the president of Child Trends, said that there was a downside to all this. "They are good for children until you get past the midpoint and everyone is overwhelmed by sheer quantity," she said. "At some point families can get too busy, but no one knows how much is too much."

"Were You Born That Way? It's not just brown eyes. Your inheritance could also include insomnia, obesity and optimism. Yet scientists are saying that genes are not—quite—destiny," by George Howe Colt and Anne Hollister, *Life*, April 1998:

In the debate over the relative power of nature and nurture, there may be no more devout believers than new parents. As my wife and I, suffused with a potent mix of awe, exhaustion and ego, gazed down at our newborn daughter in the hospital, it has hard not to feel like miniature gods with a squirming lump of figurative putty in our hands. We had long believed that people could make the world a better place, and now we firmly believed that we could make this a better baby. At home our bedside tables are swaybacked by towers of well-thumbed parents' manuals. A black-and-white Stim-Mobile, designed to sharpen visual acuity, hung over the crib. The shelves were lined with books, educational puzzles and IQ-boosting rattles. Down the line we envisioned museum visits, art lessons, ballet. And if someone had tapped us on the shoulder and told us that none of this would matter—that, in fact, if we could switch babies in the nursery and send our precious darling home with any other new parents in the hospital, as long as these parents weren't penniless, violent or drug addicted, our daughter would turn out pretty much the same . . . well, we would have thwacked that someone with a Stim-Mobile.

Does the key to who we are lie in our genes or in our family, friends and experiences? In one of the most bitter controversies of the twentieth century—the battle over nature and nurture—a wealth of new research has tipped the scales overwhelmingly toward nature. Studies of twins and advances in molecular biology have uncovered a more significant genetic component to personality than was previously known. Far from a piece of putty, say biologists, my daughter is more like a computer's motherboard, her basic personality hardwired into infinitesimal squiggles of DNA. As parents, we would have no more influence on some aspects of her behavior than we had on the color of her hair. And yet, new findings are also shedding light on how heredity and environment interact. Psychiatrists are using these findings to help patients overcome their genetic predispositions. Meanwhile, advances in genetic research and reproductive technology are leading us to the brink of some extraordinary—and terrifying—possibilities.

The moment the scales began to tip can be traced to a 1979 meeting between a steelworker named Jim Lewis and a clerical worker named Jim Springer. Identical twins separated five weeks after birth, they were raised by families 80 miles apart in Ohio. Reunited 39 years later, they would have strained the credulity of the editors of *Ripley's Believe It or Not.* Not only did both have dark hair, stand six feet tall and weigh 180 pounds, they spoke with the same inflections, moved with the same gait and made the same gestures. Both loved stock-car racing and hated baseball. Both married women named Linda, divorced them and married women named Betty. Both drove Chevrolets, drank Miller Lite, chain-smoked Salems and vacationed on the same half-mile stretch of a Florida beach. Both had elevated blood pressure, severe migraines and had undergone vasectomies. Both bit their nails. Their heart rates, brain waves and IQs were nearly identical. Their scores on personality tests were as close as if one person had taken the same test twice.

Identical twins raised in different families are a built-in research lab for measuring the relative contributions of nature and nurture. The Jims became one of 7,000 sets of twins studied by the Minnesota Center for Twin and Adoption Research, one of a half-dozen such centers in this country. Using psychological and physiological tests to compare the relative similarities of identical and fraternal twins, these centers calculate the "inheritability" of behavioral traits—the degree to which a trait in a given population is attributable to a gene rather than to the environment. They have found, for instance, that "assertiveness" is 60 percent heritable, while "the ability to be enthralled by an aesthetic experience" is 55 percent heritable.

Studying adolescents adopted in infancy, University of Virginia psychologist Sandra Scarr was surprised to find that children adopted by well-educated, professional parents performed no better in school or on intelligence tests than children who had been adopted into working-class homes. "Providing children with super environments—private schooling, museum visits, lessons and so on—makes no difference in their intelligence, adjustment or personality development," says Scarr. She concludes that if a child has "good enough parenting"—parents who aren't abusive or neglectful and provide a basic level of support—one set of parents is as good as another. "It doesn't matter whether you take the kids fishing or to a Mozart concert," says Scarr. "As long as you do it with love, almost anything you do is going to be fine and functionally equivalent."

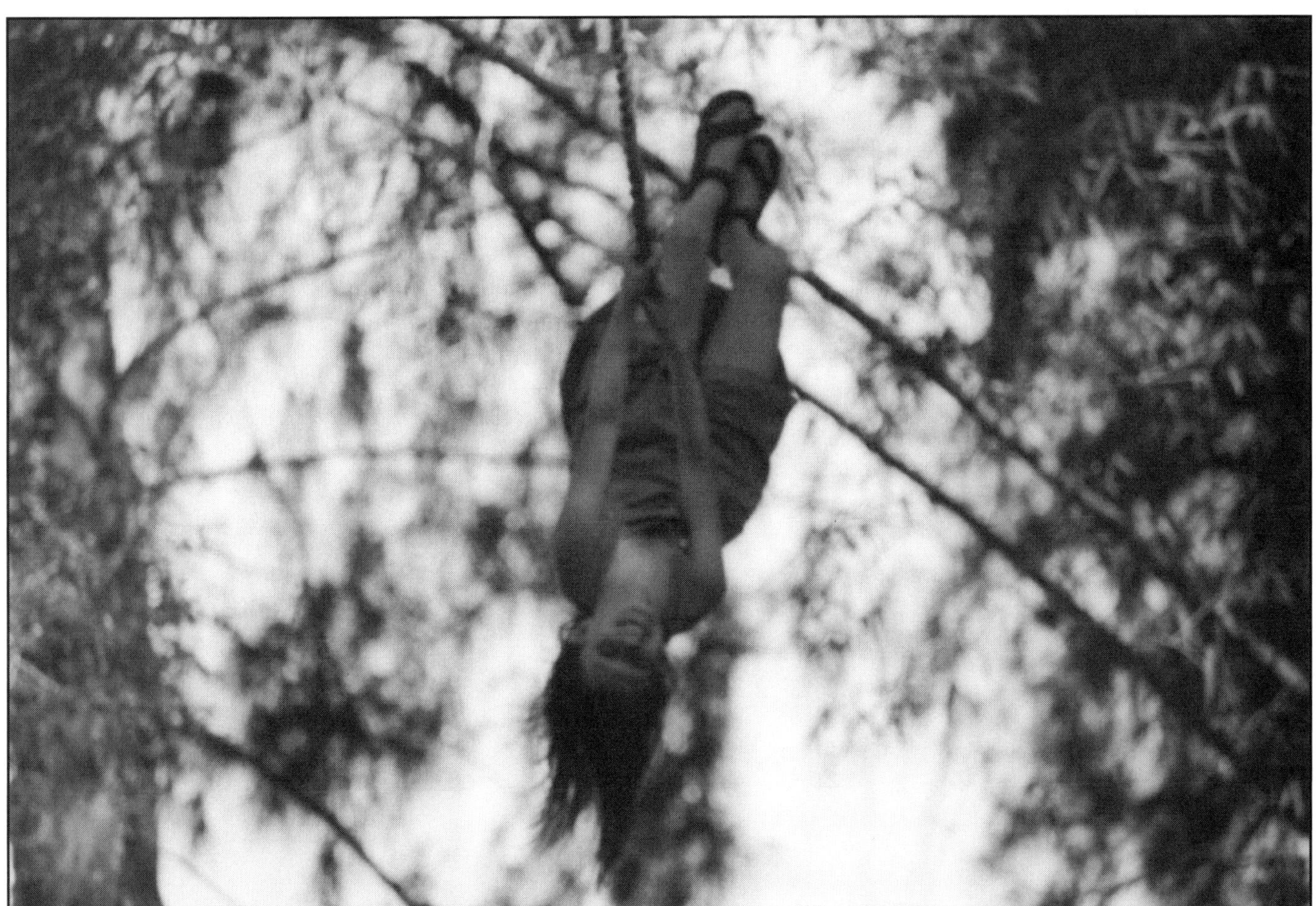

Robin has always considered herself a daredevil.

The tan you want
to touch
SEA
&SKI
SUNTAN
LOTION

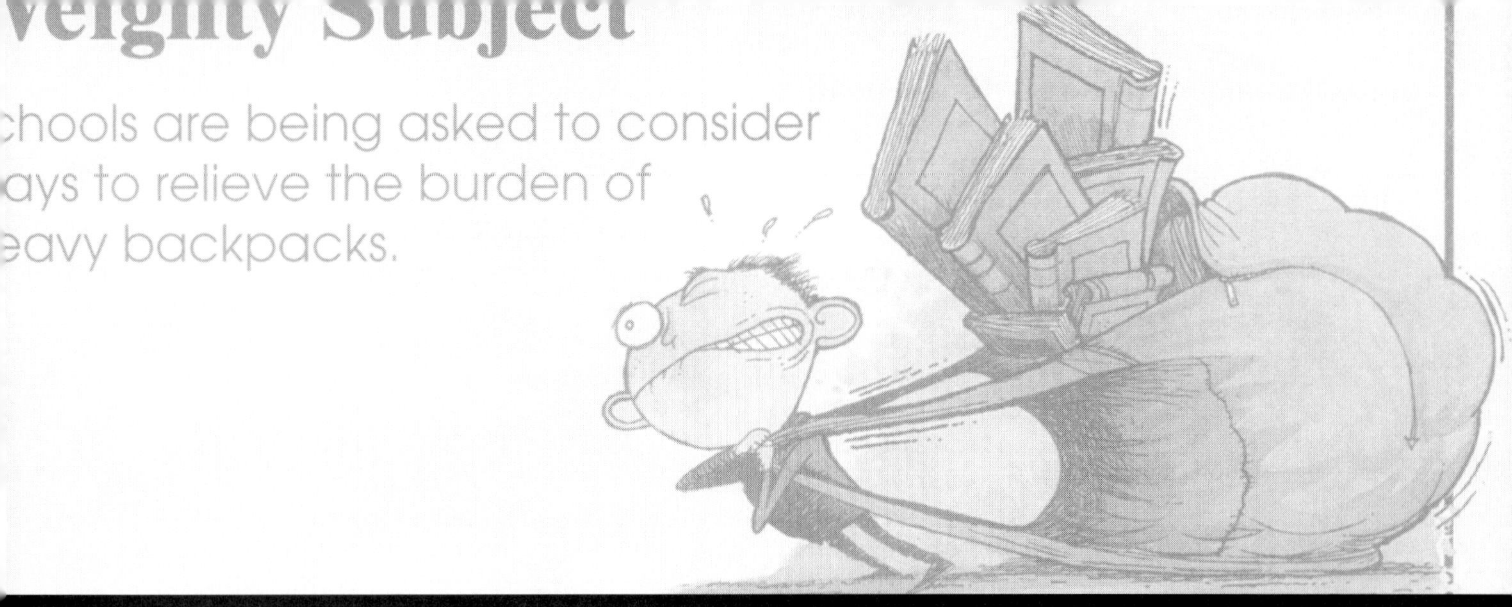

Weighty Subject
chools are being asked to consider
ays to relieve the burden of
eavy backpacks.

1999 NEWS FEATURE

"Weighty Subject, Schools are being asked to consider ways to relieve the burden of backpacks," *Governing*, July 2002:
Joan Clemons has twice undergone back surgery, which makes her sensitive to the possibility that toting heavy textbooks around school all day can be detrimental to her son Robbie. "My son is perfectly healthy," she says, "but when I saw what he was carrying to middle school, I got concerned about his back." So Clemons joined forces with other parents, teachers and administrators at Robbie's school in Sharon, Massachusetts, to alleviate the backpack burden on kids.

The school's Backpack Committee persuaded a private company to donate some binders, which they were able to sell in turn to parents. The proceeds were enough to buy extra copies of many of the textbooks used at the school, allowing kids to store one copy of each book at home and have another waiting for them in the classroom. That cut Robbie's backpack weight from 30 pounds to about 15 pounds worth of binders and gym clothes.

It was one small step, but it's more than most other schools have done to lift some of the weight off students. Textbooks have gotten bigger and heavier, while many schools do not allow students access to lockers because of safety and drug concerns. It has all added up to a daily load for middle and high school students that might strain a seasoned backcountry hiker.

"We do have research on children and adults that once you've hurt your back, you're at a higher risk for injury," says Shelly Goodgold, a professor of physical therapy at Simmons College. Goodgold readily acknowledges that there haven't been long-term studies that show direct evidence linking backpack weight to serious injuries and long-term problems in children. But she has done a study of 345 Boston-area students that found 68 percent of sixth graders were carrying more than 15 percent of their own body weight on their backs. That's the limit recommended by the American Chiropractic Association and other health groups. . . .

There aren't any obvious solutions to the backpack weight dilemma. Many schools can't afford duplicate textbooks at even a small institution. Replacing books with lighter CD-ROMs would also be expensive, especially when you factor in the necessary computer costs. Some schools have pushed for backpacks on wheels, but those cause congestion in the hallways, aren't very useful where there are stairs and are most universally dismissed by older kids as hopelessly dorky.

Indeed, fashion pressures pose real problems for juvenile backpack-wearers, from their penchant for slinging packs over one shoulder to the loose-strap look that pulls weight away from the pack and ruins posture. A teacher at Sharon Middle School came up with the idea of featuring some of the most popular kids on posters demonstrating proper and improper ways to wear backpacks. That had some effect, but since Robbie Clemons has moved on to Sharon High School, his load has grown heavier again. The school has smaller lockers, short breaks between classes that are widely spread out, and different levels of instruction taught within each grade, making textbook duplication prohibitively expensive.

What's more, high school kids aren't interested in wearing their backpacks any ergonomically correct way. "A lot of the kids have this fad where they wear it all the way down to their tush," Joan Clemons laments.

INDEX

Universal Reference Publications
Statistical & Demographic Reference Books

Working Americans 1880-1999
Volume I: The Working Class, Volume II: The Middle Class, Volume III: The Upper Class

Each of the volumes in the *Working Americans 1880-1999* series focuses on a particular class of Americans, The Working Class, The Middle Class and The Upper Class over the last 120 years. Chapters in each volume focus on one decade and profile three to five families. Family Profiles include real data on Income & Job Descriptions, Selected Prices of the Times, Annual Income, Annual Budgets, Family Finances, Life at Work, Life at Home, Life in the Community, Working Conditions, Cost of Living, Amusements and much more. Each chapter also contains an Economic Profile with Average Wages of other Professions, a selection of Typical Pricing, Key Events & Inventions, News Profiles, Articles from Local Media and Illustrations. The *Working Americans* series captures the lifestyles of each of the classes from the last twelve decades, covers a vast array of occupations and ethnic backgrounds and travels the entire nation. These interesting and useful compilations of portraits of the American Working, Middle and Upper Classes during the last 120 years will be an important addition to any high school, public or academic library reference collection.

"These interesting, unique compilations of economic and social facts, figures and graphs will support multiple research needs. They will engage and enlighten patrons in high school, public and academic library collections." –Booklist (on Volumes I and II)

Volume I: The Working Class ◆ 558 pages; Hardcover ISBN 1-891482-81-5, $135.00
Volume II: The Middle Class ◆ 591 pages; Hardcover ISBN 1-891482-72-6; $135.00
Volume III: The Upper Class ◆ 567 pages; Hardcover ISBN 1-930956-38-X, $135.00
Four Volume Set (Volumes I-IV), Hardcover ISBN 1-59237-017-9, $500.00

The Value of a Dollar – Millennium Edition

A guide to practical economy, *The Value of a Dollar* records the actual prices of thousands of items that consumers purchased from the Civil War to the present, along with facts about investment options and income opportunities. The first edition, published by Gale Research in 1994, covered the period of 1860 to 1989. This second edition has been completely redesigned and revised and now contains two new chapters, 1990-1994 and 1995-1999. Each 5-year chapter includes a Historical Snapshot, Consumer Expenditures, Investments, Selected Income, Income/Standard Jobs, Food Basket, Standard Prices and Miscellany. This interesting and useful publication will be widely used in any reference collection.

"Recommended for high school, college and public libraries." –ARBA

493 pages; Hardcover ISBN 1-891482-49-1, $135.00

Profiles of America, 2003 A Statistical Guide to All U.S. Cities, Towns and Counties

Profiles of America is the only source that pulls together, in one place, statistical, historical and descriptive information about almost every place in the United States in an easy-to-use format. This award winning reference set, now in its second edition, compiles statistics and data from over 30 different sources – the latest census information has been included along with more than nine brand new statistical topics. This Four-Volume Set details over 40,000 places, from the biggest metropolis to the smallest unincorporated hamlet, and provides statistical details and information on over 50 different topics including Geography, Climate, Population, Vital Statistics, Economy, Income, Taxes, Education, Housing, Health & Environment, Public Safety, Newspapers, Transportation, Presidential Election Results and Information Contacts or Chambers of Commerce. Profiles are arranged, for ease-of-use, by state and then by county. Each county begins with a County-Wide Overview and is followed by information for each Community in that particular county. The Community Profiles within the county are arranged alphabetically. *Profiles of America* is a virtual snapshot of America at your fingertips and a unique compilation of information that will be widely used in any reference collection.

A Library Journal Best Reference Book "
An outstanding compilation." –Library Journal

3,200 pages; Four Volume Set; Softcover ISBN 1-891482-80-7, $500.00

The American Tally, 2002/03

This important statistical handbook compiles, all in one place, comparative statistics on all U.S. cities and towns with a 10,000+ population. *The American Tally* provides statistical details on over 3,000 cities and towns and profiles how they compare with one another in Population Characteristics, Education, Language & Immigration, Income & Employment and Housing. Each section begins with an alphabetical listing of cities by state, allowing for quick access to both the statistics and relative rankings of any city. Next, the highest and lowest cities are listed in each statistic. These important, informative lists provide quick reference to which cities are at both extremes of the spectrum for each statistic. Unlike any other reference, *The American Tally* provides quick, easy access to comparative statistics – a must-have for any reference collection.

"A solid library reference." -Bookwatch

500 pages; Softcover ISBN 1-930956-29-0, $125.00

America's Top-Rated Cities, 2003

America's Top-Rated Cities provides current, comprehensive statistical information and other essential data in one easy-to-use source on the 100 "top" cities that have been cited as the best for business and living in the U.S. This handbook allows readers to see, at a glance, a concise social, business, economic, demographic and environmental profile of each city, including brief evaluative comments. In addition to detailed data on Cost of Living, Finances, Real Estate, Education, Major Employers, Media, Crime and Climate, city reports now include Housing Vacancies, Tax Audits, Bankruptcy, Presidential Election Results and more. This outstanding source of information will be widely used in any reference collection.

"The only source of its kind that brings together all of this information into one easy-to-use source. It will be beneficial to many business and public libraries." –ARBA

2,500 pages, 4 Volume Set; Softcover ISBN 1-891482-79-3, $195.00

The Comparative Guide to American Suburbs, 2001

The Comparative Guide to American Suburbs is a one-stop source for Statistics on the 2,000+ suburban communities surrounding the 50 largest metropolitan areas – their population characteristics, income levels, economy, school system and important data on how they compare to one another. Organized into 50 Metropolitan Area chapters, each chapter contains an overview of the Metropolitan Area, a detailed Map followed by a comprehensive Statistical Profile of each Suburban Community, including Contact Information, Physical Characteristics, Population Characteristics, Income, Economy, Unemployment Rate, Cost of Living, Education, Chambers of Commerce and more. Next, statistical data is sorted into Ranking Tables that rank the suburbs by twenty different criteria, including Population, Per Capita Income, Unemployment Rate, Crime Rate, Cost of Living and more. *The Comparative Guide to American Suburbs* is the best source for locating data on suburbs. Those looking to relocate, as well as those doing preliminary market research, will find this an invaluable timesaving resource.

"Public and academic libraries will find this compilation useful... The work draws together figures from many sources and will be especially helpful for job relocation decisions." – Booklist

1,681 pages; Softcover ISBN 1-930956-42-8, $130.00

America's Top-Rated Smaller Cities, 2002

A perfect companion to *America's Top-Rated Cities, America's Top-Rated Smaller Cities* provides current, comprehensive business and living profiles of smaller cities (population 25,000-99,999) that have been cited as the best for business and living in the United States. Sixty new, never-before profiled cities make up this 2002 edition of *America's Top-Rated Smaller Cities,* all are top-ranked by Population Growth, Median Income, Unemployment Rate and Crime Rate. In addition to this new selection procedure, city reports reflect the most current data available on a wide-range of statistics as well. Each includes a Background of the City, an Overview of the State Finances and statistical details on Employment & Earnings, Household Income, Unemployment Rate, Population Characteristics, Taxes, Cost of Living, Education, Health Care, Public Safety, Recreation, Media, Air & Water Quality and much more. *America's Top-Rated Smaller Cities* offers a reliable, one-stop source for statistical data that, before now, could only be found scattered in hundreds of sources. This volume is designed for a wide range of readers: individuals considering relocating a residence or business; professionals considering expanding their business or changing careers; general and market researchers; real estate consultants; human resource personnel; urban planners and investors.

"Provides current, comprehensive statistical information in one easy-to-use source... Recommended for public and academic libraries and specialized collections." –Library Journal

1,072 pages; Softcover ISBN 1-930956-67-3, $160.00

Crime in America's Top-Rated Cities, 2000

This volume includes over 20 years of crime statistics in all major crime categories: violent crimes, property crimes and total crime. *Crime in America's Top-Rated Cities* is conveniently arranged by city and covers 76 top-rated cities. *Crime in America's Top-Rated Cities* offers details that compare the number of crimes and crime rates for the city, suburbs and metro area along with national crime trends for violent, property and total crimes. Also, this handbook contains important information and statistics on Anti-Crime Programs, Crime Risk, Hate Crimes, Illegal Drugs, Law Enforcement, Correctional Facilities, Death Penalty Laws and much more. A much-needed resource for people who are relocating, business professionals, general researchers, the press, law enforcement officials and students of criminal justice.

"Data is easy to access and will save hours of searching." –Global Enforcement Review

832 pages; Softcover ISBN 1-891482-84-X, $155.00

To preview any of our Directories Risk-Free for 30 days, call (800) 562-2139 or fax to (518) 789-0556

The Environmental Resource Handbook, 2002

This brand new first edition is the most up-to-date and comprehensive source for Environmental Resources and Statistics. Section I: Resources provides detailed contact information for thousands of information sources, including Associations & Organizations, Awards & Honors, Conferences, Foundations & Grants, Environmental Health, Government Agencies, National Parks & Wildlife Refuges, Publications, Research Centers, Educational Programs, Green Product Catalogs, Consultants and much more. Section II: Statistics, provides statistics and rankings on hundreds of important topics, including Children's Environmental Index, Municipal Finances, Toxic Chemicals, Recycling, Climate, Air & Water Quality and more. This kind of up-to-date environmental data, all in one place, is not available anywhere else on the market place today. This brand new title is a must-have for all public and academic libraries as well as any organization with a primary focus on the environment.

"...the intrinsic value of the information make it worth consideration by libraries with environmental collections and environmentally concerned users." –Booklist

998 pages; Softcover ISBN 1-930956-04-5, $155.00 ◆ Online Database $300.00

Weather America, A Thirty-Year Summary of Statistical Weather Data and Rankings, 2001

This valuable resource provides extensive climatological data for over 4,000 National and Cooperative Weather Stations throughout the United States. *Weather America* begins with a new Major Storms section that details major storm events of the nation and a National Rankings section that details rankings for several data elements, such as Maximum Temperature and Precipitation. The main body of *Weather America* is organized into 50 state sections. Each section provides a Data Table on each Weather Station, organized alphabetically, that provides statistics on Maximum and Minimum Temperatures, Precipitation, Snowfall, Extreme Temperatures, Foggy Days, Humidity and more. State sections contain two brand new features in this edition – a City Index and a narrative Description of the climatic conditions of the state. Each section also includes a revised Map of the State that includes not only weather stations, but cities and towns.

"Best Reference Book of the Year." –Library Journal

2,013 pages; Softcover ISBN 1-891482-29-7, $175.00

The Comparative Guide to American Elementary & Secondary Schools, 2002/03

The only guide of its kind, this 2002/03 edition of the award winning Comparative Guide to American Elementary and Secondary Schools has been broadly expanded to offer a snapshot profile of every public school district in the United States serving 1,500 or more students – more than 5,900 districts are covered, that's almost 2,000 more than the previous edition. Organized alphabetically by district within state, each chapter begins with a Statistical Overview of the state. Each district listing includes contact information (name, address, phone number and web site) plus Grades Served, the Numbers of Students and Teachers and the Number of Regular, Special Education, Alternative and Vocational Schools in the district along with statistics on Student/Classroom Teacher Ratios, Drop Out Rates, Ethnicity, the Numbers of Librarians and Guidance Counselors and District Expenditures per student. Brand New to this edition, *The Comparative Guide to American Elementary and Secondary Schools* provides important ranking tables, both by state and nationally, for each data element. For easy navigation through this wealth of information, this handbook contains a useful City Index that lists all districts that operate schools within a city. These important comparative statistics are necessary for anyone considering relocation or doing comparative research on their own district and would be a perfect acquisition for any public library or school district library.

"This straightforward guide is an easy way to find general information. Valuable for academic and large public library collections." –ARBA

2,355 pages; Softcover ISBN 1-930956-93-2, $125.00

Sedgwick Press
Health Directories

The Complete Directory for People with Disabilities, 2003

A wealth of information, now in one comprehensive sourcebook. Completely updated for 2003, this edition contains more information than ever before, including thousands of new entries and enhancements to existing entries and thousands of additional web sites and e-mail addresses. Plus, the chapters on Camps and Rehabilitation Facilities have been extensively updated and a brand new chapter on Sub-Acute Rehabilitation Facilities has been added to this edition. This up-to-date directory is the most comprehensive resource available for people with disabilities, detailing Independent Living Centers, Rehabilitation Facilities, State & Federal Agencies, Associations, Support Groups, Periodicals & Books, Assistive Devices, Employment & Education Programs, Camps and Travel Groups. Each year, more libraries, schools, colleges, hospitals, rehabilitation centers and individuals add *The Complete Directory for People with Disabilities* to their collections, making sure that this information is readily available to the families, individuals and professionals who can benefit most from the amazing wealth of resources cataloged here.

"No other reference tool exists to meet the special needs of the disabled in one convenient resource for information." –Library Journal

1,200 pages; Softcover ISBN 1-930956-69-X, $165.00 ◆ Online Database $215.00 ◆ Online Database & Directory Combo $300.00

The Complete Directory for People with Chronic Illness, 2001/02

Thousands of hours of research have gone into this completely updated 2001/02 edition – several new chapters have been added along with thousands of new entries and enhancements to existing entries. This widely-hailed directory is structured around the 90 most prevalent chronic illnesses – from Asthma to Cancer to Wilson's Disease – and provides a comprehensive overview of the support services and information resources available for people diagnosed with a chronic illness. Each chronic illness has its own chapter and contains a brief description in layman's language, followed by important resources for National & Local Organizations, State Agencies, Newsletters, Books & Periodicals, Libraries & Research Centers, Support Groups & Hotlines, Web Sites and much more. This directory is an important resource for health care professionals, the collections of hospital and health care libraries, as well as an invaluable tool for people with a chronic illness and their support network.

"A must purchase for all hospital and health care libraries and is strongly recommended for all public library reference departments." –ARBA

1,152 pages; Softcover ISBN 1-930956-63-7, $165.00 ◆ Online Database $215.00 ◆ Online Database & Directory Combo $300.00

The Complete Learning Disabilities Directory, 2002

The 2002 Complete Learning Disabilities Directory is the most comprehensive database of Programs, Services, Curriculum Materials, Professional Meetings & Resources, Camps, Newsletters and Support Groups for teachers, students and families concerned with learning disabilities. This information-packed directory includes information about Associations & Organizations, Schools, Colleges & Testing Materials, Government Agencies, Legal Resources and much more. For quick, easy access to information, this directory contains four indexes: Entry Name Index, Subject Index and Geographic Index. With every passing year, the field of learning disabilities attracts more attention and the network of caring, committed and knowledgeable professionals grows every day. This directory is an invaluable research tool for these parents, students and professionals.

"Due to its wealth and depth of coverage, parents, teachers and others... should find this an invaluable resource." -Booklist

848 pages; Softcover ISBN 1-930956-36-3, $145.00 ◆ Online Database $195.00 ◆ Online Database & Directory Combo $280.00

The Complete Mental Health Directory, 2002

This is the most comprehensive resource covering the field of behavioral health, with critical information for both the layman and the mental health professional. For the layman, this directory offers understandable descriptions of 25 Mental Health Disorders as well as detailed information on Associations, Media, Support Groups and Mental Health Facilities. For the professional, *The Complete Mental Health Directory* offers critical and comprehensive information on Managed Care Organizations, Information Systems, Government Agencies and Provider Organizations. This comprehensive volume of needed information will be widely used in any reference collection.

"... the strength of this directory is that it consolidates widely dispersed information into a single volume." –Booklist

800 pages; Softcover ISBN 1-930956-06-1, $165.00 ◆ Online Database $215.00 ◆ Online & Directory Combo $300.00

To preview any of our Directories Risk-Free for 30 days, call (800) 562-2139 or fax to (518) 789-0556

Older Americans Information Directory, 2002/03

Completely updated for 2002/03, this Fourth Edition has been completely revised and now contains 1,000 new listings, over 8,000 updates to existing listings and over 3,000 brand new e-mail addresses and web sites. You'll find important resources for Older Americans including National, Regional, State & Local Organizations, Government Agencies, Research Centers, Libraries & Information Centers, Legal Resources, Discount Travel Information, Continuing Education Programs, Disability Aids & Assistive Devices, Health, Print Media and Electronic Media. Three indexes: Entry Index, Subject Index and Geographic Index make it easy to find just the right source of information. This comprehensive guide to resources for Older Americans will be a welcome addition to any reference collection.

"Highly recommended for academic, public, health science and consumer libraries…" –Choice

1,200 pages; Softcover ISBN 1-930956-65-7, $165.00 ◆ Online Database $215.00 ◆ Online Database & Directory Combo $300.00

The Complete Directory for Pediatric Disorders, 2002/03

This important directory provides parents and caregivers with information about Pediatric Conditions, Disorders, Diseases and Disabilities, including Blood Disorders, Bone & Spinal Disorders, Brain Defects & Abnormalities, Chromosomal Disorders, Congenital Heart Defects, Movement Disorders, Neuromuscular Disorders and Pediatric Tumors & Cancers. This carefully written directory offers: understandable Descriptions of 15 major bodily systems; Descriptions of more than 200 Disorders and a Resources Section, detailing National Agencies & Associations, State Associations, Online Services, Libraries & Resource Centers, Research Centers, Support Groups & Hotlines, Camps, Books and Periodicals. This resource will provide immediate access to information crucial to families and caregivers when coping with children's illnesses.

"Recommended for public and consumer health libraries." –Library Journal

1,120 pages; Softcover ISBN 1-930956-61-4, $165.00 ◆ Online Database $215.00 ◆ Online Database & Directory Combo $300.00

The Complete Directory for People with Rare Disorders, 2002/03

This outstanding reference is produced in conjunction with the National Organization for Rare Disorders to provide comprehensive and needed access to important information on over 1,000 rare disorders, including Cancers and Muscular, Genetic and Blood Disorders. An informative Disorder Description is provided for each of the 1,100 disorders (rare Cancers and Muscular, Genetic and Blood Disorders) followed by information on National and State Organizations dealing with a particular disorder, Umbrella Organizations that cover a wide range of disorders, the Publications that can be useful when researching a disorder and the Government Agencies to contact. Detailed and up-to-date listings contain mailing address, phone and fax numbers, web sites and e-mail addresses along with a description. For quick, easy access to information, this directory contains two indexes: Entry Name Index and Acronym/Keyword Index along with an informative Guide for Rare Disorder Advocates. The Complete Directory for People with Rare Disorders will be an invaluable tool for the thousands of families that have been struck with a rare or "orphan" disease, who feel that they have no place to turn and will be a much-used addition to the reference collection of any public or academic library.

"Quick access to information… public libraries and hospital patient libraries will find this a useful resource in directing users to support groups or agencies dealing with a rare disorder." –Booklist

726 pages; Softcover ISBN 1-891482-18-1, $165.00

Sedgwick Press
Education Directories

Educators Resource Directory, 2003/04

Educators Resource Directory is a comprehensive resource that provides the educational professional with thousands of resources and statistical data for professional development. This directory saves hours of research time by providing immediate access to Associations & Organizations, Conferences & Trade Shows, Educational Research Centers, Employment Opportunities & Teaching Abroad, School Library Services, Scholarships, Financial Resources, Professional Consultants, Computer Software & Testing Resources and much more. Plus, this comprehensive directory also includes a section on Statistics and Rankings with over 100 tables, including statistics on Average Teacher Salaries, SAT/ACT scores, Revenues & Expenditures and more. These important statistics will allow the user to see how their school rates among others, make relocation decisions and so much more. *Educators Resource Directory* will be a well-used addition to the reference collection of any school district, education department or public library.

"Recommended for all collections that serve elementary and secondary school professionals." –Choice

1,000 pages; Softcover ISBN 1-59237-002-0, $145.00 ◆ Online Database $195.00 ◆ Online Database & Directory Combo $280.00

To preview any of our Directories Risk-Free for 30 days, call (800) 562-2139 or fax to (518) 789-0556

Grey House Publishing
Business Directories

The Directory of Business Information Resources, 2002
With 100% verification, over 1,000 new listings and more than 12,000 updates, this 2002 edition of *The Directory of Business Information Resources* is the most up-to-date source for contacts in over 98 business areas – from advertising and agriculture to utilities and wholesalers. This carefully researched volume details: the Associations representing each industry; the Newsletters that keep members current; the Magazines and Journals - with their "Special Issues" - that are important to the trade, the Conventions that are "must attends," Databases, Directories and Industry Web Sites that provide access to must-have marketing resources. Includes contact names, phone & fax numbers, web sites and e-mail addresses. This one-volume resource is a gold mine of information and would be a welcome addition to any reference collection.

"This is a most useful and easy-to-use addition to any researcher's library." –The Information Professionals Institute

2,500 pages; Softcover ISBN 1-930956-75-4, $250.00 ◆ Online Database $495.00

Nations of the World, 2003 A Political, Economic and Business Handbook
This completely revised Third Edition covers all the nations of the world in an easy-to-use, single volume. Each nation is profiled in a single chapter that includes Key Facts, Political & Economic Issues, a Country Profile and Business Information. This 2003 edition has been completely updated with the latest Political and Economic data including changes since September 11, 2001 and now reflects the most current information on Politics, Travel Advisories, Economics and more. You'll find such vital information as a Country Map, Population Characteristics, Inflation, Agricultural Production, Foreign Debt, Political History, Foreign Policy, Regional Insecurity, Economics, Trade & Tourism, Historical Profile, Political Systems, Ethnicity, Languages, Media, Climate, Hotels, Chambers of Commerce, Banking, Travel Information and more. Five Regional Chapters follow the main text and include a Regional Map, an Introductory Article, Key Indicators and Currencies for the Region. Noted for its sophisticated, up-to-date and reliable compilation of political, economic and business information, this brand new edition will be an important acquisition to any public, academic or special library reference collection.

"A useful addition to both general reference collections and business collections." –RUSQ

1,700 pages; Softcover ISBN 1-930956-00-2, $135.00

The Grey House Performing Arts Directory, 2003
The Grey House Performing Arts Directory is the most comprehensive resource covering the Performing Arts. This important directory provides current information on over 8,500 Dance Companies, Instrumental Music Programs, Opera Companies, Choral Groups, Theater Companies, Performing Arts Series and Performing Arts Facilities. Plus, this edition now contains a brand new section on Artist Management Groups. In addition to mailing address, phone & fax numbers, e-mail addresses and web sites, dozens of other fields of available information include mission statement, key contacts, facilities, seating capacity, season, attendance and more. This directory also provides an important Information Resources section that covers hundreds of Performing Arts Associations, Magazines, Newsletters, Trade Shows, Directories, Databases and Industry Web Sites. Five indexes provide immediate access to this wealth of information: Entry Name, Executive Name, Performance Facilities, Geographic and Information Resources. *The Grey House Performing Arts Directory* pulls together thousands of Performing Arts Organizations, Facilities and Information Resources into an easy-to-use source – this kind of comprehensiveness and extensive detail is not available in any resource on the market place today.

"An immensely useful and user-friendly new reference tool... recommended for public, academic and certain special library reference collections." –Booklist

1,500 pages; Softcover ISBN 1-930956-87-8, $170.00 ◆ Online Database $335.00

Research Services Directory, 2001 Commercial & Corporate Research Centers
This Eighth Edition provides access to well over 7,000 independent Commercial Research Firms, Corporate Research Centers and Laboratories offering contract services for hands-on, basic or applied research. Each entry provides the company's name, mailing address, phone & fax numbers, key contacts, web site, e-mail address, as well as a company description and research and technical fields served. Four indexes provide immediate access to this wealth of information: Research Firms Index, Geographic Index, Personnel Name Index and Subject Index.

"An important source for organizations in need of information about laboratories, individuals and other facilities." –ARBA

1,309 pages; Softcover ISBN 1-891482-82-3, $395.00 ◆ Online Database $850.00

To preview any of our Directories Risk-Free for 30 days, call (800) 562-2139 or fax to (518) 789-0556

The Directory of Venture Capital Firms, 2003

This brand new Sixth Edition has been extensively updated and broadly expanded to offer direct access to over 2,800 Domestic and International Venture Capital Firms, including address, phone & fax numbers, e-mail addresses and web sites for both primary and branch locations. Entries include details on the firm's Mission Statement, Industry Group Preferences, Geographic Preferences, Average and Minimum Investments and Investment Criteria. You'll also find details that are available nowhere else, including the Firm's Portfolio Companies and extensive information on each of the firm's Managing Partners, such as Education, Professional Background and Directorships held, along with the Partner's E-mail Address. *The Directory of Venture Capital Firms* offers five important indexes: Geographic Index, Executive Name Index, Portfolio Company Index, Industry Preference Index and College & University Index. With its comprehensive coverage and detailed, extensive information on each company, *The Directory of Venture Capital Firms* is an important addition to any finance collection.

"... a better value than its principal competitor, Pratt's Guide to Venture Capital Sources. Recommended for business collections in large public, academic and business libraries." –Choice

1,300 pages; Softcover ISBN 1-930956-77-0, $450.00 ◆ Online Database $889.00

The Directory of Mail Order Catalogs, 2003

Published since 1981, this Seventeenth Edition features 100% verification of data and is the premier source of information on the mail order catalog industry. Details over 12,000 consumer catalog companies with 44 different product chapters from Animals to Toys & Games. Contains detailed contact information including e-mail addresses and web sites along with important business details such as employee size, years in business, sales volume, catalog size, number of catalogs mailed and more. Four indexes provide quick access to information: Catalog & Company Name Index, Geographic Index, Product Index and Web Sites Index.

"This is a godsend for those looking for information." –Reference Book Review

1,700 pages; Softcover ISBN 1-891482-73-4, $250.00 ◆ Online Database $495.00

The Directory of Business to Business Catalogs, 2003

The completely updated 2003 *Directory of Business to Business Catalogs*, provides details on over 6,000 suppliers of everything from computers to laboratory supplies... office products to office design... marketing resources to safety equipment... landscaping to maintenance suppliers... building construction and much more. Detailed entries offer mailing address, phone & fax numbers, e-mail addresses, web sites, key contacts, sales volume, employee size, catalog printing information and more. Jut about every kind of product a business needs in its day-to-day operations is covered in this carefully-researched volume. Three indexes are provided for at-a-glance access to information: Catalog & Company Name Index, Geographic Index and Web Sites Index.

"...an excellent choice for libraries... wishing to supplement their business supplier resources." –Booklist

800 pages; Softcover ISBN 1-891482-69-6, $165.00 ◆ Online Database $325.00

Thomas Food and Beverage Market Place, 2002/03

Thomas Food and Beverage Market Place is bigger and better than ever with thousands of new companies, thousands of updates to existing companies and two revised and enhanced product category indexes. This comprehensive directory profiles over 18,000 Food & Beverage Manufacturers, 12,000 Equipment & Supply Companies, 2,200 Transportation & Warehouse Companies, 2,000 Brokers & Wholesalers, 8,000 Importers & Exporters, 900 Industry Resources and hundreds of Mail Order Catalogs. Listings include detailed Contact Information, Sales Volumes, Key Contacts, Brand & Product Information, Packaging Details and much more. *Thomas Food and Beverage Market Place* is available as a three-volume printed set, a subscription-based Online Database via the Internet, on CD-ROM, as well as mailing lists and a licensable database.

8,500 pages, 3 Volume Set; Softcover ISBN 1-930956-95-9, $495.00 ◆ CD-ROM ISBN 1-930956-33-9, $695.00 ◆ CD-ROM & 3 Volume Set Combo ISBN 1-930956-34-7, $895.00 ◆ Online Database $695.00 ◆ Online Database & 3 Volume Set Combo, $895.00

The Grey House Safety & Security Directory, 2003

The Grey House Safety & Security Directory is the most comprehensive reference tool and buyer's guide for the safety and security industry. Published continuously since 1943 as Best's Safety & Security Directory, Grey House acquired the title in 2002. Arranged by safety topic, each chapter begins with OSHA regulations for the topic, followed by Training Articles written by top professionals in the field and Self-Inspection Checklists. Next, each topic contains Buyer's Guide sections that feature related products and services. Topics include Administration, Insurance, Employee Health Maintenance & Ergonomics, Ordinary Materials Handling, Workplace Preparation & Maintenance, Electrical Lighting & Safety, Fire & Rescue, Security and much more. Six important indexes make finding information and product manufacturers quick and easy: Geographical Index of Manufacturers and Distributors, Company Profile Index, Brand Name Index, Product Index, Index of Web Sites and Index of Advertisers. This comprehensive, up-to-date reference will provide every tool necessary to make sure a business is in compliance with OSHA regulations and locate the products and services needed to meet those regulations.

1,500 pages, 2 Volume Set; Softcover ISBN1-930956-71-1, $225.00

To preview any of our Directories Risk-Free for 30 days, call (800) 562-2139 or fax to (518) 789-0556